INTERDEPENDENCE, INTERACTION, AND CLOSE RELATIONSHIPS

Interdependence theory is a powerful and applicable theory that has shaped the study of interpersonal relationships for decades, providing foundational constructs and elucidating key assumptions within the burgeoning field of relationship science. Research guided by interdependence theory sheds light on the diverse phenomena within ongoing relationships, including the emergence of co-operation, trust, dependence, power, and relationship maintenance. At its core, interdependence theory pinpoints key elements of daily interactions that predict specific experiences and outcomes that people have in different situations. This handbook goes further to explain how interdependence theory continues to be used fruitfully in research, driving our current understanding of relational processes. We invite you to enter the world of interdependence and discover what top scholars across disciplines are discussing in their efforts to fully understand close, intimate relationships.

Laura V. Machia is Associate Professor of Psychology and Director of the Close Relationships Laboratory at Syracuse University, USA.

Christopher R. Agnew is Professor of Psychological Sciences and Associate Vice President for Research at Purdue University, USA.

Ximena B. Arriaga is Professor of Psychological Sciences at Purdue University, USA, and the Director of the Purdue Acceptance and Inclusion Consortium.

Advances in Personal Relationships

Christopher R. Agnew
Purdue University
John P. Caughlin
University of Illinois at Urbana-Champaign
C. Raymond Knee
University of Houston
Terri L. Orbuch
Oakland University

Although scholars from a variety of disciplines have written and conversed about the importance of personal relationships for decades, the emergence of personal relationships as a field of study is relatively recent. Advances in Personal Relationships represents the culmination of years of multidisciplinary and interdisciplinary work on personal relationships. Sponsored by the International Association for Relationship Research, the series offers readers cutting-edge research and theory in the field. Contributing authors are internationally known scholars from a variety of disciplines, including social psychology, clinical psychology, communication, history, sociology, gerontology, and family studies. Volumes include integrative reviews, conceptual pieces, summaries of research programs, and major theoretical works. Advances in Personal Relationships presents first-rate scholarship that is both provocative and theoretically grounded. The theoretical and empirical work described by authors will stimulate readers and advance the field by offering new ideas and retooling old ones. The series will be of interest to upper-division undergraduate students, graduate students, researchers, and practitioners.

Other Books in the Series

Attribution, Communication Behavior, and Close Relationships
Valerie Manusov and John H. Harvey, editors

Stability and Change in Relationships
Anita L. Vangelisti, Harry T. Reis, and Mary Anne Fitzpatrick, editors

Understanding Marriage: Developments in the Study of Couple Interaction
Patricia Noller and Judith A. Feeney, editors

Growing Together: Personal Relationships Across the Lifespan
Frieder R. Lang and Karen L. Fingerman, editors

Communicating Social Support
Daena J. Goldsmith

Communicating Affection: Interpersonal Behavior and Social Context
Kory Floyd

Changing Relations: Achieving Intimacy in a Time of Social Transition
Robin Goodwin

Feeling Hurt in Close Relationships
Anita L. Vangelisti, editor

Romantic Relationships in Emerging Adulthood
Frank D. Fincham and Ming Cui, editors

Responding to Intimate Violence Against Women: The Role of Informal Networks
Renate Klein

Social Influences on Romantic Relationships: Beyond the Dyad
Christopher R. Agnew, editor

Positive Approaches to Optimal Relationship Development
C. Raymond Knee and Harry T. Reis, editors

Personality and Close Relationship Processes
Stanley O. Gaines, Jr.

The Experience and Expression of Uncertainty in Close Relationships
Jennifer A. Theiss

Contemporary Studies on Relationships, Health, and Wellness
Jennifer A. Theiss and Kathryn Greene, editors

Interdependence, Interaction, and Close Relationships

Edited by
Laura V. Machia
Syracuse University

Christopher R. Agnew
Purdue University

Ximena B. Arriaga
Purdue University

CAMBRIDGE
UNIVERSITY PRESS

CAMBRIDGE
UNIVERSITY PRESS

University Printing House, Cambridge CB2 8BS, United Kingdom

One Liberty Plaza, 20th Floor, New York, NY 10006, USA

477 Williamstown Road, Port Melbourne, VIC 3207, Australia

314-321, 3rd Floor, Plot 3, Splendor Forum, Jasola District Centre, New Delhi - 110025, India

103 Penang Road, #05-06/07, Visioncrest Commercial, Singapore 238467

Cambridge University Press is part of the University of Cambridge.

It furthers the University's mission by disseminating knowledge in the pursuit of education, learning and research at the highest international levels of excellence.

www.cambridge.org
Information on this title: www.cambridge.org/9781108703659
DOI: 10.1017/9781108645836

First published 2020
First paperback edition 2022

A catalogue record for this publication is available from the British Library

ISBN 978-1-108-48096-3 Hardback
ISBN 978-1-108-70365-9 Paperback

CONTENTS

FIGURES

TABLES

CONTRIBUTORS

CHRISTOPHER R. AGNEW, Department of Psychological Sciences, Purdue University, West Lafayette, Indiana, USA

XIMENA B. ARRIAGA, Department of Psychological Sciences, Purdue University, West Lafayette, Indiana, USA

LEVI R. BAKER, Department of Psychology, University of North Carolina at Greensboro, North Carolina, USA

DANIEL BALLIET, Department of Experimental and Applied Psychology, Vrije Universiteit Amsterdam, Netherlands

ASHLYN BRADY, Department of Psychology, University of North Carolina at Greensboro, North Carolina, USA

WILLIAM J. CHOPIK, Department of Psychology, Michigan State University, USA

SIMON COLUMBUS, Department of Experimental and Applied Psychology, Vrije Universiteit Amsterdam, Netherlands

KASSANDRA CORTES, Department of Business, Wilfrid Laurier University, Ontario, Canada

STANLEY O. GAINES, JR., School of Social Sciences, Brunel University London, Uxbridge, Middlesex, United Kingdom

YUTHIKA U. GIRME, Department of Psychology, Simon Fraser University, Burnaby, British Columbia, Canada

BENJAMIN W. HADDEN, Department of Psychology, Florida Atlantic University, USA

DELETHA P. HARDIN, Department of Psychology, University of Tampa, Florida, USA

JOHN G. HOLMES, Department of Psychology, University of Waterloo, Ontario, Canada

LUCY L. HUNT, Department of Psychological Sciences, Purdue University, West Lafayette, Indiana, USA

BRITTANY K. JAKUBIAK, Department of Psychology, Syracuse University, New York, USA

MADOKA KUMASHIRO, Psychology Department, Goldsmiths, Univeristy of London, London, United Kingdom

EDWARD P. LEMAY, JR., Department of Psychology, University of Maryland, College Park, Maryland, USA

LAURA V. MACHIA, Department of Psychology, Syracuse University, New York, USA

BRENT A. MATTINGLY, Department of Psychology, Ursinus College, Collegeville, Pennsylvania, USA

KEVIN P. MCINTYRE, Department of Psychology, Trinity University, San Antonio, Texas, USA

JAMES K. MCNULTY, Department of Psychology, Florida State University, USA

SHAE MONTALVO, Department of Psychology, University of North Carolina at Greensboro, North Carolina, USA

MONIQUE S. NAKAMURA, Department of Psychology, University of Minnesota – Twin Cities, USA

BRIAN G. OGOLSKY, Department of Human Development and Family Studies, University of Illinois at Urbana-Champaign, USA

NICKOLA C. OVERALL, School of Psychology, The University of Auckland, New Zealand

ASHLEY K. RANDALL, Counseling and Counseling Psychology, Arizona State University, USA

VALENTINA RAUCH-ANDEREGG, Harvard Second Generation Study, Harvard Medical School, Boston, Massachusetts, USA

TEKISHA M. RICE, Department of Human Development and Family Studies, University of Illinois at Urbana-Champaign, USA

FRANCESCA RIGHETTI, Department of Experimental and Applied Psychology, Vrije Universiteit Amsterdam, Netherlands

JEFFRY A. SIMPSON, Department of Psychology, University of Minnesota, USA

SUSAN SPRECHER, Department of Sociology and Anthropology, Illinois State University, USA

KENNETH TAN, School of Social Sciences, Singapore Management University, Singapore

JENNIFER M. TOMLINSON, Department of Psychology, Colgate University, Hamilton, New York, USA

JOANNE V. WOOD, Department of Psychology, University of Waterloo, Ontario, Canada

ACKNOWLEDGMENTS

In 2017, Syracuse University hosted a mini-conference sponsored by the International Association for Relationship Research. Over 200 scholars came together for a weekend centered on the theme of "Interdependence, Interaction, and Relationships." For three days, scholars discussed their work in formal presentations, informal interactions between sessions, and lively conversations during happy hours. When the conference ended, it was clear that ideas surrounding interdependence remain relevant and generative and the idea for this book came to be.

Interdependence Theory (IT) – a theory first discussed more than 60 years ago – is a remarkably flexible theory that strongly influences contemporary relationship science. IT constructs underlie numerous current theories and frameworks, often in implicit ways. This volume draws IT's core to the forefront, emphasizing its contribution and explicitly highlighting its influence. Most of this influence is theoretical, but several contemporary methodological advances can also be attributed to this powerful theory. The intent of this book is to highlight IT, show how IT has shaped the field of relationship science, and foreshadow how it will continue to guide research into the future.

Hosting the conference that inspired this book required a great deal of support. We are indebted to Syracuse University, and especially to the College of Arts and Sciences, the Graduate School, and the Psychology Department for their financial support. The other members of the local organizing committee – Jennifer Tomlinson, Joy McClure, and Len Newman – provided practical and emotional support throughout the planning process, for which we are immensely grateful. Finally, we thank the International Association for Relationship Research for sponsoring the conference, and especially thank Sue Sprecher, Leah Bryant, Jeff Simpson, and Dan Perlman for their guidance.

We also wish to express our gratitude to those who helped make this book possible. First and foremost, we thank the chapter authors for their ideas, expertise, and enthusiasm for this project. We also thank John

Caughlin, Chip Knee, and Terri Orbuch for their support of the project in their roles as Advances in Personal Relationships series coeditors. Thanks also go to those at Cambridge University Press for their assistance along the way, including Janka Romero (Commissioning Editor) and Emily Watton (Editorial Assistant). Finally, we are deeply indebted to Hal Kelley and John Thibaut, whose ideas set forth the study of interdependence, and to Caryl Rusbult and her peers (John Holmes, Harry Reis, Paul Van Lange, and many others) for fostering a strong interdependence tradition. Caryl Rusbult's commitment to the advancement of interdependence theory paved the way for the ideas in this volume and continues to profoundly inspire the scholars at its helm. Over 25 years ago, Caryl concluded a paper with the words, "Interdependence theory is a fruitful basis for understanding maintenance of close relationships," (Rusbult & Buunk, 1993, p. 200). This volume is a testament to how right she was.

Laura V. Machia

Christopher R. Agnew

Ximena B. Arriaga

REFERENCE

Rusbult, C. E., & Buunk, B. (1993). Commitment processes in close relationships: An interdependence analysis. *Journal of Social and Personal Relationships*, 10, 175–204.

Introduction

LAURA V. MACHIA

> In this book is presented a theory of interpersonal relations and group functioning. The major motivation that governed this effort was a desire to give cumulative treatment to a discussion of some persistent problems in social psychology and to answer for ourselves the question: how do the data of the field look when they are arranged by their relevance to a conceptual structure that begins with relatively simple assumptions and adds further ones only as they become necessary? If it is not entirely idiosyncratic, any success along these lines might be expected to be useful both as a guide to research and in contributing some order and simplification to an increasingly bewildering congeries of fact.
>
> (Thibaut & Kelley, 1959, p. 1)

Above are the opening lines of the now-classic 1959 Interdependence Theory (IT) book by John Thibaut and Hal Kelley, *The Social Psychology of Groups*. This passage not only sets the stage for the book, telling the reader what to expect in the 300-plus pages that followed, but clairvoyantly told the field what to expect in the 60-plus years that have followed. IT has indeed been useful as a guide to research and as a way to order the myriad empirical facts uncovered about relationships, not just in social psychology, but in diverse disciplines spanning the social and behavioral sciences. In this volume, we hope once again to contribute some order and simplification to an even more increasingly robust literature, as the simple assumptions of IT remain as relevant as ever.

Interdependence Theory (IT) utilizes social psychological, economic, sociological, and learning theories to explain behavior (Thibaut & Kelley, 1959). It is a powerful theory that explains how elements of an interpersonal situation and characteristics of the people interacting combine in ways that predict specific experiences and outcomes (Rusbult & Van Lange, 2003). Research adopting this perspective has explained diverse phenomena within relationships such as cooperation, trust, dependence, power, and relationship maintenance, among others (see VanderDrift & Agnew, 2020). At its core, the theory is unchanged since its original articulation. However, its core has

1

informed empirical work spanning content areas and scientific disciplines, and that empirical work has subsequently extended the breadth of the theory in important, lasting ways.

The first part of this volume, titled "Interdependence, Situations, and Context," features four chapters that most directly focus on extending the core tenet of IT, which is that situations are central to understanding interaction and behavior (Kelley et al., 2003). All of the chapters in the first part aid in defining and understanding the power of situations and contextual factors. In Chapter 1, Columbus, Righetti, and Balliet discuss Functional Interdependence Theory, which posits that people are well-prepared to understand situations in terms of interdependence features. They review the new taxonomies and methods that allow for researchers to measure the interdependent situations people experience in their relationships. The advances summarized in this chapter allow researchers from multiple theoretical perspectives (e.g., attachment), interested in any interpersonal process (e.g., maintenance) to measure and understand how the extent of interdependence between partners contributes to the partners' behaviors and acquired outcomes.

In Chapter 2, Holmes notes that the naturally occurring costs that arise from interdependence can undermine partners' motivation to act in caring ways toward each other. He proposes that overcoming these challenges requires that partners stay perpetually focused on the long-term rewards of interdependence without being distracted by the momentary costs that occur due to interdependence. The theory summarized in this chapter allows researchers to understand and predict when and why partners will act on their self-protective goals, and when and why they will act on their pro-relationship goals.

In Chapter 3, Chopik highlights an exciting new application of geographic modeling to examine how geographical variation in social behavior can be applied to understanding close relationship processes. Not only are partners interdependent with each other, but they are interdependent with their entire social and physical space, which has predictable geographic patterns. The theory detailed in this chapter will be immensely useful for readers interested in understanding the greater geographic contexts in which interdependence arises, and the helpful primer on best methodological and visualization practices will guide readers who are interested in including geographic analyses into their existing research.

Closing the first part, in Chapter 4, Gaines and Hardin examine ethnicity and country of origin as potential contextual moderators of interdependence processes. Indeed, culture has an immense impact on social behavior. Although Thibaut and Kelley (1959) presented interdependence theory as a culturally universal perspective, it is reasonable to expect culture to affect interdependent processes in meaningful ways. Readers who are interested in how the broader culture surrounding an interdependent relationship affects that relationship's processes will benefit from Gaines and Hardin's explanation of how to develop and test hypotheses in which culture is explicitly considered in the context of interdependence.

The second and third parts of this volume are comprised of chapters that describe how empirical work has tested and extended a different aspect of IT. Specifically, people who are interdependent have outcomes that are affected by their partners' actions. As a result, partners who cooperate with each other have the potential to achieve greater outcomes than they could have as individuals, as they can combine time and resources. However, depending on others also creates vulnerabilities, particularly with others who are not caring or responsive to a person's needs. The second part of this volume is titled "Interdependence, Security, and Risk." Four chapters explore how interdependence can be a source of interpersonal security, but it also increases the risk of being rejected, hurt, or devalued by others.

In Chapter 5, Hunt, Kumashiro, and Arriaga detail how interdependent situations can influence attachment security. Some situations may activate a sense of risk and require benevolent and skilled partners to buffer insecurities. Other situations may foster a sense of worthiness or comfort with closeness and trust toward others. In that way, people learn about the risks of interdependence through being interdependent with others. In their chapter, the authors describe the Attachment Security Enhancement Model, which details how and when new experiences with risk cause people to update their expectations going forward.

In Chapter 6, Jakubiak notes that there are at least two sources of insecurity associated with close relationships: (1) those originating from the nature of interdependence itself and (2) those originating from stressors outside of the relationship. These risks are especially salient for individuals who exhibit chronic attachment insecurities. They benefit from situations in which partners can mitigate the sense of risk, facilitate continued interdependence, and encourage each other to thrive. Readers will benefit from learning about the types of supportive and affectionate partner behavior that promote security, which are crucial in understanding how interdependent processes can help partners mitigate these risks and encourage exploration.

In Chapter 7, Nakamura, Simpson, and Overall delve deeper into the association between how salient risks are to interdependent partners and what each partner can do to mitigate the perception of these risks for each other. Specifically, they detail some of the ways in which partners can successfully buffer the insecure reactions of anxious and avoidant individuals, including when, how, and why these ways work. These buffering strategies could help those for whom the risks of interdependence are especially salient to develop and maintain more "secure" environments.

Closing this part with Chapter 8, Rauch-Anderegg and Randall consider that partners' experiences of stress and coping are interdependent – one partner's stress affects the other, as does how they cope with stress. As such, dyadic coping (i.e., a joint means of regulating own and each other's emotional experiences) could be a particularly useful type of coping for stress that occurs in the context of relationships. Readers interested in interdependent processes associated with stress will benefit from reading the theoretical rationale for dyadic coping, as well as reviewing two recent empirical examples offered.

The third part of this volume, titled "Interdependence, Goal Pursuit, and Person Factors," contains four chapters that focus on the other half of the reward-risk theme of IT: the rewarding outcomes people receive as part of an interdependent unit depend on their personalities and levels of cooperation with their partners. In Chapter 9, Hadden and Girme recognize the complex nature of how interdependence affects individuals' ability to achieve their personal goals. Are personal and relational goals inherently antagonistic? Or might they be considered complementary? By providing an organizing structure in approaching this question, the literature that appears divided becomes clear: Relationships thrive when both personal and relational needs align. However, the alignment of personal and relational needs is dependent on multiple factors related to the goals, the partners, and the interaction that they describe.

In Chapter 10, Lemay extends the IT notion that the quality of interactions and relationships depends on the thoughts and feelings of both partners. He notes that people often try to manage the thoughts and feelings others have about them, and that adopting the goal to be valued by others often motivates people to enact prosocial behaviors. Demonstrating the power of interdependence, however, Lemay summarizes a wealth of research that suggests whether people do actually engage in prosocial behavior depends on whether they perceive others would value them for doing so.

In Chapter 11, Mattingly, Tomlinson, and McIntyre provide an overview of the self-expansion model through the lens of IT. The Self-Expansion Model holds that, because people form interdependent units with each other, people's senses of self are inherently connected to others' selves. This model is inherently compatible with IT, in that it is through interdependence with another person that one's sense of self changes. For example, individuals in an interdependent relationship may come to view their partners' traits (both good and bad) as if they are their own. Readers of this chapter will learn about the recent empirical developments in the self-expansion literature and how they are related to, and extend, IT.

Closing the part, in Chapter 12, Cortes and Wood detail an important process in which self-esteem and related personality traits influence whether people are able to achieve the benefits of having a close interpersonal bond (e.g., comfort, support). Specifically, people with low self-esteem generally feel that their partners are less accepting and responsive to them, which hinders their ability to achieve the positive outcomes of interdependence and cooperation. Throughout their chapter, the authors describe situations in which self-esteem affects perceptions of partner responsiveness to the detriment of those with low self-esteem.

In the final part of this volume, titled "Interdependence, Timing, and Expectations," we note that whereas IT in its original form certainly acknowledges history and future as important, its primary empirical focus is on specific, in-the-moment interactions. More recent IT work has extended this to be more explicitly longitudinal, looking at how people come to be ready for interdependence, what they expect will occur as a result of it, how they develop it, and what trajectories of interdependence may exist. The final part provides four chapters of contemporary work on these time-relevant topics.

In Chapter 13, Agnew, Hadden, and Tan postulate that timing matters in romantic relationships, as it does in all areas of life. More specifically, at any given moment in life, a person can be said to be receptive to a relationship in so far as they (a) want to be in a romantic relationship (termed relationship desirability) and (b) feel ready to be in a romantic relationship (termed relationship readiness). In their chapter, the authors detail Relationship Receptivity Theory, which demonstrates how classic IT constructs – constructs such as relational cognitions, emotions, motivations, behaviors, and outcomes – are influenced by how receptive an individual is to a relationship at a given time.

In Chapter 14, Baker, McNulty, Brady, and Montalvo summarize a substantive and important extension to IT. When predicting important relationship outcomes, the authors demonstrate the value of not only looking at how the relationship is now, as IT has always done, but also looking at how partners expect it to change in the future. The authors identify factors (e.g., plans to improve the relationship, personality, gender) that may cause partners' expected experiences to diverge from their current experiences, review theoretical and empirical work suggesting that expectations are uniquely important, and introduce a new measure of expected relationship satisfaction, alternatives, and investments designed for future research into these ideas.

In Chapter 15, Rice and Ogolsky review research on trajectories in relationships, asserting that there are countless pathways to commitment which vary by individual, relational, and contextual factors. It is important to examine the development of commitment across time, as it is key to understanding the outcomes interdependent partners receive (i.e., why some relationships end, some progress, and others cycle). To this end, the authors consider the role of expectations in the development of commitment, including how they are influenced by historical and social contexts. Readers will benefit from their methodological and analytical suggestions to study the trajectories of commitment effectively.

Finally, in the closing chapter, Chapter 16, Sprecher provides a thorough methodological and theoretical primer on how interdependence can be created in a laboratory, and what outcomes are associated with closeness. Although there are undeniably limitations in the degree to which findings from laboratory-generated interdependence can generalize to real-world interdependent relationships, creating interdependence in a laboratory can allow researchers to test various theoretically important variables in a controlled setting. Readers who are interested in narrowing in on how interdependence itself affects interpersonal interactions will benefit from this thorough, data-driven analysis.

Collectively, these sixteen chapters represent a wide and impressive foray into current IT perspectives and applications. Classic IT was formulated over half a century ago, yet it has demonstrated remarkable longevity across changing social contexts. Part of its longevity can be attributed to the fact that its originators proposed a minimal theory that precisely defined the characteristics of individuals and situations that produce particular outcomes (Thibaut & Kelley, 1959). As those change, the theory is expected to adapt as well (e.g., conflict itself does not cause any exact outcomes; however, conflict between two individuals with specific, measurable personalities in a context with particular, measurable structural constraints will reliably predict consistent outcomes). Another cause for its longevity, however, can be attributed to the fact that contemporary scholars have seen the value in extending this theory. Throughout this volume, readers will see the breadth of extensions made to IT.

It is valuable to explicitly reflect on the types of extensions that have occurred. Whereas IT has always recognized the power of a situation, contemporary scholars are becoming more and more explicit in their recognition that perhaps even more important is the power of what a person makes of a situation. In line with this contemporary extension, many of our chapters explicitly address how people think about the interdependent situations they encounter and what effect their cognitions have on their behavioral choices. Specifically, as described previously, the opening part provides four chapters that do just this (Chapters 1–4).

In addition, the field of relationship science is embracing more and more meta-theory – the combining of theoretical perspectives to more fully explain common relationship phenomena. In this volume, there are chapters explicitly dedicated to extending IT by drawing these connections. We see the strongest evidence of this move toward meta-theory in chapters that connect IT with attachment theory (Chapters 5 and 7), and self-theories (Chapters 10–12). In addition, we present chapters that present social psychological perspectives on what interdependence is (Chapters 1 and 2), as well as those that present sociological perspectives (Chapters 3 and 4), clinical psychological applications (Chapter 8), and life history approaches (Chapters 13 and 15). Collectively, the diversity of topics, author expertise, and connections drawn in the chapters that follow depict how rich and fruitful meta-theoretical approaches to relationship science are.

Finally, many of the chapters in the volume embrace the current era of methodological and statistical advancement and extend the more theoretical elements of IT to make them explicitly measurable. We present chapters depicting the myriad different methodological choices available to close relationship scholars, including experimental designs (Chapter 16), trajectory tracking (Chapter 15), self-report measures (Chapter 14), archival research (Chapter 4), and momentary assessments (Chapter 1). The importance of methods and statistics to relationship scientists is evident even in chapters not explicitly dedicated to method and statistical topics, as it sets the backdrop for how the theories were built and the findings obtained throughout this volume.

It is also valuable to explicitly reflect on the types of extensions that are likely to occur in the future. The time since Thibaut and Kelley's first seminal work has been one of rapid methodological and statistical advance. Techniques for statistically modelling context and dependence are now well-established, allowing for sophisticated treatments of entire life spaces. These spaces span time (e.g., as described in Sprecher's chapter on how closeness builds temporally, or in Agnew and colleagues chapter on how people are more or less ready for commitment at various times), place (e.g., an example of which is contained in Chopik's chapter on geographical mapping), and interaction partners (e.g., as alluded to in most chapters, but especially in Nakamura and colleagues' chapter on how partners influence each others' attachment security). One example of the kinds of outcomes we can expect from this additional sophistication is summarized by Columbus and colleagues, in Chapter 1, when they describe research measuring how strongly those in interdependent relationships' interests and power correspond. Whereas previous generations of research on interdependent processes hypothesized about the dimensions of interdependence (e.g., mutuality of dependence), current generations have the tools to actually measure those dimensions and assess the contributors and outcomes of them. This will allow for IT to expand in scope, from predominately being valuable in characterizing interdependent relationships, to being omniscient regarding the future of those interdependent relationships.

The behavioral sciences have not only advanced methodologically since Thibaut and Kelley's first IT writings, but they have also advanced theoretically. Other theories of human behavior and relationships have flourished, and now scholars are in the nascent phases of integrating these theories. In this volume, examples of this abound. For example, Hunt and colleagues examine how interdependence constructs explain change in attachment style, Mattingly and colleagues write about how interdependence can contribute to self-expansion goals, and Lemay describes how interdependent goals can shape prosocial behavior. This is truly a remarkable moment for relationship science; theories originating from diverse perspectives and built by unaffiliated scholars can easily be woven together and empirically tested using common methods. It is thus safe to say that a paradigm now exists in relationship science. That is, we now have a shared constellation of beliefs, values, and techniques that allow for those from diverse theoretical perspectives to converge on core tenets. Going forward with a paradigm, the focus of relationship scientists is likely to shift. Prior to now, research has been focused on examining fundamentals (e.g., do people have stable attachment styles? How do interdependent partners weigh the risks and rewards of interdependence?). Now, research is likely to turn its attention toward assuming these fundamentals as true and using them to solve puzzles (e.g., how do relationships stay satisfying over time?).

Collectively, this volume combines chapters from an accomplished set of scholars spanning scientific disciplines. It is our hope that organizing and reflecting on the manner in which Interdependence Theory core themes have been extended and applied can inform future research on interdependent processes and serve as a reminder of the overwhelming power of relationships, interaction, and interdependence.

REFERENCES

Kelley, H. H., Holmes, J. G., Kerr, N. L., Reis, H. T., Rusbult, C. E., & Van Lange, P. A. M. (2003). *An Atlas of Interpersonal Situations*. Cambridge: Cambridge University Press. doi.org/10.1017/CBO9780511499845

Rusbult, C. E. & Van Lange, P. A. M. (2003). Interdependence, interaction, and relationships. *Annual Review of Psychology*, 54, 351–375. doi.org/10.1146/annurev.psych.54.101601.145059

Thibaut, J. W. & Kelley, H. H. (1959). *The Social Psychology of Groups*. New York: Wiley.

VanderDrift, L. E. & Agnew, C. R. (2020). Interdependence perspectives on relationship maintenance. In B. G. Ogolsky & J. K. Monk (Eds.), *Relationship Maintenance: Theory, Process, and Context* (pp. 15–28). Cambridge: Cambridge University Press.

PART I

INTERDEPENDENCE, SITUATIONS, AND CONTEXT

Situations in Close Relationships

SIMON COLUMBUS, FRANCESCA RIGHETTI, AND
DANIEL BALLIET

Imagine Ahmed and Bouke, generally a happy couple – just their musical tastes don't match: While Ahmed prefers classical music, Bouke is more into electronica. On a particular evening, our couple feel like relaxing at home. If both were to turn on their music, there would be a cacophony that would make neither happy, so a quiet apartment could be an acceptable compromise. Still, Ahmed might be happier if he put on a rendition of a Beethoven symphony, and Bouke may not be too pained by it. Bouke's favorite Venetian Snares, in contrast, would quickly drive Ahmed out of the house.

Interdependence Theory has arisen from thinking about these types of situations partners experience together in close relationships (Kelley & Thibaut, 1978; Kelley et al., 2003; Thibaut & Kelley, 1959). Its analysis focuses on how the structure of the situation determines each partner's outcomes – their tangible and psychological costs and benefits. The theory identifies four dimensions of interdependence: mutual dependence (the degree to which partners control each other's outcomes), the basis of interdependence (whether interdependence arises from social exchange – i.e., each partner controlling the other's outcomes – or from the need for coordination on joint action), conflict of interests (the degree to which one partner's gain is the other partner's loss), and power (the degree to which one partner has more control over their counterpart's outcomes than vice-versa). In addition, two dimensions index uncertainty: information certainty (the degree to which people are certain or uncertain about the consequences of their own and the other's actions in the situation) and future interdependence (the degree to which behavior in the current situation influences interdependence in future situations) (Kelley et al., 2003).

In this chapter, we focus on mutual dependence, conflict of interests, and power. Analyzing our example along these three dimensions tells us that

This project was supported by an ERC Starting Grant (#635356) awarded to Daniel Balliet.

Ahmed and Bouke are mutually dependent: Their actions (whether to turn on their preferred music) affect their own and their partner's outcomes. There is also a degree of conflict of interests between them, as their preferred outcomes (which music is playing) do not align. Finally, we may consider that Bouke has more power in this situation than Ahmed does, as Ahmed's well-being depends more on Bouke's behavior (he'd be driven out of the house by Bouke's favorite music) than Bouke's well-being depends on Ahmed's (Bouke could live with Ahmed's choice of music, even if it's not his favorite). Yet, other situations may involve greater independence, more corresponding interests, or a different balance of power.

Interdependence Theory is uniquely positioned to answer the call to ground the science of relationships on an analysis of situations (Reis, 2008). This call suggests that even though each partner may have their own interpretation of a situation, their construal is grounded in objective features of the situation and organized along universal (or at least widely shared) dimensions. Over the last decade, situation research has made major advances in conceptualizing what a situation is, clearly distinguishing objective properties from the mental representation of situation characteristics (Rauthmann, Sherman, & Funder, 2015), and focusing its taxonomic efforts on the latter. Several new taxonomies and accompanying measures of both general and specifically social situation characteristics are now available (general: CAPTIONs, Parrigon, Woo, Tay, & Wang, 2017; DIAMONDS, Rauthmann et al., 2014; social: FIT/SIS, Balliet, Tybur, & van Lange, 2017; Gerpott, Balliet, Columbus, Molho, & de Vries, 2018; SAAP, Brown, Neel, & Sherman, 2015), and advances in experience sampling methodology make it possible to accurately measure the psychological experience of situations in daily life (for methodological introductions, see Bolger & Laurenceau, 2013; Mehl & Conner, 2013).

Most interesting to relationship researchers working in the tradition of Interdependence Theory, Functional Interdependence Theory proposes that people are able to assess their situational interdependence along the dimensions proposed by interdependence theorists (Balliet et al., 2017): Mutual dependence, coordination versus social exchange, conflict of interests, and power. A new measure – the Situational Interdependence Scale – also makes it possible to measure these perceptions (SIS, Gerpott et al., 2018).[1] Coupled with intensively longitudinal methods that sample situations from the daily lives of couples, these new theories and measures promise further insights into interdependence in close relationships.

---

[1] The SIS measures perceptions of mutual dependence, conflict of interests, and power, as well as future interdependence and information certainty, as indicated in the third section of Table 1.1. The SIS omits social exchange versus coordination given the lack of evidence that people can distinguish situations along this dimension (Gerpott et al., 2018).

In the following, we first present an overview of recent developments in situation research, introducing new taxonomies and measures that can be useful to relationship researchers. We specifically discuss Functional Interdependence Theory (Balliet et al., 2017) and the Situational Interdependence Scale (Gerpott et al., 2018), and highlight a first application in the field of relationship research (Columbus, Molho, Righetti, & Balliet, 2019). Subsequently, we discuss potential applications of measuring situational interdependence in daily life to questions related to Interdependence Theory, Attachment Theory, and relationship maintenance behaviors such as responsiveness, sacrifice, and forgiveness. We conclude by providing a broad framework for asking questions about situational interdependence in the context of close relationships.

RECENT ADVANCES IN SITUATION RESEARCH

Situation research has experienced a revival in recent years. This has been part a response to sustained calls to provide a basis for the oft-repeated claim of "the power of the situation" (Holmes, 2002; Reis, 2008), and part an attempt to substantiate accounts of personality rooted in cross-situational stability (Funder, 2001; Mischel & Shoda, 1995). The call for innovation in situation research has been answered by the development of new frameworks for studying psychological properties of situations (Balliet et al., 2017; Horstmann & Ziegler, 2016; Rauthmann et al., 2015), new measures to assess how people think about situations (Horstmann, Rauthmann, & Sherman, 2018; Molho & Balliet, 2017), and new data collection methods to access situations in daily life.

Frameworks for Studying Situation Perception

New frameworks have brought conceptual clarity to ontological questions in the study of situations. A prominent account (Rauthmann et al., 2015) distinguishes between situation cues, situation characteristics, and classes of situations as three distinct subjects of study. The distinction between cues – objective properties of the physical or social situation – and characteristics – the psychological situation constructed by the subject from external and internal inputs – distinguishes the major efforts at a situation taxonomy, and has a long history in psychological theorizing. For example, Murray (1938) distinguished between "alpha press" – the objective account of an environment's impact on a person's behavior – and "beta press" – the influence of the subject's own interpretation of the environment. Later accounts arising in the wake of the person-situation debate of the 1970s similarly distinguished between physically observable and subjective features of situations (Block & Block, 1981; Saucier, Bel-Bahar, & Fernandez, 2007).

Much attention has been paid to objective features of situations that Rauthmann et al. (2015) refer to as "cues." These features correspond to the alpha press of Murray's theory: the physical and social aspects of a situation that could be recorded by an outside observer. More recent work has disentangled situation cues into answers to five simple "W-questions": Who is with you in the situation? Which objects are present? What is happening? Where are you? When is it happening? (Pervin, 1978). In other words, situation cues can be classed into a) persons and relationships; b) objects; c) events and activities; d) locations; and e) time. Despite the intuitive appeal of this classification, however, little progress has been made toward a useful taxonomy of objective situation cues (Horstmann et al., 2018; Saucier et al., 2007).

Rather than to focus on cues, a recent wave of situation taxonomies has instead centered on psychological situation characteristics (Brown et al., 2015; Gerpott et al., 2018; Parrigon et al., 2017; Rauthmann et al., 2014). Corresponding to Murray's beta press, these are the psychologically relevant meanings of cues or abstract mental representations of psychologically meaningful variables constructed from internal and external inputs (Balliet et al., 2017; Rauthmann et al., 2015). Rauthmann et al. (2015) classify these inputs into person factors such as traits, habits, knowledge, the person's social roles, and affective or motivational states on one hand, and situation factors corresponding to the above-mentioned W-questions on the other hand. Person factors thus include both states and traits of the person (cf. Gerpott et al., 2018). In parallel, we may also distinguish more fleeting, state-like aspects of the situation and more stable (or trait-like) aspects of an environment (Asendorpf, 2015). Perennial issues in a relationship, for example, may be thought of as situation "traits" in this way. In a given situation, all of these aspects then form the input for psychological situation characteristics.

Functional Interdependence Theory Functional Interdependence Theory (FIT) is a theoretical account integrating Interdependence Theory (Kelley & Thibaut, 1978; Kelley et al., 2003) with principles of evolutionary psychology to explain why and how people are able to make sense of outcome interdependence in social situations (Balliet et al., 2017). From Interdependence Theory, it takes the major dimensions of interdependence and the idea that behavior is a consequence of the objective features of interdependence (i.e., the "structure" of a situation), together with each person's goals and expectations (Holmes, 2002). From evolutionary psychology, FIT takes a computational model of the mind, in which situation characteristics are the result of computations from cues and can in turn be fed into other computations and behavior.

Our human ancestors must have experienced a wide variety of interdependent situations in their dealings with others, and so FIT proposes that the human mind is adapted to navigating interdependent situations. This means that people are attentive to cues of interdependence in their environment and condition their behavior on their perceptions of interdependence. Indeed, people are attentive to cues of interdependence, such as others' eye gaze (Emery, 2000), nonverbal behavior (Hall, Coats, & LeBeau, 2005), and emotional expressions (e.g., Berdahl & Martorana, 2006).

Recent research shows that, more comprehensively, people respond to cues of interdependence along the multiple dimensions proposed by Interdependence Theory in both their perceptions and behavior (Gerpott et al., 2018). For example, people infer conflict of interests from a person's crossed arms (Gerpott et al., 2018), and use their counterpart's emotional expressions to tell how much power they hold in a negotiation (Columbus & Balliet, 2018; Pietroni, van Kleef, de Dreu, & Pagliaro, 2008; Pietroni, van Kleef, Rubaltelli, & Rumiati, 2009). This suggests that people are able to make use of cues in their social environment to estimate their interdependence with others in specific situations.

According to FIT, information about interdependence is organized in the form of internal regulatory variables (Tooby, Cosmides, Sell, Lieberman, & Sznycer, 2008). These variables integrate information from multiple sources, which may have the form of cues in the (social) environment – such as the presence and behavior of other people, their status, or the subject's relationship to them – but also other internal regulatory variables, such as a kinship index (Lieberman, Tooby, & Cosmides, 2007). In turn, these indices of interdependence can feed into other internal regulatory variables but also, and perhaps more importantly, impact behavior. Going back to our initial example, Ahmed may consider cues of Bouke's current mood to determine how much their musical wishes are in conflict in this situation. Concluding that Bouke seems upbeat, Ahmed may infer that his partner won't mind some Beethoven too much – their conflict of interests is limited. This perception of conflict then influences his decision to turn on the Symphony No. 3. As in this example, the internal regulatory variables proposed by FIT thus provide the link between the cues in a given situation an individual encounters and posited psychological and behavioral consequences of situational interdependence. This account can be tested and compared with other models via recent developments in situation taxonomies and the measurement of psychological characteristics of situations.

New Taxonomies and Measures

In recent years, a number of new taxonomies have been developed to classify the psychological characteristics of situations (for a historical overview, see Horstmann et al., 2018). In contrast to previous efforts in this direction, these taxonomies are also accompanied by validated measurement scales. For the first time, this makes it feasible for researchers to study the psychological representation of situations in close relationships using validated measures. New taxonomies and measures include the Situational Eight DIAMONDS (Rauthmann et al., 2014), CAPTIONs (Parrigon et al., 2017), and the Situational Interdependence Scale (SIS, Gerpott et al., 2018). Other notable developments are the Situational Affordances for Adaptive Problems measure (SAAP, Brown et al., 2015) and the Big Five Inventory of Occupational Situations (Ziegler, 2014).

These taxonomies have been developed in different ways and are motivated by different applications. Both CAPTIONs and Situation 5 were developed using a lexical approach, by sampling adjectives that apply to situations – in analogy to the development of the Big 5 and HEXACO personality factor models (Ashton & Lee, 2005; Goldberg, 1982; John, Angleitner, & Ostendorf, 1988). DIAMONDS was developed by adaptation of a personality measure (the California Adult Q-sort) to describe situations (Rauthmann et al., 2014; Wagerman & Funder, 2009). In contrast, both SIS and SAAP were developed using a theory-driven approach, informed by evolutionary theory and, in the case of the SIS, directly based on dimensions of situations posited in Interdependence Theory (Balliet et al., 2017; Gerpott et al., 2018; Kelley & Thibaut, 1978; Kelley et al., 2003). The SIS is also unique in being based on a theoretical account of how people think about interdependence in situations (Balliet et al., 2017).

Different taxonomies can be applied to different sets of situations. CAPTIONs and DIAMONDS can be used to describe all situations, whereas SIS and SAAP are designed to describe situations involving social interactions. In contrast to these rather general scales, the Situation 5 was specifically designed to be used in an occupational context. These differences in focus suggest that each taxonomy and measure may be appropriate for use in specific contexts. Moreover, integration may not result in the development of a single, overarching taxonomy, but rather in a nomological network describing the interrelations between factors in the different taxonomies (Horstmann et al., 2018). Nevertheless, it has been pointed out that there is significant overlap in the dimensions of DIAMONDS and CAPTIONs (Horstmann et al., 2018; Rauthmann & Sherman, 2017).

In contrast, the DIAMONDS and CAPTIONs dimensions do not map on the dimensions of interdependence assessed by the SIS. Indeed, correlations between DIAMONDS and SIS ratings of situations tend to be low (Gerpott et al., 2018). The SIS dimension of Conflict of Interests shows a mid-sized correlation with the DIAMONDS dimensions of Adversity and (negatively) pOsitivity. Adversity is also negatively associated with the SIS dimension of Information Certainty (Gerpott et al., 2018). Some SIS dimensions, however, such as Mutual Dependence and Power, display little, if any, correlation with

TABLE 1.1 Dimensions, descriptions, and sample items of the SIS, DIAMONDS, and CAPTIONs taxonomies and scales.

Dimensions	Description	Sample Items (Source Scale)
CAPTIONs		**28-item CAPTIONs-SF (Parrigon et al., 2017)**
Complexity	The extent to which the situation involves emotional or ethical complexity, or requires learning and deep thought.	analytical, scholarly
Adversity	The extent to which the situation is difficult and depleting and involves exertion of physical or mental resources.	stressful, tiresome
Positive Valence	The extent to which the situation involves intimacy, personal warmth, or general positivity.	cherished, heartwarming
Typicality	The extent to which the situation is common and straightforward in nature, as opposed to involving novelty and ambiguity.	regular, standard
Importance	The extent to which the situation is important for attaining one's goals.	useful, productive
humOr	The extent "to which the situation is humorous or lighthearted" (Parrigon et al., 2017, p. 656).	wacky, goofy
Negative Valence	The extent to which the situation is sinister or involves malice.	repulsive, malicious
DIAMONDS		**S8-I (Rauthmann & Sherman, 2016)**
Duty	The extent to which work or a task needs to be done.	Work has to be done.
Intellect	The extent to which the situation requires intellectual engagement or poses cognitive demands.	Deep thinking is required.
Adversity	The extent to which someone is threatened or that problems exist in the situation.	Somebody is being threatened, accused, or criticized.
Mating	The extent to which a situation is "conducive to sex, love, and romance" (Rauthmann et al., 2014, p. 708).	Potential romantic partners are present.
pOsitivity	The extent to which the situation is pleasant.	The situation is pleasant.

TABLE 1.1 (*cont.*)

Dimensions	Description	Sample Items (Source Scale)
Negativity	The extent to which the situation may give rise to negative feelings.	The situation contains negative feelings (e.g., stress, anxiety, guilt, etc.).
Deception	The extent to which there is mistrust, lying, or hostility in the situation.	Somebody is being deceived.
Sociality	The extent to which social interaction occurs and is important, especially if it is pleasant.	Social interactions are possible or required.
Situational Interdependence Scale		**10-item SIS-short (Gerpott et al., 2018)**
Mutual Dependence	The extent to which each person's outcomes depend on the other person's behavior.	What each of us does in this situation affects the other.
Conflict of Interests	The extent of conflict of interests – the degree to which one person's outcomes negatively affect the other person's outcomes.	Our preferred outcomes in this situation are conflicting.
Power	The asymmetry of dependence – the extent to which one person depends more on the other than vice-versa.	Who do you feel had more power to determine their own outcome in this situation?*
Future Interdependence	The extent to which behavior in the current situation affects the nature of future interactions.	How we behave now will have consequences for future outcomes.
Information Certainty	The extent to which each person knows how their own and the other person's actions affect each other's outcomes.	We both know what the other wants.

Note: * indicates items answered on a Likert scale, *1 = Completely the other, 3 = Both equally, 5 = Completely Myself.* All other items are answered on a standard Likert-type response scale (Strongly Agree–Strongly Disagree). See source papers for detailed instructions.

the DIAMONDS dimensions (Gerpott et al., 2018). Similarly, DIAMONDS dimensions such as Intellect and Mating are not associated with ratings on the SIS (Gerpott et al., 2018). This indicates that broad taxonomies of everyday situations, such as DIAMONDS and CAPTIONs, may measure different aspects of situations than more narrowly focused taxonomies such as the SIS.

How should a researcher choose a taxonomy of situations and the corresponding measure? Different applications may call for different uses.[2] Scales such as DIAMONDS and CAPTIONs are applicable to a broad range of everyday situations, many of which may not involve social interactions. Scales that are designed to measure interdependence (SIS) or affordances in social interactions (SAAP) may not be useable in this case. Researchers interested in relationships, however, may appreciate the theoretical grounding of the SIS in Interdependence Theory and its precision in analyzing social interactions. The dimensions of the SIS find their equivalence in constructs studied by relationship researchers, such as mutual dependence, conflict, or power, enabling an interested researcher to draw on rich theory in developing hypotheses about situational influences.

STUDYING SITUATIONS USING EXPERIMENTS
AND IN DAILY LIFE

The situations people experience throughout their daily lives can vary tremendously. A researcher studying situations will thus often be interested in intra-personal variation or consistency in motivation, cognition, and behavior across various situations. Such questions can be answered by exposing participants to different situations in the laboratory (e.g., Leikas, Lönnqvist, & Verkasalo, 2012). Yet, it may not always be clear what properties of the experimental situation are efficacious psychologically. Including scales that measure situation perception could thus help elucidate how manipulations influence behavior (e.g., Columbus, Münich, & Gerpott, 2019).

However, many relationship researchers may move beyond a lab setting to examine interactions in daily life. They may be interested in the structure of everyday experience and intra-personal variation across naturally occurring situations (i.e., an idiographic approach modeling each individual's behavior; Conner, Tennen, Fleeson, & Feldman Barrett, 2009), or in predicting future situations from past situations. New methods are making it increasingly feasible to collect data on situations in everyday life in or close to the situation. Although diary and experience sampling methods have a long history in psychological research, they have long been difficult and expensive to administer. The rise of smartphones and the mobile web, however, makes it

---

[2] The use of a specific scale may also be motivated by requirements of conciseness and the availability of translations. However, short versions exist of the DIAMONDS (eight items, one per dimension, see Rauthmann & Sherman, 2016), CAPTIONs (seven and fourteen items, one or two per dimension), and SIS (ten items, two per dimension). DIAMONDS and SIS have also been translated into several different languages. For translations of the SIS, see https:// amsterdamcooperationlab.com/sis/.

easy to administer experience sampling surveys at comparably low cost, and allow for assessment of behavior shortly after it occurs.

Ambulatory assessment methods can be broadly distinguished into diary and experience sampling studies. Diary studies involve a single, daily survey, often administered at the end of the day, similar to a classic diary. These surveys can be longer, taking up to ten minutes every day, and may even involve simple implicit measures (e.g., an IAT) or a small experimental component. Diary studies, being less taxing on participants than experience sampling, may also run longer, up to several weeks at a time.

Experience sampling, in contrast, involves several short surveys over the course of a day. A key distinction is between variable time-based, fixed time-based, and event-based sampling of situations (Conner et al., 2009). Variable time-based sampling involves surveys administered at (semi-) random times throughout the day. It reduces issues of memory bias and is well-suited for studying ongoing phenomena, such as situations or mood. Because situations are sampled randomly this way, this is the most suitable approach for studying the patterns of situations in everyday life. Fixed time-based sampling involves surveys administered on a predictable schedule. It may pose a lighter load on participants but causes greater concerns of memory bias and involves non-random sampling of situations. Consequently, fixed time-based sampling may omit situations that do not occur around the specific time of assessment. However, for relationship researchers, it may help increase the number of surveys to which both partners reply. Finally, event-sampling involves reports initiated usually by the participant every time a given event occurs. This is the best approach for studying events that have a low frequency or very specific characteristics that make them unique, either of which might be missed in time-based sampling. For example, Interdependence Theory highlights "diagnostic situations" such as (severe) conflicts of interest, and researchers interested in these situations specifically may prefer event-based sampling.

STUDYING NATURALLY OCCURRING SITUATIONS IN CLOSE RELATIONSHIPS

Studying situations in close relationships poses particular challenges. Oftentimes, a researcher may be interested in obtaining reports from both partners regarding the same situations. Different approaches may yield different rates of success with this aim, but also come with different biases.

A way to make sure partners report on the same situation is to instruct them to coordinate before making their report ("joint recall"). This may yield rates of alignment above 90 percent. However, it could also mean that partners discuss the situation before completing measures and influence each other's perception of the situation, or that they selectively choose to report particular types of situations (e.g., omitting high conflict situations). Providing partners with an anchoring time point (e.g., "the first situation after 10:00 today") may help limit the problem of selection, but some problems are likely to remain, such as outsized influence of a more powerful partner on selecting the situation to report. Moreover, asking partners to coordinate their reports is only feasible for diary studies or designs that do not involve multiple assessments throughout the day.

Another approach is to ask partners to report situations individually but contact them at the same (variable) time ("individual recall"). Partners can then be asked to report about the last situation they experienced with each other. This approach, however, can reduce the amount of available data for at least two reasons. First, there could be many instances in which partners did not experience a dyadic interaction since the previous signal. Second, even if they report on a situation, partners may report on different situations, but participants' own indication of the timing of a situation is often too unreliable to match their reports. It is then important to ask participants to briefly describe the situation and code afterwards whether they reported on the same situation. This may mean a much lower response rate than achieved with joint recall but may often be the only feasible option when using experience sampling.[3]

Situations in Close Relationships: The Interdependence in
Daily Life-Couples Study

In a first application of the Situational Interdependence Scale to relationship research, we have conducted an experience sampling study on a diverse sample of 139 Dutch couples. After an intake session, during which we assessed various personality and attitude measures as well as relationship-relevant constructs, the couples participated in a week-long experience sampling phase. During this phase, they were prompted simultaneously to complete seven short surveys a day. The surveys asked each participant to report the last situation they had experienced with their partner by answering four W-questions (When? Where? With whom? What did you do, and what happened?) and to rate the situation on the 10-item short form of the SIS, alongside some other situational measures. More details of the Interdependence in Daily Life Study are described in Columbus, Molho, Righetti, and Balliet (n.d.).

---

[3] For example, Columbus, Molho et al. (2019) contacted participants with a total of 13,622 surveys and obtained 11,122 responses. However, only 6,766 responses reported on a situation the subject had experienced with their partner. For 5,152 of these responses, both partners responded to the same survey (2,576 situation) and, of these, 3,576 responses (1,788 situations) were rated as actually involving the same situation.

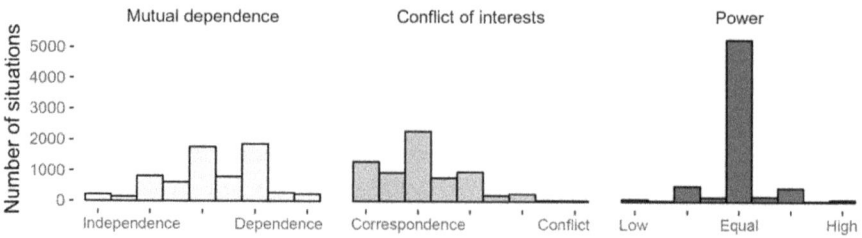

FIGURE 1.1 Distributions of perceived mutual dependence, conflict of interests, and power in interactions between romantic partners (n = 278, k = 6,766 situations)

First results reported in Columbus, Molho et al. (2019) show significant agreement between partners on their perception of the situation on the SIS, attesting to the reliability of the measure. Interestingly, greater agreement on the structure of situations predicted greater relationship satisfaction (Rentzsch, Columbus, Balliet, & Gerlach, n.d.). Couples mostly experienced situations involving corresponding interests and equal power, with significant spread in mutual dependence (see Figure 1.1). Moreover, one partner's perception of the couple's interdependence in a given situation predicted the other partner's rating of their cooperation in the situation. In particular, mutual dependence was associated with increased cooperation, and conflict of interests with decreased cooperation; power did not show a relationship with behavior. These initial results highlight the variety of interdependent situations couples experience, but also how the experience and perception of interdependence relates to relationship-relevant emotions, cognitions, and behaviors. Thus, these findings illustrate how situational measures of interdependence in daily life can answer new questions in relationship research. In the next section, we discuss potential avenues for research in the traditions of Interdependence Theory and Attachment Theory, and on relationship maintenance behaviors such as responsiveness, sacrifice, and forgiveness.

APPLICATIONS IN RELATIONSHIP RESEARCH

Theoretical Perspectives

Interdependence Theory and the Investment Model Researchers working in the tradition of Interdependence Theory (Kelley & Thibaut, 1978; Kelley et al., 2003) and its descendants, including the Investment Model (Rusbult, 1980; Rusbult, Agnew, & Arriaga, 2012; Rusbult, Martz, & Agnew, 1998), explicitly study the experience of interdependent situations in close relationships (Reis & Arriaga, 2014; Rusbult & van Lange, 2003). Their work highlights that situational, but also personal and relationship characteristics shape situation perceptions (Arriaga, 2013; Campbell, Simpson, Boldry, & Rubin,

2010; Simpson, Campbell, & Weisberg, 2006). Interdependence theory, in particular, emphasizes the transformation of situations in light of individuals' goals. It posits that individuals may consider the long-term consequences of their actions, react to norms and rules, or account for their partner's outcomes – all of which can transform the interdependence structure of a situation as they perceive it (Kelley & Thibaut, 1978; Yovetich & Rusbult, 1994). For example, a situation may appear less conflictful in light of future interactions involving opportunities for mutual gain. The Investment Model further distinguishes dependence – "the descriptive, structural state of a relationship" – from commitment – "the psychological experience of that state" (Le & Agnew, 2003, p. 38) which involves feelings of attachment and the intent to sustain the relationship (Rusbult et al., 1998, 2012).

Research using both manipulated and self-reported interdependent situations shows the effect of different dimensions of interdependence on individual and relationship outcomes. For example, both high and low power have been linked to negative affect, reduced investments and commitment, and lower relationship satisfaction (high power: Lennon, Stewart, & Ledermann, 2013; Righetti et al., 2015; low power: Murray, Holmes, & Pinkus, 2010; Simpson, Farrell, Oriña, & Rothman, 2015). Commitment – strongly related to the experience of dependence – is consistently linked to higher relationship satisfaction and relationship persistence (Le & Agnew, 2003; Le, Dove, Agnew, Korn, & Mutso, 2010). Conflict of interests is linked to negative affect and behaviors (Columbus, Molho et al., 2019; Durante, Eastwick, Finkel, Gangestad, & Simpson, 2016; Righetti, Gere, Hofmann, Visserman, & van Lange, 2016; Simpson, Rholes, & Phillips, 1996). Even coordination can be challenging to achieve in close relationships (Finkel et al., 2006). The effects of interdependent situations also carry over to future interactions, affecting whether people select to enter dependent situations with their partner (Kelley et al., 2003; Reis & Arriaga, 2014). For example, the experience of dependence and conflict may, under some circumstances, result in the escalation of commitment (Gordon, Impett, Kogan, Oveis, & Keltner, 2012; Murray & Holmes, 2009).

The Investment Model builds on the analysis of dyadic situations in Interdependence Theory. However, the model focuses on how three bases of dependence in a relationship (investment size, relationship satisfaction, and quality of alternatives) relate to the subjective experience of commitment (Rusbult, 1980; Rusbult et al., 1998, 2012). This analysis does not account for how interdependence may vary from situation to situation within a relationship. Incidentally, research in this tradition has also largely neglected the multidimensional nature of interdependence. A focus on situational interdependence can inform research on the Investment Model in at least two ways.

First, researchers may ask how the bases of dependence give rise to daily experiences of mutual dependence, conflict of interests, or power. For example, individuals who perceive their alternatives to be of higher quality than their partner does may hold more power than their partner in daily interactions. In turn, these situational experiences may translate into a sense of (lower) commitment (cf. Drigotas & Rusbult, 1992). It has been theorized that the latter effect of interdependent situations on commitment and relationship perseverance is mediated by affective responses (Rusbult & van Lange, 2003). For example, conflicts of interests may give rise to both anger and disgust (e.g., Gerpott et al., 2018). Yet, while anger often dissipates quickly, disgust may have a more long-lasting impact on relationship outcomes (Hutcherson & Gross, 2011).

Second, the experience of interdependent situations may also feed back to reshape the bases of dependence. For example, recurrently encountering conflicts of interests with one's partner may decrease relationship satisfaction, while deciding to sacrifice in such situations may increase the investment size (Righetti et al., 2016; Rusbult et al., 1998). Thus, the experience of interdependent situations may both affect and be affected by the bases of dependence postulated by the Investment Model.

Several models have sprung from interdependence theory to explain how people navigate situations involving conflict and dependence. Murray and Holmes (2009) have proposed a motivation-management theory that posits that situational conflict of interests interacts with interpersonal trust to give each partner a sense of risk, which in turn affects the pursuit of connect and self-protect goals (Cavallo, Murray, & Holmes, 2014; Murray & Holmes, 2015). One implication is that chronic interpersonal trust affects perceptions of risk and goal pursuit more strongly in situations that are low in information certainty (Murray & Holmes, 2009, 2015). Connect goals lead individuals to escalate their dependence on their partner, and to justify their commitment (Murray et al., 2009b). Self-protect goals, in contrast, lead them to withhold commitment, and escalate their partner's dependence. Each partner's responsiveness is then thought to inform updated trust (Murray et al., 2009a).

What emerges is a sophisticated account of how individual differences (e.g., self-esteem, Gomillion & Murray, 2014) and relationship history (via trust, Murray & Holmes, 2009; Murray, Holmes, Griffin, & Derrick, 2015) shape expectations about one's partner (Holmes, 2002) and the pursuit of interpersonal goals. One hypothesis is that these factors determine whether an individual will accommodate their partner in a high-conflict situation (Rusbult, Verette, Whitney, Slovik, & Lipkus, 1991; Yovetich & Rusbult, 1994). Another is that the pursuit of connect and self-protect goals should influence the degree of dependence they experience in subsequent situations, in that having connect goals will induce people to seek and encounter situations high in dependence, while having self-protection goals will induce people to seek situations low in dependence.

Attachment Theory Attachment theory has emerged from a developmental perspective to encompass relationship processes throughout the lifespan (Fraley & Shaver, 2000; Hazan & Shaver, 1987) and recent theorizing and empirical research increasingly probes intrapersonal dynamics within relationships (Arriaga, Kumashiro, Simpson, & Overall, 2017; Girme et al., 2018). Attachment styles are an important dimension of individual differences that determines the situations people seek out and how people respond to interdependent situations in the short- and long-term. They predict how comfortable individuals are with situations containing interdependence dilemmas in which they are forced to decide whether to escalate or reduce their dependence on an attachment figure (Bartz & Lydon, 2006). For example, the individual may be faced with the opportunity to express their romantic interest in the other. Such a situation is high in future interdependence (i.e., the individual's actions determine the degree and form of future interdependence with the other), but also in information uncertainty (i.e., the individual does not know whether the romantic interest is mutual). Individuals high in anxious attachment may be uncomfortable with such situations and seek to avoid them (Bartz & Lydon, 2006).

Individuals high in anxious attachment also perceive more frequent and severe conflict situations (Simpson et al., 2006), and respond more negatively to these situations, experiencing greater hurt and more negative emotions (Mikulincer & Shaver, 2005; Schoebi & Randall, 2015; Simpson et al., 1996; 2006). Attachment style also influences negative behaviors toward partners in response to dependence (Campbell, Simpson, Kashy, & Rholes, 2001) and accommodation in the face of conflict (Gaines et al., 1997). Recent work on the intrapersonal dynamics of adult attachment has also emphasized the context-dependent activation of the attachment system. This work suggests that the attachment system is particularly responsive to threatening situations, becoming activated when security needs are not met (Campbell & Marshall, 2011).

Attachment researchers have explored the relationship of trait-like adult attachment with the perceptions, selection, and response to interdependent situations. However, much of this work has focused on individual dimensions – in particular conflict – and outside a more comprehensive, multidimensional framework of interdependence. On the other hand, interdependence theorists have paid limited attention to individual differences in the perception and selection of situations. Attachment theory makes direct predictions about the perception and selection of interdependent situations. In particular, anxious attachment should predict both increased perceptions of conflict of interests (Simpson et al., 2006) and information uncertainty. Moreover, individuals high in anxious attachment might be expected to select situations involving high mutual dependence. In contrast, avoidant attachment may be associated with heightened perception of mutual dependence and avoidance of such situations. A key distinction between insecure attachment styles may be the avoidance (in avoidant individuals) versus selection (in anxious individuals) of situations in which the individual has low power relative to their partner.

Recent work has started to explore the dynamic nature of adult attachment and in particular the activation of the attachment system by situations within a relationship (Arriaga et al., 2017; Campbell & Marshall, 2011). Specifically, Arriaga et al. (2017) have proposed an attachment security enhancement model (ASEM), which posits that insecurity-triggering situations evoke attachment processes. Borrowing the concept of "diagnostic situations" from interdependence theory, ASEM posits that certain situations trigger insecurity. These are situations involving conflicts of interest, power asymmetries, or low information certainty. Insecurity, in turn, can activate a need for greater interdependence, leading to anxious thoughts and feelings, or a need for greater independence, leading to avoidant thoughts and feelings. Moreover, the repeated experience of insecurity reinforces insecure expectations – that is, negative or defensive models of the self and ambiguous or negative models of others.

This account of within-person attachment processes explicitly links short-term motivations (need for interdependence or independence) to the experience of interdependent situations. Moreover, it highlights that intrapersonal attachment processes may affect situation selection both in the short-term (as motivations are enacted) and in the long-term (as working models are revised, shaping expectations about the self and others in interdependent situations). This directly calls for the study of attachment processes grounded in the experience of situational interdependence.

Relationship Maintenance Behaviors To maintain a relationship, partners need to engage in relationship maintenance behaviors, such as being responsive, sacrificing for their partner, and forgiving slights and transgressions. Such behaviors both occur in and shape the interdependent situations partners experience together. Perceived partner responsiveness (Reis, Clark, & Holmes, 2004) encompasses a number of constructs, such as reflected appraisal, emotional rapport, and responsiveness to needs. It is "the process by which individuals come to believe that relationship partners both attend to and react supportively to central, core defining features of the self" (ibid., p. 203).

What is perceived as responsive may depend on the structure of the situation, which affords the expression of some motives but not others (de Vries, Tybur, Pollet, & van Vugt, 2016). Situations in which responsive behavior comes with a cost (i.e., which involve a conflict of interest) may especially afford the expression of responsiveness. Indeed, the effect of support and conflict behaviors depends on the nature of the situation and on the personalities of the partners, especially their attachment styles (Overall & Simpson, 2015; Overall, Girme, & Simpson, 2016; Visserman, Righetti, Impett, Keltner, & van Lange, 2018). In particular, a tendency to respond to one's own dependence with responsive behavior predicts better relationship outcomes, but only in situations where one experiences high dependence (Overall & Sibley, 2008). However, situational factors have so far received less attention than person factors. This points toward further avenues for research exploring the context-dependence of responsive behavior.

Research into the antecedents and consequences of sacrifice has largely sprung from an interdependence tradition. Indeed, this research area is directly focused on the experience of mixed-motive situations, in which individuals can forego personal gain to benefit their partner (Righetti & Impett, 2017). Variations in the degree of conflict of interests may further affect whether people sacrifice and how this is perceived by their partner. In particular, sacrifice may be less likely to occur the higher the costs are. However, partners may in turn experience greater gratitude in response to sacrifices when they acknowledge the severity of the conflict of interests. Moreover, people may be more likely to sacrifice when they perceive greater future interdependence with their partner, in hope of reciprocation in the future. Finally, individuals high in commitment and trust are more likely to sacrifice for their partner (Etcheverry & Le, 2005; Powell & van Vugt, 2003; Shallcross & Simpson, 2012; van Lange et al., 1997), whereas those high in power are less willing to do so (Righetti et al., 2015). However, these predictors were, so far, only considered as traits. Power, but also mutual dependence, do however fluctuate from situation to situation (Columbus, Molho et al., 2019), giving rise to the question of whether situational factors affect the willingness to sacrifice in similar, or perhaps rather different ways than at the trait level.

When individuals fail to accommodate their partners' needs, they may yet be forgiven – their partner's negative feelings toward them do not have to be long-lasting. At times, partners may hurt each other or transgress relationship norms. Forgiveness is then necessary to re-establish a positive relationship. A recent meta-analysis showed forgiveness to be promoted by apology and state empathy, though intent and anger made it less likely (Fehr, Gelfand, & Nag, 2010). While state variables thus proved more important in predicting forgiveness than victim dispositions, few studies have probed the effects of situation characteristics. In one study, individuals who experienced more power were more likely to forgive, an effect further magnified in highly committed relationships (Karremans & Smith, 2010). However, beyond power, other features of interdependence may also affect willingness to forgive, such as the degree of conflict of interest and future interdependence. An individual's motivation to forgive a transgression may depend on their perception of the choices their partner faced (e.g., harm may be more easily pardoned if avoiding it would have required a significant sacrifice). In addition, there may be a forward-looking motivation to forgive in order to avoid future conflict. Moreover, forgiveness itself may have effects on partners' willingness to enter mutually dependent or conflictual situations, and their behavior in such situations. For example, one study showed that forgiveness promoted later closeness and commitment (Tsang, McCullough, & Fincham, 2006).

A Structure for Research on Situations in Relationships

Durante et al. (2016) have recently proposed that relationship research relies on (implicit) assumptions that partners, overall, experience largely corresponding interests. They also propose that this distinguishes the tradition of relationship research from evolutionary perspectives, which more strongly emphasize conflicts of interest. Although Durante et al. (2016) largely conceptualize interdependence and conflict of interests at the relationship level, their work nevertheless raises the question – at the purely descriptive level – of the pattern of interdependence that partners experience in a relationship.

First evidence by Columbus, Molho et al. (2019) reveals that it is not merely an assumption that couples experience largely corresponding interests. Couples predominantly reported situations involving corresponding interests and equal power, and a wide spread of mutual dependence. Starting from these purely descriptive results, future research may address a series of research questions on the experience of situational interdependence in couples. One set of questions relates to person-situation transactions: First, are there individual differences in the perception of situations? Second, when and how do individuals and couples select, evoke, or manipulate situations (Buss, 1987, 2009)? A second set of questions relate to the effects of situations and person-situation interactions: First, do different situations give rise to different behavior? Second, do individuals and couples differ in their response to particular situations, and, if so, what are the mechanisms by which they may regulate their reactions?

Person-situation transactions encompass the ways individual differences – in particular, personality – affect the perception, selection, evocation, and manipulation of situations. We assume that individuals arrive at a particular mental representation of a situation – in the form of situation characteristics – by a process of construal that relies of cues in the social environment as well as person factors (Rauthmann et al., 2015). Individuals differ in the way they access and weight cues, leading them to perceive situations differently. Such variation may reflect attachment styles: for example, individuals high in anxious attachment perceive more frequent and more severe conflicts of interests (Simpson et al., 2006). Individuals also select situations they enter or avoid, evoke situations by (unintentionally) eliciting reactions from others, and manipulate situations by (intentionally) altering them (Buss, 1987, 2009).

Recent work inspired by interdependence and attachment theories has proposed ways in which experiences of interdependence may have short- and long-term effects on the type of situations people experience, in part because of the ways they regulate risk, commitment, and attachment (Arriaga et al., 2017; Murray & Holmes, 2009).

Interdependent situations have direct relationship-relevant outcomes, including affective and behavioral responses. Columbus, Molho et al. (2019) revealed that the interdependence structure of situations directly predicts the degree of prosocial behavior toward the partner. However, interdependent situations also cause affective responses (Gerpott et al., 2018; Righetti et al., 2016), and may trigger the motivation-management system (Murray & Holmes, 2009) and attachment processes (Arriaga et al., 2017) proposed by recent theories.

Significant progress has also been made in understanding the importance of dyadic effects, highlighting in particular the importance of responsiveness to partners' needs (Reis et al., 2004; Reis & Gable, 2015). Yet, responses to interdependent situations should be expected to differ between individuals and between couples. For example, individuals high in anxious attachment experience more hurt as a consequence of conflicts of interests (Campbell, Simpson, Boldry, & Kashy, 2005). At the level of couples, partners may also develop patterns of responses that play out over time (Rusbult & van Lange, 2003). Further research into such person- and couple-situation interactions is clearly promising.

CONCLUSION

Research in the tradition of Interdependence Theory is research rooted in an appreciation of the importance of situations (Holmes, 2002; Kelley & Thibaut, 1978; Kelley et al., 2003; Reis, 2008). New frameworks and measures, such as Functional Interdependence Theory (Balliet et al., 2017) and the Situational Interdependence Scale (Gerpott et al., 2018), open new research trajectories by allowing the assessment of interdependent situations in daily life. Embarking on these trajectories can lead to a richer understanding of how couples select, shape, and navigate their interdependent relationships.

REFERENCES

Arriaga, X. B. (2013). An interdependence theory analysis of close relationships. In J. A. Simpson & L. Campbell (Eds.), *Oxford Handbook of Close Relationships* (pp. 39–65). Oxford: Oxford University Press.

Arriaga, X. B., Kumashiro, M., Simpson, J. A., & Overall, N. C. (2017). Revising working models across time: Relationship situations that enhance attachment security. *Personality and Social Psychology Review*, 22, 71–96. doi:10.1177/1088868317705257

Asendorpf, J. B. (2015). From the psychology of situations to the psychology of environments. *European Journal of Personality*, 29, 382–432. doi:10.1002/per.2005

Ashton, M. C. & Lee, K. (2005). A defence of the lexical approach to the study of personality structure. *European Journal of Personality*, 19, 5–24. doi:10.1002/per.541

Balliet, D., Tybur, J. M., & van Lange, P. A. M. (2017). Functional Interdependence Theory: An evolutionary account of social situations. *Personality and Social Psychology Review*, 21, 361–388. doi:10.1177/1088868316657965

Bartz, J. A. & Lydon, J. E. (2006). Navigating the interdependence dilemma: Attachment goals and the use of communal norms with potential close others. *Journal of Personality and Social Psychology*, 91, 77–96. doi:10.1037/0022-3514.91.1.77

Berdahl, J. L. & Martorana, P. (2006). Effects of power on emotion and expression during a controversial group discussion. *European Journal of Social Psychology*, 36, 497–509. doi:10.1002/ejsp.354

Block, J. & Block, J. (1981). Studying situational dimensions: A grand perspective and some limited empiricism. In D. Magnusson (Ed.), *Toward a Psychology of Situations: An Interactional Perspective* (pp. 85–106). Hillsdale, NJ: Erlbaum.

Bolger, N. & Laurenceau, J.-P. (2013). *Intensive Longitudinal Methods: An Introduction to Diary and Experience Sampling Research.* New York: Guilford.

Brown, N. A., Neel, R., & Sherman, R. A. (2015). Measuring the evolutionarily important goals of situations: Situational affordances for adaptive problems. *Evolutionary Psychology*, 13, 1–15. doi:10.1177/1474704915593662

Buss, D. M. (1987). Selection, evocation, and manipulation. *Journal of Personality and Social Psychology*, 53, 1214–1221. doi:10.1037/0022-3514.53.6.1214

Buss, D. M. (2009). An evolutionary formulation of person–situation interactions. *Journal of Research in Personality*, 43, 241–242. doi:10.1016/j.jrp.2008.12.019

Campbell, L. & Marshall, T. (2011). Anxious attachment and relationship processes: An interactionist perspective. *Journal of Personality*, 79, 917–947. doi:10.1111/j.1467-6494.2011.00723.x

Campbell, L., Simpson, J. A., Boldry, J., & Kashy, D. A. (2005). Perceptions of conflict and support in romantic relationships: The role of attachment anxiety. *Journal of Personality and Social Psychology*, 88, 510–531. doi:10.1037/0022-3514.88.3.510

Campbell, L., Simpson, J. A., Boldry, J. G., & Rubin, H. (2010). Trust, variability in relationship evaluations, and relationship processes. *Journal of Personality and Social Psychology*, 99, 14–31. doi:10.1037/a0019714

Campbell, L., Simpson, J. A., Kashy, D. A., & Rholes, W. S. (2001). Attachment orientations, dependence, and behavior in a stressful situation: An application of the Actor-Partner Interdependence Model. *Journal of Social and Personal Relationships*, 18, 821–843. doi:10.1177/0265407501186005

Cavallo, J. V., Murray, S. L., & Holmes, J. G. (2014). Risk regulation in close relationships. In M. Mikulincer & P. R. Shaver (Eds.), *Mechanisms of Social Connection: From Brain to Group* (pp. 237–254). Washington, DC: American Psychological Association.

Columbus, S. & Balliet, D. (2018). [Reverse appraisal of situation characteristics in negotiations]. Unpublished raw data.

Columbus, S., Molho, C., Righetti, F., & Balliet, D. (2019). *Interdependence and Cooperation in Daily Life*. Under review.

Columbus, S., Molho, C., Righetti, F., & Balliet, D. (n.d.). *The Interdependence in Daily Life Study*. Manuscript in preparation.

Columbus, S., Münich, J., & Gerpott, F. H. (2019). *Playing a Different Game: Situation Perception Mediates Framing Effects on Cooperative Behaviour*. Preprint. Retrieved from https://psyarxiv.com/gf7kz

Conner, T. S., Tennen, H., Fleeson, W., & Feldman Barrett, L. (2009). Experience sampling methods: A modern idiographic approach to personality research. *Social and Personality Psychology Compass*, 3, 292–313. doi:10.1111/j.1751-9004.2009.00170.x

de Vries, R. E., Tybur, J. M., Pollet, T. V., & van Vugt, M. (2016). Evolution, situational affordances, and the HEXACO model of personality. *Evolution and Human Behavior*, 37, 407–421. doi:10.1016/j.evolhumbehav.2016.04.001

Drigotas, S. M. & Rusbult, C. E. (1992). Should I stay or should I go?: A dependence model of breakups. *Journal of Personality and Social Psychology*, 62, 62–87.

Durante, K. M., Eastwick, P. W., Finkel, E. J., Gangestad, S. W., & Simpson, J. A. (2016). Pair-bonded relationships and romantic alternatives: Toward an integration of evolutionary and relationship science perspectives. In J. M. Olson & M. P. Zanna (Eds.), *Advances in Experimental Social Psychology* (Vol. 53, pp. 1–74). Burlington, MA: Academic Press. doi:10.1016/bs.aesp.2015.09.001

Emery, N. J. (2000). The eyes have it: The neuroethology, function and evolution of social gaze. *Neuroscience and Biobehavioral Reviews*, 24, 581–604. doi:10.1016/S0149-7634(00)00025-7

Etcheverry, P. E. & Le, B. (2005). Thinking about commitment: Accessibility of commitment and prediction of relationship persistence, accommodation, and willingness to sacrifice. *Personal Relationships*, 12, 103–123. doi:10.1111/j.1350-4126.2005.00104.x

Fehr, R., Gelfand, M. J., & Nag, M. (2010). The road to forgiveness: A meta-analytic synthesis of its situational and dispositional correlates. *Psychological Bulletin*, 136, 894–914. doi:10.1037/a0019993

Finkel, E. J., Campbell, W. K., Brunell, A. B., Dalton, A. N., Scarbeck, S. J., & Chartrand, T. L. (2006). High-maintenance interaction: Inefficient social coordination impairs self-regulation. *Journal of Personality and Social Psychology*, 91, 456–475. doi:10.1037/0022-3514.91.3.456

Fraley, R. C. & Shaver, P. R. (2000). Adult romantic attachment: Theoretical developments, emerging controversies, and unanswered questions. *Review of General Psychology*, 4, 132–154. doi:10.1037//1089-2680.4.2.132

Funder, D. C. (2001). Personality. *Annual Review of Psychology*, 52, 197–221.

Gaines, S. O., Reis, H. T., Summers, S., Rusbult, C. E., Cox, C. L., Wexler, M. O., . . . Kurland, G. J. (1997). Impact of attachment style on reactions to accommodative dilemmas in close relationships. *Personal Relationships*, 4, 93–113. doi:10.1111/j.1475-6811.1997.tb00133.x

Gerpott, F. H., Balliet, D., Columbus, S., Molho, C., & de Vries, R. E. (2018). How do people think about interdependence? Testing a multidimensional model of subjective outcome interdependence. *Journal of Personality and Social Psychology*, 115, 716–742. doi:10.1037/pspp0000166

Girme, Y. U., Agnew, C. R., VanderDrift, L. E., Harvey, S. M., Rholes, W. S., & Simpson, J. A. (2018). The ebbs and flows of attachment: Within-person variation in attachment undermine secure individuals' relationship wellbeing across time. *Journal of Personality and Social Psychology*, 114, 397–421. doi:10.1037/pspi0000115

Goldberg, L. R. (1982). From Ace to Zombie: Some explorations in the language of personality. In C. D. Spielberger & J. N. Butcher (Eds.), *Advances in Personality Assessment* (Vol. 1, pp. 203–234). Hillsdale, NJ: Erlbaum.

Gomillion, S. & Murray, S. L. (2014). Shifting dependence: The influence of partner instrumentality and self-esteem on responses to interpersonal risk. *Personality and Social Psychology Bulletin*, 40, 57–69. doi:10.1177/0146167213503885

Gordon, A. M., Impett, E. A., Kogan, A., Oveis, C., & Keltner, D. (2012). To have and to hold: Gratitude promotes relationship maintenance in intimate bonds. *Journal of Personality and Social Psychology*, 103, 257–274. doi:10.1037/a0028723

Hall, J. A., Coats, E. J., & LeBeau, L. S. (2005). Nonverbal behavior and the vertical dimension of social relations: A meta-analysis. *Psychological Bulletin*, 131, 898–924. doi:10.1037/0033-2909.131.6.898

Hazan, C. & Shaver, P. (1987). Romantic love conceptualized as an attachment process. *Interpersonal Relations and Group Processes*, 52, 511–524. doi:10.1037/0022-3514.52.3.511

Holmes, J. G. (2002). Interpersonal Expectations as the building blocks of social cognition: An Interdependence Theory perspective. *Personal Relationships*, 9, 1–26. doi:10.1111/1475-6811.00001

Horstmann, K. T., & Ziegler, M. (2016). Situational perception: Its theoretical foundation, assessment, and links to personality. In U. Kumar (Ed.), *The Wiley Handbook of Personality Assessment* (1st ed., pp. 31–43). Oxford: Wiley Blackwell.

Horstmann, K. T., Rauthmann, J. F., & Sherman, R. A. (2018). Measurement of situational influences. In V. Zeigler-Hill & T. K. Shackelford (Eds.), *SAGE Handbook of Personality and Individual Differences*. London: Sage.

Hutcherson, C. A. & Gross, J. J. (2011). The moral emotions: A social-functionalist account of anger, disgust, and contempt. *Journal of Personality and Social Psychology*, 100, 719–737. doi:10.1037/a0022408

John, O. P., Angleitner, A., & Ostendorf, F. (1988). The lexical approach to personality: A historical review of trait taxonomic research. *European Journal of Personality*, 2, 171–203. doi:10.1002/per.2410020302

Karremans, J. C. & Smith, P. K. (2010). Having the power to forgive: When the experience of power increases interpersonal forgiveness. *Personality and Social Psychology Bulletin*, 36, 1010–1023. doi:10.1177/0146167210376761

Kelley, H. H., Holmes, J. G., Kerr, N. L., Reis, H. T., Rusbult, C. E., & van Lange, P. A. M. (2003). *An Atlas of Interpersonal Situations*. Cambridge: Cambridge University Press. doi:10.1017/CBO9780511499845

Kelley, H. H. & Thibaut, J. W. (1978). *Interpersonal Relations: A Theory of Interdependence*. New York: Wiley.

Le, B. & Agnew, C. R. (2003). Commitment and its theorized determinants: A meta-analysis of the Investment Model. *Personal Relationships*, 10, 37–57. doi:10.1111/1475-6811.00035

Le, B., Dove, N. L., Agnew, C. R., Korn, M. S., & Mutso, A. A. (2010). Predicting nonmarital romantic relationship dissolution: A meta-analytic synthesis. *Personal Relationships*, 17, 377–390. doi:10.1111/j.1475-6811.2010.01285.x

Leikas, S., Lönnqvist, J.-E., & Verkasalo, M. (2012). Persons, situations, and behaviors: Consistency and variability of different behaviors in four interpersonal situations. *Journal of Personality and Social Psychology*, 103, 1007–1022. doi:10.1037/a0030385

Lennon, C. A., Stewart, A. L., & Ledermann, T. (2013). The role of power in intimate relationships. *Journal of Social and Personal Relationships*, 30, 95–114. doi:10.1177/0265407512452990

Lieberman, D., Tooby, J., & Cosmides, L. (2007). The architecture of human kin detection. *Nature*, 445, 727–731. doi:10.1038/nature05510

Mehl, M. R. & Conner, T. S. (Eds.). (2013). *Handbook of Research Methods for Studying Daily Life*. New York: Guilford.

Mikulincer, M. & Shaver, P. R. (2005). Attachment theory and emotions in close relationships: Exploring the attachment-related dynamics of emotional reactions to relational events. *Personal Relationships*, 12, 149–168. doi:10.1111/j.1350-4126.2005.00108.x

Mischel, W. & Shoda, Y. (1995). A cognitive-affective system theory of personality: Reconceptualizing situations, dispositions, dynamics, and invariance in personality structure. *Psychological Review*, 102, 246–268. doi:10.1037/0033-295X.102.2.246

Molho, C. & Balliet, D. (2017). Navigating interdependent social situations. In J. F. Rauthmann, R. A. Sherman, & D. C. Funder (Eds.), *The Oxford Handbook of Psychological Situations*. Oxford: Oxford University Press. doi:10.1093/oxfordhb/9780190263348.013.3

Murray, H. A. (1938). *Explorations in Personality*. New York: Oxford University Press.

Murray, S. L., Aloni, M., Holmes, J. G., Derrick, J. L., Stinson, D. A., & Leder, S. (2009a). Fostering partner dependence as trust insurance: The implicit contingencies of the exchange script in close relationships. *Journal of Personality and Social Psychology*, 96, 324–348. doi:10.1037/a0012856

Murray, S. L. & Holmes, J. G. (2009). The architecture of interdependent minds: A motivation-management theory of mutual responsiveness. *Psychological Review*, 116, 908–928. doi:10.1037/a0017015

Murray, S. L. & Holmes, J. G. (2015). Maintaining mutual commitment in the face of risk. *Current Opinion in Psychology*, 1, 57–60. doi:10.1016/j.copsyc.2014.11.005

Murray, S. L., Holmes, J. G., Aloni, M., Pinkus, R. T., Derrick, J. L., & Leder, S. (2009b). Commitment insurance: Compensating for the autonomy costs of interdependence in close relationships. *Journal of Personality and Social Psychology*, 97, 256–278. doi:10.1037/a0014562

Murray, S. L., Holmes, J. G., Griffin, D. W., & Derrick, J. L. (2015). The equilibrium model of relationship maintenance. *Journal of Personality and Social Psychology*, 108, 93–113. doi:10.1037/pspi0000004

Murray, S. L., Holmes, J. G., & Pinkus, R. T. (2010). A smart unconscious? Procedural origins of automatic partner attitudes in marriage. *Journal of Experimental Social Psychology*, 46, 650–656. doi:10.1016/j.jesp.2010.03.003

Overall, N. C. & Sibley, C. G. (2008). When accommodation matters: Situational dependency within daily interactions with romantic partners. *Journal of Experimental Social Psychology*, 44, 95–104. doi:10.1016/j.jesp.2007.02.005

Overall, N. C., Girme, Y. U., & Simpson, J. A. (2016). The power of diagnostic situations: How support and conflict can foster growth and security. In C. R. Knee & H. T. Reis (Eds.), *Positive Approaches to Optimal Relationship Development* (pp. 148–170). Cambridge: Cambridge University Press.

Overall, N. C. & Simpson, J. A. (2015). Attachment and dyadic regulation processes. *Current Opinion in Psychology*, 1, 61–66. doi:10.1016/j.copsyc.2014.11.008

Parrigon, S., Woo, S. E., Tay, L., & Wang, T. (2017). CAPTION-ing the situation: A lexically-derived taxonomy of psychological situation characteristics. *Journal of Personality and Social Psychology*, 112, 642–681. doi:10.1037/pspp0000111

Pervin, L. A. (1978). Definitions, measurements, and classifications of stimuli, situations, and environments. *Human Ecology*, 6, 71–105. doi:10.1007/BF00888567

Pietroni, D., van Kleef, G. A., de Dreu, C. K. W. & Pagliaro, S. (2008). Emotions as strategic information: Effects of other's emotional expressions on fixed-pie perception, demands, and integrative behaviour in negotiations. *Journal of Experimental Social Psychology*, 44, 1444–1454. doi:10.1016/j.jesp.2008.06.007

Pietroni, D., van Kleef, G. A., Rubaltelli, E., & Rumiati, R. (2009). When happiness pays in negotiation. The interpersonal effects of "exit option": direct emotions. *Mind and Society*, 8, 77–92. doi:10.1007/s11299-008-0047-9

Powell, C. & van Vugt, M. (2003). Genuine giving or selfish sacrifice? The role of commitment and cost level upon willingness to sacrifice. *European Journal of Social Psychology*, 33, 403–412. doi:10.1002/ejsp.154

Rauthmann, J. F., Gallardo-Pujol, D., Guillaume, E. M., Todd, E., Nave, C. S., Sherman, R. A., ... Funder, D. C. (2014). The situational eight DIAMONDS: A taxonomy of major dimensions of situation characteristics. *Journal of Personality and Social Psychology*, 107, 677–718. doi:10.1037/a0037250

Rauthmann, J. F. & Sherman, R. A. (2016). Ultra-brief measures for the situational eight DIAMONDS domains. *European Journal of Psychological Assessment*, 32, 165–174. doi:10.1027/1015-5759/a000245

Rauthmann, J. F. & Sherman, R. A. (2017). The description of situations: Towards replicable domains of psychological situation characteristics. *Journal of Personality and Social Psychology*, 114, 482–488. doi:10.1037/pspp0000162

Rauthmann, J. F., Sherman, R. A., & Funder, D. C. (2015). Principles of situation research: Towards a better understanding of psychological situations. *European Journal of Personality*, 29, 363–381. doi:10.1002/per.1994

Reis, H. T. (2008). Reinvigorating the concept of situation in social psychology. *Personality and Social Psychology Review*, 12, 311–329. doi:10.1177/1088868308321721

Reis, H. T. & Arriaga, X. B. (2014). Interdependence theory and related theories. In B. Gawronski & G. V. Bodenhausen (Eds.), *Theory and Explanation in Social Psychology* (pp. 305–327). New York: Guilford.

Reis, H. T., Clark, M. S., & Holmes, J. G. (2004). Perceived partner responsiveness as an organizing construct in the study of intimacy and closeness. In D. J. Mashek & A. Aron (Eds.), *Handbook of Closeness and Intimacy*. New York: Psychology Press.

Reis, H. T. & Gable, S. L. (2015). Responsiveness. *Current Opinion in Psychology*, 1, 67–71. doi:10.1016/j.copsyc.2015.01.001

Rentzsch, K., Columbus, S., Balliet, D., & Gerlach, T. M. (n.d.). *Similarity in Situation Perception Predicts Relationship Satisfaction.* Manuscript in preparation.

Righetti, F., Gere, J., Hofmann, W., Visserman, M. L., & van Lange, P. A. M. (2016). The burden of empathy: Partners' responses to divergence of interests in daily life. *Emotion*, 16, 684–690. doi:10.1037/emo0000163

Righetti, F. & Impett, E. (2017). Sacrifice in close relationships: Motives, emotions, and relationship outcomes. *Social and Personality Psychology Compass*, 11, 1–11. doi:10.1111/spc3.12342

Righetti, F., Luchies, L. B., van Gils, S., Slotter, E. B., Witcher, B., & Kumashiro, M. (2015). The prosocial versus proself power holder: How power influences sacrifice in romantic relationships. *Personality and Social Psychology Bulletin*, 41, 779–790. doi:10.1177/0146167215579054

Rusbult, C. E. (1980). Commitment and satisfaction in romantic associations: A test of the investment model. *Journal of Experimental Social Psychology*, 16, 172–186. doi:10.1016/0022-1031(80)90007-4

Rusbult, C. E., Agnew, C. R., & Arriaga, X. B. (2012). The investment model of commitment processes. In P. A. M. van Lange, A. W. Kruglanski, & E. T. Higgins (Eds.), *Handbook of Theories of Social Psychology* (pp. 218–231). London: Sage. doi:10.4135/9781446249222.n37

Rusbult, C. E., Martz, J. M., & Agnew, C. R. (1998). The investment model scale: Measuring commitment level, satisfaction level, quality of alternatives, and investment size. *Personal Relationships*, 5, 357–387. doi:10.1111/j.1475-6811.1998.tb00177.x

Rusbult, C. E. & van Lange, P. A. M. (2003). Interdependence, interaction, and relationships. *Annual Review of Psychology*, 54, 351–375. doi:10.1146/annurev.psych.54.101601.145059

Rusbult, C. E., Verette, J., Whitney, G. A., Slovik, L. F., & Lipkus, I. (1991). Accommodation processes in close relationships: Theory and preliminary empirical evidence. *Journal of Personality and Social Psychology*, 60, 53–78.

Saucier, G., Bel-Bahar, T., & Fernandez, C. (2007). What modifies the expression of personality tendencies? Defining basic domains of situation variables. *Journal of Personality*, 75, 479–504. doi:10.1111/j.1467-6494.2007.00446.x

Schoebi, D. & Randall, A. K. (2015). Emotional dynamics in intimate relationships. *Emotion Review*, 7, 342–348. doi:10.1177/1754073915590620

Shallcross, S. L. & Simpson, J. A. (2012). Trust and responsiveness in strain-test situations: A dyadic perspective. *Journal of Personality and Social Psychology*, 102(5), 1031–1044. doi:10.1037/a0026829

Simpson, J. A., Campbell, L., & Weisberg, Y. J. (2006). Daily perceptions of conflict and support in romantic relationships: The ups and downs of anxiously attached individuals. In M. Mikulincer, & G. S. Goodman (Eds.), *Dynamics of Romantic Love: Attachment, Caregiving, and Sex* (pp. 216–239). New York: Guilford.

Simpson, J. A., Farrell, A. K., Oriña, M. M., & Rothman, A. J. (2015). Power and social influence in relationships. In M. Mikulincer, & P. R. Shaver (Eds.), *APA Handbook of Personality and Social Psychology, Volume 3: Interpersonal Relations* (pp. 393–420). Washington, DC: American Psychological Association. doi:10.1037/14344-015

Simpson, J. A., Rholes, W. S., & Phillips, D. (1996). Conflict in close relationships: An attachment perspective. *Journal of Personality and Social Psychology*, 71, 899–914. doi:10.1037/0022-3514.71.5.899

Thibaut, J. W. & Kelley, H. H. (1959). *The Social Psychology of Groups*. New York: John Wiley & Sons.

Tooby, J., Cosmides, L., Sell, A., Lieberman, D., & Sznycer, D. (2008). Internal regulatory variables and the design of human motivation: A computational and evolutionary approach. In A. J. Elliot (Ed.), *Handbook of Approach and Avoidance Motivation* (pp. 251–271). New York: Psychology Press.

Tsang, J. A., McCullough, M. E., & Fincham, F. D. (2006). The longitudinal association between forgiveness and relationship closeness and commitment. *Journal of Social and Clinical Psychology*, 25, 448–472.

van Lange, P. A. M., Rusbult, C. E., Drigotas, S. M., Arriaga, X. B., Witcher, B. S., & Cox, C. L. (1997). Willingness to sacrifice in close relationships. *Journal of Personality and Social Psychology*, 72, 1373–1395.

Visserman, M. L., Righetti, F., Impett, E. A., Keltner, D., & van Lange, P. A. M. (2018). It's the motive that counts: Perceived sacrifice motives and gratitude in romantic relationships. *Emotion*, 18, 625–637. doi:10.1037/emo0000344

Wagerman, S. A. & Funder, D. C. (2009). Personality psychology of situations. In P. J. Corr & G. Matthews (Eds.), *The Cambridge Handbook of Personality Psychology* (pp. 27–42). Cambridge: Cambridge University Press. doi:10.1017/CBO9780511596544.005

Yovetich, N. A. & Rusbult, C. E. (1994). Accommodative behavior in close relationships: Exploring transformation of motivation. *Journal of Experimental Social Psychology*, 30, 138–164.

Ziegler, M. (2014). *Big Five Inventory of Personality in Occupational Situations*. Mödling, Austria: Schuhfried GmbH.

2

The Structure of Interdependence Shapes Social Cognition in Relationships

JOHN G. HOLMES

Relationships can be immensely rewarding. When love and support is mutual, feelings of intimacy and connectedness strengthen. Partners become tuned to each other's needs and facilitate each other's goals, magnifying the considerable benefits of interdependence. This rosy picture might suggest relationships are easy. In fact, interdependence is extremely complicated and difficult (Kelley et al., 2003; Thibaut & Kelley, 1959). It involves the complex tasks of coordinating goals, maintaining fair exchange, and dealing with a partner's inevitable bad behavior. So, despite all the rewards, there will be notable costs, disappointments, and hurt feelings. There will be times when normally happy couples feel confused and out of touch. Or feel distant and let down. Or worse, angry and alienated. The issue is, in the face of such costs, how do people maintain their positive motivations and ensure the survival of the relationship?

This chapter focuses on motivated cognition. The thesis is that happy couples are motivated to find ways to get past these occasionally upsetting and costly interactions by rationalizing them and diminishing their impact on their overall feelings: they must weave a story that contains the damage and does not detract from their pursuit of the larger goal of enjoying the benefits of interdependence. Thus, the goal is to identify the cognitive processes that allow people to maintain their prosocial motivations necessary to sustain mutual commitment over time.

THE CHALLENGES OF INTERDEPENDENCE

Interdependence, by its very nature, invariably results in disruptive interactions and costly experiences. What are the most common challenges? First, coordination of goals and plans is a complex problem. If a partner impedes your personal goals and interferes with what you want to do, then how do you react? Second, equivalence in exchange is a fundamental rule in relationships.

But what happens if social exchange becomes imbalanced and partners' contributions are unequal? Finally, Caryl Rusbult once famously commented that, "Eventually, all partners behave badly." How does one accommodate or adjust to being treated poorly in ways that are not responsive to your needs?

The fundamental question becomes, how do partners reconcile the deep rewards of interdependence with its inevitable costs? I will argue that despite costly disruptions, people need to maintain strong positive feelings for their partner to motivate caring and responsive behavior. But why is that? The answer is that the core task of relationships is to maintain reciprocity of benefits to ensure the survival of the dyad. The reciprocity principle requires mutual responsiveness to each other's needs. This requirement for mutual responsiveness is an imperial goal central to survival, one that shapes social cognition. As John Anderson noted, "Thinking is for doing." Consequentially, cognition should provide adaptive solutions to problems of interdependence in ways that maintain mutual responsiveness. In terms of my ecological or functional perspective, cognition should reflect the nature of the challenges (e.g., coordination of goals) and tasks of interdependence (e.g., maintain caring for partner).

The Architecture of Interdependent Minds

The cognitive mechanisms for maintaining mutual responsiveness must essentially sustain two things. First, they must support a sense of trust, of safety in expressing needs and engaging in connection. Second, they must ensure that the partner is valued sufficiently to support feelings of commitment that motivate prosocial, caring actions. Put another way, success requires that cognitive processes coordinate one person's trust in another's commitment (e.g., to risk asking for support) with the other's actual commitment to be responsive and caring (i.e., to be supportive).

Cognitive adjustments must sustain long-term feelings of safety and value in the face of everyday costs and challenges. Essentially, this is a case of "goal shielding" from disruptive local forces (Kruglanski et al., 2002). People need cognitive solutions that allow them to "keep their eyes on the prize" – to not be distracted from implementing their broader goal of achieving mutual responsiveness by the localized costs and challenges that occur. Basically, people must rationalize the costs and not allow them to disrupt the broader goal of achieving mutual responsiveness. Such compensatory reactions to the costs of interdependence preserve feelings of safety and partner value through dissonance reduction – a case of *motivated reasoning* to neutralize problems in the relationship.

For instance, when a partner's request for help interferes with your goal to finish writing a paper, your cognition might exaggerate the partner's virtues by remembering instances when the partner supported your career. Basically, costs trigger praise in a "yes, but" type of cognitive logic. Murray and Holmes (2009) propose a set of three different if-then procedural rules that *automatically* compensate for costs and disruptions. The contention is that the mind has efficient, functional solutions to the common problems posed by interdependence: a "smart unconscious." What are these proposed if-then rules that generate adaptive reactions? They are as follows:

1. If a partner impedes one's personal goals, then resist devaluing the partner and sustain a positive image;
2. If exchange is seen as imbalanced, then contribute more to restore mutual dependence;
3. If a partner is hurtful or behaves badly, then try to accommodate and not retaliate.

These three rules are part of the cognitive toolbox that helps people maintain a stable and satisfying relationship. Essentially, cognitive working models contain the implicit know-how to promote caring interactions. We believe that these implicit reactions will function efficiently and automatically and not be controlled by more deliberative thought processes related to personality or relationship quality.

A Dual Process Perspective. Murray and Holmes (2009) proposed a dual process perspective in which the mind functions not only efficiently and automatically, as described above, but also flexibly and deliberately, to suit chronic relationship goals and motivations. Initially, automatic goal activation is primed by situational features that capture elements of risk. Executive control then permits a person, if there is the motivation and opportunity, to modify these automatic goals to better reflect a person's chronic and broader motivations (cf. the MODE model, Figure 2.1; Fazio, 1990). What determines such motivations? According to *risk regulation theory* (Murray, Holmes & Collins, 2006), interdependence with another person has risks and creates a basic tension between motivations, between connectedness or approach goals and self-protection or avoidance goals. Resolving this fundamental conflict requires a risk regulation system to prioritize these goals with

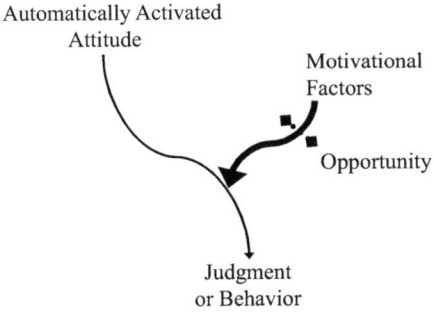

FIGURE 2.1 Fazio MODE model of the attitude-to-behavior process

the overarching aim to minimize vulnerability from being hurt given relationship circumstances.

Executive Control of Goals

According to risk regulation theory, the arbiter of this goal conflict is the level of trust in a partner's caring and commitment. A person's chronic trust level toward a partner reflects stable expectations about the partner's motivations and can shape the correction of automatic goals at the executive stage. Personality and relationship quality are predicted to influence this deliberative, thoughtful process because it involves top-down cognitive dynamics.

Chronic *high trust* reflects confident expectations about a partner's caring and likely responsiveness to one's needs. It is based on a combination of high-quality relationship experiences and personality qualities related to felt security, such as high self-esteem (HSE) or secure attachment. High SE people assume the partner values them just as highly as they value themselves, a case of naïve realism (Murray & Holmes, 2000). The agenda of high trust individuals is to facilitate connectedness and approach goals; they are generally willing to risk closeness and vulnerability because of the expectation that a partner will be responsive and interactions rewarding.

Chronic *low trust*, on the other hand, reflects uncertain expectations about a partner's caring and responsiveness (see Cortes & Wood, Chapter 12). It is based on lower quality experiences or an insecure personality, such as low SE or anxious attachment. Low SE people assume partners have doubts about their value, just as they doubt themselves. The agenda of low SE individuals is to facilitate self-protective, avoidance goals and not chance closeness and vulnerability in situations involving interpersonal risk .

ILLUSTRATIONS OF THE DUAL PROCESS MODEL FOR THREE BASIC CHALLENGES

The First Challenge: Goal Interference

Interdependence with a partner inevitably compromises one's autonomous goal pursuits: People will experience costs from goal coordination failures (see Baker et al., Chapter 14). Because of this negative experience a cognitive mechanism is needed to deflect such threats and support the implementation of connection goals. We propose an if-then rule which links costs automatically to *increased* partner valuing – a form of cognitive compensation. Its function is to sustain commitment and motivate future responsiveness in the face of local disruptions (Murray, Holmes et al., 2009).

As an illustration, participants in one investigation (Murray, Holmes et al., 2009) recalled a time in which they voiced concerns to a friend about the costs of their relationships. (In another experiment, they marked instances on a checklist where a partner interfered with their goals.) The speed with which participants associated their partner with positive traits such as "understanding" and "attractive" after recalling their autonomy concerns captured their implicit evaluations of their partners. Additionally, participants provided explicit measures of positive evaluations, as well as their optimism about the longevity and success of their relationships. Relative to control participants, those who recalled autonomy concerns displayed more positive implicit evaluations of their partners. This enhanced positivity suggests that participants' initial impulse was to justify their commitment to their partners in order to offset worries about autonomy and thereby remain engaged in the relationship. This pattern was not modified by relationship quality or trust.

However, as described previously, chronic trust influences secondary corrective processes that can overturn this goal when it is inconsistent with one's chronic motivations. For high trust people, justifying commitment is a goal consistent with their persistent connectedness strivings and, as such, secondary processes should reinforce it. For low trust people, however, such a connectedness goal runs counter to chronic self-protective motivations, so they should overturn such goals when they have sufficient ability and opportunity to do so.

An examination of participants' *explicit* reports in the aforementioned study confirmed this outcome. In this and other studies, self-esteem was used as a proxy for trust to conceal the intent of the experiment, removing a focus on how much people felt cared for and valued by the partner. Though both high SE and low SE people's *implicit* evaluations of their partners were more positive when autonomy costs were salient, their explicit evaluations diverged (see Figure 2.2). High SE people remained positive, reporting even stronger "positive illusions" than control participants about their partners and their relationships after recalling autonomy concerns. Low SE people, however, reported less positivity after recalling autonomy concerns compared to control participants. Those with low SE appeared to correct the initial impulse toward connection and, instead, deliberatively devalued their partner in an effort to guard themselves against the inherent costs and risks of greater interdependence. This pattern, depicted in Figure 2.2, is prototypical of the results across many studies: high SE individuals defensively enhance their connection to their partner in the face of a threat, while low SE individuals have a more fragile sense of confidence they are valued and distance themselves from the partner.

These conclusions were further examined in a daily diary study of newly-weds (Murray, Holmes et al., 2009). Two hundred and twenty-two couples completed diaries for 14 days in an electronic format, detailing examples of

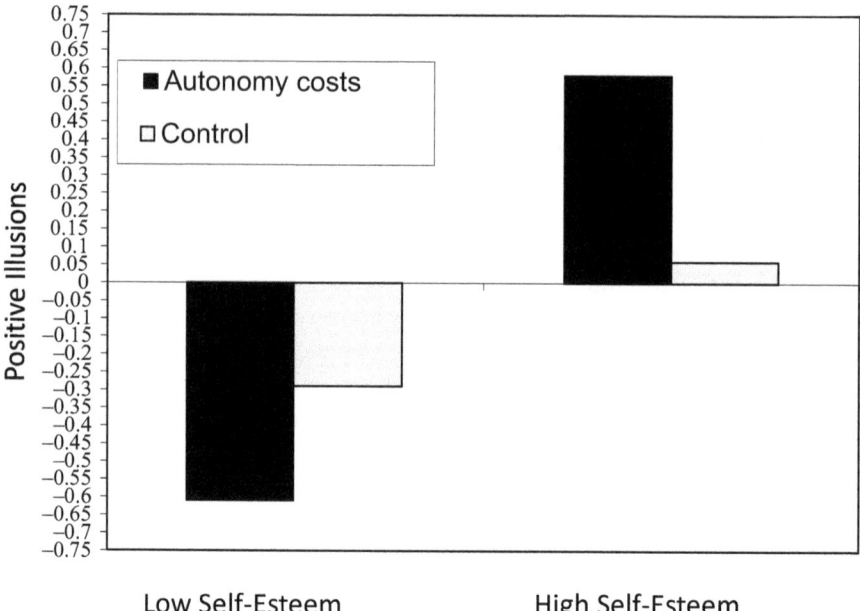

FIGURE 2.2 Flexibility – explicit illusions

autonomy costs each day ("My partner did not do something he/she had
promised to do; My partner did what he/she wanted to do rather than what
I wanted to do"). They also completed a measure of partner valuing ("in love
with my partner; my partner is a great partner"). Counterintuitively, high
trust or high SE people valued the partner all the more when a partner
interfered with their goals the previous day. Crucially, their partners reported
that they actually *behaved* more responsively when they exhibited such
motivated construal. Lower SE people failed to show this compensation
pattern; to them, a cost was just a cost.

But was this rationalization of costs adaptive over the longer term? Yes.
Commitment was indeed strengthened by compensation processes; evidence
of more cognitive compensation by a person in the daily diary actually
predicted stronger satisfaction a year later. Thus, as predicted, motivated
cognition was indeed functional in strengthening the relationship.

A Second Challenge: Unequal Exchange

Because equivalence of exchange is fundamental in relationships, when people
face circumstances where they feel inferior to their partners they confront a
serious challenge to interdependence. There are implicit but well understood
rules to social exchange. In order to maintain and develop interdependence

and obtain the benefits that accompany it, people must be sure that their partners will be responsive to their needs (Reis, Clark, & Holmes, 2004) and not take advantage of their personal vulnerabilities. Though these perceptions of responsiveness are derived from many sources (Murray, Leder et al., 2009), feeling that one is "special" and "irreplaceable" to one's partner plays a large role in forming confident expectations.

When people feel particularly valuable to their partners or believe that their partners would have a difficult time obtaining the same benefits in another relationship, they should have greater confidence that their partners will be committed to their relationship and, therefore, responsive to their most important needs. However, being made to feel inferior to one's partner may challenge the belief that one is irreplaceable. Perceptions of equality contribute a great deal to feelings of love and acceptance (Murray et al., 2005). Thus, events such as a partner's promotion that highlight one's potential inferiority should shake people's confidence in their partner's expected responsiveness, and the specter of potential rejection may begin to loom.

How can people cope with such acute feelings of inferiority? Evidence suggests that people automatically engage in goal pursuit designed to quell concerns about a partner's responsiveness by restoring their sense of irreplaceability. In one illustrative experiment, participants were implicitly primed with an exchange script that activated concerns about interpersonal matching. Participants in this exchange-priming condition evaluated personal ads in which the ostensible author emphasized his/her desire for a partner who would provide an equitable match. The results revealed that, relative to control participants, participants exposed to the exchange-priming condition reported greater worry about feeling inferior to their partners and a greater willingness to engage in behaviors that would increase their partner's dependence on them. For example, participants concerned with inferiority tried to make themselves irreplaceable to their partners by doing things such as assuming responsibility for the partner's day-to-day lives (e.g., making sure they were aware of important deadlines, managing their social schedule) and narrowing their partner's social network (Murray, Aloni et al., 2009).

This automatic response to inferiority concerns is characteristic of self-protection goals. By fostering partner dependence on their contributions, people can obtain greater assurance that their partners will remain committed to the relationship. Becoming irreplaceable lessens the likelihood that their partners will seek more beneficial outcomes in a different relationship, thereby reducing the risk of a painful rejection experience. Though this strategy may ultimately foster mutual commitment, it reflects underlying concerns about safety and self-protection rather than connection and interpersonal advancement (Higgins, 1997). This particular automatic impulse provides a "fit" with the chronic motivations of people low in chronic trust, making it unlikely to be overturned when low-trust people have the opportunity and ability to do so.

However, partner-dependence goals are more difficult for high trust people to enact, given that their chronic motivation is to pursue connection with their partners. How do high trust people resolve such goal conflict? As when regulating risk, they appear to engage executive-based corrective processes to correct for this incongruent automatic goal.

Support for this observation has been provided by an experiment similar to that described above, in which participants were once again primed with concerns about inferiority (Murray, Aloni et al., 2009). In this instance, however, the prime was more explicit (and thus subject to conscious influence) in that participants read descriptions of romantic couples married seven years earlier and were asked to predict whether they had remained married or had divorced. The couples varied in the degree to which the partners matched one another (i.e., were similar), and participants were given feedback on their predictions indicating that couples who matched to a greater degree were more likely to still be married, whereas couples who matched less well typically divorced. Following this explicit matching prime, participants reported their desire to heighten their partner's dependence on them through their contributions and to increase their own irreplaceability.

Low SE people again reported greater efforts to do this in the exchange-priming condition relative to control participants, replicating the results obtained when participants were exposed to the implicit prime. High SE participants, however, reported *less* desire to foster partner dependence when they experienced an exchange prime relative to control participants. In contrast to how they responded to the implicit prime, high SE people who faced an explicit exchange prime were able to exert secondary corrective processes, which allowed them to overturn their initial impulse to protect themselves by trying to make their partner more dependent on them. Instead, they downplayed these goals, perhaps in an effort to focus on goals aimed at developing intimacy with their partners rather than protecting themselves from possible rejection.

A field study replicated this logic, showing that following days when people felt inferior or believed they had not contributed enough, they increased their contributions to the relationship by doing more for the partner (Murray, Aloni et al., 2009). These efforts were quite functional: The partners actually reported fewer doubts about the person on such days. The if-then rule indeed served to make the partner feel more positive about the self, strengthening commitment at a point when it might potentially be flagging.

A Third Challenge: Bad Behavior

Perhaps the most difficult challenge in relationships is coming to terms with a partner's bad, selfish, or non-responsive behavior. How does one reconcile such troubling actions with the larger overall picture? Such behavior raises concerns about one's value to the partner, about trust in the partner's caring. And such behavior should indeed automatically activate self-protective automatic goals, resulting in reduced dependence, at least temporally, on someone who has harmed oneself and one's interests. Indeed, Murray, Derrick, Leder, and Holmes (2008) found evidence for such tendencies. People were asked to recall as vividly as possible a time when they felt hurt and let down by their partner, to describe in detail how it felt at the time and to rate the degree the transgression was forgiven. Compared to a control, experimental participants reacted more quickly in a lexical decision task to self-protect words such as caution, defense, protect. Importantly, this effect disappeared if the transgression had been forgiven and the risk of interdependence reduced.

In this case the automatic activation of self-protective goals would undermine the relationship, not strengthen it. The interesting issue then is whether people will overturn the impulse in order to sustain good relationship feelings. Our prediction was that HSE people would override or correct the self-protect goal in order to maintain their chronic agenda to connect. LSEs were expected to actually execute the self-protect goal and distance themselves from the partner in the face of perceptions of risk.

Such effects for HSEs are only predicted by the MODE model if people have sufficient cognitive resources to overturn impulses (Fazio, 1990). In general, chronic trust or its proxy, self-esteem, serves as the foundation of a regulatory system that inhibits or reinforces automatically activated goals to align them with chronic motivational agendas. However, in many cases, overturning conflicting goals requires people to exert considerable self-control, a task that depends on the availability of sufficient executive resources (Baumeister, Bratslavsky, Muraven, & Tice, 1998). When executive resources are impeded or taxed, people may be unable to resolve goal tension or align their goal pursuits with their chronic motivational agendas. Consequently, people high and low in chronic trust (or esteem) may be unable to employ their preferred regulatory strategies, thus negating its impact on relational self-regulation.

The idea that divergent risk regulation efforts of high and low self-esteem individuals are dependent on executive functioning was tested directly in a series of studies by Cavallo, Holmes, Fitzsimons, Murray, and Wood (2012). In one of these studies, half of the participants were exposed to a relationship threat by having them read a short passage implying that their relationship perceptions were more positive than warranted by research evidence ostensibly compiled by a number of experts over several years. Participants in a control condition read a similar passage suggesting that their relationship perceptions were generally accurate or perhaps slightly underestimated the quality of their relationships. Following this, participants' executive resources were taxed by a cognitive load manipulation.

When participants were under low cognitive load and had ample executive resources available, self-esteem predicted responses to risk as in prior research. Relative to control participants, HSEs responded counterintuitively to relationship threat by actually bolstering their feelings of connectedness, whereas LSEs reported feeling less connected to their partners. Put in self-regulatory terms, HSEs prioritized connectedness and drew psychologically closer to their partners, whereas LSEs prioritized self-protection and distanced themselves from their relationships.

However, high cognitive load mitigated the influence of self-esteem. When participants were cognitively busy and executive resources were taxed, HSEs and LSEs reported similar responses to threat and did not differ from control participants in their feelings of connectedness. That is, when participants had little ability to exert the corrective processes that would prioritize HSEs and LSEs' preferred regulatory aims, self-esteem did not predict relationship outcomes. This indicates not only that HSEs and LSEs align situational goals with their chronic motivational agendas when they can, but also that executive resources are *necessary* for implementing these preferred goals.

These results were replicated in a daily diary study of married couples (Cavallo et al., 2012). The authors examined the link between bad partner behavior one day and the person's accommodation and feelings of connection the next. They also included a measure of people's chronic working memory capacity. The daily diary slope for the compensatory "if feel rejected, accommodate" rule predicted increased satisfaction *for the partner* one year later, underlining the degree to which the rule is functional is sustaining a strong relationship! However, HSEs with poor working memory capacity were less happy, presumably because they didn't have the cognitive resources to overturn the impulse to self-protect and distance themselves from the partner. LSEs with poor capacity were actually happier: Apparently, blocking their ruminations and worries about hurt feelings and potential rejection allows them to simply experience and enjoy the everyday benefits of interdependence.

THE EQUILIBRIUM MODEL OF RELATIONSHIP MAINTENANCE

The three if-then compensation rules each serve to strengthen trust and commitment in the face of adversity. They are cognitive tools available to preserve a sense of safety and value. But are they actually activated and brought into play when commitment wavers in a relationship and is in need of strengthening to preserve mutual responsiveness? Murray, Holmes, Griffin, and Derek (2015) studied the adjustments of childless couples in first marriages. Each of the three if-then rules was indexed over a 14-day daily diary period and commitment was measured in a longitudinal design with four separate panels over three years of marriage. A composite was created to summarize overall use of the three threat mitigation strategies, and commitment change was measured compared to a person's average state.

The results showed that when commitment wavered, weakening compared to a person's average state, the implementation of the three rules increased dramatically. Further, implementing the rules had the effect of seriously strengthening commitment to the relationship. The pattern of results suggests that individuals vary on which rules are "favorites," because the particular issues that surface in their own relationship are likely to govern the rules most frequently activated. For instance, a couple may experience frequent goal interference issues if their respective goal systems are less compatible, requiring them to more commonly compensate cognitively by valuing the partner more. On the other hand, this same couple may only infrequently deal with exchange issues or accommodation to bad partner behavior, resulting in less common implementation of adaptive responses to these issues.

Thus, the three threat-mitigation rules foster stability in a relationship by providing constructive solutions to each type of "problem" posed by interdependence. These rules are automatically activated to deal with specific situational risks and consequently are only activated when specific if-threats occur in the relationship on a regular basis.

SUMMARY

In sum, regulating connection and self-protection goals that vie for motivational priority in risky interpersonal situations requires executive control, and chronic trust is often highly influential in shaping these processes. When relationship situations automatically activate these goals, high and low trust people are likely to pursue them if they are congruent with their chronic motivations. However, when these goals conflict with chronic motivational aims, people engage in controlled processes that override incongruent goals and thereby restore regulatory fit between situational goals and their broader motivations.

IMPLICATIONS

Research on motivated cognition in relationships has a short history and the implications of people's tendency to tell a positive story about their partners are seldom discussed. There are two intriguing puzzles about relationships that can be analyzed from this perspective.

The first puzzle is why most people's satisfaction ratings in their relationship tend to stay consistently high over time, until they aren't. What accounts for such optimism and the sudden fall from grace? The thesis is that motivated cognition regulates information flow and perception to fit a positive story skeleton. However, some relationship realities become too hard to stretch to fit such upbeat narratives. Eventually then, relationships begin to unravel when the stories do, when events and interactions simply do not support positive conclusions. When the stories collapse under the weight of negative evidence, positive sentiment is also likely to suddenly fall apart. The end result resembles the pattern described by "Catastrophe" theorists, when the "Black Swann" suddenly appears and destroys equilibrium.

The second puzzle involves the mystery of why the quality of everyday interaction experiences is not faithfully reflected in people's conclusions about their relationships (Murray, Holmes & Pinkus, 2010). Why might that be? The argument is that motivated cognition serves to distort the conclusions people draw to support a positive and optimism narrative, at least at the deliberative processing, propositional stage. Murray et al. (2010) had married couples complete daily diaries for three weeks, reporting on a wide variety of relationship experiences. Later in time, they found that the tenor of such experiences was not predictive of people's conclusions, such as relationship satisfaction or trust.

However, those experiences, especially those reflecting responsive or non-responsive behavior by the partner, were nicely captured by measures of people's automatic attitudes (Fazio, 1990) toward the partner. Apparently, automatic, implicit evaluations are less subject to modification in the service of motivated cognition. And importantly, if people formed negative attitudes based on negative experiences initially, those attitudes eventually undermined and colored feelings in the relationship. On a happier note, if people formed positive implicit attitudes, based on a partner's responsive behavior, those attitudes were capable of counteracting negative overall conclusions reached in the executive control phase. Those negative conclusions often were reached by low SE individuals based on their ruminations and worries, not based on actual evidence. Sometimes when reality reveals itself the story has a nice ending!

REFERENCES

Baumeister, R. F., Bratslavsky, E., Muraven, M., & Tice, D. M. (1998). Ego-depletion: Is the active self a limited resource? *Journal of Personality and Social Psychology, 74,* 1252–1265.

Cavallo, J., Holmes, J. G., Fitzsimons, G., Murray, S. L., & Wood, J. V. (2012). Managing motivational conflict: How self-esteem and executive resources influence self-regulatory responses to risk. *Journal of Personality and Social Psychology,* 103, 430–451.

Fazio, R. H. (1990). Multiple processes by which attitudes guide behavior: The MODE model as an integrative framework. In M. P. Zanna (Ed.), *Advances in Experimental Social Psychology* (Vol. 23, pp. 75–109). New York: Academic Press.

Higgins, E. T. (1997). Beyond pleasure and pain. *American Psychologist*, 52, 1280–1300.

Kelley, H. H., Holmes, J. G., Kerr, N. L., Reis, H. T., Rusbult, C. E., & Van Lange, P. A. M. (2003). *An Atlas of Interpersonal Situations*. Cambridge: Cambridge University Press.

Kruglanski, A. W., Shah, J. Y., Fishbach, A., Friedman, R., Chun, W. Y., & Sleeth-Keppler, D. (2002). A theory of goal systems. In M. P. Zanna (Ed.), *Advances in Experimental Social Psychology* (Vol. 34, pp. 331–378). San Diego, CA: Academic Press.

Murray, S. L., Aloni, M., Holmes, J. G., Derrick, J., Anthony, D., & Leder, S. (2009). Fostering partner dependence as trust insurance: The implicit contingencies of exchange in close relationships. *Journal of Personality and Social Psychology*, 96, 324–348.

Murray, S. L., Derrick, J., Leder, S., & Holmes, J. G. (2008). Balancing connectedness and self-protection goals in close relationships: A levels of processing perspective on risk regulation. *Journal of Personality and Social Psychology*, 94, 429–459.

Murray, S. L. & Holmes, J. G. (2000). Seeing the self through a partner's eyes: Why self-doubts turn into relationship insecurities. In A. Tesser, R. B. Felson, & J. M. Suls (Eds.), *Psychological Perspectives on Self and Identity* (pp. 173–198). Washington: APA Press.

Murray, S. L. & Holmes, J. G. (2009). The architecture of interdependent minds: A motivation-management theory of mutual responsiveness. *Psychological Review*, 116, 908–928.

Murray, S. L., Holmes, J. G., Aloni, M., Pinkus, R. T., Derrick, J. L., & Leder, S. (2009). Commitment-insurance: Compensating for the autonomy costs of interdependence in close relationships. *Journal of Personality and Social Psychology*, 97, 256–279.

Murray, S. L., Holmes, J. G., & Collins, N. L. (2006). Optimizing assurance: The risk regulation system in relationships. *Psychological Bulletin*, 132, 641–666.

Murray, S. L, Holmes, J. G., Griffin, D., & Derrick, J. (2015). The equilibrium model of relationship maintenance. *Journal of Personality and Social Psychology*, 108, 93–113.

Murray, S. L., Holmes, J. G., & Pinkus, R. (2010). A smart unconscious? Procedural origins of automatic partner attitudes in marriage. *Journal of Experimental Social Psychology*, 46, 650–656.

Murray, S. L., Leder, S., McClellan, J., Holmes, J. G., Pinkus, R., & Harris, B. (2009). Becoming irreplaceable: How comparisons to the partner's alternatives differentially affects low and high self-esteem people. *Journal of Experimental Social Psychology*, 45, 1180–1191.

Murray S. L., Rose, P., Holmes, J. G., Podchaski, E., Derrick, J., Bellavia, G., & Griffin, D. W. (2005). Putting the partner within reach: A dyadic perspective on felt security. *Journal of Personality and Social Psychology*, 88, 327–347.

Reis, H., Clark, M., & Holmes, J.G. (2004). Perceived partner responsiveness as an organizing construct in the study of intimacy and closeness. In D. J. Mashek & A. Aron (Eds.), *Handbook of Intimacy and Closeness* (pp. 201–225). Mahwah, NJ: Lawrence Erlbaum.

Thibaut, J. W. & Kelley, H. H. (1959). *The Social Psychology of Groups*. Oxford: John Wiley.

3

Home Is Where the Heart Is

Geographic Variation in Relational Behavior and Outcomes

WILLIAM J. CHOPIK

People often imbue inanimate objects and broader, abstract entities with personal characteristics. Places are one such entity that people imbue with anthropomorphic traits. For example, cities and towns can be described as (interpersonally) warm and welcoming or cold and hostile. These perceptions almost certainly rely on our and others' experiences with these places (or a place's reputation). But do places actually vary in these characteristics that we judge them on? Over the past 10–15 years, a renewed interest in the geographic variation of psychological and social characteristics has emerged (Rentfrow, 2014). A collection of theories, methods, and data has emerged that provides a new appreciation for how individuals and social institutions vary across physical space.

In this chapter, I will present the current thinking about geographical variation in psychological and social behavior and how it can be applied to the study of close relationships and interdependence. Much of the literature I review comes from studies examining geographic variation in individual psychological characteristics (e.g., Big Five personality traits). However, I will link each mechanism back to its implications with respect to close relationships. I will also present an overview of best methodological practices and some visualization examples to help guide readers who are interested in implementing geographic related concepts into their existing research programs.

WHY WOULD PSYCHOLOGICAL AND SOCIAL BEHAVIOR VARY GEOGRAPHICALLY?

The idea that individuals are embedded in environments and relationships that modulate their behavior is one of the hallmarks of Interdependence Theory. Some of the earliest manifestations of Interdependence Theory were

This research was supported by a grant from the National Institute of Aging (2 R03 AG054705–01A1).

rooted in more basic models for how individuals function in psychological "life spaces" (Lewin, 1936). In Lewin's initial thinking that behavior is a function of the person and their environment (i.e., $B = f(P,E)$), he purposefully distinguished the psychological interpretation of an environment from the actual physical characteristics of an environment. Such a distinction that environments and situations were rooted in individual interpretations originated from Gestalt psychology and spurred an enormous development of thinking and research on the influence of the individual differences and situations (and their interactions) for predicting behavior.

Worth noting, though, situations and environments are naturally bound to a person's geographic and physical location. The likelihood of an individual's exposure to all sorts of situations varies geographically. For example, the likelihood of experiencing a volcanic eruption is very low in East Lansing, MI. More seriously, the dating norms, characteristics (and the number) of potential dating partners, and other factors (e.g., the socioeconomic status of an area) all have implications for people's relationships and vary geographically. Indeed, connections between Lewin's original conceptualization and people and environments interacting have been extended to considering the physical environments which people and their relationships inhabit. In this way, Kelley (1991) broadened the discussion of $B = f(P,E)$ to include an individual's interaction with their "physical environment" in the broader sense – such that the range of individual actions are necessarily constrained by the psychological, and often physical, environments in which they find themselves (Chein, 1954; Heider, 1959; Koffka, 1935). Repeated patterns of interactions with one's environment eventually become imprinted on individuals, leading to reliable patterns of individual differences. Although Lewin and Kelley (and others) rarely made predictions for exactly how physical and geographic environments come to be integrated into an individual's life space, in recent years theorists have attempted to make such efforts by studying geographic variation in psychological and social behavior (Rentfrow, 2010; Rentfrow, Gosling, & Potter, 2008).

One obvious question that many people have is why psychological and social behavior would vary according to geography in the first place. According to research and theory, there are at least three explanations for why geographic variation in psychological characteristics might emerge and persist over time – selective migration, social influences, and environmental influences. Of course, each of these mechanisms is not mutually exclusive from one another and has received a considerable amount of support.

Selective Migration

Selective migration simply refers to the idea that geographic variation in part results from people moving from one place to another for a particular reason (or choosing to stay for a particular reason). There are likely an infinite number of reasons why people move to a certain place (Rossi, 1955). The reasons could be psychological – people who are outgoing and extraverted might think they would be happier living in a populous city setting than a rural, sparse setting. Others might move to a certain place with individuals who share their values, such as social or religious values. There is evidence to suggest that living among politically dissimilar others is associated with residential mobility (Motyl, 2016; Motyl, Iyer, Oishi, Trawalter, & Nosek, 2014). In other words, people tend to move to ideologically homogenous areas that align with their own values. The same can be said for many different subgroups of the population (e.g., sexual minorities, religious individuals; Hughes & Saxton, 2006; Lee, Wimark, Ortiz, & Sewell, 2018; Philbreck, 2007). With respect to relationship science, many individuals move for interpersonal reasons as well – whether it be to find (or maintain) a relationship or to escape interpersonally difficult environments. In this way, selective migration could be thought of as a more abstracted form of locomotion – a concept often employed in the Interdependence Theory literature to characterize how individuals modulate their interdependence in relationships (or even end a relationship) depending on the outcomes they are receiving (Van Lange & Visser, 1999). With respect to selective migration, individuals would be choosing to depart an area that is not providing them with a satisfaction of their psychological and relational needs.

Also under the umbrella of selective migration are choices that involve *remaining* in an area when one has a choice to leave. For example, agreeable individuals often have success in romantic and interpersonal relationships, and their migration and immobility has implications not only for themselves but the places to which they would theoretically move (Chopik & Lucas, 2019; Dyrenforth, Kashy, Donnellan, & Lucas, 2010; Jokela, 2009, 2014). Agreeable people are less likely to migrate to different places over time (and, thus, disagreeable people are more likely to move). Agreeable individuals are motivated to build strong ties in their community and relationships, which often explains their unwillingness to break those ties by moving (Boneva & Frieze, 2001; Frieze, Hansen, & Boneva, 2006). High patterns of migration early in life, and how these moves intersect with close relationships, also have implications for an individual's health and well-being. For example, introverts who reported many moves during their childhood had poorer health, lower well-being, and a higher risk of mortality (Oishi & Schimmack, 2010). The link between introversion and mortality was explained by introverts' inability to form lasting social relationships across life, especially during childhood and adolescence. These are just some of the ways in which close relationships are affected by individuals, desires to move away from (or stay in) one geographic area.

Social Influences

Social influence refers to the psychological influence that the social environment has on the formation of individual and social characteristics. Within the consideration of social influence are at least two ways that people can be influenced by their environments.

The first way people are influenced by their environment is by contagion or some transitive process through which an individual's characteristics are molded based on the people around them. For example, if someone lives around or interacts with particularly avoidantly attached people, they may become more avoidantly attached themselves. Similar processes are often found in close relationships research. Couples and interpersonal partners show a large degree of coordinated changes over time – they tend to change in similar ways with respect to their personalities, social activities, physical limitations, cognition, health, and happiness (e.g., Chopik, Kim, & Smith, 2018; Hoppmann & Gerstorf, 2009; Hoppmann, Gerstorf, & Hibbert, 2011; Neal, Durbin, Gornik, & Lo, 2017).

The second way in which geographic environments exert social influence is through the broader social characteristics of a region (beyond just the individuals that we know) that might modulate individual behavior. These include broader environmental indicators that might affect social behavior, like crime, marriage, or mortality rates. Indeed, there already exist entire ecological models that guide interpersonal behavior (Bronfenbrenner, 1977, 2005; Bronfenbrenner & Ceci, 1994; Bronfenbrenner & Evans, 2000). Ecological approaches and considerations are common in explaining the interdependence found in a variety of different social relationships (Goodfriend & Arriaga, 2018; Nuttall & Valentino, 2017). Many of these ecological models integrate insights from life history and attachment theories, such that parental availability is a signal of the unpredictability and/or harshness of an environment (Belsky, Steinberg, & Draper, 1991; Chisholm, 1996, 1999; Simpson & Belsky, 2008).

There are also plenty of other scenarios in which individuals experience a "reactance" to their social environments. In these scenarios, instead of assimilating a region's characteristics, encountering a region or group of people that are so wildly different might result in individuals changing in ways that are in opposition to prevailing trends or norms in a region. This would also be considered a form of social influence, as the source that propels change is still an individual's social environment. One example of social influence mechanisms giving rise to geographic variability is how living among dissimilar people might affect us – whether it be transmitted through individuals (e.g., arguments we have with them) or broader social characteristics of a region (e.g., the social policies or institutions). In one such study demonstrating this phenomenon, individuals who live among politically dissimilar others (e.g., a liberal individual living in a conservative county) reported higher attachment avoidance and lower perspective taking than those individuals who "fit" with their environments (Chopik & Motyl, 2016; Motyl et al., 2014). Many of the mechanisms causing "misfits" of various kinds to experience negative consequences are through reductions in a sense of belonging (Motyl, 2016). Thus, at least some geographic variation in psychological characteristics related to relationship formation and maintenance arise from social influence processes.

Environmental Influences

Environmental influence suggests that features of an individual's physical environment affect their approach toward social relationships. Admittedly, there are fewer studies examining how the physical environment could potentially affect individuals. People often take a broad conceptualization for what is considered an environmental influence, including the local terrain, population density, neighborhood characteristics (e.g., the number of hospitals), and temperature/climate (Rentfrow et al., 2008). One such example is the persistent finding that rates of violent and aggressive behavior are higher in hot climates compared to cooler climates (Anderson, 2001). However, aggression is not the only social characteristic that increases as the seasons change. One dominant theory for explaining geographic variation involves the relative prevalence of pathogens around the world (Schaller & Murray, 2008).

Along with the physiological defenses our bodies have for fighting against pathogens (Kent, Bluthé, Kelley, & Dantzer, 1992), researchers also suggest that we have similarly built up psychological and social defense systems that protect us from contracting diseases associated with increased mortality. Researchers will often examine the interpersonal behavior of individuals living in regions with historically high rates of pathogen prevalence. In one such study, unrestricted sociosexuality (e.g., an openness to uncommitted sexual activity) was lower in regions with historically high disease rates (Murray & Schaller, 2014; Schaller & Murray, 2008). Thus, even in a context in which uncommitted sexual activity might lead to greater reproductive success, individuals curb their risky sexual practices as a means of avoiding transmittable diseases. Such defenses are also seen in individual characteristics like extraversion and openness to experience as well. Climate and weather have unique places in the study of geographic variation in personal and social characteristics. Weather and climate have been used to explain phenomena as broad as mortality and disease rates and as narrow as individual levels of depression and psychopathology (Geoffroy, Bellivier, Scott, & Etain, 2014; Magnusson, 2000). The high selection pressures of exposure to such deadly diseases is also one of the reasons why such social defense systems are also seen in other species, including chimpanzees, rodents, and even tadpoles (see Murray & Schaller, 2014).

Other, more literal interpretations of physical and environmental influences also exist. One such example was a five study report by Oishi et al. (2015), finding that introverted individuals preferred and were happier in more mountainous and secluded regions in the US (e.g., shaded forests/areas). This general pattern is found whether the researchers assessed the personalities of people actually living in mountainous regions, choices about hypothetically spending time in secluded places, and participants temporarily placed in secluded locations. The idea that some people seek out environments that are more sparsely populated has direct implications for their relationships – not only the number of people they could potentially form relationships with but also the dispositions of their potential relational partners. Such person-environment "fits" partially explain why introverts are happier in countries that are more introverted (Fulmer et al., 2010). Given the implications of introversion for the formation and maintenance of close relationships (Hotard, McFatter, McWhirter, & Stegall, 1989), environmental influences could be one of the drivers of geographic variation in social characteristics (through the select distribution of introverts), but little research beyond what is mentioned here has specifically investigated this possibility.

Mutual Reinforcement of Mechanisms

Of course, in presenting each of these mechanisms that give rise to geographic variation, I do not mean to imply that they are mutually exclusive. In fact, many of these mechanisms exert their will simultaneously. A region can come to be more avoidant with respect to close relationships by virtue of (1) many avoidant people moving to that area, (2) features of the environment cultivating more avoidant tendencies, or (3) both. Indeed, many demonstrations of geographic variations cite the many factors that mold a region to be a certain way. For example, voting behavior is thought to arise from a complex interaction of initial migration tendencies, the exposure to racial/ethnic diversity, and gradual contagion of social and political attitudes across social groups over time (McCann, 2014; Rentfrow, Jost, Gosling, & Potter, 2009). Likewise, geographic areas often change as a result of population fluctuations, which change not only the people emigrating there but the host region as well (Portes & Hao, 2002; van Prooijen, Krouwel, & Emmer, 2018). Other researchers think that sociality and warmth of cities might be a function of the intellectual institutions available, the population density, and the generosity of the people living around individuals (Park & Peterson, 2010). Yet others believe that prosociality originates from the influence of social norms and economic institutions that drive the development of social characteristics over time among both countries and cities within countries (Conway, Ryder, Tweed, & Sokol, 2001; Levine, Martinez, Brase, & Sorenson, 1994; Reysen & Levine, 2014).

A Case Study: Attachment Orientation

With respect to how attachment orientation and marriage rates vary across geographic space, similar mechanisms are also at play (Schmitt et al., 2003, 2004). For example, individuals from frontier and western U.S. states tend to report higher levels of attachment avoidance (i.e., a discomfort with emotional and physical intimacy; Chopik & Motyl, 2017). Likewise, in the same report, states with a higher proportion of avoidant individuals have a lower marriage rate, smaller household sizes on average, a greater proportion of people living alone, and are less prone to prosocial behavior.

Again, we see the influence of multiple processes that might bring about such geographic variation (see Chopik & Motyl, 2017; for an expanded discussion and for a reiteration of these mechanisms). The higher levels of avoidance in frontier states could be partially explained by a combination of selective migration and social and environmental influences. Specifically, individuals in frontier states (i.e., more recently settled states) are more independent and autonomous than individuals living in the Eastern US (Kitayama, Conway, Pietromonaco, Park, & Plaut, 2010). Initial settlers of the frontier may have been more independent and less interconnected – traits that helped them adapt to new unexplored environments. As time passed, frontier states developed institutions that inculcate psychological tendencies not found in other regions of the world. As a result, these independent thinkers and avoidant individuals seek out more personal accomplishments, make more dispositional attributions, live in sparsely populated regions, and even name their children more esoteric names (Kitayama et al., 2010; Kitayama, Ishii, Imada, Takemura, & Ramaswamy, 2006; Uskul, Kitayama, & Nisbett, 2008; Varnum & Kitayama, 2011). These same states have a greater percentage of people living alone, a greater percentage of households without grandchildren, and a greater percentage of people who are self-employed (Vandello & Cohen, 1999). In this way, the selective migration of people to the frontier closely resembles what Campbell (1975) and others have referred to as a form of social evolution that outpaces more traditional forms of biological evolution to form complexity in human systems in geographic environments.

Likewise, the harsh and dangerous conditions of these environments also put ecological pressures to adopt shorter-term relationships and engage in more superficial bonds, similar to other theorizing regarding the development of attachment orientations (Belsky et al., 1991; Chisholm, 1993). Through intergenerational transmission and social contagion, the harshness of the early frontier region could lead to higher rates of avoidant attachment in the western U.S. (Belsky et al., 1991; Chopik, Edelstein, et al., 2014; Chopik, Moors, & Edelstein, 2014; Fonagy, Steele, & Steele, 1991; Fowler & Christakis, 2008). In our 2017 study, we found support for many of these ideas – frontier and western states were higher in avoidance and showed many of the more independent social institutions that would be predicted from the mechanisms discussed (e.g., lower marriage rates, more single-led households; Chopik & Motyl, 2017).[1]

THE PRACTICAL STEPS OF STUDYING GEOGRAPHIC VARIATION IN INDIVIDUAL AND SOCIAL CHARACTERISTICS

Now that I have provided an overview of the reasons why geographic variation of psychological features *might* exist, and some examples of the questions that previous research has examined, a key question concerns how researchers might go about executing studies on geography and social relationships. Of course, there is no single way to go about analyzing geographic data – the analytic approach often depends on an individual researcher's question and the data available at hand. Nevertheless, there are a few general practices that current researchers tend to adopt (and a few practices that researchers should avoid). In the following section I outline the type of data that are typically available and the various ways in which one can analyze and visually display geographic variation.

The most typical way that researchers acquire geographic data is through large scale internet projects (e.g., outofservice.com; Rentfrow et al., 2008). Common practices include analyzing data from existing representative studies or secondary data (e.g., the World Values Survey; Chopik, 2017), using administrative data (e.g., violent crime rates; Bach, Defever, Chopik, & Konrath, 2017), or going through the labor-intensive process of collecting new data or collaborating with large networks of other researchers who will collect new data (Levine et al., 1994; Moshontz et al., 2018; Schmitt et al., 2003).

Analytic Approaches

There are many ways in which one could analyze geographic data (and many newer techniques are currently in development). Nevertheless, there are a few very basic ways in which people have analyzed geographic data. The most

---

[1] Another example of how social and environmental mechanisms intersect is seen in an ethnographic study of women and children living in a small Northern Brazilian town of Timbaúba in the state of Pernambuco – a small, economically deprived town with a very high infant mortality rate (particularly those in the Alto do Cruzeiro region). Nancy Scheper-Hughes notes that names are not provided to children until they begin to walk or speak, and abandonment of children is common (Scheper-Hughes, 1985, 1993). In the years since her initial visits to the Alto do Cruzeiro, the infant mortality rate (and birth rates overall) fell dramatically – a change that could partially be attributable to a free, government-run pregnancy clinic. Not surprisingly, this change in environmental and physical circumstances changed psychological behavior as well. Mothers now "held on" tightly to every infant, given the high likelihood that they would survive and live a long, healthy life (Scheper-Hughes, 2013).

basic approach is a purely correlational analysis at the region-level. This approach involves computing the mean for each region and then using a correlation/regression analysis. For example, if we had a data set of 1,000,000 people's evaluation of their relationship satisfaction within 50 U.S. states, we would compute 50 means, each of which represents a state. From there, we would conduct a basic correlation between these means and a predictor of interest (e.g., the percentage of a state's population currently divorced). Control variables (state-level demographics) could also be included in a regression analysis, provided they are measured at the same, superordinate level. One unfortunate product of this approach is that it often collapses across within-region variability (e.g., that people's relationship satisfaction varies considerably *within* a region). Also, this approach can handicap researchers by restricting their effective sample size to 50.

A way of fully appreciating the nested structure of the data is through the use of multi-level modeling (MLM), which is used extensively by relationships researchers because of its advantages in controlling for the non-independence that arises from couples, families, and other groups. From this perspective, Level-2 predictors at the region level (e.g., the number of sunny days on average) can be used to predict individual (Level-1) responses, such as relationship satisfaction. Additional levels (e.g., regions within nations) can also be estimated (Preacher, 2011), although a typical approach is to have two levels of data. Both Level-1 and Level-2 predictors (and cross-level interactions) can be modeled in a multi-level modeling framework to test questions related to geographic variability. For example, the degree to which an individual reports deriving their relationship satisfaction from external sources (a Level-1 predictor measured in individuals) could be a moderator of the association between the number of sunny days on average (a Level-2 predictor) and relationship satisfaction (the Level-1 outcome).

Of course, researchers should be careful that they do not run afoul of the ecological fallacy when generalizing associations from one unit of analysis (individuals) to another (regions) and vice versa (Chopik, O'Brien, & Konrath, 2017; Robinson, 1950). The same can be said for associations between relationship-related constructs measured at the individual and regional level. For a hypothetical example, imagine that anxiously attached individuals are dissatisfied in their relationships on average (at the individual level). However, also imagine that, using state-level data, we paradoxically find that states with higher mean levels of anxiety also have higher mean levels of relationship satisfaction. At the individual level, attachment anxiety is negatively associated with relationship satisfaction; at the regional level, attachment anxiety is positively associated with relationship satisfaction. How would something like this be possible? This would be an illustration of Robinson's paradox, which can be common when comparing individual and aggregate correlations between variables.

This paradox of results could be driven by some sort of explanation that, in the course of aggregation, causes a correlation to differ at different units of analysis. Hypothetically, it could be the case that anxious individuals try migrating to states that have particularly successful relationships in an effort to improve their relationships (or some other reason). Thus, states that on average report high relationship satisfaction oddly also have a higher proportion of anxiously attached individuals. Such a phenomenon (however unlikely) could possibly lead to a negative correlation at the individual level (anxiously attached individuals report lower relationship satisfaction) but a positive correlation at the state level (such that states with higher relationship satisfaction also have a higher proportion of anxiously attached individuals). Although this example seems far-fetched, such paradoxes have been illustrated in many other domains that are studied at individual and regional levels of analysis, including problems discussed in sociology, political science, and epidemiology (Allport, 1924; Gelman, 2009; Van Poppel & Day, 1996). A more general problem nested within the ecological fallacy involves trying to use aggregated findings to make inferences about individuals. For example, North Dakota has the highest means of anxiety and avoidance at the state-level compared to every other U.S. state (Chopik & Motyl, 2017). However, automatically assuming that a randomly selected individual from North Dakota is less secure than a randomly selected individual from California (a more secure state) would also be a commission of this fallacy. Oftentimes, to combat the ambiguity that can arise from examining a question from multiple units of analysis, researchers will specifically employ both correlational approaches at both units of measurement and multi-level modeling within one report (see Johnson & Chopik, 2019).

From these two basic models (correlations and MLM) spring forth many additional approaches. For example, questions regarding "fit" between individuals or couples and their environments can be modeled via multilevel polynomial regressions and decomposition using response surface methodology (Chopik & Motyl, 2016; Humberg, Nestler, & Back, 2019; van Scheppingen, Chopik, Bleidorn, & Denissen, 2019; Weidmann, Schönbrodt, Ledermann, & Grob, 2017). The use of polynomial regressions allows researchers to overcome the limitations of traditional difference scores while modeling non-linear relations between variables. Such non-linear effects are a boon for relationship researchers looking to test dose-response types of questions (Girme, Overall, Simpson, & Fletcher, 2015). Using the aforementioned example of sunny days at the region-level, one could test many non-linear effects: it could be the case that the number of sunny days no long matters for relationship satisfaction after at least half of the days in a region are sunny. Likewise, maybe the effects of sunny days enhancing relationship satisfaction are only apparent when a great majority of days (75 percent) are sunny and when individuals also report low avoidance (i.e., the effect is specific to people low in avoidance when there are at 75% of sunny days). Such curvilinear effects (and further moderation effects among higher-order polynomials) can be modeled in the context of geographic data and analyses.

The use of these models are discussed extensively elsewhere (Barranti, Carlson, & Côté, 2017; Edwards, 2002, 2007), and several tools now exist for easy graphing of relationships in three-dimensional space (Edwards, 2016; Schönbrodt, 2016). In the next couple of years, additional methods for conceptualizing analytic data will emerge and become more mainstream among psychologists and relationship researchers alike, including hot spot analysis (Abson, Dougill, & Stringer, 2012), sequence analysis (Vanhoutte, Wahrendorf, & Nazroo, 2017), and many more. Several of these techniques are standard practice in fields of sociology, anthropology, public health, and geography; to my knowledge, they have yet to be applied to relationship science.

Visualization Approaches

Just as there are many different ways of analyzing geographic data, there seems to be an infinite number of ways to visualize geographic data. The different ways of visualizing data also differ in terms of the needed level of technical expertise with specific forms of graphing software. For example, ArcGIS is a popular proprietary software used by geographers to depict different forms of geographic data. The use of such programs allows researchers to display complex patterns of data overlaying maps, whether it be comparisons of different regions or how individuals move between regions (e.g., tracking commuting or mobility routes). Although software suites such as these provide a wide range of opportunities for researchers interested in geographic data analysis, the cost (and renewals) may be prohibitively expensive. Luckily, there are many open source alternatives that can serve researchers' purposes. Simply searching for open source mapping software will yield many of these available programs (e.g., QGIS, gvSIG, Whitebox GAT, SAHA GIS, etc.). Some programs even have some visualization capabilities that the average researcher might not be aware of (e.g., exporting a hotspot analysis of a map image via Qualtrics). For those who are hesitant about learning a new interface or software, there are also plenty of alternatives that are easy to implement, either through R statistical software or even in-browser point-and-click interfaces.

Figure 3.1 shows a few different relationship-related constructs graphed at different units of analysis – county, state, and country (see https://osf.io/2cfsv/ for color versions of these figures and the non-proprietary data used to produce them).

Figure 3.1(a) plots variability in positive relationships at the county level in 1,347 counties in the United States (Schwartz et al., 2013). This data from this map was derived from a project that constructed a dictionary of words

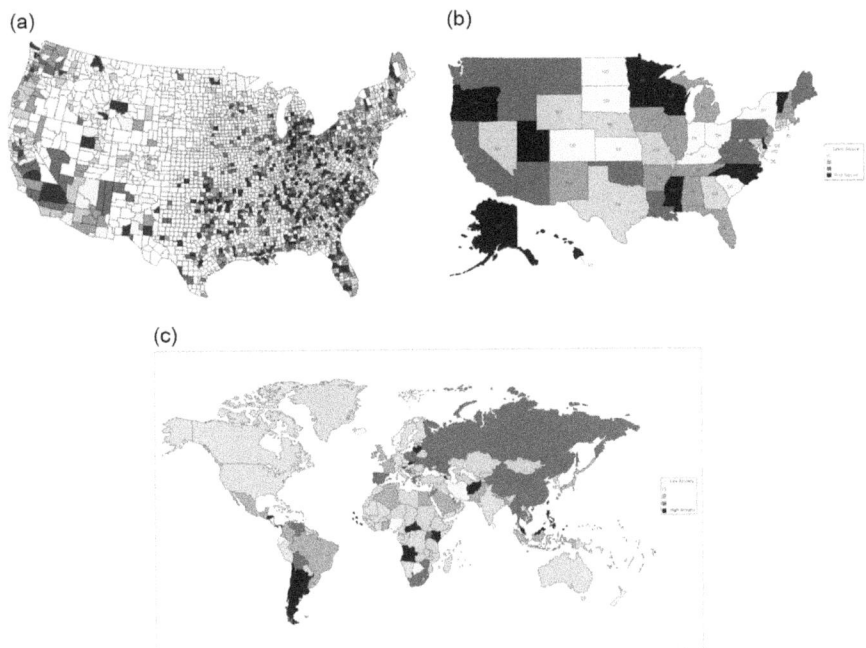

FIGURE 3.1 Geographic variation in (a) positive relationship tweets, (b) attachment security, and (c) attachment anxiety

related to positive relationships, which was then applied to 148 million tweets throughout the U.S. The researchers of this project only included counties for which there were 50,000 data points available. The darker colors represent more positive relationship-related words found in tweets. Many questions related to close relationships can be conducted at the county level. One popular outcome at such a refined unit of analysis is health (e.g., heart disease; Eichstaedt et al., 2015). To plot this graph, there are a number of R packages a researcher could use. Two of the most well documented packages are the mapproj and ggmap packages. In order to produce these maps, one merely has to run the syntax below:

```
install.packages("mapproj")
install.packages("ggmap")
require(maps) require(ggmap)
rel_data <- read.csv(file.choose())
rel_data
# data to link fips codes to county names
data(county.fips)
rel_data = merge(rel_data, county.fips, by="fips")
# Name of each county in the order we need to pass them
into map().
```

```
map_names = map("county", plot=FALSE)$names
# Create a list of variable values in the correct order for
mapping
ix = match(rel_data$polyname, map_names)
x = array(NA, length(map_names))
x[ix] = rel_data$pos_r
groups   <-   as.numeric(cut(x,   c(-Inf,   .008834,   .010142,
.011125, .012127, Inf)))
colors   =   c("#FFFF00",   "#FFBF00",   "#FF7F00",   "#FF3F00",
"#FF0000")
map("county", col=colors[groups], fill=TRUE, resolution=0,
lty=0,
projection="polyconic")
map("county", col = "black", fill = FALSE, add = TRUE, lty =
1, lwd = 0.2, projection= "polyconic")
```

Figure 3.1(b) plots variability in attachment security at the state level (using data from Chopik & Motyl, 2017). Attachment security was created by reverse scoring the anxiety and avoidance scales from the Experiences in Close Relationships Scale-Revised (ECR-R; Fraley, Waller, & Brennan, 2000) and averaging them together. These maps can be created by the same aforementioned packages. However, for illustrative purposes, this figure was made using one of the many in-browser applications available for free (i.e., www.indexmundi.com/map/creator/; map "USA"). In this way, displays of geographic data can be conducted without necessarily having extensive technical skills or even a familiarity with R. To use this particular user interface, I first "binned" the states into five groups depending on their level of attachment security. This binned information can be entered into the data tab. Worth noting, researchers could also use the full range of data and specify data/color ranges next. Then, I specified the bins and colors using the Color Ranges tab (set to five ranges; 0–1.1 for the lowest category; 1.2–2.1 for the next category). Further options regarding the map can be adjusted from this initial template. This approach is among the simplest if one wanted to plot geographic relationship data in which mean levels of a construct were compared across regions.

Figure 3.1(c) plots variability in attachment anxiety (measured with the ECR-R) around the world (see Chopik & Edelstein, 2014). This map was created using the same in-browser service as the state-level data. However, worth noting, this data set did not have all available countries. Thus, there are portions of the map that are "missing," which is not uncommon when one adopts such a broad approach (and in many studies of geographic variation). If a user leaves a country's data "blank" or "missing" in the data entry tab, then the default color used is gray for that country, signifying that the country has no available data.

I used these three examples as mere illustrations for how someone with little technical expertise could readily jump into the visualization of geographic data. However, there are several, more sophisticated programs (and even components of the R packages used above) that would likely serve researchers better in answering their research questions. In the next couple of years, the hope is that more user-friendly interfaces and open source programs become available in order to make geographic analyses in relationships research more mainstream.

Other Methodological Considerations

Level of Analysis Inherent in selecting an appropriate analytic approach is the choice and specification of the level at which a relational phenomenon is happening. For example, a researcher might be interested in how the economy and/or crime rates of an individual's environment were related to attitudes toward casual sex (a prediction possibly born out of ecological models of attachment and development; Belsky et al., 1991; Chisholm, 1996). It makes little sense to ask this type of question at the state level. States are comprised of a wide variety of cities/towns – both rural and urban, and collapsing across these entities might be equating large groups of people that probably live in disparate places within a state. An average crime rate for an entire state has few implications for people living in individual cities, where the local crime rate is more influential for their daily lives. However, other geographic variables might affect the subordinate regions rather uniformly. For example, federal policies, laws, and conditions (e.g., legalization of gay marriage, travel restrictions, GDP, cultural practices) might affect all groups in a more homogeneous way and more proximate information is not necessary. Likewise, if a researcher is interested in how migrating across regions affects their relationship process of interest, a great deal of thought needs to be put into how this question is formulated.

Given that moving within a region is more common than moving between regions, it might make more sense to examine regions that are more local to individuals. Moving from Buford, WY (a population of one person, until 2019) to Cheyenne, WY (a population of ~64,000) might have implications for an existing relationship or change the prospects of a single individual looking for a new relationship. Likewise, moving from a region with a balanced sex ratio to a region with an imbalanced sex ratio (either placing someone in the minority or majority sex of a region) would also change an individual's romantic prospects (Durante, Griskevicius, Simpson, Cantú, & Tybur, 2012). Questions like these and others might be posed by analyzing *within*, rather than *between*, the broader geographic regions that are typically studied. Another researcher might be interested in the effects of migration on social networks among refugees and immigrants as they move from one nation to another. Studies of such vulnerable groups necessarily involve a cross-country perspective because migration necessarily occurs between countries. However, an analysis of more proximal geographic regions (e.g., how immigrants from other countries move around within a US state) may not be as relevant for that particular question. As an intuitive rule of thumb, mechanisms of social and environmental influences likely occur at smaller units of analysis because people literally have to be exposed to them where they reside. If there is no clear way in which these influences affect people, it is likely not a fruitful approach to adopt. Having said that, mechanisms of selective migration can occur at many different levels of abstraction. Of course, there are plenty of exceptions to this rule of thumb. But, nevertheless, when conceptualizing how relationship processes might drive (or be driven by) geographic variation, it is important to consider the unit of analysis.

Sample Size There is some ambiguity regarding how large a sample should be in order to appropriately proceed with a geographic analysis. As a rule of thumb, it is better to have a large sample, both in terms of participants and geographic regions. Although this rule of thumb could be extended to all research questions centered around reliably estimating a mean/effect and its variability (Cohen, 1992; Simmons, Nelson, & Simonsohn, 2011), it is of particular importance when examining geographic variation, which historically has had a wide range of what is considered an appropriate sample size (Chopik et al., 2017). Regardless of the analysis a researcher employs, it is important to have enough participants in a region in order to estimate a mean that reliably represents a given region. For example, to examine relationship satisfaction among different counties in the state of Michigan, a researcher would ideally have a representative sample of participants from each of the 83 counties in the state of Michigan. Although this seems like an obvious point, actually implementing this practice can be very difficult given that some counties (cities, countries) are more populous than others. A little known secret in the literature is that the vast majority of participants in studies of geography come from predominantly urban areas (Bleidorn et al., 2016), with few studies including a sufficient number of participants from rural areas (Millward & Spinney, 2013). Thus, the extent to which relationship-related processes might vary across rural and urban contexts is currently unknown (Wenger, 1995). Representative samples in geographic research is an aspirational standard that is rarely achieved.

Further complicating the issue of sample sizes (and how to attain representative samples) is that the number of observations required to draw reliable conclusions will differ depending on the selected unit of analysis. For example, for individual-level analyses, a sample of 1,000,000 people likely provides more than enough statistical power to answer a substantive question of interest. However, if these 1,000,000 people reside in 50 states – and the process of interest is presumed to occur at the "state" level – a researcher's effective sample size is only N = 50; that is, the unit of analysis becomes states. In this way, the number of Level-1 and Level-2 units is an important distinction when one is conducting multi-level analyses (see Maas & Hox, 2005, for a more complete discussion). Although there are some methods available for answering questions with very few Level-2 (or any higher-level) units (McNeish & Stapleton, 2016), it is generally advised to have enough geographic units such that a reasonable amount of variability across higher-level units can be estimated. With too few geographic regions, variability could either be minimized or artificially inflated, giving the impression that regions vary in ways that they really do not. Nevertheless, there are oftentimes practical constraints on how many geographic regions are available (e.g., there are only 50 U.S. states or 83 counties in Michigan).

Reliability of Sampling The reliability and replicability of sampling at geographic regions can also be a point of contention, particularly when researchers want to draw broad conclusions about a geographic area. If a researcher has a large sample of individuals' relationship satisfaction information and an index of where they live (e.g., states), an additional sample from the same states (i.e., the same population) that is taken contemporaneously may not yield the same or a similar estimate. This will occur if individuals within a region exhibit relatively independent levels of the psychological variable of interest (versus non-independent or "clustered" levels). Given that the intraclass correlation (ICC) reflects the extent of non-independence among observations, the ICC can be used as a proxy to indicate the reliability of sampling. If, instead, levels of relationship satisfaction within an area are highly non-independent (e.g., grouped or clustered observations), then taking an additional sample from an area would likely produce a similar estimate. This reflects similarity among people in a geographic area (relative to people living in a different area), such that repeated sampling will yield similar results (i.e., everyone from Champaign, IL is really similar to each other [or the same on some characteristics], so random samples within a region are likely very similar).

There are additional methods for quantifying the reliability of geographic data. These include group mean reliabilities (i.e., ICC-2; Bliese, 2000) computed by splitting a sample within a region into two samples, estimating a mean for each sample, and calculating the reliability of those two means, as if they were separate observations. Another common approach is to check for different forms of measurement invariance or response styles across regions, to ensure that variability in the data cannot be attributable to people from different regions completing questionnaires differently, which can be an issue particularly in cross-cultural research (Harzing, 2006; Nye, Roberts, Saucier, & Zhou, 2008; van Herk, Poortinga, & Verhallen, 2004).

Yet another approach is to calculate spatial autocorrelations (or spatial regressions), which indicate whether neighboring geographic regions are more similar to one another than non-neighboring geographic regions. The premise of spatial dependence is very similar to other forms of non-independence. Recently, several illustrations of how to handle spatial dependency (and the consequences of not doing so) have been published (Rentfrow et al., 2013; Webster & Duffy, 2016). In the aforementioned study (Chopik & Motyl, 2017), states high in attachment avoidance tended to cluster on the frontier, suggesting some non-independence in the data that violates some of the assumptions of regression models. The methods to alleviate this issue are relatively simple to implement (Moran, 1950a, 1950b; Ward & Gleditsch, 2018). These approaches often involve creating a matrix of the geographic regions with an indicator variable for whether they do (1) or do not (0) border each other, creating a spatial weight by obtaining mean levels of a variable of interest in the neighboring/bordering regions, and then including this weight as a covariate in regression models. These approaches and others, including out-of-sample replication (Rentfrow et al., 2013), have been used to evaluate the reliability of region-level estimates and sampling.

CONCLUSION

Oftentimes, relationships are thought to be inextricable from the physical locations in which they occur. People meet sweethearts in their hometowns and colleges. They fall in love on the observation deck of the Empire State Building. There are some places where it may be easier to form and maintain relationships. Others have sentiments about physical locations (e.g., "home is where the heart is"). For example, in the Wizard of Oz, a famous mantra that Dorothy recites is, "There's no place like home," as it (and her slippers) transport her from the whimsical land of Oz to the familiar homelife in Kansas that provided her a sense of security (Morgan, 2010). Implicit is this mantra is that "home" and place mean different things to different people – Oz is not home, Kansas is. I hope that I have also given you an appreciation that individuals, places, and the interactions between people and places are not static entities over time – people move, actively shape, and are shaped by their environments. There are a number of ways that these processes might unfold, leading to geographic variation in relational characteristics over time.

In this chapter, I provided a broad overview of ways in which geographic variation in psychological and relational characteristics is conceptualized, analyzed, and visualized. Understanding and appreciating how social factors influence individuals is by no means a new or controversial idea (Lewin, 1936). An honest assessment of the current field of close relationships is that it has largely neglected environmental influences, whether occuring through indi-viduals and couples selecting environments of their own (selective migration) or being affected by their surrounding social and physical environments (e.g., social and environmental influence).

A large portion of this chapter was dedicated to providing readers with practical suggestions for how to analyze geographic factors and their implications for close relationships. Close relationships can have profound implications for individuals' health and well-being. Certainly relationships – and the individuals who comprise them – vary across contexts and geography. Whereas this notion has been implicit in Interdependence Theory since its inception, the field of relationships research is just now beginning to grapple with how external circumstances and people's subjective experiences of those circumstances affect them. Whether and to what extent such factors influence individuals is still an open question. With the increasing availability of data, means of acquiring new data, and the methods for analyzing/visualizing data, the future is bright for studying questions of close relationships from a geographic lens, whether the relationships are formed and maintained in Kansas, Oz, or anywhere else.

REFERENCES

Abson, D. J., Dougill, A. J., & Stringer, L. C. (2012). Using Principal Component Analysis for information-rich socio-ecological vulnerability mapping in Southern Africa. *Applied Geography*, 35, 515–524.

Allport, F. H. (1924). The group fallacy in relation to social science. *The Journal of Abnormal Psychology and Social Psychology*, 19, 60–73.

Anderson, C. A. (2001). Heat and violence. *Current Directions in Psychological Science*, 10, 33–38.

Bach, R. A., Defever, A. M., Chopik, W. J., & Konrath, S. H. (2017). Geographic variation in empathy: A state-level analysis. *Journal of Research in Personality*, 68, 124–130.

Barranti, M., Carlson, E. N., & Côté, S. (2017). How to test questions about similarity in personality and social psychology research: Description and empirical demonstration of response surface analysis. *Social Psychological and Personality Science*, 8, 465–475.

Belsky, J., Steinberg, L., & Draper, P. (1991). Childhood experience, interpersonal development, and reproductive strategy: An evolutionary theory of socialization. *Child Development*, 62, 647–670.

Bleidorn, W., Schönbrodt, F., Gebauer, J. E., Rentfrow, P. J., Potter, J., & Gosling, S. D. (2016). To live among like-minded others: Exploring the links between person-city personality fit and self-esteem. *Psychological Science*, 27, 419–427.

Bliese, P. D. (2000). Within-group agreement, non-independence, and reliability: Implications for data aggregation and analysis. In K. K. Klein & S. W. J. Kozlowski (Eds.), *Multilevel Theory, Research, and Methods in Organizations: Foundations, Extensions, and New Directions* (pp. 349–381). San Francisco, CA: Jossey-Bass.

Boneva, B. S. & Frieze, I. H. (2001). Toward a concept of a migrant personality. *Journal of Social Issues*, 57, 477–491.

Bronfenbrenner, U. (1977). Toward an experimental ecology of human development. *American Psychologist*, 32, 513–531.

Bronfenbrenner, U. (2005). *Making Human Beings Human: Bioecological Perspectives on Human Development*. Thousand Oaks, CA: Sage Publications Ltd.

Bronfenbrenner, U. & Ceci, S. J. (1994). Nature–nurture reconceptualized in developmental perspective: A bioecological model. *Psychological Review*, 101, 568–586.

Bronfenbrenner, U. & Evans, G. W. (2000). Developmental science in the 21st century: Emerging questions, theoretical models, research designs and empirical findings. *Social Development*, 9, 115–125.

Campbell, D. T. (1975). On the conflicts between biological and social evolution and between psychology and moral tradition. *American Psychologist*, 30, 1103–1126.

Chein, I. (1954). The environment as a determinant of behavior. *The Journal of Social Psychology*, 39, 115–127.

Chisholm, J. S. (1993). Death, hope, and sex: Life-history theory and the development of reproductive strategies. *Current Anthropology*, 34, 1–24.

Chisholm, J. S. (1996). The evolutionary ecology of attachment organization. *Human Nature*, 7, 1–38.

Chisholm, J. S. (1999). *Death, Hope and Sex: Steps to an Evolutionary Ecology of Mind and Morality*. New York: Cambridge University Press.

Chopik, W. J. (2017). Associations among relational values, support, health, and well-being across the adult lifespan. *Personal Relationships*, 24, 408–422.

Chopik, W. J. & Edelstein, R. S. (2014). Age differences in romantic attachment around the world. *Social Psychological and Personality Science*, 5, 892–900.

Chopik, W. J., Edelstein, R. S., van Anders, S. M., Wardecker, B. M., Shipman, E. L., & Samples-Steele, C. R. (2014). Too close for comfort? Adult attachment and cuddling in romantic and parent-child relationships. *Personality and Individual Differences*, 69, 212–216.

Chopik, W. J., Kim, E. S., & Smith, J. (2018). An examination of dyadic changes in optimism and physical health over time. *Health Psychology*, 37, 42–50.

Chopik, W. J. & Lucas, R. E. (2019). Actor, partner, and similarity effects of personality on global and experienced well-being. *Journal of Research in Personality*, 78, 249–261.

Chopik, W. J., Moors, A. C., & Edelstein, R. S. (2014). Maternal nurturance predicts decreases in attachment avoidance in emerging adulthood. *Journal of Research in Personality*, 53, 47–53.

Chopik, W. J. & Motyl, M. (2016). Ideological fit enhances interpersonal orientations. *Social Psychological and Personality Science*, 7, 759–768.

Chopik, W. J. & Motyl, M. (2017). Is Virginia for lovers? Geographic variation in adult attachment orientation. *Journal of Research in Personality*, 66, 38–45.

Chopik, W. J., O'Brien, E., & Konrath, S. H. (2017). Differences in empathic concern and perspective taking across 63 countries. *Journal of Cross-Cultural Psychology*, 48, 23–38.

Cohen, J. (1992). A power primer. *Psychological Bulletin*, 112, 155–159.

Conway, L. G., Ryder, A. G., Tweed, R. G., & Sokol, B. W. (2001). Intranational cultural variation: Exploring further implications of collectivism within the United States. *Journal of Cross-Cultural Psychology*, 32, 681–697.

Durante, K. M., Griskevicius, V., Simpson, J. A., Cantú, S. M., & Tybur, J. M. (2012). Sex ratio and women's career choice: Does a scarcity of men lead women to choose briefcase over baby? *Journal of Personality and Social Psychology*, 103, 121–134.

Dyrenforth, P. S., Kashy, D. A., Donnellan, M. B., & Lucas, R. E. (2010). Predicting relationship and life satisfaction from personality in nationally representative samples from three countries: The relative importance of actor, partner, and similarity effects. *Journal of Personality and Social Psychology*, 99, 690–702.

Edwards, J. R. (2002). Alternatives to difference scores: Polynomial regression analysis and response surface methodology. In F. Drasgow, & N. W. Schmitt (Eds.), *Advances in Measurement and Data Analysis* (pp. 350–400). San Francisco: Jossey-Bass.

Edwards, J. R. (2007). Polynomial regression and response surface methodology. In C. Ostroff, & T. A. Judge (Eds.), *Perspectives on Organizational Fit* (pp. 361–372). San Francisco: Jossey-Bass.

Edwards, J. R. (2016). Excel file for plotting response surfaces. Retrieved from http://public.kenan-flagler.unc.edu/faculty/edwardsj/downloads.htm

Eichstaedt, J. C., Schwartz, H. A., Kern, M. L., Park, G., Labarthe, D. R., Merchant, R. M., ... Seligman, M. E. P. (2015). Psychological language on Twitter predicts county-level heart disease mortality. *Psychological Science*, 26, 159–169.

Fonagy, P., Steele, H., & Steele, M. (1991). Maternal representations of attachment during pregnancy predict the organization of infant-mother attachment at one year of age. *Child Development*, 62, 891–905.

Fowler, J. H. & Christakis, N. A. (2008). Dynamic spread of happiness in a large social network: Longitudinal analysis over 20 years in the Framingham Heart Study. *BMJ*, 337, a2338.

Fraley, R. C., Waller, N. G., & Brennan, K. A. (2000). An item response theory analysis of self-report measures of adult attachment. *Journal of Personality and Social Psychology*, 78, 350–365.

Frieze, I. H., Hansen, S. B., & Boneva, B. (2006). The migrant personality and college students' plans for geographic mobility. *Journal of Environmental Psychology*, 26, 170–177.

Fulmer, C. A., Gelfand, M. J., Kruglanski, A. W., Kim-Prieto, C., Diener, E., Pierro, A., & Higgins, E. T. (2010). On "feeling right" in cultural contexts: How person-culture match affects self-esteem and subjective well-being. *Psychological Science*, 21, 1563–1569.

Gelman, A. (2009). *Red State, Blue State, Rich State, Poor State: Why Americans Vote the Way They Do – Expanded Edition*. Princeton, NJ: Princeton University Press.

Geoffroy, P. A., Bellivier, F., Scott, J., & Etain, B. (2014). Seasonality and bipolar disorder: A systematic review, from admission rates to seasonality of symptoms. *Journal of Affective Disorders*, 168, 210–223.

Girme, Y. U., Overall, N. C., Simpson, J. A., & Fletcher, G. J. O. (2015). "All or nothing": Attachment avoidance and the curvilinear effects of partner support. *Journal of Personality and Social Psychology*, 108, 450–475.

Goodfriend, W. & Arriaga, X. B. (2018). Cognitive reframing of intimate partner aggression: Social and contextual influences. *International Journal of Environmental Research and Public Health*, 15, 2464–2477.

Harzing, A.-W. (2006). Response styles in cross-national survey research: A 26-country study. *International Journal of Cross Cultural Management*, 6, 243–266.

Heider, F. (1959). On Lewin's methods and theory. *Journal of Social Issues*, Supplement Series, No. 13.

Hoppmann, C. A. & Gerstorf, D. (2009). Spousal interrelations in old age – A mini-review. *Gerontology*, 55, 449–459.

Hoppmann, C. A., Gerstorf, D., & Hibbert, A. (2011). Spousal associations between functional limitation and depressive symptom trajectories: Longitudinal findings from the Study of Asset and Health Dynamics Among the Oldest Old (AHEAD). *Health Psychology*, 30, 153–162.

Hotard, S. R., McFatter, R. M., McWhirter, R. M., & Stegall, M. E. (1989). Interactive effects of extraversion, neuroticism, and social relationships on subjective well-being. *Journal of Personality and Social Psychology*, 57, 321.

Hughes, A. & Saxton, P. (2006). Geographic micro-clustering of homosexual men: Implications for research and social policy. *Social Policy Journal of New Zealand*, 28, 158–178.

Humberg, S., Nestler, S., & Back, M. D. (2019). Response surface analysis in personality and social psychology: Checklist and clarifications for the case of congruence hypotheses. *Social Psychological and Personality Science*, 10, 409–419.

Johnson, D. J. & Chopik, W. J. (2019). Geographic variation in the Black-violence stereotype. *Social Psychological and Personality Science*, 10, 287–294.

Jokela, M. (2009). Personality predicts migration within and between U.S. states. *Journal of Research in Personality*, 43, 79–83.

Jokela, M. (2014). Personality and the realization of migration desires. In P. J. Rentfrow (Ed.), *Geographical Psychology: Exploring the Interaction of Environment and Behavior* (pp. 71–88). Washington, DC: American Psychological Association.

Kelley, H. H. (1991). Lewin, situations, and interdependence. *Journal of Social Issues*, 47, 211–233.

Kent, S., Bluthé, R.-M., Kelley, K. W., & Dantzer, R. (1992). Sickness behavior as a new target for drug development. *Trends in Pharmacological Sciences*, 13, 24–28.

Kitayama, S., Conway, L. G., III, Pietromonaco, P. R., Park, H., & Plaut, V. C. (2010). Ethos of independence across regions in the United States: The production-adoption model of cultural change. *American Psychologist*, 65, 559–574.

Kitayama, S., Ishii, K., Imada, T., Takemura, K., & Ramaswamy, J. (2006). Voluntary settlement and the spirit of independence: Evidence from Japan's "northern frontier." *Journal of Personality and Social Psychology*, 91, 369–384.

Koffka, K. (1935). *Principles of Gestalt Psychology*. New York: Harcourt Brace.

Lee, J. G. L., Wimark, T., Ortiz, K. S., & Sewell, K. B. (2018). Health-related regional and neighborhood correlates of sexual minority concentration: A systematic review. *PLoS ONE*, 13, e0198751-e0198751.

Levine, R. V., Martinez, T. S., Brase, G., & Sorenson, K. (1994). Helping in 36 U.S. cities. *Journal of Personality and Social Psychology*, 67, 69–82.

Lewin, K. (1936). *Principles of Topological Psychology*. New York: McGraw-Hill.

Maas, C. J. & Hox, J. J. (2005). Sufficient sample sizes for multilevel modeling. *Methodology*, 1, 86–92.

Magnusson, A. (2000). An overview of epidemiological studies on seasonal affective disorder. *Acta Psychiatrica Scandinavica*, 101, 176–184.

McCann, S. J. H. (2014). Big five personality differences and political, social, and economic conservatism: An American state-level analysis. In P. J. Rentfrow (Ed.), *Geographical Psychology: Exploring the Interaction of Environment and Behavior* (pp. 139–160). Washington, DC: American Psychological Association.

McNeish, D. & Stapleton, L. M. (2016). Modeling clustered data with very few clusters. *Multivariate Behavioral Research*, 51, 495–518.

Millward, H. & Spinney, J. (2013). Urban–rural variation in satisfaction with life: Demographic, health, and geographic predictors in Halifax, Canada. *Applied Research in Quality of Life*, 8, 279–297.

Moran, P. A. (1950a). Notes on continuous stochastic phenomena. *Biometrika*, 37, 17–23.

Moran, P. A. (1950b). A test for the serial independence of residuals. *Biometrika*, 37, 178–181.

Morgan, P. (2010). Towards a developmental theory of place attachment. *Journal of Environmental Psychology*, 30, 11–22.

Moshontz, H., Campbell, L., Ebersole, C. R., IJzerman, H., Urry, H. L., Forscher, P. S., . . . Chartier, C. R. (2018). The psychological science accelerator: Advancing psychology through a distributed collaborative network. *Advances in Methods and Practices in Psychological Science*, 1, 501–515.

Motyl, M. (2016). Liberals and conservatives are geographically dividing. In P. Valdesolo & J. Graham (Eds.), *Bridging Ideological Divides: The Claremont Symposium for Applied Social Psychology*. Los Angeles: Sage Press.

Motyl, M., Iyer, R., Oishi, S., Trawalter, S., & Nosek, B. A. (2014). How ideological migration geographically segregates groups. *Journal of Experimental Social Psychology*, 51, 1–14.

Murray, D. R. & Schaller, M. (2014). Pathogen prevalence and geographical variaion in traits and behavior. In P. J. Rentfrow (Ed.), *Geographical Psychology: Exploring the Interaction of Environment and Behavior* (pp. 51–70). Washington, DC: American Psychological Association.

Neal, J. W., Durbin, C. E., Gornik, A. E., & Lo, S. L. (2017). Codevelopment of preschoolers' temperament traits and social play networks over an entire school year. *Journal of Personality and Social Psychology*, 113, 627–640.

Nuttall, A. K. & Valentino, K. (2017). An ecological-transactional model of generational boundary dissolution across development. *Marriage & Family Review*, 53, 105–150.

Nye, C. D., Roberts, B. W., Saucier, G., & Zhou, X. (2008). Testing the measurement equivalence of personality adjective items across cultures. *Journal of Research in Personality*, 42, 1524–1536.

Oishi, S. & Schimmack, U. (2010). Residential mobility, well-being, and mortality. *Journal of Personality and Social Psychology*, 98, 980–994.

Oishi, S., Talhelm, T., & Lee, M. (2015). Personality and geography: Introverts prefer mountains. *Journal of Research in Personality*, 58, 55–68.

Park, N. & Peterson, C. (2010). Does it matter where we live?: The urban psychology of character strengths. *American Psychologist*, 65, 535–547.

Philbreck, N. (2007). *Mayflower: A Story of Courage, Community, and War*. New York: Penguin.

Portes, A. & Hao, L. (2002). The price of uniformity: Language, family and personality adjustment in the immigrant second generation. *Ethnic and Racial Studies*, 25, 889–912.

Preacher, K. J. (2011). Multilevel SEM strategies for evaluating mediation in three-level data. *Multivariate Behavioral Research*, 46, 691–731.

Rentfrow, P. J. (2010). Statewide differences in personality: Toward a psychological geography of the United States. *American Psychologist*, 65, 548–558.

Rentfrow, P. J. (2014). *Geographical Psychology: Exploring the Interaction of Environment and Behavior*. Washington, DC: American Psychological Association.

Rentfrow, P. J., Gosling, S. D., Jokela, M., Stillwell, D. J., Kosinski, M., & Potter, J. (2013). Divided we stand: Three psychological regions of the United States and their political, economic, social, and health correlates. *Journal of Personality and Social Psychology*, 105, 996–1012.

Rentfrow, P. J., Gosling, S. D., & Potter, J. (2008). A theory of the emergence, persistence, and expression of geographic variation in psychological characteristics. *Perspectives on Psychological Science*, 3, 339–369.

Rentfrow, P. J., Jost, J. T., Gosling, S. D., & Potter, J. (2009). Statewide differences in personality predict voting patterns in 1996–2004 US presidential elections. In J. T. Jost, A. C. Kay, & H. Thorisdottir (Eds.), *Social and Psychological Bases of Ideology and System Justification* (pp. 314–349). New York: Oxford University.

Reysen, S. & Levine, R. V. (2014). People, culture, and place: How place predicts helping toward strangers. In P. J. Rentfrow (Ed.), *Geographical Psychology: Exploring the Interaction of Environment and Behavior* (pp. 241–260). Washington, DC: American Psychological Association.

Robinson, W. S. (1950). Ecological correlations and the behavior of individuals. *American Sociological Review*, 15, 351–357.

Rossi, P. H. (1955). *Why Families Move: A Study in the Social Psychology of Urban Residential Mobility*. Glencoe, IL: Free Press.

Schaller, M. & Murray, D. R. (2008). Pathogens, personality, and culture: Disease prevalence predicts worldwide variability in sociosexuality, extraversion, and openness to experience. *Journal of Personality and Social Psychology*, 95, 212–221.

Scheper-Hughes, N. (1985). Culture, scarcity, and maternal thinking: Maternal detachment and infant survival in a Brazilian shantytown. *Ethos*, 13, 291–317.

Scheper-Hughes, N. (1993). *Death without Weeping: The Violence of Everyday Life in Brazil*. Berkeley, CA: University of California Press.

Scheper-Hughes, N. (2013). No more angel-babies on the Alto. *Berkeley Review of Latin American Studies*, Spring 2013, 25–31.

Schmitt, D. P., Alcalay, L., Allensworth, M., Allik, J., Ault, L., Austers, I., . . . Zupanèiè, A. (2003). Are men universally more dismissing than women? Gender differences in romantic attachment across 62 cultural regions. *Personal Relationships*, 10, 307–331.

Schmitt, D. P., Alcalay, L., Allensworth, M., Allik, J., Ault, L., Austers, I., . . . Scrimali, T. (2004). Patterns and universals of adult romantic attachment across 62 cultural regions: Are models of self and of other pancultural constructs? *Journal of Cross-Cultural Psychology*, 35, 367–402.

Schönbrodt, F. D. (2016). RSA: An R package for response surface analysis (version 0.9.10). Retrieved from https://cran.r-project.org/package=RSA

Schwartz, H. A., Eichstaedt, J. C., Kern, M. L., Dziurzynski, L., Lucas, R. E., Agrawal, M., . . . Seligman, M. E. (2013). *Characterizing geographic variation in well-being using tweets.* Paper presented at the Seventh International AAAI Conference on Weblogs and Social Media.

Simmons, J. P., Nelson, L. D., & Simonsohn, U. (2011). False-positive psychology: Undisclosed flexibility in data collection and analysis allows presenting anything as significant. *Psychological Science, 22,* 1359–1366.

Simpson, J. A. & Belsky, J. (2008). Attachment theory within a modern evolutionary framework. In J. Cassidy & P. R. Shaver (Eds.), *Handbook of Attachment: Theory, Research, and Clinical Applications* (2nd ed., pp. 131–157). New York: Guilford Press.

Uskul, A. K., Kitayama, S., & Nisbett, R. E. (2008). Ecocultural basis of cognition: Farmers and fishermen are more holistic than herders. *Proceedings of the National Academy of Sciences, 105,* 8552–8556.

van Herk, H., Poortinga, Y. H., & Verhallen, T. M. M. (2004). Response styles in rating scales: Evidence of method bias in data from six EU countries. *Journal of Cross-Cultural Psychology, 35,* 346–360.

Van Lange, P. A. & Visser, K. (1999). Locomotion in social dilemmas: How people adapt to cooperative, tit-for-tat, and noncooperative partners. *Journal of Personality and Social Psychology, 77,* 762–773.

Van Poppel, F. & Day, L. H. (1996). A test of Durkheim's theory of suicide – without committing the "ecological fallacy." *American Sociological Review, 61,* 500–507.

van Prooijen, J.-W., Krouwel, A. P. M., & Emmer, J. (2018). Ideological responses to the EU refugee crisis: The left, the right, and the extremes. *Social Psychological and Personality Science, 9,* 143–150.

van Scheppingen, M. A., Chopik, W. J., Bleidorn, W., & Denissen, J. J. A. (2019). Longitudinal actor, partner, and similarity effects of personality on well-being. *Journal of Personality and Social Psychology, 117,* e51–e70.

Vandello, J. A. & Cohen, D. (1999). Patterns of individualism and collectivism across the United States. *Journal of Personality and Social Psychology, 77,* 279–292.

Vanhoutte, B., Wahrendorf, M., & Nazroo, J. (2017). Duration, timing and order: How housing histories relate to later life wellbeing. *Longitudinal and Life Course Studies, 8,* 227–243.

Varnum, M. E. W. & Kitayama, S. (2011). What's in a name? Popular names are less common on frontiers. *Psychological Science, 22,* 176–183.

Ward, M. D. & Gleditsch, K. S. (2018). *Spatial Regression Models.* Los Angeles: Sage Publications.

Webster, G. D. & Duffy, R. D. (2016). Losing faith in the intelligence–religiosity link: New evidence for a decline effect, spatial dependence, and mediation by education and life quality. *Intelligence, 55,* 15–27.

Weidmann, R., Schönbrodt, F. D., Ledermann, T., & Grob, A. (2017). Concurrent and longitudinal dyadic polynomial regression analyses of Big Five traits and relationship satisfaction: Does similarity matter? *Journal of Research in Personality, 70,* 6–15.

Wenger, G. C. (1995). A comparison of urban with rural support networks: Liverpool and North Wales. *Ageing & Society, 15,* 59–81.

4

Ethnicity, Interdependence, and the Investment Model of Commitment Processes

STANLEY O. GAINES, JR. AND DELETHA P. HARDIN

In *The Analysis of Subjective Culture*, Triandis (1972) provided one of the earliest conceptual frameworks for understanding the potential impact of *culture* (i.e., "the [hu]man-made part of the environment"; Herskovits, 1955, p. 305) on social behavior (Fiske, Kitayama, Markus, & Nisbett, 1998). Triandis distinguished between *objective culture* (comprising physical manifestations of culture, such as tools) and *subjective culture* (comprising psychological manifestations of culture, such as norms; e.g., Triandis, 2004). In turn, Triandis emphasized *cultural values* (i.e., organized sets of beliefs that are transmitted from earlier generations to later generations within a given society, with the caveat that not all persons necessarily embrace those beliefs to the same degree within the same society; e.g., Triandis, 1995) as aspects of subjective culture that are especially likely to influence interpersonal behavior (see Heine, 2016).

In the present chapter, we contend that Triandis's (1972) conceptual framework constitutes a full-fledged theory of subjective culture, with potentially important implications for the extent to which empirical links among the constructs within Thibaut and Kelley's (1959; Kelley & Thibaut, 1978) interdependence theory in general – and Rusbult's (1980) investment model in particular – may be moderated by *ethnicity* (i.e., persons' presumed biological and/or cultural heritage; see Markus, 2008). Triandis's (1989, 1996) assumption that different ethnic groups embrace the cultural values of *individualism* (i.e., persons' orientation toward the welfare of themselves) and *collectivism* (i.e., persons' orientation toward the welfare of others instead of, or in addition to, themselves; see Gaines, 1997) to different degrees is especially important to our adaptation of Triandis's theory of subjective culture in order to understand how (if at all) culture is relevant to interdependence processes. We draw upon Le and Agnew's (2003) meta-analysis of the generalizability of Rusbult's investment model across ethnic groups in the process of evaluating Triandis's theory of subjective culture, especially the results of two studies (in order of appearance, Lin & Rusbult, 1995; and Davis & Strube,

1993) in the process of evaluating relevant evidence. In addition, we propose both a critique and a prospective revamping of Triandis's theory (drawing upon the cultural perspective on marriage as advanced by K. K. Dion & Dion, 1993; as well as the suffocation model of marriage as presented by Finkel, Hui, Carswell, & Larson, 2014) in a manner that could add conceptual insight into Rusbult's model.

AN OVERVIEW OF TRIANDIS'S THEORY OF SUBJECTIVE CULTURE

So far, we have noted Triandis's (1972) constructs of objective and subjective aspects of culture, as well as Triandis's (2004) constructs of individualism and collectivism as cultural values (keeping in mind that some of Triandis's writings refer to person-level individualism as *idiocentrism* and person-level collectivism as *allocentrism*; e.g., Triandis, 1995). However, at the core of Triandis's (1972, pp. 22–23) theory of subjective culture, one finds an intricately developed model that links distal antecedents (e.g., economic activities, social and political organizations), proximal antecedents (e.g., language, religion), basic psychological processes (e.g., cognitive learning, instrumental learning), subjective culture (e.g., cognitive structures, behavioral intentions), and consequences (e.g., developed abilities, patterns of action). Given that some critics have questioned the need for an interdisciplinary field of cultural psychology (Shweder & Sullivan, 1993), Triandis's model and broader theory of subjective culture offers considerable promise to social psychology regarding the development and testing of novel, culturally informed hypotheses concerning determinants of interpersonal behavior.

One can detect echoes of Triandis's (1972) model of antecedents and consequences of subjective cultural in other (and, arguably, better-known) models and theories of cognitive and behavioral processes within cultural psychology. For example, Markus and Kitayama's (1991) model of antecedents and consequences of self-construals, as elaborated by Fiske et al. (1998, p. 918), bears more than a passing resemblance to Triandis's earlier model (for a review of the conceptual rationale and subsequent research concerning Markus and Kitayama's model, see Matsumoto, 1999). Nevertheless, Triandis's model and underlying theory of subjective culture tend not to be cited by name within cultural psychology, possibly due to the game-changing influence of Hofstede's (1980) research and cultural dimensions theory concerning work-related values (positing an individualism-collectivism dichotomy as one of several "cultural syndromes") within the field (see Heine, 2016).

In previous chapters on culture as reflected in close relationship processes, we drew primarily upon Triandis's (1995) *Individualism and Collectivism* when we contended that 1) cultural values might serve as direct predictors of interdependence dynamics (Gaines & Hardin, 2013) and 2) ethnicity might serve as a moderator of the effects of cultural values on interdependence phenomena (Gaines & Hardin, 2018). However, in the present chapter, we delve into Triandis's (1972) *The Analysis of Subjective Culture* as we argue that interdependence processes themselves might be moderated by ethnicity *because the promotion of specific cultural values across generations may differ from one ethnic group to another*. As we shall see in the following sections, not only did Triandis (1989) speculate that "exchange theory" in general (Triandis's preferred term for the original formulation of interdependence theory by Thibaut & Kelley, 1959) is likely to be relevant to close relationship processes among those ethnic groups who presumably embrace individualism (rather than collectivism) to the greatest extent; but Triandis (1996) also speculated that the effects of rewards and costs on relationship stability in particular are likely to be significant among those ethnic groups who presumably embrace individualism (rather than collectivism) to the greatest extent.

INTERDEPENDENCE THEORY: UNIVERSAL OR LIMITED TO INDIVIDUALISTIC ETHNIC GROUPS?

Thibaut and Kelley's (1959) interdependence theory initially focused on the mutual influence that relationship partners typically exert upon each other's *behavior* (rather than each other's thoughts or feelings; see Kelley, 1997). If one were to operationalize Thibaut and Kelley's earliest version of interdependence theory solely in terms of the rewards versus costs that individuals experience within close relationships, then one might be tempted to conclude that reinforcement is the defining process of close relationships (Foa & Foa, 1974). However, even in their earliest version of interdependence theory, Thibaut and Kelley acknowledged that relationship dynamics cannot be reduced solely to partners' receipt of net profits (i.e., preponderance of rewards over costs; Berscheid, 1985). Moreover, in their major revision of interdependence theory, Kelley and Thibaut (1978) noted that many interpersonal situations may require that partners incur net losses over the short term, in order for partners to obtain net profits over the long term (Berscheid & Reis, 1998).

Prior to the 1990s (i.e., the "decade of ethnicity"; see Shweder & Sullivan, 1993), Thibaut and Kelley (1959) viewed their interdependence theory as universal in scope, generalizing across a variety of ethnic (e.g., racial, religious, and national) groups (e.g., Kelley et al. 1983/2002). However, according to Triandis's (1972) theory of subjective culture, "[w]e expect that in collectivistic cultures[,] the applicability of exchange theories will be more limited than in individualistic cultures" (Triandis, 1989, p. 509). For example, among persons from the United States, United Kingdom, France, and Germany (all of whom Triandis classified as individualistic, due to historical circumstances that ostensibly led persons in those nations to prioritize individual rights over ingroup rights), Triandis (2004) would expect reinforcement to be a defining feature of close relationship processes. Conversely, among persons from Japan, India, Russia, and Brazil (all of whom Triandis categorized as collect-ivistic, due to historical circumstances that supposedly led persons in those nations to prioritize ingroup rights over individual rights), Triandis would expect reinforcement to be irrelevant to close relationship processes.

What evidence – if any – would support Triandis's (1989) assertions concerning ethnicity as a moderator of the importance that reinforcement plays in close relationship processes? Unfortunately, Triandis did not cite any empirical research on ethnicity and reinforcement within close relationships. Instead, Triandis cited Mills and Clark's (1982) distinction between *communal* and *exchange* relationships as conceptual support (i.e., personal or emotion-ally intimate relationships are communally based, characterized by partners' attention to each other's needs; whereas social or emotionally non-intimate relationships are exchange-based, characterized by partners' attention to their own needs; see also Clark & Mills, 1979). In addition, the empirical studies that Triandis *did* cite (i.e., Triandis, Vassiliou, & Nassiakou, 1968, studies 1–3) addressed individuals' behavioral intentions alongside perceptions of social roles and social behavior in various types of social and personal relationships (e.g., greater likelihood for persons in the supposedly individualistic United States, compared to the likelihood for persons in the ostensibly part-individu-alistic/part-collectivistic Greece, to indicate a preference for behaving more positively toward ingroup versus outgroup members without regard to the social roles that particular ingroup or outgroup members occupy) – *not* individuals' receipt of rewards or costs within close relationships. Thus, we conclude that Triandis's own studies have not adequately tested Triandis's predictions concerning ethnicity as a moderator of reinforcement in close relationships.

THE INVESTMENT MODEL: UNIVERSAL OR LIMITED TO INDIVIDUALISTIC ETHNIC GROUPS?

Thibaut and Kelley's (1959) interdependence theory proposes that, in order to properly understand why some close relationships persist (whereas other close relationships fail to stand the test of time), one cannot limit one's attention to presumed covariance (e.g., a significant positive correlation) between relationship *satisfaction* (i.e., individuals' experience of positive versus negative emotions toward their partners, presumably reflecting rewards versus costs that are received within the relationships) and relation-ship stability (Rusbult, Drigotas, & Verette, 1994). Rather, at a minimum, one must add *dependence* (i.e., the extent to which individuals count on their relationships to obtain rewards versus costs) as a potential covariate of

satisfaction and relationship stability (Rusbult & Buunk, 1993). Unless individuals experience low satisfaction *and* low dependence, they will tend to
remain in their current relationships (see Rusbult & Arriaga, 2000).

According to Rusbult's (1980) *investment model*, dependence mediates
the impact of satisfaction on relationship stability (i.e., satisfaction is reflected
positively in dependence, which in turn is reflected positively in relationship
stability; Rusbult, Agnew, & Arriaga, 2012). Furthermore, individuals experience dependence subjectively as *commitment* (i.e., individual' decision to
persist in their relationships; Arriaga, 2013). In fact, commitment – rather
than dependence *per se* – emerges as the pivotal variable in Rusbult's investment model (e.g., Rusbult & Agnew, 2010). Not only is commitment positioned as the primary *consequence* of various constructs in addition to
satisfaction (e.g., perceived quality of alternatives, investment size, prescriptive support); but commitment is also positioned as the primary *antecedent* of
several constructs (e.g., accommodation, derogation of alternatives, willingness to sacrifice, perceived superiority; Gaines & Agnew, 2003).

Just as Thibaut and Kelley (1959) cast their interdependence theory as
universal in scope, so too did Rusbult (1980) view her investment model – a
direct extension of interdependence theory (Rusbult, Olsen, Davis, & Hannon, 2001) – as universal. It turns out that Triandis (1996) did not criticize the
universality of Rusbult's investment model *per se*. However, Triandis *did*
comment directly upon the universality of the presumed impact of rewards
and costs (which Rusbult treated as proxies for, if not direct influences on,
satisfaction in some of her earliest research; e.g., Rusbult 1980, 1983; Rusbult,
Johnson, & Morrow, 1986) upon individuals' maintenance versus termination
of ongoing relationships:

> *Collectivists pay much attention to the needs of members of their ingroups in determin-
> ing their social behavior. Thus, if a relationship is desirable from the point of view of the
> ingroup but costly from the point of view of the individual, [then] the individual is likely
> to stay in the relationship. Individualists pay attention to the advantages and costs of
> relationships, as described by exchange theory (Thibaut & Kelley, 1959). If the costs
> exceed the advantages, [then] individualists drop the relationship.*
>
> (Triandis, 1996, p. 409)

Given that, as noted in the preceding section, Triandis (2004) depicted
certain nations as individualistic (e.g., the United States, the United Kingdom,
France, Germany) versus collectivistic (e.g., Japan, India, Russia, Brazil), what
evidence – if any – would lend support to Triandis's (1996) claims about
ethnicity as a moderator of the direct or indirect effects of rewards and costs
upon individuals' maintenance versus termination of close relationships? As
was the case with reinforcement in general (e.g., Triandis, 1989), Triandis did
not cite any research on ethnicity and the impact of rewards or costs on
relationship stability. Instead, once again, Triandis cited Mills and Clark's
(1982) distinction between communal relationships (supposedly characteristic

of collectivistic nations, where individuals' own rewards and costs are not likely to affect relationship stability) and exchange relationships (ostensibly characteristic of individualistic nations, where individuals' own rewards and costs *are* likely to affect relationship stability). Furthermore, Triandis did not cite any of his own research as direct support for his claims about ethnicity and the impact of rewards versus costs on relationship stability. Therefore, we conclude that Triandis did not test those hypotheses from his theory of subjective culture (Triandis, 1972) that are most relevant to Rusbult's (1980) investment model.

RESULTS OF STUDIES ON THE UNIVERSALITY OF THE
INVESTMENT MODEL: EMPIRICAL CHALLENGES TO THE
THEORY OF SUBJECTIVE CULTURE

We are not aware of any studies in which relationship scientists (as distinct from cultural psychologists) have overtly applied Triandis's (1972) theory of subjective culture to tests of Rusbult's (1980) investment model across ethnic groups. However, results of Le and Agnew's (2003) meta-analysis of links among investment model variables indicated that – across several nations (i.e., the United States, the United Kingdom, the Netherlands, Israel, and Taiwan), and as expected – 1) satisfaction is a significant positive predictor of commitment; 2) *perceived quality of alternatives* (i.e., the extent to which individuals believe that they could acquire relatively high rewards and accrue relatively low costs by leaving their current relationships and entering other relationships; Van Lange & Balliet, 2015) is a significant negative predictor of commitment; and 3) *investment size* (i.e., the degree to which resources that individuals have put into their relationships are perceived as irretrievable; Agnew & VanderDrift, 2015) is a significant positive predictor of commitment. Furthermore, when Le and Agnew (2003) examined race (i.e., White versus non-White) as a potential moderator, none of the investment model links differed significantly across racial groups. The non-effect of race as a moderator concerning path coefficients within Rusbult's investment model is particularly noteworthy in light of Triandis's (1976) assertion that White persons' and Black persons' perceptions of the social environment differ qualitatively (e.g., White persons are more likely to view social interactions through an individualistic lens; whereas Black persons are more likely to view the same interactions through a collectivistic lens). Therefore, at first glance, the extant evidence provides an empirical challenge to a key tenet of Triandis's (1972) theory of subjective culture.

One might argue that Le and Agnew's (2003) general distinction between White and non-White groups is not sufficiently comparable to Triandis's (1976) specific White–Black distinction for us to question the relevance of Triandis's (1972) theory of subjective culture to the universality of links among investment model variables, even indirectly. However, Davis and Strube's (1993) study of investment model correlations among a sample of White versus Black couples – which was included in Le and Agnew's (2003) meta-analysis – *did* apply a White–Black distinction. Davis and Strube concluded that, in and of itself, race did not affect the magnitude or direction of correlations among investment model variables. One glimmer of hope regarding Triandis's theory of subjective culture can be found in a significant interaction effect involving race (the between-couples variable) and gender (the within-couples variable), such that the positive correlation between satisfaction and commitment was significant among White men, but not among Black men (a result that is consistent with Triandis's general hypothesis that the interdependence theory of Thibaut & Kelley, 1959, is applicable to "individualists" but not to "collectivists"). Nevertheless, the interaction effect raises questions of its own – for example, if race were as important to close relationship processes as Triandis's theory would predict, then why was the satisfaction-commitment correlation significant and positive among White women and Black women alike (and why were the alternatives-commitment and investment-commitment correlations significant and in the expected direction among all race/gender subgroups)? All in all, Davis and Strube's (1993) results lead us to question Triandis's assumptions about race as a moderator of interdependence processes (in this instance, correlations among investment model variables).

Additionally, one might argue that Le and Agnew's (2003) distinction between White and non-White groups emphasizes one aspect of ethnicity (i.e., race) while simultaneously de-emphasizing another aspect of ethnicity (i.e., nationality) that Triandis (2004) had identified. However, Lin and Rusbult's (1995) study of investment model correlations among a sample of American versus Taiwanese individuals – which, likewise, was included in Le and Agnew's meta-analysis – applied a variation on a U.S.–China distinction (consistent with Triandis, 1995). Lin and Rusbult concluded that, on its own, nationality (which they labelled as "culture") did not affect the magnitude or direction of correlations among investment model variables. In the absence of interaction effect tests involving nationality and gender, it appears that – among American and Taiwanese persons alike – 1) satisfaction is a significant positive correlate of commitment; 2) quality of perceived alternatives is a significant negative correlate of commitment; 3) investment size is a significant positive correlate of commitment; 4) *relationship centrality* (i.e., the extent to which individuals perceive their relationships as integral aspects of their selves; see Agnew & Etcheverry, 2006) is a significant positive correlate of commitment; and 5) *prescriptive support* (i.e., "normative support," or the extent to which individuals believe that members of their larger social networks approve of particular relationships; Gaines & Agnew, 2003) is a significant positive correlate of commitment (see also Etcheverry & Agnew, 2004, regarding "subjective norms" as comparable to prescriptive support). All things considered, Lin and Rusbult's results lead us to question Triandis's assumptions about nationality as a moderator of interdependence processes (in particular, correlations among investment model variables).

In an attempt to infuse Thibaut and Kelley's (1959) interdependence theory with constructs from cultural psychology (Gaines & Hardin, 2013), we began with a quote from Kelley et al. (2003, p. 136) that acknowledged the potential relevance of culture to interdependence processes. Given that Kelley et al. had cited Markus and Kitayama (1991), we focused on Markus and Kitayama's constructs of *independent self-construal* (i.e., individuals' mental representation of themselves as separated from significant others) and *interdependent self-construal* (i.e., individuals' mental representation of themselves as bound together with significant others; see also Fiske et al., 1998) as potentially direct influences on Rusbult's (1980) investment model variables. However, Kelley et al. (2003) did not refer overtly to direct effects of independent and/or interdependent self-construals on interdependence processes (indeed, they did not mention Markus and Kitayama's self-construal theory by name). Instead, Kelley et al. emphasized ethnicity (in the form of unspecified social groups who presumably differ in the cultural values of individualism and/or collectivism) as a moderator of interdependence processes, *when interpersonal situations are low or ambiguous in interdependence* – an important qualifier that we had not noted in our previous writings (see also Gaines & Hardin, 2018).

One conceptual problem with Triandis's (1972) theory of subjective culture is that – when one takes Triandis's focus on the original version of Thibaut and Kelley's (1959) interdependence theory into account – Triandis's theory addresses exchange but ignores *coordination* (i.e., partners' engagement in joint activities with each other, as distinct from giving or denying rewards to each other; see Kelley, 1979) in close relationships. Consequently, one might argue that Triandis's theory (as well as the research by Triandis et al. [1968] that Triandis cited in support of his theory) should not be applied to genuinely high-interdependence relationships (i.e., those relationships that are high in coordination as well as high in exchange). Instead, one might be better off examining ethnicity as a moderator of the effects of rewards and costs on satisfaction among individuals who have not made a long-term commitment to their would-be relationship partners (although such an approach would not allow one to test the full investment model of Rusbult, 1980).

Perhaps a more fundamental problem with Triandis's (1972) theory of subjective culture is that it fails to incorporate the concept of *transformation of motivation* (a process whereby individuals in high-interdependence relationships progress from acting primarily in their self-interest over the short term to acting primarily in the interest of their relationships over the long term) that serves as a centerpiece of Kelley and Thibaut's (1978) revised interdependence theory (see Kelley, 1979). Triandis's (1989, 1996) subsequent omissions of transformation of motivation from his elaborations on the theory of subjective culture lead one to wonder whether Triandis was aware of the importance of that concept to the evolution of interdependence theory. As Rusbult and colleagues increasingly explored consequences of commitment (e.g., by examining *accommodation*, or individuals' refraining from reciprocating partners' anger or criticism, instead responding in a manner that is intended to promote their relationships; Rusbult, Verette, Whitney, Slovik, & Lipkus, 1991), it became clear that transformation of motivation is an essential feature of high-interdependence relationships (Rusbult & Buunk, 1993). Therefore, we anticipate that the original formulation of Triandis's theory will not be applicable to those relationships in which transformation of motivation routinely occurs, regardless of individuals' ethnicity or presumed cultural value orientations.

REVAMPING THE THEORY OF SUBJECTIVE CULTURE

Commitment as a Manifestation of Subjective Culture

So far, our review of Triandis's (1972) theory of subjective culture has raised serious doubts concerning the utility of the theory in explaining relationship processes that have already been explained by Thibaut and Kelley's (1959) interdependence theory and Rusbult's (1980) investment model. However, rather than discard Triandis's theory entirely, we wish to consider ways in which portions of Triandis's theory can be integrated with Thibaut and Kelley's theory, bolstering both theories (and, by implication, future research in the fields of cultural psychology and relationship science) along the way. We shall focus upon Thibaut and Kelley's core construct of commitment, which potentially represents a specific manifestation of subjective culture. We hasten to add that our perspective on commitment departs from Triandis's own statements on interdependence constructs, which (as we have seen) were limited to pronouncements about the importance of rewards and costs among ostensibly individualistic ethnic groups.

Throughout the present book, fellow relationship scientists have explored the meaning, antecedents, and consequences of commitment. In the tradition of Thibaut and Kelley (1959), interdependence theorists have tended to view commitment as a unidimensional construct (see Kelley et al., 1983/2002), Nevertheless, even those interdependence theorists who conceptualize and measure commitment as one construct (most notably Rusbult, 1980) have acknowledged that commitment is a complex construct, encompassing cognition (i.e., long-term perspective), affection (i.e., psychological attachment), and behavioral intent (i.e., propensity to maintain the relationship; Rusbult et al., 2001) and reflected in various stay/leave behaviors (Le & Agnew, 2003). As it happens, within the conceptual model that forms the foundation for Triandis's (1972) theory of subjective culture, the construct of subjective culture not only includes cognition, affect, and behavioral intent but also is presumed to influence individuals' social behavior. Such overlap begs the question: Can commitment be understood as a manifestation of subjective culture?

According to Dion and Dion's (1993) cultural perspective on marriage, romantic love (a specific form of psychological attachment; see Kelley et al., 1983/2002) is more likely to serve as the basis for entering into marriage (a specific form of stay/leave behavior; see Kelley et al., 2003) among persons from individualistic ethnic groups, rather than persons from collectivistic ethnic groups. Conversely, adoption of traditional gender roles (a specific form of long-term orientation; see Kelley et al., 1983/2002) is more likely to serve as the basis for entering into marriage among persons from collectivistic ethnic groups, rather than persons from individualistic ethnic groups. Finally, within a particular ethnic group, persons may differ in the extent to which they contemplate getting married and staying married as separate prospects (a specific type of intent to persist; see Kelley et al., 2003); although such between-person variability historically has been associated with collectivistic ethnic groups, societal change in many areas of the world have resulted in increased variability from person to person concerning intent to marry and intent to divorce; see also Dion & Dion, 1996). Overall, even though Dion and Dion (1993) did not mention Triandis's (1972) theory of subjective culture or Thibaut and Kelley's (1959) interdependence theory, we believe that the Dions' cultural perspective offers a means toward conceptualizing aspects of commitment as special instances of subjective culture.

Before proceeding further, we note that unidimensional measures of commitment (e.g., Rusbult, 1983; Rusbult, Martz, & Agnew, 1998) may not allow researchers to detect the specific cultural influences on commitment that we have predicted. For that matter, it is not clear whether multidimensional measures of commitment (e.g., Adams & Jones, 1997; Stanley & Markman, 1992) necessarily would yield the cultural influences that we have predicted. Perhaps enterprising researchers could compare the goodness-of-fit regarding culturally invariant versus culturally variant models of the factor patterns for unidimensional versus multidimensional measures of commitment (via a series of multiple-group confirmatory factor analyses; see Brown, 2015), in order to determine whether commitment displays empirical (as distinct from conceptual) promise as an indicator of subjective culture.

Developing Investment Model Influences as Basic Psychological Processes

Notwithstanding differences of opinion within relationship science concerning commitment as a unidimensional versus multidimensional construct (for a review, see Rusbult, Coolsen, Kirchner, & Clarke, 2006), interdependence theorists generally agree that individuals possess a subjective sense that their relationships are generally rewarding versus costly (even if individuals do not consciously calculate running tallies of their net profits versus losses; Agnew & VanderDrift, 2018). Assuming that individuals not only learn to associate positive versus negative outcomes with their ongoing relationship interactions but also experience commitment levels that covary with those associations, one might argue that investment model influences on commitment can be interpreted as basic psychological processes – a prospect that is compatible with Triandis's (1972) theory of subjective culture. Although we have already seen that the investment model generalizes across ethnic groups, we have not considered the possibility that the *development* of certain investment model variables can vary as a function of individuals' ethnicity.

Perhaps the most obvious candidate for a basic psychological process that might be moderated by ethnicity within the context of Rusbult's (1980) investment model is satisfaction. We believe that Rusbult and Arriaga's (2000, pp. 83–84) hypothetical examples of differing *comparison levels* (CL, or the general levels of positive versus negative outcomes that individuals have learned to expect via interactions in one or more relationships across time), *comparison levels for alternatives* (CL-alt, or the lowest levels of positive versus negative outcomes that individuals are willing to accept in their current relationships, keeping in mind the possibility of more versus less favorable outcomes that individuals might experience if they were to become involved with other partners in the future), and *goodness of outcomes* (i.e., individuals' actual experience of positive versus negative outcomes in their current relationships) can serve as bases for postulating ethnicity-as-moderator effects. For example, 1) within individualistic ethnic groups, CL (reflecting a concern with personal, as opposed to group, rewards and costs; see Triandis, 1989, 1996) will tend to be *higher* than goodness of outcomes; whereas 2) within collectivistic ethnic groups, CL will tend to be *lower* than goodness of outcomes. Therefore, over time, persons in individualistic ethnic groups will be less likely to become sufficiently satisfied with their relationships to make a commitment to those relationships (let alone proceed to get married and stay married), compared to persons in collectivistic ethnic groups. However, as far as we know, our hypotheses concerning ethnicity as a moderator of developing satisfaction have not been tested.

Another, less obvious candidate for a basic psychological process that might be moderated by ethnicity from the standpoint of Rusbult's (1980) investment model is dependence. It is not clear whether dependence is best regarded as a) an aggregate of the predictors of commitment (usually limited to satisfaction, perceived quality of alternatives, and investment size); b) the functional equivalent of commitment (rather than the predictors of commitment *per se*); or c) an entity that is distinguishable from commitment or the other variables that typically are measured in studies of the investment model – the latter of which would be consistent with the view that dependence is the inverse of *power*, which in turn refers to the degree to which individuals exert influence upon their partners' receipt of rewards versus costs (e.g., Simpson, Farrell, Orina, & Rothman, 2015). For the purposes of the present chapter, the conceptualization of dependence as the inverse of power allows us to draw a parallel between 1) a portion of the model of subjective culture that Triandis (1972, pp. 22–23) articulated and 2) a portion of the model of the psychology of power that Galinsky, Rucker, and Magee (2015, p. 424) presented – namely, culture as a potential moderator of another basic psychological process (in this instance, individuals' developing sense of dependence, or lack of power). Returning to our interpretation of Rusbult and Arriaga's (2000, pp. 83–84) conceptual analysis of dependence, 1) within individualistic ethnic groups, CL-alt will tend to be even *higher* than CL; whereas 2) within collectivistic ethnic groups, CL-alt will tend to be even *lower* than CL. Thus, across time, persons in individualistic ethnic groups will be less likely to become sufficiently dependent upon their relationships to make a commitment to those relationships (let alone proceed to get married and stay married), compared to persons in collectivistic ethnic groups. However, to our knowledge, our hypotheses concerning ethnicity as a moderator of developing dependence have not been tested.

Rusbult and Arriaga's (2000) analysis of the development of satisfaction and dependence does not address the roles of CL, CL-alt, or goodness of outcomes in developing other investment model influences on commitment. However, the *suffocation model of marriage* (postulating that the trajectory of history in the United States has given rise to individuals' heightened expectations concerning the fulfilment of growth-related needs over time, in the tradition of Maslow, 1968), as presented by Finkel, Hui, et al. (2014) and Finkel, Larson, Carswell, & Hui (2014), suggests that successive generations' increase in CL within the United States has coincided with decreases in satisfaction, increases in perceived quality of alternatives, and decreases in investment size. Finkel et al. argued that, not only is their model applicable to other Western nations at the present time; but their model is likely to be applicable to Eastern nations at some point in the not-too-distance future. Thus, in terms of basic psychological processes, Finkel et al. cast their model as universal. However, as Finkel et al. acknowledged, some of their critics (e.g., Feeney & Collins, 2014; Pietromonaco & Perry-Jenkins, 2014) have contended that the suffocation model primarily describes the social-psychological experiences of White Americans – a (stereo)typical example of a individual-istic ethnic group (e.g., Triandis, 1976). In any event, the universality versus cultural specificity of the suffocation model have yet to be determined empirically.

TYING UP LOOSE ENDS: UNRESOLVED ISSUES CONCERNING INTERDEPENDENCE PROCESSES WITHIN THE THEORY OF SUBJECTIVE CULTURE

Throughout the present chapter, we have not questioned the assumption (popularly associated with Hofstede, 1980) that persons can be classified as individualistic versus collectivistic. However, results of a meta-analysis by Oyserman, Coon, and Kemmelmeier (2002; see also Oyserman, Kemmelme-ier, & Coon, 2002) indicate that, not only are scores on individualism and collectivism generally uncorrelated when surveys do not constrain respond-ents to answer in an either-or format; but individualism is especially unlikely to covary as a function of persons' race or nationality (in contrast, collectivism frequently covaries with ethnicity). We strongly advise future researchers to include measures of individualism and collectivism alongside measures of Rusbult's (1980) investment model variables (e.g., Rusbult et al., 1998) across various ethnic groups, rather than accept the individualism-collectivism dichotomy at face value.

Also, we have not questioned the assumption (popularly associated with Triandis, 1995) that – even if persons within a given ethnic group vary widely in the cultural values that they embrace – the "me-value" of individualism and the "we-value" of collectivism are the only values that should be measured. However, certain "we-values" in addition to collectivism (e.g., familism, romanticism, spiritualism) may be relevant to interdependence processes (see Gaines, 1997). We encourage future researchers to expand their concep-tion of cultural values when conducting studies of Rusbult's (1980) investment model, especially when making East-West comparisons (where the logical counterpart to individualism might be spiritualism, or persons' orientation toward the welfare of all living entities, whether natural or supernatural; see Braithwaite & Scott, 1991).

Finally, we have not questioned the assumption (which one can find in Hofstede, 1980; as well as Triandis, 1995) that race and nationality are the only aspects of ethnicity that warrant investigation. However, Cohen (2009, 2010) argued that religion deserves to be added as a culturally relevant variable. We believe that future researchers should complement Davis and Strube's (1993) study of race as a moderator, as well as Lin and Rusbult's (1995) study of nationality as a moderator, with religion as a moderator of the investment model processes that Rusbult (1980) initially viewed as universal (see also Wesselmann, VanderDrift, & Agnew, 2016).

CONCLUDING THOUGHTS

At the beginning of the present chapter, we identified Triandis's (1972) *The Analysis of Subjective Culture* as a potential blueprint for understanding the role of ethnicity in moderating interdependence processes. As we have seen, only a handful of studies (i.e., Davis & Strube, 1993; Lin & Rusbult, 1995) have addressed ethnicity as a moderator of Rusbult's (1980) investment model; and even those studies have focused exclusively upon Thibaut and Kelley's (1959) interdependence theory when testing predictions about universality of the investment model. We hope that the present chapter will spark relationship scientists' interest in Triandis's theory of subjective culture as a complement to interdependence theory in future research.

REFERENCES

Adams, J. & Jones, W. (1997). The conceptualization of marital commitment: An integrative analysis. *Journal of Personality and Social Psychology*, 72, 1177–1196.

Agnew, C. R. & Etcheverry, P. E. (2006). Cognitive interdependence considering self-in-relationship. In K. D. Vohs & E. J. Finkel (Eds.), *Self and Relationships: Connecting Intrapersonal and Interpersonal Processes* (pp. 274–293). New York: Guilford Press.

Agnew, C. R. & VanderDrift, L. E. (2015). Relationship maintenance and dissolution. In M. Mikulincer & P. R. Shaver (Eds.), *APA Handbook of Personality and Social Psychology* (Vol. 3: Interpersonal relations, pp. 581–604). Washington, DC: American Psychological Association.

Agnew, C. R. & VanderDrift, L. E. (2018). Commitment processes in personal relationship. In A. L. Vangelisti & D. Perlman (Eds.), *The Cambridge Handbook of Personal Relationships* (2nd ed., pp. 437–448). Cambridge: Cambridge University Press.

Arriaga, X. B. (2013). An interdependence theory analysis of close relationships. In J. A. Simpson & L. Campbell (Eds.), *The Oxford Handbook of Close Relationships* (pp. 39–65). Oxford: Oxford University Press.

Berscheid, E. (1985). Interpersonal attraction. In G. Lindzey & E. Aronson (Eds.), *The Handbook of Social Psychology* (3rd ed., Vol. 2, pp. 413–484). New York: Random House.

Berscheid, E. & Reis, H. T. (1998). Attraction and close relationships. In D. T. Gilbert, S. T. Fiske, & G. Lindzey (Eds.), *The Handbook of Social Psychology* (4th ed., Vol. 2, pp. 193–281). Boston: McGraw-Hill.

Braithwaite, V. A. & Scott, W. A. (1991). Values. In J. P. Robinson, P. R. Shaver, & L. S. Wrightsman (Eds.), *Measures of Personality and Social Psychological Attitudes* (pp. 661–753). San Diego: Academic Press.

Brown, T. A. (2015). *Confirmatory Factor Analysis for Applied Research* (2nd ed.). New York: Guilford.

Clark, M. S. & Mills, J. (1979). Interpersonal attraction in exchange and communal relationships. *Journal of Personality and Social Psychology*, 37, 12–24.

Cohen, A. B. (2009). Many forms of culture. *American Psychologist*, 64, 194–204.

Cohen, A. B. (2010). Just how many different forms of culture are there? *American Psychologist*, 65, 59–61.

Davis, L. E. & Strube, M. J. (1993). An assessment of romantic commitment among Black and White dating couples. *Journal of Applied Social Psychology*, 23, 212–225.

Dion, K. K. & Dion, K. L. (1993). Individualistic and collectivistic perspectives on gender and the cultural context of love and intimacy. *Journal of Social Issues*, 49(3), 53–69.

Dion, K. K. & Dion, K. L. (1996). Cultural perspectives on romantic love. *Personal Relationships*, 3, 5–17.

Etcheverry, P. E. & Agnew, C. R. (2004). Subjective norms and the prediction of romantic relationship state and fate. *Personal Relationships*, 11, 409–428.

Feeney, B. C. & Collins, N. L. (2014). Much "I do" about nothing? Ascending Mount Maslow with an oxygenated marriage. *Psychological Inquiry*, 25, 69–79.

Finkel, E. J., Hui, C, M., Carswell, K. L., & Larson, G. M. (2014). The suffocation of marriage: Climbing Mount Maslow without enough oxygen. *Psychological Inquiry*, 25, 1–41.

Finkel, E. J., Larson, G. M., Carswell, K. L., & Hui, C. M. (2014). Marriage at the summit: Response to the commentaries. *Psychological Inquiry*, 25, 120–145.

Fiske, A. P., Kitayama, S., Markus, H. R., & Nisbett, R. E. (1998). The cultural matrix of social psychology. In D. T. Gilbert, S. T. Fiske, & G. Lindzey (Eds.), *The Handbook of Social Psychology* (4th ed., Vol. 2, pp. 915–981). New York: McGraw-Hill.

Foa, U. G. & Foa, E. B. (1974). *Societal Structures of the Mind*. Springfield, IL: Charles C. Thomas.

Gaines, S. O., Jr. (1997). *Culture, Ethnicity, and Personal Relationship Processes*. New York: Routledge.

Gaines, S. O., Jr. & Agnew, C. R. (2003). Relationship maintenance in intercultural marriages: An interdependence perspective. In D. J. Canary & M. Dainton (Eds.), *Maintaining Relationships through Communication: Relational, Contextual, and Cultural Variations* (pp. 231–253). Mahwah, NJ: Erlbaum.

Gaines, S. O., Jr. & Hardin, D. P. (2013). Interdependence revisited: Perspectives from cultural psychology. In L. Campbell & J. A. Simpson (Eds.), *Oxford Handbook of Close Relationships* (pp. 553–572). Oxford: Oxford University Press.

Gaines S. O., Jr. & Hardin, D. P. (2018). Ethnicity, culture, and close relationships. In A. L. Vangelisti & D. Perlman (Eds.), *The Cambridge Handbook of Personal Relationships* (2nd ed., pp. 494–508). Cambridge: Cambridge University Press.

Galinsky, A. D., Rucker, D. D., & Magee, J. C. (2015). Power: Past findings, present considerations, and future directions. In M. Mikulincer & P. R. Shaver (Eds.), *APA Handbook of Personality and Social Psychology* (Vol. 3: Interpersonal Relationships, pp. 421–460). Washington, DC: American Psychological Association.

Heine, S. J. (2016). *Cultural Psychology* (3rd ed.). New York: W. W. Norton.

Herskovits, M. J. (1955). *Cultural Anthropology*. New York: Knopf.

Hofstede, G. (1980). *Culture's Consequences: International Differences in Work-Related Values*. Newbury Park, CA: Sage.

Kelley, H. H. (1979). *Personal Relationships: Their Structures and Processes*. Hillsdale, NJ: Erlbaum.

Kelley, H. H. (1997). The "stimulus field" for interpersonal phenomena: The source for language and thought about interpersonal events. *Personality and Social Psychology Review, 1,* 140–169.

Kelley, H. H., Berscheid, E., Christensen, A., Harvey, J. H., Huston, T. L, Levinger, G., McClintock, E., Peplau, L. A., & Peterson, D. R. (2002). *Close Relationships.* New York: Percheron Press. (Original work published in 1983)

Kelley, H. H., Holmes, J. G., Kerr, N. L., Reis, H. T., Rusbult, C. E., & Van Lange, P. A. M. (2003). *An Atlas of Interpersonal Situations.* New York: Cambridge University Press.

Kelley, H. H. & Thibaut, J. W. (1978). *Interpersonal Relations: A Theory of Interdependence.* New York: Wiley.

Le, B. & Agnew, C. R. (2003). Commitment and its theorized determinants: A meta-analysis of the investment model. *Personal Relationships, 10,* 37–57.

Lin, Y. H. W. & Rusbult, C. E. (1995). Commitment to dating relationships and cross-sex friendships in America and China: The impact of centrality of relationship, normative support, and investment model variables. *Journal of Social and Personal Relationships, 12,* 7–26.

Markus, H. R. (2008). Pride, prejudice, and ambivalence: Toward a unified theory of race and ethnicity. *American Psychologist, 63,* 651–670.

Markus, H. & Kitayama, S. (1991). Culture and the self: Implications for cognition, emotion, and motivation. *Psychological Review, 98,* 224–253.

Maslow, A. H. (1968). *Toward a Psychology of Being.* New York: Van Nostrand Reinhold.

Matsumoto, D. (1999). Culture and self: An empirical assessment of Markus and Kitayama's theory of independent and interdependent self-construals. *Asian Journal of Social Psychology, 2,* 289–310.

Mills, J. & Clark, M. S. (1982). Exchange and communal relationships. In L. Wheeler (Ed.), *Review of Personality and Social Psychology* (Vol. 3, pp. 121–144). Beverly Hills, CA: Sage.

Oyserman, D., Coon, H. M., & Kemmelmeier, M. (2002). Rethinking individualism and collectivism: Evaluation of theoretical assumptions and meta-analyses. *Psychological Bulletin, 128,* 3–72.

Oyserman, D., Kemmelmeier, M., & Coon, H. M. (2002). Cultural psychology: A new look: Reply to Bond (2002), Fiske (2002), Kitayama (2002), and Miller (2002). *Psychological Bulletin, 128,* 110–117.

Pietromonaco, P. R. & Perry-Jenkins M. (2014). Marriage in whose America? What the suffocation model misses. *Psychological Inquiry, 25,* 108–113.

Rusbult, C. E. (1980). Commitment and satisfaction in romantic associations: A test of the investment model. *Journal of Experimental Social Psychology, 16,* 172–186.

Rusbult, C. E. (1983). A longitudinal test of the investment model: The development (and deterioration) of satisfaction and commitment in heterosexual involvements. *Journal of Personality and Social Psychology, 45,* 101–117.

Rusbult, C. E. & Agnew, C. R. (2010). Prosocial motivation and behavior in close relationships. In M. Mikulincer & P. R. Shaver (Eds.), *Prosocial Motives, Emotions, and Behavior: The Better Angels of Our Nature* (pp. 327–345). Washington, DC: American Psychological Association.

Rusbult, C. E., Agnew, C. R., & Arriaga, X. B. (2012). The investment model of commitment processes. In P. A. M. Van Lange, A. W. Kruglanski, & E. T. Higgins (Eds.), *Handbook of Theories of Social Psychology* (Vol. 2, pp. 218–231). Los Angeles: Sage.

Rusbult, C. E. & Arriaga, X. B. (2000). Interdependence in personal relationships. In W. Ickes & S. Duck (Eds.), *The Social Psychology of Personal Relationships* (pp. 79–108). Chichester: John Wiley & Sons.

Rusbult, C. E. & Buunk, B. P. (1993). Commitment processes in close relationships: An interdependence analysis. *Journal of Social and Personal Relationships*, 10, 175–204.

Rusbult, C. E., Coolsen, M. K., Kirchner, J. L., & Clarke, J. A. (2006). Commitment. In A. L. Vangelisti & D. Perlman (Eds.), *The Cambridge Handbook of Personal Relationships* (pp. 615–635). Cambridge: Cambridge University Press.

Rusbult, C. E., Drigotas, S. M., & Verette, J. (1994). The investment model: An interdependence analysis of commitment processes and relationship maintenance phenomena. In D. J. Canary & L. Stafford (Eds.), *Communication and Relational Maintenance* (pp. 115–139). San Diego: Academic Press.

Rusbult, C. E., Johnson, D. J., & Morrow, G. D. (1986). Predicting satisfaction and commitment in adult romantic relationships: An assessment of the generalizability of the investment model. *Social Psychology Quarterly*, 49, 81–89.

Rusbult, C. E., Martz, J. M., & Agnew, C. R. (1998). The Investment Model Scale: Measuring commitment level, satisfaction, quality of alternatives, and investment size. *Personal Relationships*, 5, 357–391.

Rusbult, C. E., Olsen, N., Davis, J. L., & Hannon, P. A. (2001). Commitment and relationship maintenance mechanisms. In J. Harvey & A. Wentzel (Eds.), *Close Romantic Relationships: Maintenance and Enhancement* (pp. 87–113). Mahwah, NJ: Erlbaum.

Rusbult, C., Verette, J., Whitney, G., Slovik, L., & Lipkus, I. (1991). Accommodation processes in close relationships: Theory and preliminary evidence. *Journal of Personality and Social Psychology*, 60, 53–78.

Shweder, R. A. & Sullivan, M. (1993). Cultural psychology: Who needs it? *Annual Review of Psychology*, 44, 497–523.

Simpson, J. A., Farrell, A. K., Orina, M. M., & Rothman, A. J. (2015). Power and social influence in relationships. In M. Mikulincer & P. R. Shaver (Eds.), *APA Handbook of Personality and Social Psychology* (Vol. 3: Interpersonal relations, pp. 393–420). Washington, DC: American Psychological Association.

Stanley, S. M. & Markman, H. J. (1992). Assessing commitment in personal relationships. *Journal of Marriage and the Family*, 54, 595–608.

Thibaut, J. W. & Kelley, H. H. (1959). *The Social Psychology of Groups*. New York: Wiley.

Triandis, H. C. (1972). *The Analysis of Subjective Culture*. New York: Wiley-Interscience.

Triandis, H. S. (1976). *Variations in Black and White Perceptions of the Social Environment*. Urbana, IL: University of Illinois Press.

Triandis, H. C. (1989). The self and social behavior in differing cultural contexts. *Psychological Review*, 96, 506–520.

Triandis, H. C. (1995). *Individualism and Collectivism*. Boulder, CO: Westview Press.

Triandis, H. C. (1996). The psychological measurement of cultural syndromes. *American Psychologist*, 51, 407–415.

Triandis, H. C. (2004). *Culture and Social Behavior*. New York: McGraw-Hill.

Triandis, H. C., Vassiliou, V., & Nassiakou, M. (1968). Three cross-cultural studies of subjective culture. *Journal of Personality and Social Psychology*, 8, 1–42.

Van Lange, P. A. M. & Balliet, D. (2015). Interdependence theory. In M. Mikulincer & P. R. Shaver (Eds.), *APA Handbook of Personality and Social Psychology* (Vol. 3: Interpersonal relations, pp. 65–92). Washington, DC: American Psychological Association.

Wesselmann, E. D., VanderDrift, L. E., & Agnew, C. R. (2016). Religious commitment: An interdependence approach. *Psychology of Religion and Spirituality*, 8, 35–45.

PART II

INTERDEPENDENCE, SECURITY, AND RISK

5

An Interdependence Analysis of Enhancing
Attachment Security

LUCY L. HUNT, MADOKA KUMASHIRO, AND
XIMENA B. ARRIAGA

People enter relationships with desires and preconceived notions regarding what the present and future hold. Relationships, however, rarely last merely on desires and preconceived notions. They evolve based on what each person is willing and able to do for the other, and how responsive each person is to the other person's needs during key moments. For one person, the most memorable situations may be painful or aversive, such as needing support but being let down by a partner. For another person, key situations may involve feeling too many obligations, demands, and induced guilt from a partner. For yet another, the most memorable and typical situations may feature a partner who anticipates needs and can be counted on for support without being made to feel indebted or inadequate. These situations are powerful because they reveal what each partner can and will do for the other, and they shape what one can expect in a given relationship.

We suggest that interpersonal situations that affect attachment security are critically important. We provide an interdependence theory analysis of key situations that may foster a sense of attachment security toward romantic partners, especially among chronically insecure individuals. Adult attachment theorists have examined how secure and insecure orientations affect the manner in which individuals forge bonds with others and navigate future distressing or challenging situations (Hazan & Shaver, 1994; Mikulincer & Florian, 1998). Interdependence theorists are more inclined to examine the conditions that reinforce a myriad of interpersonal tendencies – such as being fair, competitive, trustworthy, and committed.

This chapter describes the Attachment Security Enhancement Model (ASEM; Arriaga, Kumashiro, Simpson, & Overall, 2018), a novel dual-process model illustrating the power of interdependent relationships to enhance

The writing of this paper was supported by funding to Madoka Kumashiro from the Economic and Social Research Council (No. ES/N013182/1) and to Ximena Arriaga from the National Science Foundation (No. 15076506).

security over time. This model integrates attachment- and interdependence-based frameworks within an overarching model of specific situations that may foster security. Understanding key situations, past and present, that may influence attachment orientations lies at the heart of the ASEM. We begin by describing hypothetical couples to exemplify relevant concepts throughout the chapter (e.g., working models, interpersonal "situations"). We then provide an overview of the ASEM, elaborate on the processes that lead attachment orientations to change, and conclude by briefly summarizing the main ideas and implications.

ATTACHMENT AND INTERDEPENDENCE THEORIES MERGED: THE IMPORTANCE OF PAST INTERPERSONAL SITUATIONS

The Nature of Adult Attachment Orientations

Early life experiences form the blueprint for fundamental beliefs about whether others can and should be trusted (e.g., whether experiences with commitment and intimacy are positive or negative). Although early experiences shape initial attachment patterns, salient new experiences may revise fundamental mental representations – the underlying beliefs, scripts, and expectations that form "working models" of self and others (Collins & Read, 1990; Pietromonaco & Carnelley, 1994). How do new experiences in adult relationships affect attachment orientations? Consider the following hypothetical individuals.

Annie's earliest memories reveal inconsistent experiences with care. Sometimes her mother did not sufficiently address Annie's individual need for attention; at other times, her mother tried to compensate for being insufficient in meeting Annie's needs, but was too effusive in her care and too involved in Annie's endeavors to the point of being intrusive. Growing up, Annie seemed to have a pattern of feeling insecure about being liked and valued by friends and close others. In adulthood, she has become preoccupied with her romantic relationships; she chronically yearns for reassurance of being desired and valued by her partners. Her concerns and preoccupation with closeness often lead to unreasonably high expectations of her partners, inevitably leading to disappointment, anger, frustration, and other negative emotional expressions. The resulting tension, conflict, and "drama" with her partners eventually strain her relationships. Annie exhibits typical features of chronic *attachment anxiety.*

In contrast, Tom does not recall many early memories, but when he does recall past experiences in early family relationships, his memories seem to bring to mind emotionally painful or distressing experiences. As he ages, he may suppress the intimate thoughts and emotions that typically occur in close relationships. Instead, he focuses on his work or hobbies and takes pride in his ability to be self-reliant. He likes being around his friends and romantic partners but, when their interactions take on emotional features, he distances himself. He also dreads interactions in which others rely on him to satisfy their needs, which inevitably occurs in long-term relationships. As he withdraws from these interactions, his partners may escalate their efforts to draw him closer but eventually withdraw as well. As a result, Tom becomes increasingly resigned to the belief that his relationships cannot last, reaffirming his expectation that he can only rely on himself. Tom exhibits typical features of chronic *attachment avoidance*.

Jesse has positive memories of her childhood, and recalls growing up in a supportive family who offered encouragement for her aspirations (e.g., trying out new hobbies and interests) and who she could turn to for comfort when things did not go well. Jesse does not become overly worried about her relationships, and she expects close others to be trustworthy. Her friendships and romantic relationships tend to be satisfying and long-lasting, and they are characterized by mutual offering of comfort and support for important goals and aspirations. Jesse exhibits typical features of chronic *attachment security*, or the general absence of anxiety or avoidance in her relationships.

These three individuals have had experiences that shape their mental representations of themselves and others. The next section describes these key mental representations in more detail.

Internal Working Models

Attachment theory highlights particularly consequential internal mental representations about the self and others – "internal working models" – that regulate attachment-relevant thoughts, feelings, expectations, and behavior. Adults typically have well-formed models of *close others* (e.g., family members, relationship partners, friends) and their *self*.

Returning to the examples above, as Annie's history demonstrates, chronic anxious-attachment orientations stem from a history of receiving inconsistent caregiving (e.g., sometimes available and other times not, or sometimes appropriate and other times overly intrusive). These experiences lead to the formation of beliefs demonstrating ambivalence about *close others* (e.g., misgivings but also hope regarding whether others will be available) and negative beliefs about the *self* (e.g., perceptions of oneself as relatively incapable or unworthy of others' positive regard); these working models characterize anxious tendencies (Bretherton, 1992). In a different vein, chronic avoidant-attachment orientations, such as Tom's, stem from a history of receiving poor, neglectful caregiving. Such experiences lead to the formation of negative beliefs about *others* (e.g., they are unreliable) and mixed, unstable beliefs about the *self* (e.g., often overly-inflated high self-esteem resulting from the need to become self-reliant); these working models characterize avoidant tendencies (Fraley, Roisman, Booth-LaForce, Owen, & Holland, 2013).

Individuals who exhibit chronic insecurities reflected in attachment anxiety and attachment avoidance tend to have worse personal and relational outcomes, compared to their secure counterparts (Mikulincer & Shaver, 2016). However, are Annie and Tom doomed to disillusionment with relationships that are unfulfilling and fraught with constant challenges or dissolution? We suggest that people like Annie and Tom need not assume they are destined to such outcomes. Instead, chronic insecurities may slowly diminish, giving way to more secure thoughts and feelings, when new relationship experiences cause insecure mental representations (i.e., working models) to change for the better. New situations are necessary to help revise negative working models of the self and others.

Attachment theory postulates that key experiences early in a person's developmental history will shape relatively stable internal working models that persist into adulthood (Mikulincer & Shaver, 2016). These working models are crucial in directing general tendencies with others. However, there also is evidence that attachment orientations can (and do) change through natural, ongoing processes in close relationships (Arriaga, Kumashiro, Finkel, VanderDrift, & Luchies, 2014; Chopik, Edelstein, & Grimm, 2019; Davila & Cobb, 2003; Kirkpatrick & Davis, 1994; Simpson, Rholes, Campbell, & Wilson, 2003). This possibility of change suggests that individuals may not be destined to a lifetime of chronic attachment insecurity. As this chapter will demonstrate, interdependence theory provides an ideal framework for understanding key interactions that drive both stability and change in a person's relational tendencies, including their working models.

An Interdependence Theory Analysis of Key Situations

Expanding on Lewin's (1936) famous formula for understanding behavior as a function of both the properties of the person and the environment, interdependence theory examines social interactions: Interaction (I) is conceived as a function of the particular features of the situation (S) and each person's (partner A and partner B) thoughts, needs, and motives regarding each other ($I = f$ [S, A, B]; Holmes, 2002; Kelley et al., 2003). The theory identifies abstract features of situations that emphasize a key dynamic: whether and how interacting partners affect what they each experience. The relevant concepts are "outcomes" – each person's state and experience derived from ongoing interactions with a partner – and "dependence" – the extent to which a person's state and experience is affected by a partner. For example, consider when Tom (person B) and his partner (person A) try to discuss an important issue (i.e., the situation). Tom's partner seeks support (i.e., person A's motive) but instead is rebuffed by Tom (i.e., person B's motive to avoid emotional situations); his partner may express disappointment and perhaps even come to rely less on Tom for support in future interactions (i.e., A's outcomes).

Many interactions are inconsequential, but certain interactions are noteworthy and lead to attributions of the causes underlying one's own and a partner's behavior. Such interactions reveal what motivates each person to do what they do; as both partners adapt to the new information, they seek certain interactions that fit with their relationship goals, avoid other situations that undermine their goals, and eventually develop patterned behaviors with each other (Kelley, 1983). Attributions and interpretations of noteworthy or "key" interactions thus either may reinforce or revise patterned behavior. The remainder of this section describes what interactions are especially noteworthy in driving attachment-relevant processes.

Some interactions are particularly important because, in addition to affecting each person's immediate outcomes, they have broader meaning and reveal each person's underlying motives. For example, Annie's current partner may be annoyed that she repeatedly starts petty arguments but, if her partner recognizes the broader meaning that she is just seeking reassurance, he may be willing to look beyond these annoyances (i.e., the immediate negative outcomes) and instead invoke sympathy that leads to delivering the reassurance she needs. If Annie recognizes that she is being annoying, she can derive several benefits, including receiving the immediate outcome of obtaining the reassurance that she sought and also detecting the broader meaning that her partner wants to do what is best for her (a pro-relationship motive). Annie may become more appreciative of the sympathy and love her partner displayed (despite her bothersome behavior) and come to realize that her needs for reassurance could cause issues in the future.

These "diagnostic" interactions provide crucial information (i.e., what Kelley referred to as "symbolic outcomes"; Kelley, 1979) about each partner's "true" motives, goals, and trustworthiness; they reveal what each person can offer in a relationship, and forecast what to expect from each other in the future (Beck & Clark, 2009; Holmes & Rempel, 1989; Reis & Arriaga, 2015; Reis & Holmes, 2012; Simpson, 2007). In the previous examples, Tom's partner learned that depending on Tom for emotional support leads to the negative outcome of disappointment, whereas Annie learned that her partner was there for her, even when she had been unreasonable. Over repeated experiences in diagnostic situations (also called "strain test" situations; Simpson, 2007), Tom's partner may seek support from others to avoid more disappointing situations with Tom, reinforcing Tom's desire to avoid closeness and engage in other avoidant tendencies. Annie, on the other hand, may come to expect to have her partner's reassurance in the future, leading her to revise her general expectations in relationships and maybe making her less preoccupied with attaining reassurance. Both examples reveal how key situations reinforce or revise existing mental representations – the working internal models – of one's relationships and one's self.

Which situations are most likely to be diagnostic of a person's underlying motives (e.g., being self-oriented versus pro-relationship oriented)? Interdependence theory suggests specific features of situations that are especially relevant. One notable feature is how much one is affected by a partner's behavior (*level of dependence*; e.g., Annie may be more strongly affected by her partner than is Tom). Another is whether an outcome affects one person more versus each partner similarly (*mutuality of dependence*; e.g., interactions may affect Annie more than they affect her partner). Power is another factor related to dependence – who controls the situation (*basis of dependence*), effectively capturing whether the situation unfolds based on coordinated actions (joint control), one's own actions (actor control), or the partner's actions (partner control).

Other features related to dependence concern synchronicity, uncertainty, and timing. Specifically, whether partners' preferences are synchronized or instead at odds with each other is important. Situations are particularly revealing when partner preferences are at odds, whereby one person's preference becomes costly or aversive to the other person (*conflict of interest*). For example, Annie wants more time together than her partner may want, and Tom avoids support situations more than his partner does; in each case, what one person prefers is at odds with the partner's preferences. The extent of *information ambiguity or uncertainty* about each person's preferences is also consequential; interpretations become increasingly subjective when motives are less certain or obvious (e.g., uncertainty over why Tom avoids discussing important issues). Finally, *timing* – whether an interaction has an immediate or delayed impact – may also reveal underlying tendencies. For example, Tom's rebuff of his partner's plea for support both disappointed and hurt his partner (an immediate, negative impact) but is also likely to lead the partner to withdraw from Tom more in the future (delayed impact).

These features are relevant to situations that trigger attachment security or insecurity. For example, certain situations are more likely to activate the attachment system in everyone. Common examples include threats of separation (real or imagined), situations requiring comfort and support, and potential costs of dependence, such as the conflict-of-interest situations briefly described (Collins & Feeney, 2000; Fraley & Shaver, 1998; Mikulincer, Gillath, & Shaver, 2002; Simpson, Rholes, & Nelligan, 1992).

Although insecurity-inducing situations can occur even among secure individuals, these individuals tend to fare better in such situations. For example, given that attachment security is associated with effective communication skills and problem-solving strategies (Gaines et al., 1997), secure partners may be able to navigate potentially challenging situations more effectively than insecure partners. Moreover, secure individuals' positive expectations that others are available and responsive, coupled with confidence that the self is a capable person worthy of love, allow them to be comfortable with dependence without threatening their sense of autonomy and control over their own fate (Feeney, 2007; Neyer, 2002; Rusbult & Van Lange, 2008). Thus, secure relationships are likely to be characterized by mutual dependence, with both partners exerting control over their own and the other person's experience to maximize positive outcomes for each other.

Despite these advantages, secure individuals sometimes do exhibit insecure behaviors. For example, someone who generally trusts others may become worried and even preoccupied because of a partner's overt and frequent flirtations with others; these moments of anxiety may be resolved by adjusting one's level of dependence until there is unambiguous information about a partner's commitment (Murray & Holmes, 2009). From an interdependence perspective, the key variables in this example concern the level of dependence and information uncertainty. Another secure person may have a partner who is experiencing substantial stress; the person might thus seek moments away from the stressed partner, at least temporarily, in order to cope with this difficult situation, which concerns increasing this person's own control ("actor control") over his/her own time.

Although secure individuals can experience momentary or short-lived insecurities ("It really hurt my feelings that she forgot my birthday. What was she thinking?"), their past experiences of being able to rely on others for care and support make it easier to recover from these moments and more quickly return to positive interactions ("She's just been really busy lately. I know she loves me"; Feeney & Collins, 2015; Salvatore, Kuo, Steele, Simpson, & Collins, 2011).

Chronically insecure individuals, on the other hand, often struggle with interdependence. They tend to respond with distrust, distress, and/or discomfort when they have to rely on others and when others must rely on them (Rusbult & Van Lange, 2003). They often exhibit relatively ineffective communication strategies and poor interpersonal problem-solving skills (Simpson, Rholes, & Phillips, 1996) that contribute to costly, negative, or painful dependence, or to uncertainty and lack of information about each other's motives (Brennan & Shaver, 1995; Collins, 1996).

In their desire to receive reassurances of love and commitment, anxious individuals often over-dramatize situations or enact other kinds of attention-seeking behaviors (Overall, Girme, Lemay, & Hammond, 2014). These situations effectively "test" whether a partner remains committed even when it is personally costly (e.g., a partner's efforts involved in providing attention or toning down drama). Partners of anxious individuals may have their pro-relationship responses tested repeatedly, which may cause their relationship satisfaction to decline (Lemay & Dudley, 2011). Particularly in trust situations, anxious individuals may develop perceptions of extreme vulnerability, low personal (actor) control, and unilateral dependence on their partner for their outcomes (Mikulincer, 1998). Moreover, given that anxious individuals are less inclined to be engaged in personal activities without their partner (Carnelley & Ruscher, 2000), their desire to be together constantly may become an issue if it interferes with the partner's desire to pursue personal or autonomous goals and activities (cf. Kumashiro, Rusbult, & Finkel, 2008). Thus, anxious individuals may inadvertently create situations that lead partners to seek distance, which in turn fuels anxious concerns over a partner abandoning them and reinforces anxious beliefs that oneself is not worthy of love or care.

In contrast, avoidant individuals place a high premium on having interactions in which they exert high personal (actor) control, often due to their generally fixed beliefs about others' unavailability, rather than on the relationship between their specific partner and the particular situation (Birnie, McClure, Lydon, & Holmberg, 2009; Holmes, 2002). As a result, partners of avoidant individuals may desire more involvement and intimacy than the avoidant partner is willing or able to provide (Lemay & Dudley, 2011). Partners may even demand change, threaten ultimatums, or feel less positive about interactions with the avoidant partner, confirming the avoidant person's belief that close relationships are not rewarding. It should be noted that avoidant individuals have learnt to suppress their need for dependence, but the innate desire for human bonds has not disappeared (Edelstein & Shaver, 2004), and avoidant individuals sometimes may react more positively than others to signs of acceptance (Carvallo & Gabriel, 2006). However, in times of distress or in situations where the avoidant individual may wish to spend more time together, partners may fail to provide the time and the care that the avoidant individual consciously or unconsciously craves, further reinforcing the belief that close others are unreliable and ultimately unfulfilling in the long run.

As the examples above demonstrate, both anxious and avoidant individuals are more likely to experience relationships in which their interpersonal preferences are less synchronized with their partners, compared to secure individuals. Anxious individuals often desire more closeness and more time together than their partners, whereas avoidant individuals tend to show the opposite tendencies. Although both are disposed to encounter more challenging situations compared to secure individuals, their differing histories of insecurity translate into predictable differences in how various situational features manifest (e.g., mutuality of dependence, basis of dependence).

The diverging experiences of those characterized as high anxiety and high avoidance are reflected in their models of self and other. For example, anxious individuals' typically low actor control stems both from their negative model of self (e.g., "She's going to leave me because I don't deserve her") and ambiguous model of others (e.g., "I hope she stays, but I doubt it"). In contrast, avoidant individuals' desire for high actor control stems both from their ambiguous model of self (e.g., "I can only count on me") and negative model of others (e.g., "If I get too close, he's going to let me down").

How, then, can such entrenched working models change for the better? Although there is considerable interest in understanding how people can become more secure in their relationships, at present non-clinical and long-term solutions remain elusive, and much of the literature on adult attachment is focused on how chronically insecure working models endure rather than on how they might be revised (Mikulincer & Shaver, 2016). This lack of information regarding attachment change led to the development of the Attachment Security Enhancement Model (ASEM; Arriaga et al., 2018), which suggests a situation-by-working model approach to bolster security. With its emphasis on situations, the ASEM draws attention to particularly relevant interactions that may revise insecure working models over time. The next sections review major ideas of the ASEM, including strategies for enhancing security.

AN OVERVIEW OF THE ATTACHMENT SECURITY ENHANCEMENT MODEL (ASEM)

The current section will provide a brief overview of the ASEM; further details of each part of the model are described in greater detail later in the chapter (also see Arriaga et al., 2018 for a more comprehensive review). The central idea is that, although people enter new relationships with deeply-ingrained tendencies reflected in their working models of self and others, new situations can adjust these working models. Specifically, how individuals manage *novel* situations with close others over time can either affirm a working model ("She's not there for me, just like nobody ever is") or revise it ("Wow – she came through! Maybe I can rely on her"). The ASEM integrates interdependence- and attachment-based frameworks to suggest how key interactions shape chronic relational tendencies – what people tend to do with each other and expect from each other. Whereas attachment theory harkens back to previous interactions and experiences as being crucial in shaping general tendencies with new partners, interdependence theory examines how current interactions within specific relationships shape current tendencies. The ASEM adopts interdependence and attachment assumptions of dyadic processes, suggesting that romantic partners affect each other's chronic tendencies in a dynamic way.

As shown in Figure 5.1, the ASEM differentiates between processes that mitigate the potentially destructive effects of momentary insecurities versus long-term processes that may revise the working models that underlie insecure tendencies. The two parts of the model work in tandem to enhance attachment security over time. In particular, the ASEM offers different pathways toward enhancing security for attachment anxiety versus avoidance. Given that chronic attachment orientations are shaped by interpersonal experiences, the model leverages the power of close romantic relationship

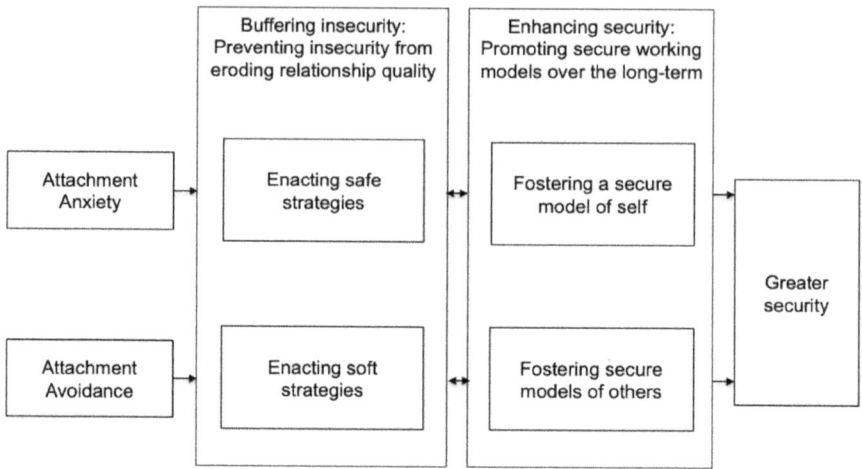

FIGURE 5.1 Revising working models across time: Relationship situations that enhance attachment security, by Arriaga, X. B., Kumashiro, M., Simpson, J. A., & Overall, N. C. (2018). Retrieved from *Personality and Social Psychology Bulletin, 22*, 71–96

partners specifically to help revise long-established internal working models that underlie attachment anxiety and avoidance dimensions (Brennan, Clark & Shaver, 1998; Fraley, Waller, & Brennan, 2000). The model targets such relationships because committed romantic partnerships are characterized by high interdependence, and partners often function as primary attachment figures in adulthood (Hazan & Shaver, 1987). It also should be noted that, just as secure parents are better able to provide responsive caregiving that give rise to raising a secure child (Jones, Cassidy, & Shaver, 2015), a secure partner may be better equipped to deliver the ASEM-based strategies compared to insecure partners who face unique struggles in relationships, such as difficulties providing support (Collins & Ford, 2010; Davila & Kashy, 2009; Feeney & Collins, 2019).

Short-term strategies for preventing insecurity from further deteriorating the quality of a relationship are shown in the right-hand column of Table 5.1. Specifically, "safe" strategies are suggested for mitigating attachment anxiety, and "soft" strategies are suggested for mitigating attachment avoidance (also see left-hand side of Figure 5.1). Importantly, these strategies can provide momentary relief of immediate insecure thoughts and feelings (e.g., feelings of uncertainty/doubt about a partner's availability, desires to withdraw during emotional interactions), but these strategies may not necessarily revise the underlying working models that sustain insecurity. Therefore, the second part of the ASEM suggests targeted situations and processes that may revise specific insecure working models over time (see right-hand side of Figure 5.1

TABLE 5.1 Sample features of insecurity and corresponding partner buffering strategies

	Recipient Insecurity Features	Effective Partner Buffering
Attachment Anxiety	*Hyperactivated responses* - Seeking reassurance of partner's commitment - Negative attributions/affect, high emotional intensity, increased drama	*Sample "safe" strategies* - Providing reassurance (e.g., emphasizing a strong and intimate bond) - Conveying commitment - De-escalating negative emotional intensity
Attachment Avoidance	*Deactivated responses* - Disengaging/withdrawal during situations characterized by emotional intensity, dependence, or partner requests for change - Prone to low commitment and discomfort with partners relying on them	*Sample "soft" strategies* - Acknowledging and respecting recipient's desire to avoid emotionally charged interactions - Being tactful about conveying how/why certain requests are reasonable - Avoiding emotional or critical tones

and right-hand side of Table 5.2). Both these momentary and long-term strategies are described in greater detail in the following two sections.

MITIGATING MOMENTARY INSECURITIES

Unsurprisingly, attachment insecurity is associated with increased conflict (Mikulincer & Shaver, 2016). Due to the differing signature characteristics associated with attachment anxiety versus avoidance, the ASEM accordingly differentiates between the suggested strategies for mitigating momentary anxious versus avoidant thoughts and feelings. This section will briefly highlight these differences (see Arriaga et al., 2018, for additional details).

Safe Strategies for Attachment Anxiety

Individuals who chronically experience anxious thoughts and feelings will often perceive more problems than is warranted, feel dependent and vulnerable, and may display overly needy or "clingy" behavior (Collins, 1996; Collins, Ford, Guichard, & Allard, 2006; Pierce & Lydon, 1998; Simpson et al., 1996). Given these issues, how can partners prevent challenging situations from spiraling out of control? As shown in Table 5.1, the ASEM suggests safe strategies to mitigate anxious thoughts and feelings (Feeney, 2004; Overall, Girme, & Simpson, 2016). Examples of safe strategies that partners can enact include

TABLE 5.2 Processes that promote a recipient's movement toward secure working models

	General Process	Situations That Foster Security
Attachment Anxiety	Confidence-building processes to foster a secure model of self - Feeling increasingly worthy and capable in *personal* domains - Increased comfort with autonomy and independence	*Sample situations that instill confidence and foster a secure model of self* - Being complimented and appreciated (e.g., partner lauds recipient, helps recipient set achievable personal goals that gradually become more challenging) - Deriving a sense of self-efficacy during challenging or distressing personal situations (e.g., partner provides praise or encouragement as recipient handles a problem/issue) - Being encouraged (and learning) to attribute personal accomplishments to one's own efforts - Feeling inspiration and autonomous support for new independent experiences
Attachment Avoidance	Positive dependence processes to foster secure models of others - Feeling increasingly valued and capable in *interpersonal* domains - Increased comfort with dependence	*Sample situations that create positive dependence and foster secure models of others* - Experiencing fun or positive interdependence, which creates positive associations with closeness (e.g., fun activities with a partner) - Feeling unexpectedly positive in interpersonal or caregiving situations assumed to be aversive - Inadvertently attaining benefits from partner support, which weakens negative associations with dependence

conveying closeness/commitment (Murray & Holmes, 2009; Murray, Holmes, & Collins, 2006; Tran & Simpson, 2009), emphasizing one's intimate bond (Murray et al., 2011), and de-escalating the anxious person's heightened negative emotions (e.g., saying "I'm here for you" or using physical touch; Jakubiak & Feeney, 2016; Kim, Feeney, & Jakubiak, 2018; Overall et al., 2014).

Soft Strategies for Attachment Avoidance

Unlike attachment anxiety, which is associated with having partners who are *intermittently* unresponsive, thus "keep[ing] hope alive" (Beckes, Simons,

Lewis, Le, & Edwards, 2017), attachment avoidance tends to be associated with the belief that others cannot be relied upon at all due to a history of experiences with *consistently* unresponsive close others. Individuals who have momentary avoidant thoughts and feelings avert emotional interactions and/or emotional support, seek distractions during challenging moments in relationships, avoid situations that require evaluating their relationship, minimize their own relational dependence on others or others' dependence on them, place a low premium on intimacy, and seek greater personal control in trust situations (Beck & Clark, 2009; Carnelley & Ruscher, 2000; Feeney & Collins, 2001; Hazan & Shaver, 1990; Mikulincer, 1998; Pietromonaco & Barrett, 1997; Ren, Arriaga, & Mahan, 2016). When an individual becomes chronically avoidant, a partner may seek greater intimacy and support, only to be met with the individual's resistance and anger (Overall, Simpson, & Struthers, 2013). Eventually partners may feel less satisfied (see Mikulincer & Shaver, 2016); they must decide whether to accept their current dissatisfaction, or instead request changes that may improve their relationship but also may cause conflict and exacerbate the other's avoidant responses.

As Table 5.1 shows, the ASEM suggests the use of "soft" strategies in making requests for change. These strategies are theorized to mitigate avoidant thoughts and feelings. Specifically, partners may respect the other's need for autonomy and alleviate an avoidant person's discomfort. Examples include respecting the person's desire to avoid emotionally-charged conversations ("Let's put a pin in this discussion until we've had a good meal and rest"), conveying why one's requests are reasonable in a matter-of-fact tone ("It's important that you involve me in decisions that also affect me"), and using distractions, sexual contact, or other tactics to effectively diffuse negative emotions (Birnbaum, Reis, Mikulincer, Gillath, & Orpaz, 2006; Little, McNulty, & Russell, 2010; Overall et al., 2013; Simpson, Winterheld, Rholes, & Oriña, 2007).

Avoidant individuals themselves report preferences for partner behaviors that reflect these strategies. For example, compared to other types of partner strategies (e.g., providing reassurance, being kind and giving), avoidant partners wish that their partners would avoid getting emotionally charged during challenging moments and instead act sensibly and reasonably when making requests (Hunt, Arriaga, & Kumashiro, 2020). However, as will be discussed in the next section, what individuals prefer when they experience insecurities may inadvertently reinforce insecure working models. Strategies to mitigate momentary insecurity may not necessarily enhance security in the longer-term.

ENHANCING ATTACHMENT SECURITY OVER TIME

The use of safe/soft strategies can address insecurity in the immediate moment to prevent further deteriorations in relationship quality. However, these strategies require continued effort by a partner. As mentioned above, partners become impatient or annoyed when they must use these strategies repeatedly, which may lead to feeling depleted and less satisfied with the relationship (Finkel & Campbell, 2001; Lemay & Clark, 2008; Lemay & Dudley, 2011; Rusbult, Verette, Whitney, Slovik, & Lipkus, 1991).

A crucial issue with relying only on safe or soft strategies is that it remains uncertain whether these strategies are sufficient to bring about revisions in insecure working models of self and others (Lavner & Bradbury, 2017). For example, safe strategies may soothe concerns about a partner's level of commitment, but continued reassurances from a partner might inadvertently reinforce high reliance on a partner to satisfy one's needs, rather than reinforce autonomy and a sense of self-efficacy. Greater dependence is unlikely to address an anxious person's chronically negative model of self. Similarly, soft strategies may condone tendencies to withdraw from interactions that are emotional or involve dependence, even when such interactions might be important in maintaining relationships. Accordingly, these strategies may not necessarily change avoidant individuals' negative models of relationships.

As shown on the right-hand side of Table 5.2, the ASEM suggests situations that may enhance an insecure partner's working models over the long-term. The second part of the model (right side of Figure 5.1) concerns ways in which partners encourage new situations that can revise insecure working models and establish a more optimal balance of dependence and autonomy (Kumashiro et al., 2008). Through new opportunities, anxious individuals may reduce their unilateral dependence on a partner and master greater levels of personal (actor) control, whereas avoidant individuals may recognize the rewards and benefits associated with dependence rather than focus on the costs. The next two sections describe these situations that may address chronic insecurities (for more details, see Arriaga et al., 2018).

Enhancing Security for Anxiously Attached Individuals

Chronic attachment anxiety primarily stems from a negative model of the self and an ambivalent model of others that feeds into the belief that the self must depend on the partner for validation of self-worth. Anxious individuals tend to be so focused on their partners and the relationship that they often miss out on opportunities for increasing their self-efficacy and self-worth. Similar to an anxious child's behavior in the "Strange Situation" paradigm (e.g., not engaging in exploratory behaviors when reunited with one's caregiver; Ainsworth, Blehar, Waters & Wall, 1978), anxious adults often fail to engage in intrinsically independent activities (Carnelley & Ruscher, 2000) in favor of focusing on their relationships. As a result, anxious individuals habitually forego opportunities to derive a sense of self-efficacy and autonomy (Deci & Ryan, 2014). Indeed, attachment anxiety shows a strong negative association with self-esteem (see Mikulincer & Shaver, 2016). Focusing on the relationship at the expense of personal pursuits makes them unilaterally dependent on their relationship for happiness, and they become overly contingent on another's approval to feel positive about themselves.

How, then, can partners enhance an anxious person's model of self? Findings from a longitudinal study revealed reductions in anxiety when partners validated and encouraged the anxious person's personal goal pursuits (Arriaga et al., 2014). The key to enhancing security for anxious individuals may then lie in a partner's ability to foster self-worth.

As shown in Table 5.2, the ASEM suggests situations that encourage greater self-confidence. Partners may encourage independent talents, abilities, and interests (e.g., "That song you wrote on the guitar was great – I want to hear more from you!"; Drigotas, 2002; Drigotas, Rusbult, Wieselquist, & Whitton, 1999; Feeney, 2004; Rusbult, Finkel, & Kumashiro, 2009; cf. Steele, 1988). Importantly, partners can be encouraging in a way that enables anxious individuals to recognize the underlying message of such confidence-building attempts. For example, low self-esteem individuals benefit more from partner compliments when instructed to think about the broader meaning behind the compliments rather than simply accepting the compliments (Marigold, Holmes, & Ross, 2007, 2010).

As anxious individuals derive a sense of self-efficacy and become more self-confident – through positive outcomes from independent pursuits, or through partner support to overcome inevitable setbacks – they will gradually come to perceive themselves as worthy of love, support, and care. As a consequence, challenging situations within the relationship may also seem less daunting or threatening, and they will have greater confidence in addressing problems both in their own endeavors and in their relationship.

Nevertheless, this process is by no means easy. Partners may have more control over the process of mitigating insecure thoughts and feelings featured in the ASEM, but less control over the self-confidence-building process of the ASEM. Bolstering self-confidence may hinge on anxious individuals having success in activities from which they can derive self-worth and learning that setbacks can lead to positive outcomes in the long run. Despite partner encouragement and support, pursuits that are too challenging or that result in failure may reinforce feelings of incompetence, or even anger at the partner for encouraging these pursuits without actively helping. In addition, anxious individuals may flatly refuse to initiate independent pursuits, or interpret a partner's encouragement of spending time on independent pursuits as the partner desiring less time together.

Thus, creating situations that effectively boost self-confidence requires a skilled and motivated partner, as it may be necessary to use safe strategies in conjunction with confidence-building strategies to buffer any resulting conflicts and help encourage more independence. Just as parents must avoid being too intrusive so that their children can learn from mistakes on their own, partners need to offer autonomous support while resisting getting too involved in order to enhance an anxious individual's self-confidence (e.g., refraining from directing the activity). This can be achieved through offering responsive and nonintrusive support (Feeney, 2004), encouraging goals that are achievable, and helping anxious individuals be less critical of themselves when they encounter setbacks (e.g., "I know it's frustrating, but I'm proud of you. And remember: Most things worth achieving involve at least some struggle. That's definitely true for me!").

Enhancing Security for Avoidantly Attached Individuals

Different situations are likely to bolster attachment security among chronic-ally avoidant individuals. As mentioned above, these individuals firmly believe that dependence is costly and that it is better to be self-sufficient and resist attempts at change. Nevertheless, the innate human need for dependence still resides within avoidant individuals. Research findings have revealed that earlier perceptions of trust in a partner predict declines in avoidance a year later (Arriaga et al., 2014), and lab-introduced exercises involving novel, light-hearted shared activities (e.g., touch yoga, short quizzes to encourage self-disclosure) reduce avoidance one month later (Stanton, Selcuk, Farrell, Slatcher, & Ong, 2017). Thus, situations that build positive interdependence and trust seem to be critical in enhancing security for individuals high in attachment avoidance.

As shown in Table 5.2, an initial step may be to increase positive dependence through introducing new, enjoyable shared experiences that help associate dependence with fun or other rewards (e.g., "Let's try out disc golf this weekend"; Aron & Aron, 1986; Girme, Overall, & Faingataa, 2014). Because avoidant individuals have a history of not being able to rely on others, using positive moments to demonstrate the opposite (i.e., that involve-ment with close others can be gratifying) will enhance models of others over time.

However, partners should not emphasize highly intimate/emotional fea-tures (e.g., Tom's partner should not mention how this new experience will bring them closer together as a couple). Emphasizing intimacy may backfire, reminding avoidant individuals of times in the past when becoming close to others was hurtful. Instead, engaging in new, fun, and exciting activities together is a low-risk way of demonstrating the benefits of close relationships. Avoidant individuals may be especially likely to respond positively to such efforts; our recent research on situations preferred by avoidant individuals (Hunt et al., 2019) demonstrates that these individuals indeed do prioritize these situational features (i.e., having fun, doing something new) over other positive features (e.g., showing trust and support, being valued). Sometimes, an external reason may be necessary to get avoidant individuals on board, such as being required to participate in fun activities as part of a study (Stanton et al., 2017).

Engaging in new, fun experiences may have benefits for the partner as well given that engaging in novel activities offers benefits to couples in general (Aron & Aron, 1986). Although avoidant individuals tend to dampen their emotional reactions, even in rewarding situations (MacDonald, Locke, Spielmann, & Joel, 2013), sharing repeated experiences that are exciting, novel, and fun may sustain the partner's relationship satisfaction.

Nevertheless, simply engaging in new activities characterized by lighthearted fun will be unlikely to improve working models of relationships over the longer term. Lasting changes require becoming less resistant of situations that involve mutual dependence, reciprocity of support provision, and trust (Arriaga et al., 2014). Although avoidant individuals tend to avoid situations that involve providing support, their negative beliefs about these situations may change during salient moments in which they experience unexpected benefits from providing support. For example, one study revealed that husbands who transitioned to fatherhood – which can be a joyous but also stressful life transition – became less avoidant over time when they provided support in caring for their infants (Simpson et al., 2003).

Avoidant individuals also react badly when they encounter situations in which they must rely on or are affected by others. However, if they inadvertently find themselves in these situations and discover that the outcome is not as negative or costly as feared, this may lead to a revision of their negative models of intimate relationships. How can partners demonstrate benefits of dependence? One study revealed that avoidant individuals reacted more positively than others when they were socially accepted (Carvallo & Gabriel, 2006), possibly because being socially accepted ran counter to their expectations of remaining distant from others. Thus, partners can capitalize on opportunities to amplify mutual appreciation, respect, and experienced benefits of dependence (e.g., Tom was pleased to overhear his partner telling her friends that his supportive behavior toward her has helped her cope with her work issues).

Unlike confidence-building situations with anxious individuals, partners of avoidant individuals may have somewhat more control over creating situations that reveal the benefits of dependence. That said, partner characteristics, such as patience, motivation, and ability, still play a large role. Partners must use a combination of enacting soft strategies to lessen partner resistance toward dependence and skillfully introducing or amplifying unexpected situations that reveal rewards of dependence (e.g., instead of directly offering help, surprise an avoidant person by taking care of an annoying errand for him/her).

OTHER INFLUENCES

So far we have focused on dyadic processes in romantic involvements that may revise insecure expressions and tendencies. Although partners may have a strong effect on a wide range of present and future attachment responses, the processes we have discussed in the ASEM alone cannot foretell how partners will react to one another in every new interaction. Attachment-relevant responses and tendencies may be affected by specific situational factors (e.g., immediately experienced emotions and motives), other individual differences (e.g., low versus high trait neuroticism), and dyadic factors (e.g., the unique combination of each partner's behaviors/motives on one another). This section describes other factors beyond interactions with a partner that may influence whether the partner processes described above are likely to enhance attachment security.

Certain individual features (e.g., personality traits) may amplify the expression of attachment responses and make them resistant to change. For example, individuals high in neuroticism tend to be more susceptible to anxious tendencies compared to those low in neuroticism (Noftle & Shaver, 2006). Another important factor concerns chronic stress: Individuals who are experiencing high stress outside of their relationship (e.g., work issues) tend to be less effective at managing stress within their relationship (i.e., "stress spillover"; Bolger, DeLongis, Kessler, & Wethington, 1989; Neff & Karney, 2004), and this external stress can give rise to insecure behaviors that are resistant to partner influence (e.g., high emotional reactivity). Moreover, individuals with particular histories (e.g., psychopathology in the self or parent, parental divorce) are more prone to fluctuations in their attachment orientations (Davila & Cobb, 2003), which may also make them resistant to partner influence.

The attachment composition within a relationship – the specific attachment pairing – is likely to affect emergent attachment responses and the viability of ASEM processes. For example, when paired with a highly avoidant individual, highly anxious individuals may eventually withdraw intimacy if their efforts to attain closeness are thwarted, just as a chronically avoidant person would be motivated to do from the outset. Alternatively, a secure partner may make a chronically avoidant person feel uniquely comfortable enough to seek closeness, but if this secure partner rebuffs or fails to reciprocate closeness (perhaps due to other factors such as mood, stress, etc.), the avoidant person may respond with anxious tendencies at first and only revert back to his or her avoidant tendencies after this uncharacteristic anxiety is suppressed. In contrast, relatively secure individuals may be more reliable in their motivations and ability to support a partner (Feeney, Collins, Van Vleet, & Tomlinson, 2013; Feeney & Thrush, 2010), which could influence a partner's effectiveness in enacting ASEM processes.

Thus, factors beyond one person's underlying attachment orientation can influence the effectiveness of the ASEM-based strategies. Together, both underlying working models that people carry into new interactions and features of the situation (e.g., stress) contribute to attachment-relevant responses in new situations.

CONCLUSION

Despite the many benefits that close relationships can provide, everyone experiences moments when they have difficulty depending on others or having others depend on them. When difficulties with interdependence occur repeatedly over time, they can give rise to chronic attachment orientations characterized by insecurity. From an interdependence theory perspective, certain situations can reveal both patterned, habitual tendencies (e.g., Annie's impulse to seek reassurance when experiencing uncertainty) as well as departures from such tendencies (e.g., Annie's willingness to act calmly when faced with uncertainty or doubt). From an attachment theory perspective, situations experienced early in life with caregivers are particularly emphasized, as these situations inform deeply rooted relational tendencies that people bring into new relationships.

Both theories provide clues to specific strategies that romantic partners can use in key situations to mitigate insecurity in the moment, reducing the destructive effects that insecurities can have on relationships. Furthermore, situations can also serve as opportunities for revising working models toward greater felt security over time. New experiences that differ from past (insecure) experiences can "update" existing working models of the self and others to become more stably secure over time. Specifically, repeated exposure to new experiences that demonstrate that one is efficacious and that close others can be trusted and even foster benefits may give rise to more secure models of the self and others.

The situation-by-working model processes form the backbone of the ASEM, which demonstrates the utility in recognizing the mutual influence of underlying relational tendencies and situational factors in predicting – and, more importantly, even improving – relational processes and outcomes. The ASEM is at the forefront of a growing body of research focusing on how partner-enacted behaviors within key situations in romantic relationships can enhance security (Arriaga et al., 2014; Farrell, Simpson, Overall, & Shallcross, 2016; Simpson et al., 2003). Long-developed insecure tendencies cannot change immediately or easily. Only repeated interactions over time that counter past experiences can result in lasting changes to deeply ingrained mental representations and patterns of behavior. Each new situation can contribute to this lasting change. Focusing on these key situations is essential, because they suggest avenues for romantic partners to change old habits for the better.

REFERENCES

Ainsworth, M. D. S., Blehar, M. C., Waters, E., & Wall, S. (1978). *Patterns of Attachment: A Psychological Study of the Strange Situation*. Hillsdale, NJ: Erlbaum.

Arriaga, X. B., Kumashiro, M., Finkel, E. J., VanderDrift, L. E., & Luchies, L. B. (2014). Filling the void: Bolstering attachment security in committed relationships. *Social Psychological and Personality Science*, 5, 398–405.

Arriaga, X. B., Kumashiro, M., Simpson, J. A., & Overall, N. C. (2018). Revising working models across time: Relationship situations that enhance attachment security. *Personality and Social Psychology Bulletin*, 22, 71–96.

Aron, A. & Aron, E. N. (1986). *Love and the Expansion of Self: Understanding Attraction and Satisfaction*. New York: Hemisphere.

Beck, L. A. & Clark, M. S. (2009). Choosing to enter or avoid diagnostic social situations. *Psychological Science*, 20, 1175–1181.

Beckes, L., Simons, K., Lewis, D., Le, A., & Edwards, W. (2017). Desperately seeking support: Negative reinforcement schedules in the formation of adult attachment associations. *Social Psychological and Personality Science*, 8, 229–238.

Birnbaum, G. E., Reis, H. T., Mikulincer, M., Gillath, O., & Orpaz, A. (2006). When sex is more than just sex: Attachment orientations, sexual experience, and relationship quality. *Journal of Personality and Social Psychology*, 91, 929–943.

Birnie, C., McClure, M. J., Lydon, J. E., & Holmberg, D. (2009). Attachment avoidance and commitment aversion: A script for relationship failure. *Personal Relationships*, 16, 79–97.

Bolger, N., DeLongis, A., Kessler, R. C., & Wethington, E. (1989). The contagion of stress across multiple roles. *Journal of Marriage and the Family*, 51, 175–183.

Brennan, K. A., Clark, C. L., & Shaver, P. R. (1998). Self-report measurement of adult attachment: An integrative overview. In J. A. Simpson & W. S. Rholes (Eds.), *Attachment Theory and Close Relationships* (pp. 46–76). New York: Guilford.

Brennan, K. A. & Shaver, P. R. (1995). Dimensions of adult attachment, affect regulation, and romantic relationship functioning. *Personality and Social Psychology Bulletin*, 21, 267–283.

Bretherton, I. (1992). The origins of attachment theory: John Bowlby and Mary Ainsworth. *Developmental Psychology*, 28, 759.

Carnelley, K. B. & Ruscher, J. B. (2000). Adult attachment and exploratory behavior in leisure. *Journal of Social Behavior and Personality*, 15, 153–165.

Carvallo, M. & Gabriel, S. (2006). No man is an island: The need to belong and dismissing avoidant attachment style. *Personality and Social Psychology Bulletin*, 32, 697–709.

Chopik, W. J., Edelstein, R. S., & Grimm, K. J. (2019). Longitudinal changes in attachment orientation over a 59-year period. *Journal of Personality and Social Psychology*, 116, 598–611.

Collins, N. L. (1996). Working models of attachment: Implications for explanation, emotion, and behavior. *Journal of Personality and Social Psychology*, 71, 810–832.

Collins, N. L. & Feeney, B. C. (2000). A safe haven: An attachment theory perspective on support seeking and caregiving in intimate relationships. *Journal of Personality and Social Psychology*, 78, 1053.

Collins, N. L. & Ford, M. B. (2010). Responding to the needs of others: The caregiving behavioral system in intimate relationships. *Journal of Social and Personal Relationships*, 27, 235–244.

Collins, N. L., Ford, M. B., Guichard, A. C., & Allard, L. M. (2006). Working models of attachment and attribution processes in intimate relationships. *Personality and Social Psychology Bulletin*, 32, 201–219.

Collins, N. L. & Read, S. J. (1990). Adult attachment, working models, and relationship quality in dating couples. *Journal of Personality and Social Psychology*, 54, 644–663.

Davila, J. & Cobb, R. (2003). Predicting change in self-reported and interviewer-assessed adult attachment: Tests of the individual difference and life stress models of attachment change. *Personality and Social Psychology Bulletin*, 29, 859–870.

Davila, J. & Kashy, D. A. (2009). Secure base processes in couples: Daily associations between support experiences and attachment security. *Journal of Family Psychology*, 23(1), 76–88.

Deci, E. L. & Ryan, R. M. (2014). Autonomy and need satisfaction in close relationships: Relationships motivation theory. In N. Weinstein (Ed.), *Human Motivation and Interpersonal Relationships: Theory, Research, and Applications* (pp. 53–73), Dordrecht, the Netherlands: Springer.

Drigotas, S. M. (2002). The Michelangelo phenomenon and personal well-being. *Journal of Personality*, 70, 59–77.

Drigotas, S. M., Rusbult, C. E., Wieselquist, J., & Whitton, S. W. (1999). Close partner as sculptor of the ideal self: Behavioral affirmation and the Michelangelo phenomenon. *Journal of Personality and Social Psychology*, 77, 293–323.

Edelstein, R. S. & Shaver, P. R. (2004). Avoidant attachment: Exploration of an oxymoron. In D. J. Mashek & A. P. Aron (Eds.), *Handbook of Closeness and Intimacy* (pp. 397–412). Mahwah, NJ: Erlbaum.

Farrell, A. K., Simpson, J. A., Overall, N. C., & Shallcross, S. L. (2016). Buffering the responses of avoidantly attached romantic partners in strain test situations. *Journal of Family Psychology*, 30, 580–591.

Feeney, B. C. (2004). A secure base: Responsive support of goal strivings and exploration in adult intimate relationships. *Journal of Personality and Social Psychology*, 87, 631–648.

Feeney, B. C. (2007). The dependency paradox in close relationships: Accepting dependence promotes independence. *Journal of Personality and Social Psychology*, 92, 268–285.

Feeney, B. C. & Collins, N. L. (2001). Predictors of caregiving in adult intimate relationships: An attachment theoretical perspective. *Journal of Personality and Social Psychology*, 80, 972–994.

Feeney, B. C. & Collins, N. L. (2015). A new look at social support: A theoretical perspective on thriving through relationships. *Personality and Social Psychology Review*, 19, 113–147.

Feeney, B. C. & Collins, N. L. (2019). The importance of relational support for attachment and exploration needs. *Current Opinion in Psychology*, 25, 182–186.

Feeney, B. C., Collins, N. L., Van Vleet, M., & Tomlinson, J. M. (2013). Motivations for providing a secure base: Links with attachment orientation and secure base support behavior. *Attachment & Human Development*, 15, 261–280.

Feeney, B. C. & Thrush, R. L. (2010). Relationship influences on exploration in adulthood: The characteristics and function of a secure base. *Journal of Personality and Social Psychology*, 98, 57–76.

Finkel, E. J. & Campbell, W. K. (2001). Self-control and accommodation in close relationships: An interdependence analysis. *Journal of Personality and Social Psychology*, 81, 263–277.

Fraley, R. C., Roisman, G. I., Booth-LaForce, C., Owen, M. T., & Holland, A. S. (2013). Interpersonal and genetic origins of adult attachment styles: A longitudinal study from infancy to early adulthood. *Journal of Personality and Social Psychology*, 104, 817.

Fraley, R. C. & Shaver, P. R. (1998). Airport separations: A naturalistic study of adult attachment dynamics in separating couples. *Journal of Personality and Social Psychology*, 75, 1198.

Fraley, R. C., Waller, N. G., & Brennan, K. A. (2000). An item response theory analysis of self-report measures of adult attachment. *Journal of Personality and Social Psychology*, 78, 350–365.

Gaines Jr., S. O., Reis, H. T., Summers, S., Rusbult, C. E., Cox, C. L., Wexler, M. O., . . . Kurland, G. J. (1997). Impact of attachment style on reactions to accommodative dilemmas in close relationships. *Personal Relationships*, 4, 93–113.

Girme, Y. U., Overall, N. C., & Faingataa, S. (2014). "Date nights" take two: The maintenance function of shared relationship activities. *Personal Relationships*, 21, 125–149.

Hazan, C. & Shaver, P. R. (1987). Romantic love conceptualized as an attachment process. *Journal of Personality and Social Psychology*, 52, 511–524.

Hazan, C. & Shaver, P. R. (1990). Love and work: An attachment-theoretical perspective. *Journal of Personality and Social Psychology*, 59, 270–280.

Hazan, C. & Shaver, P. R. (1994). Attachment as an organizational framework for research on close relationships. *Psychological Inquiry*, 5, 1–22.

Holmes, J. G. (2002). Interpersonal expectations as the building blocks of social cognition: An interdependence theory analysis. *Personal Relationships*, 9, 1–26.

Holmes, J. G. & Rempel, J. K. (1989). Trust in close relationships. In C. Hendrick (Ed.), *Review of Personality and Social Psychology* (Vol. 10, pp. 187–220). London: Sage.

Hunt, L. L., Arriaga, X. B., & Kumashiro, M. (2020). *"Tell Me What You Want, What You Really Really Want": Preferences within Attachment-Relevant Situations.* Manuscript in preparation.

Jakubiak, B. K. & Feeney, B. C. (2016). A sense of security: Touch promotes state attachment security. *Social Psychological and Personality Science*, 7, 745–753.

Jones, J. D., Cassidy, J., & Shaver, P. R. (2015). Parents' self-reported attachment styles: A review of links with parenting behaviors, emotions, and cognitions. *Personality and Social Psychology Review*, 19(1), 44–76.

Kelley, H. H. (1979). *Personal Relationships: Their Structures and Processes.* Hillsdale, NJ: Lawrence Erlbaum.

Kelley, H. H. (1983). The situational origins of human tendencies: A further reason for the formal analysis of structure. *Personality and Social Psychology Bulletin*, 9, 8–30.

Kelley, H. H., Holmes, J. G., Kerr, N. L., Reis, H. T., Rusbult, C. E., & Van Lange, P. A. M. (2003). *An Atlas of Interpersonal Situations*. Cambridge: Cambridge University Press.

Kim, K. J., Feeney, B. C., & Jakubiak, B. K. (2018). Touch reduces romantic jealousy in the anxiously attached. *Journal of Social and Personal Relationships*, 35, 1019–1041.

Kirkpatrick, L. A. & Davis, K. E. (1994). Attachment style, gender, and relationship stability: A longitudinal analysis. *Journal of Personality and Social Psychology*, 66, 502–512.

Kumashiro, M., Rusbult, C. E., & Finkel, E. J. (2008). Navigating personal and relational concerns: The quest for equilibrium. *Journal of Personality and Social Psychology*, 95, 94–110.

Lavner, J. A. & Bradbury, T. N. (2017). Protecting relationships from stress. *Current Opinion in Psychology*, 13, 11–14.

Lemay, E. P., Jr. & Clark, M. S. (2008). "You're just saying that:" Contingencies of self-worth, suspicion, and authenticity in the interpersonal affirmation process. *Journal of Experimental Social Psychology*, 44, 1376–1382.

Lemay, E. P., Jr. & Dudley, K. L. (2011). Caution: Fragile! Regulating the interpersonal security of chronically insecure partners. *Journal of Personality and Social Psychology*, 100, 681–702.

Lewin, K. (1936). *Principles of Topological Psychology*. New York: McGraw-Hill.

Little, K. C., McNulty, J. K., & Russell, V. M. (2010). Sex buffers intimates against the negative implications of attachment insecurity. *Personality and Social Psychology Bulletin*, 36, 484–498.

MacDonald, G., Locke, K. D., Spielmann, S. S., & Joel, S. (2013). Insecure attachment predicts ambivalent social threat and reward perceptions in romantic relationships. *Journal of Social and Personal Relationships*, 30, 647–661.

Marigold, D. C., Holmes, J. G., & Ross, M. (2007). More than words: Reframing compliments from romantic partners fosters security in low self-esteem individuals. *Journal of Personality and Social Psychology*, 92, 232–248.

Marigold, D. C., Holmes, J. G., & Ross, M. (2010). Fostering relationship resilience: An intervention for low self-esteem individuals. *Journal of Experimental Social Psychology*, 46, 624–630.

Mikulincer, M. (1998). Attachment working models and the sense of trust: An exploration of interaction goals and affect regulation. *Journal of Personality and Social Psychology*, 74, 1209–1224.

Mikulincer, M. & Florian, V. (1998). The relationship between adult attachment styles and emotional and cognitive reactions to stressful events. In J. A. Simpson & W. S. Rholes (Eds.), *Attachment Theory and Close Relationships* (pp. 143–165). New York: Guilford.

Mikulincer, M., Gillath, O., & Shaver, P. R. (2002). Activation of the attachment system in adulthood: Threat-related primes increase the accessibility of mental representations of attachment figures. *Journal of Personality and Social Psychology*, 83, 881.

Mikulincer, M. & Shaver, P. R. (2016). *Attachment in Adulthood: Structure, Dynamics, and Change* (2nd ed.). New York: Guildford.

Murray, S. L. & Holmes, J. G. (2009). The architecture of interdependent minds: A motivation-management theory of mutual responsiveness. *Psychological Review*, 116, 908–928.

Murray, S. L., Holmes, J. G., & Collins, N. L. (2006). Optimizing assurances: The risk regulation system in relationships. *Psychological Bulletin*, 132, 641–666.

Murray, S. L., Pinkus, R. T., Holmes, J. G., Harris, B., Gomillion, S., Aloni, M., . . . Leder, S. (2011). Signaling when (and when not) to be cautious and self-protective: Impulsive and reflective trust in close relationships. *Journal of Personality and Social Psychology*, 101, 485.

Neff, L. A. & Karney, B. R. (2004). How does context affect intimate relationships? Linking external stress and cognitive processes within marriage. *Personality and Social Psychology Bulletin*, 30, 134–148.

Neyer, F. J. (2002). The dyadic interdependence of attachment security and dependency: A conceptual replication across older twin pairs and younger couples. *Journal of Social and Personal Relationships*, 19, 483–503.

Noftle, E. E. & Shaver, P. R. (2006). Attachment dimensions and the big five personality traits: Associations and comparative ability to predict relationship quality. *Journal of Research in Personality*, 40, 179–208.

Overall, N. C., Girme, Y. U., Lemay, E. P., Jr., & Hammond, M. T. (2014). Attachment anxiety and reactions to relationship threat: The benefits and costs of inducing guilt in romantic partners. *Journal of Personality and Social Psychology*, 106, 235–256.

Overall, N. C., Girme, Y. U., & Simpson, J. A. (2016). The power of diagnostic situations: How support and conflict can foster growth and security. In C. R. Knee & H. T. Reis (Eds.), *Positive Approaches to Optimal Development* (pp. 148–170). Cambridge: Cambridge University Press.

Overall, N. C., Simpson, J. A., & Struthers, H. (2013). Buffering attachment-related avoidance: Softening emotional and behavioral defenses during conflict discussions. *Journal of Personality and Social Psychology*, 104, 854–871.

Pierce, T. & Lydon, J. (1998). Priming relational schemas: Effects of contextually activated and chronically accessible interpersonal expectations on responses to a stressful event. *Journal of Personality and Social Psychology*, 75, 1441–1448.

Pietromonaco, P. R. & Barrett, L. F. (1997). Working models of attachment and daily social interactions. *Journal of Personality and Social Psychology*, 73, 1409–1423.

Pietromonaco, P. R. & Carnelley, K. B. (1994). Gender and working models of attachment: Consequences for perceptions of self and romantic relationships. *Personal Relationships*, 1, 63–82.

Reis, H. T. & Arriaga, X. B. (2015). Interdependence theory. In B. Gawronski & G. Bodenhausen (Eds.), *Theory and Explanation in Social Psychology* (pp. 305–327). New York, NY: Guilford Press.

Reis, H. T. & Holmes, J. G. (2012). Perspectives on the situation. In K. Deaux & M. Snyder (Eds.), *The Oxford Handbook of Personality and Social Psychology* (pp. 64–92). New York: Oxford University Press.

Ren, D., Arriaga, X. B., & Mahan, E. R. (2016). Attachment insecurity and perceived importance of relational features. *Journal of Social and Personal Relationships*, 34, 446–466.

Rusbult, C. E., Finkel, E. J., & Kumashiro, M. (2009). The Michelangelo phenomenon. *Current Directions in Psychological Science*, 18, 305–309.

Rusbult, C. E. & Van Lange, P. A. M. (2003). Interdependence, interaction, and relationships. *Annual Review of Psychology*, 54, 351–375.

Rusbult, C. E. & Van Lange, P. A. (2008). Why we need interdependence theory. *Social and Personality Psychology Compass*, 2, 2049–2070.

Rusbult, C. E., Verette, J., Whitney, G. A., Slovik, L. F., & Lipkus, I. (1991). Accommodation processes in close relationships: Theory and preliminary empirical evidence. *Journal of Personality and Social Psychology*, 60, 53–78.

Salvatore, J. E., Kuo, S. I., Steele, R. D., Simpson, J. A., & Collins, W. A. (2011). Recovering from conflict in romantic relationships: A developmental perspective. *Psychological Science*, 22, 376–383.

Simpson, J. A. (2007). Psychological foundations of trust. *Current Directions in Psychological Science*, 16, 264–268.

Simpson, J. A., Rholes, W. S., Campbell, L., & Wilson, C. L. (2003). Changes in attachment orientations across the transition to parenthood. *Journal of Experimental Social Psychology*, 39, 317–331.

Simpson, J. A., Rholes, W. S., & Nelligan, J. S. (1992). Support seeking and support giving within couples in an anxiety-provoking situation: The role of attachment styles. *Journal of Personality and Social Psychology*, 62, 434–446.

Simpson, J. A., Rholes, W. S., & Phillips, D. (1996). Conflict in close relationships: An attachment perspective. *Journal of Personality and Social Psychology*, 71, 899–914.

Simpson, J. A., Winterheld, H. A., Rholes, S. R., & Oriña, M. M. (2007). Working models of attachment and reactions to different forms of caregiving from romantic partners. *Journal of Personality and Social Psychology*, 93, 466–477.

Stanton, S., Selcuk, E., Farrell, A. K., Slatcher, R. B., & Ong, A. D. (2017). Partner responsiveness predicts all-cause mortality via daily negative affect reactivity: A 20-year longitudinal study. *Psychosomatic Medicine*, 79, A148.

Steele, C. M. (1988). The psychology of self-affirmation: Sustaining the integrity of the self. In L. Berkowitz & L. Berkowitz (Eds.), *Advances in Experimental Social Psychology: Vol. 21. Social Psychological Studies of the Self: Perspectives and Programs* (pp. 261–302). San Diego, CA: Academic.

Tran, S. & Simpson, J. A. (2009). Prorelationship maintenance behaviors: The joint roles of attachment and commitment. *Journal of Personality and Social Psychology*, 97, 685–698.

6

Safe and Secure

How Interdependent Close Relationships Mitigate Risks and Ease Insecurities

BRITTANY K. JAKUBIAK

At a weekly get together, Sarah listens as a friend describes how her long-term boyfriend broke up with her unexpectedly, leaving her single after she invested several years into their relationship. Another friend describes a fight she had with her spouse because he bought them tickets to a horror movie he wanted to see but knew she wouldn't enjoy. A third friend complains that his partner expects him to sacrifice but never reciprocates by making sacrifices of her own. Sarah remains silent, thinking that she would certainly have had a story to share if she were still dating her ex-boyfriend, Ryan. Throughout their relationship, Sarah worried constantly that Ryan was losing interest, and Sarah and Ryan repeatedly fought about her jealousy. Listening to her friends' relationship struggles, Sarah wonders whether she's better off staying single than continuing to search for a partner. She always imagined herself marrying, but the idea of someone controlling her weekend plans or having the power to upend her life makes singlehood sound more desirable. Yet, despite the distress Sarah's friends' relationships cause them, Sarah also remembers times when she envied her friends because of their supportive partners. Sarah can recall how one friend's partner supported her through her father's passing and how another friend's partner encouraged him to apply to law school despite his concerns about student loans. Sarah would be ready to settle down if she could find someone trustworthy, someone worth the risk.

Although this situation is fictitious, the relationship processes described are based on reality. This chapter will review the myriad risks individuals face when they form romantic relationships, as well as the ways that partners can regulate those relational risks by behaving responsively and affectionately. Some individuals, like Sarah, are especially concerned with relational risks; this chapter will describe how individual differences in attachment orientation impact perceived relational risks and how partners of insecurely attached individuals can regulate attachment insecurity and relational risk perception. As Sarah's story highlights, close relationships influence how individuals experience external risks (e.g., stressors, risky opportunities) as well. This chapter will also review empirical research demonstrating that responsive partner behavior allows individuals to thrive outside of their relationships by regulating external risks. Finally, this chapter will conclude with suggestions for future research.

Relational Risks in Close (Romantic) Relationships

As Sarah's example illustrates, close relationships entail risk. Risk is unavoidable because close relationships are defined by *interdependence*: individuals' mutual influence of one another's thoughts, feelings, and behavior over time (Holmes, 2002; Kelley et al., 2003). Being interdependent means giving up some control over one's "outcomes" (i.e., positive and negative consequences; Kelley et al., 2003) to another person, a proposition that is inherently risky (Murray, Holmes, & Collins, 2006). In the example above, Sarah's friends are dissatisfied because their own outcomes were negatively affected by their partners' behaviors (e.g., ignoring preferences for weekend plans, terminating the relationship).

Relational risks – the risks associated with forming and maintaining relationships – abound. For example, any time that partners' interests diverge, there is a risk that one couple-member may act unilaterally to benefit him/herself and disregard the other's wishes. Although a partner's disregard for movie preferences poses a relatively minor risk, there are likely to be more serious consequences for shared "outcomes" when partners disregard preferences related to major financial issues, relocation decisions, or child-related practices. Additional relational risks include the possibility that partners may be unresponsive to one another's requests for support, may take advantage of one another's forgiveness by continuing to behave unkindly, may require one another to sacrifice without sacrificing themselves, may be unfaithful, or may dissolve the relationship (e.g., Cavallo, Murray, & Holmes, 2013; Murray, Derrick, Leder, & Holmes, 2008; Murray et al., 2006; Strelan, Crabb, Chan, & Jones, 2017). Relational risks are salient when people make the initial decision to enter an interdependent relationship, and relational risks continue to accrue over time as individuals invest in their relationships. Any investment (e.g., time, personal disclosures, monetary resources) poses a potential risk because these investments will be lost or divided if the relationship ends (Goodfriend & Agnew, 2008; Rusbult, 1983).

Despite these and many other potential relational risks, individuals choose to pursue, invest in, and maintain close relationships. According to risk regulation theory (Murray et al., 2006), individuals are simultaneously motivated by *relationship-promotion goals* (i.e., invest in close relationships) and *self-protection goals* (i.e., avoid close relationships) due to a fundamental need for social connection and the desire to avoid the risks that relationships carry (Baumeister & Leary, 1995). To resolve the conflict between these contradictory goals, people evaluate the risks in specific interpersonal situations and invest in relationships only when the risks are perceived as sufficiently low. To evaluate the level of risk in a particular situation, individuals use an "appraisal rule" to evaluate their partner's regard (see Murray et al., 2006, 2008). To take a calculated risk, individuals should invest only if they determine that their partner values them and is likely to consider and protect their interests in future interactions. As described by Murray et al. (2006), individuals evaluate characteristics of the partner (e.g., "Is this person caring?"), characteristics of the self (e.g., "Am I the kind of person who is likely to be cared for?"), and characteristics of the dyadic relationship (e.g., "Is this person likely to care for me?") in making these appraisals. By considering these questions, individuals estimate the likelihood that a partner will be accepting (low risk) versus rejecting (high risk) and decide whether to prioritize self-protection or relationship-promotion goals accordingly (Murray et al., 2006, 2008).

Researchers typically use the term "trust" to explain this process (e.g., Holmes, 2002; Holmes & Rempel, 1989; Rempel, Holmes, & Zanna, 1985). Individuals trust their partners when they believe they "can count on [the] partner to care for them and be responsive to their needs, now and in the future" (Holmes & Rempel, 1989, p. 188). Trust signals that they can safely prioritize connection goals and invest in their relationships (Cavallo et al., 2013; Holmes, 2002). In one demonstration of this process, people who reported high levels of trust behaved more constructively than people with lower levels of trust during laboratory "strain-tests" (i.e., major goal conflict situations; Shallcross & Simpson, 2012). In another study in which couples discussed relationship transgressions together (another situation that requires balancing connection and protection goals), individuals who exhibited more trust in their partners reported greater intimacy after discussing a transgression and disengaged less during the discussion than individuals who trusted their partners less (Khalifian & Barry, 2016). As these examples demonstrate, trust in a partner's positive regard and responsiveness allows individuals to take the calculated risk of becoming interdependent and maintaining interdependence to reap relational benefits (e.g., Holmes & Rempel, 1989; Murray, Bellavia, Rose, & Griffin, 2003; Rempel, Ross, & Holmes, 2001).

Partner Regulation of Relational Risks

Individuals consider the characteristics of the partner, the self, and the dyadic relationship to evaluate the level of risk in a particular situation (e.g., Murray et al., 2006). Therefore, partners can promote trust (i.e., shape the perceived relational risks) by demonstrating dispositional caring and a motivation to behave responsively (e.g., understanding, caring; Reis & Clark, 2013; Reis & Gable, 2015) in interpersonal situations.

Some situations (termed "interdependence dilemmas") are uniquely diagnostic of the partner's regard and underlying motivations. Interdependence dilemmas entail "non-corresponding outcomes" or "conflicting interests" so that couple-members' goals are at odds and both partners' goals cannot be satisfied simultaneously (e.g., Holmes & Rempel, 1989; Kelley et al., 2003; Rusbult & Van Lange, 2003; Van Lange & Rusbult, 2012). In these situations, couple-members could behave unresponsively (pursue self-interests) or responsively (attempt to compromise). Individuals can assess their partner's motivations during interdependence dilemmas because being responsive in these situations is costly and requires sacrifice. Partners who set aside their self-interests and behave responsively demonstrate that they are trustworthy and that the relationship entails relatively low risk moving forward.

Responsive partner behavior in interdependence dilemmas has indeed been shown to provide diagnostic information and impact trust in empirical studies (see Simpson, 2007a, for review). For example, individuals report greater trust when partners accommodate (rather than retaliate), are willing to sacrifice, and forgive an individual for his or her transgression (Wieselquist, 2009; Wieselquist, Rusbult, Foster, & Agnew, 1999). Accommodation, sacrifice, and forgiveness all require a partner to override his/her fundamental self-interest, so each behavior demonstrates positive regard and favorable underlying motivations.

Although interdependence dilemmas provide valuable diagnostic situations, other situations/behaviors can also reveal a partner's motives. Indeed, researchers recently highlighted the importance of everyday situations for developing interpersonal perceptions. For instance, Lakey and Orehek (2011) proposed relational regulation theory, which suggests that people develop the perception that support is available to them primarily through "ordinary action and shared activity" rather than specific, directed support (Lakey, 2013, p. 717). In other words, commonplace interactions may provide information about the partner's motivations even without the partner needing to sacrifice or provide costly support. Relatedly, recent empirical research demonstrated that a partner's enthusiastic response when an individual shared positive events (i.e., capitalization) was more strongly associated with the individual feeling supported than was a partner's support concerning negative events (Gable, Gosnell, Maisel, & Strachman, 2012).

Consistent with these perspectives, everyday positive interpersonal interactions should also provide diagnostic information. Specifically, direct communication of affection should promote the perception that one is caring, trustworthy, and will be responsive in the future to mitigate relational risks. Affectionate communication is defined as "an individual's intention and overt enactment or expression of feelings of closeness, care, and fondness for another" (Floyd & Morman, 1998, p. 145). Individuals communicate affection through verbal statements (e.g., saying "I love you"), active touch (e.g., kissing, hugging), passive touch (e.g., resting a hand on one's partner), and behaving considerately (e.g., celebrating birthdays and accomplishments).

According to affection exchange theory (e.g., Floyd, 2002, 2006a), receiving and providing affectionate communication promotes physical and psychological health and enhances relationship quality. Several studies by Floyd and colleagues provide support for this theory (e.g., Floyd, 2006b; Floyd & Hesse, 2014; Floyd, Pauley, & Hesse, 2010; Floyd & Riforgiate, 2008; Floyd et al., 2005, 2007a, 2007b, 2009; Pauley, Floyd, & Hesse, 2014). Receiving and providing affection independently predicted individual and relational well-being benefits (e.g., Floyd et al., 2005) and helped individuals to manage stress (e.g., Floyd, 2006b). Experimental investigations also demonstrated that engaging in affectionate communication led to decreases in stress, faster stress recovery, and increases in relationship quality (Floyd et al., 2007a, 2009). Accordingly, individuals who provide affection to or receive affection from their partners may be buffered from perceived relational risks because they are less reactive to stressors in general and because they come to view their relationships more favorably.

Physical touch, one form of affectionate communication, may be especially effective in mitigating relational risks by communicating a partner's love, care, and future responsiveness. Touch may be particularly potent, compared to other forms of affectionate communication, because it produces a visceral, physiological reaction in addition to the psychological interpretation of affection common to all forms of affectionate communication (Jakubiak & Feeney, 2017). Specifically, affectionate touch is processed by a specialized class of nerve receptors called C tactile afferents (CT afferents) that activate reward areas of the brain, and it results in the release of oxytocin and endogenous opioids (e.g., Machin & Dunbar, 2011; McGlone, Wessberg, & Olausson, 2014; Morrison, 2012; Morrison, Löken, & Olausson, 2010). These physiological responses to affectionate touch buffer stress, which could make individuals less reactive to relational risks more generally (Gibbs, 1986; Heinrichs, Baumgartner, Kirschbaum, & Ehlert, 2003; Kubzanski, Berry Mendes, Appleton, Block, & Adler, 2013; Smith & Wang, 2012). Additionally, oxytocin has been shown to enhance perceptions of a partner's responsiveness (Algoe, Kurtz, & Grewen, 2017), which could more directly alter perceived relational risks by influencing specific perceptions of a partner's behavior.

In a recent theoretical perspective on affectionate touch in adulthood, Jakubiak and Feeney (2017) proposed that affectionate touch may promote relational well-being in part because it encourages individuals to evaluate their relationships as less risky and increase interdependence. Jakubiak and Feeney (2017) proposed that enhanced felt security, in particular, allows individuals who receive touch to prioritize relationship-promotion goals. Felt security is defined as a feeling of safety and calm that results from the perception that one is cared for and accepted (Collins & Feeney, 2004a; Sroufe & Waters, 1977). According to attachment theory, individuals develop chronic attachment security through repeated experiences in which others are responsive (Baldwin, 1992; Bowlby, 1969/1982); momentary felt security (or state security) instead results from individual experiences in which caregivers communicate their love and care (Mikulincer & Shaver, 2007a). Felt security and trust are closely related constructs (Holmes, 2002). Individuals who feel that they can trust their partners to be responsive and accepting in the future feel safe, and feeling safe with one's partner enables one to trust that a partner will be responsive in the future (e.g., Jakubiak & Feeney, 2017; Simpson, 2007a, 2007b).

Empirical evidence demonstrates that receiving affectionate touch promotes state security/trust. In one set of experiments, Jakubiak and Feeney (2016a) found that individuals who were assigned to receive touch from their romantic partners subsequently reported greater state security/trust than individuals who were not assigned to receive touch. Relatedly, Debrot, Shoebi, Perrez, and Horn (2013) demonstrated that receiving touch on a daily basis predicts changes in psychological intimacy (another construct closely related to trust and measured almost identically to felt security).

Therefore, providing affectionate touch is one way that partners might regulate relational risks by saliently and viscerally communicating their positive regard and pro-relational motivation. In doing so, affectionate touch should enable individuals to avoid stress and prioritize their relationships (rather than self-protection) in situations that trigger relational threat). In a recent demonstration of this idea, couple members who were randomly assigned to hold hands with one another during a conflict discussion a) self-reported and exhibited less stress and b) behaved more constructively while discussing the conflict than couples randomly assigned to hold neutral objects (Jakubiak & Feeney, 2019). Engaging in touch may have mitigated perceived relational risks so that individuals could avoid stress and prioritize compromise, emotional support, and accepting responsibility without fear that their partners would take advantage of them.

Like affectionate touch, sexual activity might also mitigate relational risks so long as it communicates affection. Recent research suggests that the benefits of engaging in frequent sex may be explained by the role that sex has in promoting affectionate moments (Debrot, Meuwly, Muise, Impett, & Schoebi, 2017). Engaging in sex should also enhance trust when couple members use sexual activity as an opportunity to behave responsively and demonstrate that they are motivated to meet one another's needs (Gadassi et al., 2016; Muise & Impett, 2015).

Individual Differences in the Perception of and Mitigation of Relational Risks

In addition to partner appraisals, self-appraisals also shape relational risk perception (Murray et al., 2006). Therefore, characteristics of an individual that impact the extent to which he/she believes that he/she is likely to be cared for will impact risk perception as well. Indeed, individuals have chronic dispositional tendencies to trust (or not to trust) others (e.g., Holmes & Rempel, 1989; Simpson, 2007a, 2007b). A particularly relevant individual characteristic is attachment orientation (Ainsworth, Blehar, Waters, & Wall, 1978; Bowlby, 1969/1982, 1973, 1980; Mikulincer & Shaver, 2007b; Mikulincer, Shaver, & Pereg, 2003). Attachment orientations are scripts or schemas that organize past experiences with caregivers and significant, close others to form expectations about others' availability and responsiveness and one's own ability to effectively seek and receive support (e.g., Baldwin, 1992; Mikulincer & Shaver, 2007b).

Trait attachment orientations are organized in two-dimensional space, with each dimension representing one of two forms of attachment insecurity: attachment anxiety and attachment avoidance. Attachment anxiety is characterized by a strong desire for closeness, persistent worries about one's relationships, concerns about being rejected or unloved, and the use of hyperactivating strategies (e.g., clinging, support-seeking) during distress (Mikulincer et al., 2003; Mikulincer & Shaver, 2007b). Alternatively, attachment avoidance is characterized by a desire to maintain emotional distance, compulsive self-reliance, and deactivating strategies (e.g., distancing, withdrawing) during distress (Mikulincer et al., 2003; Mikulincer & Shaver, 2007b). Individuals who have low attachment anxiety and low attachment avoidance are considered to be "securely attached" (i.e., comfortable with closeness and independence).

Whereas securely attached individuals evaluate relational risks realistically, individuals who are insecurely attached (high on the attachment anxiety and/or attachment avoidance dimensions) are especially sensitive to relational risks. According to Simpson and Rholes' (1994, 2012) attachment diathesis-stress models, negative relational events (e.g., conflict, abandonment), which cause distress for all people, are particularly distressing for individuals who are high in attachment anxiety because they ruminate about such events. Anxiously attached individuals also chronically underestimate their partner's regard and willingness to be responsive in the future (Simpson & Rholes, 2012); thus, they chronically overestimate relational risks. As a result, anxiously attached individuals become distressed and behave in self-protective, relationship-damaging ways in situations that trigger relational threat (e.g., Overall, Girme, Lemay, & Hammond, 2014; Overall & Simpson, 2015). For example, anxiously attached individuals behave less positively toward their partners than other individuals while discussing major relationship problems (Simpson, Rholes, & Phillips, 1996), and anxiously attached individuals report the greatest jealousy and maladaptive jealous behavior (e.g., Buunk, 1997; Guerrero & Afifi, 1998; Guerrero & Andersen, 1998).

Avoidantly attached people are also especially sensitive to relational risks, but their insecurity manifests differently. Based on a history of interacting with unresponsive caregivers, avoidantly attached individuals are uncomfortable with dependence and avoid closeness and vulnerability (e.g., Mikulincer & Shaver, 2007b). Although all individuals have competing relationship-promotion and self-protection goals (Murray et al., 2006, but see Hadden & Girme, Chapter 9), avoidantly attached individuals suppress their relationship-promotion goals and are defensively self-reliant (e.g., Simpson & Rholes, 2012). They do not seek support from partners, withdraw when partners seek closeness or support, and become angry when partners try to influence them by requesting a change (e.g., Collins & Feeney, 2000; Mikulincer, 1998; Overall & Simpson, 2015; Overall, Simpson, & Struthers, 2013). Perhaps unsurprisingly then, attachment avoidance is associated with lower relationship satisfaction and connectedness (Li & Chan, 2012).

Because relational risks are elevated for insecurely attached individuals, responsive partner behavior may be especially useful to mitigate their perceived risks. People high in anxious and avoidant attachment perceive different risks, so partner risk mitigation strategies also differ. This idea is termed "dyadic regulation" of attachment (see Nakamura, Simpson, & Overall, Chapter 7; also see Overall & Lemay, 2015; Overall & Simpson, 2015; Simpson & Overall, 2014). Anxiously attached individuals are concerned with the stability of their relationships, so partners regulate attachment anxiety by behaving affectionately and communicating their commitment. For example, although anxiously attached individuals typically behave destructively during situations that could threaten their relationships, anxiously attached individuals behaved more constructively during interdependence dilemmas when they believed that their partners were committed (Tran & Simpson, 2009).

In a more direct demonstration of this regulation process, anxiously attached individuals who were randomly assigned to receive affectionate touch from their romantic partners during a jealousy-inducing laboratory manipulation experienced less jealousy and reported more positive affect than individuals randomly assigned to receive another security-enhancing intervention or no intervention (Kim, Feeney, & Jakubiak, 2018). Although attachment anxiety predicted more extreme jealousy overall, the relationship between participants' attachment anxiety and jealousy was reduced for individuals who received touch, which suggests that the partners mitigated relational risk by providing reassuring touch (Kim et al., 2018). Although the dyadic regulation in this study was manipulated, other research indicates that partners do strategically attempt to regulate attachment anxiety. Specifically, partners of anxiously attached individuals have been shown to exaggerate their affection and hide negative sentiments (Lemay & Dudley, 2011). By doing so, partners help to reduce the perceived risks of engaging in the relationship so that anxiously attached individuals can more successfully navigate relationship situations.

To regulate attachment avoidance, partners instead use strategies that "soften" their influence and downplay dependence to reduce the relational risks relevant to avoidance (see Overall & Lemay, 2015). These regulation attempts are effective; for example, Overall et al. (2013) demonstrated that avoidantly attached individuals exhibited less anger and withdrew from discussions less when their partners validated their viewpoints, acknowledged their efforts to change, and were sensitive to their autonomy needs. In a related study, Farrell, Simpson, Overall, and Shallcross (2016) found that partners of avoidantly attached individuals regulated their avoidance using similar softening strategies during strain tests. Partners buffered attachment avoidance by expressing confidence that the avoidantly attached individual would behave responsively and by acknowledging the avoidantly attached individual's sacrifices (Farrell et al., 2016).

Avoidantly attached individuals' partners can also mitigate relational risk by communicating positive regard, affection, and support so long as they communicate in a way that is sensitive to avoidantly attached individuals' desire for autonomy. For instance, avoidantly attached individuals were receptive to practical partner support (e.g., advice, suggestions) but unreceptive to emotional support (e.g., encouragement, nurturance; Girme, Overall, Simpson, & Fletcher, 2015; Simpson, Winterheld, Rholes, & Oriña, 2007). Practical support may demonstrate a partner's responsiveness while avoiding extreme closeness. A recent report also indicates that intimacy-promoting behaviors (i.e., reminiscing about positive partner experiences, the partner demonstrating love, partner yoga) buffer insecurity for avoidantly attached individuals (Stanton, Campbell, & Pink, 2017). These experiences improved affect and relationship quality, increased self-disclosure, and reduced attachment avoidance over time in a sample of avoidantly attached individuals (Stanton et al., 2017). Accordingly, partner regulation does not only buffer perceived relational risk and the resulting self-protective, destructive relational behaviors, responsive partner behaviors can reduce attachment insecurity itself.

A recent theoretical perspective – built on a set of exciting empirical findings – suggests that partners are instrumental in promoting security and reducing insecurity immediately and over time (Arriaga, Kumashiro, Finkel, VanderDrift, & Luchies, 2014; Arriaga, Kumashiro, Simpson, & Overall, 2017; see Hunt, Kumashiro, & Arriaga, Chapter 5). Partners reduce attachment insecurity in the moment by providing reassurance (for attachment anxiety) or using softening strategies (for attachment avoidance), each of which reduces the immediate source of distress. However, to reduce chronic insecurity over time, partners must modify insecure working models by behaving in ways that shift insecurely attached individuals' chronic expectations. Partners reduce anxious attachment by enhancing the model of self (e.g., encouraging exploration), whereas partners reduce avoidant attachment by enhancing the model of others (e.g., being dependable; Arriaga et al., 2014). This research suggests that partners can mitigate even chronically perceived relational risks.

EXTERNAL RISKS AND INTERPERSONAL RISK MITIGATION

Partner Regulation of External Risks

Relational risks are not the only risks that partners regulate. As outlined by John Bowlby in his original writings on attachment theory, close others mitigate external risks to allow individuals to cope with adversity and to grow and learn outside of adversity (Bowlby, 1969/1982, 1973, 1988). Specifically, two key functions of attachment figures (parents in childhood, romantic partners in adulthood; Hazan & Shaver, 1987) are 1) to restore a feeling of security when individuals encounter external threats ("safe haven function"), and 2) to encourage individuals to explore the environment ("secure base function"; Bowlby, 1969/1982, 1973, 1988). In a recent elaboration of this idea, Feeney and Collins (2015) explicated how support from close others allows individuals to thrive through adversity and through participation in life opportunities outside of adversity. In both contexts, depending on partners enables individuals to thrive by mitigating actual and perceived external risks (Feeney, Van Vleet, & Jakubiak, 2015).

Adversity and External Threat Perception The psychological tradition of stress research emphasizes that people respond to external stressors differently, based on their unique appraisals of the threat that the stressor poses and the resources available to cope with the stressor (Cohen, Gianaros, & Manuck, 2016; Lazarus & Folkman, 1987). Close others (e.g., attachment figures) can contribute to coping resources and reduce the perception of stressors as threatening by demonstrating their availability and willingness to provide support. Consistent with this idea, social baseline theory proposes that the environment is fundamentally less risky when individuals are embedded in social networks because (1) risks are distributed across network members and (2) close others provide direct assistance and resources that enable coping with environmental threats (Beckes & Coan, 2011; Coan & Sbarra, 2015). The latter function (termed "load sharing") is akin to social support, the provision of resources or encouragement (e.g., Cohen & Wills, 1985).

Like load sharing, people expect to receive social support from close others with whom they are interdependent more than from distant acquaintances (Beckes & Coan, 2011). Thus, risking interdependence with romantic partners carries the benefit of alleviating external risks. There is extensive research demonstrating that close others who provide responsive support during adversity help individuals to cope effectively (Collins & Feeney, 2000, 2010; DeVries, Glasper, & Detillion, 2003; Feeney & Collins, 2015; Kane, McCall, Collins, & Blascovich, 2012; Mikulincer & Shaver, 2009; Uchino, 2009). For example, receiving responsive support from one's partner while discussing a personal stressor predicted greater felt security and short-term improvements in mood (Collins & Feeney, 2000). Additionally, a recent study suggests that partner support protects individuals' emotional and physical well-being as they enter old age (Feeney & Jakubiak, 2018). Fears about aging were associated with decreases in well-being over one year, but individuals who received responsive partner support did not experience these declines (Feeney & Jakubiak, 2018).

Specific support behaviors – including affectionate behavior – also help individuals to cope with external threats and mitigate external risk perception. For example, individuals who held a close other's hand under the threat of shock experienced less neurological threat activation than individuals who faced the threat alone (Brown, Beckes, Allen, & Coan, 2017; Coan, Schaefer, & Davidson, 2006). Even imagining receiving supportive touch from one's romantic partner buffered stress and pain (Jakubiak & Feeney, 2016b). Relatedly, individuals who reported more intimacy in daily life were less reactive to daily stressors (Ditzen, Hoppmann, & Klumb, 2008). According to a recent theory, intimate and affectionate relationship interactions constitute a relational resource that promotes resilience to external threats (Afifi, Merrill, & Davis, 2016).

The beneficial role of close others is also well established in the health psychology literature in the context of health threats (Helgeson & Zajdel, 2017). Partners facilitate coping by providing tangible assistance that reduces the actual health threat and by offering comfort that reduces perceived threat. Couples who cope communally (i.e., view an illness as "our problem and our responsibility" and collaborate to address the problem) also experience better adjustment than couples who cope independently (e.g., Helgeson, Jakubiak, Seltman, Hausmann, & Korytkowski, 2017; Helgeson, Jakubiak, Van Vleet, & Zajdel, 2018).

Exploration and External Threat Perception Although Bowlby also proposed a second function of attachment relationships – facilitating exploration – this function has been less extensively studied than the safe haven function (Feeney & Collins, 2015). Like adversity, exploration entails external risk, though the type and degree of risk differs. Exploration is defined as "motivated autonomous engagement with the physical or social environment … such that the outcome is uncertain" (Jakubiak & Feeney, 2016c, p. 319). Because the outcome is uncertain, exploration is risky. When individuals pursue opportunities or goals, they may face physical risks (e.g., injury), social risks (e.g., rejection), or psychological risks (e.g., failure, disappointment, embarrassment, shame). Proximal and supportive close others reduce these risks and thereby encourage individuals to accept opportunities for growth (Feeney, 2004; Feeney & Collins, 2015; Feeney, Van Vleet, Jakubiak, & Tomlinson, 2017; Jakubiak & Feeney, 2016c).

Support for exploration is termed secure base support (or more broadly "relational catalyst support"), and it entails a) helping individuals to view opportunities as challenges rather than threats, b) expressing enthusiasm for opportunities, c) providing encouragement and instrumental support, d) demonstrating availability, and e) avoiding intrusiveness (Crowell et al., 2002; Feeney, 2004; Feeney & Collins, 2015; Feeney & Thrush, 2010; Feeney et al., 2017). Several empirical studies have demonstrated that receiving secure base support fosters exploration. Individuals who received secure base support perceived that they were more capable and that their goals were more achievable than individuals who received less support (Feeney, 2004, 2007; Tomlinson, Feeney, & Van Vleet, 2016). Additionally, individuals who received secure base support were more likely to accept specific opportunities for growth and engaged in greater pursuit of personal goals than individuals who received less support (Feeney, 2007; Feeney et al., 2017). Finally, individuals who received secure base support made more progress on their personal goals on the same day and the next day (Jakubiak & Feeney, 2016c), and they were more likely to achieve their goals over time than individuals who received less support (e.g., Brunstein, Dangelmayer, & Schultheiss, 1996; Girme, Overall, & Simpson, 2013; Koestner, Powers, Carbonneau, Milyavskaya, & Chua, 2012; Overall, Fletcher, & Simpson, 2010).

Secure base support is beneficial because it enables individuals to accept opportunities and pursue goals without excessive concern for risks. For example, individuals who received secure base support reported greater enthusiasm for and enjoyment during exploration, which suggests that they were less concerned about potential risks than individuals who received less support (Feeney & Thrush, 2010). Secure base support may also enable goal achievement because it enables individuals to persist in spite of obstacles because the risks of failure and disappointment are reduced (Feeney & Thrush, 2010). Receiving secure base support not only encourages exploration, it also has benefits for support-recipients' individual well-being and their relationships. For example, individuals who received support for their goals reported more positive mood, greater self-esteem, and greater increases in relationship quality over time than individuals who received less secure base support (Feeney, 2004; Feeney & Thrush, 2010; Jakubiak & Feeney, 2016c; Overall et al., 2010).

Affectionate behavior may also be effective in encouraging exploration, although only one set of studies has tested this hypothesis to date. In one experiment, individuals who imagined receiving touch from their partners were more likely to accept an opportunity to complete a challenging task than individuals who imagined receiving verbal support (Jakubiak & Feeney, 2016b). In a second experiment, individuals who imagined receiving touch from their partners viewed stressful, evaluative laboratory tasks with greater enthusiasm than participants who imagined receiving verbal support or imagined something neutral (Jakubiak & Feeney, 2016b). These studies suggest that reminders of a partner's affection may reduce the perceived risks associated with stressful and difficult tasks to encourage individuals to engage with them enthusiastically.

Individual Differences in Perception of and Mitigation of External Risks

Although close others mitigate external risks for all individuals to some degree, individuals differ in their perception of external risks and the extent to which close others are able to mitigate these risks by providing support. Again, attachment orientation is an important individual difference in this regard. According to Simpson and Rholes' (1994, 2012) diathesis-stress model, avoidantly attached individuals should be particularly upset by external sources of stress because they desire support but are hesitant to seek it. Indeed, avoidant women sought less support during adversity than other women, especially when they were more distressed (Simpson, Rholes, & Nelligan, 1992). Similarly, avoidantly attached individuals have been shown to hide their distress from their partners to avoid burdening their partners, especially when they are highly committed (Winterheld, 2017). Without support to defray risks of exploration, avoidantly attached individuals have lower expectations about the likelihood of goal attainment and put less effort into initiating and maintaining goal-directed behavior (Orehek, Vazeou-Nieuwenhuis, Quick, & Weaverling, 2017).

Although avoidantly attached individuals may be especially vulnerable to external risks, both anxiously and avoidantly attached individuals engage in less exploration than more securely attached individuals because they lack a secure base from which to explore (e.g., Green & Campbell, 2000; Jakubiak & Feeney, 2016c). For example, anxiously and avoidantly attached individuals made less progress on their daily goals than individuals who were low in attachment insecurity (Jakubiak & Feeney, 2016c). Anxiously attached individuals, in particular, may have difficulty engaging in exploration because they are excessively concerned with maintaining their relationships. In fact, anxiously attached individuals (to a greater extent than others) evaluate potential exploration opportunities to ensure that their partner would approve (Orehek et al., 2017).

Research suggests that partner support is also less effective in reducing external risks during adversity and exploration for insecurely attached individuals because they have chronic expectations that close others will not be available and supportive. Insecurely attached individuals interpreted ambiguous support more negatively and benefited from it less than other individuals (e.g., Collins & Feeney, 2004b). Whereas responsive support may overcome insecurely attached individuals chronic expectations that support is unavailable, they interpret ambiguous support in line with their expectations. Secure base support was also less effective in encouraging daily exploration for anxiously attached individuals than for individuals low in anxious attachment

(Jakubiak & Feeney, 2016c). Because anxiously attached individuals are especially vigilant for relational risks, they may misinterpret a partner's support for goals as an attempt to pull away and prioritize the relationship rather than personal pursuits.

Just as partners can regulate relational risks by regulating insecurity (e.g., Simpson & Overall, 2014), partners may be able to mitigate external risks for insecurely attached individuals by providing support that is sensitive to insecurely attached individuals' chronic insecurities. For instance, partners of avoidantly attached individuals mitigate external risks by providing high, rather than moderate, levels of support (Girme et al., 2015). Anxiously attached individuals were not similarly soothed by high levels of support (Girme et al., 2015), which suggests that additional research should investigate strategies by which partners can regulate external risks for anxiously attached individuals.

FUTURE DIRECTIONS

Accumulating research indicates that close others mitigate both relational and external risks; however, a great deal about these processes remains unknown. One key future direction is to investigate how partner regulation affects partners themselves. Partner regulation has clear benefits for individuals (support-recipients), but might engaging in continual partner regulation carry costs for partners (support-providers)? Is it too much to ask that a partner regulate one's insecurities within the relationship, help one overcome adversity, and support one's goals?

Some theorists have described meeting partners needs as burdensome and taxing and suggested that extensive support provision has negative implications (Finkel, Hui, Carswell, & Larson, 2014). Consistent with this theory, individuals with insecurely attached partners experienced greater physiological threat while anticipating having a discussion with their partner than individuals with securely attached partners (Peters, Overall, Girme, & Jamieson, 2017). Partners of insecurely attached individuals may anticipate needing to buffer their partners' insecurity during the discussion and experience distress themselves. Another study indicated that buffering a partner's insecurity predicts decreases in relationship satisfaction over time (Lemay & Dudley, 2011). Research on caregiving in the context of chronic illness also suggests costs of long-term support provision (Vitaliano, Zhang, & Scanlan, 2003). However, other theorists have argued that support provision is beneficial for individuals (e.g., Inagaki & Orehek, 2017), and empirical research demonstrates short-term benefits of caregiving (Inagaki & Eisenberger, 2016). Future research should investigate whether mitigating relational and external risks carry costs for support-providers. If support-provision is costly, it will be advantageous to identify forms of support that are less costly to provide.

Relatedly, future research should investigate whether individuals can regulate relational and external risks themselves or use other individuals (besides their romantic partners) to regulate risk. For example, Murray and Holmes (2015) identified three "if-then rules" that individuals use to maintain commitment to their relationships even when confronted with perceived relational risks. These strategies represent an alternative to direct partner regulation, and they ultimately serve the same purpose. If individuals (especially insecurely attached individuals) enact these if-then rules, they may be able to rely less on their partners for risk regulation and avoid over-burdening their partners.

In conclusion, close relationships have great potential to regulate relational and external risks. Although most existing research has highlighted partner responsiveness during interdependence dilemmas (e.g., strain tests, conflicts) to mitigate relational risk, new lines of research highlight affectionate behaviors as another way to develop trust and encourage individuals to invest in their close relationships. Responsive partner support and affectionate behavior similarly help individuals to thrive in the context of adversity and outside of adversity, by facilitating exploration and personal growth.

REFERENCES

Afifi, A. D., Merrill, A. F., & Davis, S. (2016). The theory of resilience and relational load. *Personal Relationships*, 23, 663–683. doi:10.1111/pere.12159

Ainsworth, M. D. S., Blehar, M. C., Waters, E., & Wall, S. (1978). *Patterns of Attachment: A Psychological Study of the Strange Situation*. Hillsdale, NJ: Erlbaum.

Algoe, S. B., Kurtz, L. E., & Grewen, K. (2017). Oxytocin and social bonds: The role of oxytocin in perceptions of romantic partners' bonding behavior. *Psychological Science*, 28, 1763–1772. doi:10.1177/0956797617716922

Arriaga, X. B., Kumashiro, M., Finkel, E. J., VanderDrift, L. E., & Luchies, L. B. (2014). Filling the void: Bolstering attachment security in committed relationships. *Social Psychological and Personality Science*, 5, 398–406. doi:10.1177/1948550613509287

Arriaga, X. B., Kumashiro, M., Simpson, J. A., & Overall, N. C. (2017). Revising working models across time: Relationship situations that enhance attachment security. *Personality and Social Psychology Review*, 22, 71–96. doi:10.1177/1088868317705257

Baldwin, M. W. (1992). Relational schemas and the processing of social information. *Psychological Bulletin*, 112, 461–484.

Baumeister, R. F. & Leary, M. R. (1995). The need to belong: Desire for interpersonal attachments as a fundamental human motivation. *Psychological Bulletin*, 117, 497.

Beckes, L. & Coan, J. A. (2011). Social baseline theory: The role of social proximity in emotion and economy of action. *Social and Personality Psychology Compass*, 5, 976–988. doi:10.1111/j.1751-9004.2011.00400.x

Bowlby, J. (1969/1982). *Attachment and Loss: Vol. 1 Attachment* (2nd ed.). New York: Basic Books.

Bowlby, J. (1973). *Attachment and Loss: Vol. 2 Separation, Anxiety, and Anger.* New York: Basic Books.

Bowlby, J. (1980). *Attachment and Loss: Vol. 3 Sadness and Depression.* New York: Basic Books.

Bowlby, J. (1988). *A Secure Base: Parent–Child Attachment and Healthy Human Development.* New York: Basic Books.

Brown, C. L., Beckes, L., Allen, J. P., & Coan, J. A. (2017). Subjective general health and the social regulation of hypothalamic activity. *Psychosomatic Medicine, 79,* 670–673. doi:10.1097/PSY.0000000000000468

Brunstein, J. C., Dangelmayer, G., & Schultheiss, O. C. (1996). Personal goals and social support in close relationships: Effects on relationship mood and marital satisfaction. *Journal of Personality and Social Psychology, 71,* 1006–1019. doi:10.1037//0022-3514.71.5.1006

Buunk, B. P. (1997). Personality, birth order and attachment styles as related to various types of jealousy. *Personality and Individual Differences, 23,* 997–1006. doi:10.1016/S0191-8869(97)00136-0

Cavallo, J. V., Murray, S. L., & Holmes, J. G. (2013). Risk regulation in close relationships. In J. A. Simpson & L. Campbell (Eds.), *The Oxford Handbook of Close Relationships* (pp. 116–136). New York: Oxford University Press. doi:10.1017/CBO9781107415324.004

Coan, J. A. & Sbarra, D. A. (2015). Social baseline theory: The social regulation of risk and effort. *Current Opinion in Psychology, 1,* 87–91. doi:10.1016/j.copsyc.2014.12.021

Coan, J. A., Schaefer, H. S., & Davidson, R. J. (2006). Lending a hand: Social regulation of the neural response to threat. *Psychological Science, 17,* 1032–1039.

Cohen, S., Gianaros, P. J., & Manuck, S. B. (2016). A stage model of stress and disease. *Perspectives on Psychological Science, 11,* 456–463. doi:10.1177/1745691616646305

Cohen, S. & Wills, T. A. (1985). Stress, social support, and the buffering hypothesis. *Psychological Bulletin, 98,* 310–357. Retrieved from www.ncbi.nlm.nih.gov/pubmed/3901065

Collins, N. L. & Feeney, B. C. (2000). A safe haven: An attachment theory perspective on support seeking and caregiving in intimate relationships. *Journal of Personality and Social Psychology, 78,* 1053–1073. doi:10.1037/0022-3514.78.6.1053

Collins, N. L., & Feeney, B. C. (2004a). An attachment theory perspective on closeness and intimacy. In D. Mashek & A. Aron (Eds.), *Handbook of Closeness and Intimacy* (pp. 163–187). Mahwah, NJ: Erlbaum.

Collins, N. L. & Feeney, B. C. (2004b). Working models of attachment shape perceptions of social support: Evidence from experimental and observational studies. *Journal of Personality and Social Psychology, 87,* 363–383. doi:10.1037/0022-3514.87.3.363

Collins, N. L. & Feeney, B. C. (2010). An attachment theoretical perspective on social support dynamics in couples: Normative processes and individual differences. In K. Sullivan & J. Davila (Eds.), *Support Processes in Intimate Relationships* (pp. 89–120). New York: Oxford University Press.

Crowell, J. A., Treboux, D., Gao, Y., Fyffe, C., Pan, H., & Waters, E. (2002). Assessing secure base behavior in adulthood: Development of a measure, links to adult attachment representations, and relations to couples' communication and reports of relationships. *Developmental Psychology*, 38, 679–693. doi:10.1037/0012-1649.38.5.679

Debrot, A., Meuwly, N., Muise, A., Impett, E. A., & Schoebi, D. (2017). More than just sex: Affection mediates the association between sexual activity and well-being. *Personality and Social Psychology Bulletin*, 43, 287–299. doi:10.1177/0146167216684124

Debrot, A., Schoebi, D., Perrez, M., & Horn, A. B. (2013). Touch as an interpersonal emotion regulation process in couples' daily lives: The mediating role of psychological intimacy. *Personality and Social Psychology Bulletin*, 39, 1373–1385. doi:10.1177/0146167213497592

DeVries, A. C., Glasper, E. R., & Detillion, C. E. (2003). Social modulation of stress responses. *Physiology and Behavior*, 79, 399–407. doi:10.1016/S0031-9384(03)00152-5

Ditzen, B., Hoppmann, C., & Klumb, P. (2008). Positive couple interactions and daily cortisol: On the stress-protecting role of intimacy. *Psychosomatic Medicine*, 70, 883–889. doi:10.1097/PSY.0b013e318185c4fc

Farrell, A. K., Simpson, J. A., Overall, N. C., & Shallcross, S. L. (2016). Buffering the responses of avoidantly attached romantic partners in strain test situations. *Journal of Family Psychology*, 30, 580–591. doi:10.1037/fam0000186

Feeney, B. C. (2004). A secure base: Responsive support of goal strivings and exploration in adult intimate relationships. *Journal of Personality and Social Psychology*, 87, 631–648. doi:10.1037/0022-3514.87.5.631

Feeney, B. C. (2007). The dependency paradox in close relationships: Accepting dependence promotes independence. *Journal of Personality and Social Psychology*, 92, 268–285. doi:10.1037/0022-3514.92.2.268

Feeney, B. C. & Collins, N. L. (2015). A new look at social support: A theoretical perspective on thriving through relationships. *Personality and Social Psychology Review*, 19, 113–147. doi:10.1177/1088868314544222

Feeney, B. C. & Jakubiak, B. K. (2018, March). Spousal support for fears about aging and goal strivings predict wellbeing in older adulthood. Paper presented at the Society for Personality and Social Psychology Annual Convention, Atlanta, Georgia.

Feeney, B. C. & Thrush, R. L. (2010). Relationship influences on exploration in adulthood: the characteristics and function of a secure base. *Journal of Personality and Social Psychology*, 98, 57–76. doi:10.1037/a0016961

Feeney, B. C., Van Vleet, M., & Jakubiak, B. K. (2015). An attachment-theoretical perspective on optimal dependence in close relationships. In J. A. Simpson & W. S. Rholes (Eds.), *Attachment Theory and Research: New Directions and Emerging Themes* (pp. 195–233). New York: Guilford Press.

Feeney, B. C., Van Vleet, M., Jakubiak, B. K., & Tomlinson, J. M. (2017). Predicting the pursuit and support of challenging life opportunities. *Personality and Social Psychology Bulletin*, 43, 1171–1187. doi:10.1177/0146167217708575

Finkel, E. J., Hui, C. M., Carswell, K. L., & Larson, G. M. (2014). The suffocation of marriage: Climbing Mount Maslow without enough oxygen. *Psychological Inquiry*, 25, 1–41. doi:10.1080/1047840X.2014.863723

Floyd, K. (2002). Human affection exchange: V. Attributes of the highly affectionate. *Communication Quarterly*, 50, 135–152. doi:10.1080/01463370209385653

Floyd, K. (2006a). *Communicating Affection: Interpersonal Behavior and Social Context*. Cambridge: Cambridge University Press. doi:10.4324/9780511606649

Floyd, K. (2006b). Human affection exchange: XII. Affectionate communication is associated with diurnal variation in salivary free cortisol. *Western Journal of Communication*, 70, 47–63. doi:10.1080/10570310500506649

Floyd, K., Boren, J. P., Hannawa, A. F., Hesse, C., McEwan, B., & Veksler, A. E. (2009). Kissing in marital and cohabiting relationships: Effects on blood lipids, stress, and relationship satisfaction. *Western Journal of Communication*, 73, 113–133. doi:10.1080/10570310902856071

Floyd, K., Hess, J. A., Miczo, L. A., Halone, K. K., Mikkelson, A. C., & Tusing, K. J. (2005). Human affection exchange: VIII. Further evidence of the benefits of expressed affection. *Communication Quarterly*, 53, 285–303. doi:10.1080/01463370500101071

Floyd, K. & Hesse, C. (2014). Affectionate communication can suppress immunity: Trait affection predicts antibodies to latent Epstein-Barr virus. *Southern Communication Journal*, 79, 2–13. doi:10.1080/1041794X.2013.858178

Floyd, K., Mikkelson, A. C., Tafoya, M. A., Farinelli, L., La Valley, A. G., Judd, J., ... Wilson, J. (2007a). Human affection exchange: XIII. Affectionate communication accelerates neuroendocrine stress recovery. *Health Communication*, 22, 123–132.

Floyd, K., Mikkelson, A. C., Tafoya, M. A., Farinelli, L., La Valley, A. G., Judd, J., ... Wilson, J. (2007b). Human affection exchange: XIV. Relational affection predicts resting heart rate and free cortisol secretion during acute stress. *Behavioral Medicine*, 32, 151–156. doi:10.3200/BMED.32.4.151-156

Floyd, K. & Morman, M. (1998). The measurement of affectionate communication. *Communication Quarterly*, 46, 144–162. doi:0.1080/01463379809370092

Floyd, K., Pauley, P. M., & Hesse, C. (2010). State and trait affectionate communication buffer adults' stress reactions. *Communication Monographs*, 77, 618–636. doi:10.1080/03637751.2010.498792

Floyd, K. & Riforgiate, S. (2008). Affectionate communication received from spouses predicts stress hormone levels in healthy adults. *Communication Monographs*, 75, 351–368. doi:10.1080/03637750802512371

Gable, S. L., Gosnell, C. L., Maisel, N. C., & Strachman, A. (2012). Safely testing the alarm: Close others' responses to personal positive events. *Journal of Personality and Social Psychology*, 103, 963–981. doi:10.1037/a0029488

Gadassi, R., Bar-Nahum, L. E., Newhouse, S., Anderson, R., Heiman, J. R., Rafaeli, E., & Janssen, E. (2016). Perceived partner responsiveness mediates the association between sexual and marital satisfaction: A daily diary study in newlywed couples. *Archives of Sexual Behavior*, 45, 109–120. doi:10.1007/s10508-014-0448-2

Gibbs, D. M. (1986). Vasopressin and oxytocin: Hypothalamic modulators of the stress response: a review. *Psychoneuroendocrinology*, 11, 131–139. doi:10.1016/0306-4530(86)90048-X

Girme, Y. U., Overall, N. C., & Simpson, J. A. (2013). When visibility matters: Short-term versus long-term costs and benefits of visible and invisible support. *Personality & Social Psychology Bulletin*, 39, 1441–1454. doi:10.1177/0146167213497802

Girme, Y. U., Overall, N., Simpson, J. A., & Fletcher, G. (2015). "All or nothing": Attachment avoidance and the curvilinear effects of partner support. *Journal of Personality and Social Psychology*, 108, 450–475. doi:10.1037/a0038866

Goodfriend, W. & Agnew, C. R. (2008). Sunken costs and desired plans: Examining different types of investments in close relationships. *Personality and Social Psychology Bulletin*, 34, 1639–1652.

Green, J. D. & Campbell, W. K. (2000). Attachment and exploration in adults: Chronic and contextual accessibility. *Personality and Social Psychology Bulletin*, 26, 452–461. doi:10.1177/0146167200266004

Guerrero, L. K. & Afifi, W. A. (1998). Communicative responses to jealousy as a function of self-esteem and relationship maintenance goals: A test of Bryson's dual motivation model. *Communication Reports*, 11, 111–122. doi:10.1080/08934219809367693

Guerrero, L. K. & Andersen, P. A. (1998). The dark side of jealousy and envy: Desire, delusion, desperation, and destructive communication. In B. H. Spitzberg & W. R. Cupach (Eds.), *The Dark Side of Relationships* (pp. 33–70). Mahwah, NJ: Lawrence Erlbaum Associates.

Hazan, C. & Shaver, P. (1987). Romantic love conceptualized as an attachment process. *Journal of Personality and Social Psychology*, 52, 511–524. doi:10.1037/0022-3514.52.3.511

Heinrichs, M., Baumgartner, T., Kirschbaum, C., & Ehlert, U. (2003). Social support and oxytocin interact to suppress cortisol and subjective responses to psychosocial stress. *Biological Psychiatry*, 54, 1389–1398. doi:10.1016/S0006-3223(03)00465-7

Helgeson, V. S., Jakubiak, B. K., Seltman, H., Hausmann, L., & Korytkowski, M. (2017). Implicit and explicit communal coping in couples with recently diagnosed type 2 diabetes. *Journal of Social and Personal Relationships*, 34, 1099–1121. doi:10.1177/0265407516669604

Helgeson, V. S., Jakubiak, B. K., Van Vleet, M., & Zajdel, M. (2018). Communal coping and adjustment to chronic illness: Theory update and evidence. *Personality and Social Psychology Review*, 22, 170–195. doi:10.1177/1088868317735767

Helgeson, V. S. & Zajdel, M. (2017). Adjusting to chronic health conditions. *Annual Review of Psychology*, 68, 545–571. doi:10.1146/annurev-psych-010416-044014

Holmes, J. G. (2002). Interpersonal expectations as the building blocks of social cognition: An interdependence theory perspective. *Personal Relationships*, 9, 1–26. doi:10.1111/1475-6811.00001

Holmes, J. G. & Rempel, J. K. (1989). Trust in close relationships. In C. Hendrick (Ed.), *Review of Personality and Social Psychology, Vol. 10. Close Relationships* (pp. 187–220). Thousand Oaks, CA: Sage Publications, Inc.

Inagaki, T. K. & Eisenberger, N. I. (2016). Giving support to others reduces sympathetic nervous system-related responses to stress. *Psychophysiology*, 53, 427–435. doi:10.1111/psyp.12578

Inagaki, T. K. & Orehek, E. (2017). On the benefits of giving social support: When, why, and how support providers gain by caring for others. *Current Directions in Psychological Science*, 26, 109–113. doi:10.1177/0963721416686212

Jakubiak, B. K. & Feeney, B. C. (2016a). A sense of security: Touch promotes state attachment security. *Social Psychological and Personality Science*, 7, 745–753. doi:10.1177/1948550616646427

Jakubiak, B. K. & Feeney, B. C. (2016b). Keep in touch: The effects of imagined touch support on stress and exploration. *Journal of Experimental Social Psychology*, 65, 59–67. doi:10.1016/j.jesp.2016.04.001

Jakubiak, B. K. & Feeney, B. C. (2016c). Daily goal progress is facilitated by spousal support and promotes psychological, physical, and relational well-being through-out adulthood. *Journal of Personality and Social Psychology*, 111, 317–340. doi:10.1037/pspi0000062.supp

Jakubiak, B. K. & Feeney, B. C. (2017). Affectionate touch to promote relational, psychological, and physical well-being in adulthood: A theoretical model and review of the research. *Personality and Social Psychology Review*, 21, 228–252. doi:10.1177/1088868316650307

Jakubiak, B. K. & Feeney, B. C. (2019). Hand-in-hand combat: Affectionate touch promotes relational well-being and buffers stress during conflict. *Personality and Social Psychology Bulletin*, 45, 431–446.

Kane, H. S., McCall, C., Collins, N. L., & Blascovich, J. (2012). Mere presence is not enough: Responsive support in a virtual world. *Journal of Experimental Social Psychology*, 48, 37–44. doi:10.1016/j.jesp.2011.07.001

Kelley, H. K., Holmes, J. G., Kerr, N. L., Reis, H. T., Rusbult, C. E., & Van Lange, P. A. M. (2003). *An Atlas of Interpersonal Situations*. New York: Cambridge University Press.

Khalifian, C. E. & Barry, R. A. (2016). Trust, attachment, and mindfulness influence intimacy and disengagement during newlyweds' discussions of relationship transgressions. *Journal of Family Psychology*, 30, 592–601. doi:10.1037/fam0000194

Kim, K. J., Feeney, B. C., & Jakubiak, B. K. (2018). Touch reduces romantic jealousy in the anxiously attached. *Journal of Social and Personal Relationships*, 35, 1019–1041. doi:10.1177/0265407517702012

Koestner, R., Powers, T. A., Carbonneau, N., Milyavskaya, M., & Chua, S. N. (2012). Distinguishing autonomous and directive forms of goal support: Their effects on goal progress, relationship quality, and subjective well-being. *Personality and Social Psychology Bulletin*, 38, 1609–1620. doi:10.1177/0146167212457075

Kubzanski, L. D., Berry Mendes, W., Appleton, A. A., Block, J., & Adler, G. K. (2013). A heartfelt response: Oxytocin effects on response to social stress in men and women. *Biological Psychology*, 90, 1–9. doi:10.1016/j.biopsycho.2012.02.010.A

Lakey, B. (2013). Social support processes in relationships. In J. Simpson & J. Campbell (Eds.), *The Oxford Handbook of Close Relationships* (pp. 711–728). New York: Oxford University Press.

Lakey, B. & Orehek, E. (2011). Relational regulation theory: a new approach to explain the link between perceived social support and mental health. *Psychological Review*, 118, 482–495. doi:10.1037/a0023477

Lazarus, R. S. & Folkman, S. (1987). Transactional theory and research on emotions and coping. *European Journal of Personality*, 1, 141–169. doi:10.1002/per.2410010304

Lemay, E. P. & Dudley, K. L. (2011). Caution: Fragile! Regulating the interpersonal security of chronically insecure partners. *Journal of Personality and Social Psychology*, 100, 681–702. doi:10.1037/a0021655

Li, T. & Chan, D. K. S. (2012). How anxious and avoidant attachment affect romantic relationship quality differently: A meta-analytic review. *European Journal of Social Psychology*, 42, 406–419. doi:10.1002/ejsp.1842

Machin, A. J. & Dunbar, R. I. (2011). The brain opioid theory of social attachment: a review of the evidence. *Behaviour*, 148, 985–1025. doi:10.1163/000579511X596624

McGlone, F., Wessberg, J., & Olausson, H. (2014). Discriminative and affective touch: Sensing and feeling. *Neuron*, 82, 737–755. doi:10.1016/j.neuron.2014.05.001

Mikulincer, M. (1998). Adult attachment style and individual differences in functional versus dysfunctional experiences of anger. *Journal of Personality and Social Psychology*, 74, 513–524. doi:10.1037//0022-3514.74.2.513

Mikulincer, M. & Shaver, P. R. (2007a). Boosting attachment security to promote mental health, prosocial values, and inter-group tolerance. *Psychological Inquiry*, 18, 139–156.

Mikulincer, M. & Shaver, P. R. (2007b). Attachment theory and research: Core concepts, basic principles, conceptual bridges. In A. A. Kruglanski & E. T. Higgins (Eds.), *Social Psychology: Handbook of Basic Principles* (2nd ed., pp. 650–677). New York: Guilford.

Mikulincer, M. & Shaver, P. R. (2009). An attachment and behavioral systems perspective on social support. *Journal of Social and Personal Relationships*, 26, 7–19. doi:10.1177/0265407509105518

Mikulincer, M., Shaver, P., & Pereg, D. (2003). Attachment theory and affect regulation: The dynamics, development, and cognitive consequences of attachment-related strategies. *Motivation and Emotion*, 27, 77.

Morrison, I. (2012). CT afferents. *Current Biology*, 22, R77–R78. doi:10.1016/j.cub.2011.11.032

Morrison, I., Löken, L. S., & Olausson, H. (2010). The skin as a social organ. *Experimental Brain Research*, 204, 305–314. doi:10.1007/s00221-009-2007-y

Muise, A. & Impett, E. A. (2015). Good, giving, and game: The relationship benefits of communal sexual motivation. *Social Psychological and Personality Science*, 6, 164–172. doi:10.1177/1948550614553641

Murray, S. L., Bellavia, G. M., Rose, P., & Griffin, D. W. (2003). Once hurt, twice hurtful: How perceived regard regulates daily marital interactions. *Journal of Personality and Social Psychology*, 84, 126–147. doi:10.1037/0022-3514.84.1.126

Murray, S. L., Derrick, J. L., Leder, S., & Holmes, J. G. (2008). Balancing connectedness and self-protection goals in close relationships: A levels-of-processing perspective on risk regulation. *Journal of Personality and Social Psychology*, 94, 429–459. doi:10.1037/0022-3514.94.3.429

Murray, S. L. & Holmes, J. G. (2015). Maintaining mutual commitment in the face of risk. *Current Opinion in Psychology*, 1, 57–60. doi:10.1016/j.copsyc.2014.11.005

Murray, S. L., Holmes, J. G., & Collins, N. L. (2006). Optimizing assurance: The risk regulation system in relationships. *Psychological Bulletin*, 132, 641–666. doi:10.1037/0033-2909.132.5.641

Orehek, E., Vazeou-Nieuwenhuis, A., Quick, E., & Weaverling, G. C. (2017). Attachment and self-regulation. *Personality and Social Psychology Bulletin*, 43, 365–380. doi:10.1177/0146167216685292

Overall, N. C., Fletcher, G. J. O., & Simpson, J. A. (2010). Helping each other grow: Romantic partner support, self-improvement, and relationship quality. *Personality and Social Psychology Bulletin*, 36, 1496–1513. doi:10.1177/0146167210383045

Overall, N. C., Girme, Y. U., Lemay, E. P., & Hammond, M. D. (2014). Attachment anxiety and reactions to relationship threat: The benefits and costs of inducing guilt in romantic partners. *Journal of Personality and Social Psychology*, 106, 235–256. doi:10.1037/a0034371

Overall, N. C. & Lemay, E. P. (2015). Attachment and dyadic regulation processes. In J. A. Simpson & W. S. Rholes (Eds.), *Attachment Theory and Research: New Directions and Emerging Themes* (pp. 145–169). New York: Guilford Press.

Overall, N. C. & Simpson, J. A. (2015). Attachment and dyadic regulation processes. *Current Opinion in Psychology*, 1, 61–66. doi:10.1016/j.copsyc.2014.11.008

Overall, N. C., Simpson, J. A., & Struthers, H. (2013). Buffering attachment-related avoidance: Softening emotional and behavioral defenses during conflict discussions. *Journal of Personality and Social Psychology*, 104, 854–871. doi:10.1037/a0031798

Pauley, P. M., Floyd, K., & Hesse, C. (2014). The stress-buffering effects of a brief dyadic interaction before an acute stressor. *Health Communication*, 30, 646–659. doi:10.1080/10410236.2014.888385

Peters, B. J., Overall, N. C., Girme, Y. U., & Jamieson, J. P. (2017). Partners' attachment insecurity predicts greater physiological threat in anticipation of attachment-relevant interactions. *Journal of Social and Personal Relationships*. doi:10.1177/0265407517734655

Reis, H. T. & Clark, M. S. (2013). Responsiveness. In J. A. Simpson & L. Campbell (Eds.), *The Oxford Handbook of Close Relationships* (pp. 400–423). New York: Oxford University Press.

Reis, H. T. & Gable, S. L. (2015). Responsiveness. *Current Opinion in Psychology*, 1, 67–71. doi:10.1016/j.copsyc.2015.01.001

Rempel, J. K., Holmes, J. G., & Zanna, M. P. (1985). Trust in close relationships. *Journal of Personality and Social Psychology*, 49, 95–112. doi:10.1037/0022-3514.49.1.95

Rempel, J. K., Ross, M., & Holmes, J. G. (2001). Trust and communicated attributions in close relationships. *Journal of Personality and Social Psychology*, 81, 57–64. doi:10.1037/0022-3514.81.1.57

Rusbult, C. E. (1983). A longitudinal test of the investment model: The development (and deterioration) of satisfaction and commitment in heterosexual involvements. *Journal of Personality and Social Psychology*, 45, 101–117.

Rusbult, C. E. & Van Lange, P. A. M. (2003). Interdependence, interaction, and relationships. *Annual Review of Psychology*, 54, 351–375. doi:10.1146/annurev.psych.54.101601.145059

Shallcross, S. L. & Simpson, J. A. (2012). Trust and responsiveness in strain-test situations: A dyadic perspective. *Journal of Personality and Social Psychology*, 102, 1031–1044. doi.org/10.1037/a0026829

Simpson, J. A. (2007a). Foundation of interpersonal trust. In A. A. Kruglanski & E. T. Higgins (Eds.), *Social Psychology: Handbook of Basic Principles* (2nd ed., pp. 587–607). New York: Guilford.

Simpson, J. A. (2007b). Psychological foundations of trust. *Current Directions in Psychological Science*, 16, 264–268.

Simpson, J. A. & Overall, N. C. (2014). Partner buffering of attachment insecurity. *Current Directions in Psychological Science*, 23, 54–59. doi:10.1177/0963721413510933

Simpson, J. A. & Rholes, W. S. (1994). Stress and secure base relationships in adulthood. In K. Bartholomew & D. Perlman (Eds.), *Advances in Personal Relationships* (Vol. 5, pp. 181–204). London: Kingsley.

Simpson, J. A. & Rholes, W. S. (2012). Adult attachment orientations, stress, and romantic relationships. In P. Devine & A. Plant (Eds.), *Advances in Experimental Social Psychology* (Vol. 45, pp. 279–328). Burlington: Academic Press. doi:10.1016/B978-0-12-394286-9.00006-8

Simpson, J. A., Rholes, W. S., & Nelligan, J. S. (1992). Support seeking and support giving within couples in an anxiety-provoking situation: The role of attachment styles. *Journal of Personality and Social Psychology*, 62, 434–446. doi:10.1037/0022-3514.62.3.434

Simpson, J. A., Rholes, W. S., & Phillips, D. (1996). Conflict in close relationships: An attachment perspective. *Journal of Personality and Social Psychology*, 71, 899–914. doi:10.1037/0022-3514.71.5.899

Simpson, J. A., Winterheld, H. A., Rholes, W. S., & Oriña, M. M. (2007). Working models of attachment and reactions to different forms of caregiving from romantic partners. *Journal of Personality and Social Psychology*, 93, 466–477. doi:10.1037/0022-3514.93.3.466

Smith, A. S. & Wang, Z. (2012). Salubrious effects of oxytocin on social stress-induced deficits. *Hormones and Behavior*, 61, 320–330. doi:10.1016/j.yhbeh.2011.11.010

Sroufe, L. A. & Waters, E. (1977). Attachment as an organizational construct. *Child Development*, 48, 1184. doi:10.2307/1128475

Stanton, S. C. E., Campbell, L., & Pink, J. C. (2017). Benefits of positive relationship experiences for avoidantly attached individuals. *Journal of Personality and Social Psychology*, 113, 568–588. doi:10.1037/pspi0000098

Strelan, P., Crabb, S., Chan, D., & Jones, L. (2017). Lay perspectives on the costs and risks of forgiving. *Personal Relationships*, 24, 392–407. doi:10.1111/pere.12189

Tomlinson, J. M., Feeney, B. C., & Van Vleet, M. (2016). A longitudinal investigation of relational catalyst support of goal strivings. *The Journal of Positive Psychology*, 11, 246–257. doi:10.1080/17439760.2015.1048815

Tran, S. & Simpson, J. A. (2009). Prorelationship maintenance behaviors: The joint roles of attachment and commitment. *Journal of Personality and Social Psychology*, 97, 685–698. doi:10.1037/a0016418

Uchino, B. N. (2009). Understanding the links between social support and physical health. *Perspectives on Psychological Science*, 4, 236–255.

Van Lange, P. A. M. & Rusbult, C. E. (2012). Interdependence theory. In P. A. M. Van Lange, A. W. Kruglanski, & E. T. Higgins (Eds.), *Handbook of Theories of Social Psychology* (pp. 251–272). Thousand Oaks, CA: Sage Publications.

Vitaliano, P. P., Zhang, J. P., & Scanlan, J. M. (2003). Is caregiving hazardous to one's physical health? A meta-analysis. *Psychological Bulletin*, 129, 946–972.

Wieselquist, J. (2009). Interpersonal forgiveness, trust, and the investment model of commitment. *Journal of Social and Personal Relationships*, 26, 531–548. doi:10.1177/0265407509347931

Wieselquist, J., Rusbult, C. E., Foster, C. A., & Agnew, C. R. (1999). Commitment, pro-relationship behavior, and trust in close relationships. *Journal of Personality and Social Psychology, 77*, 942–966. doi:10.1037//0022-3514.77.5.942

Winterheld, H. A. (2017). Hiding feelings for whose sake? Attachment avoidance, relationship connectedness, and protective buffering intentions. *Emotion, 17*, 965–980. doi:10.1037/emo0000291

7

Partner Buffering in Interdependent Relationships

An Attachment Perspective

MONIQUE S. NAKAMURA, JEFFRY A. SIMPSON, AND
NICKOLA C. OVERALL

Insecurely attached people tend to have difficulties resolving relationship issues, regulating their negative emotions, and maintaining satisfying relationships. Recent theory and research, however, has begun to identify ways in which the romantic partners of insecurely attached people may be able to buffer (or soothe) these difficulties, especially in stressful situations or during difficult interactions involving interdependence between partners. In this chapter, we canvass the most recent theoretical and empirical literature on partner buffering in intimate relationships and we outline various ways in which partners may be able to meet the needs and assuage the concerns of insecure individuals, resulting in better relationship outcomes and improved satisfaction over time.

To address these goals, we begin by discussing some foundational principles of attachment theory along with the two primary forms of attachment insecurity (anxiety and avoidance). We then describe recent models that focus on partner buffering and discuss an updated process model that describes how partner buffering works in interdependent relationships. After doing so, we review the small but growing empirical literature on partner buffering and discuss current findings in relation to the process model of partner buffering. Finally, we identify possible directions for future research on this important, rapidly expanding topic in relationship science.

ATTACHMENT THEORY AND ORIENTATIONS

According to attachment theory (Bowlby, 1969, 1973, 1980, 1988), humans evolved to remain in close proximity to, and form strong attachment bonds with, their primary caregivers (i.e., attachment figures) because individuals who possessed these behavioral and emotional tendencies were more likely to survive and eventually reproduce. When feeling threatened, distressed, or overly challenged, children (as well as adolescents and adults) rely on the attachment bonds they have forged with their attachment figures not only to promote safety, but also to enhance their sense of felt security and well-being (Sroufe & Waters, 1977). The nature of these attachment bonds, however, depends in part on the way in which individuals have been treated by different attachment figures over the course of their lives (Ainsworth, Blehar, Waters, & Wall, 1978; Bowlby, 1969, 1973; Johnson, Dweck, & Chen, 2007; Main, Kaplan, & Cassidy, 1985), which shapes the internal working models they develop of themselves and close others (e.g., current and future attachment figures). Internal working models are comprised of episodic memories associated with prior and current attachment figures, the emotional content of past attachment-related experiences with specific attachment figures, and generalized beliefs, attitudes, and values regarding what partners should and should not do as well as what close relationships should be like (Collins & Read, 1990; Pietromonaco & Carnelley, 1994). Once developed, working models guide how individuals think, feel, and behave, especially in stressful situations that activate (or turn on) the attachment system (Mikulincer & Shaver, 2003; Simpson & Rholes, 1994, 2012).

Individuals who have received responsive, reliable care and support from prior attachment figures (e.g., parents, close friends, romantic partners) typically develop secure working models characterized by positive views of the self (i.e., as someone deserving of love and respect) and positive views/ expectations of others (i.e., that attachment figures will provide appropriate comfort and support when needed). Due to the nature of their working models, when securely attached individuals feel threatened, stressed, or overly challenged, they utilize "problem-focused" coping strategies, whereby they turn to their partners for support and assistance, which typically dissipates their negative affect and allows them to experience increased closeness and intimacy with their partners over time (Mikulincer & Shaver, 2007).

Insecurely attached individuals, on the other hand, have different working models and, therefore, cope with stress differently. Anxiously attached people harbor negative views of themselves as relationship partners and hopeful yet conflicted views/expectations that their partners will provide sufficient care and support when it is needed. As a result, they are hypervigilant to signs of abandonment and crave greater closeness to and acceptance from their partners, due in part to their prior experiences of receiving inconsistent care and support (Mikulincer & Shaver, 2003). In response to this hyperactivation of the attachment system, anxiously attached people monitor and demand considerable attention from their partners and rely on ruminative, emotion-focused coping strategies, which keep them feeling insecure and can be detrimental to their partners and relationships (Downey, Freitas, Michaelis, & Khouri, 1998).

Avoidantly attached individuals hold negative and cynical views of their partners and either positive or negative views of themselves as relationship partners (Bartholomew & Horowitz, 1991). They are particularly sensitive to potential threats to their independence and autonomy, and cope with such threats by withdrawing emotionally or becoming rigidly self-reliant, due in large part to their prior experiences with rejecting or distant attachment figures (Pietromonaco & Feldman Barrett, 1997). When stressed, avoidantly attached people are less inclined to seek and give support to their partners (Simpson, Rholes, & Nelligan, 1992), which reflects their use of avoidance coping strategies. By deactivating their attachment system and distancing themselves from their partners in stressful situations, avoidantly attached individuals are able to maintain independence and autonomy and regulate their negative emotions (Mikulincer & Shaver, 2003).

Both types of attachment insecurity tend to weaken relationships by lowering relationship satisfaction, escalating relationship problems, and inhibiting positive experiences (Mikulincer & Shaver, 2007). The romantic partners of insecurely attached people can, however, play a key role in dampening the negative reactions of insecure individuals. We now summarize recent partner buffering models and the current empirical literature on how partners buffer the negative outcomes associated with attachment insecurity.

ATTACHMENT PARTNER BUFFERING MODELS

Most of the research conducted on attachment insecurity has adopted an individual-centered viewpoint in which partners are rarely considered. Recent work, however, has shifted to a more dyadic and interdependent conceptualization of attachment processes, especially when couples are under stress (see Simpson & Rholes, 2012, 2017, for reviews). By broadening the theoretical scope to include *both* partners and their interaction patterns, researchers can not only identify how partners reciprocally affect each other but the most effective ways in which partners can buffer attachment anxiety and avoidance in relationships. Several models have outlined some of the primary interpersonal processes through which partner buffering can occur.

Simpson and Overall (2014) proposed the Dyadic Regulation Model of Insecurity Buffering, which highlights how partner buffering can occur during stressful, attachment-relevant dyadic interactions. According to this model, when insecure individuals encounter a stressful or threatening event, their attachment system and insecurities are activated. The non-distressed partner (i.e., the agent) can then attempt to down-regulate the distress experienced by insecure individuals (i.e., the target) by enacting specific partner buffering behaviors (either deliberately or automatically without thought or planning) to soothe him/her. Buffering behaviors can include accommodating the target's wishes or needs, validating the target's viewpoints, and/or providing some form of support to help the target regulate his/her thoughts and emotions more constructively.

Successful partner buffering is more likely to occur when the agent's support is responsive to the particular needs of the target – that is, when the agent "matches" and addresses the target's attachment-relevant needs, motives, and concerns. This happens when individuals are highly responsive to the needs, motives, and concerns of their partners. For anxiously attached targets, buffering behaviors reassuring them that they are loved and supported should be particularly effective, such as providing strong emotional support, directly accommodating to their wishes and needs, and/or easing their concerns regarding loss or abandonment. For avoidantly attached targets, in contrast, buffering behaviors that allow them to maintain autonomy and independence should be most beneficial, such as providing instrumental support by discussing practical solutions to distressing problems, using "soft" influence tactics when trying to motivate change in problematic features of the avoidant partner, or meeting their needs while still allowing them to remain autonomous (also see Overall & Simpson, 2015).

If the agent's buffering attempts are successful, targets should report greater felt-security, which in turn should result in less distress, better emotion regulation, and more constructive behavior by the target. If this pattern, which can be described as mutual cyclical growth (Wieselquist, Rusbult, Foster, & Agnew, 1999), occurs repeatedly over time, positive longer-term outcomes should follow, including targets feeling more positively about themselves, targets evaluating the relationship more positively, and agents also evaluating the relationship more positively.

Building on Simpson and Overall (2014), Arriaga, Kumashiro, Simpson, and Overall (2018) developed the Attachment Security Enhancement Model, which further integrates partner buffering and security enhancement processes. According to this model, there are two broad buffering strategies: safe strategies (that should work for anxiously attached individuals) and soft strategies (that should work for avoidantly attached individuals). Safe strategies assuage attachment anxiety by calming the target through clear displays of strong, unwavering commitment (e.g., Tran & Simpson, 2009). Soft strategies assuage attachment avoidance by allowing the target to step away from a problem or issue without negative repercussions or by making requests of targets in a less emotionally-laden, more matter-of-fact manner (e.g., Farrell, Simpson, Overall, & Shallcross, 2016; Overall, Simpson, & Struthers, 2013). All of these strategies are geared to alleviate the momentary insecurities of highly anxious and highly avoidant targets that arise in threatening or distressing situations.

To generate greater long-term attachment security, Arriaga et al. (2018) describe additional security enhancement strategies that can be employed in situations that do not involve conflict or relationship-relevant distress. For anxiously attached people, for example, experiences that instill greater self-confidence or more positive models of self should reduce their

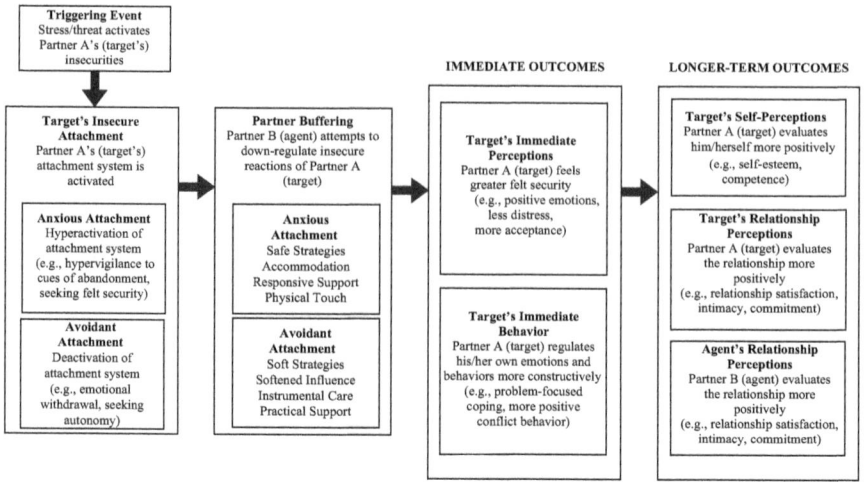

FIGURE 7.1 The revised dyadic regulation model of insecurity buffering. The revised model outlines how certain types of events activate the attachment systems of insecurely attached individuals (targets), which results in specific reactions depending on the target's form of attachment insecurity. Agents (i.e., the partners of targets) can buffer insecurely attached targets by engaging in specific buffering strategies. Partner buffering that addresses the needs, motives, and concerns of anxious or avoidant targets should generate positive immediate outcomes and, eventually, positive long-term outcomes in both the target and the agent

hyperactivation tendencies. For avoidantly attached individuals, experiences that facilitate stronger emotional connection to their partners or more positive models of their partners should reduce their deactivation tendencies. Thus, immediate partner buffering strategies and longer-term security enhancement strategies are likely to work in tandem to both reduce attachment insecurity and increase attachment security across time, ultimately yielding benefits for both partners as well as their relationship.

In order to synthesize these models and account for recent partner buffering findings (reviewed below), we propose a slightly revised and expanded version of Simpson and Overall's (2014) Dyadic Regulation Model of Attachment Insecurity. As shown in Figure 7.1, some triggering event initially activates a target's attachment system, which generates hyperactivation in anxiously attached individuals and deactivation in avoidantly attached individuals. Partners (or agents) may then buffer the target by providing the type and amount of comfort/support that matches the target's form of attachment insecurity. Because anxiously attached targets need greater closeness in order to allay their felt insecurity, agents should enact safe strategies, which include accommodation, responsive emotional support, and physical touch (see Jakubiak, Chapter 6) to down-regulate the target's negative state.

The partners of avoidantly attached targets, in contrast, should enact soft strategies, which include softened (attenuated) influence attempts and instrumental or practical forms of support. This should help avoidant targets feel as if they still have some degree of autonomy and independence while being helped or supported by their partners. If these patterns occur repeatedly over time, partner buffering should lead targets to generally feel more accepted, less distressed, and better able to regulate their emotions more constructively. Across time, these outcomes should generate higher levels of self-esteem and greater competence along with higher levels of intimacy, commitment, and relationship satisfaction in both targets and agents.

EMPIRICAL RESEARCH ON EFFECTIVE PARTNER BUFFERING STRATEGIES

Several studies have examined the effectiveness of various strategies/tactics that, from a theoretical standpoint, should buffer insecurely attached partners, especially during stressful couple conflict discussions. In most romantic relationships, major conflicts are often threatening situations capable of triggering the attachment system in one or both partners, providing a good context in which to investigate partner buffering processes and outcomes. We now summarize key partner buffering findings in the current empirical literature, several of which are relevant to some of the paths depicted in Figure 7.1.

Anxious Attachment

Much of the research on buffering anxiously attached individuals has been conducted outside the context of interpersonal conflict. Lemay and Clark (2008), for example, found that when people harbor insecurities about their partner's actual regard for them, as anxiously attached people often do, they frequently express their insecurity and emotional vulnerability, which can lead their partners to perceive them as vulnerable. The partners of insecure individuals may then try to express positive sentiments, which insecure individuals may interpret as inauthentic, making their partners feel as if they are "walking on eggshells." These authenticity doubts typically perpetuate this cycle of insecurity. Lemay and Clark (2008) suggested that this cycle can be disrupted by helping insecure targets (i.e., those being buffered) defocus or consider other factors that could be affecting the agent's (i.e., the bufferer's) evaluation of the target. By altering these cognitive distortions with the help of agents, targets can begin to recognize and acknowledge positive behaviors enacted by agents as authentic. Additionally, perceived goal validation also reduces attachment anxiety across three years via changes in partner trust

(Arriaga, Kumashiro, Finkel, VanderDrift, & Luchies, 2014), and sexual satisfaction also appears to buffer anxiously attached partners from declines in marital satisfaction (Little, McNulty, & Russell, 2010). Although these findings pertain to situations other than conflict, shifting appraisals, providing goal validation, increasing trust, and improving sexual satisfaction are avenues agents can possibly utilize to buffer insecure targets.

Several studies have also investigated buffering anxiously attached people in conflict. As mentioned previously, when anxiously attached people experience conflict with their romantic partners, they usually perceive higher levels of negativity from their partners and yearn to gain reassurance by drawing their partners closer emotionally. Tran and Simpson (2009) observed (video recorded) married partners discussing negative habits that each partner wanted to change in the other to improve the relationship. In each discussion, they assessed each partner's degree of felt security, their emotional reactions, and their constructive accommodation behaviors (e.g., taking the partner's feelings/views into account, reassuring the partner when s/he was distressed, working collaboratively to do what was best for the partner or relationship; Rusbult, Verette, Whitney, Slovik, & Likpus, 1991). Tran and Simpson found that anxiously attached individuals did, in fact, express more negative emotions and display fewer accommodation behaviors in these discussions. However, when their *partners* displayed more constructive accommodation behaviors and reported being more committed in the relationship, anxiously attached individuals felt relatively more positive emotions and greater acceptance. Greater partner accommodation and commitment, in other words, helped anxiously attached individuals regulate their negative emotions more constructively and feel more secure during these discussions.

Similar kinds of effects have been documented for physical touch. Jakubiak and Feeney (2016) conducted two experiments on the effects of touch from a friend or a romantic partner on feelings of attachment security. When participants imagined receiving touch from a friend or a romantic partner, they had greater accessibility to secure words (e.g., love, comfort) on a later memory task. In the second study, participants received physically affectionate touch from their romantic partners, which produced greater state security compared to participants who did not receive touch. Both of these effects, however, emerged only for securely and anxiously attached people, not avoidantly attached ones.

Avoidant Attachment

Unlike anxiously attached people, avoidant individuals frequently withdraw in distressing situations, especially when their autonomy and independence are threatened. Simpson, Winterheld, Rholes, and Oriña (2007) observed (video recorded) romantic partners as they tried to resolve their most important relationship problem. Compared to securely attached care recipients, avoidantly attached recipients were rated as more calmed when they received instrumental care (e.g., advice or suggestions for how to solve the problem, discussing the problem in a rational, logical way), whereas emotional care (e.g., encouraging recipients to talk about their emotions and experiences, expressing emotional support to them) calmed securely attached individuals the most. Expanding on these findings, Girme, Overall, Simpson, and Fletcher (2015) have documented a curvilinear effect of practical support, such that low-to-moderate levels of practical support offered to avoidantly attached people are associated with negative outcomes, but as practical support shifts toward moderate-to-high levels, avoidantly attached people experience more positive outcomes (e.g., less distress, less perceived partner control/criticism, less distancing, greater self-efficacy).

In addition to instrumental or practical support, soft influence tactics should also soothe avoidantly attached people. Indeed, Overall et al. (2013) observed (video recorded) couples discussing problems in which one partner (the agent) wanted to change a problematic feature of the other partner (the target), which should threaten most avoidant people. Behavioral coding of the agent's use of soft influence tactics (e.g., being sensitive to the target's autonomy needs, acknowledging the target's efforts/good qualities) indicated that avoidantly attached individuals did, in fact, report feeling angrier and withdrew more during these discussions. However, avoidantly attached targets whose partners displayed softer influence tactics were less angry and less withdrawn compared to those whose partners did not display soft influence tactics. These more positive responses, in turn, were associated with better conflict resolution as rated by coders.

Additionally, asking avoidantly attached people to make major personal sacrifices should elicit defensiveness due to the possible constraints that such requests might impose on their independence and autonomy. However, two types of buffering behaviors – expressing confidence that avoidant partners will make the requested sacrifice, and acknowledging and giving credit for the sacrifice – appear to be effective at reducing negative reactions in avoidant people. Farrell et al. (2016) observed (video recorded) couples as they discussed major strain-test issues. Even though avoidantly attached partners were less accommodating in general when asked to make a sacrifice and reported lower trust and commitment, when partners expressed greater confidence in their ability to make the sacrifice and acknowledged their efforts, avoidant individuals reacted more positively.

Partner buffering has also been examined in clinically distressed couples. Johnson and her colleagues, for example, have integrated attachment theory into clinical practice through Emotionally Focused Therapy (EFT). Moser, Johnson, Dalgleish, Lafontaine, Wiebe, and Tasca (2016) have investigated the effects of EFT on changes in attachment insecurity across time, focusing on blamer softening (in which the "blaming" partner, who has been harmed or betrayed, is vulnerable while expressing fears of emotional or physical abandonment as the "withdrawing" partner, who often is the source of harm or betrayal, attempts to respond with warmth, empathy, and acceptance). When couples engaged in blamer softening, couples (both the "blaming" and "withdrawing" partner) experienced significant decreases in relationship-specific attachment avoidance, decreases in relationship-specific attachment anxiety, and increases in relationship satisfaction pre- to post-therapy.

FUTURE DIRECTIONS OF PARTNER BUFFERING

Based on the findings of partner buffering research, the general effectiveness of matching buffering strategies to the specific motives, needs, and concerns of insecurely attached partners given their type of insecurity is fairly well supported. Future research, however, could appreciably extend what we currently know by examining potential moderators of these partner buffering effects, identify who is more versus less likely to "burnout" from enacting prolonged partner buffering, and clarifying differences between EFT (which applies mainly to highly distressed couples) and our model (which is geared to couples who tend to be less distressed).

Accounting for the History of Insecure Targets and Agents

Some targets are bound to be easier to buffer than others. We conjecture that the effects of partner buffering on targets could be moderated by their relationship history (e.g., targets' earlier attachment relationships, their current relationship with their romantic partner, and previous attachment-relevant experiences in romantic relationships). If, for example, insecure targets were securely attached to their parents in childhood, they may be easier to buffer than insecure targets who were insecurely attached to one or both of their parents. Agents (i.e., those doing the buffering) may be able to utilize targets' prior secure attachment history to their advantage when attempting to buffer them. If insecure targets had secure attachments during childhood, agents might be able to draw upon these positive experiences and help targets think about times when their parent(s) reacted responsively to them during difficult situations.

Indirect evidence supporting the possible efficacy of this approach comes from studies that have investigated attachment security priming (see Gillath & Karantzas, 2019, for a review). Repeatedly priming secure attachment concepts decreases attachment anxiety, increases positive self-views, and increases positive relationship evaluations for up to five days post-priming (Carnelley & Rowe, 2007). Hudson and Fraley (2018) have also found that repeatedly priming attachment security across four months produces fairly stable decreases in attachment anxiety. Buffering by attempting to prime insecure partners with memories or images of attachment security could, therefore, improve long-term personal and relational outcomes by instilling more positive self and relationship evaluations. Carnelley and Rowe (2007), however, also found that, among participants experimentally primed with attachment security, securely attached individuals were *more* likely to shift their relationship expectations in a positive direction than insecurely attached people were. Thus, even though insecure targets who had secure attachment figures in the past may be easier to buffer than insecure targets who experienced only insecure attachment figures, doing so may still be relatively challenging.

In addition to the history of the target's attachment, the attachment security of the agent may be an emergent property that influences the effectiveness of buffering insecurely attached partners. While our model describes how agents can buffer their partner's insecurity, it does not focus on the attachment orientation of the agents themselves. If agents are also insecurely attached, they may have more difficulty regulating their own emotions along with their partner's emotions, especially in highly stressful situations. Employing the strategies outlined in our model assumes that agents can effectively regulate their own emotions well enough and long enough to provide appropriate care to their distressed insecure partners. But when insecure agents must deal with targets who are highly dysregulated and responding in highly maladaptive ways, the two partners may feed off of each other's emotionally dysregulated state, preventing both partners from down-regulating their heightened distress. Some evidence supports this claim. Particularly for anxious wives and avoidant husbands, insecure dyads respond to the anticipation of conflict with greater cortisol reactivity, anxious wives have greater difficulty recognizing their avoidant husband's distress during conflict, and avoidant husbands have greater difficulty constructively expressing their need for support (Beck, Pietromonaco, DeBuse, Powers, & Sayer, 2013).

Accounting for Agent Burnout

If agents buffer their target partners well and consistently over time, insecurely attached targets may learn to regulate their negative emotions more constructively, which should improve relationship satisfaction for both targets and agents. Oftentimes, however, the buffering attempts of agents may not be effective because of their lack of skill or knowledge regarding how to help their insecure partners reduce their distress and function better. Moreover, targets may perceive agents' buffering attempts as insincere or disingenuous, which could increase targets' distress and dysfunction (Lemay & Dudley,

2011). This could create a cycle of mutual cyclical deterioration in which: a) targets communicate their needs less effectively by exaggerating their negative emotions, elevate their demands for reassurance, or perceive their partners more negatively, which b) leads agents to perceive that their attempts to quell the target's concerns are not being acknowledged or are not working, which c) then motivates agents to reduce their buffering attempts. If agents' buffering attempts repeatedly fail, they are likely to burn out and terminate all attempts to console their insecure partners.

Certain relationships or partners may be more prone to burning out. The partner buffering model shown in Figure 7.1 assumes that agents may be capable of enacting certain strategies that can effectively down-regulate their partner's insecure reactions. At the beginning of relationships or when they are relatively new, if agents are not buffering their partners properly or their strategies do not downregulate their partner's distress, agents may still remain hopeful about long-term prospects of the relationship. But as time passes, ineffective partner buffering may start to weigh negatively on both the target and the agent, which could manifest in reductions of buffering behavior across time, feelings of frustration, exhaustion or being undervalued, and general withdrawal from the relationships. By contrast, effective partner buffering may reinforce continued buffering efforts, build competence and feelings of relational value and engagement.

Relational factors may also play a role in partner burnout, particularly commitment. Being highly committed might protect against partner burnout. People who are more committed tend to be more willing to sacrifice in order to benefit their partner and relationship (Van Lange et al., 1997), suggesting that highly committed agents may on average be less prone to burning out over time. Although most agents are likely to eventually tire from constantly trying to buffer their partners, especially if it is to no avail, agents who are more committed may be more willing to make and endure this long-term sacrifice. The willingness to sacrifice may also depend on the agent's attachment orientation. Avoidantly attached individuals, for example, are less inclined to make sacrifices for their relationships and may also be more susceptible to burnout (Farrell et al., 2016).

Ties with Emotionally Focused Therapy

Emotionally Focused Therapy (EFT) (Johnson, 2004), which is grounded in attachment theory, addresses attachment insecurity concerns in distressed couples. EFT and our model both highlight the importance of incorporating attachment principles to help partners regulate their negative emotions in order to behave more constructively and increase relationship satisfaction. Several concepts in EFT align well with some of the processes outlined in our model, but there are some key differences, including the dyadic conceptualization of the processes that unfold between partners, the source of the problem or conflict, its severity, and how distress is best alleviated.

To identify the similarities between EFT and our model, one must understand the therapeutic steps of EFT in relation to our model. In EFT, the first therapeutic step is cycle de-escalation, whereby the therapist helps the couple recognize the destructive cycle in which the partners typically engage that maintains distress and sustains attachment insecurity (Johnson, 2004). This step is relevant to the portion of our model that outlines how attachment insecurity is triggered and the subsequent behavior that insecurely attached targets normally display.

The second therapeutic step in EFT involves restructuring the couple's interaction patterns (Johnson, 2004), which is related to the partner buffering section in our model. In this second step, both partners learn to enact strategies that help each other regulate their emotions more constructively during difficult conversations in order to break habitual demand-withdrawal patterns of communication. Two techniques are taught as part of this step: withdrawer re-engagement, and blamer softening. Withdrawer re-engagement encourages disclosing attachment needs and fears of rejection while still being available and responsive to the partner's needs and concerns. Blamer softening encourages expressing feelings from a position of vulnerability without blame or criticism. Similarly, our model focuses on the enactment of strategies that ought to mitigate attachment insecurities and concerns in targets, leading to immediate outcomes in which feelings are communicated more accurately and emotions are experienced more constructively.

Despite these similarities, there are several differences between the two frameworks. First, EFT directly addresses how *both* partners have contributed to the problem/conflict and can possibly contribute to its solution. In EFT, for example, the therapist focuses on the communication patterns and emotional expression of both partners while taking into account each partner's attachment history. In our model, the focus is on two fairly separate roles: the partner in the potential buffering role (the agent), and the partner who is being buffered (the target). Moreover, our model does not directly consider the agent's attachment history or how the agent is affected by the target's emotional and behavioral reactions when distressed.

In addition, EFT specifically addresses demand-withdrawal patterns, whereby one partner usually blames or criticizes the other partner, which then leads the other partner to shut down or withdraw from the conversation (Christensen, 1988). This pattern of communication is frequently seen in distressed couples. Indeed, many couples treated with EFT have a history of one partner betraying the other, meaning that the primary source of distress is often tied to the partner who did the betraying. To complicate matters, one or both partners may also be struggling with mental health issues, which exacerbates the negative communication patterns commonly witnessed in clinical populations. Unlike EFT, our model does not focus on specific communication patterns, and it applies to distressing situations in which one partner both is and is not the primary source of distress, such as problems at work, conflicts with friends or family, and difficulties making important decisions. Finally, the issues that generate distress are often not as severe as those that occur for couples undergoing EFT.

Because the source of conflict and severity of issues differ between EFT and our model, the buffering strategies employed also differ to some extent. EFT therapists, for example, encourage couples to experience and recognize their negative affect and dysfunctional communication patterns during some therapy sessions. Doing so allows both partners to experience a state of vulnerability, which can instigate change in their attachment working models. Inducing vulnerability is especially important for relationships characterized by severe transgressions or betrayals because it often facilitates their improvement. Our model, by comparison, suggests that agents should typically try to downregulate targets immediately, instead of allowing them to experience or escalate negative feelings when they feel distressed. Among couples with less severe problems, many agents may be able to buffer targets without being adversely affected by the target's dysregulation, especially if agents are not responsible for the target's distress. Agents who can continue to manage their emotions well and construct-ively should be able to provide better, more appropriate support to their insecurely attached partners. Particularly when problems are less chronic and severe, allowing targets to remain distressed may only escalate the target's dysregulation, making it even harder for agents to buffer them effectively.

Acknowledging differences between EFT and our model may help clarify the direction in which future research on partner buffering might head. Because the goal in our model is for agents to buffer targets, the agent's attachment history and the outcomes of their prior buffering attempts are not included in our model. These important variables, however, are more directly addressed and considered in EFT. In addition, future studies should examine how the attachment insecurity of agents affects the success of their buffering behavior and how buffering targets impacts the agent's likelihood of burning out over time. Finally, for conflicts in which an agent has betrayed a target or that involve severe issues (e.g., domestic violence, chronic substance use), it will be important to determine whether the specific buffering strategies outlined in our model are still effective.

CONCLUSIONS

The last 10 years has seen a surge of research adopting a dyadic perspective to understand attachment insecurity better. Partner buffering is one of the most important demonstrations of the value of a dyadic perspective because it reveals how the negative outcomes associated with one partner's attachment insecurity can be buffered by partners who enact strategies that down-regulate insecure reactions during stressful interactions. The growing literature has identified specific partner buffering behaviors that appear to reduce attachment insecurity and improve relationship outcomes. Taking a dyadic perspective, however, also involves considering the strengths, weaknesses, and potential burnout of partners who engage in buffering. Therapeutic models that focus on dyadic patterns, such as EFT, provide valuable insights into how buffering may be maximized by helping *both* partners develop effective strategies that work together to improve attachment dynamics in relationships.

REFERENCES

Ainsworth, M. D. S., Blehar, M. C., Waters, E., & Wall, S. (1978). *Patterns of Attachment: A Psychological Study of the Strange Situation.* Oxford: Lawrence Erlbaum.

Arriaga, X. B., Kumashiro, M., Finkel, E. J., VanderDrift, L. E., & Luchies, L. B. (2014). Filling the void: Bolstering attachment security in committed relationships. *Social Psychological and Personality Science,* 5, 398–406. doi:10.1177/1948550613509287

Arriaga, X. B., Kumashiro, M., Simpson, J. A., & Overall, N. C. (2018). Revising working models across time: Relationship situations that enhance attachment security. *Personality and Social Psychology Review,* 22, 71–96. doi:10.1177/1088868317705257

Bartholomew, K. & Horowitz, L. M. (1991). Attachment styles among young adults: A test of a four-category model. *Journal of Personality and Social Psychology,* 61, 226–244. doi:10.1037/0022-3514.61.2.226

Beck, L. A., Pietromonaco, P. R., DeBuse, C. J., Powers, S. I., & Sayer, A. G. (2013). Spouses' attachment pairings predict neuroendocrine, behavioral, and psychological responses to marital conflict. *Journal of Personality and Social Psychology,* 105, 388–424. doi:10.1037/a0033056

Bowlby, J. (1969). *Attachment and Loss: Vol. 1: Attachment.* New York: Basic Books.

Bowlby, J. (1973). *Attachment and Loss: Vol. 2: Separation.* New York: Basic Books.

Bowlby, J. (1980). *Attachment and Loss: Vol. 3: Loss.* New York: Basic Books.

Bowlby, J. (1988). *A Secure Base: Clinical Applications of Attachment Theory.* London: Routledge.

Carnelley, K. B. & Rowe, A. C. (2007). Repeated priming of attachment security influences later views of self and relationships. *Personal Relationships,* 14, 307–320. doi:10.1111/j.1475-6811.2007.00156.x

Christensen, A. (1988). Dysfunctional interaction patterns in couples. In P. Noller, & M. A. Fitzpatrick (Eds.), *Perspectives on Marital Interaction* (pp. 31–52). Clevedon: Multilingual Matters.

Collins, N. L. & Read, S. J. (1990). Adult attachment, working models, and relationship quality in dating couples. *Journal of Personality and Social Psychology,* 58, 644–663. doi:10.1037/0022-3514.58.4.644

Downey, G., Freitas, A. L., Michaelis, B., & Khouri, H. (1998). The self-fulfilling prophecy in close relationships: Rejection sensitivity and rejection by romantic partners. *Journal of Personality and Social Psychology*, 75, 545–560. doi:10.1037/0022-3514.75.2.545

Farrell, A. K., Simpson, J. A., Overall, N. C., & Shallcross, S. L. (2016). Buffering the responses of avoidantly attached romantic partners in strain test situations. *Journal of Family Psychology*, 30, 580–591. doi:10.1037/fam0000186

Gillath, O. & Karantzas, G. (2019). Attachment security priming: A systematic review. *Current Opinion in Psychology*, 25, 86–95. doi:10.1016/j.copsyc.2018.03.001

Girme, Y. U., Overall, N. C., Simpson, J. A., & Fletcher, G. J. O. (2015). "All or nothing": Attachment avoidance and the curvilinear effects of partner support. *Journal of Personality and Social Psychology*, 108, 450–475. doi:10.1037/a0038866

Hudson, N. W. & Fraley, R. C. (2018). Moving toward greater security: The effects of repeatedly priming attachment security and anxiety. *Journal of Research in Personality*, 74, 147–157. doi:10.1016/j.jrp.2018.04.002

Jakubiak, B. K. & Feeney, B. C. (2016). A sense of security: Touch promotes state attachment security. *Social Psychological and Personality Science*, 7, 745–753. doi:10.1177/1948550616646427

Johnson, S. (2004). *The Practice of Emotionally Focused Couple Therapy* (1st/2nd ed.). New York: Brunner-Routledge.

Johnson, S. C., Dweck, C. S., & Chen, F. S. (2007). Evidence for infants' internal working models of attachment. *Psychological Science*, 18, 501–502. doi:10.1111/j.1467-9280.2007.01929.x

Lemay, E. P., Jr. & Clark, M. S. (2008). "Walking on eggshells": How expressing relationship insecurities perpetuates them. *Journal of Personality and Social Psychology*, 95, 420–441. doi:10.1037/0022-3514.95.2.420

Lemay, E. P., Jr. & Dudley, K. L. (2011). Caution: Fragile! Regulating the interpersonal security of chronically insecure partners. *Journal of Personality and Social Psychology*, 100, 681–702. doi:10.1037/a0021655

Little, K. C., McNulty, J. K., & Russell, V. M. (2010). Sex buffers intimates against the negative implications of attachment insecurity. *Personality and Social Psychology Bulletin*, 36, 484–498. doi:10.1177/0146167209352494

Main, M., Kaplan, N., & Cassidy, J. (1985). Security in infancy, childhood, and adulthood: A move to the level of representation. *Monographs of the Society for Research in Child Development*, 50, 66–104. doi:10.2307/3333827

Mikulincer, M. & Shaver, P. R. (2003). The attachment behavioral system in adulthood: Activation, psychodynamics, and interpersonal processes. In M. Zanna (Ed.), *Advances in Experimental Social Psychology* (Vol. 35). New York: Academic Press.

Mikulincer, M. & Shaver, P. R. (2007). *Attachment in Adulthood: Structure, Dynamics, and Change*. New York: Guilford Press.

Moser, M. B., Johnson, S. M., Dalgleish, T. L., Lafontaine, M., Wiebe, S. A., & Tasca, G. A. (2016). Changes in relationship-specific attachment in emotionally focused couple therapy. *Journal of Marital and Family Therapy*, 42, 231–245. doi:10.1111/jmft.12139

Overall, N. C. & Simpson, J. A. (2015). Attachment and dyadic regulation processes. *Current Opinion in Psychology*, 1, 61–66. doi:10.1016/j.copsyc.2014.11.008

Overall, N. C., Simpson, J. A., & Struthers, H. (2013). Buffering attachment-related avoidance: Softening emotional and behavioral defenses during conflict discussions. *Journal of Personality and Social Psychology*, 104, 854–871. doi:10.1037/a0031798

Pietromonaco, P. R. & Carnelley, K. B. (1994). Gender and working models of attachment: Consequences for perceptions of self and romantic relationships. *Personal Relationships*, 1, 63–82. doi:10.1111/j.1475-6811.1994.tb00055.x

Pietromonaco, P. R. & Feldman Barrett, L. (1997). Working models of attachment and daily social interactions. *Journal of Personality and Social Psychology*, 73, 1409–1423. doi:10.1037/0022-3514.73.6.1409

Rusbult, C. E., Verette, J., Whitney, G. A., Slovik, L. F., & Lipkus, I. (1991). Accommodation processes in close relationships: Theory and preliminary empirical evidence. *Journal of Personality and Social Psychology*, 60, 53–78. doi:10.1037/0022-3514.60.1.53

Simpson, J. A. & Overall, N. C. (2014). Partner buffering of attachment insecurity. *Current Directions in Psychological Science*, 23, 54–59. doi:10.1177/0963721413510933

Simpson, J. A. & Rholes, W. S. (1994). Stress and secure base relationships in adulthood: Attachment processes in adulthood. In K. Bartholomew & D. Perlman (Eds.), *Advances in Personal Relationships: Attachment Processes in Adulthood* (Vol. 5, pp. 181–204). London: Kingsley.

Simpson, J. A. & Rholes, W. S. (2012). Adult attachment orientations, stress, and romantic relationships. *Advances in Experimental Social Psychology*, 45, 279–328. doi:10.1016/B978-0-12-394286-9.00006-8

Simpson, J. A. & Rholes, W. S. (2017). Adult attachment, stress, and romantic relationships. *Current Opinion in Psychology*, 13, 19–24. doi:10.1016/j.copsyc.2016.04.006

Simpson, J. A., Rholes, W. S., & Nelligan, J. S. (1992). Support seeking and support giving within couples in an anxiety-provoking situation: The role of attachment styles. *Journal of Personality and Social Psychology*, 62, 434–446. doi:10.1037/0022-3514.62.3.434

Simpson, J. A., Winterheld, H. A., Rholes, W. S., & Oriña, M. M. (2007). Working models of attachment and reactions to different forms of caregiving from romantic partners. *Journal of Personality and Social Psychology*, 93, 466–477. doi:10.1037/0022-3514.93.3.466

Sroufe, L. A. & Waters, E. (1977). Attachment as an organizational construct. *Child Development*, 48, 1184–1199. doi:10.2307/1128475

Tran, S. & Simpson, J. A. (2009). Prorelationship maintenance behaviors: The joint roles of attachment and commitment. *Journal of Personality and Social Psychology*, 97, 685–698. doi:10.1037/a0016418

Van Lange, P. A. M., Rusbult, C. E., Drigotas, S. M., Arriaga, X. B., Witcher, B. S., & Cox, C. L. (1997). Willingness to sacrifice in close relationships. *Journal of Personality and Social Psychology*, 72, 1373–1395. doi:10.1037/0022-3514.72.6.1373

Wieselquist, J., Rusbult, C. E., Foster, C. A., & Agnew, C. R. (1999). Commitment, prorelationship behavior, and trust in close relationships. *Journal of Personality and Social Psychology*, 77, 942–966. doi:10.1037/0022-3514.77.5.942

8

Stress as a Risk Factor to Well-Being

Role of Dyadic Coping

VALENTINA RAUCH-ANDEREGG AND ASHLEY K. RANDALL

Family systems theorists have long argued that the experiences between members in a system are interdependent (see Gladding, 2015); however, biological and psychological theorists have not necessarily adopted this approach when conceptualizing specific social experiences, such as stress (Selye, 1974). As such, stress has long been considered an *intra*personal experience, one that arises out of the imbalance between the demands of one's environment and their resources (Lazarus & Folkman, 1984).

Hill's (1958) ABC-X model offered a conceptualization of the association between a family's members individual stressful experience and its effect on family crises, yet did not consider the interdependence between family members' experiences or how the experience of one family member's stress may be relational in nature (affecting others in the family). For example, partners in a same-gender relationship may be reluctant to show public displays of affection for fear of discrimination due to their sexual minority status (e.g., Brady, 2017) or one partner may struggle with their expectations of being a first-time parent and attentive partner (e.g., Halford, Petch, & Creedy, 2015). According to Selye, (1974), the evaluation of such experiences as stressful (or not) are influenced by an individual's personal characteristics, such as their personality, and by the situation itself.

To date, a majority of research has focused on the individual experience of stress and its associations with individual well-being (e.g., Ganster & Rosen, 2013; Juster, McEwen, & Lupien, 2010; McEwen, 2008). However, relational scholars have long viewed one's social environment as an important element to understand one's experiences (Bodenmann, 2000; Bodenmann & Randall, 2013), especially given the interdependence between partners' experiences (Bradbury & Karney, 2014). In the section that follows, we present how stress can impact romantic partners as interdependent dyads, how they can jointly cope with stress, and important directions for future research in understanding partners' interdependent stress and coping processes.

DEFINING STRESS AS A RELATIONAL CONSTRUCT

Stress in close relationships can be best understood by identifying the *locus*, *intensity*, and *duration* of the stress (Randall & Bodenmann, 2009). Stress can originate from outside (*external*) or inside (*internal*) one's relationship. Common external stressors include stress from school or work obligations, social contacts, or free time (Ledermann, Bodenmann, Rudaz, & Bradbury, 2010; Milek, Randall, Nussbeck, Breitenstein, & Bodenmann, 2017; Neff & Karney, 2004). Additionally, some individuals may experience additional external stressors due to their minority status, such as increased experience of discrimination because of one's sexual orientation (Meyer, 2003). Stress can also originate within the relationship, such as differences of opinions with one's partner, annoying habits of the partner, or differing relational goals (Falconier, Nussbeck, Bodenmann, Schneider, & Bradbury, 2015; Lau, Randall, & Duran, 2019; Ledermann et al., 2010).

Importantly, an individual's experience of (external) stress can impact their partner's experience as well. First, the stressful feelings from one partner can crossover to the other partner (stress crossover; Totenhagen, Serido, Curran, & Butler, 2012), causing stress in both partners (e.g., Totenhagen, Randall, Cooper, Tao, & Walsh, 2017). Second, the experience of an external stress can spill over into the relationship causing internal stress. This is known as *stress spillover* (Neff & Karney, 2004). For example, if one partner experiences discrimination at work due to their sexual minority status, this may cause the partner to shut down at home in an attempt to individually cope with this stress (e.g., Totenhagen, Randall, & Lloyd, 2018). As an additional example, if one partner had a stressful day because the baby cried all day, this may lead to lower sexual activity between the partners, as well as reduced relationship satisfaction (Bodenmann, Atkins, Schär, & Poffet, 2010).

Irrespective of the origin of the stress, stress can also be categorized based on its intensity and duration. Specifically, the occurrence of stress can be considered relatively *minor* (e.g., daily hassles; Bodenmann et al., 2010; Falconier, Nussbeck, et al., 2015) or *major* in nature (e.g., the experience of a chronic illness or major life event; Meier, Bodenmann, Moergeli, & Jenewein, 2011). Additionally, these stressors can last for a short time period, such as over a week (*acute*), or a long time period, such as over months or years (*chronic*). Understanding the various conceptualizations of stress based on its locus, intensity, and duration help relational scholars further understand the specific stressors couples and families may face, as well as possible unique implications for couples' stress and coping processes.

PARTNERS' COPING WITH STRESS

Based on principles of couples' interdependence, the *systemic-transactional model* (STM; Bodenmann, 1997, 2005) is built upon the core assumption that partners' stress and coping are an interdependent process. The STM helps conceptualize how the stress of one partner can affect the other, and how the partners can work together to cope with the stress. The assumptions of the STM can be best described in the metaphor of partners rowing in a boat: the boat can only move if partners row in synchrony, which relies on the coordination and resources of both partners. While stress has been shown to be linked with adverse relationship outcomes (Randall & Bodenmann, 2009, 2017), engaging in positive dyadic coping, as a joint means of regulating own and each other's emotional experiences, has been found to be positively associated with high relationship functioning for couples around the world (see Falconier, Jackson, Hilpert, & Bodenmann, 2015 for a meta-analytic review; Falconier, Randall, & Bodenmann, 2016).

The purpose of this chapter is to present new research extending the STM (Bodenmann, 1997, 2005). First, we present research on the experience of external stressors, such as the experience of minority stress for same-gender couples. Second, we present research on the experience of an internal stress such as the experience of a birth of a child. For both, we provide a short review on the associations between these types of stress and well-being, and then offer promising directions in applying the STM to understand how couples can cope with these stressors as a relational maintenance strategy (Randall & Messerschmitt, 2019).

ASSOCIATIONS BETWEEN STRESS AND WELL-BEING

Not surprisingly, the experience of stress can have deleterious effects on a variety of health indices and outcomes. Specifically, stress can impact the immune system by making individuals more vulnerable to infectious diseases (Ader, 2001). In addition, stress has been shown to negatively affect health behaviors, such as diet and exercise, or sleep quality, and also health problems, such as high blood pressure and high blood sugar (Clark et al., 2011; Kiecolt-Glaser et al., 2005). Although a wealth of literature exists on the well-documented negative association between stress and individual well-being (Glaser & Kiecolt-Glaser, 2005), here we present literature on the experience of two specific stressors: the experience of minority stress for same-gender couples, and the stress associated with the transition to parenthood.

Sexual Minority Stress

Although stress is common for all individuals, some individuals may experience additional stressors due to their minority status (Meyer, 1995, 2003). For example, sexual minority individuals (i.e., individuals who identify as lesbian, gay, or bisexual) may experience discrimination in the workplace (Otis, Rostosky, Riggle, & Hamrin, 2006) or a lack of family support due to their marginalized sexual identity (see Rostosky & Riggle, 2017 for a review). The experience of sexual minority stress has been found to be associated with negative mental and physical health outcomes (e.g., Frost, Lehavot, & Meyer, 2015; Meyer, 2003). Furthermore, the repeated exposure to such stressors can lead to negative internal thoughts about one's sexual orientation (internalized homophobia; Meyer & Dean, 1998). Recently, research by Totenhagen et al. (2018) extended theoretical work on the vulnerability-stress adaptation model (Karney & Bradbury, 1995). Their research found support for conceptualizing internalized homophobia as an enduring vulnerability that may disproportionally affect sexual minority individuals. Specifically, based on 14–day daily diaries from 81 same-gender couples their research revealed that, on days when individuals reported higher levels of internalized homophobia, they also reported greater daily stress. This research adds to the previous literature that has shown feelings of internalized homophobia to be associated with an increase in attempted suicide (e.g., Hammelman, 1993) and symptoms of anxiety and depression (Igartua, Gill, & Montoro, 2003; Newcomb & Mustanski, 2010). As such, the increased exposure to and experience of sexual minority stressors may be an important mechanism behind the association between internalized homophobia and indices of individual well-being.

Transition to Parenthood Stress

Many couples find the transition to parenthood to be stressful and highly demanding (e.g., Doss, Cicila, Hsueh, Morrison, & Carhart, 2014), as the birth of a child can add up to 40 hours of extra work per week for a couple (Halford et al., 2015). For heterosexual couples, research has shown that women, on average, do about 75 percent to 80 percent of the extra work placed on them after childbirth (e.g., Bianchi, Milkie, Sayer, & Robinson, 2000), while men often focus more on their careers and paid work (Baxter, Hewitt, & Haynes, 2008). Although partners spend about the same time on housework before pregnancy, for heterosexual couples, the shift to more "traditional family roles" after childbirth may be more salient for some couples, which may lead to feelings of relationship dissatisfaction (e.g., Twenge, Campbell, & Foster, 2003).

In addition to the shift of roles in the family, another frequent source of potential stress is the lack of sleep, which is almost universal for parents with young children (Medina, Lederhos, & Lillis, 2009). Sleep deprivation has been shown to be linked with lower individual well-being, such as the presence of depression symptoms (Cottrell & Khan, 2005; Parfitt & Ayers, 2014; Tomfohr, Buliga, Letourneau, Campbell, & Giesbrecht, 2015). A study with 46 women and 40 men from England revealed that sleep deprivation was significantly associated with postnatal mental health problems, including symptoms of anxiety and depression (Parfitt & Ayers, 2014). In heterosexual couples, women seem to be more vulnerable to emotional difficulties throughout the perinatal phase as they often report higher anxiety and depression compared to men (O'Hara & Wisner, 2014; Vismara et al., 2016). Furthermore, the time spent with friends and family or engaging in physical activities also decreases after the birth of a child (Claxton & Perry-Jenkins, 2008). This decrease in extracurricular activity has been found to be particularly harmful on relationship functioning, as decreased time spent between partners is positively associated with marital disagreements and decreased relationship satisfaction (Hatch & Bulcroft, 2004; Kilbourne, Howell, & England, 1990). Taken together, while the birth of a first child can be an exciting time, it is also filled with many changes that can cause stress.

Stress and Relational Well-Being

Satisfying relationships are known to be beneficial for one's mental and physical health (see for an overview Robles, Slatcher, Trombello, & McGinn, 2014). While these findings have been demonstrated among young, middle-aged, and elderly individuals in a heterosexual relationships (Waldinger & Schulz, 2010), limited research exists on these associations for same-gender couples, which is an important area for future research. A possible explanation for the associations between positive, satisfying relationships and health benefits might be that relationship satisfaction is related to lower stress and better cardiovascular functioning (Holt-Lunstad, Birmingham, & Jones, 2008), whereas dissatisfaction can be associated with negative interactions that trigger the psychophysiological stress system, which in turn increases health risks (Robles & Kiecolt-Glaser, 2003).

As noted above, an individual's stress experience can be conceptualized as a dyadic construct: It may originate and crossover from the partner (Totenhagen et al., 2012) or spillover from individual factors that are external to the relationship (Neff & Karney, 2004). Cross-sectional research has shown stress spillover to be associated with decreased relationship quality and communication in heterosexual couples (Bodenmann, Ledermann, & Bradbury, 2007; Bolger, DeLongis, Kessler, & Wethington, 1989; Schulz, Cowan, Cowan, & Brennan, 2004), and to be linked with decreases in relationship functioning over time (Bodenmann & Cina, 2006; Karney, Story, & Bradbury, 2005).

Sexual Minority Stress Sexual minority individual's experience of stress can be affected by relation dynamics, insomuch as the relationship itself is "socially stigmatized or marginalized in some way" (LeBlanc, Frost, & Wight, 2015, p. 8). LeBlanc et al. (2015) proposed a conceptual framework to understand couple-level minority stress. Specifically, their framework highlights how each partner's individual-level minority stressors (e.g., experiences of internalized homophobia, stigma, and discrimination) are associated with not only their own but also their partner's mental health (e.g., mood disorders, substance use, and suicide risk), and joint perceptions of relational stress (e.g., conflict, sexual dysfunction, and relationship dissatisfaction). Furthermore, LeBlanc et al. (2015) posit that the associations of individual-level stressors with individual and relational well-being may be mediated by couple-level minority stress (e.g., stigma, discrimination, and concealment). However, additional research applying this model is in its infancy.

For those in a romantic relationship, experiences of minority stress may not only affect the individual who experienced the stress, but their relational partner as well (Doyle & Molix, 2015; Rostosky & Riggle, 2002; Totenhagen et al., 2017). For example, recent research by Totenhagen et al. (2017) revealed that, on days when men in a same-gender relationship experience greater sexual-minority stress, they report a decrease in relationship quality the following day; however, this effect was not found for women in a same-sex relationship, perhaps due to their (women's) greater propensity to disclose their stressful experiences. Furthermore, Rostosky and Riggle's (2017) conceptual review on the associations between minority stress and relationship outcomes found that feelings of internalized homophobia were associated with lower relationship investment (Greene & Britton, 2015), relationship satisfaction (Cohen & Byers, 2015; Lewis, Milletich, Derlega, & Padilla, 2014), greater physical aggression (Milletich, Gumienny, Kelley, & D'Lima, 2014), and decreased perceptions of partner support (Khaddouma, Norona, & Whitton, 2015). Taken together, both theory and research suggest that the experience of sexual minority stressors can be considered relational in nature and reflect interdependent processes affecting both partners in the relationship.

Transition to Parenthood The transition to parenthood brings many changes for expecting parents, as noted above. Given this, is it not surprising that first-time parents report declines in relationship satisfaction during the first two years after the birth of their child (Mitnick, Heyman, & Smith Slep, 2009). The decline in relationship satisfaction over time is steeper and more rapid than it is for childless couples (Lawrence, Rothman, Cobb, Rothman, & Bradbury, 2008), and can persist for up to seven years (Keizer & Schenk, 2012). Spending less time together as a couple is associated with a decline of couple communication, an increased rate of relationship conflicts (Claxton & Perry-Jenkins, 2008; Curran, Hazen, Jacobvitz, & Sasaki, 2006; Kluwer & Johnson, 2007), and reduced intimacy (Claxton & Perry-Jenkins, 2008; Dew & Wilcox, 2011). Additionally, partners may experience a loss of libido and decreased frequency of sexual intercourse (Hipp, Kane Low, & van Anders, 2012; Parfitt & Ayers, 2014), especially as they adjust to being first-time parents. Women feel less supported by their partner than men do across the transition to parenthood (Rholes, Simpson, Campbell, & Grich, 2001), and men's reports also suggest they support their partner less during this time (Simpson, Rholes, Campbell, Tran, & Wilson, 2003).

Coping with Stress: Role of Dyadic Coping

Bodenmann's (1995, 2005) systemic-transactional model (STM) posits that couples' stress and coping experiences are interdependent. The interdependence between partners' experiences can be first demonstrated when partners communicate their stress to one another, either verbally (e.g., "I am stressed" or "I am feeling overwhelmed") or nonverbally (e.g., shutting down or sighing). One partner's non-verbal (implicit) communication of stress is thought to leave room for misunderstanding by the non-stressed partner. For example, one partner's sigh can be misinterpreted as boredom or fatigue, rather than as a signal of needing to talk or feel supported. Emphasis in dyadic coping is placed on verbal (explicit) stress communication that alleviates stress; stressed partners who explicit communicate their experience of stress are more likely to be understood by the non-stressed partner and to get support that matches the needs of the stressed partner (Bodenmann, 2000, 2015).

Specific Types of Dyadic Coping Partners' dyadic coping behaviors are displayed following the (stressed) partner's communication of stress. Specifically, partners can choose to respond either positively or negatively (see Figure 8.1; Bodenmann, 1997). Positive dyadic coping includes: problem-focused, emotion-focused, delegated, and common dyadic coping. Specifically, *problem-focused supportive dyadic* coping refers to the ways in which partners can help problem-solve with one another about how to cope with the stress (e.g., "Perhaps you could meditate or take a bath to feel better?"). *Emotion focused supportive dyadic* coping refers to ways in which partners

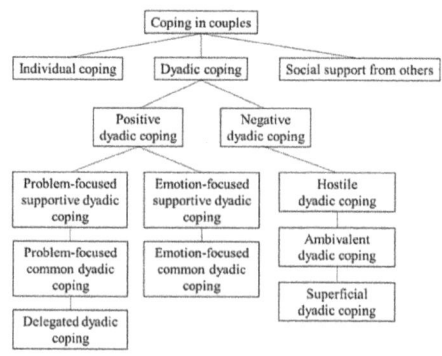

FIGURE 8.1 Conceptualization of types of dyadic coping in couples

can provide empathy or understanding (e.g., "I can understand how experiencing this made you feel hurt or upset. I would be upset too!"). *Delegated dyadic coping* refers to situations in which the stressed partner asks the non-stressed partner to do something in order to reduce their stress (e.g. "Perhaps you could run the errands, so I can sleep and recover from the crying baby last night"). Lastly, *common dyadic coping* occurs when both partners are affected by the same stressor (e.g., sleep deprivation because of the crying baby) and attempt to cope together as a unit (e.g., "It is a tough time, but we are a team and will manage this situation together").

Unfortunately, partners can also respond negatively to their partner's stress. *Negative dyadic coping* subsumes all coping forms that are not helpful (i.e., ambivalent, superficial, and hostile dyadic coping). *Ambivalent dyadic coping* occurs when support is being provided but the non-stressed partner sees the support as unnecessary (e.g., "I don't understand how you are stressed about this, but I can help if it would make you feel better"), while *superficial dyadic coping* refers to supportive behavior that is provided with an unmotivated attitude (e.g., "I guess we can go out tonight to help you feel better, even though I was hoping to watch TV tonight"). *Hostile dyadic coping* refers to negative and destructive behaviors (verbally and non-verbally), such as labelling a partner's stress as trivial, laughing at the partner, or devaluing the partner (e.g., "Seriously?! You should be able to handle a situation like this").

Efficacy of Engaging in Dyadic Coping Engaging in positive dyadic coping has been found to be associated with the reduction of stress for both partners, the increased feelings of we-ness, increased trust, and greater relationship satisfaction (e.g., Bodenmann, Meuwly, & Kayser, 2011; Papp & Witt, 2010) in both different-gender (Falconier, Jackson, et al., 2015) and same-gender couples (Meuwly, Feinstein, Davila, Nuñez, & Bodenmann, 2013; Randall, Tao, Totenhagen, Walsh, & Cooper, 2017; Randall, Totenhagen, Walsh, Adams, & Tao, 2017). Despite the wealth of research on dyadic coping, until recently, there has been a lack of literature examining dyadic coping in couples coping with specific stressors, such as sexual minority stress and stress associated with the transition to parenthood. Here we present some initial evidence on the associations between stress and well-being, as moderated by dyadic coping.

Sexual Minority Stress Despite prior research to suggest minority individuals experience greater stress compared to their heterosexual counterparts, Weaver (2014) found that, compared to heterosexual individuals, individuals who identified as lesbian or gay reported less perceived stress. The author suggested that one of the reasons why sexual minorities may perceive less stress may have to do with the fact that they have greater dyadic coping skills, although, to date, no research has directly examined potential differences between heterosexual and same-sex couples' coping behaviors within the same study.

Randall and colleagues have expanded upon Weaver's (2014) study to examine same-gender couples' experiences of stress and dyadic coping, and resulting implications for individual and relational well-being. Based on a sample of 95 same-gender couples (64 female–female dyads; 31 male–male dyads) their research has shown perceived partners' supportive dyadic coping to be negatively associated with reported symptoms of depression and anxiety (Randall, Tao, et al., 2017; Tao, Randall, & Totenhagen, in press).

These studies provide initial evidence for the importance of examining how sexual minority couples may experience and cope with stress in the context of their relationship, although additional research is sorely needed. We expand upon this in the Future Directions section.

Transition to Parenthood Given that the transition to parenthood is a stressful period in a couple's life, investigating partners' resources for coping with such stressors, such as engaging in dyadic coping, seems important (Halford et al., 2015). Using a sample of 78 couples who were about to become parents, Molgora, Acquati, Fenaroli, and Saita (2018) found that stress communication and common dyadic coping were positively associated with relationship satisfaction (both actor and partner effects). Despite this initial study, research investigating the beneficial effects of dyadic coping on relationship functioning during the transition to parenthood is sparse. To address this gap in the literature, Bodenmann and colleagues launched a longitudinal study with 307 Swiss heterosexual couples examining the development of couples' relationships across the transition to parenthood. Additionally, the goal of this study was to examine the effectiveness of a new intervention program called *Couple Care and Coping Program* (CCC-P). CCC-P is a blend of the two evidence-based relationship education programs, *Couples Coping Enhancement Training* (CCET; Bodenmann & Shantinath, 2004) and *Couple CARE for Parents* (Halford, Moore, Wilson, Farrugia, & Dyer, 2004). CCET focuses on teaching couples about how stress can impact their relationship and how to engage in dyadic coping to combat the detrimental effects of these stressors. In contrast, Couple CARE for Parents specifically targets the needs of becoming parents by focusing on different relationship competencies (e.g., communication and self-regulation in relationships), as well as shaping realistic expectations about the transition to parenthood.

CCC-P combines the content of these two existing programs by teaching couples about expectations during the transition to parenthood, self-regulation in relationships (i.e., a process whereby each partner assesses their relationship behaviors, sets self-change goals, and implements self-change to enhance their couple relationship), and dyadic coping. CCC-P includes five home-visits around the birth of the first child, which are done by midwives. An initial investigation revealed that, for men and women, common and supportive dyadic coping did not change during pregnancy; rather, they decreased significantly after birth (Rauch-Anderegg, Kuhn, Milek, Halford, & Bodenmann, 2019). This seems to indicate that parents with a young child may have diminished resources to engage in dyadic coping and support each other during such a demanding, and transitionary period. In the same study, Rauch-Anderegg et al. (2019) found males' supportive dyadic coping to predict their female partners' relationship satisfaction across the transition to parenthood, despite the general decline in dyadic coping across the transition to parenthood. This partner-effect seems to highlight the interdependence between partners' experiences and provides further evidence for the associations between positive dyadic coping and relationship satisfaction, as demonstrated among couples who are not transitioning to parenthood (Falconier, Jackson, et al., 2015). However, results based on a study with Swiss couples transitioning to parenthood unveiled that lower prenatal dyadic coping does not accelerate the decline of relationship satisfaction, whereas circumstantial risk (i.e., unplanned pregnancy, divorce in the family of origin, low income, low education, intimate partner aggression) does predict future relationship dissatisfaction among women (Rauch-Anderegg, Nieuwenboom, Halford, & Bodenmann, under revision). Among women who received CCC-P, circumstantial risk did not predict changes in relationship satisfaction across the transition to parenthood.

Couples transitioning to parenthood are likely to report being dissatisfied in their relationship (Mitnick et al., 2009), and intervention programs only lead to small mean effect sizes in mitigating these effects (see for an overview; Pinquart & Teubert, 2010). Therefore, a promising area for future research is to further investigate the risk and protective factors associated with relationship satisfaction. Dyadic coping might be a protective factor that could be strengthened with an intervention, as shown in studies for couples who are not transitioning to parenthood (Bodenmann & Shantinath, 2004). If this could also be achieved in couples transitioning to parenthood, fewer couples becoming parents would be at risk for low relationship satisfaction and its consequences, and children would be more likely to have sensitive parents. Additionally, it would be helpful to identify the optimal phase to teach parents about dyadic coping during the transition to parenthood (the second trimester, right after birth, etc.), as some phases may be more optimal than others. Furthermore, additional research is needed to understand the experience of non-heterosexual couples transitioning to parenthood (Glazer, 2014; Goldberg, Kinkler, Moyer, & Weber, 2014).

CONCLUSIONS AND FUTURE DIRECTIONS

In this chapter, we have reviewed evidence on stress as a risk factor to both individual and relational well-being as it pertains to the experience of two specific stressors: minority stress and stress associated with the transition to parenthood. Additionally, we provided evidence that, although partners' stress experiences are linked, they can engage in (positive) dyadic coping to counteract some of its negative effects. Despite the novel extension of the systemic transactional model (Bodenmann, 1995, 2005) to these specific populations and contexts, there are important directions for future research in understanding partners' interdependent stress and coping processes.

First, we suggest that future research should focus on partners' different expectations regarding dyadic coping across different experiences. While some individuals may prefer that their partner engage in emotion-focused dyadic coping, others may prefer problem-focused dyadic coping; however, this may depend on the type of stressor that is experienced and contextual factors such as life-stage. Preferences for coping when faced with specific stressors, and during specific life-stages, have not yet been examined. In a similar vein, there might be phases/situations of very high stress (e.g., the transition to parenthood) when couples may not have the resources to engage in dyadic coping and therefore do not expect support from their partner, or when couples may have a strong desire for specific forms of dyadic coping to strengthen their feeling of we-ness. One way this can be examined is by administering the Dyadic Coping Inventory (DCI; Bodenmann, 2008). The DCI is a 37 item self-report inventory designed to assess for stress and coping behaviors of one's self (self) and perceptions of the partner's behavior (partner). The DCI provides two ways of computing a fairness-variable: The *equity index* refers to each partner's perceived equity in dyadic coping (subtracting the self-reported received support from the self-reported provided support), while the *reciprocity index* captures the fairness between both partners' dyadic coping efforts (subtracting the self-reported received/provided support from partner A from the self-reported received/provided support from partner B). Both indices represent a within-person index of fairness in dyadic coping, which reflects principles in social exchange and interdependence theory (Kelley & Thibaut, 1978; Miller, 2017); examining associations related to the costs and benefits of engaging in dyadic coping may be an important area for future research. For example, Meier et al. (accepted) are using data based on 307 heterosexual couples to investigate the link between fairness in dyadic coping and depressive symptoms in becoming parents. Findings to date suggest that perceived equity in dyadic coping is associated with fewer depressive symptoms in a curvilinear manner, such that the more balance women perceived in the dyadic coping efforts of themselves and their male partners, the lower the women's depressive symptoms.

Second, we propose that increased attention be placed on collecting and analyzing ecological momentary assessment (EMA) data, which will allow for researchers to further understand "life as lived" (Bolger, Davis, & Rafaeli, 2003, p. 579). For example, Lau and colleagues (2019) used real-time interaction data taken from forty-one heterosexual romantic partner dyads to examine how partners' (verbal and non-verbal) responses may impact perceived interaction quality. Results from this study showed that when one partner communicated stress, the other partner responded with language use indicative of different types of dyadic coping (Lau, Randall & Duran 2019). As such, collecting additional behavioral or physiological data would provide a more objective perspective on questions about the process and efficacy of dyadic coping. Data taken from real-time assessment could possibly be used to help teach couples the types of dyadic coping that are most effective citations (similar to biofeedback; Schwartz & Andrasik, 2017). Furthermore, the collection of biological data may help researchers and clinicians understand if there is a certain threshold within which dyadic coping can occur (i.e., if stress is too high, there are no internal resources to engage in dyadic coping; see Ditzen et al., 2009; Ditzen, Hahlweg, Fehm-Wolfsdorf, & Baucom, 2011). Together, EMA and biological and physiological measures help to avoid potential biases in self-report assessments.

Third, we propose that increased attention be placed on understanding the temporal dynamics associated with providing and engaging in dyadic coping (e.g., Kuhn, Milek, Meuwly, Bradbury, & Bodenmann, 2017). For example, it would be helpful to understand the communication patterns between the stressed and non-stressed partner to gain further insight into the timing of when and the types of dyadic coping that are beneficial to indices of individual and relational well-being. Specifically, future research could examine whether the non-stressed partner responds immediately to the stress expression or is delayed in responding (e.g., over seconds or minutes), and the degree to which the support provided matches the needs of the stressed partner to yield benefits.

Lastly, although recent research on the applications of the systemic transactional model (Bodenmann, 1997, 2005) with marginalized populations (primarily sexual minority individuals) support the well-documented associations between positive dyadic coping and well-being (see meta-analysis by Falconier, Jackson, et al., 2015), to date there is limited research that has been conducted with other marginalized groups, such as racial or ethnic minority couples. Additionally, there is a dearth of research on the "darker side" of coping (i.e., couples who report engaging in negative dyadic coping). Bodenmann (1995) posits that engaging in negative dyadic coping can be detrimental for the couples feeling of we-ness, especially when the stressed partner does self-disclose their "deeper" emotions. This leaves the stressed partner vulnerable to their partner's reactions. Future research could investigate the general effects of negative dyadic coping on individual (e.g., anxiety and depression) and relational outcomes (e.g., relationship satisfaction, stability, we-ness) and if timing and/or frequency is more detrimental to couples' relationship well-being – for example, if negative dyadic coping after having shared very deep emotions is more detrimental than after having shared more superficial emotions, or if frequent slightly negative dyadic coping behavior is more destructive than a single very intensive negative experience. Asking these questions can help to understand which may be more detrimental; daily reports of superficial (negative) dyadic coping when the partner is not really listening, or having a partner's first report of a stressful situation being met with hostility (e.g., "Seriously?! As a professional you should be able to handle this situation.").

In sum, this chapter provided evidence that given partners' interdependence, stress has detrimental effects on both individual and relational well-being, and to cope with stress partners can engage in (positive) dyadic coping. Recent applications of the systemic transactional model (Bodenmann, 1997, 2005) shed light on how partners can engage in positive dyadic coping, especially when experiencing sexual minority stress and stress associated with the transition to parenthood. Understanding how partners' interdependence contributes to their joint stress and coping processes provides additional evidence on how couples' engagement in relationship maintenance behaviors, such as dyadic coping, may lead to well-being across the life-span (Randall & Messerschmitt, in press).

REFERENCES

Ader, R. (2001). Psychoneuroimmunology. *Current Directions in Psychological Science*, 10, 94–98. doi:10.1111/1467-8721.00124

Baxter, J., Hewitt, B., & Haynes, M. (2008). Life course transitions and housework: Marriage, parenthood, and time on housework. *Journal of Marriage and Family*, 70, 259–272. doi:10.1111/j.1741-3737.2008.00479.x

Bianchi, S. M., Milkie, M. A., Sayer, L. C., & Robinson, J. P. (2000). Is anyone doing the housework? Trends in the gender division of household labor. *Social Forces*, 79, 191–228. doi:10.2307/2675569

Bodenmann, G. (1995). A systemic-transactional conceptualization of stress and coping in couples. *Swiss Journal of Psychology / Schweizerische Zeitschrift Für Psychologie / Revue Suisse de Psychologie*, 54, 34–49.

Bodenmann, G. (1997). Dyadic coping: A systemic-transactional view of stress and coping among couples: Theory and empirical findings. *European Review of Applied Psychology*, 47, 137–141.

Bodenmann, G. (2000). *Stress und Coping bei Paaren [Stress and Coping in Couples]*. Göttingen: Hogrefe.

Bodenmann, G. (2005). Dyadic coping and its significance for marital functioning. In Tracey A. Revenson, K. Kayser, & G. Bodenmann (Eds.), *Couples Coping with Stress: Emerging Perspectives on Dyadic Coping* (pp. 33–49). Washington, D.C.: American Psychological Association.

Bodenmann, G. (2008). *Dyadisches Coping Inventar (DCI)*. Bern: Huber. Retrieved from www.zora.uzh.ch/6249/

Bodenmann, G. (2015). *Bevor der Stress uns scheidet: Resilienz in der Partnerschaft.* Bern: Verlag Hans Huber.

Bodenmann, G., Atkins, D. C., Schär, M., & Poffet, V. (2010). The association between daily stress and sexual activity. *Journal of Family Psychology*, 24, 271–279. doi:10.1037/a0019365

Bodenmann, G. & Cina, A. (2006). Stress and coping among stable-satisfied, stable-distressed and separated/divorced Swiss couples. *Journal of Divorce & Remarriage*, 44, 71–89. doi:10.1300/J087v44n01_04

Bodenmann, G., Ledermann, T., & Bradbury, T. N. (2007). Stress, sex, and satisfaction in marriage. *Personal Relationships*, 14, 551–569. doi:10.1111/j.1475-6811.2007.00171.x

Bodenmann, G., Meuwly, N., & Kayser, K. (2011). Two conceptualizations of dyadic coping and their potential for predicting relationship quality and individual well-being: A comparison. *European Psychologist*, 16, 255–266. doi:10.1027/1016-9040/a000068

Bodenmann, G. & Randall, A. K. (2013). Close relationships in psychiatric disorders. *Current Opinion in Psychiatry*, 26, 464–467. doi:10.1097/YCO.0b013e3283642de7

Bodenmann, G. & Shantinath, S. D. (2004). The Couples Coping Enhancement Training (CCET): A new approach to prevention of marital distress based upon stress and coping. *Family Relations*, 53, 477–484. doi:10.1111/j.0197-6664.2004.00056.x

Bolger, N., Davis, A., & Rafaeli, E. (2003). Diary methods: Capturing life as it is lived. *Annual Review of Psychology*, 54, 579–616. doi:10.1146/annurev.psych.54.101601.145030

Bolger, N., DeLongis, A., Kessler, R. C., & Wethington, E. (1989). The contagion of stress across multiple roles. *Journal of Marriage and the Family*, 51, 175–183. doi:10.2307/352378

Bradbury, T. N. & Karney, B. R. (2014). *Intimate Relationships (2nd ed.).* New York: W. W. Norton & Company.

Brady, J. P. (2017). *The Effects of Perceived Danger, Fear of Heterosexism, and Internalized Homone Gativity on Public Displays of Affection Among Gender and Sexual Minorities.* Chicago, Illinois: The Paul University, College of Science and Health. Retrieved from http://via.library.depaul.edu/csh_etd/235

Clark, M. M., Warren, B. A., Hagen, P. T., Johnson, B. D., Jenkins, S. M., Werneburg, B. L., & Olsen, K. D. (2011). Stress level, health behaviors, and quality of life in employees joining a wellness center. *American Journal of Health Promotion*, 26, 21–25. doi:10.4278/ajhp.090821-QUAN-272

Claxton, A. & Perry-Jenkins, M. (2008). No fun anymore: Leisure and marital quality across the transition to parenthood. *Journal of Marriage and the Family*, 70, 28–43. doi:10.1111/j.1741-3737.2007.00459.x

Cohen, J. N. & Byers, E. S. (2015). Minority stress, protective factors, and sexual functioning of women in a same-sex relationship. *Psychology of Sexual Orientation and Gender Diversity*, 2, 391–403. doi:10.1037/sgd0000108

Cottrell, L. & Khan, A. (2005). Impact of childhood epilepsy on maternal sleep and socioemotional functioning. *Clinical Pediatrics*, 44, 613–616. doi:10.1177/000992280504400709

Curran, M., Hazen, N., Jacobvitz, D., & Sasaki, T. (2006). How representations of the parental marriage predict marital emotional attunement during the transition to parenthood. *Journal of Family Psychology*, 20, 477–484. doi:10.1037/0893-3200.20.3.477

Dew, J. & Wilcox, W. B. (2011). If momma ain't happy: Explaining declines in marital satisfaction among new mothers. *Journal of Marriage and Family*, 73, 1–12. doi:10.1111/j.1741-3737.2010.00782.x

Ditzen, B., Hahlweg, K., Fehm-Wolfsdorf, G., & Baucom, D. (2011). Assisting couples to develop healthy relationships: Effects of couples relationship education on cortisol. *Psychoneuroendocrinology*, 36, 597–607. doi:10.1016/j.psyneuen.2010.07.019

Ditzen, B., Schaer, M., Gabriel, B., Bodenmann, G., Ehlert, U., & Heinrichs, M. (2009). Intranasal oxytocin increases positive communication and reduces cortisol levels during couple conflict. *Biological Psychiatry*, 65, 728–731. doi:10.1016/j.biopsych.2008.10.011

Doss, B. D., Cicila, L. N., Hsueh, A. C., Morrison, K. R., & Carhart, K. (2014). A randomized controlled trial of brief coparenting and relationship interventions during the transition to parenthood. *Journal of Family Psychology*, 28, 483–494. doi:10.1037/a0037311

Doyle, D. M. & Molix, L. (2015). Social stigma and sexual minorities' romantic relationship functioning: A meta-analytic review. *Personality and Social Psychology Bulletin*, 41, 1363–1381. doi:10.1177/0146167215594592

Falconier, M. K., Jackson, J. B., Hilpert, P., & Bodenmann, G. (2015). Dyadic coping and relationship satisfaction: A meta-analysis. *Clinical Psychology Review*, 42, 28–46. doi:10.1016/j.cpr.2015.07.002

Falconier, M. K., Nussbeck, F., Bodenmann, G., Schneider, H., & Bradbury, T. (2015). Stress from daily hassles in couples: Its effects on intradyadic stress, relationship satisfaction, and physical and psychological well-being. *Journal of Marital and Family Therapy*, 41, 221–235. doi:10.1111/jmft.12073

Falconier, M. K., Randall, A. K., & Bodenmann, G. (Eds.) (2016). *Couples Coping with Stress: A Cross-Cultural Perspective*. New York: Routledge.

Frost, D. M., Lehavot, K., & Meyer, I. H. (2015). Minority stress and physical health among sexual minority individuals. *Journal of Behavioral Medicine*, 38, 1–8. doi:10.1007/s10865-013-9523-8

Ganster, D. C. & Rosen, C. C. (2013). Work stress and employee health: A multidisciplinary review. *Journal of Management*, 39, 1085–1122. doi:10.1177/0149206313475815

Gladding, S. T. (2015). *Family Therapy: History, Theory, and Practice* (6th ed.). Boston: Pearson.

Glaser, R. & Kiecolt-Glaser, J. K. (2005). Stress-induced immune dysfunction: Implications for health. *Nature Reviews Immunology*, 5, 243–251. doi:10.1038/nri1571

Glazer, D. (2014). LGBT transitions to parenthood. *Journal of Gay & Lesbian Mental Health*, 18, 213–221. doi:10.1080/19359705.2014.883668

Goldberg, A. E., Kinkler, L. A., Moyer, A. M., & Weber, E. (2014). Intimate relationship challenges in early parenthood among lesbian, gay, and heterosexual couples adopting via the child welfare system. *Professional Psychology: Research and Practice*, 45, 221–230. doi:10.1037/a0037443

Greene, D. C. & Britton, P. J. (2015). Predicting relationship commitment in gay men: Contributions of vicarious shame and internalized homophobia to the investment model. *Psychology of Men & Masculinity*, 16, 78–87. doi:10.1037/a0034988

Halford, W. K., Moore, E., Wilson, K. L., Farrugia, C., & Dyer, C. (2004). Benefits of flexible delivery relationship education: An evaluation of the Couple CARE Program. *Family Relations*, 53, 469–476. doi:10.1111/j.0197-6664.2004.00055.x

Halford, W. K., Petch, J., & Creedy, D. K. (2015). *Clinical Guide to Helping New Parents: The Couple CARE for Parents Program*. New York: Springer.

Hammelman, T. L. (1993). Gay and lesbian youth: Contributing factors to serious attempts or considerations of suicide. *Journal of Gay & Lesbian Psychotherapy*, 2, 77–89. doi:10.1300/J236v02n01_06

Hatch, L. R. & Bulcroft, K. (2004). Does long-term marriage bring less frequent disagreements?: Five explanatory frameworks. *Journal of Family Issues*, 25, 465–495. doi:10.1177/0192513X03257766

Hill, R. (1958). Generic features of families under stress. *Social Casework*, 39, 139–150. doi:10.1177/1044389458039002-318

Hipp, L. E., Kane Low, L., & van Anders, S. M. (2012). Exploring women's postpartum sexuality: Social, psychological, relational, and birth-related contextual factors. *The Journal of Sexual Medicine*, 9, 2330–2341. doi:10.1111/j.1743-6109.2012.02804.x

Holt-Lunstad, J., Birmingham, W., & Jones, B. Q. (2008). Is there something unique about marriage? The relative impact of marital status, relationship quality, and network social support on ambulatory blood pressure and mental health. *Annals of Behavioral Medicine*, 35, 239–244. doi:10.1007/s12160-008-9018-y

Igartua, K. J., Gill, K., & Montoro, R. (2003). Internalized homophobia: A factor in depression, anxiety, and suicide in the gay and lesbian population. *Canadian Journal of Community Mental Health*, 22, 15–30. doi:10.7870/cjcmh-2003-0011

Juster, R.-P., McEwen, B. S., & Lupien, S. J. (2010). Allostatic load biomarkers of chronic stress and impact on health and cognition. *Neuroscience & Biobehavioral Reviews*, 35, 2–16. doi:10.1016/j.neubiorev.2009.10.002

Karney, B. R. & Bradbury, T. N. (1995). The longitudinal course of marital quality and stability: A review of theory, method, and research. *Psychological Bulletin*, 118, 3–34.

Karney, B. R., Story, L. B., & Bradbury, T. N. (2005). Marriages in context: Interactions between chronic and acute stress among newlyweds. In T. A. Revenson, K. Kayser, & G. Bodenmann (Eds.), *Couples Coping with Stress: Emerging Perspectives on Dyadic Coping* (pp. 13–32). Washington, D.C.: American Psychological Association.

Keizer, R. & Schenk, N. (2012). Becoming a parent and relationship satisfaction: A longitudinal dyadic perspective. *Journal of Marriage and Family*, 74, 759–773. doi:10.1111/j.1741-3737.2012.00991.x

Kelley, H. H. & Thibaut, J. W. (1978). *Interpersonal Relations: A Theory of Interdependence*. New York: Wiley.

Khaddouma, A., Norona, J. C., & Whitton, S. W. (2015). Individual, couple, and contextual factors associated with same-sex relationship instability. *Couple and Family Psychology: Research and Practice*, 4, 106–125. doi:10.1037/cfp0000043

Kiecolt-Glaser, J. K., Loving, T. J., Stowell, J. R., Malarkey, W. B., Lemeshow, S., Dickinson, S. L., & Glaser, R. (2005). Hostile marital interactions, proinflammatory cytokine production, and wound healing. *Archives of General Psychiatry*, 62, 1377–1384. doi:10.1001/archpsyc.62.12.1377

Kilbourne, B. S., Howell, F., & England, P. (1990). A measurement model for subjective marital solidarity: Invariance across time, gender, and life cycle stage. *Social Science Research*, 19, 62–81. doi:10.1016/0049-089X(90)90015-B

Kluwer, E. S. & Johnson, M. D. (2007). Conflict frequency and relationship quality across the transition to parenthood. *Journal of Marriage & Family*, 69, 1089–1106. doi:10.1111/j.1741-3737.2007.00434.x

Kuhn, R., Milek, A., Meuwly, N., Bradbury, T. N., & Bodenmann, G. (2017). Zooming in: A microanalysis of couples' dyadic coping conversations after experimentally induced stress. *Journal of Family Psychology*, 31, 1063–1073. doi:10.1037/fam0000354

Lau, K. H., Randall, A. K., & Duran, N. D. (2019). Examining the effects of couples' real-time stress and coping processes on interaction quality: Language use as a mediator. *Frontiers: Personality and Social Psychology*, 9, 2598. doi:10.3389/fpsyg.2018.02598

Lawrence, E., Rothman, A. D., Cobb, R. J., Rothman, M. T., & Bradbury, T. N. (2008). Marital satisfaction across the transition to parenthood. *Journal of Family Psychology*, 22, 41–50. doi:10.1037/0893-3200.22.1.41

Lazarus, R. & Folkman, S. (1984). *Stress, Appraisal, and Coping*. New York: Springer.

LeBlanc, A. J., Frost, D. M., & Wight, R. G. (2015). Minority stress and stress proliferation among same-sex and other marginalized couples. *Journal of Marriage and Family*, 77, 40–59. doi:10.1111/jomf.12160

Ledermann, T., Bodenmann, G., Rudaz, M., & Bradbury, T. N. (2010). Stress, communication, and marital quality in couples. *Family Relations*, 59, 195–206. doi:10.1111/j.1741-3729.2010.00595.x

Lewis, R. J., Milletich, R. J., Derlega, V. J., & Padilla, M. A. (2014). Sexual minority stressors and psychological aggression in lesbian women's intimate relationships: The mediating roles of rumination and relationship satisfaction. *Psychology of Women Quarterly*, 38, 535–550. doi:10.1177/0361684313517866

McEwen, B. S. (2008). Central effects of stress hormones in health and disease: Understanding the protective and damaging effects of stress and stress mediators. *European Journal of Pharmacology*, 583, 174–185. doi:10.1016/j.ejphar.2007.11.071

Medina, A. M., Lederhos, C. L., & Lillis, T. A. (2009). Sleep disruption and decline in marital satisfaction across the transition to parenthood. *Families, Systems, & Health*, 27, 153–160. doi:10.1037/a0015762

Meier, C., Bodenmann, G., Moergeli, H., & Jenewein, J. (2011). Dyadic coping, quality of life, and psychological distress among chronic obstructive pulmonary disease patients and their partners. *International Journal of Chronic Obstructive Pulmonary Disease*, 6, 583–596. doi:10.2147/COPD.S24508

Meier, F., Milek, A., Rauch-Anderegg, V., Benz-Fragniere, C., Nieuwenboom, W., Schmid, H., & Bodenmann, G. (submitted). Fair enough? Decreased fairness in dyadic coping across the transition to parenthood associated with depression of first-time parents. PLOS ONE.

Meuwly, N., Feinstein, B. A., Davila, J., Nuñez, D. G., & Bodenmann, G. (2013). Relationship quality among swiss women in opposite-sex versus same-sex romantic relationships. *Swiss Journal of Psychology*, 72, 229–233. doi:10.1024/1421-0185/a000115

Meyer, I. H. (1995). Minority stress and mental health in gay men. *Journal of Health and Social Behavior*, 36, 38–56.

Meyer, I. H. (2003). Prejudice, social stress, and mental health in lesbian, gay, and bisexual populations: Conceptual issues and research evidence. *Psychological Bulletin*, 129, 674–697. doi:10.1037/0033-2909.129.5.674

Meyer, I. H. & Dean, L. (1998). Internalized homophobia, intimacy, and sexual behavior among gay and bisexual men. In Gregory M. Herek (Ed.), *Stigma and Sexual Orientation: Understanding Prejudice against Lesbians, Gay Men, and Bisexuals* (pp. 160–186). Thousand Oaks, CA: SAGE Publications, Inc. doi:10.4135/9781452243818.n8

Milek, A., Randall, A. K., Nussbeck, F. W., Breitenstein, C. J., & Bodenmann, G. (2017). Deleterious effects of stress on time spent together and parents' relationship satisfaction. *Journal of Couple & Relationship Therapy*, 16, 210–231. doi:10.1080/15332691.2016.1238799

Miller, R. S. (2017). *Intimate Relationships* (8th ed.). Dubuque: McGraw-Hill Education.

Milletich, R. J., Gumienny, L. A., Kelley, M. L., & D'Lima, G. M. (2014). Predictors of women's same-sex partner violence perpetration. *Journal of Family Violence*, 29, 653–664. doi:10.1007/s10896-014-9620-7

Mitnick, D. M., Heyman, R. E., & Smith Slep, A. M. (2009). Changes in relationship satisfaction across the transition to parenthood: A meta-analysis. *Journal of Family Psychology*, 23, 848–852. doi:10.1037/a0017004

Molgora, S., Acquati, C., Fenaroli, V., & Saita, E. (2018). Dyadic coping and marital adjustment during pregnancy: A cross-sectional study of Italian couples expecting their first child. *International Journal of Psychology*, 54, 277–285. doi:10.1002/ijop.12476

Neff, L. & Karney, B. R. (2004). How does context affect intimate relationships? Linking external stress and cognitive processes within marriage. *Personality and Social Psychology Bulletin*, 30, 134–148. doi:10.1177/0146167203255984

Newcomb, M. E. & Mustanski, B. (2010). Internalized homophobia and internalizing mental health problems: A meta-analytic review. *Clinical Psychology Review*, 30, 1019–1029. doi:10.1016/j.cpr.2010.07.003

O'Hara, M. W. & Wisner, K. L. (2014). Perinatal mental illness: Definition, description and aetiology. *Best Practice & Research Clinical Obstetrics & Gynaecology*, 28, 3–12. doi:10.1016/j.bpobgyn.2013.09.002

Otis, M. D., Rostosky, S. S., Riggle, E. D. B., & Hamrin, R. (2006). Stress and relationship quality in same-sex couples. *Journal of Social and Personal Relationships*, 23, 81–99. doi:10.1177/0265407506060179

Papp, L. M. & Witt, N. L. (2010). Romantic partners' individual coping strategies and dyadic coping: Implications for relationship functioning. *Journal of Family Psychology*, 24, 551–559. doi:10.1037/a0020836

Parfitt, Y. & Ayers, S. (2014). Transition to parenthood and mental health in first-time parents. *Infant Mental Health Journal*, 35, 263–273. doi:10.1002/imhj.21443

Pinquart, M. & Teubert, D. (2010). Effects of parenting education with expectant and new parents: A meta-analysis. *Journal of Family Psychology*, 24, 316–327. doi:10.1037/a0019691

Randall, A. K. & Bodenmann, G. (2009). The role of stress on close relationships and marital satisfaction. *Clinical Psychology Review*, 29, 105–115. doi:10.1016/j.cpr.2008.10.004

Randall, A. K. & Bodenmann, G. (2017). Stress and its associations with relationship satisfaction. *Current Opinion in Psychology*, 13, 96–106. doi:10.1016/j.copsyc.2016.05.010

Randall, A. K. & Messerschmitt, S. (2019). Dyadic coping as relationship maintenance. In B. Ogolsky & J. K. Monk (Eds.), Relationship maintenance: Theory, process, and context (pp. 178–193). Cambridge University Press.

Randall, A. K., Tao, C., Totenhagen, C. J., Walsh, K. J., & Cooper, A. N. (2017). Associations between sexual orientation discrimination and depression among same-sex couples: Moderating effects of dyadic coping. *Journal of Couple & Relationship Therapy*, 16, 325–345. doi:10.1080/15332691.2016.1253520

Randall, A. K., Totenhagen, C. J., Walsh, K. J., Adams, C., & Tao, C. (2017). Coping with workplace minority stress: Associations between dyadic coping and anxiety among women in same-sex relationships. *Journal of Lesbian Studies*, 21, 70–87. doi:10.1080/10894160.2016.1142353

Rauch-Anderegg, V., Kuhn, R., Milek, A., Halford, W. K., & Bodenmann, G. (2019). Relationship Behaviors across the Transition to Parenthood. *Journal of Family Issues*. 0192513X1987886-. doi: 10.1177/0192513x19878864

Rauch-Anderegg, V., Nieuwenboom, W., Halford, W. K., & Bodenmann, G. (submitted). The effect of prenatal dyadic coping and other risk factors on couples' relationship satisfaction across the transition to parenthood. PLOS ONE.

Rholes, W. S., Simpson, J. A., Campbell, L., & Grich, J. (2001). Adult attachment and the transition to parenthood. *Journal of Personality and Social Psychology*, 81, 421–435. doi:10.1037/0022-3514.81.3.421

Robles, T. F. & Kiecolt-Glaser, J. K. (2003). The physiology of marriage: Pathways to health. *Physiology & Behavior*, 79, 409–416. doi:10.1016/S0031-9384(03)00160-4

Robles, T. F., Slatcher, R. B., Trombello, J. M., & McGinn, M. M. (2014). Marital quality and health: A meta-analytic review. *Psychological Bulletin*, 140, 140–187. doi:10.1037/a0031859

Rostosky, S. S. & Riggle, E. D. B. (2002). "Out" at work: The relation of actor and partner workplace policy and internalized homophobia to disclosure status. *Journal of Counseling Psychology*, 49, 411–419. doi:10.1037/0022-0167.49.4.411

Rostosky, S. S. & Riggle, E. D. B. (2017). Same-sex couple relationship strengths: A review and synthesis of the empirical literature (2000–2016). *Psychology of Sexual Orientation and Gender Diversity*, 4, 1–13. doi:10.1037/sgd0000216

Schulz, M. S., Cowan, P. A., Cowan, C. P., & Brennan, R. T. (2004). Coming home upset: Gender, marital satisfaction, and the daily spillover of workday experience into couple interactions. *Journal of Family Psychology*, 18, 250–263. doi:10.1037/0893-3200.18.1.250

Schwartz, M. S. & Andrasik, F. (2017). *Biofeedback: A Practitioner's Guide.* New York: Guilford Press.

Selye, H. (1974). *Stress without Distress*. Philadelphia, PA: Lippincott.

Simpson, J. A., Rholes, W. S., Campbell, L., Tran, S., & Wilson, C. L. (2003). Adult attachment, the transition to parenthood, and depressive symptoms. *Journal of Personality and Social Psychology*, 84, 1172–1187. doi:10.1037/0022-3514.84.6.1172

Tao, C., Randall, A. K., & Totenhagen, C. T. (in press). Family reactions to partner stress and depression in same-sex couples: A dyadic examination of the moderating effects of dyadic coping. In J. Theiss & K. Greene (Eds.), *Relationships, Health, and Well-ness*.

Tomfohr, L. M., Buliga, E., Letourneau, N. L., Campbell, T. S., & Giesbrecht, G. F. (2015). Trajectories of sleep quality and associations with mood during the perinatal period. *Sleep*, 38, 1237–1245. doi:10.5665/sleep.4900

Totenhagen, C. J., Randall, A. K., Cooper, A. N., Tao, C., & Walsh, K. J. (2017). Stress spillover and crossover in same-sex couples: Concurrent and lagged daily effects. *Journal of GLBT Family Studies*, 13, 236–256. doi:10.1080/1550428X.2016.1203273

Totenhagen, C. J., Randall, A. K., & Lloyd, K. (2018). Stress and relationship functioning in same-sex couples: The vulnerabilities of internalized homophobia and outness. *Family Relations*, 67, 399–413. doi:10.1111/fare.12311

Totenhagen, C. J., Serido, J., Curran, M. A., & Butler, E. A. (2012). Daily hassles and uplifts: A diary study on understanding relationship quality. *Journal of Family Psychology*, 26, 719–728. doi:10.1037/a0029628

Twenge, J. M., Campbell, W. K., & Foster, C. A. (2003). Parenthood and marital satisfaction: A meta-analytic review. *Journal of Marriage and Family*, 65, 574–583. doi:10.1111/j.1741-3737.2003.00574.x

Vismara, L., Rollè, L., Agostini, F., Sechi, C., Fenaroli, V., Molgora, S., . . . Tambelli, R. (2016). Perinatal parenting stress, anxiety, and depression outcomes in first-time mothers and fathers: A 3- to 6-months postpartum follow-up study. *Frontiers in Psychology*, 7, 938. doi:10.3389/fpsyg.2016.00938

Waldinger, R. J. & Schulz, M. S. (2010). What's love got to do with it? Social functioning, perceived health, and daily happiness in married octogenarians. *Psychology and Aging*, 25, 422–431. doi:10.1037/a0019087

Weaver, K. M. (2014). *An Investigation of Gay Male, Lesbian, and Transgender Dyadic Coping in Romantic Relationships*. Louisville, KY: Spalding University.

PART III

INTERDEPENDENCE, GOAL PURSUIT, AND PERSON FACTORS

9

Autonomous Interdependence

A Complementary Understanding of Personal and Relational Needs in Interdependent Relationships

BENJAMIN W. HADDEN AND YUTHIKA U. GIRME

> Love is generally confused with dependence. Those of us who have grown in true love know that we can love only in proportion to our capacity for independence.
>
> Mr. Fred Rogers, *The World According to Mister Rogers*

Romantic relationships are highly interdependent systems that require people to navigate between their own personal interests, their partner's personal interests, and the interests of the relationship (Kelley & Thibaut, 1978; Rusbult & Agnew, 2010; Rusbult & Van Lange, 1996; Thibaut & Kelley, 1959; Van Lange & Rusbult, 2012). Because of this, one predominant line of research in relationship science focuses on situations in which personal and relational needs are opposed to each other, such as when interdependence comes at the expense of personal autonomy and agency (Feeney, 2007; Kumashiro, Rusbult, & Finkel, 2008; Visserman, Righetti, Kumashiro, & Van Lange, 2017). As noted by the late Mr. Rogers, however, personal and relational needs may be more complementary. Indeed, other perspectives in relationship science acknowledge that interdependent relationships are actually potent sources for the fulfillment of not just relational needs for intimacy, but also for personal needs that allow people to integrate and express their true selves and to effectively pursue personal goals (e.g., Knee, Hadden, Porter, & Rodriguez, 2013; Orehek & Forest, 2016). But how can personal and relational needs be both antagonistic *and* complementary?

In this chapter, we seek to organize and integrate these perspectives to highlight that whether needs are antagonistic or complementary depend on important factors. More specifically, we present a framework that contends that relationships thrive when both personal and relational needs align. However, the alignment of personal and relational needs cannot be taken for granted, and is dependent on a number of factors. To develop a better understanding of when and why needs align, we discuss (a) the distinction between personal and relational as a distinction between volitional and obligation-driven activities, (b) dyadic coordination of needs across both couple members, and (c) how to manage people's existing beliefs and expectations that pit personal and relational needs against each other. Overall, this chapter aims to shed light on the complexities of coordinating personal and relational needs in highly interdependent relationships.

WHAT ARE PERSONAL AND RELATIONAL NEEDS?

The concept of basic psychological needs – innate psychological nutriments that are essential for ongoing psychological growth, integrity, and well-being (Deci & Ryan, 2000) – has long been of interest to psychologists (Baumeister & Leary, 1995; Freud, 1920; Maslow, 1954; McDougall, 1908; Murray, 1938; Reis, Sheldon, Gable, Roscoe, & Ryan, 2000). Modern psychological perspectives have largely adopted an organismic perspective of basic psychological needs, in which needs are defined as the essential building blocks of optimal development that serve to organize and motivate behavior (see Baumeister & Leary, 1995; Deci & Ryan, 2000; Ryan & Deci, 2000). When psychological needs are met, people have a more integrated self-concept (i.e., behaviors are seen as more consistent with one's true self; Deci & Ryan, 2000), and experience more harmony and wellbeing. When needs are unmet or thwarted, people will experience a fragmented self-concept, lower wellbeing, and the development of various psychopathologies (Deci & Ryan, 2000). The organismic perspective of basic psychological needs is a dynamic model, suggesting that needs both motivate behavior and explain outcomes depending on the relative degree to which they are satisfied versus thwarted. Although researchers have proposed various basic psychological needs across most major theoretical perspectives (e.g., Aron & Aron 1997; Baumeister & Leary, 2005; Bowlby, 1969; Deci & Ryan, 2000; Feeney & Collins, 2015), for the purposes of this chapter it is important to note that most needs can be categorized as either a *personal* need for volition or a *relational* need for intimacy (e.g., Deci & Ryan, 2000; Kumashiro et al., 2008; VanderDrift & Agnew, 2012).

To understand the distinction between personal and relational needs, take a minute to imagine your perfect day. What are you picturing? Although people's specific answers are likely to differ, we would wager that two common themes emerge across responses: volitional behaviors that are meaningful and relational experiences with close others. On the one hand, you are likely thinking about activities or goal pursuits that are enjoyable or meaningful to you. These activities are something you freely engage in without feeling pressured. Maybe you see yourself sipping fine New Zealand wine or watching a late afternoon thunderstorm. Perhaps your perfect day involves pursuing goals, such as completing a 5k run or writing this chapter. Whatever the activities, they are likely pursuits that satisfy personal needs which provide you with a sense of volition, autonomy, and agency (Deci &

Ryan, 2000; Heintzelman & King, 2014), and contribute to feelings of personal growth and a sense of meaning (Aron & Aron, 1996; Feeney & Thrush, 2010). This conceptualization of personal needs is a central unifying construct that has been referred to across several psychological fields. For example, self-determination theory refers to autonomy, a sense that one has free choice to express their "true self" without fear of rejection or judgment. Attachment theory similarly argues that people have a need for independent exploration, engaging in new and novel activities of their choice (Bowlby, 1969; Feeney & Collins, 2015; Feeney & Thrush, 2010). Self-expansion theory argues that engaging in novel and fun activities helps to expand people's self-concept (Aron & Aron, 1996). Central to all of these perspectives is that individuals feel a sense of uncoerced volition and free choice to pursue in given activities, and that engaging in these types of activities are crucial for personal development and wellbeing.

On the other hand, it is also likely that you imagine spending your day with close friends, family, or a romantic partner. Maybe you see yourself having dinner with some friends or going for a stroll on the beach with a romantic partner. Perhaps your day involves pursuing relationship goals, such as taking a dance class or going on vacation together. Whatever the activities, these relational experiences likely satisfy feelings of intimacy and belongingness, which contribute to feelings of closeness and love (Aron & Aron 1997; Reis & Shaver, 1988). Indeed, close relationships are arguably the cornerstone of our lives, and, similar to our description of volition as a personal need, the fundamental need for intimacy in close relationships has served as a unifying construct across many psychological theories and perspectives. For instance, Baumeister and Leary (1995) referred to the need to belong and reviewed extensive evidence on belongingness as a vital human motivation. Self-determination theory similarly posits a need for relatedness or feelings of close personal connections (Deci & Ryan, 2000). The need for relatedness also derives from perspectives on intimacy and closeness, which reflects reciprocal responsiveness in relationships that lead individuals to feeling understood, validated, and cared for (Reis & Patrick, 1996). Finally, attachment theory refers to a need for responsive caregivers who provide feelings of a safe haven and secure base as fundamental to normative development and interpersonal functioning (Bowlby, 1969; Collins & Feeney, 2004; Hazan & Shaver, 1994).

Overall, decades of research outline that people have two basic overarching needs, a *personal* need for volition reflected in feelings of choicefulness and agency, and a *relational* need for interdependence reflected in feelings of closeness and intimacy in our close relationships. Importantly, both volition and interdependence uniquely contribute to wellness and thriving (Deci & Ryan, 2000; Feeney & Collins, 2015), and both serve as strong motivators of behavior. The importance of personal needs on the one hand and relational needs on the other can create an apparent dilemma in intimate relationships:

how do people navigate the challenge of feeling volitional while also building intimacy by meeting the needs of their partner and relationship? Unfortunately, the current discussion of personal and relational needs is largely disorganized, with research lines focusing on adopting either an antagonistic perspective in which personal and relational needs are pitted against each other, and other lines of research adopting a more complementary perspective in which personal and relational needs work together to maximize outcomes. In the following sections, we review the antagonistic and complementary views of personal and relational needs, before integrating these perspectives to identify factors that foster complementary processes in order to maximize optimal development.

AN ANTAGONISTIC PERSPECTIVE OF PERSONAL VERSUS RELATIONAL NEEDS

The apparent conundrum in balancing personal versus relational needs underlies on common theoretical perspective that there are substantial personal costs associated with maintaining highly interdependent relationships and, as such, that interdependence and independence are mutually exclusive (Kumashiro et al., 2008; Visserman et al., 2017). In other words, focusing on intimacy within the relationship means forgoing volition, or focusing on volition means neglecting the relationship. Holding this belief has a number of consequences for how people approach intimate relationships. For instance, single individuals avoid intimate relationships that conflict with the pursuit of personal needs and goals, as demonstrated by societal trends in which single people are rebuffing committed relationships and delaying marriages in order to prioritize their personal aspirations and goals (Copen, Daniels, Vespa, & Mosher, 2012). In fact, by avoiding conflicts and disagreements that are inevitable in relationships, single people high in avoidance social goals experience better life satisfaction (Girme, Overall, Faingataa & Sibley, 2016). Single people also report that singlehood offers many personal benefits that are unavailable when in a relationship, including more volition, autonomy, financial independence, and opportunities for better social networking and sexual experiences (Stein, 1975; Wang & Abbott, 2013). Single people also report more diverse social networks and better quality relationships with their family and friends compared to coupled people who are presumably restricted by the demands of spending time with their partner (Sarkisian & Gerstel, 2016).

Some relationships research has also implicitly accepted this premise, with several theories baking it into their premise. For instance, researchers have suggested that people have to work hard to balance personal versus relationship needs. According to this perspective, people have a finite amount of time and resources, and prioritizing personal needs and goals (e.g., training for a marathon) undermines the time and energy that could be spent fulfilling relational needs and goals (e.g., making a romantic dinner for your partner; Kumashiro et al., 2008; Visserman et al., 2017). In such contexts where people are forced to pit personal and relational needs against each other, people do, in fact, seek to achieve an equilibrium in their personal versus relational experiences (Kumashiro et al., 2008). Individuals who are told, for example, that they are over-dedicated to personal needs, or report that their personal needs interfere with the needs of their partner or relationship, are more motivated to restore balance by prioritizing their relational needs (Kumashiro et al., 2008). However, managing this balance is challenging, and individuals require considerable self-control in order to obtain an optimal balance (Visserman et al., 2017).

Several relationship theories and perspectives also focus explicitly on contexts in which partners' immediate self-interests conflict with each other, in which partners have to "give up" some of their personal needs in order to maintain healthy and satisfying relationships (Kelley & Thibaut, 1978; Thibaut & Kelley, 1959). According to interdependence theory, for instance, when people experience a conflict between their and their partner's immediate self-interests, they need to inhibit self-interested impulses in order to activate relationship-orientated goals and behave in ways that are best for the relationship (Kelley & Thibaut, 1978; Thibaut & Kelley, 1959). Based on this perspective, an extensive body of work in the relationship maintenance literature has demonstrated that individuals frequently hold back their thoughts and feelings in order to accommodate their partner's needs or behaviors (Rusbult, Verette, Whitney, Slovik, & Lipkus, 1991), make personal sacrifices for the sake of their partner's happiness or future goals (Van Lange et al., 1997), forgive their partners' hurtful transgressions at the cost of their own self-respect (Luchies, Finkel, McNulty, & Kumashiro, 2010), and derogate attractive alternatives to remain committed (or show others their commitment) to their current relationship (Johnson & Rusbult, 1989; Rusbult & Buunk, 1993). Furthermore, these relationship maintenance behaviors require self-regulation to inhibit self-oriented impulses (Finkel & Campbell, 2001; Finkel & Fitzsimons, 2011; Pronk, Karremans, Overbeek, Vermulst, & Wigboldus, 2010; Ritter, Karremans, & van Schie, 2010), which again highlights the challenge in balancing personal autonomy in highly interdependent relationships.

Taken together, prominent lines of research highlight an antagonistic view of personal and relationship needs, focusing on situations in which individuals often have to choose between fulfilling one or the other. The natural extension of this perspective is that optimal management of this presumed "conflict" involves strategies such as carefully balancing personal versus relationship needs (Kumashiro et al., 2008; Visserman et al., 2017), giving up personal needs in order to fulfill the needs of partners' or the relationship (Rusbult et al., 1991; Van Lange et al., 1997), or forgoing interdependent relationships altogether in order to prioritize personal needs and goals (Copen et al., 2012; Tan, Agnew, & Hadden, 2020). In other words, these lines of research highlight situations in which individuals may feel the need to choose whether they will prioritize their sense of agency and volition or their sense of interdependence and intimacy with others.

A COMPLEMENTARY PERSPECTIVE OF PERSONAL AND RELATIONAL NEEDS

Other lines of research emphasize a more harmonious view of personal and relational needs in romantic relationships, focusing on how romantic relationships are potent sources for the satisfaction of both volition and intimacy. These perspectives emphasize that, in well-functioning relationships, personal and relational needs are complementary and cyclically reinforce each other. First, we note that prior research has consistently found that personal and relational needs have been observed to be highly correlated (Deci & Ryan, 2014). For instance, daily diary research has found that when people experience satisfaction of various personal needs that reflect volition on a given day – such as authenticity, autonomy, or meaning in life – they are also likely to experience especially high levels of connection and relatedness to others (Hadden & Smith, 2019; Heppner et al., 2008; Reis et al., 2000; Ryan, Bernstein, & Brown, 2010). This suggests that, far from being a source of frustration for personal needs, interacting with close others helps facilitate the satisfaction of relational needs and feelings of volition, autonomy, and meaning. Daily diary research is particularly important for the complementary perspective being advanced in this chapter because these studies indicate that it is not simply the case that some people are better at strategically balancing their needs and thus experience greater personal and relational need satisfaction overall, but rather that personal and relational needs *co-occur* on the same day and situations and interactions that fulfill personal needs tend to simultaneously satisfy relational needs as well, and vice versa.

Co-occurrence of relational and personal needs is also well-observed within close relationships, such that relationships which fulfill personal needs simultaneously fulfill relational needs, and vice versa. If a given relationship satisfies an individuals' need for autonomy and competence, individuals also tend to report a greater sense of relatedness and security with that partner (La Guardia, Ryan, Couchman, & Deci, 2000; Patrick, Knee, Canevello, & Lonsbary, 2007). Related research on authenticity in relationships has similarly found that, when people feel authentic to themselves in their relationships, they are also likely to feel more connected to their romantic partners (Brunell et al., 2010). These co-occurrences exist at both the between-person level and the daily level, such that when people experience more autonomy and competence within their romantic relationships, they also feel more relatedness (Patrick et al., 2007). Similarly, this is also the case across different close relationships, such that if a relationship with a given person fulfills autonomy more than other close relationships in that person's life, it is also likely to fulfill relatedness to a greater extent as well (La Guardia et al., 2000).

Cyclical Nature of Personal and Relational Needs

Why is it that satisfaction of personal and relational needs tend to co-occur within romantic relationships? We suggest that there is a cyclical feedback loop between personal and relational needs, such that feelings of volition and autonomous functioning in relationships are necessary for true feelings of connection with romantic partners. Previous empirical and theoretical work outlines how, when individuals are volitionally engaged in their relationship, they are more confident in their own self-worth and do not feel that their "ego" is on the line, satisfying personal needs for competency and agency (see Hodgins & Knee, 2002 for a review). Similarly, people with higher evaluations of their self-worth are confident their partners can be trusted to react responsively, which results in people feeling comfortable with relying on and being vulnerable with their partners (Murray, Holmes, & Collins, 2006). This sense of relative security allows people to invest in and express their needs to their partners without worrying about whether such expressions will be accepted by their partner (Brunell et al., 2010; Canevello & Crocker, 2010; Hodgins & Knee, 2002; Knee, Lonsbary, Canevello, & Patrick, 2005; La Guardia et al., 2000; La Guardia & Patrick, 2008). Such a sense of self-worth and security is important for facilitating more direct and open communication of individuals' dependency needs, such as more directly expressing needs for support from their romantic partners (Don & Hammond, 2017; Murray et al., 2006; Murray, Holmes, & Griffin, 2000).

Importantly, self-disclosing important aspects of oneself creates the opportunity for increased intimacy and closeness with partners. For instance, the interpersonal process model of intimacy describes how the intimacy process is initiated when an individual self-discloses personal information to their partner (Reis & Patrick, 1996; Reis & Shaver, 1988). Key to this process is that when an individual self-discloses, their partner reacts responsively by acknowledging and validating the individual. Importantly, in order for individuals to experience increases in intimacy, the information they disclose has to be meaningful and personally relevant (Reis & Patrick, 1996; Reis & Shaver, 1988). Research has also found that emotional disclosure is more important than factual disclosure (Morton, 1978; Reis & Patrick, 1996), because emotional disclosure allows "for the most core aspects of the self to be known, understood, and validated by another" (Laurenceau, Rivera, Schaffer, & Pietromonaco, 2004, p. 63). That is, the act of revealing personally relevant information increases intimacy to the extent that an individual feels that they are revealing their authentic "true self."

Further, and demonstrating the feedback loop between relational and personal needs, feeling understood and validated by romantic partners encourages people to recognize and express their truest selves (Knee et al., 2013; Laurenceau, Barrett, & Rovine, 2005; Reis & Patrick, 1996). For instance, the degree to which partners respond to self-disclosure with unconditional positive regard and nonjudgmental acceptance of disclosures and of dependency needs increases people's feelings of volition and agency as they are encouraged to reveal more of themselves in the future (Laurenceau et al., 2004). Indeed, feeling that one cannot disclose personally relevant information results in lower feelings of volition and agency because individuals feel restricted in how authentic they can be in the relationship (Uysal, Lin, & Knee, 2010). Other relationship theories, such as attachment theory, also highlight how romantic relationships function as a base from which people can grow in meaningful ways by developing new skills and pursue important personal goals (Bowlby, 1969; Hazan & Shaver, 1994). For instance, people turn to their partners (who serve as "safe havens") for comfort and security during stressful situations (Mikulincer & Shaver, 2007). Notably, when partners are accepting of individuals' needs and offer responsive support, individuals experience increases in autonomous functioning. In one study, the more partners were accepting of an individual's need for support for a personal goal, the more likely individuals were to feel capable, engage in more independent functioning, and make progress toward their personal goals six months later (Feeney, 2007). This work highlights how romantic partners can serve to increase volition and autonomous functioning by facilitating the recognition and development of abilities and the encouragement of independent exploration and goal pursuits (Bolger, Zuckerman, & Kessler, 2000; Deci & Ryan, 2014; Feeney & Collins, 2015; Feeney & Thrush, 2010).

In turn, interactions with partners that help individuals grow in meaningful ways provide a basis for continued intimacy and relationship satisfaction. For instance, support that facilitates the effective pursuit of personal goals leads to higher perceived relationship quality (Orehek & Forest, 2016; Orehek, Forest, & Wingrove, 2018). Further, self-expansion theory (Aron & Aron, 1996; Xu, Lewandowski, & Aron, 2016) details a process by which novel activities with partners allow us to develop new skills, which then promotes relationship satisfaction. According to self-expansion theory, people have fundamental personal needs to expand their resources, perspectives, and abilities. Individuals need to grow in personally meaningful ways, develop new skills, and hone existing skills. Self-expansion theory also emphasizes that people can satisfy personal needs for growth by including close others within their self-concept, thereby assimilating the traits and characteristics of the partner into their own self-concept and experiencing greater cognitive interdependence (Agnew, Van Lange, Rusbult, & Langston, 1998). Indeed, several experiments have found that people allocate resources to a close other as they would to themselves instead of as they would to a stranger, and tend to process information about close others as if it is about themselves (e.g., Aron, Aron, Tudor, & Nelson, 1991). As such, satisfying relational needs by increasing cognitive interdependence – merging their identity with their partners – facilitates agency, competence, and growth. Self-expansion theory also emphasizes that satisfying romantic relationships are those in which partners engage in novel and challenging activities together (Xu et al., 2016).

In this sense, romantic relationships serve not just to facilitate the satisfaction of relational needs for close connections, but also as potent sources of personal need satisfaction. Moreover, rather than a sense of closeness and intimacy with one's romantic partner creating a sense of dependence that hinders people's sense of personal growth and feelings of choicefulness, agency, and volition, optimally functioning romantic relationships actually encourage such feelings (Aron & Aron, 1997; Feeney, 2007; Knee et al., 2013). As such, research on self-disclosure supports a cyclical model, in which individuals come to feel greater closeness and connection with their partner only to the extent to which they are able to fully invest their core self into the relationship, and that they feel such free expressions are supported by their partner.

Taken together, there is strong and consistent evidence across literatures and theories that personal and relational needs are highly complementary, often co-occurring such that relationships that satisfy one type of need will often satisfy the other, while relationships that thwart one type will thwart the other. Further, the body of research across a number of theoretical perspectives converges on the notion that not only are feelings of volition and feelings of intimacy not mutually exclusive, but rather, that they facilitate each other via a positive feedback loop. When people allow themselves to be vulnerable with their partners, to seek or accept help and advice, and engage in novel activities with their partners, they create opportunities to grow closer with their partners, which ultimately allows their partners to affirm and validate people's true selves and support their personal goal strivings.

INTEGRATING ANTAGONISTIC AND COMPLEMENTARY PERSPECTIVES

When understanding how people foster their personal needs within interdependent relationships, two predominant perspectives emerge: an *antagonistic perspective* that pits personal and relational needs against one another, and a *complementary perspective* in which personal and relational needs work in a cyclical feedback loop to foster optimal development. We do not believe that one perspective is more correct. Rather, we contend that these two perspectives can be readily integrated to produce a more holistic view that highlights whether personal and relational needs work together or against one another depends on important relational factors. For example, we first acknowledge that not all personal activities are volitional (e.g., going to an unfulfilling job), and that the true distinction for balance is not between personal versus relational needs but rather between obligation-driven activities and volitional activities. Second, we note that the processes of mutual facilitation of personal needs for volition and relational needs for interdependence within romantic relationships are neither inevitable nor automatic. Rather, relationships are a fundamentally dyadic phenomenon that require the coordination of both partners' needs at any given point in time. Third, we recognize the importance of people's existing beliefs and expectations, and use attachment insecurities as one example of how individuals' characteristics can shape perceptions of personal and relational needs within romantic relationships.

Personal and Relational Needs in Volitional versus Obligatory Activities

Because time, resources, and energy are limited, people must carefully prioritize their goals and seek a balance across various domains of their life (Kumashiro et al., 2008). People need to go to work to earn money, take care of household chores, spend time with friends, and pursue other personal goals they set for themselves. When in a highly interdependent romantic relationship, people must also devote significant time and attention to relationship activities and goals. However, prior research drawing on the antagonistic view has often conflated a balance between fulfilling personal needs for volition and relational needs for interdependence with a balance between activities pursued because of obligations that may not fulfill people's psychological needs (e.g., work) and activities pursued because of genuine interest that fulfill psychological needs (e.g., hobbies). That is, the domain of a given activity or goal (e.g., personal versus relational) does not cleanly line up with the degree to which it fulfills psychological needs (e.g., volition or dependence). In fact, intimate relationships themselves vary in the degree to which they are volitionally experienced versus seen as obligations (Knee et al., 2013). As we discussed above, when relationships are felt as volitional, they also satisfy feelings of relatedness, and vice versa (Patrick et al., 2007).

We suggest that a more useful distinction is between *obligational* and *volitional* activities (Deci & Ryan, 2000). Research has consistently shown that many activities that are sometimes referred to as "personal," such as work or chores, are obligations which tend to thwart both personal needs for volition and relational needs for intimacy. For example, people often experience stifling of both personal needs and relational needs during the work week and higher fulfillment of both on weekends (Reis et al., 2000; Ryan et al., 2010). On weekdays, when daily activities revolve primarily around work, personal and relational needs are thwarted, whereas these needs are more satisfied on weekends when leisure, hobbies, and socializing are primary foci. This "weekend effect" is perhaps obvious regarding the fulfillment of relational needs – but what about the fulfillment of personal needs? On workdays, an individual is focused on achieving work-related goals with colleagues rather than romantic partners or other close others, and any socializing with colleagues is itself treated as secondary. Although domains such as work are certainly personal in that they are typically done without one's romantic partner, such activities are, for many people, not freely chosen and often do not imbue a particularly high sense of volition, meaning, or authenticity (Reis et al., 2000).

However, other "personal" activities, such as leisure, are often done in conjunction with either romantic partners, friends, or family. Indeed, as noted above, engaging in fun and stimulating activities with romantic partners is beneficial for feelings of both volition and interdependence (Aron & Aron, 1996; Aron, Lewandowski, Mashek, & Aron, 2013). That is why when you imagined your perfect day at the beginning of this chapter, you likely imagined engaging in personal leisure activities with a romantic partner, friends, or family. Indeed, people often engage in joint relationship activities (e.g., movies, sporting activities, concerts, hobbies, etc.) that can be motivated for self, partner, or relationship reasons (Girme, Overall, & Faingataa, 2014). Even if you imagined an independent activity, research has shown that, when pursued independently, active partner support for hobbies enhances the degree to which individuals experience growth (Fivecoat, Tomlinson, Aron, & Caprariello, 2015). As such, romantic partners (and other close relationship partners more generally) play instrumental and vital roles in how much "personal" leisure activities, hobbies, and goals facilitate personal needs.

Of course, this is not to say that we can or even should get all of our need satisfaction from romantic partners. We cannot spend all of our time with our romantic partners, and maintaining a strong and robust social network with friends and family is vital not just for our personal wellbeing but also our romantic relationships (Agnew, 2014; Finkel, Hui, Carswell, & Larson, 2014). Thus, although it is important for people to balance their time and resources to maximizing thriving (e.g., Kumashiro et al., 2008), balance might more precisely refer to how people optimally attend to various domains of their life, including pressures created by society (e.g., spending time with family members they dislike; working for the sake of a paycheck) and more enjoyable leisure activities (e.g., spending time with a beloved romantic partner; engaging in hobbies), rather than prioritizing personal versus relational needs at any given moment.

Dyadic Coordination of Needs

Relationships are a fundamentally dyadic phenomenon that require the coordination of both partners' needs at any given point in time. Given the need to balance domains of life such as work, financial pressures, and people's social networks with one's romantic relationship, it is not always the case that partner's interests and resources will align. Take, for instance, a situation in which an individual has had a rough day at work and needs reassurance from their partner. However, their partner has to attend an important social event and is unable to provide the needed support. In such a case, the individual may have to forgo receiving support until their partner has the adequate resources and time. Alternatively, their partner may choose to sacrifice their other social commitment in order to stay home and provide the needed support. Or take another situation in which couple members have an argument, and one individual is overly critical. Their partner can respond by insulting or criticizing the individual in return, or they can defuse the situation by calmly telling the individual that they are especially hurt by what was just said. All couple members must make sacrifices or accommodate each other's missteps from time to time in order to preserve relationships, with both partners forgoing some self-interest, such as giving up time with other friends, engaging in an undesirable activity, or forgiving transgressions.

Ultimately, pro-relationship behaviors are beneficial for the success of relationships as couple members tend to each other's needs and develop intimacy (Righetti & Impett, 2017; Van Lange et al., 1997). However, although putting a partner's interests before one's own may be beneficial in the long-term, it can have mixed effects in the short-term. For example, partners who sacrifice often feel ambivalent about the sacrifice, feeling both joy and contentment at having done something good for their partners, as well as negative emotions such as irritation or resentment and seeing the relationship as an impediment to their own more immediate desires (Righetti & Impett, 2017). When couple members' interests are misaligned, voicing frustration is potentially damaging to the relationship and to partners' willingness to express their needs in the future (Feeney, 2007), but not speaking up may result in long-term frustration for oneself (Overall, Fletcher, Simpson, & Sibley, 2009). At the same time, suppressing such feelings is associated with lower feelings of authenticity and volition (Impett et al., 2012). Thus, when couple members' interests diverge – perhaps because of different desires or demands from other life contexts – people may feel a conflict between their immediate sense of volition and their closeness with their partner, such that they must prioritize either their relationship or their free expression.

The dynamics of a given relationship play an influential role in whether apparent mismatch between partners' needs in a given moment lead to a divergence between volition and interdependence. That is, optimal relational functioning relies on partners' responses and engagement across interactions, and whether couple members feel they can freely express themselves without fear of creating distance between themselves and their partner depends on how partners typically react (Knee & Reis, 2016). When feeling frustrated following a sacrifice, for instance, both the manner in which an individual voices their frustration (e.g., gently and constructively; Gottman, 1994; Rusbult, Drigotas, & Verette, 1994) and the degree to which partners react with understanding rather than critically and defensively (Deci & Ryan, 2014; Feeney, 2007; Knee et al., 2013; Knee, Hadden, & Baker, 2016; Rusbult et al., 1994) will determine the trajectory of the relationship over time. In other words, when people provide unconditional positive regard, they facilitate the intimacy-building process (Reis & Shaver, 1988), encouraging their partners' self-expression in the future. However, when people only provide conditional positive regard, withholding support and acceptance only when the individual meets some expectation or level of approval, needs for volition and interdependence are pitted against one another. When people are afraid their partners will respond negatively to intimate self-disclosure or support seeking, they are forced to choose between freely expressing themselves on one hand and risking rejection by their partner on the other.

Attachment Insecurity and Individual Differences in Need Fulfillment

Finally, partners bring with themselves life histories, lay theories, and insecurities about romantic relationships (Bowlby, 1973; Mikulincer & Shaver, 2015). These beliefs about close others play a key role in how insecure individuals manage their personal versus relational needs in intimate relationships. Unlike secure individuals who are comfortable with dependence in highly interdependent relationships, insecure individuals tend to pit their independence and interdependence needs against each other. Individuals high in *attachment avoidance* assume that close others will be unavailable or undependable (Bowlby, 1973; Mikulincer & Shaver, 2015) and, to prevent further rejection, they prioritize their independence and self-reliance over intimacy (Arriaga, Kumashiro, Finkel, VanderDrift, & Luchies, 2014; Ren, Arriaga & Mahan, 2017; Tan, Overall, & Taylor, 2012). In contrast, individuals high in *attachment anxiety* believe that they are not worthy of love (Bowlby, 1973; Mikulincer & Shaver, 2015). To establish and maintain a sense of felt security, highly anxious individuals prioritize intimacy and closeness over independence in their relationships (Mikulincer & Shaver, 2015; Ren et al., 2017).

Unfortunately, because insecure individuals prioritize either their independence or interdependence in relationships, they hinder the process of mutual facilitation of personal relational needs, ultimately resulting in lower relationship satisfaction, commitment, trust, and intimacy (Hadden, Smith & Webster, 2014; Mikulincer & Shaver, 2015; Simpson, 1990) as well as personal wellbeing, including higher self-criticism, anxiety, and depressive symptoms, and lower self-efficacy and achievement of personal goals (Cantazaro & Wei, 2010; Feeney, 2004; Shaver, Schachner, & Mikulincer, 2005). In fact, although highly avoidant individuals desire greater autonomy and independence, they tend to report a lack of autonomy in close relationships (Girme, Overall, & Hammond, 2019; Hadden, Rodriguez, Knee, DiBello, & Baker, 2016; La Guardia et al., 2000). Similarly, although highly anxious individuals yearn for intimacy at the expense of independence, they experience lower feelings of closeness and intimacy in their relationships (Hadden et al., 2016; La Guardia et al., 2000; Simpson, 1990).

Research has shown, however, that a complementary view of personal and relational needs can provide a roadmap for downregulating insecure individuals' defensive reactions and insecurities. For example, the Attachment Security Enhancement Model (Arriaga, Kumashiro, Simpson, & Overall, 2018) outlines that, in order to restore long-term security, partners of insecure people should facilitate the needs of insecure individuals that they try to rebuff (for related work on Dyadic Regulation Model of Insecurity Buffering see Overall & Simpson, 2015; Simpson & Overall, 2014). That is, avoidant individuals who reject intimacy require evidence of trust and their partners' availability, and that they can engage in enjoyable activities with their partner without feeling restricted or hindered (thus facilitating interdependence). Anxious individuals, meanwhile, require an opportunity to thrive in personal domains (thus facilitating independence; Arriaga et al., 2018).

Supporting this perspective, avoidant individuals report greater self-efficacy, more positive evaluations of their partners, and lower avoidance over time when they experience dependence safely, such as when partners demonstrate their availability and trustworthiness (Arriaga et al., 2014; Girme, Overall, Simpson, & Fletcher, 2015) or when avoidant individuals engage in relationship-enhancing activities (Stanton, Campbell, & Pink, 2017). In fact, highlighting the complementary view of personal and relational needs, partners' autonomy-sensitive support facilitates highly avoidant individuals' autonomy, which actually helps avoidant individuals commit to their relationships over time (Girme et al., 2019). Similarly, anxious individuals experience lower attachment anxiety over time when given an opportunity to pursue their personal goals, such as when partners facilitate anxious individuals' personal goal pursuits and broader sense of competence (Arriaga et al., 2014; Marigold, Holmes, & Ross, 2007). In essence, insecure individuals can become more secure over time when they come to recognize the mutually reinforcing, rather than mutually exclusive, nature of personal and relational needs.

CONCLUSION

People have fundamental and powerful needs for both personal volition and relational dependence, the fulfillment of which may at first glance appear mutually exclusive in the context of highly interdependent romantic relationships. In this chapter, we drew from a broad array of empirical evidence and theoretical perspectives to propose that, far from being mutually exclusive, volition and dependence are in fact mutually fulfilling and highly complementary processes. That is, that feelings of volition in the context of one's relationship are necessary for the development of intimacy, facilitating a number of known beneficial processes. In turn, such vulnerable actions allow partners to respond in ways that affirm each other, facilitate trust that partners will be accepting in the future, and allow individuals to effectively pursue independent goals. Of course, such processes are not inevitable; dyadic and extra-relational dynamics may hinder the cyclical process of personal and relational need fulfillment either by interrupting the process or by causing partners to perceive a divergence between personal and relational needs. Ultimately, rather than adopting an antagonistic view and seeking to balance volition versus dependence, people (and their relationships) are better off when partners adopt a complementary view and facilitate both volition and dependence.

REFERENCES

Agnew, C. R. (Ed.) (2014). *Social Influences on Romantic Relationships: Beyond the Dyad.* Cambridge: Cambridge University Press.

Agnew, C. R., Van Lange, P. A. M., Rusbult, C. E., & Langston, C. A. (1998). Cognitive interdependence: Commitment and the mental representation of close relationships. *Journal of Personality and Social Psychology, 74,* 939–954.

Aron, A. & Aron, E. N. (1997). Self-expansion motivation and including other in the self. In S. Duck (Ed.), *Handbook of Personal Relationships: Theory, Research and Interventions* (pp. 251–270). Hoboken, NJ: John Wiley & Sons Inc.

Aron, A., Aron, E. N., Tudor, M., & Nelson, G. (1991). Close relationships as including other in the self. *Journal of Personality and Social Psychology, 60,* 241–253.

Aron, A., Lewandowski, G. W., Jr., Mashek, D., & Aron, E. N. (2013). The self-expansion model of motivation and cognition in close relationships. In J. A. Simpson & L. Campbell (Eds.), *Oxford Library of Psychology. The Oxford Handbook of Close Relationships* (pp. 90–115). New York: Oxford University Press.

Aron, E. N. & Aron, A. (1996). Love and the expansion of the self: The state of the model. *Personal Relationships, 3,* 45–58.

Arriaga, X. B., Kumashiro, M., Finkel, E. J., VanderDrift, L. E., & Luchies, L. B. (2014). Filling the void: Bolstering attachment security in committed relationships. *Social Psychological and Personality Science, 5,* 398–406.

Arriaga, X. B., Kumashiro, M., Simpson, J. A., & Overall, N. C. (2018). Revising working models across time: Relationship situations that enhance attachment security. *Personality and Social Psychology Review, 22,* 71–96.

Baumeister, R. F. & Leary, M. R. (1995). The need to belong: Desire for interpersonal attachments as a fundamental human motivation. *Psychological Bulletin*, 117, 497–529.

Bolger, N., Zuckerman, A., & Kessler, R. C. (2000). Invisible support and adjustment to stress. *Journal of Personality and Social Psychology*, 79, 953–961.

Bowlby, J. (1969). *Attachment and Loss: Vol. 1. Attachment.* New York: Basic Books.

Bowlby, J. (1973). *Attachment and Loss: Vol. 2. Separation.* New York: Basic Books.

Brunell, A. B., Kernis, M. H., Goldman, B. M., Heppner, W., Davis, P., Cascio, E. V., & Webster, G. D. (2010). Dispositional authenticity and romantic relationship functioning. *Personality and Individual Differences*, 48, 900–905.

Cantazaro, A. & Wei, M. (2010). Adult attachment, dependence, self-criticism, and depressive symptoms: A test of a mediational model. *Journal of Personality*, 78, 1135–1162.

Canevello, A. & Crocker, J. (2010). Creating good relationships: Responsiveness, relationship quality, and interpersonal goals. *Journal of Personality and Social Psychology*, 99, 78–106.

Collins, N. L. & Feeney, B. C. (2004). Working models of attachment shape perceptions of social support: Evidence from experimental and observational studies. *Journal of Personality and Social Psychology*, 87, 363–383.

Copen, C. E., Daniels, K., Vespa, J., & Mosher, W. D. (2012). *First marriages in the United States: Data from the 2006–2010 National Survey of Family Growth. National Health Statistics Reports. Number 49.* Hyattsville, MD: National Center for Health Statistics.

Deci, E. L. & Ryan, R. M. (2000). The 'what' and 'why' of goal pursuits: Human needs and the self-determination of behavior. *Psychological Inquiry*, 11, 227–268.

Deci, E. L. & Ryan, R. M. (2014). Autonomy and need satisfaction in close relationships: Relationships Motivation Theory. In N. Weinstein (Ed.), *Human Motivation and Interpersonal Relationships* (pp. 53–73). New York: Springer.

Don, B. P. & Hammond, M. D. (2017). Social support in intimate relationships: The role of relationship autonomy. *Personality and Social Psychology Bulletin*, 43, 1112–1124.

Feeney, B. C. (2004). A secure base: Responsive support of goal strivings and exploration in adult intimate relationships. *Journal of Personality and Social Psychology*, 87, 631–648.

Feeney, B. C. (2007). The dependency paradox in close relationships: Accepting dependence promotes independence. *Journal of Personality and Social Psychology*, 92, 268–285.

Feeney, B. C. & Collins, N. L. (2015). A new look at social support: A theoretical perspective on thriving through relationships. *Personality and Social Psychology Review*, 19, 113–147.

Feeney, B. C. & Thrush, R. L. (2010). Relationship influences on exploration in adulthood: The characteristics and function of a secure base. *Journal of Personality and Social Psychology*, 98, 57–76.

Finkel, E. J. & Campbell, W. K. (2001). Self-control and accommodation in close relationships: An interdependence analysis. *Journal of Personality and Social Psychology*, 81, 263–277.

Finkel, E. J. & Fitzsimons, G. M. (2011). The effects of social relationships on self-regulation. In K. D. Vohs & R. F. Baumeister (Eds.), *Handbook of Self-Regulation: Research, Theory, and Applications* (pp. 390–406). New York: Guilford Press.

Finkel, E. J., Hui, C. M., Carswell, K. L., & Larson, G. M. (2014). The suffocation of marriage: Climbing Mount Maslow without enough oxygen. *Psychological Inquiry*, 25, 1–41.

Fivecoat, H. C., Tomlinson, J. M., Aron, A., & Caprariello, P. A. (2015). Partner support for individual self-expansion opportunities: Effects on relationship satisfaction in long-term couples. *Journal of Social and Personal Relationships*, 32, 368–385.

Freud, S. (1920). *A General Introduction to Psychoanalysis*. New York: Horace Liveright.

Girme, Y. U., Overall, N. C., & Faingataa, S. (2014). "Date nights" take two: The maintenance function of shared relationship activities. *Personal Relationships*, 21, 125–149.

Girme, Y. U., Overall, N. C, Faingataa, S., & Sibley, C. G. (2016). Happily single: The link between relationship status and wellbeing depends on avoidance and approach social goals. *Social Personality and Psychological Science*, 7, 122–130.

Girme, Y. U., Overall, N. C., & Hammond, M. D. (2019). Facilitating autonomy in interdependent relationships: Invisible support facilitates highly avoidant individuals' autonomy. *Journal of Family Psychology*, 33, 154–165.

Girme, Y. U., Overall, N. C., Simpson, J. A., & Fletcher, G. O. (2015). "All or nothing": Attachment avoidance and the curvilinear effects of partner support. *Journal of Personality and Social Psychology*, 108, 450–475.

Gottman, J. M. (1994). *What Predicts Divorce? The Relationship between Marital Processes and Marital Outcomes*. Hillsdale, NJ: Lawrence Erlbaum Associates, Inc.

Hadden, B. W., Rodriguez, L. M., Knee, C. R., DiBello, A. M., & Baker, Z. G. (2016). An actor–partner interdependence model of attachment and need fulfillment in romantic dyads. *Social Psychological and Personality Science*, 7, 349–357.

Hadden, B. W. & Smith, C. V. (2019). I gotta say, today was a good (and meaningful) day: Daily meaning in life as a potential basic psychological need. *Journal of Happiness Studies*, 20, 185–202.

Hadden, B. W., Smith, C. V., & Webster, G. D. (2014). Relationship duration moderates associations between attachment and relationship quality: Meta-analytic support for the temporal adult romantic attachment model. *Personality and Social Psychology Review*, 18, 42–58.

Hazan, C. & Shaver, P. R. (1994). Attachment as an organizational framework for research on close relationships. *Psychological Inquiry*, 5, 1–22.

Heintzelman, S. J. & King, L. A. (2014). Life is pretty meaningful. *American Psychologist*, 69, 561–574.

Heppner, W. L., Kernis, M. H., Nezlek, J. B., Foster, J., Lakey, C. E., & Goldman, B. M. (2008). Within-person relationships among daily self-esteem, need satisfaction, and authenticity. *Psychological Science*, 19, 1140–1145.

Hodgins, H. S. & Knee, C. R. (2002). The integrating self and conscious experience. In E. L. Deci & R. M. Ryan (Eds.), *Handbook of Self-Determination Research* (pp. 87–100). Rochester, NY: University of Rochester Press.

Impett, E. A., Kogan, A., English, T., John, O., Oveis, C., Gordon, A. M., & Keltner, D. (2012). Suppression sours sacrifice: Emotional and relational costs of suppressing emotions in romantic relationships. *Personality and Social Psychology Bulletin*, 38, 707–720.

Johnson, D. J. & Rusbult, C. E. (1989). Resisting temptation: Devaluation of alternative partners as a means of maintaining commitment in close relationships. *Journal of Personality and Social Psychology*, 57, 967–980.

Kelley, H. H. & Thibaut, J. W. (1978). *Interpersonal Relations: A Theory of Interdependence*. New York: Wiley.

Knee, C. R., Hadden, B. W., & Baker, Z. (2016). Optimal relationships as mutual fulfillment of self-determination theory's basic psychological needs. In C. R. Knee & H. T. Reis (Eds.), *Positive Approaches to Optimal Relationship Development* (pp. 30–55). Cambridge: Cambridge University Press.

Knee, C. R., Hadden, B. W., Porter, B., & Rodriguez, L. M. (2013). Self-determination theory and romantic relationship processes. *Personality and Social Psychology Review*, 17, 307–324.

Knee, C. R., Lonsbary, C., Canevello, A., & Patrick, H. (2005). Self-determination and conflict in romantic relationships. *Journal of Personality and Social Psychology*, 89, 997–1009.

Knee, R. C. & Reis, H. T. (Eds.) (2016). *Positive Approaches to Optimal Relationship Development*. Cambridge: Cambridge University Press.

Kumashiro, M., Rusbult, C. E., & Finkel, E. J. (2008). Navigating personal and relational concerns: The quest for equilibrium. *Journal of Personality and Social Psychology*, 95, 94–110.

La Guardia, J. G. & Patrick, H. (2008). Self-determination theory as a fundamental theory of close relationships. *Canadian Psychology/Psychologie Canadienne*, 49, 201–209.

La Guardia, J. G., Ryan, R. M., Couchman, C. E., & Deci, E. L. (2000). Within-person variation in security of attachment: A self-determination theory perspective on attachment, need fulfillment, and well-being. *Journal of Personality and Social Psychology*, 79, 367–384.

Laurenceau, J.-P., Barrett, L. F., & Rovine, M. J. (2005). The interpersonal process model of intimacy in marriage: A daily-diary and multilevel modeling approach. *Journal of Family Psychology*, 19, 314–323.

Laurenceau, J.-P., Rivera, L. M., Schaffer, A. R., & Pietromonaco, P. R. (2004). Intimacy as an interpersonal process: Current status and future directions. In D. J. Mashek & A. P. Aron (Eds.), *Handbook of Closeness and Intimacy* (pp. 61–78). Mahwah, NJ: Lawrence Erlbaum Associates Publishers.

Luchies, L. B., Finkel, E. J., McNulty, J. K., & Kumashiro, M. (2010). The doormat effect: When forgiving erodes self-respect and self-concept clarity. *Journal of Personality and Social Psychology*, 98, 734–749.

Marigold, D. C., Holmes, J. G., & Ross, M. (2007). More than words: Reframing compliments from romantic partners fosters security in low self-esteem individuals. *Journal of Personality and Social Psychology*, 92, 232–248.

Maslow, A. H. (1954). *Motivation and Personality*. Oxford: Harpers.

McDougall, W. (1908). *An Introduction to Social Psychology*. New York: Methuen.

Mikulincer, M. & Shaver, P. R. (2007). *Attachment in Adulthood: Structure, Dynamics, and Change.* New York: Guilford Press.

Mikulincer, M. & Shaver, P. R. (2015). The psychological effects of the contextual activation of security-enhancing mental representations in adulthood. *Current Opinion in Psychology*, 1, 18–21.

Morton, T. L. (1978). Intimacy and reciprocity of exchange: A comparison of spouses and strangers. *Journal of Personality and Social Psychology*, 36, 72–81.

Murray, H. A. (1938). *Explorations in Personality.* New York: Oxford University Press.

Murray, S. L., Holmes, J. G., & Collins, N. L. (2006). Optimizing assurance: The risk regulation system in relationships. *Psychological Bulletin*, 132, 641–666.

Murray, S. L., Holmes, J. G., & Griffin, D. W. (2000). Self-esteem and the quest for felt security: How perceived regard regulates attachment processes. *Journal of Personality and Social Psychology*, 78, 478–498.

Orehek, E. & Forest, A. L. (2016). When people serve as means to goals: Implications of a motivational account of close relationships. *Current Directions in Psychological Science*, 25, 79–84.

Orehek, E., Forest, A. L., & Wingrove, S. (2018). People as means to multiple goals: Implications for interpersonal relationships. *Personality and Social Psychology Bulletin*, 44, 1487–1501.

Overall, N. C., Fletcher, G. J. O., Simpson, J. A., & Sibley, C. G. (2009). Regulating partners in intimate relationships: The costs and benefits of different communication strategies. *Journal of Personality and Social Psychology*, 96, 620–639.

Overall, N. C. & Simpson, J. A. (2015). Attachment and dyadic regulation processes. *Current Opinion in Psychology*, 1, 61–66.

Patrick, H., Knee, C. R., Canevello, A., & Lonsbary, C. (2007). The role of need fulfillment in relationship functioning and well-being: A self-determination theory perspective. *Journal of Personality and Social Psychology*, 92, 434–457.

Pronk, T. M., Karremans, J. C., Overbeek, G., Vermulst, A. A., & Wigboldus, D. H. J. (2010). What it takes to forgive: When and why executive functioning facilitates forgiveness. *Journal of Personality and Social Psychology*, 98, 119–131.

Ren, D., Arriaga, X. B., & Mahan, E. R. (2017). Attachment insecurity and perceived importance of relational features. *Journal of Social and Personal Relationships*, 34, 446–466.

Reis, H. T. & Patrick, B. C. (1996). Attachment and intimacy: Component processes. In E. T. Higgins & A. W. Kruglanski (Eds.), *Social Psychology: Handbook of Basic Principles* (pp. 523–563). New York: Guilford Press.

Reis, H. T. & Shaver, P. (1988). Intimacy as an interpersonal process. In S. Duck, D. F. Hay, S. E. Hobfoll, W. Ickes, & B. M. Montgomery (Eds.), *Handbook of Personal Relationships: Theory, Research and Interventions* (pp. 367–389). Oxford: John Wiley & Sons.

Reis, H. T., Sheldon, K. M., Gable, S. L., Roscoe, J., & Ryan, R. M. (2000). Daily well-being: The role of autonomy, competence, and relatedness. *Personality and Social Psychology Bulletin*, 26, 419–435.

Righetti, F. & Impett, E. (2017). Sacrifice in close relationships: Motives, emotions, and relationship outcomes. *Social and Personality Psychology Compass*, 11, e12342

Ritter, S. M., Karremans, J. C., & van Schie, H. T. (2010). The role of self-regulation in derogating attractive alternatives. *Journal of Experimental Social Psychology*, 46, 631–637.

Rusbult, C. E. & Agnew, C. R. (2010). Prosocial motivation and behavior in close relationships. In M. Mikulincer & P. R. Shaver (Eds.), *Prosocial Motives, Emotions, and Behavior: The Better Angels of Our Nature* (pp. 327–345). Washington, DC: American Psychological Association.

Rusbult, C. E. & Buunk, B. P. (1993). Commitment processes in close relationships: An interdependence analysis. *Journal of Social and Personal Relationships*, 10, 175–204.

Rusbult, C. E., Drigotas, S. M., & Verette, J. (1994). The investment model: An interdependence analysis of commitment processes and relationship maintenance phenomena. In D. J. Canary & L. Stafford (Eds.), *Communication and Relational Maintenance* (pp. 115–139). San Diego, CA: Academic Press.

Rusbult, C. E. & Van Lange, P. A. M. (1996). Interdependence processes. In E. T. Higgins & A. W. Kruglanski (Eds.), *Social Psychology: Handbook of Basic Principles* (pp. 564–596). New York: Guilford Press.

Rusbult, C. E., Verette, J., Whitney, G. A., Slovik, L. F., & Lipkus, I. (1991). Accommodation processes in close relationships: Theory and preliminary empirical evidence. *Journal of Personality and Social Psychology*, 60, 53–78.

Ryan, R. M., Bernstein, J. H., & Brown, K. W. (2010). Weekends, work, and well-being: Psychological need satisfactions and day of the week effects on mood, vitality, and physical symptoms. *Journal of Social and Clinical Psychology*, 29, 95–122.

Ryan, R. M. & Deci, E. L. (2000). Self-determination theory and the facilitation of intrinsic motivation, social development, and well-being. *American Psychologist*, 55, 68–78.

Sarkisian, N. & Gerstel, N. (2016). Does singlehood isolate or integrate? Examining the link between marital status and ties to kin, friends, and neighbors. *Journal of Social and Personal Relationships*, 33, 361–384.

Shaver, P. R., Schachner, D. A., & Mikulincer, M. (2005). Attachment style, excessive reassurance seeking, relationship processes, and depression. *Personality and Social Psychology Bulletin*, 31, 343–359.

Simpson, J. A. (1990). Influence of attachment styles on romantic relationships. *Journal of Personality and Social Psychology*, 59, 971–980.

Simpson, J. A. & Overall, N. C. (2014). Partner buffering of attachment insecurity. *Current Directions in Psychological Science*, 23, 54–59.

Stanton, S. C. E., Campbell, L., & Pink, J. C. (2017). Benefits of positive relationship experiences for avoidantly attached individuals. *Journal of Personality and Social Psychology*, 113, 568–588.

Stein, P. J. (1975). Singlehood: An alternative to marriage. *The Family Coordinator*, 24, 489–503.

Tan, K., Agnew, C. R., & Hadden, B. W. (2020). Seeking and ensuring interdependence: Desiring commitment and the strategic initiation and maintenance of close relationships. *Personality and Social Psychology Bulletin*, 46, 36–50.

Tan, R., Overall, N. C., & Taylor, J. K. (2012). Let's talk about us: Attachment, relationship-focused disclosure, and relationship quality. *Personal Relationships*, 19, 521–534.

Thibaut, J. W. & Kelly, H. H. (1959). *The Social Psychology of Groups*. Oxford: John Wiley.

Uysal, A., Lin, H. L., & Knee, C. R. (2010). The role of need satisfaction in self-concealment and well-being. *Personality and Social Psychology Bulletin*, 36, 187–199.

Van Lange, P. A. M. & Rusbult, C. E. (2012). Interdependence theory. In P. A. M. Van Lange, A. W. Kruglanski, & E. T. Higgins (Eds.), *Handbook of Theories of Social Psychology* (Vol. 2, pp. 251–272). Thousand Oaks, CA: Sage. doi:10.4135/9781446249222.n39

Van Lange, P. A. M., Rusbult, C. E., Drigotas, S. M., Arriaga, X. B., Witcher, B. S., & Cox, C. L. (1997). Willingness to sacrifice in close relationships. *Journal of Personality and Social Psychology*, 72, 1373–1395.

VanderDrift, L. E. & Agnew, C. R. (2012). Need fulfillment and stay–leave behavior: On the diagnosticity of personal and relational needs. *Journal of Social and Personal Relationships*, 29, 228–245.

Visserman, M. L., Righetti, F., Kumashiro, M., & Van Lange, P. A. M. (2017). Me or us? Self-control promotes a healthy balance between personal and relationship concerns. *Social Psychological and Personality Science*, 8, 55–65.

Wang, H. & Abbott, D. A. (2013). Waiting for Mr. Right: The meaning of being a single educated Chinese female over 30 in Beijing and Guangzhou. *Women's Studies International Forum*, 40, 222–229.

Xu, X., Lewandowski, G. W., & Aron, A. (2016). The self-expansion model and optimal relationship development. In C. R. Knee & H. T. Reis (Eds.), *Positive Approaches to Optimal Relationship Development* (pp. 79–100). Cambridge: Cambridge University Press.

10

Pursuing Interpersonal Value

An Interdependence Perspective

EDWARD P. LEMAY, JR.

The success of our interpersonal interactions and relationships often depends on how we are viewed by others. Others' impressions of us can determine whether we are approached, helped, and invited, or, conversely, avoided, neglected, and excluded. Their evaluations can determine whether a close relationship flourishes and persists. Given their interpersonal significance, it should come as no surprise that people often care about the impressions and evaluations others have of them, and often try to create positive impressions (Goffman, 1959; Leary, 1994; Leary & Baumeister, 2000; Schlenker, 2003). This concern with how others view the self can be found across all levels of acquaintanceship. In the early stages of relationship formation, people often monitor the behavior of potential relationship partners for signs of their interest in and regard for them, such as whether potential partners seem to care about their needs, reciprocate prosocial gestures, and have positive evaluations of their qualities (Clark, Dubash, & Mills, 1998; Condon & Crano, 1988; Lydon, Jamieson, & Holmes, 1997). Within the context of established close relationships, people report wanting their partners to view them positively in many domains, even more positively then they view themselves (Murray, Holmes, & Griffin, 2000). This is particularly true in domains that are relevant to the partner's approval (e.g., physical attractiveness for dating partners). In these domains, people are especially likely to engage in self-presentation to elicit positive evaluations from their partners (Swann, Bosson, & Pelham, 2002). These findings suggest that most people care about their *relational value* – the extent to which they are viewed as valuable relationship partners (Leary & Baumeister, 2000) – and make efforts to maintain it.

The current chapter describes a new program of research examining *interpersonal value goals* and their role in interpersonal relationships. Interpersonal value goals are goals to be valued as a relationship partner, which may be activated in both romantic and platonic relationship contexts. They include goals to receive positive evaluations, liking, inclusion, or approval from others, the receipt of which suggests that others are interested in forming or maintaining a social bond. Within close relationships, interpersonal value goals may also include goals to have partners who are committed to maintaining a relationship with the self, who express their commitment through prosocial acts, and who follow communal norms for close relationships (Clark & Mills, 2011). These are all indicators that others desire to forge or maintain close relationships with the self and, therefore, that one is valued as a relationship partner. Importantly, interpersonal value goals are distinct from desires to connect with others, as reflected in constructs such as attraction, communal motivation, and relationship commitment (e.g., Berscheid & Walster, 1978; Clark & Mills, 2011; Rusbult & Buunk, 1993). Interpersonal value goals most directly concern what people want from others, rather than how people feel about others, and they are much less frequently studied relative to these other constructs. Below I outline novel hypotheses regarding interpersonal value goals and describe how these predictions diverge from constructs that appear to be related. Then I describe recent empirical tests of these predictions.

INTERPERSONAL VALUE GOALS, INTERACTION, AND RELATIONSHIPS

The adoption of interpersonal value goals may have far-reaching effects on social interactions and relationships, shaping each person's thoughts, motivations, and behaviors.

Interpersonal value goals may motivate prosocial behavior and interpersonal responsiveness, which are behaviors that convey care, positive regard, and understanding (Reis, Clark, & Holmes, 2004). That is, people who want to be valued by others may engage in behaviors that appear prosocial and responsive to others' needs. Both interdependence and learning theories may be useful for understanding why adopting interpersonal value goals should have this prosocial effect. According to interdependence theory and related perspectives, people's ability to satisfy their goals is often dependent on the behaviors of relationship partners, and so achievement of personal goals may often require coordinating with partners, maintaining satisfying relationships with partners over time, and persuading partners to enact behaviors that will be conducive to goal achievement (Fitzsimons, Finkel, & Vandellen, 2015; Kelley & Thibaut, 1978; Reis & Arriaga, 2015; Rusbult & Van Lange, 2003). In such cases, satisfying one's own goals may often require satisfying goals or contingencies held by a relationship partner. This is particularly true for the goal to be valued by partners, a goal whose achievement is ultimately entirely dependent on the partner's responses. In other words, the goal to be valued reflects high dependence and partner control (Rusbult & Van Lange, 2003).

Learning theories (e.g., Bandura, 1977a, 1977b) are useful for understanding why, in the context of this dependence, people typically choose prosocial behavior as a means to persuade their partners to value them. Through their history of interaction with others, most people should have learned that prosocial behavior elicits others' positive sentiments. Indeed, many studies suggest that other people respond to prosocial behavior with positive regard, reciprocated prosocial behavior, and other indicators that they value prosocial individuals (Buunk & Schaufeli, 1999; Gouldner, 1960; Kenny & la Voie, 1982; Murray, Holmes, & Collins, 2006; Reis et al., 2004). Hence, most people should have had many experiences in which others responded to their prosocial behavior by communicating that they are valued. This should be particularly true in communal relationships, relationships in which members are expected to enact prosocial and supportive acts, which characterizes most close relationships (Clark & Lemay, 2010). People may also learn that prosocial behavior is valued by observing real or fictitious relationships involving other people (Bandura, Ross, & Ross, 1963; Cialdini, Baumann, & Kenrick, 1981; Prot et al., 2014). For example, people may observe prosocial actors receiving acceptance and favors on television, or observe the way relationship partners praise the prosocial behaviors of other people in their social networks.

After an accumulation of these learning experiences, most people may eventually endorse a lay theory (i.e., an explicit belief about the world) positing that enacting prosocial behavior is an effective way to persuade others to value the self. This belief, in turn, may guide people to enact prosocial behaviors when they try to be valued by others. Indeed, beliefs about the degree to which actions can satisfy goals, or "utility beliefs," tend to guide the strategies people select to accomplish their goals (Eccles & Wigfield, 2002). For example, given that John had many interactions in which his kindness was rewarded with signs that he is valued by others, he should develop explicit beliefs that being kind is a useful way to get others to value him. Consequently, he may rely on kindness as a strategy when he wants to be valued by Mary.

Through repeated interactions with particular partners, people may also learn the contingencies that must be met to be valued by those specific partners. When Mary's expressions of her valuing of John depend on John's enactment of prosocial behavior toward Mary, John may develop beliefs, perhaps often unconscious or unarticulated beliefs, that enacting prosocial behavior is a useful strategy to be valued by Mary. Over time, these beliefs may automatically impel John to enact prosocial behavior when his goals to be valued by Mary are activated. This prediction is consistent with learning theories, which suggest that people come to enact behaviors that have been directly or vicariously rewarded in the past, particularly when they are seeking those rewards in the present (Bandura, 1977a; Batson & Powell, 2003; Cialdini et al., 1981). Furthermore, this prediction is consistent with interdependence theoretical perspectives positing that people often enact prosocial behavior as a result of overlearned contingencies, social norms, and awareness of the implications of their prosocial behavior for satisfying their own needs (Kelley & Thibaut, 1985). People may not be aware of the impact of these learning experiences on their decisions to use prosocial behavior as a strategy to be valued by their partners. The structure of interdependence can shape behavior even when people are not aware of its influence (Reis & Arriaga, 2015).

Due to these learning experiences, interpersonal value goals may also elicit prosocial, other-oriented motivations. Although the goal to be valued by others seems to most directly reflect self-interest (i.e., a concern with obtaining something of value from others for the self) (Crocker, Canevello, & Brown, 2017), it may typically activate prosocial goals that involve consideration of others' welfare. For example, people who want to be valued may become motivated to care for a relationship partner's needs, termed communal motivation (Clark & Lemay, 2010). Similarly, they may adopt compassionate goals, which are goals to enact behaviors that will benefit others' welfare (Crocker & Canevello, 2008). They may adopt these goals because they have learned from prior interactions that others respond positively to prosocial motivation. Given that prosocial behavior and motivation bolster relationship quality (Clark & Lemay, 2010; Crocker et al., 2017; Le, Impett, Lemay, Muise, & Tskhay, 2018; Lemay, Clark, & Feeney, 2007; Reis et al., 2004), these prosocial responses may serve as pathways through which adopting interpersonal value goals can improve the quality of relationships.

This prediction that one type of goal can activate another is consistent with Goal Systems Theory, which posits that goals activate subordinate goals that serve as means to their fulfillment (Kruglanski et al., 2002). The possibility that prosocial goals may be activated by a desire to be valued is also congruent with interdependence perspectives suggesting that, because self-interest is dependent on partner responses within interdependent relationships, pursuit of self-interested motives can cause people to care for their partner's needs and promote their partner's welfare, and give rise to genuine altruistic motivations (Kelley & Thibaut, 1985; Reis & Arriaga, 2015). For example, people may become motivated to care for others or enact pro-relationship behaviors as indirect ways of satisfying the goal of maintaining relationships that are personally rewarding (Van Lange et al., 1997; Yovetich & Rusbult, 1994). They may not even be aware of the self-centered origins of their prosocial motivation due to the automatic and unconscious nature through which people apply overlearned social rules (Bargh, 1994; Kelley & Thibaut, 1985; Reis & Arriaga, 2015). Hence, people may adopt communal motivation or compassionate goals when they want to be valued by their partner and feel entirely altruistic throughout the process.

Interpersonal value goals may also produce positive illusions in relationships. People tend to see the world in ways that confirm their own desires

(Kunda, 1990), and this extends to their perceptions of their interpersonal relationships (Gagne & Lydon, 2001; Lemay & Clark, 2015; Murray, Holmes, & Griffin, 1996; Rusbult, Van Lange, Wildschut, Yovetich, & Verette, 2000). Given this readiness to see relationships in desired ways, people who want to be valued by others may often come to believe that they are valued. That is, they may exaggerate their partner's positive regard, care, or commitment, and perceive their partner's behaviors as reflecting more of these sentiments than what might be inferred by impartial observers. In turn, given that feeling confident in a partner's regard, care, and commitment often bolsters relationship quality (Lemay & Clark, 2015; Murray et al., 2000; Reis et al., 2004), these positive illusions could have downstream benefits for relationships.

Beyond these within-person effects, the goal to be valued may also have *interpersonal effects*. Specifically, by pursuing positive regard or acceptance from others, people may elicit more positive evaluations and prosocial motivations in others. This may occur because, according to the predictions outlined above, people who want to be valued enact prosocial behaviors and adopt prosocial goals. In turn, given that prosocial responses typically elicit positive sentiments and reciprocation of prosocial behaviors in others (Buunk & Schaufeli, 1999; Gouldner, 1960; Kenny & la Voie, 1982; Murray et al., 2006; Reis et al., 2004), partners who are the beneficiaries of these prosocial responses should develop more positive regard, desires to forge or maintain bonds, and motivations to reciprocate with prosocial behaviors of their own. Furthermore, people who adopt the goal to be valued may enact more idiosyncratic behaviors that are tuned to a particular partner, including behaviors that meet the partner's idiosyncratic needs, desires, and evaluative standards. Through these mechanisms, interpersonal value goals may often be successfully pursued; people who want to be valued may often achieve this goal. Of course, this process rests on people's ability to identify and enact behaviors that render them more valuable to others. In some cases, this may not be true (e.g., someone who uses warmth as a means to be valued by a partner who does not respond positively to warmth). In such cases, the pursuit of interpersonal value may be unsuccessful in eliciting positive sentiments in partners. Knowledge of the contingencies of interpersonal value in the immediate situation, and an ability to satisfy those contingencies, may often be important for successfully pursuing interpersonal value goals.

OTHER PERSPECTIVES SUGGESTING HARMFUL CONSEQUENCES OF INTERPERSONAL VALUE GOALS

Other lines of research suggest that people experience strained interpersonal relationships when they care about, or try to manage, how they are viewed by others. However, in each case, the measure of this construct does not appear to assess interpersonal value goals in isolation. Although other examples could be described, in the following section I describe two that seem to most explicitly imply that adopting the goal to be valued is destructive.

Feeney, Noller, and Hanrahan (1994) developed a measure that they entitled "need for approval," which was described as assessing respondents' needs for acceptance and confirmation from others (Fossati et al., 2003). In contrast to the predictions outlined above for interpersonal value goals, greater need for approval, as assessed with this measure, was associated with lower marital commitment (Ehrenberg, Robertson, & Pringle, 2012), greater discomfort with closeness (Bekker, Bachrach, & Croon, 2007; Corcoran & Mallinckrodt, 2000; Karantzas, Feeney, & Wilkinson, 2010), less security in relationships (Bekker et al., 2007; Corcoran & Mallinckrodt, 2000; Feeney et al., 1994; Karantzas et al., 2010), ineffective conflict resolution styles (Corcoran & Mallinckrodt, 2000), and passive-aggressive behavior (Bekker et al., 2007). A close look at the measure, however, suggests that it assesses much more than the need for approval, such as the inability to make independent decisions (including the item, "I find it hard to make a decision unless I know what other people think"), low self-esteem (including the item, "Sometimes I think I am no good at all"), and doubts about one's interpersonal value (including the item, "I wonder why people would want to be involved with me") (Feeney et al., 1994; Karantzas et al., 2010). These other constructs, rather than a desire for approval, may drive these negative effects. Indeed, low self-esteem and doubts about one's value have been associated with reduced relationship quality, such as perceived devaluation by partners and derogation of partners (Murray et al., 2006). People who score high on this need for approval measure may have an insatiable desire to be valued – wanting others' approval but usually believing that they do not have it. In addition, their chronic doubts may render them so sensitive to interpersonal devaluation that their partners learn that they must be extraordinarily cautious around them and withhold criticism, which can undermine relationship quality (Lemay & Dudley, 2011). Insecurity about being valued is distinct from the goal to be valued, and I expect that, when they are not confounded, the goal to be valued usually has benefits for relationships.

Research on self-image goals provides another example of findings that, on the surface, suggest that it is destructive to pursue positive regard from others or try to manage others' views of the self. According to Crocker and Canevello (2008), self-image goals are goals to construct, maintain, or defend desired public and private images of the self to obtain something for the self. This construct seems similar to interpersonal value goals. Indeed, the measure of self-image goals used in most of this research includes items that seem to overlap with interpersonal value goals, such as items assessing goals to avoid rejection, avoid criticism, and get others to acknowledge one's positive qualities, and self-image goals have been described in similar ways, such as "approach goals to obtain status or approval" (Erickson et al., 2018, p. 2) and goals for others to "see oneself as valuable and worthy" (Duarte & Pinto-Gouveia, 2015, p. 810). Furthermore, according to Canevello and Crocker (2015), "when people have self-image goals, they try to manage how others see them and convince others that they possess desirable qualities and lack undesirable qualities to get what they want from others" (p. 620). This seems to be what people typically do when they have goals to be valued by others, such as goals to be liked, evaluated positively, or accepted, all of which suggest wanting something from others and, often, a need to demonstrate desirable qualities to obtain these outcomes. However, in contrast to the predictions outlined above, adopting self-image goals has been associated with low interpersonal trust (Crocker & Canevello, 2008), reduced perceptions of social support (Crocker & Canevello, 2008), more interpersonal conflict (Crocker & Canevello, 2008; Moeller, Crocker, & Bushman, 2009), reduced responsive-ness in relationsihps (Canevello & Crocker, 2010; Hadden & Knee, 2015), more negative regard for others (Canevello & Crocker, 2011), and lower relationship quality (Canevello & Crocker, 2010).

Once again, however, a close look at the measure used in this work suggests that it is different from interpersonal value goals. The measure appears to include items assessing goals to avoid imperfections ("avoid the possibility of being wrong"; "avoid taking risks or making mistakes"; "avoid showing your weaknesses"), and goals to dominate others ("convince others that you are right"; "get others to do things my way"), which are not the same constructs as goals to be viewed positively or manage others impressions. Furthermore, prior research on both perfectionism (Hewitt et al., 2003; Lopez & Rice, 2006; Mackinnon et al., 2012) and dominance (Hamby, 1996; Reis et al., 2004; Sadikaj, Moskowitz, & Zuroff, 2016) suggests that these constructs are associated with poor psychological and interpersonal functioning. Given the inclusion of these types of items, self-image goals may have more negative effects relative to interpersonal value goals.

In fact, in many cases, people who want to be valued by others may behave in ways that are antithetical to perfectionistic and dominant behavior. For example, people who want to be valued by others sometimes reveal their mistakes to appear modest (Tice, Butler, Muraven, & Stillwell, 1995), disclose vulnerabilities so they seem humble, so others known them, or to elicit support (Clark & Finkel, 2005; Collins & Feeney, 2000; Hack-enbracht & Tamir, 2010; Laurenceau, Barrett, & Pietromonaco, 1998), and yield to others' wishes and agree with their opinions (Chen, Shechter, & Chaiken, 1996; Gordon, 1996; Jones, 1964). Hence, it seems clear that pursuing interpersonal value is distinct from self-image goals, may not consistently elicit the tactics included in the self-image goals measure, and may have distinct effects on many relationship outcomes. In the following section, I summarize a new program of research that has tested some of these ideas.

EXPERIMENTAL STUDIES EXAMINING CONSEQUENCES OF INTERPERSONAL VALUE GOALS

Three experimental studies supported predictions regarding prosocial consequences of goals to create a positive impression in others. In the first study, a sample of undergraduate college students completed measures with regard to a casual acquaintance under two levels of a within-subjects goal manipulation. In the high impression management condition, participants were instructed to adopt the goal of trying to get the acquaintance to "view you in a desirable way so that he/she approves of you, wants to include you in his/her activities, and wants to be your friend." In the low impression management condition, participants instead adopted the goal of "not caring what [acquaintance name] thinks of you, and being uninterested in making any particular impression on this person." Participants completed a measure of compassionate goals (e.g., "I want to make a positive difference in his/her life"; Crocker & Canevello, 2008) and responsiveness (e.g., "I want to make this person feel valued as a person"; Canevello & Crocker, 2010) toward the acquaintance under each of these goal instructions. Consistent with the view that impression management goals foster, rather than undermine, prosocial orientation, compassionate goals and responsiveness intentions were higher when completed under high, relative to low, impression management instructions. When participants assumed that they wanted to create a positive impression, they more readily endorsed compassionate goals and intentions to be responsive.

Two additional studies examined the effects of interpersonal value goals in ongoing social interaction. Participants were asked to engage in a video recorded interaction with a stranger in one study, and with a known relationship partner (i.e., friends or romantic partners) in the other study. In both studies, one member of each pair was randomly assigned to the role of "actor," and the other was assigned as "partner." Actors were further randomly assigned to the control condition or the impression management condition. Actors in the impression management conditions were instructed to adopt a goal to manage impressions during their interaction with their study partner, including the goal to try to be liked by the other (in the study of stranger interactions) and the goal to earn positive regard from the other (in the study of known partner interactions). Actors in the control conditions, and all partners, did not receive special instructions. After the interaction, actors and partners completed a battery of self-report measures. In addition, a panel of objective observers who were blind to experimental condition viewed the recorded interactions and made judgments regarding actors' behavior. The observers rated actors on their responsive behavior during the interaction, such as warm and friendly behavior, expressing positive regard, and listening to their partners.

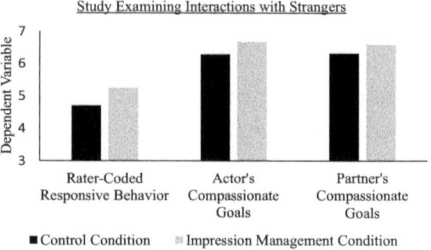

FIGURE 10.1 Responsive behavior and compassionate goals as a function of experimental condition during interactions with strangers

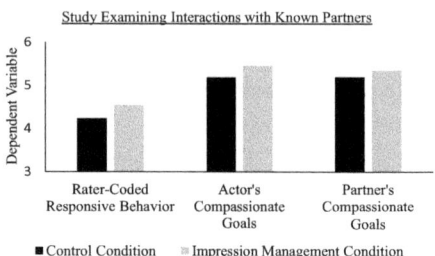

FIGURE 10.2 Responsive behavior and compassionate goals as a function of experimental condition during interactions with known partners

Results are presented in Figures 10.1 and 10.2. In both studies, actors instructed to adopt impression management goals were viewed as significantly more responsive by the objective observers, relative to actors in the control condition. Actors in the impression management condition also reported significantly more compassionate goals in both studies following the interaction, suggesting that their goal to be valued triggered other-oriented goals to care for the partner's welfare. Furthermore, partners interacting with these actors reported marginally higher compassionate goals toward actors (Study 1) and positive regard for actors (Study 2) in the impression management condition than toward actors in the control condition. These results suggest that the goal to persuade others to develop positive impressions of oneself elicits prosocial behavior, prosocial motivation, and more positive responses in partners. Although not all effects reached conventional significance levels, none of the effects supported the alternative argument that trying to manage others' impressions elicits negative responses in partners.

Additional analyses tested predictions regarding positive illusions. As discussed earlier, people who want to be valued by others may develop illusions that they are valued. In the experimental study of interactions with strangers, actors reported on their perceptions of the interaction partner's attraction to them and compassionate goals toward them. Relative to actors in the control condition, actors in the impression management goal condition reported greater confidence (marginally significant) that partners were attracted to them, and thought that partners more strongly endorsed compassionate goals toward them (significant). Importantly, this was the case even after statistically controlling for the interaction partner's self-reported attraction and compassionate goals toward actors, which suggests that actors' adoption of impression management goals biased their perceptions of partners' attraction and compassionate goals. These results suggest that actors who were trying to be viewed positively were more confident that they were, in fact, viewed positively, independently of whether they actually were viewed more positively. This pattern suggests wishful thinking. In the study of interactions with known partners, this effect emerged for women, but not for men. Women were more confident in their partner's positive regard when they were trying to be valued by them, relative to women in the control condition.

In both of these interaction studies, actors also completed Crocker and Canevello's (2008) measure of self-image goals with regard to the interaction. In neither study did actors report significantly stronger adoption of self-image goals when they were instructed to manage a positive impression, relative to actors in the control condition. These results suggest a distinction between adopting impression management goals and the tactics represented in the self-image goals measure.

CONSEQUENCES OF INTERPERSONAL VALUE GOALS IN EVERYDAY LIFE

The interaction studies described above support the view that trying to be valued by others elicits increased prosocial behavior and compassionate goals using experimental methods, which are useful for establishing causal effects of interpersonal value goals. However, the studies took place in a laboratory, which may create concerns that the findings do not generalize to everyday social interactions. Hence, I sought to test the predictions in a more ecologically valid context using daily experience sampling methodology, a method that permits examination of naturally occurring interpersonal experiences in the context of everyday life. Both members of 200 romantic relationships reported on their relationship experiences each day for fourteen days. Participants completed items assessing their daily adoption of interpersonal value goals (e.g., "Today, I wanted [partner name] to view me positively"; "Today I wanted my partner to be committed to our relationship"), and items from the self-image goals scale to assess daily self-image goals (e.g., "Today, in my relationship with [partner name], I wanted to avoid the possibility of being wrong"; "Today, I wanted to get [partner name] to do things my way"). They also reported on their prosocial behavior toward their partner each day, such as considerate, warm, and supportive behaviors, their compassionate goals toward their partner, and their global evaluation of their partner.

Predictions were tested using actor–partner interdependence models (Kenny, Kashy, & Cook, 2006). In these models, the goals reported by both partners were modeled as predicting each partner's outcome variables, which allows for examining both intrapersonal and interpersonal effects of goals. For example, does John's goal to be positively regarded by Mary on a particular day predict John's own prosocial behavior toward Mary on that day? Does John's goal also predict Mary's prosocial behavior toward John on that day? Results from these models largely supported the predictions outlined above. Participants were more likely to adopt compassionate goals and enact prosocial behavior on days when they were trying to be valued by their partners. In addition, they were more likely to adopt compassionate goals, enact prosocial behavior, and evaluate their partners positively on days when their partner was trying to be valued by them. These latter effects suggest that, when people are trying to be valued by their partners, they effectively elicit prosocial behavior and more positive sentiments from their partners. The pattern of results was the same regardless of whether I examined just the pursuit of positive regard, or whether I also included other indicators of wanting to be valued by others in the index (e.g., wanting others' commitment and care).

One of the limitations of these findings is that they are associations between variables measured at the same time, which are vulnerable to a variety of alternative explanations involving reversed causation and common causal variables. Prospective effects provide more convincing evidence while addressing some of these alternative explanations. In the prospective models, goals adopted on each day (day d) were modeled as predicting change in outcomes measured the following day (day $d+1$). These models also supported predictions. Participants who tried to be valued by their partners on a particular day were more likely to enact prosocial behavior and adopt compassionate goals the following day. In addition, their partners were more likely to adopt compassionate goals and evaluate them positively the following day.

Daily self-image goals (items adapted from Crocker & Canevello, 2008) were controlled in all of these analyses, which had a nearly opposite pattern of effects. For example, those who adopted self-image goals on a given day were less likely to enact prosocial behavior that day. Furthermore, they had partners who evaluated them more negatively and were lower in compassionate goals. These results support the prediction that self-image goals and the goal to be valued have distinct effects on interpersonal processes.

Additional analyses found support for predictions regarding the biasing effects of interpersonal value goals on cognition. Participants who wanted to be valued by their partners on a particular day felt more confident that they were positively regarded and cared for by their partners on that day, and this effect was found even after controlling for their partner's self-reported sentiments. In other words, participants felt more valued when they wanted to be valued, a pattern suggesting wishful thinking.

I also examined potential reversed causal effects in which daily prosocial behavior and compassionate goals predict increases in adoption of interpersonal value goals the following day. These effects may reflect the fact that, when people invest in their relationships, such as by adopting compassionate goals and enacting prosocial behavior, it increases their felt dependence on the relationship (Rusbult & Buunk, 1993), which then heightens their desire to be valued by their partners. If this were the case, it would suggest mutually reinforcing processes in which the goal to be valued both contributes to and arises from prosocial responses to partners. I found evidence supporting such reversed effects. People who were especially prosocial to their partners or adopted compassionate goals on a particular day were especially likely to want to be valued by their partners the following day. Different results were obtained for self-image goals. People who adopted compassionate goals on a particular day tended to decrease in their adoption of self-image goals the following day. Perhaps these individuals became disinterested in adopting harmful self-image goals (i.e., perfectionism, dominance) after their prosocial responses because these responses gave them reason to expect that their partners were satisfied with them, or functioned as a form of investment in the relationship that bolstered a desire for intimacy and harmony. These results suggest mutually reinforcing links between interpersonal value goals, but not self-image goals, and prosocial motivation. Interpersonal value goals appear to heighten people's tendencies to invest in their relationships via prosocial responses to their partners, which appears to reinforce the desire to be valued by partners. These processes may partially explain the temporal stability of interpersonal value goals over time. Interpersonal value goals may be stable over time, in part because the prosocial means people enact to pursue interpersonal value constitute a type of relationship investment that reinforces the expectancy and importance of being valued by the partner.

EVIDENCE FOR MECHANISMS

People may enact prosocial behavior when they want to be positively regarded by others because they have observed many social interactions in which prosocial behavior was rewarded with positive responses from others, leading them to adopt lay theories, or explicit beliefs, that prosocial behavior is an effective means of earning positive evaluation from others. In turn, these beliefs may guide people into selecting prosocial behavior as a strategy when they want to be valued by others.

The daily experience study described above provided support for these predictions. I developed a new measure assessing participants' endorsement of lay theories positing that prosocial behavior elicits positive sentiments in others (e.g., "Behaving in a helpful or supportive way will get others to like you"; "Being kind and considerate toward others is a reliable way to earn their acceptance"). Supporting the view that most people endorse these lay theories, the average score on this measure was well above the scale midpoint, reflecting general agreement with these statements. Indeed, only a few participants tended to disagree with them. Furthermore, endorsement of these lay theories moderated the effects of interpersonal value goals. Daily adoption of interpersonal value goals was associated with prosocial behavior and adoption of compassionate goals more strongly for participants who strongly endorsed these lay theories, relative to participants whose endorsement was weaker. These results suggest that explicit lay theories regarding the instrumentality of prosocial behavior, in terms of its ability to increase the extent to which others value the self, motivate prosocial behavior when people want to be valued by others.

As described earlier, experiences within specific relationships may also be important in shaping how people pursue the goal of being valued by partners. When Mary regularly rewards John's prosocial behavior with expressions of affection, pleasure, and positive regard, John may come to associate his prosocial behavior with being valued by Mary, and therefore enact prosocial behavior when he wants Mary to value him. The 14-day daily diary study described above was used to test this possibility. Using the first 7 days of data, I calculated several indices capturing the extent to which participants had partners who rewarded their daily prosocial behavior. Specifically, I calculated three within-dyad correlations capturing association across the seven days between the actor's self-reported daily enactment of prosocial behavior and a) the partner's daily sentiments (i.e., care, positive regard, and acceptance) toward the actor; b) the partner's self-reported daily reciprocation of prosocial behavior toward the actor; and c) the partner's self-reported daily emotional response toward the actor (including feeling happy, content, and satisfied). These three within-dyad correlations were averaged to create a person-level index of partner reinforcement. When John scored higher on this measure, it suggests that Mary exhibited a contingent pattern of responding across the seven days in which she rewarded John's elevated daily prosocial behavior with positive sentiments, reciprocated prosocial behavior, and positive emotion on the day. The average score on this index was significantly greater than zero, suggesting that most participants had partners who reinforced their prosocial behavior. However, there was also a great deal of variability in this partner reinforcement index, suggesting that some participants had partners who did not reward prosocial behavior.

Next, I examined whether this index of partner reinforcement during the first week moderated the link between daily interpersonal value goals and

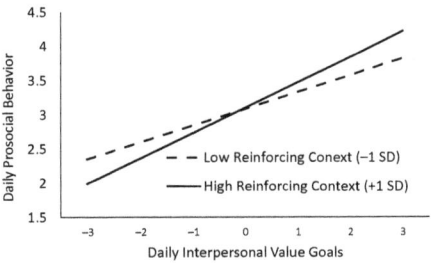

FIGURE 10.3 Effects of daily interpersonal value goals on prosocial behavior as a function of reinforcing relationship context (contingency between daily prosocial behavior and partner valuing the prior week)

daily enactment of prosocial behavior in the second week. Results are depicted in Figure 10.3. As predicted, the effect of daily interpersonal value goals on prosocial behavior was stronger for participants who had highly reinforcing partners. That is, John was particularly likely to enact prosocial behavior on days when he wanted to be valued by Mary when Mary tended to reward John's prosocial behavior with signs that she valued him the prior week. These results suggest that the relationship context shaped how participants pursued their goals to be valued by their partners; they were especially likely to enact prosocial behavior as a means to be valued by partners when they were immersed in relationship contexts in which prosocial behavior was indeed an effective means of being valued.

WHO ADOPTS INTERPERSONAL VALUE GOALS? THE ROLE OF RELATIONSHIP COMMITMENT

Within the context of established close relationships, adoption of the goal to be valued by partners may often be driven by relationship commitment. Relationship commitment involves a desire for the relationship to persist, psychological attachment to the relationship, and a long-term orientation to the relationship (i.e., envisioning that one will be in the relationship in the distant future) (Arriaga & Agnew, 2001; Rusbult, 1983; Rusbult & Buunk, 1993). According to interdependence theoretical perspectives (Kelley & Thibaut, 1978; Rusbult & Buunk, 1993; Rusbult & Van Lange, 2003), once people become committed, they exhibit a *transformation of motivation* in which they become motivated to maintain the welfare of their relationship. Consistent with this prediction, commitment is associated with willingness to sacrifice personal goals to maintain the relationship (Van Lange et al., 1997), enactment of prosocial behaviors during conflicts (Rusbult, Verette, Whitney, Slovik, & Lipkus, 1991), derogation of tempting alternative partners (Johnson & Rusbult, 1989), willingness to forgive partners' transgressions (Finkel,

Rusbult, Kumashiro, & Hannon, 2002), and reduced infidelity (Drigotas, Safstrom, & Gentilia, 1999).

Being valued by partners may be viewed as important to ensuring the quality and stability of the relationship. After all, partners who view the self as a valuable relationship partner may be more motivated to enact pro-relationship behaviors and maintain the relationship. Hence, the transform-ation of motivation that accompanies commitment, and that includes striving to maintain the welfare of the relationship, may often include adoption of the goal to be valued by partners. These considerations suggest that relationship commitment should be an important driver of the adoption of interpersonal value goals.

To test these ideas, in the daily diary study described above, I measured commitment at the start of the study using an adaption of the commitment subscale of the Investment Model Scale (Rusbult, Martz, & Agnew, 1998). In addition, I measured daily experiences of commitment during the daily diary phase of the study (e.g., "Today, to what extent did you feel committed to your relationship with your partner"). Both individual differences in commit-ment, and daily fluctuations in commitment, positively and significantly predicted daily adoption of interpersonal value goals. The effect of individual differences in commitment suggests that more committed individuals, as measured at the start of the study, reported stronger adoption of the goal to be valued by their partners, averaged across the daily assessments. The effect of daily commitment suggests that participants especially wanted to be valued on days when they were especially committed to their relationships. These results support the prediction that relationship commitment can prompt people to seek to be valued by their partners. Of course, the goal to be valued may also extend beyond the context of committed, close relationships. For example, people may want to be valued by new acquaintances and others who are not close relationship partners (e.g., coworkers or supervisors for many people) for reasons other than commitment (e.g., anticipating the develop-ment of a close relationship, self-esteem enhancement, tangible rewards of being valued, like a raise or promotion). But these results suggest that the pro-relationship motivation that is associated with commitment may be one factor that encourages adoption of the goal to be valued.

SUMMARY AND CONCLUSIONS

Receiving acceptance, positive regard, care, and commitment from others is critical to meeting fundamental needs for belonging (Baumeister & Leary, 1995), and is central to the quality of social interactions and relationships (Clark & Lemay, 2010; Murray et al., 2006; Reis et al., 2004). However, little is known regarding how the goal to be valued by others impacts the quality of interactions and relationships. In this chapter, I summarized a new program of research examining the consequences of trying to be valued by others. Experimental and daily diary studies suggest that, when people try to be valued by others, such as earning others' positive regard, commitment, or care, they enact more prosocial behavior and adopt compassionate goals. Hence, adopting the goal to be valued, which technically reflects self-interest, often triggered other-focused goals and prosocial behaviors that typically bolster relationship quality. Consistent with Interdependence Theory (Kelley & Thibaut, 1985; Reis & Arriaga, 2015), these results suggest a robust positive association between pursuing self-interested goals of being valued by others and other-oriented goals to care for others' welfare.

Social learning of interdependence may account for these processes. Through their history of observing interactions and relationships characterized by reciprocity and positive responses to prosocial behavior, people may develop lay theories positing that prosocial behavior is an effective means of pursuing positive regard from others, which may guide the adoption of prosocial tactics when people want to be valued by others. Learning of contingencies within specific relationships may also inform the selection of prosocial tactics as a means to be valued by others. That is, some people have relationship partners who are especially rewarding when they enact prosocial behavior, such as by expressing more warmth, positive emotion, and positive regard. People who are immersed in these relationship contexts may be particularly likely to view prosocial behavior as useful in getting their partners to value them. Links between interpersonal value goals and prosocial behavior may be especially strong for these individuals. Recent results support both mechanisms. The goal to be valued by others was especially predictive of prosocial behavior when people endorsed explicit beliefs that prosocial behavior leads people to be valued by others. Independently of this effect, the goal to be valued was especially predictive of prosocial behavior when people had reinforcing partners who valued them on days they enacted prosocial behavior. These results may suggest that both explicit and general beliefs regarding interdependence, as well as the pattern of interdependence within specific relationships, can shape whether people use prosocial behavior to satisfy self-interested goals to be valued, consistent with Kelley and Thibaut's (1985) argument that knowledge of interdependence and social norms shapes people's enactment of prosocial behavior.

Pursuing the goal to be valued appeared to usually be successful, eliciting more compassionate goals and positive evaluations in partners. Pursuing the goal to be valued was also associated with more confidence in being valued by partners. Hence, interpersonal value goals appeared to bolster relationship quality through several pathways.

More committed individuals were more likely to adopt interpersonal value goals, suggesting that trying to be valued by partners may be the outcome of a desire to maintain the quality of interdependent relationships. Indeed, maintaining a partner's positive regard for the self may be an important way of ensuring relationship quality. In addition, people who enacted prosocial behaviors and adopted prosocial motivations (i.e., compassionate goals) toward partners, indicators that they have invested in their relationships, increased over time in their adoption of interpersonal value goals. Hence, interpersonal value goals and relationship investment may have a mutually reinforcing relationship – people who want to be valued invest in their relationships and treat their partners well, which bolsters their desire to be valued.

The current chapter suggests that, as a result of learning the rules of interdependence, striving to be valued promotes, rather than undermines, prosocial behavior and caring for others' welfare, and, ultimately, the quality of interdependent interactions and relationships.

REFERENCES

Arriaga, X. B. & Agnew, C. R. (2001). Being committed: Affective, cognitive, and conative components of relationship commitment. *Personality and Social Psychology Bulletin*, 27, 1190–1203.

Bandura, A. (1977a). *Social Learning Theory*. Upper Saddle River, NJ: Prentice Hall.

Bandura, A. (1977b). Self-efficacy: Toward a unifying theory of behavioral change. *Psychological Review*, 84, 191–215.

Bandura, A., Ross, D., & Ross, S. A. (1963). Vicarious reinforcement and imitative learning. *Journal of Abnormal and Social Psychology*, 67, 601–607.

Bargh, J. A. (1994). The four horsemen of automaticity: Awareness, intention, efficiency, and control in social cognition. In J. R. S. Wyer & T. K. Srull (Eds.), *Handbook of Social Cognition* (2nd ed., pp. 1–40). Hillsdale, NJ: Erlbaum.

Batson, C. D. & Powell, A. A. (2003). Altruism and prosocial behavior. In T. Millon & M. J. Lerner (Eds.), *Handbook of Psychology: Personality and Social Psychology* (Vol. 5, pp. 463–484). Hoboken, NJ: John Wiley & Sons.

Baumeister, R. F. & Leary, M. R. (1995). The need to belong: Desire for interpersonal attachments as a fundamental human motivation. *Psychological Bulletin*, 117, 497–529.

Bekker, M. H., Bachrach, N., & Croon, M. A. (2007). The relationships of antisocial behavior with attachment styles, autonomy-connectedness, and alexithymia. *Journal of Clinical Psychology*, 63, 507–527.

Berscheid, E. & Walster, E. (1978). *Interpersonal Attraction*. Reading, MA: Addison-Wesley.

Buunk, B. P. & Schaufeli, W. B. (1999). Reciprocity in interpersonal relationships: An evolutionary perspective on its importance for health and well-being. *European Review of Social Psychology*, 10, 259–291.

Canevello, A. & Crocker, J. (2010). Creating good relationships: Responsiveness, relationship quality, and interpersonal goals. *Journal of Personality and Social Psychology*, 99, 78–106.

Canevello, A. & Crocker, J. (2011). Interpersonal goals, others' regard for the self, and self-esteem: The paradoxical consequences of self-image and compassionate goals. *European Journal of Social Psychology*, 41, 422–434.

Canevello, A. & Crocker, J. (2015). How self-image and compassionate goals shape intrapsychic experiences. *Social and Personality Psychology Compass*, 9, 620–629.

Chen, S., Shechter, D. & Chaiken, S. (1996). Getting at the truth or getting along: Accuracy-versus impression-motivated heuristic and systematic processing. *Journal of Personality and Social Psychology*, 71, 262–275.

Cialdini, R. B., Baumann, D. J., & Kenrick, D. T. (1981). Insights from sadness: A three-step model of the development of altruism as hedonism. *Developmental Review*, 1, 207–223.

Clark, M. S., Dubash, P., & Mills, J. (1998). Interest in another's consideration of one's needs in communal and exchange relationships. *Journal of Experimental Social Psychology*, 34, 246–264.

Clark, M. S. & Finkel, E. J. (2005). Willingness to express emotion: The impact of relationship type, communal orientation, and their interaction. *Personal Relationships*, 12, 169–180.

Clark, M. S. & Lemay, E. P., Jr. (2010). Close relationships. In S. T. Fiske, D. T. Gilbert, & G. Lindzey (Eds.), *Handbook of Social Psychology* (5th ed., Vol. 2, pp. 898–940). New York: Wiley.

Clark, M. S. & Mills, J. R. (2011). A theory of communal (and exchange) relationships. In P. A. M. V. Lange, A. W. Kruglanski, & E. T. Higgins (Eds.), *Handbook of Theories of Social Psychology* (pp. 232–250). Los Angeles, CA: Sage Publications.

Collins, N. L. & Feeney, B. C. (2000). A safe haven: An attachment theory perspective on support seeking and caregiving in intimate relationships. *Journal of Personality and Social Psychology*, 78, 1053–1073.

Condon, J. W. & Crano, W. D. (1988). Inferred evaluation and the relation between attitude similarity and interpersonal attraction. *Journal of Personality and Social Psychology*, 54, 789–797.

Corcoran, K. O. C. & Mallinckrodt, B. (2000). Adult attachment, self-efficacy, perspective taking, and conflict resolution. *Journal of Counseling & Development*, 78, 473–483.

Crocker, J. & Canevello, A. (2008). Creating and undermining social support in communal relationships: The role of compassionate and self-image goals. *Journal of Personality and Social Psychology*, 95, 555–575.

Crocker, J., Canevello, A., & Brown, A. A. (2017). Social motivation: Costs and benefits of selfishness and otherishness. *Annual Review of Psychology*, 68, 299–325.

Drigotas, S. M., Safstrom, C. A., & Gentilia, T. (1999). An investment model prediction of dating infidelity. *Journal of Personality and Social Psychology*, 77, 509–524.

Duarte, J. & Pinto-Gouveia, J. (2015). Focusing on self or others has different consequences for psychological well-being: A longitudinal study of the effects of distinct interpersonal goals. *Journal of Social and Clinical Psychology*, 34, 809–825.

Eccles, J. S. & Wigfield, A. (2002). Motivational beliefs, values, and goals. *Annual Review of Psychology*, 53, 109–132.

Ehrenberg, M. F., Robertson, M., & Pringle, J. (2012). Attachment style and marital commitment in the context of remarriage. *Journal of Divorce & Remarriage*, 53, 204–219.

Erickson, T. M., Granillo, M. T., Crocker, J., Abelson, J. L., Reas, H. E., & Quach, C. M. (2018). Compassionate and self-image goals as interpersonal maintenance factors in clinical depression and anxiety. *Journal of Clinical Psychology*, 74, 608–625.

Feeney, J. A., Noller, P., & Hanrahan, M. (1994). Assessing adult attachment. In M. B. Sperling & W. H. Berman (Eds.), *Attachment in Adults: Clinical and Developmental Perspectives* (pp. 128–152). New York: Guilford Press.

Finkel, E. J., Rusbult, C. E., Kumashiro, M., & Hannon, P. A. (2002). Dealing with betrayal in close relationships: Does commitment promote forgiveness? *Journal of Personality and Social Psychology*, 82, 956–974.

Fitzsimons, G. M., Finkel, E. J., & Vandellen, M. R. (2015). Transactive goal dynamics. *Psychological Review*, 122, 648–673.

Fossati, A., Feeney, J. A., Donati, D., Donini, M., Novella, L., Bagnato, M., . . . Maffei, C. (2003). On the dimensionality of the Attachment Style Questionnaire in Italian clinical and nonclinical participants. *Journal of Social and Personal Relationships*, 20, 55–79.

Gagne, F. M. & Lydon, J. E. (2001). Mindset and relationship illusions: The moderating effects of domain specificity and relationship commitment. *Personality and Social Psychology Bulletin*, 27, 1144–1155.

Goffman, E. (1959). *The Presentation of Self in Everyday Life*. Oxford: Doubleday.

Gordon, R. A. (1996). Impact of ingratiation on judgments and evaluations: A meta-analytic investigation. *Journal of Personality and Social Psychology*, 71, 54–70.

Gouldner, A. W. (1960). The norm of reciprocity: A preliminary statement. *American Sociological Review*, 25, 161–178.

Hackenbracht, J. & Tamir, M. (2010). Preferences for sadness when eliciting help: Instrumental motives in sadness regulation. *Motivation and Emotion*, 34, 306–315.

Hadden, B. W. & Knee, C. R. (2015). Who am I in it for? Interpersonal goals and secure base support. *Self and Identity*, 14, 675–691.

Hamby, S. L. (1996). The dominance scale: Preliminary psychometric properties. *Violence and Victims*, 11, 199–212.

Hewitt, P. L., Flett, G. L., Sherry, S. B., Habke, M., Parkin, M., Lam, R. W., . . . Stein, M. B. (2003). The interpersonal expression of perfection: Perfectionistic self-presentation and psychological distress. *Journal of Personality and Social Psychology*, 84, 1303–1325.

Johnson, D. J. & Rusbult, C. E. (1989). Resisting temptation: Devaluation of alternative partners as a means of maintaining commitment in close relationships. *Journal of Personality and Social Psychology*, 57, 967–980.

Jones, E. E. (1964). *Ingratiation*. New York: Appleton-Century-Crofts.

Karantzas, G. C., Feeney, J. A., & Wilkinson, R. (2010). Is less more? Confirmatory factor analysis of the Attachment Style Questionnaires. *Journal of Social and Personal Relationships*, 27, 749–780.

Kelley, H. H. & Thibaut, J. W. (1978). *Interpersonal Relations: A Theory of Interdependence*. New York: Wiley.

Kelley, H. H. & Thibaut, J. W. (1985). Self-interest, science, and cynicism. *Journal of Social and Clinical Psychology*, 3, 26–32.

Kenny, D. A., Kashy, D. A., & Cook, W. L. (2006). *Dyadic Data Analysis*. New York: Guilford Press.

Kenny, D. A. & la Voie, L. (1982). Reciprocity of interpersonal attraction: A confirmed hypothesis. *Social Psychology Quarterly*, 45, 54–58.

Kruglanski, A. W., Shah, J. Y., Fishbach, A., Friedman, R., Chun, W. Y., & Sleeth-Keppler, D. (2002). A theory of goal systems. *Advances in Experimental Social Psychology*, 34, 331–378.

Kunda, Z. (1990). The case for motivated reasoning. *Psychological Bulletin*, 108(3), 480–498.

Laurenceau, J.-P., Barrett, L. F., & Pietromonaco, P. R. (1998). Intimacy as an interpersonal process: The importance of self-disclosure, partner disclosure, and perceived partner prosocialness in interpersonal exchanges. *Journal of Personality and Social Psychology*, 74, 1238–1251.

Le, B. M., Impett, E. A., Lemay Jr, E. P., Muise, A., & Tskhay, K. O. (2018). Communal motivation and well-being in interpersonal relationships: An integrative review and meta-analysis. *Psychological Bulletin*, 144, 1–25.

Leary, M. R. (1994). *Self-Presentation: Impression Management and Interpersonal Behavior*. Dubusque, IA: Brown & Benchmark.

Leary, M. R. & Baumeister, R. F. (2000). The nature and function of self-esteem: Sociometer theory. In M. P. Zanna (Ed.), *Advances in Experimental Social Psychology* (Vol. 32, pp. 1–62). San Diego, CA: Academic Press.

Lemay, E. P. & Clark, M. S. (2015). Motivated cognition in relationships. *Current Opinion in Psychology*, 1, 72–75.

Lemay, E. P., Jr., Clark, M. S., & Feeney, B. C. (2007). Projection of prosocialness to needs and the construction of satisfying communal relationships. *Journal of Personality and Social Psychology*, 92, 834–853.

Lemay, E. P., Jr. & Dudley, K. L. (2011). Caution: Fragile! Regulating the interpersonal security of chronically insecure partners. *Journal of Personality and Social Psychology*, 100, 681–702.

Lopez, F. G. & Rice, K. G. (2006). Preliminary development and validation of a measure of relationship authenticity. *Journal of Counseling Psychology*, 53, 362–371.

Lydon, J. E., Jamieson, D. W., & Holmes, J. G. (1997). The meaning of social interactions in the transition from acquaintanceship to friendship. *Journal of Personality and Social Psychology*, 73, 536–548.

Mackinnon, S. P., Sherry, S. B., Antony, M. M., Stewart, S. H., Sherry, D. L., & Hartling, N. (2012). Caught in a bad romance: Perfectionism, conflict, and depression in romantic relationships. *Journal of Family Psychology*, 26, 215–225.

Moeller, S. J., Crocker, J., & Bushman, B. J. (2009). Creating hostility and conflict: Effects of entitlement and self-image goals. *Journal of Experimental Social Psychology*, 45, 448–452.

Murray, S. L., Holmes, J. G., & Collins, N. L. (2006). Optimizing assurance: The risk regulation system in relationships. *Psychological Bulletin*, 132, 641–666.

Murray, S. L., Holmes, J. G., & Griffin, D. W. (1996). The benefits of positive illusions: Idealization and the construction of satisfaction in close relationships. *Journal of Personality and Social Psychology*, 70, 79–98.

Murray, S. L., Holmes, J. G., & Griffin, D. W. (2000). Self-esteem and the quest for felt security: How perceived regard regulates attachment processes. *Journal of Personality and Social Psychology*, 78, 478–498.

Prot, S., Gentile, D. A., Anderson, C. A., Suzuki, K., Swing, E., Lim, K. M., . . . Liuqing, W. (2014). Long-term relations among prosocial-media use, empathy, and pro-social behavior. *Psychological Science*, 25, 358–368.

Reis, H. T. & Arriaga, X. B. (2015). Interdependence theory and related theories. In B. Gawronski & G. Bodenhausen (Eds.), *Theory and Explanation in Social Psychology* (pp. 305–327). New York: Guilford Press.

Reis, H. T., Clark, M. S., & Holmes, J. G. (2004). Perceived partner prosocialness as an organizing construct in the study of intimacy and closeness. In D. J. Mashek & A. P. Aron (Eds.), *Handbook of Closeness and Intimacy* (pp. 201–225). Mahwah, NJ: Lawrence Erlbaum Associates.

Rusbult, C. E. (1983). A longitudinal test of the investment model: The development (and deterioration) of satisfaction and commitment in heterosexual involve-ments. *Journal of Personality and Social Psychology*, 45, 101–117.

Rusbult, C. E. & Buunk, B. P. (1993). Commitment processes in close relationships: An interdependence analysis. *Journal of Social and Personal Relationships*, 10, 175–204.

Rusbult, C. E., Van Lange, P. A. M., Wildschut, T., Yovetich, N. A., & Verette, J. (2000). Perceived superiority in close relationships: Why it exists and persists. *Journal of Personality and Social Psychology*, 79, 521–545.

Rusbult, C. E., Martz, J. M., & Agnew, C. R. (1998). The Investment Model Scale: Measuring commitment level, satisfaction level, quality of alternatives, and investment size. *Personal Relationships*, 5, 357–391.

Rusbult, C. E. & Van Lange, P. A. (2003). Interdependence, interaction, and relation-ships. *Annual Review of Psychology*, 54, 351–375.

Rusbult, C. E., Verette, J., Whitney, G. A., Slovik, L. F., & Lipkus, I. (1991). Accom-modation processes in close relationships: Theory and preliminary empirical evidence. *Journal of Personality and Social Psychology*, 60, 53–78.

Sadikaj, G., Moskowitz, D., & Zuroff, D. C. (2016). Negative affective reaction to partner's dominant behavior influences satisfaction with romantic relationship. *Journal of Social and Personal Relationships*, 34, 1324–1346.

Schlenker, B. R. (2003). Self-presentation. In M. R. Leary & J. P. Tangney (Eds.), *Handbook of Self and Identity* (pp. 492–518). New York: Guilford Press.

Swann, W. B., Jr., Bosson, J. K., & Pelham, B. W. (2002). Different partners, different selves: Strategic verification of circumscribed identities. *Personality and Social Psychology Bulletin*, 28, 1215–1228.

Tice, D. M., Butler, J. L., Muraven, M. B., & Stillwell, A. M. (1995). When modesty prevails: Differential favorability of self-presentation to friends and strangers. *Journal of Personality and Social Psychology*, 69, 1120–1138.

Van Lange, P. A. M., Rusbult, C. E., Drigotas, S. M., Arriaga, X. B., Witcher, B. S., & Cox, C. L. (1997). Willingness to sacrifice in close relationships. *Journal of Personality and Social Psychology*, 72, 1373–1395.

Yovetich, N. A. & Rusbult, C. E. (1994). Accommodative behavior in close relation-ships: Exploring transformation of motivation. *Journal of Experimental Social Psychology*, 30, 138–164.

11

Advances in Self-Expansion

BRENT A. MATTINGLY, JENNIFER M. TOMLINSON, AND
KEVIN P. MCINTYRE

The self-expansion model, broadly defined, is a theoretical framework which explains a process in which individuals broaden the content and diversity of their self-concepts by acquiring or augmenting identities, perspectives, capabilities, and resources (Aron, Lewandowski, Mashek, & Aron, 2013). Early theorizing between the mid-1980s and early 2000s regarding the self-expansion process suggested that individuals were fundamentally motivated to increase their self-efficacy and that a central way in which this was accomplished was by literally expanding the size of the self-concept by increasing the number of identities, perspectives, capabilities, and resources they possess (e.g., Aron & Aron, 1986; Aron et al., 2013; Aron, Norman, & Aron, 1998). Though there are several ways in which individuals could expand the self-concept, such as individual pursuits (e.g., Mattingly & Lewandowski, 2014), the self-expansion model argues that close relationships are the primary way in which individuals experience self-expansion (Aron et al., 2013). This early work on self-expansion greatly impacted the field of relationship science, as it represented a major theoretical advancement and linked disparate literatures within social psychology; for example, seminal work on the inclusion of other in the self component of self-expansion (Aron, Aron, & Smollan, 1992) has been cited over 3,600 times since its publication. Nevertheless, there have been substantial advances in the literature that have both broadened and deepened our understanding of the self-expansion model.

Recently, researchers have slightly refined the definition of self-expansion while retaining several central features. In particular, recent research tends to define the self-expansion process as a *cognitive reorganization of the self-concept* which may involve both the acquisition and augmentation of self-concept content (e.g., Gordon & Luo, 2011; Mattingly, McIntyre, & Selterman, 2018; McIntyre, Mattingly, & Lewandowski, 2017), therefore capturing a wider range of self-concept changes (i.e., an individual would not need to acquire new self-concept content for self-expansion to occur, but rather could further develop existing self-concept content).

In the current chapter, we consider how self-expansion can be under-stood through the lens of Interdependence Theory (for an overview, see the Introduction), such that, as individuals change their sense of self to incorpor-ate aspects of their partner, they experience a transformation of motivation. This, in turn, changes both how partners perceive the interaction as well as how they choose to respond to it. We view the self-expansion model and Interdependence Theory as complementary approaches in understanding both individuals' motivations toward and behavior within their relationships. To address this idea, the chapter is divided into three distinct parts in which we focus on the recent empirical developments in the self-expansion literature and how they are related to Interdependence Theory. In part 1, we discuss cognitive and motivational precursors (i.e., antecedents) to the self-expansion process. In part 2, we review recent research regarding the defining character-istics of self-expansion, as well as how it differs from other relationship-induced self-concept changes. In part 3, we discuss various inter- and intra-personal outcomes of self-expansion.

PRECURSORS OF SELF-EXPANSION

Though the majority of research on self-expansion has examined the internal mechanisms of the self-expansion process (see What Defines and Differenti-ates the Self-Expansion Process?) as well as downstream relationship out-comes, such as relationship quality and maintenance behaviors (see Relational and Individual Outcomes of Self-Expansion), substantially less work has been done examining the antecedents of self-expansion. In this section, we review three motivational and cognitive precursors of self-expansion that have garnered empirical attention in recent years. We also highlight the ways in which these precursors can be understood in terms of Interdependence Theory in that individuals arrive at relationships with pre-existing dispos-itions that influence relationship dynamics (Agnew & Le, 2015).

Approach Motivation

Much of the early work on self-expansion defined the process as being fundamentally motivated (e.g., Aron et al., 2013); however, until recently, no research had examined the nature of this underlying motivation. Using the hedonic principle as an organizing framework (i.e., that individuals are motivated to seek pleasure [approach motivation] and avoid pain [avoidance motivation]; Higgins, 1998), Mattingly, McIntyre, and Lewandowski (2012) posited that self-expansion is rooted in approach motivation, such that individuals high in approach motivation (i.e., those seeking to maximize rewards) should be more likely to seek and experience self-expansion as a way to build their self-efficacy. In Interdependence Theory terminology, this guiding motivation is consistent with individuals seeking to maximize their own rewards ("MaxOwn") prior to shifting their focus toward partner and relationship interests (i.e., transformation of motivation). Across their first three studies (Studies 1, 2a, and 2b), Mattingly et al. (2012) found robust evidence that approach (but not avoidance) motivation was positively correlated with self-expansion in romantic relationships. In a fourth study (Study 3), single participants were randomly presented with a hypothetical romantic partner who provided ample or few opportunities for self-expansion. Notably, those high in approach motivation were significantly more interested in forming a relationship with the target who provided ample (vs. few) self-expansion opportunities, whereas those low in approach motivation were equally interested in the two hypothetical targets. This suggests that approach motivation sensitizes individuals to self-expansion (cf. Hilaire, 2013), whereas avoidance motivation does not. Furthermore, this effect has been replicated when examining friendship formation, such that approach-motivated individuals are more likely to desire friendships with others who provide ample (vs. few) self-expansion opportunities (Lewandowski, Mattingly, McIntyre, & Acri, 2016).

This ability of approach motivation to sensitize individuals to self-expansion opportunities has important implications in the formation and maintenance of relationships. That is, beyond attracting individuals to partners who provide self-expansion opportunities (Mattingly et al., 2012), approach motivation also drives individuals' relationship-enhancing behaviors. Specifically, Walker and Harasymchuk (2017) found that individuals with approach-motivated relationship goals were more likely to plan dates with their partners that were self-expanding in nature (i.e., novel and exciting). Moreover, in a follow-up session one week later, approach-motivated individuals reported that they were more likely to have engaged in these self-expanding dates with their partners. Taken together with Mattingly et al.'s (2012) and Lewandowski et al.'s (2016) findings, this evidence indicates that approach-motivated individuals are more likely to seek others who provide self-expansion, plan and engage in self-expanding dates with their romantic partners, and have relationships high in self-expansion. Examined through the lens of Interdependence Theory, this research suggests that there is a motivation rooted in self-interest that ultimately leads individuals to focus on the effective situation and engage in behaviors that benefit the partner and relationship as a whole (e.g., Kelley & Thibaut, 1978).

Implicit Theories of Relationships

In addition to motivational orientations, individuals also possess beliefs about relationships that serve to promote and foster self-expansion. Specifically, individuals with strong growth beliefs tend to view relationships as malleable and developing over time, and view challenges as opportunities to strengthen their relationships presumably because they have experienced a transformation of motivation. Conversely, individuals with strong destiny beliefs tend to believe that romantic partners are either compatible or incompatible and that relationships are either successful or unsuccessful from the beginning; that is, they view relationships as relatively fixed (Franiuk, Cohen, & Pomerantz, 2002; Knee, 1998; Knee, Patrick, & Lonsbary, 2003). In turn, individuals who possess strong growth beliefs likely seek opportunities to cultivate their relationship whereas those who possess strong destiny beliefs are more motivated to evaluate the viability of a relationship (Knee et al., 2003). In this way, growth beliefs are likely to operate in a similar manner as approach motivation, and there is evidence that beliefs about growth and incremental development are associated with approach motivation (Burnette, O'Boyle, VanEpps, Pollack, & Finkel, 2013).

Accordingly, recent work by Mattingly, McIntyre, Knee, and Loving (2019) has examined the hypothesis that growth beliefs, but not destiny beliefs, may foster relationship self-expansion. In two cross-sectional studies (Studies 1 and 3), this hypothesis was supported – growth beliefs positively predicted self-expansion, whereas destiny beliefs did not. In a longitudinal examination of individuals in early stage relationships (Study 2), Mattingly et al. (2019) further found that increases in growth beliefs over a nine-month period predicted subsequent relationship self-expansion, indicating that individuals who began endorsing growth beliefs to a greater degree also reported that their relationships were more self-expanding. Notably, changes in self-expansion did not predict subsequent growth beliefs, indicating that individuals were not merely changing their beliefs based upon the self-expanding nature of their relationship. This suggests that growth beliefs likely temporally precede the planning and enacting of self-expanding activities as well as the self-expansion experience.

Self-Concept Clarity

A defining aspect of self-expansion is that an individual's self-concept is changed in some substantive way, whether through the acquisition of new traits and identities or the reorganization of existing content (Aron et al., 2013; McIntyre et al, 2017). However, such changes to the self-concept may only be embraced by those who already have a clear sense of self, as individuals who are uncertain about themselves may view self-concept changes to be threatening as they potentially destabilize these individuals' already tenuous sense of self. More succinctly put, self-concept clarity – the degree to which individuals have clearly defined, confidently held, and internally consistent self-concepts (Campbell et al., 1996; Lodi-Smith & DeMarree, 2017) – also predicts the degree to which individuals seek and experience self-expansion in their relationships.

In the first test of this hypothesis, Lewandowski, Nardone, and Raines (2010, Study 1) had romantically-involved participants self-report their self-concept clarity and the degree of inclusion of other in the self experienced in their relationship (which is one way in which individuals can self-expand; Aron et al., 2013; Mattingly & Lewandowski, 2014). Consistent with the prediction that those with a clear self-concept would be more likely to self-expand, Lewandowski et al. (2010) found a positive correlation between self-concept clarity and inclusion of other in the self. To demonstrate the direction of this effect in a second study, Lewandowski et al. (2010, Study 2) experimentally manipulated individuals' self-concept clarity by having participants describe instances in which they behaved consistently (high self-concept clarity) or inconsistently (low self-concept clarity) with who they viewed themselves to be. Again supporting predictions, participants manipulated to have high (vs. low) self-concept clarity reported greater inclusion of other in the self. However, one limitation of these studies is that both samples relied on individuals already in romantic relationships; thus, it is plausible that heightened self-concept clarity simply made individuals *feel* as if their relationship possessed self-expansion.

Thus, to more directly test the hypothesis that self-concept clarity serves as a precursor to self-concept change, Emery, Walsh, and Slotter (2015, Study 1) had a sample of single individuals complete measures of self-concept clarity and *interest* in self-expansion. As predicted, individuals with clearer self-concepts reported greater interest in self-expanding, an effect that was conceptually replicated by Mattingly and McIntyre (2018). Next, Emery et al. (2015, Study 2) experimentally manipulated self-concept clarity by having individuals indicate their self-concept traits that were consistent (high self-concept clarity) or in conflict (low self-concept clarity) with one another. Individuals manipulated to have high self-concept clarity were significantly more interested in self-expanding, relative to those low in self-concept clarity. In the strongest test of the hypothesis, Emery et al. (2015, Study 3) again experimentally manipulated self-concept clarity and then had single participants complete a dating profile task. Specifically, participants viewed a potential romantic partner whose profile was manipulated to contain a self-concept attribute that participants had previously rejected in a pre-testing session (i.e., participants had previously indicated that they did not possess this trait as part of their self-concept). As predicted, those high (vs. low) in self-concept clarity were more likely to spontaneously incorporate and endorse this previously rejected self-concept attribute into their self-concepts, and this effect was especially strong when participants were motivated to meet the potential romantic partner.

Beyond high self-concept clarity fostering self-expansion, low self-concept clarity may actually inhibit the self-expansion process. Specifically, individuals low in self-concept clarity are less likely to support a partner's self-concept change (Jakubiak & Tomlinson, in press), as they assume that they too would need to change (Emery, Gardner, Finkel, & Carswell, 2018). Therefore, individuals who exhibit self-concept confusion tend to both avoid self-expansion and try to prevent situations that might require self-change. This hesitancy to experience self-expansion by people low in self-concept clarity may ultimately impair their relationships overall, in that they are missing out on all of the benefits of self-expansion (described in Relational and Individual Outcomes of Self-Expansion). Importantly, Interdependence Theory supports the notion that partners can actively encourage and facilitate one another's self-change, such that they both move closer to their ideal selves (Drigotas, Rusbult, Wieselquist, & Whitton, 1999). However, people low in self-concept clarity may be hesitant to embrace these changes both in themselves and in their partners, as they see these changes as potential threats to their underdeveloped self-concepts (e.g., DiDonato & Krueger, 2010). Thus, people low in self-concept clarity may be slower, or less likely, to experience a transformation of motivation in that they are less likely to develop closeness with their partner (Lewandowski et al, 2010) and affirm their partners' self-growth (DiDonato & Krueger, 2010).

Summary

Interdependence theory highlights the importance of interpersonal orientations that lead to individuals experiencing a transformation of motivation. Recent research on the precursors of self-expansion (i.e., approach motivation, implicit theories of relationships, self-concept clarity) supports the notion that self-expansion is a desirable outcome of relationships that fosters interdependence. However, individual traits must be considered in concert with relational dynamics and situational forces to fully understand desirable relationship outcomes such as satisfaction, commitment, and pro-relationship behaviors. There are likely several additional factors (e.g., internal states, relational dynamics, situational forces) that also precede the self-expansion experience. For example, having a partner who provides support for an individual's growth can strengthen both individual (e.g., self-expansion) and relational (e.g., closeness) well-being (Aron et al., 2013).

WHAT DEFINES AND DIFFERENTIATES THE SELF-EXPANSION PROCESS?

Next, we turn our focus to recent research that has further refined the self-expansion model by differentiating self-expansion from other ways in which relationships might influence the self and by identifying the elements needed (or not needed) for self-expanding activities. In addition, we discuss the ways in which self-expansion is similar to and different from other positive relationship processes.

How Self-Expansion Changes the Self-Concept

One recent advance to the self-expansion model has been to specify the type of self-concept changes that occur as part of the self-expansion process. According to the two-dimensional model of relationship-induced self-concept change, it is possible to differentiate between the direction of self-concept change (i.e., increase vs. decrease) and the valence of self-concept content (i.e., positive vs. negative) in identifying the ways in which relationships can influence the self (Mattingly, Lewandowski, & McIntyre, 2014; McIntyre, Mattingly, & Lewandowski, 2015). In particular, self-expansion occurs within a relationship when a romantic partner, or aspects of the relationship, lead individuals to experience *increases in positive* self-concept content. This framework has been useful in emphasizing that self-expansion should ultimately result in the net gain of positive self-concept content, which the individual views positively. For example, in the moment, it may be very challenging to climb a mountain with one's partner but, as a result of engaging in this experience, one might gain a broader perspective and feel a sense of accomplishment that would increase positive feelings, capabilities, and identities about the self and the relationship. These changes to the self-concept, especially early on in a relationship when self-expansion may be most potent, may help individuals experience a transformation of motivation as they start out with the goal of maximizing benefits to the self and transition to the goal of maximizing benefits for the relationship.

This process of self-expansion is therefore conceptually and empirically distinct from self-change that emerges from other combinations of the direction and valence dimensions. For example, relationships that decrease positive self-concept content, in contrast, would be considered to result in self-contraction (Mattingly et al., 2014), meaning that one loses interest or access to positive aspects of the self as a result of the relationship. Beyond positive self-concept content, individuals may also experience changes to negative self-concept content. Self-pruning occurs when the relationship leads individuals to decrease the negative aspects of self-concept, whereas self-adulteration occurs when individuals experience an increase in the number of negative self-concept attributes. Self-expansion and self-pruning are associated with positive relationship outcomes due to the overall self-concept becoming more positive (i.e., the gain of positive or loss of negative both improve the overall self-concept), whereas self-contraction and self-adulteration are associated with negative outcomes due to the self-concept degrading (McIntyre et al., 2015).

How Is Self-Expansion Different from Related Positive Relationship Processes?

The *Michelangelo phenomenon* (Drigotas et al., 1999) is a related process that also results in the augmentation of self-concept content. According to research on the Michelangelo phenomenon, relationship partners affirm aspects of the individual's ideal self, which in turn sculpts, shapes, and ultimately improves the individual's self-concept (Cheung & Gardner, 2016; DiDonato & Krueger, 2010; Drigotas et al., 1999). By metaphorically chiseling away undesirable aspects of the self-concept "stone" and reshaping the existing aspects, partners help reveal the individual's ideal form. In this way, individuals' transformation of motivation leads them to focus on maximizing benefits for relationship partners (e.g., enabling partners to achieve their ideal selves). Having a partner who recognizes one's ideal form is important across age groups and becomes even more closely tied to satisfaction as people age (Bühler, Weidmann, Kumashiro, & Grob, 2019). Put into the language of the two-dimensional model of relationship-induced self-concept change, Michelangelo-like partners promote both self-expansion and self-pruning. Though no research that we are aware of has considered both the Michelangelo phenomenon and self-expansion model in the same study, we view perceived partner affirmation as one potential way in which self-expansion could occur.

Inclusion of other in the self (Aron, Aron, Tudor, & Nelson, 1991) is another related but distinct process that considers the degree of self–other overlap between partners. Inclusion of the other in the self is one way in which self-expansion might occur, but inclusion of the other in the self and self-expansion are not interchangeable constructs. Inclusion of the other in the self can be a precursor to self-expansion, whereby partners expand by gaining access to novel perspectives, resources, identities, and capabilities from their relationships, as well as a consequence of self-expanding activities (Aron et al., 2013). Research in this area suggests that people treat close others similarly to the self (Aron et al., 1991), resulting in more difficulty differentiating the self and the other in a variety of reaction time tasks (e.g. Ketay, Beck, Riela, Bailey, & Aron, 2019). Inclusion of the other in the self is thought to occur primarily in the early stages of relationship development when rapid self-expansion occurs (Aron, Paris, & Aron, 1995), thus resulting in a transformation of motivation and subsequently cognitive interdependence (Agnew, Van Lange, Rusbult, & Langston, 1998). In contrast, participation in certain shared activities would be the most common source of self-expansion within established relationships (Strong & Aron, 2006).

Self-Expanding Activities: Separating Expansion from Arousal

Typically, self-expanding activities have been defined as shared activities engaged with a romantic partner that are exciting, novel, and/or challenging

(Aron et al., 2013; Strong & Aron, 2006). In fact, a variety of experimental, intervention, and daily diary studies have found benefits for participation in self-expanding activities in ongoing relationships (e.g. Aron, Norman, Aron, McKenna, & Heyman, 2000; Coulter & Malouff, 2013; Girme, Overall, & Faingataa, 2014; Graham, 2008; Muise et al., 2019; Reissman, Aron, & Bergen, 1993). Though it is clear that self-expanding activities are integral to staving off relationship boredom (Harasymchuk, Cloutier, Peetz, & Lebreton, 2017), considerably less research has considered what elements are needed to maximize the benefits of shared activities.

Intervention studies considering the effects of self-expanding activities have typically used the term "exciting activities" when asking couples to participate in self-expanding activities on their own time in comparison to couples who have participated in either "pleasant" and/or no activities together (Coulter & Malouff, 2013; Reissman et al., 1993). Other experimental studies have focused on novel and arousing activities in comparison to mundane activities (Aron et al., 2000, Studies 3–5). A recent experiment focused on novel and exciting activities in comparison to pleasant and familiar activities or no activities, bringing novelty to the foreground (Muise et al., 2019; Study 3). All of these studies show clear, consistent, and robust benefits for participation in self-expanding activities, but it is not yet clear whether these components are distinguishable (e.g., novelty, challenge, arousal, or excitement). However, which component is most beneficial may not be as important as whether self–other connectedness increases, as individuals who treat the partner's outcomes as their own will ultimately behave in a pro-relationship manner (e.g., Agnew & Le, 2015; Aron et al., 1991).

One question that researchers have sought to answer is if physical arousal is needed for self-expanding activities, as many of the activities used in previous studies are exciting and have an arousal component (e.g. Aron et al., 2000; Studies 3–5). Lewandowski and Aron (2004) first differentiated self-expansion (defined here as novelty/challenge) from arousal in a sample of opposite sex stranger pairs, finding that arousal predicted attraction, whereas novelty/challenge during an activity did not. However, another study using similar methodology with pairs in ongoing relationships (both married couples and friends) found that perceived self-expansion (defined here as fun/interesting) predicted both relationship and individual well-being above and beyond the effects of arousal (Tomlinson, Hughes, Lewandowski, Aron, & Geyer, 2019). Based on data obtained from an experiment and two cross-sectional studies, perceptions of fun/interest (above and beyond arousal) within activities done with a friend or partner predicted relationship satisfaction, closeness, self-expansion, and positive affect. Thus, it seems that arousal plays a role in early stage relationships but that it is not as important in ongoing relationships. This suggests that self-expanding activities do not necessarily need to have a physically arousing component. Indeed, one study on individual self-expansion found that a mental task almost completely devoid of arousal was effective in creating a sense of self-expansion, providing further evidence that arousal is not a necessary component of the self-expansion experience (Mattingly & Lewandowski, 2013b; Study 2).

Another recent advance in the understanding of what makes self-expanding activities work (or not work) is research that has identified individual differences that influence the efficacy. At the individual level, Graham and Harf (2015) found that there seems to be an optimal level of challenge depending on the skill level of the individual. In particular, if an activity is too challenging, people might become frustrated, doubt their capabilities (i.e., self-contraction), internalize beliefs of failure (i.e., self-adulteration), and fail to reap the benefits of self-expansion. At the couple level, Girme et al. (2014) found that it was necessary for both partners to be dedicated to shared activities for those activities to effectively benefit the relationship (e.g., "Max-Joint"). Thus, in addition to understanding which aspects are most beneficial for self-expanding activities, there are also likely to be characteristics of the individual or couple that influence their effectiveness.

Summary

Recent theoretical advances to the self-expansion model have further refined the definitions of both self-expansion itself and self-expanding activities. Such advances are important because they make it clear what is or is not self-expanding, and also make it easier to clearly communicate the applied implications of our science to the public. This work has a lot of potential applications, and fine-tuning theoretical understanding will make it easier for practitioners, for example, to know what to recommend to couples who may be struggling. In addition, carefully specifying the behaviors that produce self-expansion motivation is helpful in theory-building, as it will allow researchers to more carefully pinpoint what types of situations or interactions will be the most likely to produce self-expansion. In turn, this will enable researchers to more accurately predict what other downstream outcomes the interactions will have. Knowing more about the nature of self-expansion may allow researchers to identify how particular aspects of self-expansion might relate to specific outcomes. For example, novelty within a self-expanding activity may increase satisfaction because it could potentially result in perceived superiority within the relationship (Rusbult, Van Lange, Wildschut, Yovetich, & Verrete, 2000). Overall, from an Interdependence Theory perspective, this research specifies the nature of the given situations that promotes self-expansion as a vehicle for the transformation of motivation, such that tendencies to select certain types of shared (e.g., cooperative) activities might influence outcomes.

RELATIONAL AND INDIVIDUAL OUTCOMES OF SELF-EXPANSION

One of the primary advances in the literature on self-expansion is the identification of the wide range of benefits that self-expansion confers on romantic relationships as well as on the individual partners within relationships. Next, we describe the extant literature examining outcomes of self-expansion, differentiating between relationship outcomes and individual outcomes.

Relationship Quality: Satisfaction and Commitment

Relationships that are perceived as more self-expanding are also seen as more satisfying and higher in commitment. This basic association has been supported using a variety of methodologies, including cross-sectional self-report studies (e.g., Cloutier & Peetz, 2017; Mattingly et al., 2014; Nardone, Lewandowski, & Le, 2008), experimental studies using behavioral manipulations of self-expansion (e.g., Aron et al., 2000; Reissman et al., 1993), and longitudinal studies (McIntyre et al., 2015). For example, Coulter and Malouff (2013) randomly assigned couples to either a four-week self-expansion intervention or a waiting list control condition. Following four weeks of completing self-expanding activities with their partner, participants reported significantly greater relationship quality, as well as increased positive affect, compared to those in the waiting list condition. Other research extends this general association between self-expansion and relationship satisfaction by demonstrating that partner support for self-expansion can also have benefits for relationship satisfaction. In a study by Fivecoat, Tomlinson, Aron, and Caprariello (2015), participants expected to complete either a self-expanding task or a stressful task. While waiting to begin the task, experimenters sent participants messages via computer that were purportedly from their partner. These messages were manipulated to provide either active support (e.g., "I bet you'll be really good at that") or passive support (e.g., "I'll talk to you in a little while"). Participants then completed a measure of relationship satisfaction. Results of this work revealed that receiving active support prior to completing self-expanding activities increased relationship satisfaction, relative to passive support. This suggests that supporting a partner's self-expansion is beneficial for both the individuals within the relationship and the relationship as a whole.

Beyond overall assessments of relationship satisfaction, several lines of recent evidence suggest that self-expansion within relationships also has implications for sexual satisfaction. First, self-expansion is positively associated with passionate love, which is characterized by an intense longing and physical desire for one's partner (Mattingly et al., 2014; Sheets, 2014). Second, relational self-expansion positively correlates with sexual satisfaction (Frost, McClelland, & Dettmann, 2017; Shukusky, McIntyre, & Mattingly, 2017). Third, couples engaging in daily self-expanding activities together reported greater sexual desire and sexual satisfaction within their relationships (Muise et al., 2019). These findings reveal a potentially important function that self-expansion plays for romantic relationships. Although declines in passionate love and sexual interest are common in long-term relationships (Acevedo & Aron, 2009), self-expansion may buffer relationships from experiencing these reductions. One key reason why self-expansion may help keep the romantic spark alive within relationships is that self-expansion is associated with sexual growth beliefs (Shukusky et al., 2017). Sexual growth beliefs, like growth beliefs in general, characterize the belief that sexual incompatibilities and difficulties are problems to be overcome, and can ultimately strengthen the relationship (Maxwell et al., 2017). Sexual growth beliefs are positively associated with both sexual satisfaction and relationship quality (Maxwell et al., 2017), but recent work suggests that this association is mediated by self-expansion (Shukusky et al., 2017).

Relationship Stability and Longevity

Given that self-expansion buffers relationships from the onset of boredom, and boredom increases the likelihood of dissolution (Acevedo & Aron, 2009; Harasymchuk et al., 2017), it seems likely that self-expansion is associated with relationship longevity. This idea has been assumed in the literature and supported indirectly, but has only recently been shown empirically. Past work, for example, has found that relational boredom, often thought to set in when self-expansion declines within a relationship, predicts reduced satisfaction (Tsapelas, Aron, & Orbuch, 2009). Similarly, meta-analyses reveal that inclusion of other in self is negatively associated with relationship dissolution (Le, Dove, Agnew, Korn, & Mutso, 2010). Importantly, recent longitudinal evidence provides the first known evidence that perceived self-expansion within a relationship increases the likelihood that couples stay together. Mattingly et al. (2019, Study 2) performed a 9-month longitudinal investigation using a community sample of early-stage romantic relationships. Because some of the relationships dissolved between the baseline and final measurements, the authors were able to perform a binary logistic regression using self-expansion as the predictor and relationship status as the outcome. Results revealed that self-expansion levels at baseline significantly predicted relationship status nine months later, and for each unit increase in self-expansion at baseline (measured on a nine-point scale), relationships were 36 percent more likely to be intact at the final measurement.

Relationship Maintenance

Beyond being associated with increased relationship and sexual satisfaction, one reason why self-expansion may promote relationship longevity is that self-expansion increases the likelihood that individuals hold relationship-enhancing cognitions and motivations, and, ultimately, enact more relationship maintenance behaviors. For example, individuals who report greater inclusion of other in self also tend to exhibit greater positivity and openness with their partners, provide their partner with more positive assurances, and engage in more shared tasks with their partners (Ledbetter, Stassen-Ferrara, & Dowd, 2013). Additionally, evidence suggests that experiencing self-expansion within a relationship is associated with greater willingness to sacrifice and an increased tendency to respond to a partner's transgressions with forgiveness (McIntyre et al., 2015), indicating that self-expanded individuals have experienced a transformation of motivation and are placing partner interests ahead of self-interests. Moreover, self-expansion is associated with reduced attention to alternatives (McIntyre et al., 2015; VanderDrift, Lewandowski, & Agnew, 2011) and, correspondingly, is associated with reduced sexual and emotional infidelity (Mattingly et al., 2014; VanderDrift et al., 2011).

Fostering Relationship Closeness

The inclusion-of-other-in-self principle suggests that a primary way that individuals experience self-expansion occurs in close relationships when individuals include aspects of their partner into their own sense of self (Aron et al., 2013). As individuals incorporate partner's traits, perspectives, identities, and resources into their self-concept, they should experience greater levels of closeness, and presumably greater similarity, with their partner, and this was a focus of much of the early work on self-expansion (e.g., Aron et al., 2000; Reissman et al., 1993). More recent evidence also suggests that couples who engage in self-expanding activities experience enhanced closeness. For example, research shows that shared participation in extreme sports, such as skydiving, predicts relationship closeness (Frye, 2018). Other work examines the roles that hormones play in affecting perceptions of closeness in new relationships. People with social anxieties experience a dysregulation of the hormone cortisol that can inhibit the experience of self-expansion that occurs during relationship formation (Ketay, Welker, Beck, Thorson, & Slatcher, 2019). Moreover, initial interactions that foster self-expansion, characterized by high self-disclosure, lead to greater perceptions of closeness, especially for those low in cortisol (Ketay, Welker, & Slatcher, 2017).

Individual Outcomes

A cornerstone of the self-expansion model is the assumption that relationship-induced self-expansion may not only have benefits for relationships, but also for the individuals within those relationships (Aron et al.,

2013). Indeed, one of the early findings in the research on self-expansion was that individuals reporting that they had recently fallen in love reported significantly larger self-concepts, as well as increased self-esteem (Aron et al., 1995). More recently, work has examined a variety of individual outcomes of relational self-expansion. Research reveals that self-expansion is associated with individual perceptions of need fulfillment, including intimacy needs, companionship needs, security needs, emotional-involvement needs (Lewandowski & Ackerman, 2006), and the basic psychological needs of autonomy, competence, and relatedness, which are important components of self-determination (McIntyre, Mattingly, & Lewandowski, 2018). Moreover, individuals high in attachment anxiety are more likely to include their partners into their self, presumably to assuage their fear of abandonment (Slotter & Gardner, 2012).

Another line of research on individual outcomes of self-expansion examines the association between self-expansion and self-efficacy. Early theorizing regarding the self-expansion model specified that individuals are motivated to engage in self-expanding activities (of which close relationships are but one example) in order to enhance their ability to accomplish goals and overall sense of self-efficacy (Aron et al., 2013). Mattingly and Lewandowski (2013a) provided the first direct test of the idea that self-expansion is associated with increased self-efficacy. Results from a series of studies revealed that self-concept size (an indirect measure of self-expansion) is positively correlated with self-efficacy. Not surprisingly, given that self-expansion is associated with greater self-efficacy, it is also associated with more successful goal pursuit. In particular, research shows that self-expansion increases the effort that individuals exert on difficult tasks (Mattingly & Lewandowski, 2013b), enhances individuals' ability to quit smoking (Xu, Floyd, Westmaas, & Aron, 2010), and increases their adherence to weight-loss programs (Xu et al., 2017).

Summary

Though well-studied in the early days of self-expansion research, there continue to be empirical advances in exploring the consequences and outcomes of the self-expansion process (e.g., sexual satisfaction, relationship longevity, need fulfillment, behavioral adherence). Additional research should examine moderators of the self-expansion process, such as when self-expansion may be particularly impactful for individuals and relationships, as there are undoubtedly individual differences and situational factors that play a role. For example, at the individual difference level, Ketay and Beck (2017) identified attachment anxiety as a potential moderator of the self-expansion process. At the situational level, individuals who have recently experienced a self-expanding event may be more likely to identify additional self-expanding opportunities due to the salience of self-expansion as a desirable outcome.

FUTURE DIRECTIONS AND CONCLUDING REMARKS

The first two decades of work on the self-expansion model revolutionized the ways in which scholars considered the dynamic interplay between self and relationships. The model generated conceptually interesting and methodologically rigorous empirical work. The research reviewed in this chapter advances the literature on self-expansion by describing the precursors of self-expansion, differentiating self-expansion from other forms of relationship-induced self-concept change, identifying the necessary components of the self-expansion process, and examining novel inter- and intrapersonal outcomes. Importantly, this work informs, and is informed by, Interdependence Theory in that self-expansion is itself a precursor of interdependence and simultaneously a consequence of interdependent processes.

Though recent work has broadened and deepened the self-expansion model, there are many avenues of empirical investigation that remain relatively untapped. For example, though research indicates that self-expansion is associated with various relationship outcomes, including dissolution, future research should examine whether self-expansion predicts the progression through various relationship stages (e.g., the development of interdependence, changes in relationship status, cohabiting, marriage), relationship trajectories (e.g., on-again/off-again relationship churning; Dailey, Pfeister, Jin, Beck, & Clark, 2009), and coping with and recovering from relationship conflict. It is also important to note that the majority of research on self-expansion in relationships has focused on couples in relatively early-stage relationships. It would deepen the theory to understand how self-expansion processes occur in other types of relationships in which interdependence can occur, such as friendships (e.g., Lewandowski et al., 2016; Tomlinson et al., 2019) and in a variety of stages of life and relationship lengths (e.g., in retirement and older adulthood; Tomlinson & Feeney, 2016).

Additionally, future research should explore moderators of the self-expansion process, as well as how self-expansion may moderate relationship processes. Emerging work has shown that individuals may only seek self-expansion under certain conditions (e.g., individuals who are approach-motivated, growth-oriented, and high in self-concept clarity). However, there are myriad individual differences (e.g., personality traits, attachment, rejection sensitivity) and relationship characteristics (e.g., partner responsiveness, asymmetrical commitment, relationship identification) that may also promote or inhibit self-expansion. For example, individuals high in rejection sensitivity (Downey, Freitas, Michaelis, & Khouri, 1998) may shy away from novelty and challenge as a way of avoiding incorporating a partner's traits into their own self-concept for fear of having to navigate self-concept confusion if the relationship were to end.

Beyond its importance to the close relationships literature, self-expansion is also beginning to be applied to various social and non-social domains. One area that seems ripe for future work is the application of the self-expansion principles into clinical and counseling psychology. Researchers and clinicians could develop self-expansion-based interventions that potentially benefit interdependent relationships at both the individual and couple level (e.g., Carson, Carson, Gil, & Baucom, 2007; Coulter & Malouff, 2013). Future research should examine the efficacy of these interventions, as well as their possible long-term benefits. Another potentially fruitful application of the self-expansion model is intergroup relations. Just as individuals experience self-expansion with romantic partners, they may also experience self-expansion by interacting with members of outgroups (Dys-Steenbergen, Wright, & Aron, 2016). By definition, interacting with individuals with different backgrounds, perspectives, and identities lays the groundwork for self-expansion, and subsequently interdependence, to potentially occur. There has also been little cross-cultural work on self-expansion processes, which could be important for potential applications to reduce intergroup conflict.

Overall, there have been many recent advances to the self-expansion model that have identified precursors, necessary components, and outcomes of the self-expansion process, yet there is still much to be examined (see Mattingly, McIntyre, & Lewandowski, in press, for a review). Future work should explicitly look for additional connections with Interdependence Theory and other generative theories such as attachment theory, perceived partner responsiveness, and capitalization, to name but a few. Accordingly, self-expansion will likely be an important theoretical model for years to come.

REFERENCES

Acevedo, B. P. & Aron, A. (2009). Does a long-term relationship kill romantic love? *Review of General Psychology*, 13, 59–65.

Agnew, C. R. & Le, B. (2015). Prosocial behavior in close relationships: An interdependence approach. In D. A. Schroeder & W. G. Graziano (Eds.), *The Oxford Handbook of Prosocial Behavior* (pp. 362–375). New York: Oxford University Press. doi:10.1093/oxfordhb/9780195399813.013.021

Agnew, C. R., Van Lange, P. A. M., Rusbult, C. E., & Langston, C. A. (1998). Cognitive interdependence: Commitment and the mental representation of close relationships. *Journal of Personality and Social Psychology*, 74, 939–954.

Aron, A. & Aron, E. N. (1986). *Love as the Expansion of Self: Understanding Attraction and Satisfaction*. New York: Hemisphere.

Aron, A., Aron, E. N., & Smollan, D. (1992). Inclusion of other in the self scale and the structure of interpersonal closeness. *Journal of Personality and Social Psychology*, 63, 596–612.

Aron, A., Aron, E. N., Tudor, M., & Nelson, G. (1991). Close relationships as including other in the self. *Journal of Personality and Social Psychology*, 60, 241–253.

Aron, A., Lewandowski, G. W., Jr., Mashek, D., & Aron, E. N. (2013). The self-expansion model of motivation and cognition in close relationships. In J. A. Simpson & L. Campbell (Eds.), *The Oxford Handbook of Close Relationships* (pp. 90–105). New York: Oxford University Press.

Aron, A., Norman, C. C., & Aron, E. N. (1998). The self-expansion model and motivation. *Representative Research in Social Psychology*, 22, 1–13.

Aron, A., Norman, C. C., Aron, E. N., McKenna, C., & Heyman, R. E. (2000). Couples' shared participation in novel and arousing activities and experienced relationship quality. *Journal of Personality and Social Psychology*, 78, 273–284.

Aron, A., Paris, M., & Aron, E. N. (1995). Falling in love: Prospective studies of self-concept change. *Journal of Personality and Social Psychology*, 69, 1102–1112.

Bühler, J. L., Weidmann, R., Kumashiro, M., & Grob, A. (2019). Does Michelangelo care about age? An adult life-span perspective on the Michelangelo phenomenon. *Journal of Social and Personal Relationships*, 36(4), 1392–1412.

Burnette, J. L., O'Boyle, E. H., VanEpps, E. M., Pollack, J. M., & Finkel, E. J. (2013). Mind-sets matter: A meta-analytic review of implicit theories and self-regulation. *Psychological Bulletin*, 139, 655–701.

Campbell, J. D., Trapnell, P. D, Heine, S. J., Katz, I. M., Lavallee, L. F., & Lehmann, D. R. (1996). Self-concept clarity: Measurement, personality correlates and cultural boundaries. *Journal of Personality and Social Psychology*, 70, 141–156.

Carson, J. W., Carson, K. M., Gil, K. M., & Baucom, D. H. (2007). Self-expansion as a mediator of relationship improvements in a mindfulness intervention. *Journal of Marriage and Family Therapy*, 33, 517–528.

Cheung, E. O. & Gardner, W. L. (2016). With a little help from my friends: Understanding how social networks influence the pursuit of the ideal self. *Self and Identity*, 15, 662–682.

Cloutier, A. & Peetz, J. (2017). People, they are a changin': The links between anticipating change and romantic relationship quality. *Journal of Social and Personal Relationships*, 34, 676–698.

Coulter, K. & Malouff, J. M. (2013). Effects of an intervention designed to enhance romantic relationship excitement: A randomized-control trial. *Couple and Family Psychology: Research and Practice*, 2, 34–44.

Dailey, R. M., Pfiester, A., Jin, B., Beck, G., & Clark, G. (2009). On-again/off-again dating relationships: How are they different from other dating relationships? *Personal Relationships*, 16, 23–47.

DiDonato, T. E. & Krueger, J. I. (2010). Interpersonal affirmation and self-authenticity: A test of Rogers's self-growth hypothesis. *Self and Identity*, 9, 322–336.

Downey, G., Freitas, A. L., Michaelis, B., & Khouri, H. (1998). The self-fulfilling prophecy in close relationships: Rejection sensitivity and rejection by romantic partners. *Journal of Personality and Social Psychology*, 75, 545–560.

Drigotas, S. M., Rusbult, C. E., Wieselquist, J., & Whitton, S. W. (1999). Close partner as sculptor of the ideal self: Behavioral affirmation and the Michelangelo phenomenon. *Journal of Personality and Social Psychology*, 77, 293–323.

Dys-Steenbergen, O., Wright, S. C., & Aron, A. (2016). Self-expansion motivation improves cross-group interactions and enhances self-growth. *Group Processes & Intergroup Relations*, 19, 60–71.

Emery, L. F., Gardner, W. L., Finkel, E. J., & Carswell, K. L. (2018). "You've changed": Low self-concept clarity predicts lack of support for partner change. *Personality and Social Psychology Bulletin*, 44, 318–331.

Emery, L. F., Walsh, C., & Slotter, E. B. (2015). Knowing who you are and adding to it: Reduced self-concept clarity predicts reduced self-expansion. *Social Psychological and Personality Science, 6,* 259–266.

Fivecoat, H. C., Tomlinson, J. M., Aron, A., & Caprariello, P. A. (2015). Partner support for individual self-expansion opportunities: Effects on relationship satisfaction in long-term couples. *Journal of Social and Personal Relationships, 32,* 368–385.

Franiuk, R., Cohen, D., & Pomerantz, E. M. (2002). Implicit theories of relationships: Implications for relationship satisfaction and longevity. *Personal Relationships, 9,* 345–367.

Frost, D. M., McClelland, S. I., & Dettmann, M. (2017). Sexual closeness discrepancies: What they are and why they matter for sexual well-being in romantic relationships. *Archives of Sexual Behavior, 46,* 2353–2364.

Frye, N. E. (2018). "Let's do *what* together?!" Shared activity perceptions and relationship closeness. *Leisure Sciences, 40,* 374–386.

Girme, Y. U., Overall, N. C., & Faingataa, S. (2014). "Date nights" take two: The maintenance function of shared relationship activities. *Personal Relationships, 21,* 125–149.

Gordon, C. L. & Luo, S. (2011). The Personal Expansion Questionnaire: Measuring one's tendency to expand through novelty and augmentation. *Personality and Individual Differences, 51,* 89–94.

Graham, J. M. (2008). Self-expansion and flow in couples' momentary experiences: An experience sampling study. *Journal of Personality and Social Psychology, 95,* 679–694.

Graham, J. M. & Harf, M. R. (2015). Self-expansion and flow: The roles of challenge, skill, affect, and activation. *Personal Relationships, 22,* 45–64.

Harasymchuk, C., Cloutier, A., Peetz, J., & Lebreton, J. (2017). Spicing up the relationship? The effects of relational boredom on shared activities. *Journal of Social and Personal Relationships, 34,* 833–854.

Higgins, E. T. (1998). Promotion and prevention: Regulatory focus as a motivational principle. *Advances in Social Psychology, 30,* 1–46.

Hilaire, N. M. (2013). *Self-expansion motivation and romantic liking in relationship initiation* (Master's thesis). Retrieved from https://ir.library.illinoisstate.edu/etd/59/

Jakubiak, B. K. & Tomlinson, J. M. (in press). The role of social support in promoting self-development. In B. A. Mattingly, K. P. McIntyre, & G. W. Lewandowski, Jr. (Eds.), *Interpersonal Relationships and the Self-Concept.* Cham, Switzerland: Springer.

Kelley, H. H. & Thibaut, J. W. (1978). *Interpersonal Relations: A Theory of Interdependence.* New York: Wiley.

Ketay, S. & Beck, L. A. (2017). Attachment predicts cortisol response and closeness in dyadic social interaction. *Psychoneuroendocrinology, 80,* 114–121.

Ketay, S., Beck, L. A., Riela, S., Bailey, C., & Aron, A. (2019). Seeing you in me: Preliminary evidence for perceptual overlap between self and close others. *Journal of Social and Personal Relationships, 36,* 2474–2486. doi:10.1177/0265407518788702.

Ketay, S., Welker, K. M., Beck, L. A., Thorson, K. R., & Slatcher, R. B. (2019). Social anxiety, cortisol, and early-stage friendship. *Journal of Social and Personal Relationships, 36,* 1954–1974. doi:10.1177/0265407518774915

Ketay, S., Welker, K. M., & Slatcher, R. B. (2017). The roles of testosterone and cortisol in friendship formation. *Psychoneuroendocrinology*, 76, 88–96.

Knee, C. R. (1998). Implicit theories of relationships: Assessment and prediction of romantic relationship initiation, coping, and longevity. *Journal of Personality and Social Psychology*, 74, 360–370.

Knee, C. R., Patrick, H., & Lonsbary, C. (2003). Implicit theories of relationships: Orientations toward evaluation and cultivation. *Personality and Social Psychology Review*, 7, 41–55.

Le, B., Dove, N. L., Agnew, C. R., Korn, M. S., & Mutso, A. A. (2010). Predicting nonmarital romantic relationship dissolution: A meta-analytic synthesis. *Personal Relationships*, 17, 377–390.

Ledbetter, A. M., Stassen-Ferrara, H. M., & Dowd, M. M. (2013). Comparing equity and self-expansion theory approaches to relationship maintenance. *Personal Relationships*, 20, 38–51.

Lewandowski, G. W., Jr. & Ackerman, R. A. (2006). Something's missing: Need fulfillment and self-expansion as predictors of susceptibility to infidelity. *Journal of Social Psychology*, 146, 389–403.

Lewandowski, G. W., Jr. & Aron, A. P. (2004). Distinguishing arousal from novelty and challenge in initial romantic attraction. *Social Behavior and Personality: An International Journal*, 32, 361–372.

Lewandowski, G. W., Jr., Mattingly, B. A., McIntyre, K. P., & Acri, L. (2016). *That's what friends are for: Self-expansion's role in friendship*. Unpublished manuscript.

Lewandowski, G. W., Jr., Nardone, N., & Raines, A. J. (2010). The role of self-concept clarity in relationship quality. *Self and Identity*, 9, 416–433.

Lodi-Smith, J. & DeMarree, K. G. (Eds.). (2017). *Self-Concept Clarity: Perspectives on Assessment, Research, and Applications*. New York: Springer.

Mattingly, B. A. & Lewandowski, G. W., Jr. (2013a). An expanded self is a more capable self: The association between self-concept size and self-efficacy. *Self and Identity*, 12, 621–634.

Mattingly, B. A. & Lewandowski, G. W., Jr. (2013b). The power of one: Benefits of individual self-expansion. *Journal of Positive Psychology*, 8, 12–22.

Mattingly, B. A. & Lewandowski, G. W., Jr. (2014). Broadening horizons: Self-expansion in relational and non-relational contexts. *Social and Personality Psychology Compass*, 8, 30–40.

Mattingly, B. A., Lewandowski, G. W, Jr., & McIntyre, K. P. (2014). "You make me a better/worse person": A two-dimensional model of relationship self-change. *Personal Relationships*, 21, 176–190.

Mattingly, B. A. & McIntyre, K. P. (2018, July). Authentically Us: Relational Self-Change Mediates the Association Between Self-Knowledge and Relationship Quality. Presentation at the 2018 International Association for Relationship Research Conference, Fort Collins, CO.

Mattingly, B. A., McIntyre, K. P., Knee, C. R., & Loving, T. J. (2019). Implicit theories of relationships and self-expansion: Implications for relationship functioning. *Journal of Social and Personal Relationships*, 36, 1579–1599.

Mattingly, B. A., McIntyre, K. P., & Lewandowski, G. W., Jr. (2012). Approach motivation and the expansion of self in close relationships. *Personal Relationships*, 19, 113–127.

Mattingly, B. A., McIntyre, K. P., & Lewandowski, G. W., Jr. (Eds.) (in press) *Interpersonal Relationships and the Self-Concept*. Cham, Switzerland: Springer.

Mattingly, B. A., McIntyre, K. P., & Selterman, D. F. (2018). Individual differences and romantic relationships: Bidirectional influences on self and relational processes. In V. Zeigler-Hill and T. K. Shackelford (Eds.), *The SAGE Handbook of Personality and Individual Differences: Volume 2. Origins of Personality and Individual Differences* (pp. 402–430). Thousand Oaks, CA: SAGE.

Maxwell, J. A., Muise, A., MacDonald, G., Day, L C., Rosen, N. O., & Impett, E. A. (2017). How implicit theories of sexuality shape sexual and relationship well-being. *Journal of Personality and Social Psychology, 112,* 238–279.

McIntyre, K. P., Mattingly, B. A., & Lewandowski, G. W., Jr. (2015). When "we" changes "me": The two-dimensional model of relational self-change and relationship outcomes. *Journal of Social and Personal Relationships, 32,* 857–878.

McIntyre, K. P., Mattingly, B. A., & Lewandowski, G. W., Jr. (2017). Self-concept clarity and romantic relationships. In J. Lodi-Smith & K. DeMarree (Eds.), *Self-Concept Clarity: Perspectives on Assessment, Research, and Applications* (pp. 107–124). New York: Springer.

McIntyre, K. P., Mattingly, B. A., & Lewandowski, G. W., Jr. (2018). *Self-expansion and basic psychological needs.* Unpublished manuscript.

Muise, A., Harasymchuk, C., Day. L. C., Bacev-Giles, C., Gere, J., & Impett, E. A. (2019). Broadening your horizons: Self-expanding activities promote desire and satisfaction in established romantic relationships. *Journal of Personality and Social Psychology, 116,* 237–258.

Nardone, N., Lewandowski, G. W., Jr., & Le, B. (2008, February). The Relation of Self-Expansion to Well-Being and Relationship Quality. Presentation at the 2008 annual meeting of the Society for Personality and Social Psychology, Albuquerque, NM.

Reissman, C., Aron, A., & Bergen, M. R. (1993). Shared activities and marital satisfaction: Causal directions and self-expansion versus boredom. *Journal of Social and Personal Relationships, 10,* 243–254.

Rusbult, C. E., Van Lange, P. A. M., Wildschut, T., Yovetich, N. A., & Verette, J. (2000). Perceived superiority in close relationships: Why it exists and persists. *Journal of Personality and Social Psychology, 79,* 521–545.

Sheets, V. L. (2014). Passion for life: Self-expansion and passionate love across the lifespan. *Journal of Social and Personal Relationships, 31,* 958–974.

Shukusky, J., McIntyre, K. P., & Mattingly, B. A. (2017, November). Those Who Play Together, Stay Together: Self-Expansion Predicts Sexual Satisfaction. Presentation at the 2017 annual meeting of the Society for the Scientific Study of Sexuality, Atlanta, GA.

Slotter, E. B. & Gardner, W. L. (2012). How needing you changes me: The influence of attachment anxiety on self-concept malleability in romantic relationships. *Self and Identity, 11,* 386–408.

Strong, G. & Aron, A. (2006). The effect of shared participation in novel and challenging activities on experienced relationship quality: Is it mediated by high positive affect? In K. D. Vohs & E. J. Finkel (Eds.), *Self and Relationships:*

Connecting Intrapersonal and Interpersonal Processes (pp. 342–359). New York: Guilford Press.

Tomlinson, J. M. & Feeney, B. C. (2016). Helping Each Other Grow: Benefits of Partner Support for Self-Expansion in Retirement. Poster presented at the Society for Personality and Social Psychology Annual Meeting. San Diego, CA.

Tomlinson, J. M., Hughes, E. K., Lewandowski, G. W., Jr., Aron, A., & Geyer, R. (2019). Do shared self-expanding activities have to be physically arousing? *Journal of Social and Personal Relationships*, 36, 2781–2801.

Tsapelas, I., Aron, A., & Orbuch, T. (2009). Marital boredom now predicts less satisfaction 9 years later. *Psychological Science*, 20, 543–545.

VanderDrift, L. E., Lewandowski, G. W., Jr., & Agnew, C. R. (2011). Reduced self-expansion in current romance and interest in relationship alternatives. *Journal of Social and Personal Relationships*, 28, 356–373.

Walker, D. & Harasymchuk, C. (2017, June). Plan a Date! Self-Expanding Relationship Activities and the Role of Approach Relationship Goals. Presentation at the 2017 International Association for Relationship Research Mini-Conference, Syracuse, NY.

Xu, X., Floyd, A. H. L., Westmaas, J. L., & Aron, A. (2010). Self-expansion and smoking abstinence. *Addictive Behaviors*, 35, 295–301.

Xu, X., Leahey, T. M., Boguszewski, K., Krupel, K., Kent, K. A., & Wing, R. R. (2017). Self-expansion is associated with better adherence and behavioral weight loss in adults. *Annals of Behavioral Medicine*, 51, 13–17.

12

Self-Esteem, Negative Expressivity, and Partner Responsiveness

KASSANDRA CORTES AND JOANNE V. WOOD

Everyone has bad days. Being scolded by a boss, failing to reach a goal, or arguing with a sibling are all negative experiences that can feel stressful or painful. Fortunately, people can turn to their romantic partners during difficult times. But, unfortunately, not everyone feels supported or cared for by their partners. Compared to people with high self-esteem (HSEs), people with low self-esteem (LSEs) generally feel that their partners are less accepting and responsive to them (Cameron, Holmes, & Vorauer, 2009; Cameron, Stinson, Gaetz, & Balchen, 2010; Gaucher et al., 2012; Murray, Holmes, & Griffin, 2000; Murray, Holmes, Griffin, Bellavia, & Rose, 2001; Murray, Holmes, MacDonald, & Ellsworth, 1998).

A widespread assumption in the literature has been that LSEs' perceptions of their partner's lower responsiveness are "all in their heads" – a projection of their own insecurities – and that LSEs' partners are actually just as responsive as HSEs' partners. Some evidence supports this assumption (e.g., Baumeister, Campbell, Kreuger, & Vohs, 2003; Lakey & Cassady, 1990; Murray et al., 2000, 2001). Contrary to this assumption and this evidence, however, we describe research demonstrating that, in specific interactions, LSEs' partners are indeed less responsive than are HSEs' partners to disclosers' negative self-disclosures. We review evidence for the role of self-esteem in global and specific perceptions of responsiveness and actual received partner responsiveness, discuss reasons for such findings, and suggest future work to untangle mechanisms accounting for LSEs' lower received responsiveness. We end by discussing implications for close relationships.

SELF-DISCLOSURE AND RESPONSIVENESS

Engaging in self-disclosure – expressing one's inner feelings and experiences to others – is beneficial for both the self and relationships (Reis & Shaver, 1988). People tend to feel a sense of relief after they have self-disclosed to another person (Pennebaker, Zech, & Rime, 2001), and people who engage in intimate disclosures tend to be liked more than those who disclose less (Collins & Miller, 1994). Furthermore, those who engage in intimate self-disclosure with their romantic partners tend to feel closer to their partners and to rate their relationships more positively (Laurenceau, Barrett, & Pietromonaco, 1998; Sprecher & Hendrick, 2004). Recent research also suggests that being prompted to self-disclose has interpersonal benefits (Cortes & Wood, 2019; Huang, Yeomans, Brooks, Minson, & Gino, 2017). When people are asked questions by others, they tend to like those others more (Huang et al., 2017), and feel more cared for (Cortes & Wood, 2019).

However, self-disclosure is an interdependent process, so the consequences of self-disclosure also depend on the type of response given by the partner. According to Reis and Shaver's (1988) interpersonal model of intimacy, partner responsiveness – the degree to which partners respond with caring, understanding, and validation to one's disclosures – determines whether the self-disclosure will enhance intimacy and whether one will self-disclose again with that partner. Responsiveness is viewed by relationship researchers as a core feature of close, satisfying relationships (Reis, 2007; Reis & Clark, 2013; Reis, Clark, & Holmes, 2004; Reis & Shaver, 1988). Some researchers have argued that responsiveness is even more central to intimacy than self-disclosure itself (Laurenceau et al., 1998). Higher responsiveness promotes intimacy (Laurenceau et al., 1998; Reis & Shaver, 1988), predicts greater relationship satisfaction, commitment, and feelings of security (Collins & Feeney, 2000; Kane et al., 2007; Laurenceau, et al., 1998; Reis et al., 2004), and enhances sexual well-being (Birnbaum & Reis, 2012). Importantly, certain personality factors predict perceptions of partner responsiveness (e.g., see Reis et al., 2004), including self-esteem.

SELF-ESTEEM AND RESPONSIVENESS

The idea emphasized by interdependence theorists, that romantic partners mutually influence each other's experiences and outcomes (Kelley, 1979; Thibaut & Kelley, 1959), is clearly evident in research on how self-esteem affects self-disclosure and responsiveness (e.g., Wood & Forest, 2016). How people feel about themselves – their feelings of self-worth – profoundly affects how they think and behave in their romantic relationships (e.g., Baldwin, 1992; Murray, Griffin, Rose, & Bellavia, 2003; Murray, Holmes & Collins, 2006; Murray et al., 2000, 2001; Rusbult, Morrow, & Johnson, 1987). People with low self-esteem do not value themselves as much as do people with high self-esteem (Leary & MacDonald, 2003). In relationships, LSEs are less confident than HSEs that their partners love them (Murray et al., 2001). LSEs are also more doubtful that their partners view them positively than are HSEs.

Compared to HSEs, LSEs also feel that their partners are less accepting, less understanding, and less responsive to their needs (Murray et al., 2000) and as providing less social support (e.g., Cameron et al., 2009; Vinokur, Schul, & Caplan, 1987). These relationship insecurities lead LSEs to feel worse about their partners and their relationships (Murray et al., 1998).

Are LSEs' Pessimistic Partner Perceptions Warranted?

Are these less favorable perceptions on the part of LSEs warranted? A widespread, albeit often implicit, assumption in the literature has been that LSEs' partners are not truly less caring and responsive but that, instead, LSEs' underestimates are "all in their heads" – a projection of their own insecurities. For instance, when participants' own perceptions of their partner's views of them were compared with their partners' actual perceptions, the results revealed that HSEs were accurate, but that LSEs dramatically underestimated their partner's views of them and love for them (Murray et al., 2000, 2001). The authors concluded that LSEs' insecurities are unwarranted:

Rather than simply and accurately reflecting a romantic partner's true regard, percep-tions of this regard are in large part a projection, reflecting self-perceived worthiness of love (a type of false consensus effect) ... individuals with higher self-esteem correctly believed their partners saw them relatively positively, whereas intimates with lower self-esteem incorrectly believed their partners saw them relatively negatively.

(Murray et al., 2000, p. 494)

In a paper reviewing the associations between self-esteem and various outcomes (e.g., performance, popularity, health), Baumeister and colleagues concluded that self-esteem strongly predicts perceptions, but not objective outcomes. The authors stated that differences in perceptions of LSEs versus HSEs are mostly untrue, including interpersonal domains: "People high in self-esteem regard themselves as better liked and more popular than others, but most of these advantages exist mainly in their own minds, and objective data (such as ratings by peers) generally fail to confirm them" (Baumeister et al., 2003, p. 36). Indeed, other research supports the idea that motivated bias affects interpretations of one's own behavior and partner behavior (Lakey & Orehek, 2011; see Reis & Gable, 2015): LSEs and rejection-sensitive individuals perceive their partner's slightly negative or ambiguous behaviors as signs of rejection and lack of caring (Downey, Freitas, Michaelis, & Khouri, 1998; Murray, Bellavia, Rose, & Griffin, 2003). LSEs also perceive less acceptance than HSEs, even when given the same acceptance cues (through friendly behavior) from a confederate (Cameron et al., 2010).

How might LSEs' unwarranted insecurities generalize to perceptions of responsiveness to specific negative self-disclosures? The research cited above focused on global perceptions of partner acceptance and responsiveness, rather than responsiveness to disclosures about particular events. However, we can draw on the social support literature because of its relevance to responsiveness. Additionally, because self-esteem is strongly linked to a number of other personality traits (i.e., attachment insecurity, rejection sensitivity, and neuroticism), we can draw on research examining those traits in the context of social support. The social support literature suggests that peoples' beliefs and expectations about support affect their perceptions of support (Lemay, Clark, & Feeney, 2007). These beliefs can stem from their personalities or from their general beliefs about the self as worthy of acceptance and caring (Carmichael, Tsai, Smith, Caprariello, & Reis, 2007; Cutrona, 1996; Fraley & Shaver, 2000; Sarason, Pierce, & Sarason, 1990), and may not correspond well with the actual support they received, as measured objectively (Baldwin, 1992; Pierce, Sarason, & Sarason, 1992). A review by Dunkel-Schetter and Bennett (1990) concluded that "subjective perceptions of support are more strongly tied to personality than to social experience" (Reis et al., 2004, p. 211). For example, one study found that LSEs reported perceiving less social support available to them in general than HSEs, but that participants' reports of enacted support received by others in the past month was uncorrelated with self-esteem (Lakey & Cassady, 1990). Similarly, another study found that, when revealing a personal flaw, LSEs perceived written messages from their partner as less supportive than HSEs, but self-esteem did not predict objective coders' ratings of support (Cameron et al., 2009).

In another study conducted by Collins and Feeney (2004), couples were brought into the lab and separated to complete individual tasks. One member of the couple was assigned to give a stressful speech that would be videotaped and rated by others. Couples were told they would have the opportunity to interact by sending brief notes throughout the study. Unbeknownst to the speech-giver, his/her partner was asked by the experimenter to act as a confederate and to write a scripted note. When speech-givers who were insecurely attached (which is highly linked to LSE) received scripted low-support messages (e.g., "Your speech was a little hard to follow, but I guess you did the best you could under the circumstances") they perceived the feedback as *less* supportive than did secure people. Even when messages are identical, then, personality or beliefs about the self can lead people to different perceptions of how supportive those messages are.

Is It Really All in LSEs' Heads?

The research reviewed above suggests that LSEs misperceive partner responsiveness due to their unwarranted relationship insecurities. This interpretation of LSEs' perceptions of weak partner responsiveness – that they are "all in their heads" – seems to be the accepted view among researchers. However, some evidence also points to the opposite conclusion: That there may be some truth to LSEs' more unfavorable perceptions. LSEs' partners may actually be, to some extent, less responsive than HSEs' partners.

Perceptions of Social Support Are Grounded in Reality It is possible that even if LSEs' perceptions of their partner's *global* regard for them is off-base – even if their beliefs about the extent of their partners' regard, love, and valuing underestimate their partners' actual regard, love, and valuing – LSEs' perceptions about their partner's responsiveness to them in *specific* daily interactions may not be off-base. Interdependence theorists highlight that past interactions with partners help people to calibrate their expectations about what to expect from partners in future interactions (Arriaga, 2013; Kelley, 1991; Rusbult & Van Lange, 2003). Therefore, LSEs' partners may have been unresponsive in specific interactions in the past, and these moments may have given substance to their inaccurate global perceptions.

In line with this idea is evidence that perceptions of social support are grounded in reality (Cutrona, Hessling, & Suhr, 1997). Several laboratory observation studies have demonstrated an association between peoples' perceptions of partner support and independent observers' ratings of provided support (see Reis & Clark, 2013 for a review). For example, Collins and Feeney (2000) found that when couples discussed an issue that one partner was facing, disclosing partners' perceptions of the support provided by their partner correlated with observers' ratings of support provided by the partner. Other research has shown that discloser reports of the support they have received from a partner align with the partner reports of the support they have enacted (Canevello & Crocker, 2010; see Clark & Lemay, 2010, for a review). Moreover, these associations between perceptions of support and objective support do not appear to be moderated by individual differences (Downey et al., 1998; Levy, Ayduk, & Downey, 2001). For example, in the Collins and Feeney (2000) dyadic laboratory study, attachment security did not moderate the degree to which support seekers' perceptions of support were correlated with objective ratings of support. If attachment security did not moderate the association between perceived and actual support, there is good reason to believe that self-esteem (which, again, is correlated with attachment security) would not moderate that association either. Thus, LSEs' reports of support are as likely as HSEs' reports of support to be correlated with coders' and partners' reports, suggesting that LSEs' perceptions about their partner's support may be grounded in reality.

At the same time, this evidence that LSEs' reports of support are correlated with more objective indices of support does not necessarily imply that LSEs are *accurate* in their perceptions. LSEs' and more objective sources' judgments may be correlated, but they may differ in their average ratings. That is, both LSEs and objective raters may recognize true differences in partner support, agreeing that some partners are more supportive and some are less supportive, but on average, LSEs may be biased negatively, such that LSEs' mean ratings may be lower than the mean of others' ratings (Overall, Fletcher, & Kenny, 2012).

Characteristics of LSEs That Could Lower Partners' Responsiveness Disclosing about negative events does not happen in a temporal vacuum: Partners have histories of interactions together that likely shape the way they respond in current interactions (Rusbult & Van Lange, 2003). Therefore, another reason we suspect that LSEs may have partners who actually are less responsive than HSEs' partners involves certain characteristics that LSEs have that may deter their partners from being more responsive. These characteristics have been shown to be associated with lower partner responsiveness, First, LSEs tend to express more negativity than HSEs (Wood & Forest, 2016). They complain more, express more unpleasant emotions like anxiety and sadness, and dwell on unpleasant events. Their Facebook status updates are more negative than HSEs' (Forest & Wood, 2012). In turn, actors' self-esteem seemed to yield partner effects: When people express negativity frequently, others like them less (Forest & Wood, 2012). Especially important to the present topic is evidence that people who express negativity frequently receive less responsiveness to specific instances of negativity (Forest, Kille, Wood, & Holmes, 2014). For example, if Sam, who expresses negativity on a daily basis to his partner Julie, comes home after a bad day at work and complains, Julie will be less responsive than if Sam did not regularly express so much negativity. It's like the "boy who cried wolf;" when someone expresses negativity a lot, loved ones take instances of negativity less seriously. Loved ones also appear to disengage, seemingly to avoid the burden of constantly providing support (Forest et al., 2014). Thus, because LSEs express more negativity than HSEs, and people who express a lot of negativity generally receive less responsiveness, there is good reason to believe LSEs receive less responsiveness. We suspect that the association between actor self-esteem and partner responsiveness would be especially likely to emerge in relationships with greater interdependence (as is the case in romantic relationships) because partners have a history of interactions together.

A second characteristic of LSEs that may lead their partners to be less responsive is that, overall, their partners tend to be less satisfied with the relationship than the partners of HSEs (Wood, Hogle, & McClellan, 2009). Satisfied partners tend to provide more support and responsiveness than less satisfied partners (e.g., Collins & Feeney, 2000). If lower satisfaction breeds lower responsiveness, then, we can expect that LSEs tend to receive less responsiveness from their partners than do HSEs.

Two additional but intertwined characteristics of LSEs may lead their partners to be less responsive than HSEs' partners. One characteristic is that, on average, LSEs expect less responsiveness from their partners. LSEs trust their partners less than HSEs do – meaning that they have less confidence that their partners care for them and will be responsive (McCarthy, Wood, Holmes, 2017; Murray et al., 2000; Reis et al., 2004). When people chronically have lower trust in their partner and expect less responsiveness, they react to acute feelings of insecurity differently than do people higher in trust. Many risk regulation studies have found that, in such instances, HSEs or higher-trust people draw closer to their partners, whereas LSEs or lower-trust people tend to self-protect (Murray et al., 1998, 2006). For example, LSEs distance themselves or derogate their partners or relationship in order to avoid further rejection and hurt.

How do these two characteristics – low expectations for responsiveness and tendency to self-protect – play out when insecure, lower-trust people want support and responsiveness from their partners? In a set of studies, McCarthy et al. (2017) found that when people experienced an unfavorable event outside the home, those who were lower in trust for their partner were less likely to disclose that event to their partners and to seek their partner's support. McCarthy et al. (2017) interpreted this finding to mean that people lower in trust were projecting unwarranted insecurities onto their partners: Because they feared their partners' reactions, they self-protectively inhibited their self-disclosures. However, it is also possible that their lower trust was based in part on past experience with their partners who actually *were* less responsive in diagnostic situations (Holmes & Rempel, 1989). In either case – whether lower trust is due to unwarranted insecurities or rooted in experiences with poorly-responding partners – refraining from self-disclosing about the negative events of the day may well worsen the relationship, leading one partner to not receive needed support, and depriving both partners of a chance to build intimacy.

In addition to failing to openly self-disclose, insecure people can behave more antagonistically toward their partners. Downey and colleagues have examined this phenomenon in their research on people who are especially sensitive to rejection (which is associated with low self-esteem). During conflicts with their partners, women high (vs. low) in rejection-sensitivity were more likely to anticipate that their partner would be unresponsive. The highly rejection-sensitive women also exhibited maladaptive behaviors during conflict, such as mocking the partner or making statements that implied a negative mindset or motivation of the partner. These behaviors then ended up eliciting less responsiveness from partners (Downey et al., 1998; Levy et al., 2001). The highly rejection-sensitive women perceived their partners to be unsupportive and, indeed, their partners were rated by independent observers as more unsupportive than those of low rejection-sensitivity women (Downey et al., 1998). Downey et al. (1998) argued that these conflict interactions unfolded as a self-fulfilling prophecy: When rejection-sensitive women expected low responsiveness, their self-protectiveness led them to behave antagonistically toward their partners, which brought about the very lack of responsiveness that they expected. Thus, although LSEs and other insecure people hold a strong desire to avoid rejection and to feel loved and valued, they often engage in exactly the kinds of behaviors that breed disliking and lower responsiveness (Wood & Forest, 2016).

Previous research suggests, then, that LSEs have four characteristics that may lead to lower responsiveness in their partners: they express a lot of negativity, which is not received well by others (Forest & Wood, 2012; Sommers, 1984); they have less satisfied partners (Wood et al., 2009), who generally provide less responsiveness than more satisfied partners (Collins & Feeney, 2000); and they have low expectations for responsiveness, which often leads them to behave self-protectively, either by being guarded or antagonistic, which leads partners to be less responsive.

In sum, some evidence suggests that LSEs underestimate their partner's responsiveness (e.g., Murray et al., 2000, 2001), whereas other evidence suggests that LSEs may indeed receive less responsiveness than HSEs (e.g., Downey et al., 1998). Below, we present work that directly examined how discloser's self-esteem is associated with listener's responsiveness, to determine whether LSEs really do elicit less responsiveness from their partners than HSEs. The specific context we examined involves self-disclosures when the topics to be disclosed (or not) are about unpleasant events external to the relationship.

A DIRECT INVESTIGATION OF SELF-ESTEEM AND PARTNER RESPONSIVENESS TO NEGATIVE SELF-DISCLOSURES

We examined the hypothesis that when self-disclosing about a negative event, LSEs perceive and actually receive less responsiveness from their partners than do HSEs (Cortes & Wood, 2018). We specifically examined negative self-disclosures about events or experiences that occurred outside of the relationship – such as having a bad day at work – when the partner was absent. Past work has mostly examined how couples react to conflict within their relationships ("inside" events). Less is known about how personality, and specifically self-esteem, affects how people express themselves, and what kind of responsiveness they receive, to events that occur outside of the relationship. Although this can be a risky context, it may be safer for both parties, on average, than conflict-ridden discussions about events inside the relationship. For example, for events that occur outside the relationship, listeners may not be motivated to defend their own past behavior.

In one study, we asked one member of the couple (the discloser) to indicate how responsive his/her partner typically is to his/her negative self-disclosures (perceived partner responsiveness). The other partner (the listener) was asked to indicate how responsive s/he typically is to his/her partner's negative self-disclosures (partner's reported actual responsiveness). We then examined LSEs' and HSEs' perceptions of their partners' responsiveness to their negative self-disclosures, and compared each with partners' reports of partners' own typical level of responsiveness. Both disclosers and listeners reported lower responsiveness when the discloser was low (vs. high) in self-esteem, suggesting that LSE disclosers were perceiving less responsive behavior and, most importantly, that partners verified LSEs' perceptions.

In another study, we brought couples into the lab, separated them, and created a negative rejection experience for one partner (the discloser). Specifically, the participant assigned to the role of discloser underwent an unpleasant rejection experience by playing a game called Cyberball (Williams & Jarvis, 2006), an online ball-tossing game shown to induce feelings of social exclusion (Williams et al., 2002). Following the Cyberball paradigm, participants were told that we were interested in their mental visualization skills and that they would play an online ball-tossing game with other participants who were logged on at the same time. After throwing a ball to a player, participants received the ball back once, but then never again for the reminder of the game. The virtual players were preprogrammed to exclude the participant by tossing the ball only to each other and not the participant, leaving the participant out for two minutes. Participants, on average, felt fairly rejected while playing, and self-esteem did not predict feelings of rejection.

Couples were then brought together and asked to discuss their experiences with the study so far for a total of six minutes. Couples were left in the room alone and were secretly videotaped. We had independent raters code for the level of responsiveness from the listener (i.e., how understanding, validating, and caring the listener was) to the disclosers' disclosures about their rejection experience. Coders rated partners of LSEs as less responsive than partners of HSEs. Taken together, we found support for the hypothesis that LSEs' pessimistic perceptions of their partner's responsiveness is not all in their heads: Partners of LSEs were indeed less responsive than partners of HSEs to their negative self-disclosures, as rated by themselves, by their partners, and by objective observers.

WHY DO LSES ELICIT LESS RESPONSIVENESS THAN HSES?

When disclosing about negative events that occur in a partner's absence, LSEs receive less responsiveness from their partners than do HSEs. What can explain such differences in received responsiveness? One possibility is that LSEs' partners' simply underestimate how upset their partners truly are, so they fail to provide high responsiveness because they do not realize that their partners need it.

A second possibility is that, as we suggested when we identified characteristics of LSEs that may discourage responsiveness in partners, LSEs' manner of disclosing unpleasant events may play a role. Because LSEs are likely more fearful than HSEs that their partners will not be understanding and responsive to them, it may be difficult for LSEs to be direct and open when soliciting support. LSEs may express their negativity in indirect ways (e.g., giving subtle hints that something is wrong), making it difficult for their partners to be responsive. When people solicit support in more direct ways (e.g., giving details of the problem), they receive better responses from caregivers (Collins & Feeney, 2000).

Although not directly related to how people disclose unpleasant events external to the relationship, some work has suggested that insecure people generally have more maladaptive expressivity styles in interpersonal contexts. The most direct evidence comes from Collins and Feeney's (2000) study on how partners discussed problems. When participants were asked to discuss a problem with their partner in the lab, insecure people (those high in avoidant attachment) were less direct (e.g., hinting, sulking) in sharing their problems with their romantic partners. In addition, past research has shown that insecure people tend to express more disruptive, uncooperative behavior during joint problem-solving tasks with friends (Zimmerman, Maier, Winter, & Grossmann, 2001) and express more anger and defensiveness during discussions about changes partners would like to see (Overall, Simpson, & Struthers, 2013). As reviewed earlier, women high in rejection sensitivity express anger during conflicts with partners in maladaptive ways – compared to women low in rejection sensitivity, they are more likely to derogate or mock their partners, to display nonverbal gestures that communicate displeasure or disapproval, and to act sad and whiny, for example (Downey et al., 1998).

Other work supports the idea that LSEs may be afraid to self-disclose directly because they are worried about their partner's responsiveness. Specifically, Lemay and colleagues showed that insecure people know that their partners sometimes "walk on eggshells" to avoid hurting them (Lemay & Clark, 2008a; Lemay & Dudley, 2011). That is, insecure people recognize that their partners try to assuage their insecurities, so they sometimes view their partners' reassurance and praise as inauthentic. Indeed, partners of insecure people report being less authentic to their partners than do partners of secure people (Lemay & Clark, 2008b; Lemay & Dudley, 2009). If LSEs anticipate getting an inauthentic response from their partners, they may be less inclined to express themselves directly.

We have begun to test all of these possibilities. Our preliminary results suggest that partners of LSEs are less responsive than partners of HSEs not because of misperceptions – partners of LSEs do recognize their partners' distress – but because of *how* LSEs self-disclosed. When presented with a scenario about getting into an argument with a best friend, LSE disclosers and partners of LSEs both reported that LSEs would disclose about the unpleasant event more indirectly and less honestly compared to HSEs. For example, LSEs were less likely than HSEs to indicate that they would be open and honest about what happened in the event and about how they were feeling. LSEs were more likely than HSEs to say that they would give subtle hints that something is wrong (e.g., mope around, sigh). LSEs (vs. HSEs) also reported being more likely to act like nothing was wrong when it really was, to hope their partner would press for more information, and to assume their partner should know something is wrong. Clinical psychologists have put such a "mindreading is expected" reaction at the top of their list of dysfunctional beliefs (see Epstein & Baucom, 2002, for a review).

Because past work has shown that direct expression elicits more responsiveness (Collins & Feeney, 2000), and there is initial evidence that LSEs are less direct than HSEs when expressing negativity, LSEs' disclosure strategies could very well explain why partners of LSEs are less responsive than partners of HSEs. However, another possibility, one which we did not test, is that LSEs are not the only ones responsible for their partners' poorer response-giving. Perhaps the partners of LSEs differ from the partners of HSEs from the outset. Perhaps they are less willing to convey responsiveness and care. Research has found that LSEs have lower partner standards and lower mating aspirations than HSEs (Hirschberger, Florian, & Mikulincer, 2002). Similarly, compared to secure people, less secure people are more willing to compromise their romantic standards and to stay in relationships that do not satisfy their needs (e.g., Slotter & Finkel, 2009). If LSEs indeed do have relatively unresponsive partners, it is possible that LSEs do not openly disclose their negative events not because they are expecting mindreading but, instead, they may be trying to downplay the issue or mute their reactions because their past experiences self-disclosing about negative events have led to unpleasant reactions from their partners.

Finally, there is work showing that insecure people tend to be poorer support givers (Collins & Feeney, 2000; Simpson, Rholes, Orina, & Grich, 2002). If LSEs are less responsive to their partners, their partners may be less responsive to them in return. Future research should further examine the mechanisms accounting for LSEs' lower likelihood than HSEs of receiving high responsiveness from their partners.

WHAT IF IT'S NOT ALL IN LSES' HEADS?

Feeling that a partner is highly responsive is critical to maintaining intimate and happy relationships (Laurenceau et al., 1998; Reis & Shaver, 1988). In the past, researchers have pointed the finger at LSEs as the likely cause for their lower quality relationships: ". . . persons with low self-esteem often underestimate their partners' regard and acceptance, a process that may instigate cycles of relationship deterioration" (Reis et al., 2004, p. 207). However, our evidence suggests that LSEs may not be the only culprits: LSEs' partners are in fact less responsive than the partners of HSEs (Cortes & Wood, 2018). Because responsiveness is integral to the well-being of relationships, LSEs' partners' lower responsiveness may also contribute to cycles of relationship deterioration (Levy et al., 2001). Our research suggests that the reason LSEs have poorer quality relationships is likely an interdependent process. When considering the cyclical process between actor's self-esteem and partner's responsiveness, it is tempting to view self-esteem as the stable attribute that then produces lower responsiveness from a partner, given that self-esteem is a relatively stable trait (Trzesniewski, Donnellan, & Robins, 2003). However, it is also possible that LSEs form lower self-esteem from their partner's lack of responsiveness during interactions over time (Kelley, 1983). Future research should focus on a) the partners of LSEs, not just LSEs themselves, when trying to understand why LSEs have poorer relationships than HSEs, and b) how actor's self-esteem may shift over time as a function of the partner's responsiveness.

Global versus Specific Perceptions

Although past research has shown that LSEs hold unwarranted global negative perceptions of their partner's regard for them (e.g., Lakey & Cassady, 1990; Murray et al., 2000, 2001), our work demonstrates that when it comes to specific dyadic interactions in which partners self-disclose about unpleasant events external to the relationship, partners of LSEs truly are less responsive than partners of HSEs (Cortes & Wood, 2018). Perhaps LSEs misperceive how much their partners globally love and care for them because they take the lower responsiveness they receive from their partners in specific dyadic interactions to mean they are less loved by their partner. Partners of LSEs may not realize that how they respond to their disclosing partner's negative self-disclosures affects their partner's perceptions of their overall love. Future research should examine how daily interactions affect global perceptions of love and care and how that association may depend on self-esteem.

Responsiveness and Personal Well-Being

Improving partner responsiveness may enhance not only people's relationships, but also their personal well-being. Research has shown that perceived partner responsiveness predicts the likelihood of quitting smoking, even above and beyond support for quitting and relationship satisfaction (Britton, Hadad, & Derrick, 2019). Higher perceptions of partner responsiveness has also been linked to lower alcohol intake (Derrick, Houston, & Ethier, 2017), lower depression (Ibarra-Rovillard & Kuiper, 2011), and even lower mortality risk (Selcuk & Ong, 2013). Because LSEs are already more susceptible to some of these harmful outcomes (e.g., Sowislo & Orth, 2013), it is possible that their partner's lower responsiveness is either exacerbating LSEs' hurt feelings or habits, or decreasing the chances that LSEs can improve. If LSEs receive more responsiveness from their partners, they may reap personal benefits, in addition to relationship benefits.

FUTURE RESEARCH

It will be important for future research to further examine the role of self-esteem in types of expressivity and perceived and received partner responsiveness. Future work should explore the boundary conditions under which LSEs elicit less (or perhaps more) support from partners, the conditions that beget more or less accuracy in received responsiveness, and how specific support contexts bleed into feelings of relationship well-being. How partners react to disclosures likely depends on a number of factors such as a) the content of the disclosure, which could be positive versus negative, revealing a personal flaw versus a negative encounter, or something that occurred in the relationship or external to the relationship, b) characteristics of the partner (e.g., personality traits, mood), and c) the climate of the relationship (e.g., when the relationship is under threat versus thriving). In the following two sections, we outline specific future directions that we see as important next steps in broadening the field's understanding of how self-esteem, responsiveness, and their dynamics help or hinder relationships.

Self-Esteem Complementarity

Much of the research to date examining how self-esteem predicts responsiveness in relationships focuses on the attributes of one partner in the dyad. Future research should examine self-esteem and responsiveness in the context of close relationships from an interdependent perspective, taking into account both partners' self-esteem and responsiveness during mutual interactions (Kelley, 1979; Thibaut & Kelley, 1959). For instance, do LSEs' partners' attributes affect responsiveness? Because there is little to no correlation between the self-esteem levels of romantic partners (Murray at al., 2000; see also Gattis, Berns, Simpson, & Christensen, 2004), partners' self-esteem may interact to predict how couples support each other. Perhaps partners of LSEs are less responsive only to the extent that they are lower in self-esteem or attachment security themselves (Collins & Feeney, 2000). Alternatively, it is possible that a more counterintuitive finding could emerge: Perhaps partners provide more responsiveness to LSEs when those partners are lower in self-esteem than higher in self-esteem. LSE listeners may more readily recognize LSEs' indirect attempts to gain support and may be more understanding of them, because they may empathize with the need to self-protect. It would be interesting for future research to examine these possibilities.

Target Interventions

Future research should also compare interventions targeting either a) increasing partners of LSEs' responsiveness to their partners' disclosures, or b) improving LSEs' manner of expressing desire for support. Perhaps if partners of LSEs are more responsive to their self-disclosures, LSEs will not feel the need to adopt cautious and indirect expression strategies in future self-disclosures. Research has shown that partners of insecure people can help attenuate their insecure partner's maladaptive patterns during conflict discussions. Overall et al. (2013) had couples discuss changes they wanted seen in their partner. During discussions in which an avoidantly attached person was the target of desired change, when partners acted sensitively and softened communication during the discussion, the avoidantly attached person experienced less anger and withdrawal, which led to a more successful conversation. This work suggests that partners of insecure people can help buffer against insecure disclosers' maladaptive patterns. If partners of LSEs were trained to engage in similar strategies, perhaps their relationships could be improved. Alternatively, if LSEs are taught to self-disclose in more direct and open ways, perhaps partners of LSEs will be more responsive. If LSEs receive as much responsiveness from their partners as HSEs, and express as directly and openly as HSEs, perhaps they will come to be as satisfied in their relationships as HSEs.

CONCLUSION

Everyone has bad days. A potential silver lining to a bad day is bonding with a partner over it. Sharing one's experiences with a partner and receiving a caring, validating, and understanding response in return promotes intimacy and happier relationships. Unfortunately, LSEs do not receive as much responsiveness from their partners as do HSEs when disclosing their unpleasant experiences. Researchers have suggested that LSEs' underestimation of their partners' regard and acceptance contributes to negative cycles of relationship deterioration (Murray et al., 1998), but it may also be the case that partners' lower responsiveness to LSEs' negative self-disclosures contributes to their poorer relationships. Future research should explore the mechanisms underlying why LSEs receive less responsiveness from their partners than HSEs receive, taking into account both the disclosers' actions – what LSEs might be doing to discourage partner responsiveness – and the receiver – what can be done to encourage more responsiveness in LSEs' partners. Such research would take the field one step closer to understanding how to improve LSEs' lower quality relationships.

REFERENCES

Arriaga, X. B. (2013). An interdependence theory analysis of close relationships. In J. A. Simpson & L. Campbell (Eds.), *The Oxford Handbook of Close Relationships* (pp. 39–65). New York: Oxford University Press.

Baldwin, M. W. (1992). Relational schemas and the processing of social information. *Psychological Bulletin*, 112, 461–484. doi:10.1037/0033-2909.112.3.461

Baumeister, R. F., Campbell, J. D., Krueger, J. I., & Vohs, K. D. (2003). Does high self-esteem cause better performance, interpersonal success, happiness, or healthier lifestyles? *Psychological Science in the Public Interest*, 4, 1–44. doi:10.1111/1529-1006.01431

Birnbaum, G. E. & Reis, H. T. (2012). When does responsiveness pique sexual interest? Attachment and sexual desire in initial acquaintanceships. *Personality and Social Psychology Bulletin*, 38, 946–958. doi:10.1177/0146167212441028

Britton, M., Hadad, S., & Derrick, J. L. (2019). Perceived partner responsiveness predicts smoking cessation in single-smoker couples. *Addictive Behaviors*, 88, 122–128. doi:10.1016/j.addbeh.2018.08.026

Cameron, J. J., Holmes, J. G., & Vorauer, J. D. (2009). When self-disclosure goes awry: Negative consequences of revealing personal failures for lower self-esteem individuals. *Journal of Experimental Social Psychology*, 45, 217–222. doi:10.1016/j.jesp.2008.09.009

Cameron, J. J., Stinson, D. A., Gaetz, R., & Balchen, S. (2010). Acceptance is in the eye of the beholder: Self-esteem and motivated perceptions of acceptance from the opposite sex. *Journal of Personality and Social Psychology*, 99, 513–529. doi:10.1111/1529-1006.01431

Canevello, A. & Crocker, J. (2010). Creating good relationships: Responsiveness, relationship quality, and interpersonal goals. *Journal of Personality and Social Psychology*, 99, 78–106. doi:10.1037/a0018186

Carmichael, C. L., Tsai, F.-F., Smith, S. M., Caprariello, P. A., & Reis, H. T. (2007). The self and intimate relationships. In C. Sedikides & S. Spencer (Eds.), *The Self* (pp. 285–309). New York: Psychology Press.

Clark, M. S. & Lemay, E. P. (2010). Close relationships. In S. T. Fiske & D. Gilbert (Eds.), *Handbook of Social Psychology* (pp. 898–940). New York: Oxford University Press.

Collins, N. L. & Feeney, B. C. (2000). A safe haven: An attachment theory perspective on support seeking and caregiving in intimate relationships. *Journal of Personality and Social Psychology*, 78, 1053–1073. doi:10.1037/0022-3514.78.6.1053

Collins, N. L. & Feeney, B. C. (2004). Working models of attachment shape perceptions of social support: Evidence from experimental and observational studies. *Journal of Personality and Social Psychology*, 87, 363–383. doi:10.1037/0022-3514.87.3.363

Collins, N. L. & Miller, L. C. (1994). Self-disclosure and liking: A meta-analytic review. *Psychological Bulletin*, 116, 457–475. doi:10.1037/0033-2909.116.3.457

Cortes, K. & Wood, J. V. (2018). Is it really "all in their heads"? How self-esteem predicts partner responsiveness. *Journal of Personality*, 86, 990–1002. doi:10.1111/jopy.12370

Cortes, K. & Wood, J. V. (2019). How was your day? Conveying care, but under the radar, for people lower in trust. *Journal of Experimental Social Psychology*, 83, 11–22. doi:10.1016/j.jesp.2019.03.003

Cutrona, C. E. (1996). Social support as a determinant of marital quality: The interplay of negative and supportive behaviors. In G. R. Pierce, B. R. Sarason, & I. G. Sarason (Eds.), *Handbook of Social Support and the Family* (pp. 173–194). New York: Plenum Press.

Cutrona, C. E., Hessling, R. M., & Suhr, J. A. (1997). The influence of husband and wife personality on marital social support interactions. *Personal Relationships*, 4, 379–393. doi:10.1111/j.1475-6811.1997.tb00152.x

Derrick, J., Houston, R., & Ethier, D. (2017). Perceived partner responsiveness moderates the effect of partner-specific stressors on alcohol urge in an experimental study. *Alcoholism-Clinical and Experimental Research*, 41, 153A.

Downey, G., Freitas, A. L., Michaelis, B., & Khouri, H. (1998). The self-fulfilling prophecy in close relationships: Rejection sensitivity and rejection by romantic partners. *Journal of Personality and Social Psychology*, 75, 545–560. doi:10.1037/0022-3514.75.2.545

Dunkel-Schetter, C. & Bennett, T. L. (1990). Differentiating the cognitive and behavioral aspects of social support. In B. R. Sarason, I. G. Sarason, & G. R. Pierce (Eds.), *Social Support: An Interactional View* (pp. 267–296). Oxford : John Wiley & Sons.

Epstein, N. B. & Baucom, D. H. (2002). *Enhanced Cognitive-Behavioral Therapy for Couples: A Contextual Approach*. Washington, DC: American Psychological Association.

Forest, A. L., Kille, D. R., Wood, J. V., & Holmes, J. G. (2014). Discount and disengage: How chronic negative expressivity undermines partner responsiveness to negative disclosures. *Journal of Personality and Social Psychology*, 107, 1013–1032. doi:10.1037/a0038163

Forest, A. L. & Wood, J. V. (2012). When social networking is not working: Individuals with low self-esteem recognize but do not reap the benefits of self-disclosure on Facebook. *Psychological Science*, 23, 295–302. doi:10.1177/0956797611429709

Fraley, C. R. & Shaver, P. R. (2000). Adult romantic attachment: Theoretical developments, emerging controversies, and unanswered questions. *Review of General Psychology*, 4, 132–154. doi:10.1037/1089-2680.4.2.132

Gattis, K. S., Berns, S., Simpson, L. E., & Christensen, A. (2004). Birds of a feather or strange birds? Ties among personality dimensions, similarity, and marital quality. *Journal of Family Psychology*, 18(4), 564–574. doi:10.1037/0893-3200.18.4.564

Gaucher, D., Wood, J. V., Stinson, D. A., Forest, A. L., Holmes, J. G., & Logel, C. (2012). Perceived regard explains self-esteem differences in expressivity. *Personality and Social Psychology Bulletin*, 38, 1144–1156. doi:10.1177/0146167212445790

Hirschberger, G., Florian, V., & Mikulincer, M. (2002). The anxiety buffering function of close relationships: Mortality salience effects on the readiness to compromise mate selection standards. *European Journal of Social Psychology*, 32, 609–625. doi:10.1002/ejsp.110

Holmes, J. G. & Rempel, J. K. (1989). Trust in close relationships. In C. Hendrick (Ed.), *Review of Personality and Social Psychology: Close Relationships* (Vol. 10, pp. 187–219). Newbury Park, CA: Sage.

Huang, K., Yeomans, M., Brooks, A. W., Minson, J., & Gino, F. (2017). It doesn't hurt to ask: Question-asking increases liking. *Journal of Personality and Social Psychology*, 113, 430–452. doi:10.1037/pspi0000097

Ibarra-Rovillard, M. S. & Kuiper, N. A. (2011). Social support and social negativity findings in depression: Perceived responsiveness to basic psychological needs. *Clinical Psychology Review*, 31, 342–352. doi:10.1016/j.cpr.2011.01.005

Kane, H. S., Jaremka, L. M., Guichard, A. C., Ford, M. B., Collins, N. L., & Feeney, B. C. (2007). Feeling supported and feeling satisfied: How one partner's attachment style predicts the other partner's relationship experiences. *Journal of Social and Personal Relationships*, 24, 535–555. doi:10.1177/0265407507079245

Kelley, H. H. (1979). *Personal Relationships: Their Structures and Properties*. Hillsdale, NJ: Erlbaum.

Kelley, H. H. (1983). Analyzing close relationships. In H. H. Kelley, E. Berscheid, A. Christensen, J. H. Harvey, T. L. Huston, G. Levinger, . . . D. R. Peterson (Eds.), *Close Relationships* (pp. 20–67). New York: W. H. Freeman.

Kelley, H. H. (1991). Lewin, situations, and interdependence. *Journal of Social Issues*, 47, 211–233.

Lakey, B. & Cassady, P. B. (1990). Cognitive processes in perceived social support. *Journal of Personality and Social Psychology*, 59, 337–343. doi:10.1037/0022-3514.59.2.337

Lakey, B. & Orehek, E. (2011). Relational regulation theory: A new approach to explain the link between perceived social support and mental health. *Psychological Review*, 118, 482–495. doi:10.1037/a0023477

Laurenceau, J. P., Barrett, L. F., & Pietromonaco, P. R. (1998). Intimacy as an interpersonal process: The importance of self-disclosure, partner disclosure, and perceived partner responsiveness in interpersonal exchanges. *Journal of Personality and Social Psychology*, 74, 1238–1251. doi:10.1037//0022-3514.74.5.1238

Leary, M. R. & MacDonald, G. (2003). Individual differences in trait self-esteem: A theoretical integration. In M. Leary & J. Tangney (Eds.), *Handbook of Self and Identity* (pp. 401–418). New York: Guilford Press.

Lemay, E. P. & Clark, M. S. (2008a). "Walking on Eggshells": How expressing relationship insecurities perpetuates them. *Journal of Personality and Social Psychology*, 95, 420–441. doi:10.1037/0022-3514.95.2.420

Lemay, E. P. & Clark, M. S. (2008b). "You're just saying that." Contingencies of self-worth, suspicion, and authenticity in the interpersonal affirmation process. *Journal of Experimental Social Psychology*, 44, 1376–1382. doi:10.1016/j.jesp.2008.05.001

Lemay, E. P., Clark, M. S., & Feeney, B. C. (2007). Projection of responsiveness to needs and the construction of satisfying communal relationships. *Journal of Personality and Social Psychology*, 92, 834–853. doi:10.1037/0022-3514.92.5.834

Lemay, E. & Dudley, K. L. (2009). Implications of reflected appraisals of interpersonal insecurity for suspicion and power. *Personality and Social Psychology Bulletin*, 35, 1672–1686. doi:10.1177/0146167209348380

Lemay, E. P. & Dudley, K. L. (2011). Caution: Fragile! Regulating the interpersonal security of chronically insecure partners. *Journal of Personality and Social Psychology*, 100, 681–702. doi:10.1037/a0021655

Levy, S. R., Ayduk, O., & Downey, G. (2001). The role of rejection sensitivity in people's relationships with significant others and valued social groups. In M. R. Leary (Ed.), *Interpersonal Rejection* (pp. 251–289). New York: Oxford University Press.

McCarthy, M. H., Wood, J. V., & Holmes, J. G. (2017). Dispositional pathways to trust: Self-esteem and agreeableness interact to predict trust and negative emotional disclosure. *Journal of Personality and Social Psychology*, 113, 95–116. doi:10.1037/pspi0000093

Murray, S. L., Bellavia, G. M., Rose, P., & Griffin, D. W. (2003). Once hurt, twice hurtful: How perceived regard regulates daily marital interactions. *Journal of Personality and Social Psychology*, 84, 126–147. doi:10.1037/0022-3514.84.1.126

Murray, S. L., Griffin, D. W., Rose, P., & Bellavia, G. M. (2003). Calibrating the sociometer: The relational contingencies of self-esteem. *Journal of Personality and Social Psychology*, 85, 63–84. doi:10.1037/0022-3514.85.1.63

Murray, S. L., Holmes, J. G., & Collins, N. L. (2006). Optimizing assurance: The risk regulation system in relationships. *Psychological Bulletin*, 132, 641–666. doi:10.1037/0033-2909.132.5.641

Murray, S. L., Holmes, J. G., & Griffin, D. W. (2000). Self-esteem and the quest for felt security: How perceived regard regulates attachment processes. *Journal of Personality and Social Psychology*, 78, 478–498. doi:10.1037/0022-3514.78.3.478

Murray, S. L., Holmes, J. G., Griffin, D. W., Bellavia, G., & Rose, P. (2001). The mismeasure of love: How self-doubt contaminates relationship beliefs. *Personality and Social Psychology Bulletin*, 27, 423–436. doi:10.1177/0146167201274004

Murray, S. L., Holmes, J. G., MacDonald, G., & Ellsworth, P. C. (1998). Through the looking glass darkly? When self-doubts turn into relationship insecurities. *Journal of Personality and Social Psychology*, 75, 1459–1480. doi:10.1037/0022-3514.75.6.1459

Overall, N. C., Fletcher, G. J. O., & Kenny, D. A. (2012). When bias and insecurity promote accuracy: Mean-level bias and tracking accuracy in couples' conflict discussions. *Personality and Social Psychology Bulletin*, 38, 642–655. doi:10.1177/0146167211432764

Overall, N. C., Simpson, J. A., & Struthers, H. (2013). Buffering attachment avoidance: Softening emotional and behavioral defenses during conflict discussions. *Journal of Personality and Social Psychology*, 104, 854–871. doi:10.1037/a0031798

Pennebaker, J. W., Zech, E., & Rimé, B. (2001). Disclosing and sharing emotion: Psychological, social, and health consequences. In M. S. Stroebe, R. O. Hansson, W. Stroebe, & H. Schut (Eds.), *Handbook of Bereavement Research: 102 Consequences, Coping, and Care* (pp. 517–544). Washington, DC: American Psychological Association.

Pierce, G. R., Sarason, B. R., & Sarason, I. G. (1992). General and specific support expectations and stress as predictors of perceived supportiveness: An experimental study. *Journal of Personality and Social Psychology*, 63, 297–307. doi:10.1037/0022-3514.63.2.297

Reis, H. T. (2007). Steps toward the ripening of relationship science. *Personal Relationships*, 14, 1–23. doi:10.1111/j.1475-6811.2006.00139.x

Reis, H. T. & Clark, M. S. (2013). Responsiveness. In J. A. Simpson & L. Campbell (Eds.), *The Oxford Handbook of Close Relationships* (pp. 400–423). New York: Oxford University Press.

Reis, H. T., Clark, M. S., & Holmes, J. G. (2004). Perceived partner responsiveness as an organizing construct in the study of closeness and intimacy. In D. J. Mashek & A. Aron (Eds.), *Handbook of Closeness and Intimacy* (pp. 201–225). Mahwah, NJ: Erlbaum.

Reis, H. T. & Gable, S. L. (2015). Responsiveness. *Current Opinion in Psychology*, 1, 67–71. doi:10.1016/j.copsyc.2015.01.001

Reis, H. T. & Shaver, P. (1988). Intimacy as an interpersonal process. In S. W. Duck (Ed.), *Handbook of Personal Relationships* (pp. 367–389). Oxford: Wiley & Sons.

Rusbult, C. E., Morrow, G. D., & Johnson, D. J. (1987). Self-esteem and problem-solving behaviour in close relationships. *British Journal of Social Psychology*, 26, 293–303. doi:10.1111/j.2044-8309.1987.tb00792.x

Rusbult, C. E. & Van Lange, P. A. M. (2003). Interdependence, interaction, and relationships. *Annual Review of Psychology*, 54, 351–375. doi:10.1146/annurev.psych.54.101601.145059

Sarason, B. R., Pierce, G. R., & Sarason, I. G. (1990). Social support: The sense of acceptance and the role of relationships. In B. R. Sarason, I. G. Sarason, & G. R. Pierce (Eds.), *Social Support: An Interactional View* (pp. 97–128). Oxford: John Wiley & Sons.

Selcuk, E. & Ong, A. D. (2013). Perceived partner responsiveness moderates the association between received emotional support and all-cause mortality. *Health Psychology*, 32, 231–235. doi:10.1037/a0028276

Simpson, J., Rholes, W., Oriña, M., & Grich, J. (2002). Working models of attachment, support giving, and support seeking in a stressful situation. *Personality and Social Psychology Bulletin*, 28, 598–608. doi:10.1177/0146167202288004

Slotter, E. B. & Finkel, E. J. (2009). The strange case of sustained dedication to an unfulfilling relationship: Predicting commitment and breakup from attachment anxiety and need fulfillment within relationships. *Personality and Social Psychology Bulletin*, 35, 85–100. doi:10.1177/0146167208325244

Sommers, S. (1984). Reported emotions and conventions of emotionality among college students. *Journal of Personality and Social Psychology*, 46, 207–215. doi:10.1037/0022-3514.46.1.207

Sowislo, J. F. & Orth, U. (2013). Does low self-esteem predict depression and anxiety? A meta-analysis of longitudinal studies. *Psychological Bulletin*, 139, 213–240. doi:10.1037/a0028931

Sprecher, S. & Hendrick, S. S. (2004). Self-disclosure in intimate relationships: Associations with individual and relationship characteristics over time. *Journal of Social and Clinical Psychology*, 23, 857–877. Retrieved from http://search.proquest.com.proxy.lib.uwaterloo.ca/docview/38037511?accountid=14906

Thibaut, J. W. & Kelley, H. H. (1959). *The Social Psychology of Groups*. New York: Wiley.

Trzesniewski, K. H., Donnellan, M. B., & Robins, R. W. (2003). Stability of self-esteem across the life span. *Journal of Personality and Social Psychology*, 84, 205–220. doi:10.1037/0022-3514.84.1.205

Vinokur, A., Schul, Y., & Caplan, R. D. (1987). Determinants of perceived social support: Interpersonal transactions, personal outlook, and transient affective states. *Journal of Personality and Social Psychology*, 53, 1137–1145. doi:10.1037/0022-3514.53.6.1137

Williams, K. D., Govan, C. L., Croker, V., Tynan, D., Cruickshank, M., & Lam, A. (2002). Investigations into differences between social- and cyberostracism. *Group Dynamics: Theory, Research, and Practice*, 6, 65–77. doi:10.1037/1089-2699.6.1.65

Williams, K. D. & Jarvis, B. (2006). Cyberball: A program for use in research on interpersonal ostracism and acceptance. *Behavior Research Methods*, 38, 174–180. doi:10.3758/BF03192765

Wood, J. V. & Forest, A. L. (2016). Self-protective yet self-defeating: The paradox of low self-esteem people's self-disclosures. In J. M. Olson & M. P. Zanna (Eds.), *Advances in Experimental Social Psychology* (Vol. 53, pp. 131–181). Cambridge, MA: Academic Press.

Wood, J. V., Hogle, A., & McClellan, J. (2009). Self-esteem and relationships. In H. Reis & S. Sprecher (Eds.), *Encyclopedia of Human Relationships*, (Vol. 3, pp. 1422–1425). Thousand Oaks, CA: Sage.

Zimmermann, P., Maier, M. A., Winter, M., & Grossmann, K. E. (2001). Attachment and adolescents' emotion regulation during a joint problem-solving task with a friend. *International Journal of Behavioral Development*, 25, 331–343. doi:10.1080/01650250143000157

PART IV

INTERDEPENDENCE, TIMING, AND EXPECTATIONS

13

Relationship Receptivity Theory

Timing and Interdependent Relationships

CHRISTOPHER R. AGNEW, BENJAMIN W. HADDEN, AND
KENNETH TAN

It has been said that timing is everything in life. Although that may be an overstatement, we would agree that timing is of critical importance in the formation, maintenance, and stability of close, interdependent relationships. For example, research has examined the notion of time in relationships by focusing on relationship length and stability (Rusbult, Olsen, Davis, & Hannon, 2001), examining long-term and short-term mating strategies as associated with one's reproductive goals (Buss & Schmidt, 1993), and, with respect to methodological approaches, conducting longitudinal studies to track relationship dynamics over time (e.g., Huston, Caughlin, Houts, Smith, & George, 2001). This chapter describes a *new* approach for understanding time in close relationships, focused on one's perceived appropriateness of timing for an involvement.

When is the "right time" for one to be involved in a relationship? Certainly, answers to this question are subjective and may take into account a constellation of factors. The emphasis on timing, encapsulated within relationship relativity theory as detailed in this chapter, is fundamentally different from traditional approaches to understanding various relational processes. Traditional foci tend to emphasize the importance and centrality of person-specific factors, such as one's attachment orientation (e.g., Mikulincer & Shaver, 2007) or agreeableness (e.g., Graziano & Tobin, 2009), or relationship-specific factors, such as satisfaction with a particular partnership (e.g., Karney & Bradbury, 1995) or accommodating a specific partner's transgressions (e.g., Rusbult, Verette, Whitney, Slovik, & Lipkus, 1991). Both person and relationship factors are of critical importance to understanding relationships and have added greatly to our knowledge of how relationships work. Complementing such approaches, this chapter describes why a consideration of timing also matters. We define critical components of relationship receptivity, discuss the waxing, waning, and synchronicity of receptivity, posit key antecedents to and consequences of receptivity, and lay out exciting possible future directions for research.

There are theories that are guided by significant consideration of event timing. Particularly relevant to our consideration of relationship receptivity is life history theory, which provides a framework for understanding how organisms allocate limited resources and time to pursue reproductive and existential success in the context of adapting to their current environment. With respect to humans, events that impact reproduction include sexual maturity, reproductive timing, and finding a potential partner, but these must be weighed against other events such as investing in personal growth (e.g., skill accumulation).

To ensure success in different environments, different energy allocation patterns are needed. These energy allocation strategies can be "fast," which is characterized by having an increased focus on the present, or "slow," which is characterized by investment in the future with little immediate benefit. "Fast" strategies are adaptive when the current environment is harsh and the future is unpredictable, whereas "slow" strategies are adaptive in opposite conditions where high returns can be expected in the future (Del Giudice, Gangestad, & Kaplan, 2015; Kenrick & Griskevicius, 2015). With respect to finding a potential partner, environmental contexts have been shown to impact on sociosexuality and mating orientation, with harsher contexts predicting less restricted sociosexuality and less long-term mating orientation (Sng, Neuberg, Varnum, & Kenrick, 2017). These strategies may underlie feelings of receptivity. The general notion of receptivity may be best thought of as combining both where a person considers themselves "now" and the qualities (or desired qualities) of a given partner(ship). Ultimately, when a person feels the time is right in their life and a given partnership is perceived as meeting essential needs, the result should be a particularly stable relationship.

Although timing matters in relationships, a critical question is *what* has to be at the right time with respect to relationship involvement. What informs a sense that now is the right time? We consider this question as we describe critical components of relationship receptivity: relationship desirability and relationship readiness.

COMPONENTS OF RELATIONSHIP RECEPTIVITY: DESIRABILITY AND READINESS

Relationship receptivity theory centers on the proposition that perceived appropriateness of personal timing is consequential for relationship cognitions, behavior, and stability (Agnew, 2014a). At any given time, a person is more or less receptive to relationship involvement throughout their lifetime. That is, a person has a sense of whether or not they a) want to be in a close relationship (termed *relationship desirability*) and b) feel ready to be in a close relationship (termed *relationship readiness*).

This sense of desire can be in reference to a short-term involvement, where one is interested in a close relationship of limited duration (e.g., as encapsulated in the desirability thought "I'd really like to be close to someone tonight"). It can also be in reference to a long-term involvement, where one is interested in a close relationship of long or unending involvement (e.g., as encapsulated in the desirability thought "I want to settle down for good"). A person may also feel at any given time more or less ready to be involved in a relationship with someone else, whether that be readiness for involvement for a brief period (e.g., as encapsulated in the readiness thought "I'm ready to be close to someone tonight") or for the "long haul" (e.g., as encapsulated in the readiness thought "I'm ready to settle down"). Consistent with our past work on long-term commitment processes (cf. Agnew & VanderDrift, 2018), our theorizing and work to date has focused on long-term receptivity, while acknowledging that feelings of short-term receptivity can and should be a focus of inquiry.

Relationship Desirability

At any given time, some people want to be involved in a romantic relationship and others do not. We refer to wanting to be involved in a relationship as *relationship desirability*, defined as the subjective desire to be involved in a relationship at a given time (Tan, Agnew, & Hadden, in press). Relationship desirability is not defined with respect to involvement with a specific individual *per se*; rather, it is with respect to one's own sense that involvement currently in a relationship is desirable for the self. It may best be considered as akin to a general attitude toward relationships, where a person varies in their relative positivity or negativity toward relational involvement in the moment (Tan et al., 2020).

With respect to desire for a long-term relationship, rather than focusing on personal attitudes toward relationship involvement in general, past research has focused on examining the *level* of commitment to a given relationship (Agnew & VanderDrift, 2018; Le & Agnew, 2003). As we have pointed out in recent work (Tan et al., 2020), with respect to longer-term committed relationships which we refer to as *commitment desirability*, current approaches to investigating commitment do not measure the extent to which individuals desire and/or seek committed relationships. Commitment desirability can be considered a general disposition toward relationship involvement, whereas commitment level represents a relationship-specific variable that indexes perceptions with respect to a specific involvement.

Desiring romantic partners and consequently having sex and reproducing are adaptive for survival as compared to remaining single, consistent with evolutionary theorizing (Pillsworth & Haselton, 2005). Moreover, people tend to evidence a strong need to belong, desiring meaningful associations with others, which has been found to be associated with physical and psychological well-being (Baumeister & Leary, 1995) and its absence associated with negative consequences (e.g., House, Landis, & Umberson, 1988). However, relationship desirability goes beyond only focusing on broad social needs and the desire for sex, social connection, and intimacy. An interdependence perspective provides a nice complement to theorizing concerning relationship desirability, as it offers a clear understanding as to why individuals rely on romantic relationships to attain desired outcomes.

Interdependence theory conceptualizes the ways in which outcomes for the self and others are evaluated, including broader considerations that accompany the pursuit of self-interest (Rusbult & Van Lange, 2003). It posits that individuals in a relationship are cognizant of both positive and negative outcomes that arise from mutual dependence. It also acknowledges that past experiences and patterns of social interactions with others can influence current desires and beliefs concerning the desirability of commitment (Simpson, Collins, & Salvatore, 2011; Van Lange, Otten, De Bruin, & Joireman, 1997). For example, experiences in previous relationships with romantic partners (e.g., a tortuous breakup) can influence the development of one's mental model regarding the desirability of relationship involvement.

The desiring of a relationship can ebb and flow throughout one's life. There are times when one is particularly desirous of involvement with another, and times when that is the last thing a person wants. It is easy to imagine a teenager wanting to be involved in a relationship, if for no other reason than being surrounded by admired peers who are pairing off. It is also easy to imagine that same person 50 years later having just lost a spouse and not at all desirous of forming a new close romantic bond. As such, flexibility in the extent to which one desires relationships can be functional insofar as it reflects adaptation to the situations one confronts. A basic premise with respect to a consideration of desirability and timing in relationships is that, without desire at a given time, a relationship (at least a voluntary one) is unlikely to form, be maintained, or last.

Relationship Readiness

In addition to considering whether one desires a relationship at a given time, one may also take into account one's relative sense of readiness for an involvement, defined as the subjective sense that the current time is or is not "right" for one to be involved in a relationship. Indeed, even if a person wants to be involved, they may not feel particularly ready to engage in a close relationship with another. The general notion of readiness has been featured in a number of psychological theories, though to our knowledge only in limited reference to close relationships and not in reference to the level of relationship commitment or stability. For example, the construct is prominent in the literature on learning. Learning readiness is a component of Thorndike's (1913, 1932) classic theory of learning. In his theory, Thorndike posited his law of readiness, whereby behavior is influenced by the relative readiness or unreadiness of a response (Thorndike, 1932). Similarly, Bruner's (1966) theory of instruction includes readiness as one of its four elements, along with structure, sequence, and motivation. Instructors need to be cognizant of a learner's predisposition and past experiences, and how they give rise to relative readiness to go "beyond the information given" (Bruner, 1973). Relatedly, Bandura's social learning theory is also characterized by a consideration of one's motivation and readiness to take action (Bandura, 1986). In summary, being ready enables individual learning and action.

Beyond learning and educational realms, readiness has also been featured in the organizational development literature. For example, Weiner (2009) described the construct of organizational readiness to change, which is both multi-faceted and multi-level, and may give rise to desired movement toward improvements in large corporate entities. Moreover, in political science, Pruitt (2007) has also highlighted readiness as an important component in the success of diplomatic initiatives. When adversaries have reached a point where they feel they are ready to work together, they are more likely to reach a negotiated settlement (Schiff, 2013).

One can also look to the health psychology literature to find the construct of readiness. For example, it is a central component within the Stages of Change Model (also referred to as the Transtheoretical Model; Prochaska & DiClemente, 2005). In this model, developed in part to better assist individuals to make desired changes in their health-relevant behaviors, a person can be placed in one of five stages with respect to their relative readiness for change: precontemplation (not thinking about change), contemplation (thinking about change), preparation (getting ready for change), action, and maintenance. Hundreds of studies attest to the empirical value of the readiness concept in accounting for behavior change (for meta-analytic support, see Norcross, Krebs, & Prochaska, 2011). Readiness cognitions are seen as both a necessary precursor to initial action and as a key ingredient underlying change and maintenance processes. This latter role is particularly relevant to our hypothesized role of the construct in accounting for relational maintenance and behavior. The general notion of readiness has been featured in a number of psychological theories, though to our knowledge only in limited reference to close relationships and not in reference to the level of relationship commitment or stability.

We refer to feeling ready to be in a longer-term committed relationship as *commitment readiness*. A basic premise with respect to readiness and timing in relationships is that, when commitment readiness is higher, both in general and within-person, a person is more likely to think and take actions conducive to the development and maintenance of a committed involvement. In this way, readiness influences relationship outcomes.

We would not argue that relationship desirability and relationship readiness are the only factors that influence one's sense of relationship receptivity. However, both are important in defining *when* a person is most likely to be receptive to forming, maintaining, and continuing in a close relationship. When both of these factors are high, one is more likely to form, maintain, and continue a relationship; conversely, when both are low, one is less likely.

How might these two components best be considered together, conceptually? It is possible that desirability is a necessary precursor for readiness. That is, one may not need to consider if they feel ready for a relationship if they do not want one. In considering the combination of these particular factors, one might look to the dual process literature in social psychology to address this question (Chaiken & Trope, 1999; Gawronski & Creighton, 2013). In particular, one may turn to phenomenon-specific dual process theories that have been proposed to understand attitudinal and persuasion processes, such as the elaboration likelihood model (ELM; Petty & Cacioppo, 1986), the heuristic systematic model (HSM; Chaiken, 1987), and the motivation and opportunity as determinants model (MODE; Fazio, 1990). A central notion in these models is that cognitive elaboration occurs along a continuum determined by how motivated and able one is to engage in effortful information processing (Gawronski & Creighton, 2013). Both motivation and ability can be said to underlie relationship receptivity and its theorized determinants. Relationship desirability taps a motivational element underlying relational thought and action toward fulfilling the goal of being in a relationship. Relationship readiness taps one's (perceived) ability to be in a relationship, assessing whether one currently has the necessary skills, knowledge, or focus to enter and/or maintain an involvement.

TIME AND TIMING: THE WAXING, WANING, AND
SYNCHRONICITY OF RECEPTIVITY

A person may feel receptive to a relationship at any given moment and at different periods throughout their lifetime. Changes in receptivity, in both onset and duration, are to be expected throughout the life course. Receptivity onset may be the result of predictable development changes. For example, part of normative adolescent development includes greater interest in forming close relationships with others, particularly romantic partners (e.g., Davies and Windle, 2000; Meier & Allen, 2009). The onset of a change in receptivity may also result from life events. The recent death of a beloved spouse is likely to result in exceptionally low receptivity. In contrast, involvement in an acrimonious relationship may result in one's receptivity rising, as one considers viable alternatives to the current partner. The duration of feeling receptive may also change with any given period of receptivity experienced.

For some people, a period of feeling receptive may last a very short time, while others may find themselves constantly feeling receptive to a relationship.

Of course, being highly receptive does not mean that one will be successful in forming or maintaining a relationship. It takes two to tango and at least two to form a relationship. During periods of maximum receptivity, when both desire and readiness are peaked, one's receptivity can only be optimally met when paired with similar levels of receptivity in another person. For a relationship to form and be maintained, it requires that individual receptivity levels match to some degree. With respect to dyadic relationships, we would hold that a relationship characterized by two individuals both wanting a relationship and feeling ready for one is more likely to succeed (i.e., remain stable) than a relationship where one of the two individuals is significantly lower in either relationship desire or readiness).

ANTECEDENTS OF COMMITMENT RECEPTIVITY

What gives rise to feeling receptive to a long-term committed relationship? Prior to attempting to answer this question, it is important to first differentiate the sense of receptivity from its theorized origins. That is, one may feel receptive at a specific time but that feeling does not directly or indirectly imply a particular antecedent or set of antecedent conditions. Multiple factors may influence one's current feelings of receptivity. Here we offer and describe three general factors underlying a constellation of more specific antecedents with respect to receptivity to a committed relationship: 1) past experiences in a committed relationship, 2) preferences and expectations regarding a committed relationship, and 3) outside pressures for involvement in a committed relationship.

Past Experiences in a Committed Relationship

Following from our past work on relationship commitment processes (e.g., Agnew, Loving, & Drigotas, 2001; Agnew, Van Lange, Rusbult, & Langston, 1998; Besikci, Agnew, & Yildirim, 2016; Etcheverry & Agnew, 2004; Goodfriend & Agnew, 2008; Le & Agnew, 2003; Lehmiller & Agnew, 2006; Tan & Agnew, 2016; VanderDrift & Agnew, 2014), our receptivity work to date has focused on the sense of desire and readiness for a long-term relationship, or wanting and feeling ready to commit to a relationship for the foreseeable future. All major theories of close relationships highlight the role of past experiences in one's current thoughts, feelings, and actions in relationships. For example, attachment theory focuses on early experiences with one's caregivers as influencing one's current view of self and others (Mikulincer & Shaver, 2007). Interdependence theory also holds that one's current relational expectations are guided by one's past relational experiences (Arriaga, 2013).

General Past Relationship Satisfaction Consistent with foundational principles from interdependence theory (Thibaut & Kelly, 1959), one is more likely to feel receptive to a relationship if they generally derived more versus less satisfaction in their past relationships. This notion is rooted in the interdependence theory concept of comparison level (or CL), defined as one's expectations for relationship outcomes based on one's past relational experiences. It is also in line with models of readiness in other domains, such as health behaviors (Prochaska & DiClemente, 2005), in which readiness is associated with more perceived benefits than costs associated with the change (Prochaska & DiClemente, 2005). If the outcomes one has received in relationships in the past have generally been positive, one should be higher in receptivity. The opposite should be true if one's past relationship outcomes have tended to be negative.

Being Over Past Relationships A person is also more likely to feel receptive to a new relationship if they feel that they are "over" past relationships, particularly dissatisfying ones. From an ego depletion perspective, a person whose cognitive resources continue to be directed toward a past partner is limited with respect to what they can devote to a new partnership. Moreover, past research has demonstrated that when one is left by one's partner (sometimes, uncharitably, referred to as being "dumped") as opposed to freely choosing to leave a partner, one is likely to experience the dissolution differently, including retaining more pluralistic thoughts with respect to the partner and relationship (cf., retaining a sense of cognitive interdependence; Agnew, 2000; Agnew et al., 1998). This continued sense of connection to a past partner is likely associated with lower receptivity to forming a new relationship.

Clarity in Preferred Partner Characteristics If one does not know what they are looking for in a partner (e.g., specific characteristics), they may be less likely to be receptive to forming a committed relationship. A person may feel reluctant to make decisions regarding committing to a specific partner if they are unsure what features of a partner to identify as appealing. Conversely, knowing what one wants should increase one's sense of receptivity. For example, one characteristic that has been shown to be important with regards to clarity is perceived partner commitment (Arriaga, Reed, Goodfriend, & Agnew, 2006; Tan et al., 2020). Perceiving that one's partner or potential partner is committed alleviates uncertainty about the potential success of a relationship (Owen et al., 2014). Moreover, from an ideals-matching perspective (Fletcher, Simpson, & Thomas, 2000), being unsure of one's ideals may make it more difficult to identify high quality romantic partners, making one less receptive to a committed relationship.

Sufficient Relationship Experience A person is more likely to be receptive to a committed relationship if the person feels that they have finished "sowing their wild oats" or have experienced a sufficient number of past relationships and feel ready to settle into a long-term relationship. In contrast, commitment receptivity may be lower among those who have not had enough relationship experiences in their life already, and do not want to be denied new or varied experiences by becoming involved in a committed relationship.

Preferences and Expectations Regarding a Committed Relationship

Receptivity also takes into account one's own personal preferences and expectations regarding relationship involvement. A person's tendency to be involved in a relationship, their current emphasis on self versus others, their expectations for future relationship satisfaction, and their perception of viable alternate partners may all play a role in determining one's receptivity to relational involvement.

Tendency to Be in a Relationship People vary in the extent to which they prefer to be involved in a committed involvement and have been involved throughout their life. Some people seem to always be involved with a partner (including "serial monogamists"), while others rarely so. These are people who are most likely to be chronically high in desirability. We would expect receptivity to be higher among those who prefer engaging in close relationships versus those who prefer to not be involved.

Current Emphasis on Me versus We There are times in one's life when one feels particularly insular and not desirous of or ready for a committed relationship. Focusing on self-development may interfere with one's willingness and ability to form and maintain a close relationship with others (VanderDrift & Agnew, 2014). This may be as a result of career stage (e.g., needing to concentrate on work to fulfill career aspirations) or during particular developmental periods (e.g., during childhood).

Expectations for Future Satisfaction If one believes that a relationship will be satisfying, one is more likely to feel receptive to both initiating and continuing an involvement. As described above, past relationship satisfaction promotes readiness by increasing perceptions of rewards and costs associated with romantic involvement. In light of recent work showing that relationship expectations are associated with current commitment level (Baker, McNulty, & VanderDrift, 2017; Lemay, 2016), it is likely that expectations about the likelihood of romantic relationships to be more rewarding and less costly should result in higher feelings of readiness and desire for a long-term relationship. In this sense, past satisfaction may influence readiness specifically via future expectations.

Weighing Current versus Future Alternatives If one believes that by waiting to become involved in a committed relationship one will obtain better outcomes versus entering a relationship now, one is likely to be less receptive currently. Research on decision-making in relationships has long included a consideration of one's possible alternatives as guiding one's evaluations of current partner options (Thibaut & Kelly, 1959). For example, the interdependence concept of comparison level for alternatives (or CLalt) refers to the outcomes one would receive if the next best alternative to the current relationship was chosen. The distance between current outcomes received and CLalt represents one's relative dependence on the current partnership. The greater one's dependence on a current partner, the less receptive one should be to pursuing a new one.

Outside Pressures for Involvement in a Committed Relationship

Relationships are also influenced by those beyond a given dyad (Agnew, 2014b). Social network members often have opinions or advice as to whether one should be involved and with whom (Agnew et al., 2001). The relationships of others may also provide a model for the appropriateness of being in a particular kind of relationship.

Commitment in Friends' Relationships One's social network environment is likely to indirectly influence whether one is more or less receptive to a committed relationship via modeling processes (Agnew, 2014b). For example, one's social network may be composed of friends who themselves are not involved in committed relationships. This network configuration does not support a descriptive norm toward being in a committed relationship. Conversely, the opposite may be the case: All of one's friends may be paired up, leading a person to feel that they, too, should be involved in a close relationship.

Commitment Norms in Family A person's family environment may also predispose one to be more or less receptive to becoming involved in a committed relationship (Sinclair, Hood, & Wright, 2014). If one's family environment features a predominance of committed relationships, it is likely to drive a sense that such relationships are normative and desirable. In contrast, if committed relationships are few and far between among one's family members, a person may feel less receptive to forming a committed relationship themselves.

Peer Pressure to Commit Beyond observing the relationships of friends, one may feel pressure from friends to be involved in a committed relationship (Wright & Sinclair, 2012). The opposite, of course, may also be the case: One's friends may frown upon forming a committed relationship, which may have the effect of lowering one's own receptivity to commitment.

Family Pressure to Commit Family pressures may also propel one to enter into a relationship, even if one would prefer not to do so. Endless books and films chronicle parents or grandparents who wish for their offspring to "settle down" with a particular partner (e.g., *The Big Sick*; Apatow & Showalter, 2017). Moreover, it remains common in some cultures for family members to intervene in forming a committed relationship (e.g., arranged marriages; Allendorf & Pandian, 2016).

Additional Receptivity Antecedents

The preceding list of antecedents is not exhaustive. Beyond these three general factors fueling feelings of relationship receptivity, there are other antecedents which likely play a role, including physiological perceptions (e.g., feeling too old, physically, for a relationship), hormonal urges (e.g., wanting to "spread one's seed"; Gangestad & Simpson, 2000), and concerns about a finite period for childbearing (e.g., motivated by the perception that one's "biological clock" is ticking away). Moreover, emotions may influence one's relationship receptivity. For example, fear of being or remaining single may motivate an individual to be higher in receptivity to enter a relationship (Spielmann et al., 2013). Another antecedent that might influence receptivity is one's socioeconomic class or status. On the one hand, individuals who are lower in social class might see a committed relationship as more desirous given the opportunity to gain resources via a partner (Sng et al., 2017). On the other hand, it is possible that individuals might instead be less desirous of a committed relationship because of the uncertainty of such relationships (Emery & Le, 2014).

CONSEQUENCES OF RECEPTIVITY

There are multiple consequences of receptivity for both those who are currently single and seeking to form a relationship and for those who are currently involved and working to maintain a relationship. Our recent empirical efforts have investigated the components of receptivity in both instances.

Among those who are single, receptivity is associated with multiple processes involved in relationship formation (Hadden, Agnew, & Tan, 2018). First, as single individuals feel increasingly ready for a committed romantic relationship, increasingly they possess relationship cognitions about forming a relationship, such as contemplating dating and holding positive views about closeness with a romantic partner (Hadden et al., 2018; Studies 1 and 2). Readiness among single people is also associated with a variety of relationship pursuit behaviors, such as paying more attention to appearance, and with reporting behaviors known to facilitate relationship formation, such as expressing romantic desire, maintaining close physical contact, playfully teasing, or overtly flirting with someone with whom they are interested (Buss, 1989; Clark, Shaver, & Abrahams, 1999; Lemay & Wolf, 2016).

In addition, feelings of readiness among single individuals predict a higher likelihood of entering a romantic relationship within the next several months (Hadden et al., 2018; Study 3). Moreover, compared to single individuals who are less ready, those who expressed greater readiness were more satisfied with and invested in a later relationship, which, in turn, predicted higher commitment to the relationship. Essentially, readiness plays a role in whether or not people will give the relationship a chance to succeed.

We have also posited that desirability is associated with single individuals wanting to ensure that they would enter into relationships that had a higher chance of success. We found that single individuals who were higher in feelings of desirability expressed more romantic interest in targets who themselves also expressed interest in having a long-term as opposed to a short-term relationship. They also thought that their potential relationship with these targets would be more successful. Interestingly, this desire for partners who matched their high levels of commitment desirability did not diminish, even when the targets were described as being less than ideal in terms of their responsiveness (Tan et al., 2020; Study 3).

Among those who are already coupled, receptivity has been examined with respect to relationship maintenance and stability. With respect to main effects, readiness has been found to be significantly associated with the level of commitment and with the stability of an ongoing relationship over time (Agnew, Hadden, & Tan, 2019). It is also positively associated with various relationship maintenance mechanisms, including greater self-disclosure (Sprecher & Hendrick, 2004), greater accommodation of partner transgressions (Rusbult, Bissonnette, Arriaga, & Cox, 1998), and greater sacrifice of individual preferences for the sake of the relationship (Van Lange, Rusbult, Drigotas, Arriaga, Witcher, & Cox, 1997). Moreover, it has been found to be negatively associated with dissolution consideration (VanderDrift, Agnew, & Wilson, 2009). Readiness also significantly moderates the known associations of commitment level with maintenance, and moderates commitment level in predicting leave behavior (Agnew et al., 2019), such that higher commitment paired with higher readiness yields significantly greater enactment of various maintenance behaviors and a lower likelihood of leave behavior. We postulate, but have yet to examine, that two individuals who have similarly high levels of receptivity simultaneously will be more likely to remain in a stable relationship than individuals who differ substantively in the level of readiness at a given time.

A similar picture emerged for desirability in coupled individuals as compared to single individuals. As mentioned earlier, crucial in our theorizing is that the goal of having a successful relationship stems from feelings of desirability, and individuals strategically look to reduce uncertainty by discerning their partner's level of commitment to facilitate their own goal of a sustained commitment. Hence, we hypothesized and found that individuals higher in desirability had higher expectations of relationship stability and more positive cognitions promoting relationship maintenance, especially when they perceived that their romantic partner was high in commitment (Tan et al., 2020, Studies 1 & 2).

FUTURE DIRECTIONS FOR RESEARCH ON RECEPTIVITY

There are a number of fascinating directions for future research on receptivity. In the remainder of this chapter we outline just a few and encourage interested readers to cultivate additional research directions with respect to timing in relationships.

Influence on Partner Selection Standards and Perceptions of Partner Virtues/Faults

When a person feels particularly receptive to a relationship, it may influence how they perceive potential romantic partners. Think about meeting the "wrong" person at the "right" time. One could imagine that a person who greatly desires and feels ready for a relationship would be more willing to "settle" for a less than ideal partner. Heightened receptivity could potentially lower one's standards regarding what is an acceptable partner; thus, receptivity may result in a different threshold of partner acceptability. This is especially possible if a person feels compelled to be receptive (e.g., to avoid negative outcomes of not being in a relationship, because of pressure to commit, due to a finite childbearing period).

Another perspective worthy of investigation regarding receptivity and partner selection comes from the decision-making literature. One notable way in which people differ in their decision-making is the extent to which they labor over and attempt to maximize their outcomes, that is, the extent to which they are "satisficers" (making choices that meet standards without having to attain the best) or "maximizers" (aiming to make the best possible choice as well as continuing to exhaust all possible alternatives; Schwarz et al., 2002). Crucially, maximizers experience more regret and less satisfaction with their choices (Schwarz et al., 2002). This is especially relevant with respect to relationship partner selection, where maximizers cannot consider all possible partners and, subsequently, may question whether their choice was best. Put into context, maximizers who are receptive might not pursue partners who are less than ideal to fulfill their goals of being in a relationship, which might lead to poorer outcomes from remaining single. It is also possible that maximizers who are receptive and have already chosen a partner continue to attend to potential alternatives, which might lead to negative outcomes for their ongoing relationship.

Those higher in receptivity are likely to view their partner's faults and transgressions differently than those lower in receptivity. If a person highly desires a committed relationship, then they are more likely to be accepting of partner shortcomings, largely as a result of wanting the relationship to work given their goals. They are motivated to give their partner (perceptual) breaks in order to sustain a relationship. In this way, highly receptive people see the world through rose colored glasses (Murray, Holmes, & Griffin, 1996).

Own and Other's Perceptions of One's Receptivity

It is unclear whether people truly have insight into their readiness and whether others' views of a person's receptivity align. Retrospectively, people might think they were receptive because they are currently in a good relationship, but at initiation may have felt less sure. Alternatively, they may recognize that they were unsure of their readiness, but with the benefit of hindsight can see that the timing really was right. As such, the narrative of readiness may be an important feature of maintaining relationships. Indeed, early qualitative work by Aron and colleagues (Aron, Dutton, Aron, & Iverson, 1989; Riela, Rodriguez, Aron, Xu, & Acevado, 2010) found that, upon reflecting upon why they fell in love with their current partner, between one-third and two-thirds of participants mentioned timing and readiness as being a factor that led them to fall in love with their partner. Of course, these findings may in part be retrospective storytelling, but they nonetheless suggest that coming to think of oneself as ready is an important part of relationship formation and maintenance, wherein people who feel the time is right are able and willing to fall in love.

Relatedly, are people cognizant of factors associated with successful long-term relationships? Relational scholars may, understandably, assume that people are aware of the kinds of thoughts and actions associated with optimal relationships (Knee & Reis, 2016). For example, a willingness to sacrifice one's own preferred behaviors for the partner's sake is known to be associated with greater relationship stability (Van Lange, Rusbult et al., 1997). Similarly, being a responsive partner is linked to relationship success (Reis, Clark, & Holmes, 2004). The extent to which a person is aware of such factors and actively thinks and behaves consistent with them is an open question. One needs to both feel receptive and know what is necessary for a committed relationship to flourish. People are more or less comfortable with engaging in self-sacrificial behaviors for a partner. Feeling receptive is not isomorphic with truly being ready to do what must be done to sustain a relationship. That is, feeling ready does not automatically imply a "successful relationship."

Receptivity may also be related to the degree to which people view relationships as in line with their personal goals, and the degree to which personal autonomy and relationship behaviors are complementary rather than in opposition. As mentioned previously, receptivity is likely linked to the degree to which relationships are viewed as more rewarding and less costly, partly due to perceiving inherently relational experiences, such as closeness, as beneficial. However, it is also possible that people feel especially ready when they see alignment between their relational needs and other domains of their lives. People hold many lay theories about how relationships function, such as with respect to growth and destiny beliefs (Knee, 1998). Some research suggests that people also hold lay beliefs about the degree to which intimate relationships conflict with the pursuit of personal needs and goals, as demonstrated by single people reporting avoidance of committed relationships in order to prioritize personal aspirations and goals (Copen, Daniels, Vespa, & Mosher, 2012). Holding such views would likely hamper the degree to which an individual feels ready for a committed relationship, *especially* when they are actively pursuing important personal goals such as career aspirations. On the other hand, when people view a relationship as supportive or instrumental to their goals (e.g., Orehek, Forest, & Wingrove, 2018), they will feel more ready as it aligns with other aspects of their lives.

Past research has shown that those involved in a relationship do not always perceive its dynamics in the same way as those outside of the relationship (e.g., social network member perceptions; Agnew et al., 2001). This may be due to biased impressions about the relationships held by those within it. This may mean, then, that social network members may be in a better position to evaluate the relative receptivity of a person than is the person him or herself. One can imagine a situation in which a person thinks they are ready to commit, but their friends and family completely disagree with this self-assessment.

One factor that may reduce the extent to which a person's own sense of receptivity is associated with relationship formation is mate value. Mate value may act as a facilitator (or barrier) of receptivity as it influences the mate selection process. There is reason to believe that a person's own (perceived) mate value is fundamental in influencing their approach to obtaining mates, as self-perceived mate value can act as a filter in attending to information about prospective mates (Kavanagh, Fletcher, & Ellis, 2014). For example, it is possible that an individual who has low self-perceived mate value will be less receptive to relationships as they might believe that they are unable to attract mates and are unwilling to risk rejection in their pursuit. This might be especially salient if they are also maximizers, with an unwillingness to compromise their standards for mate selection.

Receptivity and Well-Being

One other potentially useful area of future receptivity research regards how levels of receptivity are associated with psychological wellbeing as a result of being in or out of a relationship. It has been traditionally thought that people in romantic relationships (those who are married, in particular) experience better psychological wellbeing than those who are single (Diener, Gohm, Suh, & Oishi, 2000). Recently this has been called into question, with an increased focus on the quality of relationships being the underlying factor regarding whether relationships are beneficial or detrimental to wellbeing (Holt-Lunstad, Birmingham, & Jones, 2008). One of the primary drawbacks of this approach, however, is that it treats single people as a homogenous group, to which others involved in relationships of varying relationship qualities are compared.

How might the relationship quality of single people vary? When considering receptivity, single and involved individuals may have similarities with respect to the quality of their relationships and wellbeing. Specifically, the association between relationship status and wellbeing may well be diminished (or possibly reversed) depending on levels of readiness or desirability. In this sense, single individuals who are not ready or who do not desire a relationship should be happier than singles who are ready or who desire a relationship. Those who feel highly desirous, in particular, however, may experience a degree of goal thwarting (Emmons, 1996), as they want a relationship but are not in one. On the other hand, individuals who are not receptive to a relationship but find themselves in one may be worse off than those who are more receptive. In particular, people who feel less ready, but nonetheless find themselves in a relationship, may be overwhelmed by the demands of a relationship.

Influence of Dissolution on Receptivity: Life after Love

The major theme of RRT is the unique focus on timing, in addition to a consideration of relationship-specific and person-specific factors. Given this, it is worth considering how relationship dissolution can influence feelings of readiness. Breakups are associated with profound emotional and psychological distress (Rhoades, Kamp Dush, Atkins, Stanley, & Markman, 2011; Sbarra & Emery, 2005; Slotter, Gardner, & Finkel, 2010) and it is reasonable to expect that breakups would have a dampening effect on feelings of readiness. Breakup likely leads to temporarily low feelings of receptivity for a new committed romantic relationship, such that people experience acute decreases in commitment readiness following breakup. However, they typically recover from breakup-related distress over time. Why would we expect a recovery period following breakup in which people feel temporarily low levels of readiness for a new committed relationship? The strong negative emotions and disruption to one's sense of self caused by the end of a romantic relationship likely leads to a temporary aversion to the intimacy and vulnerability involved with closer romantic relationships. Moreover, breakup may not necessarily involve a complete decoupling and end of psychological attachment to romantic partners (e.g., Agnew, Arriaga, & Wilson, 2008; Agnew & VanderDrift, 2015; Tan, Agnew, VanderDrift, & Harvey, 2015). It is natural for people to experience emotional longing, psychological attachment to former partners, and even feelings of anger and desire for revenge after relationships have ended (e.g., Barbara & Dion, 2000; Barber & Cooper, 2014; Davis et al., 2003; Saffrey & Ehrenberg, 2007; Sbarra & Emery, 2005; Spielmann, MacDonald, & Wilson, 2009; Tan et al., 2015). Additionally, given the trade-offs people often have to make between personal and relational goals in romantic relationships (Kumashiro, Rusbult, & Finkel, 2008; Vander-Drift & Agnew, 2014), people may feel they need time single to rebuild their sense of self and pursue personal goals before focusing on building a new partnership with another.

Receptivity at Key Stages of Relationship Development

Thus far, we have largely considered readiness for romantic relationships at a relatively abstract level: readiness for commitment *in general*. But relationships can also be conceptualized at more concrete levels as a series of interactions, situations, and stages over time. Indeed, some research has attempted to map out a normative sequence of concrete relationship events, such as saying "I love you" to a partner, meeting each other's family and friends, and moving in together (Eastwick, Keneski, Morgan, McDonald, & Huang, 2018). Readiness may be applicable to these more concrete relationship development behaviors as well. In particular, it would be interesting to understand what makes individuals more or less ready for any single event, and how readiness for an event develops over time. Does readiness to, for instance, saying "I love you" to a partner mean someone is more likely to engage in that behavior? What about reactions when one's partner says it first, prompting the person to say it back before they may feel ready to do so? (cf. Joel, Teper, & MacDonald, 2014). Thus, feelings of readiness for concrete relationship events or transitions may be a particularly important aspect of relationship development.

THE TIME HAS COME

The time is past due for an active, thoughtful consideration of the role of timing in understanding formation, maintenance, and stability of interdependent relationships. Such consideration differs from past approaches to the study of interpersonal relationships (Agnew, 2014a). As highlighted here, most relational scholars study either aspects of a person (or persons) or of the relationship itself in attempting to understand why people think, feel, or behave in various ways in their relationships or to understand why relationships start, continue, or end (Finkel, Simpson, & Eastwick, 2017; Karney & Bradbury, 1995). The emphasis on individual, dyadic, and external forces have characterized much of relationship research, but the role, if any, of timing of the relationship within a person's (or persons') life has not been explicitly considered. Throughout this chapter, we have suggested that the role of timing is crucial in understanding relationships, but it has been barely researched. This chapter presents relationship receptivity theory, one attempt to explicate the importance of timing in understanding relational processes. We hope that the novel hypotheses derived from the theory will spark new interest among researchers and that the results from hypothesis tests will further enrich our understanding of the role of timing in interpersonal relationships.

REFERENCES

Agnew, C. R. (2000). Cognitive interdependence and the experience of relationship loss. In J. H. Harvey & E. D. Miller (Eds.), *Loss and Trauma: General and Close Relationship Perspectives* (pp. 385–398). Philadelphia, PA: Brunner-Routledge.

Agnew, C. R. (2014a). Relationship Receptivity: Commitment in a Changing World. Invited keynote address presented at the 2014 International Association of Relationship Research Conference, Melbourne, Australia.

Agnew, C. R. (Ed.) (2014b). *Social Influences on Romantic Relationships: Beyond the Dyad.* Cambridge: Cambridge University Press.

Agnew, C. R., Arriaga, X. B., & Wilson, J. E. (2008). Committed to what? Using the Bases of Relational Commitment Model to understand continuity and changes in social relationships. In J. P. Forgas & J. Fitness (Eds.), *Social Relationships: Cognitive, Affective and Motivational Processes* (pp. 147–164). New York: Psychology Press.

Agnew, C. R., Hadden, B. W., & Tan, K. (2019). It's about time: Readiness, commitment and stability in close relationships. *Social Psychological and Personality Science*, 10, 1046–1055.

Agnew, C. R., Loving, T. J., & Drigotas, S. M. (2001). Substituting the forest for the trees: Social networks and the prediction of romantic relationship state and fate. *Journal of Personality and Social Psychology*, 81, 1042–1057.

Agnew, C. R., Van Lange, P. A. M., Rusbult, C. E., & Langston, C. A. (1998). Cognitive interdependence: Commitment and the mental representation of close relationships. *Journal of Personality and Social Psychology*, 74, 939–954.

Agnew, C. R. & VanderDrift, L. E. (2015). Relationship maintenance and dissolution. In M. Mikulincer & P. R. Shaver (Eds.), *APA Handbook of Personality and Social Psychology: Vol. 3. Interpersonal Relations* (pp. 581–604). Washington, DC: American Psychological Association.

Agnew, C. R. & VanderDrift, L. E. (2018). Commitment processes in personal relationship. In A. L. Vangelisti & D. Perlman (Eds.), *The Cambridge Handbook of Personal Relationships* (2nd ed., pp. 437–448). Cambridge: Cambridge University Press.

Allendorf, K. & Pandian, R. K. (2016). The decline of arranged marriage? Marital change and continuity in India. *Population and Development Review*, 42, 435–464.

Apatow, J. (Producer) & Showalter, M. (Director). (2017). *The Big Sick* [Motion Picture]. United States: Apatow Productions.

Aron, A., Dutton, D. G., Aron, E. N., & Iverson, A. (1989). Experiences of falling in love. *Journal of Social and Personal Relationships*, 6, 243–257.

Arriaga, X. B. (2013). An interdependence theory analysis of close relationships. In J. A. Simpson & L. Campbell (Eds.), *Oxford Library of Psychology. The Oxford Handbook of Close Relationships* (pp. 39–65). New York: Oxford University Press.

Arriaga, X. B., Reed, J., Goodfriend, W., & Agnew, C. R. (2006). Relationship perceptions and persistence: Do fluctuations in perceived partner commitment undermine dating relationships? *Journal of Personality and Social Psychology*, 91, 1045–1065.

Baker, L. R., McNulty, J. K., & VanderDrift, L. E. (2017). Expectations for future relationship satisfaction: Unique sources and critical implications for commitment. *Journal of Experimental Psychology: General*, 146, 700–721.

Bandura, A. (1986). *Social Foundations of Thought and Action: A Social Cognitive Theory*. Englewood Cliffs, NJ: Prentice Hall.

Barbara, A. M. & Dion, K. L. (2000). Breaking up is hard to do, especially for strongly "preoccupied" lovers. *Journal of Personal and Interpersonal Loss*, 5, 315–342.

Barber, L. L. & Cooper, M. L. (2014). Rebound sex: Sexual motives and behaviors following a relationship breakup. *Archives of Sexual Behavior*, 43, 251–265.

Baumeister, R. F. & Leary, M. R. (1995). The need to belong: Desire for interpersonal attachments as a fundamental human motivation. *Psychological Bulletin*, 117, 497–529.

Besikci, E., Agnew, C. R., & Yildirim, A. (2016). It's my partner, deal with it: Rejection sensitivity, normative beliefs, and commitment. *Personal Relationships*, 23, 384–395.

Bruner, J. S. (1966). *Toward a Theory of Instruction*. Cambridge, MA: Harvard University Press.

Bruner, J. S. (1973). Reception strategies in concept attainment. In J. S. Bruner & J. M. Anglin (Eds.), *Beyond the Information Given: Studies in the Psychology of Knowing*. New York: Norton.

Buss, D. M. (1989). Sex differences in human mate preferences: Evolutionary hypotheses tested in 37 cultures. *Behavioral and Brain Sciences*, 12, 1–49.

Buss, D. M. & Schmidt, D. P. (1993). Sexual strategies theory: An evolutionary perspective on human mating. *Psychological Review*, 100, 204–232.

Chaiken, S. (1987). The heuristic model of persuasion. In M. P. Zanna, J. M. Olsen, & C. P, Herman (Eds.), *Social Influence: The Ontario Symposium* (Vol. 5, pp. 3–39). Hillsdale, NJ: Erlbaum.

Chaiken, S. & Trope, Y., (Eds.) (1999). *Dual-Process Theories in Social Psychology*, New York: Guilford Press.

Clark, C. L., Shaver, P. R., & Abrahams, M. F. (1999). Strategic behaviors in romantic relationship initiation. *Personality and Social Psychology Bulletin*, 25, 707–720.

Copen, C. E., Daniels, K., Vespa, J., & Mosher, W. D. (2012). First marriages in the United States: Data from the 2006–2010 National Survey of Family Growth. *National Health Statistics Report*, 49, 1–21.

Davies, P. T. & Windle, M. (2000). Middle adolescents' dating pathways and psychosocial adjustment. *Merrill-Palmer Quarterly*, 46, 90–118.

Davis, D., Shaver, P. R., & Vernon, M. L. (2003). Physical, emotional, and behavioral reactions to breaking up: The roles of gender, age, environmental involvement, and attachment style. *Personality and Social Psychology Bulletin*, 29, 971–884.

Del Giudice, M., Gangestad, S. W., & Kaplan, H. S. (2015). Life history theory and evolutionary psychology. In D. M. Buss (Ed.), *The Handbook of Evolutionary Psychology* (2nd ed., pp. 88–114). New York: Wiley and Sons.

Diener, E., Gohm, C. L., Suh, E., & Oishi, S. (2000). Similarity of the relations between marital status and well-being across cultures. *Journal of Cross-Cultural Psychology*, 31, 419–436.

Eastwick, P. W., Keneski, E., Morgan, T. A., McDonald, M. A. & Huang, S. A. (2018). What do short-term and long-term relationships look like? Building the relationship coordination and strategic timing (ReCAST) model. *Journal of Experimental Psychology: General*, 5, 747–781.

Emery, L. F. & Le, B. (2014). Imagining the white picket fence: Social class, future plans, and romantic relationship quality. *Social Psychological and Personality Science*, 5, 653–661.

Emmons, R. A. (1996). Striving and feeling: Personal goals and subjective well-being. In P. M. Gollwitzer & J. A. Bargh (Eds.), *The Psychology of Action: Linking Cognition and Motivation and Behavior* (pp. 313–337). New York: Guilford Press.

Etcheverry, P. E. & Agnew, C. R. (2004). Subjective norms and the prediction of romantic relationship state and fate. *Personal Relationships*, 11, 409–428.

Fazio, R. H. (1990). Multiple processes by which attitudes guide behavior: The MODE model as an integrative framework. *Advances in Experimental Social Psychology*, 23, 75–109.

Finkel, E. J., Simpson, J. A., & Eastwick, P. W. (2017). The psychology of close relationships: Fourteen core principles. *Annual Review of Psychology*, 68, 383–411.

Fletcher, G. J. O., Simpson, J. A., & Thomas, G. (2000). Ideals, perceptions and evaluations in early relationship development. *Journal of Personality and Social Psychology*, 79, 933–940.

Gangestad, S. W. & Simpson, J. A. (2000). The evolution of human mating: trade-offs and strategic pluralism. *Behavioral and Brain Sciences*, 23, 573–587.

Gawronski, B. & Creighton, L. A. (2013). Dual process theories. In D. E. Carlston (Ed.), *The Oxford Handbook of Social Cognition* (pp. 282–312). New York: Oxford University Press.

Goodfriend, W. & Agnew, C. R. (2008). Sunken costs and desired plans: Examining different types of investments in close relationships. *Personality and Social Psychology Bulletin*, 34, 1639–1652.

Graziano, W. G. & Tobin, R. M. (2009). Agreeableness. In M. Leary & R. H. Hoyle (Eds.), *Handbook of Individual Differences in Social Behavior* (pp. 46–61). New York: The Guilford Press.

Hadden, B. W., Agnew, C. R.., & Tan, K. (2018). Commitment readiness and relationship formation. *Personality and Social Psychology Bulletin*, 44, 1242–1257.

Holt-Lunstad, J., Birmingham, W. & Jones, B. Q. (2008). Is there something unique about marriage? The relative impact of marital status, relationship quality, and network social support on ambulatory blood pressure and mental health. *Annals of Behavioral Medicine*, 35, 239–244.

House, J. S., Landis, K. R., & Umberson, D. (1988). Social relationships and health. *Science*, 241, 540–545.

Huston, T. L., Caughlin, J. P., Houts, R. M., Smith, S. E., & George, L. J. (2001). The connubial crucible: Newlywed years as predictors of marital delight, distress, and divorce. *Journal of Personality and Social Psychology*, 80, 237–252.

Joel, S., Teper, R., & MacDonald, G. (2014). People overestimate their willingness to reject potential romantic partners by overlooking their concern for others. *Psychological Science*, 25, 2233–2240.

Karney, B. R. & Bradbury, T. N. (1995). The longitudinal course of marital quality and stability: A review of theory, method and research. *Psychological Bulletin*, 118, 3–34.

Kavanagh, P. S., Fletcher, G. J., & Ellis, B. J. (2014). The mating sociometer and attractive others: a double-edged sword in romantic relationships. *Journal of Social Psychology*, 154, 126–141.

Kenrick, D. T. & Griskevicius, V. (2015). Life history, fundamental motives, and sexual competition. *Current Opinion in Psychology*, 1, 40–44.

Knee, C. R. (1998). Implicit theories of relationships: Assessment and prediction of romantic relationship initiation, coping and longevity. *Journal of Personality and Social Psychology*, 74, 360–370.

Knee, C. R. & Reis, H. T. (Eds.). (2016). *Positive Approaches to Optimal Relationship Development*. New York: Cambridge University Press.

Kumashiro, M., Rusbult, C. E., & Finkel, E. J. (2008). Navigating personal and relational concerns: The quest for equilibrium. *Journal of Personality and Social Psychology*, 95, 94–110.

Le, B. & Agnew, C. R. (2003). Commitment and its theorized determinants: A meta-analysis of the Investment Model. *Personal Relationships*, 10, 37–57.

Lehmiller, J. J. & Agnew, C. R. (2006). Marginalized relationships: The impact of social disapproval on romantic relationship commitment. *Personality and Social Psychology Bulletin*, 32, 40–51.

Lemay, E. P., Jr. (2016). The forecast model of relationship commitment. *Journal of Personality and Social Psychology*, 111, 34–52.

Lemay, E. P. & Wolf, N. R. (2016). Projection of romantic and sexual desire in opposite-sex friendships: How wishful thinking creates a self-fulfilling prophecy. *Personality and Social Psychology Bulletin*, 42, 864–878.

Meier, A. & Allen, G. (2009). Romantic relationships from adolescence to young adulthood: Evidence from the National Longitudinal Study of Adolescent Health. *The Sociological Quarterly*, 50, 308–335.

Mikulincer, M. & Shaver, P. R. (2007). *Attachment in Adulthood: Structure, Dynamics, and Change*. New York: Guilford Press.

Murray, S. L., Holmes, J. G., & Griffin, D. W. (1996). The benefits of positive illusions: Idealization and the construction of satisfaction in close relationships. *Journal of Personality and Social Psychology*, 70, 79–98.

Norcross, J. C., Krebs, P. M., and Prochaska, J. O. (2011). Stages of change. *Journal of Clinical Psychology*, 67, 143–154.

Orehek, E., Forest, A. L., & Wingrove, S. (2018). People as means to multiple goals: Implications for interpersonal relationships. *Personality and Social Psychology Bulletin*, 44, 1487–1501.

Owen, K., Rhoades, G., Shuck, B., Fincham, F. D., Stanley, S., Markman, H., & Knopp, K. (2014). Commitment uncertainty: A theoretical overview. *Couple and Family Psychology: Research and Practice*, 3, 207–219.

Petty, R. E. & Cacioppo, J. T. (1986). The elaboration likelihood model of persuasion. *Advances in Experimental Social Psychology*, 19, 123–205.

Pillsworth, E. G. & Haselton, M. G. (2005). The evolution of coupling. *Psychological Inquiry*, 16, 98–104.

Prochaska, J. O. & DiClemente, C. C. (2005). The transtheoretical approach. In J. C. Norcross & M. R. Goldfried (Eds.), *Handbook of Psychotherapy Integration* (2nd ed., pp. 147–171). New York: Oxford University Press.

Pruitt, D. G. (2007). Readiness theory and the Northern Ireland conflict. *American Behavioral Scientist*, 50, 1520–1541.

Reis, H. T., Clark, M. S., & Holmes, J. G. (2004). Perceived partner responsiveness as an organizing construct in the study of intimacy and closeness. In D. J. Mashek & A. P. Aron (Eds.), *Handbook of Closeness and Intimacy* (pp. 201–225). Mahwah, NJ: Erlbaum.

Rhoades, G. K., Kamp Dush, C. M., Atkins, D. C., Stanley, S. M., & Markman, H. J. (2011). Breaking up is hard to do: The impact of unmarried relationship dissolution on mental health and life satisfaction. *Journal of Family Psychology*, 25, 366–374.

Riela, S., Rodriguez, G., Aron, A., Xu, X., & Acevado, B. P. (2010). Experiences of falling in love: Investigating culture, ethnicity, gender, and speed. *Journal of Social and Personal Relationships*, 27, 473–493.

Rusbult, C. E., Bissonnette, V. I., Arriaga, X. B., & Cox, C. L. (1998). Accommodation processes during the early years of marriage. In T. N. Bradbury (Ed.), *The Developmental Course of Marital Dysfunction* (pp. 74–113). New York: Cambridge University Press.

Rusbult, C. E., Olsen, N., Davis, J. L., & Hannon, P. A. (2001). Commitment and relationship maintenance mechanisms. In J. Harvey & A. Wenzel (Eds.), *Close Relationships: Maintenance and Enhancement* (pp. 87–113). Mahwah, NJ: Erlbaum.

Rusbult, C. E. & Van Lange, P. A. M. (2003). Interdependence, interaction, and relationships. *Annual Review of Psychology*, 54, 351–375.

Rusbult, C. E., Verette, J., Whitney, G. A., Slovik, L. F., & Lipkus, I. (1991). Accommodation processes in close relationships: Theory and preliminary empirical evidence. *Journal of Personality and Social Psychology*, 60, 53–78.

Saffrey, C. & Ehrenberg, M. (2007). When thinking hurts: Attachment, rumination, and postrelationship adjustment. *Personal Relationships*, 14, 351–368.

Sbarra, D. A. & Emery, R. E. (2005). The emotional sequelae of nonmarital relationship dissolution: Analysis of change and intraindividual variability over time. *Personal Relationships*, 12, 213–232.

Schiff, A. (2013). On success in peace processes: Readiness theory and the Aceh peace process. *Peace and Conflict Studies*, 20(1), Article 2.

Schwarz, B. Ward, A., Monterosso, J., Lyubomirksy, S., White, K., & Lehman, D. R. (2002). Maximizing versus satisficing: Happiness is matter of choice. *Journal of Personality and Social Psychology*, 83, 1178–1197.

Simpson, J. A., Collins, W. A., & Salvatore, J. E. (2011). The impact of early interpersonal experience on adult romantic relationship functioning: Recent findings from the Minnesota longitudinal study of risk and adaptation. *Current Directions in Psychological Science*, 20, 355–359.

Sinclair, H. C., Hood, K. B., & Wright, B. L. (2014). Revisiting the Romeo and Juliet effect: Reexamining the links between social network opinions and romantic relationship outcomes. *Social Psychology*, 45, 170–178.

Slotter, E. B., Gardner, W. L., & Finkel, E. J. (2010). Who am I without you? The influence of romantic breakup on the self-concept. *Personality and Social Psychology Bulletin*, 36, 147–160.

Sng, O., Neuberg, S. L., Varnum, M. E. W., & Kenrick, D. T. (2017). The crowded life is a slow life: Population density and life history strategy. *Journal of Personality and Social Psychology*, 112, 736–754.

Spielmann, S. S., MacDonald, G., Maxwell, J. A., Joel, S., Peragine, D., Muise, A., & Impett, E. A. (2013). Settling for less out of fear of being single. *Journal of Personality and Social Psychology*, 105, 1049–1073.

Spielmann, S. S., MacDonald, G., & Wilson, A. E. (2009). On the rebound: Focusing on someone new helps anxiously attached individuals let go of ex-partners. *Personality and Social Psychology Bulletin*, 35, 1382–1394.

Sprecher, S. & Hendrick, S. S. (2004). Self-disclosure in intimate relationships: Associations with individual and relationship characteristics over time. *Journal of Social and Clinical Psychology*, 23, 857–877.

Tan, K. & Agnew, C. R. (2016). Ease of retrieval effects on relationship commitment: The role of future plans. *Personality and Social Psychology Bulletin*, 42, 161–171.

Tan, K., Agnew, C. R., & Hadden, B. W. (2020). Seeking and ensuring interdependence: Desiring commitment and the strategic initiation and maintenance of close relationships. *Personality and Social Psychology Bulletin*, 46, 36–50.

Tan, K., Agnew, C. R., VanderDrift, L. E., & Harvey, S. M. (2015). Committed to us: Predicting relationship closeness following nonmarital romantic relationship breakup. *Journal of Social and Personal Relationships*, 32, 456–471.

Thibaut, J. W. & Kelly, H. H. (1959). *The Social Psychology of Groups*. Oxford: John Wiley.

Thorndike, E. (1999) [1913]. *Education Psychology*. New York: Routledge.

Thorndike, E. (1932). *The Fundamentals of Learning*. New York: Teachers College Press.

Van Lange, P. A. M., Otten, W., De Bruin, E. M. N., & Joireman, J. A. (1997). Development of prosocial, individualistic, and competitive orientations: Theory and preliminary evidence. *Journal of Personality and Social Psychology*, 73, 733–746.

Van Lange, P. A. M., Rusbult, C. E., Drigotas, S. M., Arriaga, X. B., Witcher, B. S., & Cox, C. L. (1997). Willingness to sacrifice in close relationships. *Journal of Personality and Social Psychology*, 72, 1373–1395.

VanderDrift, L. E. & Agnew, C. R. (2014). Relational consequences of personal goal pursuits. *Journal of Personality and Social Psychology*, 106, 927–940.

VanderDrift, L. E., Agnew, C. R., & Wilson, J. E. (2009). Nonmarital romantic relationship commitment and leave behavior: The mediating role of dissolution consideration. *Personality and Social Psychology Bulletin*, 35, 1220–1232.

Weiner, B. J. (2009). A theory of organizational readiness for change. *Implementation Science*, 4, 67.

Wright, B. L. & Sinclair, H. C. (2012). Pulling the strings: Effects of friend and parent opinions on dating choices. *Personal Relationships*, 19, 743–758.

14

A New Measure of Expected Relationship Satisfaction, Alternatives, and Investment Supports an Expectations Model of Interdependence

LEVI R. BAKER, JAMES K. MCNULTY, ASHLYN BRADY, AND
SHAE MONTALVO

When I (the first author) was an undergraduate, my roommate was in a long-distance romantic relationship that regularly involved conflict. For several hours almost every night, I would overhear my roommate arguing with his girlfriend over the phone. Not only did he do little to hide the conflict, he often directly spoke about how unhappy they were together. Given such events, I predicted my roommate and his girlfriend would eventually break up. Nevertheless, in stark contrast to my prediction, just before graduation my roommate revealed that he had proposed to her and that they were engaged to become married. Stunned by the news, I asked him why he would propose to someone that made him so unhappy. He explained that he was confident that they would argue less once they lived together because many of their arguments resulted from not spending enough time together. Moreover, he noted that there would be fewer opportunities to meet new single women once he left college and began working in a largely male-dominated industry.

As an aspiring relationship researcher, I looked to one of the most influential relationship theories – interdependence theory – to better understand why my roommate proposed to his girlfriend. Although classic interdependence perspectives (e.g., Kelley & Thibaut, 1978; Thibaut & Kelley, 1959) integrated many of the constructs relevant to his decision, it failed to account for his decision. More specifically, whereas interdependence theory suggests that people should be more committed to their relationships to the extent that they a) are currently satisfied with the relationship and b) perceive they currently have few alternatives to the relationship, my roommate was highly committed despite a) being currently unhappy with his relationship and b) attending a university with many desirable alternative partners. In fact, his decision seemed to be influenced more by his interpersonal expectations for

These authors contributed equally to this work.

the future (e.g., expected satisfaction, expected alternatives) than his beliefs about the present or past.

In this chapter, we a) integrate a growing body of research highlighting the importance of expectations for decision-making into existing interdependence perspectives on close relationships and b) describe a new measure that assesses expected aspects of interdependence to assist with future research. To this end, this first section briefly reviews the primary tenets of interdependence theory. The second section reviews theory and research suggesting that decisions are often determined more by expectations than by current or previous experiences, thus suggesting that current interdependence perspectives may be incomplete to the extent that they emphasize intimates' beliefs about the present or past over their expectations for the future. The third section identifies unique sources of relationship expectations that may lead such expectations to diverge from beliefs about the present or past. The fourth and fifth sections present the methods and results of a study that validated a new measure of expected satisfaction, alternatives, and investments. Finally, the sixth section discusses how this measure can be used in future research and the implications of this study for interdependence theory.

BRIEF OVERVIEW OF INTERDEPENDENCE THEORY

Interdependence theory is one of the most established and influential theories in relationship science (see Finkel & Simpson, 2015) and specifically accounts for why people commit to maintaining close relationships and thus remain in those relationships. According to classic conceptualizations of this theory (e.g., Kelley & Thibaut, 1978; Thibaut & Kelley, 1959), intimates are more committed to a relationship, and thus more likely to remain in that relationship, to the extent that the relationship is currently satisfying and they believe the relationship is better than their current alternatives to the relationship. Rusbult's (1980) investment model later expanded on this theory by suggesting that intimates' previous investments of time and resources also contribute to their commitment to, and thus the longevity of, their relationships. A consistent body of research supports these ideas. Most notably, a recent meta-analysis (Tran, Judge, & Kashima, 2019; see also, Le & Agnew, 2003) of 202 samples revealed that commitment is strongly positively associated with both relationship satisfaction ($r = .65$) and investments ($r = .53$) and negatively associated with perceived alternatives ($r = -.43$).

COMMITMENT SHOULD DEPEND MORE ON EXPECTED INTERDEPENDENCE

Nevertheless, a growing body of research suggests that decisions are influenced more by expected outcomes than by present or past outcomes; thus, interdependence theory may be enhanced by extending beyond present or past beliefs to include interpersonal expectations about the future. For example, expectancy-value theories (Atkinson, 1957; Feather, 1982) and supporting research (for reviews, see Gilbert & Wilson, 2007; Seligman, Railton, Baumeister, & Sripada, 2013; Wigfield, Tonks, & Klauda, 2009) suggest that people base their decisions primarily on the extent to which they expect possible options will lead to desired results. Further, a growing body of research that has directly compared the influence of current and expected emotions and evaluations concluded that behavior is often influenced more by expected, rather than current, outcomes (Bushman, Baumeister, & Phillips, 2001; DeWall, Baumeister, Chester, & Bushman, 2016; Freedman, Wallington, & Bless, 1967; Gross, 1998; Manucia, Baumann, & Cialdini, 1984; Mellers, Schwartz, & Ritov, 1999; Resulaj, Kiani, Wolpert, & Shadlen, 2009; Silverman, 1967; Tice, Bratslavsky, & Baumeister, 2001; Vogel, Wester, Wei, & Boysen, 2005; for review, see Baumeister, Vohs, DeWall, & Zhang, 2007). Most notably, DeWall et al. (2016) conducted a meta-analysis of 413 samples that examined the implications of current and anticipated emotions and reported that only 22 percent of studies reported significant associations between current emotions and behavior, whereas 90 percent of studies reported significant associations between expected emotions and behavior.

In regard to factors that promote decisions to remain or leave a relationship, then, expectations about future satisfaction, alternatives, and investment may serve distinct functions that are ultimately more relevant to commitment-related decisions compared to the functions served by present or past relationship satisfaction, alternatives, and investments. First, with respect to satisfaction, a primary function of emotions is to make individuals aware of whether or not their needs and goals are being met (see Carver & Scheier, 1998); thus, intimates' current satisfaction with a relationship should signal the extent to which their relationships do or do not currently fulfill their interpersonal needs and goals. Although recognizing that a relationship is unfulfilling may at times motivate intimates to leave their relationships, many remain in their relationships despite their current dissatisfaction (Arriaga, 2001; McNulty & Karney, 2001; McNulty, O'Mara, & Karney, 2008) and opt to attempt to improve the quality of the relationship instead. In contrast, expected emotions function to inform decisions about the future (Dennett, 1991; see Olson, Roese, & Zanna, 1996); thus, intimates' expected relationship satisfaction should guide their decision to remain in or leave their relationships. Accordingly, a series of studies conducted by Baker, McNulty, and VanderDrift (2017) directly supported the idea that expected satisfaction is a more functional and proximal predictor of commitment than is current satisfaction. In particular, five cross-sectional, experimental, and longitudinal studies demonstrated that expected satisfaction was a stronger predictor of a) relationship commitment, b) relationship maintenance behaviors that signal commitment (e.g., devaluing attractive alternative partners), and

c) relationship stability than was current satisfaction. In one study, for example, intimates were led to believe that their relationships were either currently satisfying or unsatisfying and would be either satisfying or unsatisfying in the future. Although intimates who were led to believe their relationships were currently satisfying were more committed than were intimates who were led to believe their relationships were currently unsatisfying, the expected satisfaction manipulation was a stronger predictor of commitment than was the current satisfaction manipulation.

Second, there is reason to believe that expected alternatives are similarly relevant to commitment-related decisions. In particular, given that there can be costs to investing the time, effort, and resources necessary to maintain a close relationship (Baker, McNulty, Overall, Lambert, & Fincham, 2013), intimates may become less committed to maintaining a relationship if they believe they will have more desirable options available to them in the future. In contrast, intimates who believe they will have fewer desirable options in the future may become more committed to their current relationship so they do not eventually lose that relationship and are forced to contend with those limited options. Although we are unaware of research or theory that supports these ideas within the context of close relationships, several theories outside of the realm of close relationships suggest that commitment increases when people perceive they will have limited options available in the future. For example, research on scarcity (e.g., Lynn, 1991, 1992) suggests that people are more willing to purchase a product if they believe that product will be unavailable in the future, suggesting that current commitment increases when people believe their options will be limited in the future. Similarly, and more directly relevant, Rosato's (2016) consumer loss-aversion model suggests that consumers' expectations about the future availability of a product affects their current commitment to that product, such that consumers are more likely to commit to products if they believe that the alternatives to those products will not be available in the future.

Finally, there is reason to expect that expected investments are similarly relevant to commitment-related decisions. Ajzen, Czasch, and Flood's (2009) model of intentions suggests that the intention to implement goal-directed behaviors increases commitment toward achieving those goals (see also Gollwitzer, 1999), and thus planning to maintain relationships by investing time and resources into those relationships should increase intimates' commitment to maintaining those relationships. Sheeran, Webb, and Gollwitzer (2005) provided support for this idea outside of the context of close relationships by demonstrating that people who developed plans to implement goal-relevant behaviors (e.g., studying for an exam) became more committed to achieving their goals than did people who did not plan to engage in those goal-relevant behaviors. Research examining this within the context of close relationships also supports this idea. In particular, Goodfriend and Agnew

(2008) demonstrated in one cross-sectional and one longitudinal study that intimates' planned investments were a significantly stronger predictor of commitment, the likelihood of future relationship dissolution, and the likelihood of starting a new relationship with a different partner than were past investments.

PREDICTORS OF EXPECTED SATISFACTION, ALTERNATIVES, AND INVESTMENTS

If expected satisfaction, alternatives, and investments are stronger and more proximal determinants of commitment, why has a consistent body of research demonstrated that current satisfaction, alternatives, and investments are robust and strong predictors of relationship commitment? We posit that these associations emerged because current experiences indirectly influence commitment by first shaping expectations for the future. In particular, previous research has demonstrated that expectations are often partially based on prior experience (Olson et al., 1996) and people often do not expect drastic changes in their lives (Quoidbach, Gilbert, & Wilson, 2013). Further, consistent with the idea that intimates' expectations for the future should be partially determined by their current and past experiences, previous research has demonstrated that intimates' current satisfaction affects their expected satisfaction (Baker, McNulty, & VanderDrift, 2017; Lemay, 2016; Lemay, Lin, & Muir, 2015; McNulty & Karney, 2002, 2004; Neff & Geers, 2013) and their current investments predict their expected investments (Goodfriend & Agnew, 2008), although we are unaware of research that has examined whether current alternatives predict expected alternatives.

Importantly, though, although people typically do not expect drastic changes in their relationships, numerous factors may still cause them to expect that their satisfaction, alternatives, and investments will increase or decrease in the future. One such factor is anticipated life events. In particular, people might anticipate moving closer or farther away from a partner, beginning to cohabitate with a partner, becoming engaged or married, having a child, becoming ill, beginning a new job, losing a job, or moving to a new residence, and anticipating events such as these may cause them to expect changes in their relationship satisfaction, the desirability of alternative relationships, or the amount they will need to invest in their relationships. Research on the transition to parenthood, for example, suggests that people often expect that becoming a new parent will require substantial investments (Biehle & Mickelson, 2012) and may decrease their relationship satisfaction (Lawrence, Nylen, & Cobb, 2007). Anticipating becoming a new parent may also lead people, especially women, to believe that they will be a less desirable to alternative partners (see Buss & Schmitt, 1993) and, thus, expecting to become a parent may lead intimates to expect that they will have fewer desirable relationship alternatives in the future. Similarly, intimates often expect that getting married will increase their relationship satisfaction (Laner & Russell, 1995), the need for greater relational investments (Poortman & Mills, 2012), and their desirability to alternative partners (Brase & Guy, 2004).

Planning to improve the quality of the relationship may also cause intimates to expect that their satisfaction and investments will increase in the future. For example, intimates often intend to act more positively around their partners (Stafford, 2011), provide their partners with support (Feeney & Collins, 2014), attempt to resolve their relationship problems (Overall, Fletcher, Simpson, & Sibley, 2009), or seek therapy (Doss, Simpson, & Christensen, 2004). Given that such plans are formed with the goal of strengthening the relationship, it is not surprising that people expect their relationship satisfaction will increase to the extent that they plan to improve their relationships (Baker et al., 2017). Nevertheless, such behaviors often require considerable time and effort (e.g., Silliman & Schumm, 1999), and thus intimates should expect that such plans will increase the amount they will invest into their relationships.

Planning to share novel experiences with their partners may similarly cause intimates to expect that their satisfaction will increase in the future. In particular, a consistent body of research suggests that intimates who engage in novel experiences with their partners, such as traveling, pursuing unfamiliar recreational activities, discussing new ideas, or trying a new restaurant, tend to remain more satisfied with those partners than do intimates who have more routine experiences (see Aron, Norman, Aron, & Lewandowski, 2002). In particular, novel experiences tend to increase physiological arousal and when people associate arousal or positive affect with their partners, they often experience increased feelings of passionate love toward their partners (Dutton & Aron, 1974; see also McNulty, Olson, Jones, & Acosta, 2017). Given that intimates are often aware of the benefits of shared novel experiences (Dion & Dion, 1996), intimates who expect to engage in these experiences should expect to become more satisfied with their relationships compared to intimates who expect to have more routine experiences.

Finally, individual differences may cause intimates to expect that their satisfaction, alternatives, and investments will increase or decrease in the future. Regarding satisfaction, individuals who believe they can successfully resolve their relationships conflicts (i.e., those with high relationship self-efficacy) should expect to resolve problems that are diminishing their satisfaction (Baker & McNulty, 2010) and thus should expect their relationship satisfaction will increase over time. In contrast, insecurely attached individuals tend to doubt their partners' responsiveness (see Shaver & Mikulincer, 2002) and thus may expect their relationship quality to decrease. Further, regarding investments, whereas anxiously attached individuals respond to such doubts by investing more into their relationships, avoidantly attached individuals respond by investing less (Feeney & Karantzas, 2017) and thus insecurely attached individuals may expect their investments to change over time. Regarding alternatives, individuals with high self-esteem tend to believe their mate value is high (Brase & Guy, 2004) and thus may be particularly likely to expect increases in desirable alternative partners. Finally, given that women's mate value depends more on their physical attractiveness, which tends to decrease over time, and men's mate value depends more on their status and resources, which tend to increase over time (Buss & Schmitt, 1993), women may be more likely to expect their alternatives will decrease whereas men may be more likely to expect their alternatives will increase.

DEVELOPING AND VALIDATING THE EXPECTED
INTERDEPENDENCE SCALE: METHODS

In order to directly test these ideas in an effort to advance future research on the growing topic of relationship expectations, we developed a new measure – the Expected Interdependence Scale (EIS) – to assess expected relationship satisfaction, alternatives, and investments. Given the volume of research (see Le & Agnew, 2003) that has used the Investment Model Scale (IMS; Rusbult, Martz, & Agnew, 1998), this new measure was based on the IMS to allow for direct comparisons of current and expected satisfaction, alternatives, and investments. We conducted one study consisting of two independent samples to develop the scale and provide evidence for its psychometric properties.

Method

Participants Two independent samples of participants who were in a romantic relationship for at least three months were recruited for this study. Sample 1 consisted of ninety-nine individuals (thirty-four men, sixty-five women) who were recruited using the Mechanical Turk service on amazon.com (MTurk). Sample 2 consisted of 116 individuals (twenty-four men, ninety-two women) who were recruited from a medium-sized university in the southeastern United States.

Participants from Sample 1 were 37 years old (SD = 12.51). Forty-nine (50%) participants were married, thirty-five (35%) reported they were in an exclusive relationship, ten (10%) reported they were engaged, and five (5%) reported they were in a casual relationship. The majority of participants (n = 77; 78%) identified as White or Caucasian, eight (8%) identified as Black or African American, seven (7%) identified as Asian, four (4%) identified as Hispanic or Latino/a, and the remaining three (3%) identified as another ethnicity or two or more ethnicities. The majority of participants (n = 91;

92%) identified as heterosexual, four (4%) identified as bisexual, two (2%) identified as gay or lesbian, and two (2%) identified as other.

Participants from Sample 2 were 19.10 years old (SD = 2.67). Seventy-seven (66%) participants reported they were in an exclusive relationship, thirty-three (28%) reported they were in a casual relationship, four (3%) reported they were engaged, one (1%) was married, and one (1%) did not respond. Forty-nine (42%) identified as White or Caucasian, thirty-four (29%) identified as Black or African American, eleven (10%) identified as Hispanic or Latino/a, eleven (10%) identified as Asian, one (1%) identified as American Indian or Alaska Native, and the remaining ten (9%) identified as another ethnicity or two or more ethnicities. The majority of participants (n = 92; 79%) identified as heterosexual, eleven (10%) identified as bisexual, seven (6%) identified as gay or lesbian, and six (5%) identified as other or did not respond.

Procedure All procedures were approved by the Institutional Review Board where the research was conducted. Participants in Study 1 received $0.50 and participants in Study 2 received partial course credit for completing the study online. Participants completed the following measures, which were presented through the university's online participation site, after providing informed consent. The order that the scales were presented was randomized; however, items within each scale were not randomized.

Measures

Current Satisfaction, Alternatives, Investments, and Commitment Participants completed the IMS to assess their current relationship satisfaction, alternatives, investments, and commitment. The IMS is comprised of seven subscales that assess specific facets of participants' current a) satisfaction (e.g., "my partner fulfills my needs for intimacy (sharing personal thoughts, secrets, etc.)"), b) alternatives (e.g., "my needs for intimacy (sharing personal thoughts, secrets, etc.) could be fulfilled in alternative relationships"), and c) investments (e.g., "I have invested a great deal of time in our relationship"), as well as participants' global current d) satisfaction (e.g., "I feel satisfied with our relationship"), e) alternatives (e.g., "the people other than my partner with whom I might become involved are very appealing"), f) investments (e.g., "I have put a great deal into our relationship that I would lose if the relationship were to end"), and g) commitment (e.g., "I am committed to maintaining my relationship with my partner"). Participants use a four-point scale (1 = Do not agree at all, 4 = Agree completely) to respond to the specific facet subscales and a nine-point scale (1 = Do not agree at all, 9 = Agree completely) to respond to the global subscales. Appropriate items were reversed, and all items were summed. Internal consistency was adequate (α's = .82–.93).

Expected Satisfaction, Alternatives, and Investments We developed the EIS to assess participants' expected relationship satisfaction, alternatives, and investments. This measure was developed by modifying the instructions and items on the IMS to assess expected rather than current relationship beliefs. We maintained parallel structure with the IMS as much as possible to allow researchers to use the EIS in conjunction with the IMS to directly compare the determinants and implications of current versus expected aspects of interdependence. As such, the EIS is similarly compromised of six subscales that assess specific facets of participants' expected a) satisfaction (e.g., "I expect that my partner will fulfill my needs for intimacy (sharing personal thoughts, secrets, etc.) in the future"), b) alternatives (e.g., "I expect that my needs for intimacy (sharing personal thoughts, secrets, etc.) could be fulfilled in alternative relationships in the future"), and c) investments (e.g., "I expect that I will invest a great deal of time in our relationship in the future"), as well as participants' expected global d) satisfaction (e.g., "I expect that I will feel satisfied with our relationship in the future"), e) alternatives (e.g., "I expect that in the future, the people other than my partner with whom I might become involved will be very appealing"), and f) investments (e.g., "I expect that in the future, I will put a great deal into our relationship that I would lose if the relationship were to end"). Participants similarly use a four-point scale (1 = Do not agree at all, 4 = Agree completely) to respond to the specific facet subscales and a nine-point scale (1 = Do not agree at all, 9 = Agree completely) to respond to the global subscales. Given that commitment is a future-oriented construct that reflects people's desire to continue a relationship into the future, we expected that intimates' expected commitment would not diverge from their current commitment and thus did not assess expected commitment. All items, instructions for participants, and scoring instructions can be obtained from the first author (www.closerelationshipslab.com).

Anticipated Life Events Participants completed a modified version of the Life Experiences Survey (LES; Sarason, Johnson, & Siegel, 1978; see Neff & Broady, 2011) to assess their anticipated life events. This version of the LES asked participants whether or not they believed that sixty-three major life events across nine domains (e.g., health, legal, finances) would occur over the next year. Because the impact of each event may differ across participants (e.g., some may believe that a new job will harm their relationship, others may believe it will benefit their relationship), participants were asked three supplemental questions for each event that assessed the extent to which they expected the event to affect their a) relationship quality (1 = this will make my relationship with my romantic partner much worse, 4 = this will not affect my relationship with my romantic partner, 7 = this will make my relationship with my romantic partner much better), b) relationship alternatives (1 = this will greatly decrease the desirability of other people who want to start a relationship with me, 4 = this will not affect the desirability of other people who want to start a relationship with me, 7 = this will greatly increase the desirability of other people who want to start a relationship with me), and c) their relationship investments (1 = this will greatly decrease the amount of time, attention, and/or effort I need to put into my relationship, 4 = this will not affect the time, attention, and/or effort I need to put into my relationship, 7 = this will greatly increase the amount of time, attention, and/or effort I need to put into my relationship).

Plans to Improve the Relationship Participants reported the extent to which they planned to improve five specific aspects of their relationship (e.g., intimacy, companionship, security) from 1 (do not plan to improve) to 7 (do plan to improve). All items were summed. Internal consistency was high (coefficient alpha was .93).

Anticipated Shared Novel Experiences Participants responded to four items from the Curiosity and Exploration Inventory (Kashdan, Rose, & Fincham, 2004) that were modified to assess the extent to which participants expected to share novel experiences with their partners (i.e., "I expect that I will have many new experiences with my partner," "I will have many opportunities to challenge myself and grow as a person with my partner," "In the future, I will encounter many unfamiliar people, events, and places with my partner," "I expect that I will have many challenging experiences with my partner") from 1 (strongly disagree) to 7 (strongly agree). All items were summed. Internal consistency was adequate ($\alpha = .76$).

Expected Mate Value Participants completed a modified version of the Mate Value Inventory (Kirsner, Figueredo, & Jacobs, 2003) to assess their expected future mate value. This measure requires individuals to report the extent to which they believe ten malleable attributes (e.g., attractive face, healthy, has financial resources, social status, successful) will describe themselves in the future, using a 7-point scale (1 = low on this attribute, 7 = high on this attribute). All items were summed. Internal consistency was adequate ($\alpha = .95$).

Individual Differences Participants completed the Rosenberg self-esteem scale (Rosenberg 1965; ten items that range from 1–4; $\alpha = .91$), the Experiences in Close Relationships-Short Form (Wei, Russell, Mallinckrodt, & Vogel, 2007; twelve items that range from 1–7; $\alpha = .78$ for attachment anxiety and .83 for attachment avoidance) to assess attachment anxiety and avoidance, and a relationship self-efficacy scale (Bradbury, 1989; seven items that range from 1–5; α = .86).

Psychometric Properties of the Scale

Initial reliability statistics indicated high internal consistency within each subscale of the EIS (facets of satisfaction α = .95, alternatives α = .96, and investments α = .91; and global satisfaction α = .95, alternatives α = .94, and investments α = .90). Item-total correlations ranged from .65 to .92; the majority of items (73%) yielded item-total correlations > .80.

Confirmatory Factor Analysis

To establish the discriminant validity of each subscale, the EIS was submitted to a confirmatory factor analysis (CFA) using Amos 24 (Arbuckle, 2016) using a six-factor model in which each of the subscales' five items loaded onto the corresponding subscales' latent factor. Model fit indexes indicated that the six-factor model sufficiently fit the data. First, the Minimum Fit Function (MFF) χ^2, which should possess a ratio to degrees of freedom (df) of less than 3, was 2.01. Second, the Comparative Fit Index (CFI), which should be at least .90, was .95. Finally, the Root Mean Square Error of Approximation (RMSEA), which should be less than .08, was .07 (for additional information about recommended model-fit thresholds, see Hu & Bentler, 1999). Factor loadings, means, and SDs for the thirty items can be found in Table 14.1. Subscale correlations can be found in Table 14.2.

Predictors of Expectations of Interdependence

First, to address the prediction that intimates' expectations of each of the three aspects of interdependence would be partially determined by their current aspects of interdependence, we examined the relationships between the six subscales of the IMS and the six subscales of the EIS. Consistent with predictions, each of these expectations for the future were positively associated with current assessments of interdependence (facets of satisfaction, r = .71, p < .01; facets of alternatives, r = .51, p < .01; facets of investments, r = .64, p < .01; global satisfaction, r = .70, p < .01; global alternatives, r = .73, p < .01; global investments, r = .54, p < .01).

Next, to identify the unique determinants of expected aspects of interdependence that may cause those expected aspects to diverge from current aspects of interdependence, a series of multiple regression analyses were conducted in

TABLE 14.1 EIS items, standardized factor loadings, and descriptive statistics of each item

Item	Factor Loading	M	SD
Facet Satisfaction			
I expect my partner will fulfill my needs for intimacy (sharing personal thoughts, secrets, etc.) in the future.	.91**	3.53	.75
I expect my partner will fulfill my needs for companionship (doing things together, enjoying each other's company, etc.) in the future.	.90**	3.51	.77
I expect my partner will fulfill my sexual needs (holding hands, kissing, etc.) in the future.	.82**	3.47	.82
I expect my partner will fulfill my needs for security (feeling trusting, comfortable in a stable relationship, etc.) in the future.	.88**	3.55	.74
I expect my partner will fulfill my needs for emotional involvement (feeling emotionally attached, feeling good when another feels good, etc.) in the future.	.93**	3.55	.71
Global Satisfaction			
I expect that I will feel satisfied with our relationship in the future.	.93**	7.76	1.87
I expect that my relationship will be much better than others' relationships in the future.	.81**	7.43	1.98
I expect that my relationship will be close to ideal in the future.	.86**	7.51	1.91
I expect that our relationship will make me very happy in the future.	.95**	7.90	1.79
I expect that our relationship will do a good job of fulfilling my needs for intimacy, companionship, etc. in the future.	.96**	7.88	1.77
Facet Alternatives			
I expect that my needs for intimacy (sharing personal thoughts, secrets, etc.) could be fulfilled in alternative relationships in the future.	.94**	2.06	1.09
I expect that my needs for companionship (doing things together, enjoying each other's company, etc.) could be fulfilled in alternative relationships in the future.	.92**	2.09	1.09
I expect that my sexual needs (holding hands, kissing, etc.) could be fulfilled in alternative relationships in the future.	.77**	1.90	1.13
I expect that my needs for security (feeling trusting, comfortable in a stable relationship, etc.) could be fulfilled in alternative relationships in the future.	.95**	2.01	1.09
I expect that my needs for emotional involvement (feeling emotionally attached, feeling good when another feels good, etc.) could be fulfilled in alternative relationships in the future.	.95**	2.07	1.10

TABLE 14.1 *(cont.)*

Item	Factor Loading	M	SD
Global Alternatives			
I expect that the people other than my partner with whom I might become involved will be very appealing in the future.	.86**	3.62	2.84
I expect that my alternatives to our relationship will be close to ideal (dating another, spending time with friends or on my own, etc.) in the future.	.85**	3.73	2.79
I expect that if I wasn't dating my partner, I would do fine – I would find another appealing person to date in the future.	.81**	4.52	2.90
I expect that my alternatives will be attractive to me (dating another, spending time with friends or on my own, etc.) in the future.	.89**	3.84	2.92
I expect that my needs for intimacy, companionship, etc., could easily be fulfilled in an alternative relationship in the future.	.91**	3.72	2.84
Facet Investments			
I expect that I will invest a great deal of time in our relationship in the future.	.90**	3.48	.71
I expect that I will tell my partner many private things about myself (I will disclose secrets to him/her) in the future.	.85**	3.56	.71
I expect that my partner and I will have an intellectual life together in the future that would be difficult to replace.	.88**	3.48	.80
I expect that my sense of personal identity (who I am) will be linked to my partner and our relationship in the future.	.74**	3.29	.94
I expect that my partner and I will share many memories in the future.	.77**	3.64	.68
Global Investments			
I expect that I will put a great deal into our relationship in the future that I would lose if the relationship were to end.	.84**	7.35	2.16
I expect that many aspects of my life will become linked to my partner (recreational activities, etc.) in the future, and I would lose all of this if we were to break up.	.79**	6.95	2.32
I expect that I will feel very involved in our relationship in the future – like I will have put a great deal into it.	.90**	7.56	1.98
I expect that my relationships with friends and family members would be complicated if my partner and I were to break up (e.g., partner will be friends with people I care about) in the future.	.66**	6.35	2.74
I expect that, compared to other people I know, I will invest a great deal in my relationship with my partner in the future.	.83**	7.47	1.92

Note. Items were based on the Investment Model Scale (Rusbult et al., 1998); ** *p* < .01.

TABLE 14.2 Subscale descriptive statistics and correlations for the EIS

	1	2	3	4	5	6
Facet satisfaction (1)	–					
Global satisfaction (2)	.93**	–				
Facet alternatives (3)	−.30**	−.31**	–			
Global alternatives (4)	−.43**	−.45**	.78**	–		
Facet investments (5)	.82**	.84**	−.32**	−.52**	–	
Global investments (6)	.60**	.68**	−.27**	−.41**	.74**	–
M	3.52	7.69	2.02	3.89	3.49	7.14
SD	.69	1.73	1.01	2.54	.66	1.88

which each expected aspect of interdependence (e.g., expected global satisfaction) was regressed onto the current aspect of interdependence (e.g., current global satisfaction) and one of the factors we predicted would affect expectations (e.g., self-esteem). Results can be found in Table 14.3. First, regarding satisfaction, intimates expected their relationship satisfaction would increase to the extent that they had high relationship self-efficacy, expected to share novel experiences with their partners, planned to improve their relationship, and were low in attachment avoidance. Second, regarding alternatives, intimates expected their relationship alternatives would increase to the extent that they had high self-esteem, were low in attachment avoidance, expected their mate value to increase, had low relationship self-efficacy, and were male. Finally, regarding investments, intimates expected their relationship investments would increase to the extent that they expected to share novel experiences with their partners, planned to improve their relationship, anticipated life events that would require investments, and were high in self-efficacy and low in attachment avoidance.

Implications of Expectations of Interdependence for Commitment

Finally, to examine whether the expected aspects of interdependence were stronger predictors of relationship commitment than were the current aspects of interdependence, we conducted two additional multiple regression analyses that regressed relationship commitment onto both the current and expected versions of either the facets of satisfaction, alternatives, and investments or global satisfaction, alternatives, and investments. Results can be found in Table 14.4. As illustrated there, current facets of alternatives and investments, as well as expected facets of satisfaction, alternatives, and investments were associated with relationship commitment. Although expected alternatives were not a significantly stronger predictor than were current alternatives, $z = .74, p = .46$, nor were expected investments a significantly stronger predictor than were current investments, $z = .30, p = .76$, expected satisfaction was a significantly stronger predictor than was current satisfaction, $z = 2.39, p = .02$.

TABLE 14.3 Predictors of expected satisfaction, alternatives, and investments

	Facets of Satisfaction			Global Satisfaction		
	b	p	r	b	p	r
Life events (satisfaction)	.01	.12	.11	.03	.14	.10
Life events (alternatives)	−.00	.62	.03	−.02	.35	−.07
Life events (investments)	.01	.15	.10	.05	.04*	.14
Plans to improve relationship	.04	.08	.12	.18	.01**	.20
Anticipated novel experiences	.28	.01**	.39	.81	.01**	.46
Expected mate value	.03	.12	.11	.04	.39	.06
Self-esteem	.02	.45	.05	.01	.88	.10
Attachment anxiety	−.03	.23	−.08	−.02	.79	−.02
Attachment avoidance	−.11	.01**	−.25	−.25	.01**	−.22
Self-efficacy	.15	.01**	.31	.41	.01**	.35
Gender	.42	.26	.08	1.22	.20	.09

	Facets of Alternatives			Global Alternatives		
	b	p	r	b	p	r
Life events (satisfaction)	−.01	.68	−.03	−.05	.10	−.11
Life events (alternatives)	.02	.17	.09	.00	.92	.01
Life events (investments)	.00	.85	.01	−.04	.23	−.08
Plans to improve relationship	.08	.06	.13	−.03	.78	−.02
Anticipated novel experiences	−.16	.04*	−.14	−.35	.03*	−.15
Expected mate value	.05	.09	.12	.16	.01*	.18
Self-esteem	.12	.02*	.16	.26	.01*	.18
Attachment anxiety	−.01	.83	−.02	−.05	.61	−.04
Attachment avoidance	.10	.06	.13	.30	.01**	.21
Self-efficacy	−.12	.03*	−.15	−.27	.01*	−.18
Gender	−2.32	.01**	−.24	−2.95	.03*	−.15

	Facets of Investments			Global Investments		
	b	p	r	b	p	r
Life events (satisfaction)	.02	.09	.12	.02	.61	.03
Life events (alternatives)	−.00	.84	−.01	.01	.85	.01
Life events (investments)	.02	.02*	.16	.07	.01*	.17
Plans to improve relationship	.10	.01**	.27	.16	.05*	.14
Anticipated novel experiences	.25	.01**	.35	.67	.01**	.31
Expected mate value	.02	.22	.08	.02	.75	.02
Self-esteem	.02	.54	.04	−.01	.95	−.00
Attachment anxiety	−.02	.41	−.06	−.03	.69	−.03
Attachment avoidance	−.13	.01**	−.29	−.42	.01**	−.30
Self-efficacy	.16	.01**	.35	.31	.01**	.23
Gender	.32	.42	.06	.12	.92	.00

Note. * $p < .05$; ** $p < .01$.

Similarly, current global alternatives and investments, as well as expected global satisfaction, alternatives, and investments were associated with relationship commitment. Although expected alternatives were not a significantly stronger predictor than were current alternatives, $z = −.59$, $p = .55$, nor were

TABLE 14.4 Effects of current and expected satisfaction, alternatives, and investments on current commitment level

	Facets Subscales			Global Subscales		
	b	*p*	*r*	*b*	*p*	*r*
Current satisfaction	.27	.29	.07	.06	.54	.04
Current alternatives	−0.30	.02	.16	−.18	.01	.19
Current investments	.57	.01	.18	.13	.06	.13
Expected satisfaction	1.12	.01	.30	.64	.01	.45
Expected alternatives	−.38	.01	.23	−.12	.05	.14
Expected investments	.77	.01	.20	.15	.04	.14

expected investments a significantly stronger predictor than were current investments, $z = .08$, $p = .94$, expected satisfaction was a significantly stronger predictor than was current satisfaction, $z = 4.53$, $p < .01$.

IMPLICATIONS AND FUTURE DIRECTIONS

In this chapter, we have presented a new measure – the Expected Interdependence Scale (EIS) – that was developed to advance future research on the topic of relationship expectations. To allow for comparisons between the relative effects of expected and current aspects of interdependence, this new measure was based on a widely used measure of current satisfaction, alternatives, and investments (IMS; Rusbult et al., 1998). The current study revealed that EIS had sufficient psychometric properties and thus can be used in future research to further examine the implications of relationship expectations. For example, given that interdependence theory has been used to explain when intimates think (e.g., positive illusions, devaluing alternatives) and behave (e.g., accommodation, forgiveness, sacrifice) in ways that maintain close relationships (for review, see Rusbult, Olsen, Davis, & Hannon, 2001), future research might use this new measure to examine whether expected aspects of interdependence similarly predict relationship maintenance thoughts and behaviors more than current aspects of interdependence. Consistent with this idea, Baker et al. (2017; Study 5) demonstrated that the extent to which intimates' devalued attractive alternative partners was determined more by their expected relationship satisfaction than their current satisfaction. Similarly, interdependence theory has been used to predict when intimates will leave abusive relationships (e.g., Rusbult & Martz, 1995). Future research might benefit by using the current measure to examine whether expected aspects of interdependence predict the decision to leave an abusive relationship more so than current aspects of interdependence (for initial indirect evidence, see Baker, Cobb, McNulty, Lambert, & Fincham, 2016).

Further, through the process of developing and validating this measure, we identified several different factors that are associated with intimates expecting that their future interdependence would diverge from their current interdependence. First, intimates who planned to improve the quality of their relationship and planned to share novel experiences with their partners expected both their satisfaction and their investments to increase in the future. Second, intimates high in attachment avoidance expected their satisfaction, alternatives, and investments to decrease in the future. Third, intimates who believe they are able to successfully resolve their relationship conflicts (i.e., are high in relationship self-efficacy) expected their satisfaction and investments to increase, and their alternatives to decrease. Fourth, in contrast, intimates high in self-esteem expected their alternatives to increase. Finally, consistent with evolutionary predictions, whereas men expected their alternatives to increase, women expected their alternative to decrease. Future research may benefit by continuing to identify factors that lead intimates to believe that their satisfaction, alternatives, and investments will increase or decrease in the future. For example, shy individuals not only tend to doubt their ability to maintain their relationships (Baker & McNulty, 2010), but also doubt their attractiveness to potential partners and thus may be more likely than non-shy individuals to expect their relationship satisfaction, alternatives, and investments to decrease. In contrast, people who are more optimistic expect better interpersonal outcomes (Alarcon, Bowling, & Khazon, 2013) and thus may expect to not only be more satisfied with their relationships in the future, but also have more desirable options available to them as well.

We also provided additional evidence that expected aspects of interdependence play a unique and often stronger role in determining commitment. More specifically, the current study revealed that although current satisfaction was strongly associated with commitment, which was consistent with a large body of previous research (for review, see Le & Agnew, 2003), current satisfaction was also strongly associated with expected satisfaction and ultimately was a weaker predictor of commitment than was expected satisfaction, which is consistent with recent research (i.e., Baker et al., 2017; Lemay, 2016). However, inconsistent with predictions, neither expected alternatives, nor expected investments were significantly stronger predictors of commitment than were current alternatives and past investments. This latter null result was also inconsistent with previous research (i.e., Goodfriend & Agnew, 2008) that demonstrated that future investments were a stronger predictor of commitment than were past investments. Differences in how these constructs were assessed may account for these seemingly inconsistent results; in particular, Goodfriend and Agnew (2008) asked participants to report the extent to which they *planned* to invest in their relationship, which reflect active plans that may be influenced by their motivation to maintain their relationship, whereas participants in the current study reported the extent to which they *expected* to invest in their relationship, which may reflect passive expectations. Regardless, it is worth noting that both expected alternatives and expected investments significantly predicted commitment in the current study after controlling for current alternatives and past investments, suggesting that these expected aspects of interdependence serve unique functions when intimates make commitment-related decisions.

These results, along with a growing body of research highlighting the importance of relationship expectations (e.g., Baker et al., 2017; Lemay, 2016; Lemay et al., 2015; Little, McNulty, & Russell, 2010; McNulty, 2008; McNulty & Fisher, 2008; McNulty & Karney, 2002, 2004; Neff & Geers, 2013; see Holmes, 2002), suggest the need to expand interdependence theory to include intimates' expectations for the future. Although interdependence theory (e.g., Rusbult, 1980; Thibaut & Kelley, 1959) has been the predominant theory to account for intimates' commitment to, and decision to remain in, their relationships, interdependence theory has focused primarily on current and past experiences within the relationship and has largely ignored intimates' expectations for the future (with some important exceptions; cf. Goodfriend & Agnew, 2008). Given that recent research suggests that expected outcomes often influence the decision-making process more than current outcomes do (for review, see Baumeister et al., 2007; DeWall et al., 2016), we propose a revision to interdependence theory that posits that current, past, and expected outcomes provide unique information that independently affect intimates' current commitment level and stay–leave decisions. First, whereas current satisfaction should signal the extent to which relationships are fulfilling intimates' interpersonal needs, expected satisfaction should signal the extent to which relationships will ultimately meet those needs in the future and thus should guide the decision to continue that relationship in the future and thus experience those outcomes. Second, whereas current alternatives should signal whether intimates currently have more desirable options than their current relationships, expected alternative should signal to intimates whether they should commit now to investing time and resources into a relationship to safeguard a relationship that may ultimately be more or less rewarding than the options they will have in the future. Finally, whereas current and past investments should signal to intimates what they would lose if the relationship was to end, intentions also serve as psychological investments (see Ajzen et al., 2009), and thus plans to invest in a relationship should also motivate intimates to remain in those relationships. In sum, intimates consider not only their past and current relationship experiences, they also envision how their relationships will affect them in the future. Such prospection serves an important role in their decision to maintain their relationships, and thus interdependence theory should be expanded to recognize the important role of relationship expectations.

REFERENCES

Ajzen, I., Czasch, C., & Flood, M. G. (2009). From intentions to behavior: Implementation intention, commitment, and conscientiousness. *Journal of Applied Social Psychology, 39*, 1356–1372.

Alarcon, G. M., Bowling, N. A., & Khazon, S. (2013). Great expectations: A meta-analytic examination of optimism and hope. *Personality and Individual Differences*, 54, 821–827.

Arbuckle, J. L. (2016). Amos (Version 24.0) [Computer Program]. Chicago: IBM SPSS.

Aron, A., Norman, C. C., Aron, E. N., & Lewandowski, G. (2002). Shared participation in self-expanding activities: Positive effects on experienced martial quality. In P. Noller, J. A. Feeney, P. Noller, & J. A. Feeney (Eds.), *Understanding Marriage: Developments in the Study of Couple Interaction* (pp. 177–194). New York: Cambridge University Press.

Arriaga, X. B. (2001). The ups and downs of dating: Fluctuations in satisfaction in newly-formed romantic relationships. *Journal of Personality and Social Psychology*, 80, 754–765.

Atkinson, J. W. (1957). Motivational determinants of risk-taking behavior. *Psychological Review*, 64, 359–372.

Baker, L. R., Cobb, R. A., McNulty, J. K., Lambert, N. M., & Fincham, F. D. (2016). Remaining in a situationally aggressive relationship: The role of relationship self-efficacy. *Personal Relationships*, 23, 591–604.

Baker, L. R. & McNulty, J. K. (2010). Shyness and marriage: Does shyness shape even established relationships? *Personality and Social Psychology Bulletin*, 36, 665–676

Baker, L. R., McNulty, J. K., Overall, N. C., Lambert, N. M., & Fincham, F. D. (2013). How do relationship maintenance behaviors affect individual well-being?: A contextual perspective. *Social Psychological and Personality Science*, 4, 282–289.

Baker, L. R., McNulty, J.K., & VanderDrift, L.E. (2017). Expectations for future relationship satisfaction: Unique sources and critical implications for commitment. *Journal of Experimental Psychology: General*, 146, 700–721.

Baumeister, R. F., Vohs, K. D., DeWall, C. N., & Zhang, L. (2007). How emotion shapes behavior: Feedback, anticipation, and reflection, rather than direct causation. *Personality and Social Psychology Review*, 11, 167–203.

Biehle, S. N. & Mickelson, K. D. (2012). First-time parents' expectations about the division of childcare and play. *Journal of Family Psychology*, 26, 36–45.

Bradbury, T. N. (1989). *Cognition, emotion, and interaction in distressed and nondistressed marriages* (Unpublished doctoral dissertation). University of Illinois at Urbana-Champaign.

Brase, G. L. & Guy, E. C. (2004). The demographics of mate value and self-esteem. *Personality and Individual Differences*, 36, 471–484.

Bushman, B. J., Baumeister, R. F., & Phillips, C. M. (2001). Do people aggress to improve their mood? Catharsis beliefs, affect regulation opportunity, and aggressive responding. *Journal of Personality and Social Psychology*, 81, 17–32.

Buss, D. M. & Schmitt, D. P. (1993). Sexual strategies theory: An evolutionary perspective on human mating. *Psychological Review*, 100, 204–232.

Carver, C. S. & Scheier, M. F. (1998). *On the Self-Regulation of Behavior*. New York: Cambridge University Press.

Dennett, D. C. (1991). *Consciousness Explained*. New York: Little, Brown and Co.

DeWall, C. N., Baumeister, R. F., Chester, D. S., & Bushman, B. J. (2016). How often does currently felt emotion predict social behavior and judgment? A meta-analytic test of two theories. *Emotion Review*, 8, 136–143.

Dion, K. K. & Dion, K. L. (1996). Cultural perspectives on romantic love. *Personal Relationships*, 3, 5–17.

Doss, B. D., Simpson, L. E., & Christensen, A. (2004). Why do couples seek marital therapy? *Professional Psychology: Research and Practice*, 35, 608–614.

Dutton, D. G. & Aron, A. P. (1974). Some evidence for heightened sexual attraction under conditions of high anxiety. *Journal of Personality and Social Psychology*, 30, 510–517.

Feather, N. T. (1982). Expectancy-value approaches: Present status and future directions. In N. T. Feather (Ed.), *Expectations and Actions: Expectancy-Value Models in Psychology*. Hillsdale, NJ: Erlbaum.

Feeney, B. C. & Collins, N. L. (2014). A theoretical perspective on the importance of social connections for thriving. In M. Mikulincer & P. R. Shaver (Eds.), *Mechanisms of Social Connection: From Brain to Group* (pp. 291–314). Washington, DC: American Psychological Association.

Feeney, J. A. & Karantzas, G. C. (2017). Couple conflict: Insights from an attachment perspective. *Current Opinion in Psychology*, 13, 60–64.

Finkel, E. J. & Simpson, J. A. (2015). Relationship science, 2015. *Current Opinion in Psychology*, 1, 5–9.

Freedman, J. L., Wallington, S. A., & Bless, E. (1967). Compliance without pressure: The effect of guilt. *Journal of Personality and Social Psychology*, 7, 117–124.

Gilbert, D. T. & Wilson, T. D. (2007). Prospection: Experiencing the future. *Science*, 317, 1351–1354.

Gollwitzer, P. M. (1999). Implementation intentions: Strong effects of simple plans. *American Psychologist*, 54, 493–503.

Goodfriend, W. & Agnew, C. R. (2008). Sunken costs and desired plans: Examining different types of investments in close relationships. *Personality and Social Psychology Bulletin*, 34, 1639–1652.

Gross, J. J. (1998). The emerging field of emotion regulation: An integrative review. *Review of General Psychology*, 2, 271–299.

Holmes, J. G. (2002). Interpersonal expectations as the building blocks of social cognition: An interdependence theory perspective. *Personal Relationships*, 9, 1–26.

Hu, L. & Bentler, P. M. (1999). Cutoff criteria for fit indexes in covariance structure analysis: Conventional criteria versus new alternatives. *Structural Equation Modeling*, 6, 1–55.

Kashdan, T. B., Rose, P., & Fincham, F. D. (2004). Curiosity and exploration: Facilitating positive subjective experiences and personal growth opportunities. *Journal of Personality Assessment*, 82, 291–305.

Kelley, H. H. & Thibaut, J. W. (1978). *Interpersonal Relations: A Theory of Interdependence*. New York: Wiley.

Kirsner, B. R., Figueredo, A. J., & Jacobs, W. J. (2003). Self, friends, and lovers: Structural relations among Beck Depression Inventory scores and perceived mate values. *Journal of Affective Disorders*, 75, 131–148.

Laner, M. R. & Russell, J. N. (1995). Marital expectations and level of premarital involvement: Does marriage education make a difference? *Teaching Sociology*, 23, 28–34.

Lawrence, E., Nylen, K., & Cobb, R. J. (2007). Prenatal expectations and marital satisfaction over the transition to parenthood. *Journal of Family Psychology*, 21, 155–164.

Le, B. & Agnew, C. R. (2003). Commitment and its theorized determinants: A meta-analysis of the investment model. *Personal Relationships*, 10, 37–57.

Lemay, E. P., Jr. (2016). The forecast model of relationship commitment. *Journal of Personality and Social Psychology*, 111, 34–52.

Lemay, E. P., Jr., Lin, J. L., & Muir, H. J. (2015). Daily affective and behavioral forecasts in romantic relationships: Seeing tomorrow through the lens of today. *Personality and Social Psychology Bulletin*, 41, 1005–1019.

Little, K. C., McNulty, J. K., & Russell, V. M. (2010). Sex buffers intimates against the negative implications of attachment insecurity. *Personality and Social Psychology Bulletin*, 36, 484–498.

Lynn, M. (1991). Scarcity effects on value: A quantitative review of the commodity theory literature. *Psychology and Marketing*, 8, 43–57.

Lynn, M. (1992). Scarcity's enhancement of desirability: The role of naive economic theories. *Basic and Applied Social Psychology*, 13, 67–78.

Manucia, G. K., Baumann, D. J., & Cialdini, R. B. (1984). Mood influences on helping: Direct effects or side effects? *Journal of Personality and Social Psychology*, 46, 357–364.

McNulty, J. K. (2008). Neuroticism and interpersonal negativity: The independent contributions of perceptions and behaviors. *Personality and Social Psychology Bulletin*, 34, 1439–1450.

McNulty, J. K. & Fisher, T. D. (2008). Gender differences in response to sexual expectancies and changes in sexual frequency: A short-term longitudinal study of sexual satisfaction in newlywed married couples. *Archives of Sexual Behavior*, 37, 229–240.

McNulty, J. K. & Karney, B. R. (2001). Attributions in marriage: Integrating specific and global evaluations of a relationship. *Personality and Social Psychology Bulletin*, 27, 943–955.

McNulty, J. K. & Karney, B. R. (2002). Expectancy confirmation in appraisals of marital interactions. *Personality and Social Psychology Bulletin*, 28, 764–775.

McNulty, J. K. & Karney, B. R. (2004). Positive expectations in the early years of marriage: Should couples expect the best or brace for the worst? *Journal of Personality and Social Psychology*, 86, 729–743.

McNulty, J. K., O'Mara, E. M., & Karney B. R. (2008). Benevolent cognitions as a strategy of relationship maintenance: "Don't sweat the small stuff" but it is not all small stuff. *Journal of Personality and Social Psychology*, 94, 631–646.

McNulty, J. K., Olson, M. A., Jones, R. E., & Acosta, L. M. (2017). Automatic associations between one's partner and one's affect as the proximal mechanism of change in relationship satisfaction: Evidence from evaluative conditioning. *Psychological Science*, 28, 1031–1040.

Mellers, B., Schwartz, A., & Ritov, I. (1999). Emotion-based choice. *Journal of Experimental Psychology: General*, 128, 332–345.

Neff, L. A. & Broady, E. F. (2011). Stress resilience in early marriage: Can practice make perfect? *Journal of Personality and Social Psychology*, 101, 1050–1067.

Neff, L. A. & Geers, A. L. (2013). Optimistic expectations in early marriage: A resource or vulnerability for adaptive relationship functioning? *Journal of Personality and Social Psychology*, 105, 38–60.

Olson, J. M., Roese, N. J., & Zanna, M. P. (1996). Expectancies. In E. T. Higgins & A. W. Kruglan- ski (Eds.), *Social Psychology: Handbook of Basic Principles* (pp. 211–238). New York: Guilford Press.

Overall, N. C., Fletcher, G. O., Simpson, J. A., & Sibley, C. G. (2009). Regulating partners in intimate relationships: The costs and benefits of different communication strategies. *Journal of Personality and Social Psychology*, 96, 620–639.

Poortman, A. & Mills, M. (2012). Investments in marriage and cohabitation: The role of legal and interpersonal commitment. *Journal of Marriage and Family*, 74, 357–376.

Quoidbach, J., Gilbert, D. T., & Wilson, T. D. (2013). The end of history illusion. *Science*, 339, 96–98.

Resulaj, A., Kiani, R., Wolpert, D. M., & Shadlen, M. N. (2009). Changes of mind in decision-making. *Nature*, 461, 263–266.

Rosato, A. (2016). Selling substitute goods to loss-averse consumers: Limited availability, bargains, and rip-offs. *RAND Journal of Economics*, 47, 709–733.

Rosenberg, M. (1965). *Society and the Adolescent Self-Image*. Princeton, NJ: Princeton University Press.

Rusbult, C. E. (1980). Satisfaction and commitment in friendships. *Representative Research in Social Psychology*, 11, 96–105.

Rusbult, C. E. & Martz, J. M. (1995). Remaining in an abusive relationship: An investment model analysis of nonvoluntary dependence. *Personality and Social Psychology Bulletin*, 21, 558–571.

Rusbult, C. E., Martz, J. M., & Agnew, C. R. (1998). The Investment Model Scale: Measuring commitment level, satisfaction level, quality of alternatives, and investment size. *Personal Relationships*, 5, 357–391.

Rusbult, C. E., Olsen, N., Davis, J. L., & Hannon, P. (2001). Commitment and relationship maintenance mechanisms. In J. H. Harvey & A. Wenzel (Eds.), *Close Romantic Relationships: Maintenance and Enhancement* (pp. 87–113). Mahwah, NJ: Erlbaum.

Sarason, I. G., Johnson, J. H., & Siegel, J. M. (1978). Assessing the impact of life changes: Development of the Life Experiences Survey. *Journal of Consulting and Clinical Psychology*, 46, 932–946.

Seligman, M. P., Railton, P., Baumeister, R. F., & Sripada, C. (2013). Navigating into the future or driven by the past. *Perspectives on Psychological Science*, 8, 119–141.

Shaver, P. R. & Mikulincer, M. (2002). Attachment-related psychodynamics. *Attachment & Human Development*, 4, 133–161.

Sheeran, P., Webb, T. L., & Gollwitzer, P. M. (2005). The interplay between goal intentions and implementation intentions. *Personality and Social Psychology Bulletin*, 31, 87–98.

Silliman, B. & Schumm, W. R. (1999). Improving practice in marriage preparation. *Journal of Sex & Marital Therapy*, 25, 23–43.

Silverman, I. W. (1967). Incidence of guilt reactions in children. *Journal of Personality and Social Psychology*, 7, 338–340.

Stafford, L. (2011). Measuring relationship maintenance behaviors: Critique and development of the revised relationship maintenance behavior scale. *Journal of Social and Personal Relationships*, 28, 278–303.

Thibaut, J. W. & Kelley, H. H. (1959). *The Social Psychology of Groups*. Oxford: John Wiley.

Tice, D. M., Bratslavsky, E., & Baumeister, R. F. (2001). Emotional distress regulation takes precedence over impulse control: If you feel bad, do it! *Journal of Personality and Social Psychology*, 80, 53–67.

Tran, P., Judge, M., & Kashima, Y. (2019). Commitment in relationships: An updated meta-analysis of the investment model. *Personal Relationships*, 26, 158–180.

Vogel, D. L., Wester, S. R., Wei, M., & Boysen, G. A. (2005). The role of outcome expectations and attitudes on decisions to seek professional help. *Journal of Counseling Psychology*, 52, 459–470.

Wei, M., Russell, D. W., Mallinckrodt, B., & Vogel, D. L. (2007). The Experiences in Close Relationship Scale (ECR)-short form: Reliability, validity, and factor structure. *Journal of Personality Assessment*, 88, 187–204.

Wigfield, A., Tonks, S., & Klauda, S. L. (2009). Expectancy-value theory. In K. R. Wenzel, A. Wigfield, K. R. Wenzel, & A. Wigfield (Eds.), *Handbook of Motivation at School* (pp. 55–75). New York: Routledge.

15

Relationship Expectations about the Commitment to Wed

A Contextual Analysis

TEKISHA M. RICE AND BRIAN G. OGOLSKY

Romantic partners may become primary attachment figures, providing support and security as relationships develop (Hazan & Shaver, 1987). However, partners also may create strain, and not all romantic relationships continue. Individuals' relationship expectations may influence assessments of how and why commitment changes as well as expectations for future involvement. Examining the development of commitment is key to understanding why some relationships end, some progress, and others cycle. To this end, this chapter considers the role of expectations in the development of a particular type of commitment: commitment to wed.

We begin by exploring the context of dating and marriage as relevant for examining the development of commitment. Next, we review prominent methods for assessing commitment to marriage and review foundational and contemporary research in the area. We contribute to this literature by reflecting on its relevance across three decades since its genesis, and we consider the crucial role of historical changes in relationship expectations as they relate to marriage. In doing so, we encourage the inclusion of contextual and intersectional perspectives in understanding the commitment to wed, and we suggest methodological and analytical ways to effectively address these factors in future research.

WHY FOCUS ON COMMITMENT TO WED?

Romantic relationships take on a uniquely intense affective orientation that distinguishes them from other forms of voluntary relationships (e.g., friendships). Indeed, expectations for closeness between romantic partners tend to be higher than expectations of friends (Fuhrman, Flannagan, & Matamoros, 2009). Marriage, in particular, reflects a distinctive institution in which partners indefinitely commit themselves to one another. Doing so is uniquely characterized by increasing levels of interdependence and the deepening of commitment both to the partner as an individual and to the relationship itself. Interdependence theory (Kelley & Thibaut, 1978; Thibaut & Kelley, 1959) posits that relationship advancement is, in part, dependent on an individual's comparison level (CL) and comparison level for alternatives (CL-alt). These comparison levels reflect expectations of current and prospective relationships, respectively, and are based on socialized beliefs about how relationships should develop. Thus, an individual is more likely to be committed when it seems likely that a current relationship will continue to meet or even exceed the individual's expectations and/or when current relationship experiences exceed the expected benefits of an alternative arrangement (i.e., a different relationship or being single).

The concept of commitment is particularly suited to romantic relationships (Fehr, 1999) and is generally described as the decisions and desires associated with the belief that a relationship will last (Johnson, 1999; Rusbult, 1983; Surra & Hughes, 1997). However, research often confounds commitment with its predictive components (Surra, Hughes, & Jacquet, 1999). Psychological attachment, for example, is conceptualized as both a predictor, feature, and outcome of relationship commitment (Rusbult, 1983). Operationalizations of commitment to wed, however, distinguish between commitment and its predictive factors by integrating the "particular events, conditions, and interactions that partners themselves say are relevant to commitment and the meaning they make of them" (Surra & Hughes, 1997, p. 7). Doing so allows researchers to examine associations between properties of developing commitment and their related implications for the relationship. Surra and Hughes (1997) argue that the commitment to marry is related yet distinct from global commitment due to the moral, social, legal, and structural constraints associated with the union. Instead, commitment to wed "concerns partners' conceptions of the likelihood that they will form and maintain a marriage to a partner" (p. 6). Critiques of this approach center on the assumed conflation of "chance of marriage"[1] with marital commitment. Indeed, rather than assessing marital commitment, popular methods instead assess commitment to a particular behavior – in this case, marriage – although this distinction has remained largely implicit. This approach has advantages over survey methods by integrating objective and subjective assessments of causal variables in relationship development and outcomes.

MAPPING RELATIONSHIP TRAJECTORIES VIA GRAPHING

Seeking to temporally understand the events and circumstances leading to marriage, early research relied on the adaptations of the retrospective

[1] The terms "commitment to wed," "chance of marriage," "likelihood of marriage," and "probability of marriage" are used interchangeably throughout this chapter.

interview technique to map commitment trajectories. These data allowed partners to construct graphs of their relationship history as a series of time-ordered changes in marital probability (Huston, Surra, Fitzgerald, & Cate, 1981). Individuals were presented a blank graph with relationship length in months on the x-axis and chance of marriage on the y-axis. In approximating the chance of marriage, participants were told to consider their own as well as their partners' feelings about marrying. Partners were informed that changes in marital probability were not "indicator[s] of how much you wanted to marry or how much you were in love" (p. 65). After indicating the beginning of the relationship on the graph, interviewers asked "at what month were you first aware that the chance of marriage was different . . . what was the chance of marriage at that time?" (p. 65). The time at which the chance of marriage changed reflected a *turning point* within the relationship. Respondents then indicated the shape of the line connecting the two points by describing whether the change was sudden or gradual. At the same time, the interviewer probed about why the chance of marriage changed. The interviewer and respondent repeated this procedure until the graph was complete to the current point of the relationship (or up to the wedding date).

By guiding the construction of relationship graphs, partners could indicate key turning points in the relationship and provide information to derive variables regarding the level of commitment and variability in the level of commitment over time. Capturing this variability is critical as commitment is considered relatively stable, displaying incremental and uniform change over time. Dramatic or inconsistent changes in commitment to marriage might reflect patterns of instability in the relationship. Therefore, the graphing procedure services the study of commitment by integrating longitudinal assessments of turning points with response data. Similar to methods for attaining life histories (see Freedman, Thornton, Camburn, Alwin, & Young-DeMarco, 1988), the mapping procedure provides a valuable bird's eye view of the relationship, allowing scholars to see the full course of a relationship – complete with peaks, valleys, stagnations, and associated events. Doing so captures the dynamic direction, frequency, and magnitude of commitment changes in relation to participants' expectations for how the relationship should develop and subjective accounts why the changes occurred.

Typologies of Relationship Development Derived from Mapping

By capturing variation in the direction, frequency, and magnitude of commitment changes, the relationship mapping procedure allows for the explication of distinct trajectories of changes in commitment. This distinction adds to the scholarly understanding of relationship development and untimely demise. An ambitious group of scholars tackled this task by examining longitudinal changes in commitment to marriage among daters (Cate,

Huston, and Nesselroade, 1986; Huston et al., 1981; Surra, 1985). Ethically, randomly assigning partners to dissolve was (and remains) unfeasible; however, because the graphing procedure serves as a somewhat natural experiment, opportunities to capture the trajectories of relationships that dissolved emerged as well. In this section, we review the history of research on typologies of relationship development. This chronological overview is intended to highlight changing perspectives on the utility of relationship typologies.

Early research examining trajectories toward marriage relied on retrospective reports from married individuals. Four pathways of commitment to wed were distinguished: accelerated, accelerated-arrested, prolonged, and intermediate (Huston et al., 1981; Surra, 1985). *Accelerated* trajectories displayed a rapid increase to certainty of marriage and were characterized by lower levels of conflict and relationship maintenance. These partners were more likely to engage in leisure together and became increasingly interdependent over time. Similarly, *accelerated-arrested* trajectories displayed higher initial levels of marriage probability. These relationships had a rapid increase in probability of marriage and regressed just before reaching certainty, complemented with a decrease in joint network activities. Accelerated and accelerated-arrested relationships had relatively shorter pre-marital phases and a comparatively higher index of upturns in chance of marriage (Surra, 1985). *Prolonged* partners displayed a slow progression to a high probability of marriage characterized by relatively more engagement in joint network activities. Similar to the accelerated relationships, prolonged partnerships participated in much leisure together; however, they displayed less pre-marital interdependence relative to the accelerated pathways. *Intermediate* trajectories developed at a moderate rate relative to prolonged and accelerated types and displayed turbulence during the final shift to 100 percent chance of marriage (Huston et al., 1981). These partners engaged in fewer activities together and spent more time alone. Similarly, Cate et al. (1986) identified three patterns of relationship trajectories. The first trajectory reflected a slow progression toward commitment to wed, characterized by frequent upturns and downturns, ambivalence, and conflict. The second trajectory displayed a rapid progression to commitment to wed characterized by less conflict and maintenance. Finally, the third trajectory progressed at a rate between the prior two and was characterized by less conflict and ambivalence than the first.

Although scholars could successfully distinguish trajectories of commitment development, a more meaningful and holistic characterization of relationships in terms of how commitment to wed developed was lacking. Marriage is accompanied by expectations of commitment as reflected in fidelity, unwavering support, and perseverance during turmoil (Hampel & Vangelisti, 2008). Therefore, continued participation in dating and marital relationships is likely driven by individuals' expectations that the relationship will succeed, and the probability of relationship survival can, in part, be accounted for by the extent to which those expectations are met (Baker, McNulty, & VanderDrift, 2017; Vannier & O'Sullivan, 2017a). Explanations for changes in commitment to wed, then, reflect socialized expectations for behaviors within and the progression of romantic relationships. Such attributions are positively related to feelings of happiness, love, and commitment (Fletcher, Fincham, Cramer, & Heron, 1987).

Reasons for Changes in Commitment to Wed

Although commitment reflects a comparatively stable relationship characteristic, as a process, its development may vary widely, undoubtedly due, in part, to individuals' reconciliation of their current relationship experiences with embedded beliefs about marriage (Surra & Bartell, 2001). As a challenge to monolithic perspectives of the development of commitment, Surra and Bartell (2001) launched a line of research that accounted for partners' own assessments of how and why commitment to marriage changed throughout their relationships. Doing so expanded traditional conceptualizations of commitment to consider partners' navigation of their own relationship realities with their relationship beliefs. Thus, precipitous or oscillating trajectories accompanied by contradictory reasons may pose an empirical puzzle that provides critical opportunities for understanding the influence of perception and expectation in the commitment processes.

Following the graphing procedure detailed above, participants attached reasons to their self-identified turning points. After describing turning points and the shapes of the lines connecting them, individuals were instructed to "Tell me, in as specific terms as possible, what happened from [date at beginning of turning point] to [date at end of turning point] that made the chance of marriage go [up/down]." Interviewers then asked "Is there anything else that happened from [date] to [date] that made the chance of marriage change?" until the participant responded "no" (Surra, 1985). The responses were coded into twenty-nine[2] themes that fall under four broad categories: interpersonal normative, individual, dyadic, and social network (see Table 15.1).

Interpersonal normative reasons include those that reflect individuals' beliefs or standards about the appropriateness of marriage for a particular life stage, the degree to which they or their partners were marriageable, and the expected depth of involvement given existing relationship schemas. Often connected with prior relationship experiences, interpersonal normative

---

[2] Surra (1987) devised a nineteen category coding scheme that was collapsed to fourteen in Surra, Arizzi, and Asmussen (1988) and expanded to twenty-nine following a larger study (Surra, 1995).

TABLE 15.1 Reasons for changes in the commitment to wed

Reasons	Definition	Example
Interpersonal Normative	Reasons that reflect an evaluation of the partner or the relationship against some internalized belief or standard for what partnerships are like	
Positive or negative predisposition to wed	Statements on a) the desirability of relationship stage (e.g., dating, engagement) given life stage (age, education status) and b) beliefs about premarital or marital relationships	"Well, just getting older and not getting any younger, we just thought taking the next couple steps toward marriage would be the right thing . . . at least prepare to . . . get ready to get married" "I experienced some of those negative feelings [about getting married] myself, and just realized how deeply rooted his feelings were against marriage"
Standards for partnership (un)met	Expectations of the self, partner, or both partners regarding ideal characteristics for a dating/ marriage partner or relationship	"I realized he would be the perfect mate for me . . . Just the thought that there was no chance of me finding anyone that was better for me than [him]" "I thought she was a little bit immature for me"
Individual	References to characteristics of the self that affect the relationship or behaviors performed by partners independent of one another	
Person's or Other's individual behaviors	Actual or implied behaviors performed by partners in the absence of one another	"I moved out, and that's when he [didn't] work and [was] always home, and I work a lot"
Positive or negative self-attributions	Actual, anticipated, and imagined beliefs about the self	"I found myself, and became more comfortable with myself" "I just haven't been feeling very well, physically, and so that makes me very irritated"
Dyadic	Statements concerning interactions between partners and partners' beliefs about those interactions	
Positive or negative changes in stage	Interactions resulting in a redefinition of the relationship as more or less involved	"We started dating seriously" "Both of us decided to date other people, and end our relationship"
Conflict	Exchanges of negative affect, tension, hostility, or over fighting between partners	"We got into an argument and he left for a few hours, and we stayed mad at each other for a couple of days"

TABLE 15.1 *(cont.)*

Reasons	Definition	Example
Positive or negative self or partner-disclosure	Interactions involving an exchange of information with a special meaning or that contained a new meaning where the content or impact was positive or negative	"I just mentioned talking about marriage ... and after that [we] went from neither one of us ever talking about [marriage] to at least one of us talking about it" "He told me how his ex-girlfriends had come here to visit him as a surprise"
Absence of self or partner-disclosure	Interactions where special or new information was not expressed when one or both partners believed it should have been	"He just stopped saying 'I'm never gonna get married'"
Behavioral interdependence	Actual, discussed, planned, and implied dyadic interaction	"We were spending every night together and planning everything out, coordinating our schedules ... practically living together already"
Absence of behavioral interdependence	References to perceived lack or insufficiency of dyadic activity engagement	"We stopped seeing each other as much ... I started working again and he started working again and we didn't have that much free time on our hands. We were both so tired that we never saw each other"
Positive or negative behavioral-response interdependence	Instances where one partner's voluntary action initiates a positive or negative behavioral or attributional response from the other partner	"She went on her trip and ... about a week into the trip I started to really miss her" "Seeing him drinking frustrates me ... he doesn't know when to [stop]"
Positive or negative attribution about partnership	Positive or negative attributions about the partner, relationship, or self in relation to the partner	"We're just so much alike, we like the same things and [are] pretty serious about finding somebody, and we get along great, we're really good friends too" "I was becoming less and less confident that our relationship was gonna last"
Social Network	Statements concerning partners' actual and anticipated interactions with network members	
One partner's interaction with others	One partner's actual or lack of independent interaction or activities with network members	"My mom says that I should really break it off, because she sees the emotional stress it puts on me"

TABLE 15.1 (*cont.*)

Reasons	Definition	Example
Both partners' interaction with others	Both partners' actual or lack of joint interaction with network members	"We went down to her folks' house and I got to meet her parents"
Network interaction independent of partners	Interactions among network members independent of dating partners	"My best friend got married this weekend, and [his] friends are getting married next weekend"
Positive or negative involvement with alternative partners	Actual or anticipated involvement with or attributions and reactions to alternative dating partners that promote/increase or deter/decrease relationship involvement	"He was still fighting with his fiancé and on New Year's they called off the wedding" "I spent all this time not committed to her and seeing other girls as options arose"
Positive or negative social comparison	Positive or negative attributions about the relationships against other close relationships	"I've dated a lot of guys and he's probably one of the nicest guys I've met, that's why this is my longest relationship" "He just reminds me a lot of my dad, and he has my dad's bad posture and doesn't stand up straight"
Positive or negative network attribution	Partners' attributions about members of or interactions within social networks	"I was becoming involved with her daughter and it was very fulfilling" "I felt like his roommate was just trying to break us up"
Circumstantial	Anticipated or unanticipated events external to either partner and the relationship for which partners perceive having little to no control over	"She barely missed the grade that she needed to stay [in school] because she was a provisional student ... so she had to transfer"

Note: The examples presented are illustrative and represent 28 of the 464 participants across all phases of the study.

reasons included positive and negative predispositions to wed as well as standards for partnership being met or unmet. Positive predispositions to wed indicated a clear positive inclination to marry, whereas negative predispositions reflected fear about involvement or generally less inclination toward relationships. For example, a person might associate the transition from college student to college graduate with an analogous relationship transition from dating to engagement. Additionally, individuals evaluated themselves, their relationship partner, and relationship itself against expectations about what was ideal or desirable in a relationship. Standards for partnership were considered to be met when a person's relationship experiences mapped on to existing expectations; standards for partnership were considered unmet when actual experiences were incongruent with individuals' ideal expectations. For example, someone might describe their partner as "all I ever wanted in a person" or the relationship as not having essential characteristics (e.g., love, commitment). These overarching beliefs guide how partners interpret and make attributions about relationship events (Knee & Petty, 2013), as well as how they behave within the relationship (Ajzen & Fishbein, 2005). Such expectations are likely garnered from prior relationship experiences (Bradbury &, Fincham 1990; Fletcher & Thomas, 1996) and may influence relationship quality (Amato & Rogers, 1999), commitment, maintenance, and perceived quality of alternatives (Riggio & Weiser, 2008).

Individual reasons include positive and negative attributions about the presence or absence of characteristics and independent behaviors of either partner. Individuals made positive or negative self-attributions based on how they believed their own characteristics influenced the relationship. For example, one participant described how they had not been feeling well and, in turn, were irritable in their interactions with their partner (see Table 15.1). Behaviors done independent of the partner and network members that contributed to changes in the commitment to wed were also included in this category. Reasons leading to self-attributions may reflect enduring vulnerabilities that influence partners' ability to navigate relationship challenges (Karney & Bradbury, 1995). An avoidant attachment orientation, for example, is associated with expecting relationship failure which, in turn, undermines commitment experiences and inhibits relationship development (Birnie, Joy McClure, Lydon, & Holmberg, 2009). Reasons related to independent behavior, however, may differentially influence partners' relationship experiences, as prior research has documented gender differences in the perception and impact of shared time on relationship well-being (Gager & Sanchez, 2003)

Dyadic reasons for change in the commitment to wed comprised the most subcategories and reflected interactions between partners and beliefs about those interactions. Positive or negative changes in relationship stage reflect mutual redefinitions of the relationship as more or less involved (e.g., "We decided to end our relationship"). Conflict indicated the exchange of negativity between partners. Positive and negative disclosures from either partner refer to special or new information being shared that is distinctively positive or negative in its context (e.g., "His ex-girlfriend came to visit"). Behavioral interdependence reflected the coordination of behaviors between partners, whereas its absence indicated violated expectations regarding a deficiency of time spent together (e.g., "We were spending every night together"). Behavioral-response interdependence may be positive or negative and describes when one partner attributes intention to the behavior of the other partner (e.g., "Seeing him drinking frustrates me"). Other reasons reflected positive or negative attributions about the relationship itself (e.g., "I was becoming less confident that our relationship was gonna last"). The exchange of information and behaviors, and the associated responses, reflect the foundational concepts of interdependence theory (Rusbult & Arriaga, 1997) such that partners co-construct each other's relationship experiences. Based on these interactions, individuals may reframe their expectations of their partner and the relationship (Huston, 2000) and reevaluate the probability of marriage.

Romantic relationships are embedded within networks of friends, family, and other network members (Huston, 2000; Sprecher, Felmlee, Schmeeckle, & Shu, 2006). Thus, it is not surprising that consideration of social networks would provide meaningful reasons for changing expectations of partners. *Social network reasons* reflected partners' interactions or lack thereof with independent or mutual networks as well as anticipated reactions of network members. Included in this category are positive and negative involvement with alternative dating partners that, respectively, promote or interfere with involvement in the current relationship. For example, one participant reflected on their parent's disapproval of the relationship (see Table 15.1). Social comparison, on the other hand, refers to positive or negative evaluations of the partnership relative to network members (e.g., "he just reminds me a lot of my dad ... he has my dad's bad posture"). Positive and negative network attributions are also included in this category and involve attributions from either partner about network interactions or from network members about either the partner or the relationship as a whole. For example, one participant discussed how interacting with his partner's daughter had been beneficial for their relationship (see Table 15.1). Finally, circumstantial reasons were associated with factors external to the relationship, which partners had little to no control over (e.g., military deployment). These reasons likely contribute to the development of a couple identity (Johnson, Caughlin, & Huston, 1999) and experiences of uncertainty (Berger, & Calabrese, 1975). Moreover, social networks contribute to relationship persistence (Felmlee, 2001) and are positioned as sources of influence through which partners maintain their relationships.

Each of these broad categories represent driving forces behind why people progressed, regressed, or maintained in their likelihood of marriage. The expectations underlying reasons for changes in the commitment to wed are likely dormant until a relevant expectancy violation occurs (Huston, 2000). However, when attended to, these expectations spur re-evaluations of current relationship events and have significance for how a relationship progresses. Based on properties of change in commitment to wed, and the reasons explicated by Surra (1995), scholars began to interrogate the role of subjective reasons for changes in the commitment to wed in order to more meaningfully distinguish relationship trajectories.

Pathways of Commitment to Wed: Integrating Subjective Influences

Surra et al. (1999) advanced a model of commitment centered on subjective accounts for changes in the chance of marriage as the most proximal predictor of changes in commitment. In an initial test of the association between subjective reasons for commitment and the development of marital relationships, Surra et al. (1988) identified three broad categories of reasons for changes in the commitment to wed: 1) interpersonal normative, capturing standards and benchmarks of what a relationship should be like at a particular stage; 2) dyadic, reflecting statements about partners interactions; and 3) social network, representing statements about interactions with others or external influences. Of these, dyadic reasons for changes in commitment composed the majority of reasons, with 99 percent of the sample specifically reporting subjective interdependence at least once. Although interpersonal normative reasons appeared the least frequently, they remained salient for some participants' relationship trajectories, launching them into marriage to meet personal expectations about the appropriate timing of marriage. Interpersonal normative reasons were associated with shorter relationships that progressed in a fashion similar to accelerated and accelerated-arrested relationships identified from previous studies (e.g., Huston et al., 1981; Surra, 1985). Dyadic reasons were associated with trajectories composed of fewer turning points and slow progression, although the chance of marriage was higher during the dating stage. In particular, behavioral interdependence was associated with positive turning points whereas disclosures were associated with rapid changes. Most social network reasons were associated with rapidly progressing trajectories; however, reasons related to alternative partners were associated with moderate declines and indicated slowly progressing, turbulent relationships with relatively low marital probability when seriously dating.

Based on these findings, Surra and colleagues advanced two commitment pathways: relationship-driven and event-driven commitments. *Relationship-driven commitments* were hypothesized to develop based on changes in individuals' perceptions of the quality of the relationship, whereas *event-driven commitments* developed as external forces prompted frequent and salient re-evaluations of the relationships. Surra and Hughes (1997) compared these pathways and found that relationship-driven commitments reflected positive changes in the assessment of the relationship, largely attributable to time spent together, mutual engagement in activities, and positive views about the relationship. Partners in these relationships, which slowly but smoothly progressed to high marital probability, were more satisfied over time. Alternatively, event-driven relationships displayed sharp increases and declines in commitment driven by conflict and partners' interaction in separate social networks. Future studies further described event-driven partnerships as more ambivalent and more likely to make self-attributions regarding relationship problems (Surra & Gray, 2000).

Despite research suggesting that developmental trajectories predict subsequent relationship outcomes (Huston, Caughlin, Houts, Smith, & George, 2001), relationship-driven and event-driven trajectories remained indistinguishable in measures of passionate and friendship-based love as well as in the likelihood of relationship progression and dissolution. The lack of predictive power of the typologies seriously constrained their contribution to the literature. Notably, the history of research mapping relationship trajectories had successfully distinguished a number of relationship trajectories. This theoretical and empirical dilemma begged for a reconceptualization of how reasons for changes in the commitment to marriage clustered to meaningfully predict relationship outcomes.

Following prior research, Ogolsky, Surra, and Monk (2016) drew from theories of positive relational beliefs, hesitation about involvement, and compatibility, to reconceptualize how partners' reasons for commitment to wed contributed to changes in its development. Using retrospective accounts from dating partners, Ogolsky et al. (2016) connected the proportion of downturns in the chance of marriage, the magnitude of change in upturns and downturns, and seven categories of reasons with accounts of change in commitment to marriage. The reasons for changes in commitment to wed in this study included conflict, behavioral interdependence, positive dyadic attributions, negative dyadic attributions, separate network interaction, joint network interaction, and positive network attributions (see Table 15.1). These scholars identified four pathways that successfully predicted relationship outcomes: dramatic, conflict-ridden, socially-involved, and partner focused.

Individuals in dramatic relationships reported a high proportion of downturns in commitment that stemmed from negative dyadic attributions, separate network interactions, and lower behavioral interdependence. These relationships were characterized by ambivalence, less passionate love, and less satisfaction. Most notably, dramatic trajectories were twice as likely to result in dissolution relative to other pathways. These findings indicate that dramatic partnerships reflect successful compatibility testing, where incompatibilities in partners' leisure activities, coupled with higher levels of passionate love and more worries about marriage, may stall partners' progression toward marriage.

Conflict-ridden trajectories had a high proportion and magnitude of declines in commitment; however, the majority of these downturns were associated with conflict. These partners were more likely to remain at a specific relationship stage and, thus, no more likely to dissolve than dramatic partners, highlighting the importance of accounting for subjective reasons for changes in commitment.

Socially-involved partners displayed a low incidence of dissolution, reflected in a lower proportion of downturns in chance of marriage and little ambivalence or worries about marriage compared to individuals in dramatic and conflict-ridden relationships. These relationships were characterized by more friendship-based love and higher levels of satisfaction. Reasons for changes in commitment were largely attributed to joint network involvement and positive network attributions.

Finally, partner-focused commitments were distinguished from other trajectories due to the high number of reasons concerning behavioral inter-dependence in the relative absence of joint network interactions. These partnerships had high levels of satisfaction and were characterized by mutual leisure engagement and more conscientiousness. Partner-focused commitments were more likely to advance in status (i.e., progress from casually to seriously dating) than dramatic commitments, and partners attributed these changes to time spent together rather than time spent with social networks. In sum, connecting subjective reasons for changes in the likelihood of marriage with relationship characteristics highlighted the utility of multiple theoretical perspectives in explaining the diverse ways in which relationships develop.

This historical overview culminates with recent research that successfully used participants' subjective accounts for changes in the chance of marriage to meaningfully characterize and distinguish trajectories of commitment to marriage (Ogolsky et al., 2016). Appraisals of change within the relationship are tied to the socialized expectations generated from relationship scripts. With the exception of individual reasons, interpersonal normative reasons may serve as a broader overarching framework for how partners conceptualize why changes in the likelihood of marriage occur. For example, dyadic reasons generally reflect the extent to which expectations are met or unmet for the quantity and quality of partners' interactions. Likewise, reasons related to social networks reflect expectations about a) the degree to which partners should jointly versus independently engage with one another's network members, and b) the value of network members' evaluations of the suitability of the relationship.

Relationship scripts (expectations about key relational events and the order in which they should take place; Ginsburg, 1988) considered in concert with assumptions of interdependence theory inform how expectations may shape relationship trajectories and outcomes. Such scripts provide a sense of certainty that a relationship is progressing in a desired direction (Murray, Lamarche, Gomillion, Seery, & Kondrak, 2017), and minimize potential violations of expectations (Mongeau, Carey, & Williams, 1998). Holmberg and MacKenzie (2002), for example, found that perceptions of one's own relationship as progressing in a way that aligns with normative expectations predicted aspects of relationship well-being. Unmet expectations, however, may represent threats to relationship longevity as they are negatively associated with perceptions of commitment, specifically when the expectancy violation emerges from comparisons between an alternative and current relationship (rather than a current and ideal relationship; Vannier & O'Sullivan, 2017b). Accordingly, comparisons between relationship expectations and current relationship experiences can contribute to partners' assessments of relationship quality, thus allowing them to enact strategies that reconcile gaps in comparison levels (Holmberg & MacKenzie, 2002).

RELATIONSHIP MAINTENANCE AND EXPECTATIONS IN RELATIONSHIP DEVELOPMENT

Relationship maintenance represents one way individuals may negotiate the threat that expectation discrepancies present to relationships. Relationship maintenance refers to the diverse ways that partners keep their relationships going. Partners may individually or interactively enact strategies that preserve the relationship by either mitigating threats or enhancing the relationship. The integrative model of relationship maintenance (Ogolsky, Monk, Rice, Theisen, & Maniotes, 2017) would approach unmet expectations as opportunities to mitigate a relationship threat. According to the model, cognitively reframing expectancy violations through derogation of alternatives, idealization, or positive attributions may buffer against the negative effects of unmet expectations on commitment and relationship development. Likewise, managing conflict that arises from discrepant expectations, forgiving one's partner for violating relationship expectations, integrating current relationship experiences into one's expectations,[3] and engaging in dyadic coping may also buffer the influence of unmet expectations on relationship outcomes. As expectancy violations are resolved, partners may continue to engage in these maintenance strategies as a means of relationship enhancement.

The model, however, neglects communication as a key means of threat mitigation. Indeed, research suggests that expectations may be a driving force in information seeking behaviors and the management of relational uncertainty (Bell & Buerkel-Rothfuss, 1990; Knobloch & Solomon, 2002). The mixed findings on relationship talk (i.e., partners' open discussion about the state of their relationship; see Badr, Acitelli, & Taylor, 2008; Finkenauer & Hazam, 2000; c.f. Knobloch, & Theiss, 2011), however, blur our understanding of communicative behaviors as effective strategies for mitigating the threat of expectation violations. Our logic suggests that communicating about relationship expectations may reduce the likelihood of expectancy violations

---

[3] We qualify the integration of current experiences with relationship expectations by highlighting the notable exception of intimate partner violence, where engaging in relationship maintenance (e.g., downplaying aggression) may prolong a relationship that is personally harmful (see Arriaga, Capezza, Goodfriend, & Allsop, 2018).

becoming reasons for regressive changes in the commitment to wed. Given that relationship maintenance may decrease over time as partners grow into routine patterns of interaction, its influence on partners' reasons for changes in the likelihood of marriage also remains a fruitful avenue for future research. Notably, partners may also face expectancy violations concerning relationship maintenance, which have implications for satisfaction (Dainton, 2000).

IMPORTANCE OF HISTORICAL CONTEXT IN UNDERSTANDING RELATIONSHIP EXPECTATIONS

Most individuals form expectations about their commitment to wed (e.g., no expectation, high expectation), and these expectations may change across time. Despite the relatively universal desire to marry, there is substantial variation in how these expectations are experienced, how they develop and relate to other relational constructs, and in the meaning attributed to them across relationship contexts. Notably, the changing legal context of marriage in the US highlights the importance of historical context when considering expectations in relationship development.

Traditionally, the transition to marriage marked adulthood and served as a system for hierarchically organizing families within the social and economic world. However, contemporary approaches center on emotional fulfillment as the primary feasible goal of marriage (Coontz, 2004).[4] Challenges to institutional discrimination have led to the extension of marriage to same-sex couples; however, this expansion may be accompanied by pressure to marry, even when not desired (Lannutti, 2007). Relatedly, the struggle for marriage equality exposed the many legal benefits of marriage. Thus, as same-sex partners take advantage of marriage equality, modern developments in the expectations of marriage as an institution and reasons for marriage are likely to occur. To illustrate, we provide descriptive data from a study of the personal and relational implications of the transition to marriage equality (see Table 15.1; Ogolsky, Monk, Rice, & Oswald, 2018).

Reasons for Changes in Commitment to Wed after Marriage Equality

The study was designed to examine how federal, state, and local marriage recognition influenced personal and relational wellbeing for individuals in different-sex and same-sex relationships. Over 500 individuals initially

---

[4] We acknowledge Finkel, Hui, Carswell, and Larson's (2014) contention that people enter marriage with much larger goals in mind, such as self-actualization. However, from our perspective, emotional fulfillment represents the highest *expected* and *attainable* demand placed on relationships across time, racial/ethnic, cultural, economic, and social contexts.

provided online data prior to federal marriage recognition and were followed for a year afterward (see Ogolsky, Monk, Rice, & Oswald, 2019 for a fuller description of the study). We examine data from a subsample of individuals dating same-sex partners who provided reasons for changes in their chance of marriage between waves two (two weeks after legal recognition) and three (four months after legal recognition). These individuals (n = 45) were demographically similar to the larger sample: mostly white (86%), a slight female majority (52%), and in their relationships for approximately seven years. We condensed the relationship mapping procedure into two key questions to capture changes in marital probability: "Right now, what is the chance that you will marry your partner?" and "What is the reason for your current chance of marriage?" Three months after the legal recognition of same-sex marriage, nineteen individuals decreased in their chance of marriage, seventeen increased, and nine reported no change. Five of those who reported no change indicated 100 percent expectation of marriage at both time points. The remaining four either reported low (5%, n = 2) or high (90%, n = 2) commitment to marrying their partner at both time points.

Reasons for changes in marital probability partially mapped on to the domains explicated by Surra (1995). Social networks exerted a clear influence on individuals' evaluations of the likelihood of marriage. For example, one participant stated "It would make living together a lot smoother with her parents," and another described: "Her father is a very older White, Republican, Catholic man and he did not take the news of us very well. My partner and I have talked about marriage and it is something that we want to happen but her family is important to her so we are waiting to put that on the table for discussion at a later date." These reflections suggest that network approval remains an important consideration for relationship progression. In addition, normative expectations (e.g., "We've been together for a while"), dyadic interaction (e.g., "We are a wonderful, cohesive couple ... and work great as a team"), and circumstances beyond partners' control (e.g., "His health is very, very bad") constituted reasons for changes in the chance of marriage. However, statements regarding the legitimacy of the relationship or benefits associated with the legal status of marriage also emerged. One participant stated, "Same sex marriage is now legal in all fifty states, so now that we qualify for benefits, we will most likely be married." Another participant was uninterested in marriage immediately after the federal decision ("I am generally against the institution of marriage, and I have thought for a long time that I would not enter into marriage, despite wanting or having long-term and monogamous relationships") but later identified the legal status as beneficial ("healthcare access or being in a better legal position to take care of my partner").

This glimpse of response data largely aligns with reasons for turning points explicated in the literature on the development of commitment to marriage. However, reasons regarding the legitimacy and the benefits of the legal status fall outside of Surra's (1985) coding scheme. Relatedly, the struggle for sexual minorities to gain access to marriage may have elevated the expectation of legal benefits associated with marriage, particularly for partners in same-sex relationships. Thus, although love also represented a reason for changes in the likelihood of marriage, notable consideration may be given to the legitimacy or myriad benefits of the legal status. We explored this hypothesis in the same sample by examining changes in two variables three months before federal marriage recognition and one year post recognition: "Legally, I feel (or I would feel) better off being married" and "Generally, I feel (or would feel) better off being married." On average, people generally expected marriage to provide the same benefits before and after its legal recognition. However, participants perceived marriage to be more legally, than generally, beneficial both before and after its legal recognition. Moreover, after same-sex partners were granted access to marriage, participants perceived more legal benefits of the institution than before its legalization.

These preliminary descriptive findings suggest that, although love still plays an important role, for some individuals, expectations of marriage are indeed shifting toward a legal benefits perspective. The salience of legal benefits may require a cognitive integration of these benefits into their working relationship models of what to expect of, as well as reasons to commit to, marriage. Although speculative, such a shift may contribute to partners' assessments of changes in commitment to marriage. Indeed, prior to the federal recognition of same-sex relationships, LGBTQ individuals with access to marriage found themselves reevaluating their perceptions of ideal characteristics of romantic partners in terms of whether a partner would be "marriage material" (Lannutti, 2007). Thus, expectations of a suitable partner, and of the relationship as a whole, may have shifted in response to unexpected desires to wed. In addition, questions regarding the relevance of assessing commitment to marriage remain as discussions of the deinstitutionalization of marriage continue (e.g., Lauer & Yodanis, 2010) and as perceptions of marriage as a heteronormative institution that polices romantic interactions disinterests both different-sex and same-sex couples from participating in traditional marriage (e.g., Pew Research Center, 2014; see also Monk & Ogolsky, 2019). These issues present important directions for future research.

FUTURE DIRECTIONS

To this point we have reviewed historical and contemporary perspectives on mapping relationship trajectories and how interdependence contributes to trajectory development by explicating reasons for changes in the commitment to wed. As with most fields, however, limitations remain that pose important directions for future research. We focus on well documented limitations, grounding them in extant literature, and make recommendations for future research. These limitations focus on accounting for the meaningfulness of intersectional perspectives and future directions focus on methodological concerns.

Integrating Intersectionality: Accounting for Meaningful Variation in Relationship Experiences and Relationship Expectations

As we have suggested in the previous section, the changing social and political views on marriage provide a critical context in which expectations surrounding the reasons for development of commitment to marriage may arise. However, contexts for understanding variations are endless and, thus, many underdeveloped areas remain. It is beyond the scope of this chapter to review how relationship expectations coalesce with reasons for changes in the commitment to marriage across various contexts; however, we argue that scholars should be attending to and exploring the potentially fruitful ways in which universal relationship processes may vary by context. Indeed, the expectations individuals hold about relationship development and commitment are integrally related to their social positions (Holmberg & Veroff, 1996). Likewise, intersectional perspectives highlight that the combination of social positions of any one individual (and thus, the variety of social positions represented within a partnership) may contribute to how people experience and assign meaning to their relationships (Few-Demo, 2014). Yet, relationship scholars have lagged in explaining the variations in how people experience and assign meaning to their relationships. To this end, we provide illustrative empirical examples that highlight how expectations of romantic relationship and reasons for changes in the commitment to marriage may vary by context.

A common critique of the relationship literature as a whole is that it may rely too much on samples of white college-age students. This may limit the generalizability of what is known about important processes in developing romantic relationships, and suggests a need for future research with more representative samples. Studies that tackle more diverse samples often do so by comparing individuals by race and/or gender along the Black/White and Female/Male dichotomies. Such research importantly highlights between-group differences in relationships but may lead to oversimplified and negative framings of non-dominant groups (e.g., Dilworth-Anderson, Burton, & Turner, 1993). In order to gain a more complete understanding of relationship development, scholars must conduct within-group inquiry more consistently to capture the heterogeneity between *and* within groups. We draw from literature on African American romantic relationships and gender differences in relationships to illustrate how intersecting social positions can shape expectations of relationship partners generally and expectations of marriage specifically.

Intersecting with Race Early research on African American romantic relationships was heavily critiqued for its deficit-based approach, positioning African American relationships as less satisfying, less stable, and less likely to endure (Dilworth-Anderson et al., 1993). Structural barriers to relationship commitment and maintenance centered on gender differences in the availability of marriage partners, such as the statement that African American women outnumber available men (Furstenburg, 2009). Institutional discrimination is most often considered the culprit of the gender gap, in that African American men are disproportionately more likely to face financial instability, earlier mortality, and incarceration. These factors may constrain comparison levels and contribute to African Americans being among the least likely to marry and most likely to divorce (Cherlin, 2010). Despite these probabilities, African Americans continue to value and desire marriage (Harknett & McLanahan, 2004; Huston & Melz, 2004). Among those who are married, partners report expecting effective premarital communication, a balance of autonomy and dyadic interaction, as well as congruence in marital expectations and religious values (Vaterlaus, Skogrand, Chaney, & Gahagan, 2017). In fact, some scholars suggest that African Americans may expect that they will not wed because marriage is held in such high regard that some individuals perceive it as an unattainable goal (Collins & Perry, 2015; Gibson-Davis, Edin, & McLanahan, 2005).

These relationship dynamics are often complicated by the intersections of class and gender. Cultural ideals around women's independence, for example, may contribute to women's ambivalence about marriage (Barros-Gomes & Baptist, 2014). Moreover, early exposure to the disadvantages associated with institutional discrimination (e.g., harsh parenting, family instability, economic hardship, discrimination, and crime) contribute to the development of negative relationship schemas in emerging adulthood that promote more negative views of marriage (Simons, Simons, Lei, & Landor, 2012). These findings were particularly salient among African American men who are often positioned as less willing to commit to long-term relationships (Towner, Dolcini, & Harper, 2015). Such perspectives may constitute barriers to commitment, which is critical to African Americans' decision to marry (Chaney, 2014). Likewise, financial stability and spirituality exert a notable influence on whether African Americans progress from dating to marriage (Allen & Olson, 2001; Barr & Simons, 2012; Collins & Perry, 2015; Fincham & Beach, 2014) and reflect normative reasons for probable changes in the commitment to wed. Within-group evaluations of changes in the commitment to wed among African Americans might reveal meaningful patterns of reasons for changes in the commitment to wed centered on structural and relational issues that emerge from institutionalized racial discrimination.

Intersecting with Gender Gender also represents a social position, often oversimplified in relationship research. Expectations around gender, its intersections with other social positions, and subsequent implications of reasons for changes in the commitment to wed remain a fruitful avenue for future research. Relationships where one partner is transgender further highlight the pervasiveness of gender performance, as gender-related microaggressions permeated how partners interacted with one another and others, and constituted reasons for regressions in relationship development (Pulice-Farrow, Brown, & Galupo, 2017). Expectations for gender roles in heterosexual relationships may be influenced, in part, by consumption of romantic media content that is associated with idealistic marital expectations (Segrin & Nabi, 2002), lower marital commitment, perceiving better quality relationship alternatives, and more costs of marriage (Osborn, 2012). However, social positions intersecting with gender may influence the degree to which individuals hold and are able to satisfy such expectations. At the intersection of gender and class, for example, lower income men and women were found to hold relationship expectations similar to those of middle-class couples regarding egalitarian roles in parenting, housework, and income (Sherman, 2017). For example, men described expectations for providing financially for their partners; however, the inflexible hours associated with low-wage employment and lack of employment opportunities undermined men's ability to fulfill these expectations. Individuals expressed frustration with partners when these expectations remained unmet and began to question the value of romantic relationships (Sherman, 2017).

Gender differences also permeate the degree to which relationship expectations are met. Men's intention to marry, for example, seems to influence whether partners will eventually marry (Guzzo, 2009). Indeed, research suggests that even when partners have similar relationship standards, women are less likely to have their standards met (Afifi, Joseph, & Aldeis, 2012).

Accounting for Intersectional and Contextual Variations

We identify three ways to account meaningfully for contextual and intersectional variations in relationship development. First, within-group analyses evade a deficiency bias by highlighting heterogeneity. Doing so skirts scholars' tendency to describe non-dominant groups as having monolithic relationship experiences. Second, person-centered analyses, rather than variable-centered analyses, group individuals that have similar variable patterns. These analyses may be beneficial in considering intersectional relationship experiences by also explicating unique developmental relationship trajectories that emerge from intersecting social positions. Finally, employing mixed methods not only expands the types of questions scholars can ask, but also allows researchers to account for interactions between specific contexts, intersecting identities, and relationship experiences. Such strategies advance the field of relationship science by challenging the post-positivist assumptions that dominate the field and highlighting the empirical, theoretical, and practical significance of varying relationship experiences.

CONCLUSION

In this chapter, we reviewed a line of research examining relationship trajectories with an eye toward the role of expectations. We question whether reasons for changes in the commitment to wed remain relevant more than three decades later, given the rapid shifts in the structure and societal function of marriage. In doing so, we contribute to this body of literature by presenting descriptive results addressing socio-political reasons for changes in the commitment to wed and the perceived general and legal benefits of marriage among romantically-involved LGB individuals during the transition to marriage equality. We assert that intersectional approaches are meaningful avenues for future research given that such variations may influence the interdependence process by modifying relationship expectations through comparison levels and comparison levels for alternatives. We concluded by suggesting analytical and methodological approaches that allow scholars to meaningfully account for intersectional and contextual variations in expectations of relationships and relationship progression. Our hope is that, having read this chapter, novice and senior scholars will be inspired to embrace the empirical challenge of acknowledging the time-bound contexts of relationship development in concert with other contextual and intersectional experiences.

REFERENCES

Afifi, T. D., Joseph, A., & Aldeis, D. (2012). The "standards for openness hypothesis": Why women find (conflict) avoidance more dissatisfying than men. *Journal of Social and Personal Relationships*, 29, 102–125. doi:10.1177/0265407511420193

Ajzen, I. & Fishbein, M. (2005). The influence of attitudes on behavior. In D. Albarracín, B. T. Johnson, & M. P. Zanna (Eds.), *Handbook of Attitudes and Attitude Change* (pp. 173–221). Hillsdale, NJ: Erlbaum.

Allen, W. D. & Olson, D. H. (2001). Five types of African-American marriages. *Journal of Marital and Family Therapy*, 27, 301–314. doi: 10.1111/j.1752-0606.2001.tb00326.x

Amato, P. R. & Rogers, S. J. (1999). Do attitudes toward divorce affect marital quality? *Journal of Family Issues*, 20, 69–86. doi:10.1177/019251399020001004

Arriaga, X. B., Capezza, N. M., Goodfriend, W., & Allsop, K. E. (2018). The invisible harm of downplaying a romantic partner's aggression. *Current Directions in Psychological Science*, 27, 275–280. doi:10.1177/0963721417754198

Badr, H., Acitelli, L. K., & Taylor, C. L. C. (2008). Does talking about their relationship affect couples' marital and psychological adjustment to lung cancer? *Journal of Cancer Survivorship*, 2, 53–64. doi:10.1007/s11764-008-0044-3

Baker, L. R., McNulty, J. K., & VanderDrift, L. E. (2017). Expectations for future relationship satisfaction: Unique sources and critical implications for commitment. *Journal of Experimental Psychology: General*, 146, 700–721. doi:10.1037/xge0000299

Barr, A. B. & Simons, R. L. (2012). Marriage expectations among African American couples in early adulthood: A dyadic analysis. *Journal of Marriage and Family*, 74, 726–742. doi:10.1111/j.1741-3737.2012.00985.x

Barros-Gomes, P. & Baptist, J. (2014). Black women's ambivalence about marriage: A voice-centered relational approach. *Journal of Couple & Relationship Therapy*, 13, 284–311. doi:10.1080/15332691.2014.929064

Bell, R. A. & Buerkel-Rothfuss, N. L. (1990). S(he) loves me, s(he) loves me not: Predictors of relational information-seeking in courtship and beyond. *Communication Quarterly*, 38, 64–82. doi:10.1080/01463379009369742

Berger, C. R. & Calabrese, R. J. (1975). Some explorations in initial interaction and beyond: Toward a developmental theory of interpersonal communication. *Human Communication Research*, 1, 99–112.

Birnie, C., Joy McClure, M., Lydon, J. E., & Holmberg, D. (2009). Attachment avoidance and commitment aversion: A script for relationship failure. *Personal Relationships*, 16, 79–97. doi: 10.1111/j.1475-6811.2009.01211.x

Bradbury, T. N. & Fincham, F. D. (1990). Attributions in marriage: Review and critique. *Psychological Bulletin*, 107, 3–33. doi: 10.1037/0033-2909.107.1.3

Cate, R. M., Huston, T. L., & Nesselroade, J. R. (1986). Premarital relationships: Toward the identification of alternative pathways to marriage. *Journal of Social and Clinical Psychology*, 4, 3–22. doi: 10.1521/jscp.1986.4.1.3

Chaney, C. (2014). "No matter what, good or bad, love is still there": Motivations for romantic commitment among Black cohabiting couples. *Marriage & Family Review*, 50, 216–245. doi:10.1080/01494929.2013.851056

Cherlin, A. J. (2010). Demographic trends in the United States: A review of research in the 2000s. *Journal of Marriage and Family*, 72, 403–419. doi:10.1111/j.1741-3737.2010.00710.x

Collins, W. L. & Perry, A. R. (2015). Black men's perspectives on the role of the black church in healthy relationship promotion and family stability. *Social Work and Christianity*, 42, 430–448. doi:10.1177/000312240406900603

Coontz, S. (2004). The world historical transformation of marriage. *Journal of Marriage and Family*, 66, 974–979. doi:10.1111/j.0022-2445.2004.00067.x

Dainton, M. (2000). Maintenance behaviors, expectations for maintenance, and satisfaction: Linking comparison levels to relational maintenance strategies. *Journal of Social and Personal Relationships*, 17, 827–842. doi:10.1177/0265407500176007

Dilworth-Anderson, P., Burton, L., & Turner, W. (1993). The importance of values in the study of culturally diverse families. *Family Relations*, 42, 238–242. doi:10.2307/585551

Fehr, B. (1999). Laypeople's conceptions of commitment. *Journal of Personality and Social Psychology*, 76, 90–103. doi:10.1037/0022-3514.76.1.90

Felmlee, D. H. (2001). No couple is an island: A social network perspective on dyadic stability. *Social Forces*, 79, 1259–1287. doi:10.1353/sof.2001.0039

Few-Demo, A. L. (2014). Intersectionality as the "new" critical approach in feminist family studies: Evolving racial/ethnic feminisms and critical race theories. *Journal of Family Theory & Review*, 6, 169–183. doi:10.1111/jftr.12039

Fincham, F. D. & Beach, S. R. (2014). I say a little prayer for you: Praying for partner increases commitment in romantic relationships. *Journal of Family Psychology*, 28, 587–593. doi:10.1037/a0034999

Finkel, E. J., Hui, C. M., Carswell, K. L., & Larson, G. M. (2014). The suffocation of marriage: Climbing Mount Maslow without enough oxygen. *Psychological Inquiry*, 25, 1–41. doi:10.1080/1047840X.2014.863723

Finkenauer, C. & Hazam, H. (2000). Disclosure and secrecy in marriage: Do both contribute to marital satisfaction? *Journal of Social and Personal Relationships*, 17, 245–263. doi:10.1177/0265407500172005

Fletcher, G. J. O. & Thomas, G. (1996). Close relationship lay theories: Their structure and function. In G. J. O. Fletcher & J. Fitness (Eds.), *Knowledge Structures in Close Relationships: A Social Psychological Approach* (pp. 3–24). Mahwah, NJ: Lawrence Erlbaum Associates Publishers.

Fletcher, G. J. O., Fincham, F. D., Cramer, L., & Heron, N. (1987). The role of attributions in the development of dating relationships. *Journal of Personality and Social Psychology*, 53, 481–489. doi:10.1037/0022-3514.53.3.481

Freedman, D., Thornton, A., Camburn, D., Alwin, D., & Young-DeMarco, L. (1988). The life history calendar: A technique for collecting retrospective data. In C. C. Clogg (Ed.), *Sociological Methodology* (Vol. 18, pp. 37–68). San Francisco, CA: Jossey-Bass.

Fuhrman, R. W., Flannagan, D., & Matamoros, M. (2009). Behavior expectations in cross-sex friendships, same-sex friendships, and romantic relationships. *Personal Relationships*, 16, 575–595. doi:10.1111/j.1475-6811.2009.01240.x

Furstenberg, F. F. (2009). If Moynihan had only known: Race, class, and family change in the late twentieth century. *The Annals of the American Academy of Political and Social Science*, 621, 94–110. doi:10.1177/0002716208324866

Gager, C. T. & Sanchez, L. (2003). Two as one? Couples' perceptions of time spent together, marital quality, and the risk of divorce. *Journal of Family Issues*, 24, 21–50. doi:10.1177/0192513X02238519

Gibson-Davis, C. M., Edin, K., & McLanahan, S. (2005). High hopes but even higher expectations: The retreat from marriage among low-income couples. *Journal of Marriage and Family*, 67, 1301–1312. doi:10.1111/j.1741-3737.2005.00218.x

Ginsburg, G. P. (1988). Rules, scripts and prototypes in personal relationships. In S. Duck, D. F. Hay, S. E. Hobfoll, W. Ickes, & B. M. Montgomery (Eds.), *Handbook of Personal Relationships: Theory, Research and Interventions* (pp. 23–39). Oxford: John Wiley & Sons.

Guzzo, K. B. (2009). Marital intentions and the stability of first cohabitations. *Journal of Family Issues*, 30, 179–205. doi:10.1177/0192513X08323694

Hampel, A. D. & Vangelisti, A. L. (2008). Commitment expectations in romantic relationships: Application of a prototype interaction-pattern model. *Personal Relationships*, 15, 81–102. doi:10.1111/j.1475-6811.2007.00186.x

Harknett, K. & McLanahan, S. S. (2004). Racial and ethnic differences in marriage after the birth of a child. *American Sociological Review*, 69, 790–811. doi:10.1177/000312240406900603

Hazan, C. & Shaver, P. (1987). Romantic love conceptualized as an attachment process. *Journal of Personality and Social Psychology*, 52, 511–524. doi:10.1037/0022-3514.52.3.511

Holmberg, D. & MacKenzie, S. (2002). So far, so good: Scripts for romantic relationship development as predictors of relational well-being. *Journal of Social and Personal Relationships*, 19, 777–796. doi:10.1177/0265407502196003

Holmberg, D. & Veroff, J. (1996). Rewriting relationship memories: The effects of courtship and wedding scripts. In G. J. P. Fletcher & J. Fitness (Eds.), *Knowledge Structures in Close Relationships: A Social Psychological Approach* (pp. 345–368). Mahwah, NJ: Lawrence Erlbaum Associates Publishers.

Huston, T. L. (2000). The social ecology of marriage and other intimate unions. *Journal of Marriage and Family*, 62, 298–320. doi:10.1111/j.1741-3737.2000.00298.x

Huston, T. L. & Melz, H. (2004). The case for (promoting) marriage: The devil is in the details. *Journal of Marriage and Family*, 66, 943–958. doi:10.1111/j.0022-2445.2004.00064.x

Huston, T. L., Caughlin, J. P., Houts, R. M., Smith, S. E., & George, L. J. (2001). The connubial crucible: Newlywed years as predictors of marital delight, distress, and divorce. *Journal of Personality and Social Psychology*, 80, 237–252. doi:10.1037/0022-3514.80.2.237

Huston, T. L., Surra, C., Fitzgerald, N., & Cate, R. (1981). From courtship to marriage: Mate selection as an interpersonal process. In S. Duck & R. Gilmour (Eds.), *Personal Relationships: Vol. 2. Developing Personal Relationships* (pp. 53–88). London: Academic Press.

Johnson, M. P. (1999). Personal, moral, and structural commitment to relationships. In W. H. Jones & J. M. Adams (Eds.), *Handbook of Interpersonal Commitment and Relationship Stability* (pp. 73–87). New York: Plenum Press.

Johnson, M. P., Caughlin, J., & Huston, T. (1999). The tripartite nature of marital commitment: Personal, moral, and structural reasons to stay married. *Journal of Marriage and Family*, 61, 160–177. doi:10.2307/353891

Karney, B. R. & Bradbury, T. N. (1995). The longitudinal course of marital quality and stability: A review of theory, methods, and research. *Psychological Bulletin*, 118, 3–34. doi:10.1037/0033-2909.118.1.3

Kelley, H. & Thibaut, J. (1978). *Interpersonal Relations: A Theory of Interdependence.* New York: John Wiley & Sons.

Knee, C. R. & Petty, K. N. (2013). Implicit theories of relationships: Destiny and growth beliefs. In J. Simpson & L. Campbell (Eds.), *The Oxford Handbook of Close Relationships* (pp. 183–199). New York: Oxford University Press: doi:10.1093/oxfordhb/9780195398694.013.0009

Knobloch, L. K. & Solomon, D. H. (2002). Information seeking beyond initial interaction: Negotiating relational uncertainty within close relationships. *Human Communication Research*, 28, 243–257. doi:10.1111/j.1468-2958.2002.tb00806.x

Knobloch, L. K. & Theiss, J. A. (2011). Relational uncertainty and relationship talk within courtship: A longitudinal actor–partner interdependence model. *Communication Monographs*, 78, 3–26. doi:10.1037/a0024063

Lannutti, P. J. (2007). The influence of same-sex marriage on the understanding of same-sex relationships. *Journal of Homosexuality*, 53, 135–151. doi:10.1111/j.1540-4560.2011.01697.x

Lauer, S. & Yodanis, C. (2010). The deinstitutionalization of marriage revisited: A new institutional approach to marriage. *Journal of Family Theory & Review*, 2, 58–72. doi:10.1111/j.1756-2589.2010.00039.x

Mongeau, P. A., Carey, C. M., & Williams, M. L. M. (1998). First date initiation and enactment: An expectancy violation approach. In D. J. Canary & K. Dindia (Eds.), *Sex Differences and Similarities in Communication: Critical Investigations of Sex and Gender in Interaction* (pp. 413–426). Mahwah, NJ: Lawrence Erlbaum Associates.

Monk, J. K. & Ogolsky, B. G. (2019). Contextual relational uncertainty model: Understanding ambiguity in a changing sociopolitical context of marriage. *Journal of Family Theory and Review*, 11, 243–261. doi: 10.1111/jftr.12325

Murray, S. L., Lamarche, V. M., Gomillion, S., Seery, M. D., & Kondrak, C. (2017). In defense of commitment: The curative power of violated expectations. *Journal of Personality and Social Psychology*, 113, 697–729. doi:10.1037/pspi0000102

Ogolsky, B. G., Monk, J. K., Rice, T. M., & Oswald, R. F. (2018). As the states turned: Implications of the changing legal context of same-sex marriage on well-being. *Journal of Social and Personal Relationships*, 36, 3219–3238. doi:10.1177/0265407518816883

Ogolsky, B. G., Monk, J. K., Rice, T. M., & Oswald, R. F. (2019). Personal well-being across the transition to marriage equality: A longitudinal analysis. *Journal of Family Psychology*, 33, 422–432. doi:10.1037/fam0000504.

Ogolsky, B. G., Monk, J. K., Rice, T. M., Theisen, J. C., & Maniotes, C. R. (2017). Relationship maintenance: A review of research on romantic relationships. *Journal of Family Theory & Review*, 9, 275–306. doi:10.1111/jftr.12205

Ogolsky, B. G., Surra, C. A., & Monk, J. K. (2016). Pathways of commitment to wed: The development and dissolution of romantic relationships. *Journal of Marriage and Family*, 78, 293–310. doi:10.1111/jomf.12260

Osborn, J. L. (2012). When TV and marriage meet: A social exchange analysis of the impact of television viewing on marital satisfaction and commitment. *Mass Communication and Society*, 15, 739–757. doi:10.1080/15205436.2011.618900

Pew Research Center. (2014). *Record share of Americans have never married as values, economics and gender patterns change*. Retrieved from www.pewsocialtrends.org/2014/09/24/record-share-of-americans-have-never-married/#will-todays-never-married-adults-eventually-marry

Pulice-Farrow, L., Brown, T. D., & Galupo, M. P. (2017). Transgender microaggressions in the context of romantic relationships. *Psychology of Sexual Orientation and Gender Diversity*, 4, 362–373. doi:10.1037/sgd0000238

Riggio, H. R. & Weiser, D. A. (2008). Attitudes toward marriage: Embeddedness and outcomes in personal relationships. *Personal Relationships*, 15, 123–140. doi:10.1111/j.1475-6811.2007.00188.x

Rusbult, C. & Arriaga, X. (1997). Interdependence theory. In S. Duck (Ed.), *Handbook of Personal Relationships* (2nd ed., pp. 221–250). London: Wiley.

Rusbult, C. E. (1983). A longitudinal test of the investment model: The development (and deterioration) of satisfaction and commitment in heterosexual involvements. *Journal of Personality and Social Psychology*, 45, 101–117. doi:10.1037/0022-3514.45.1.101

Segrin, C. & Nabi, R. L. (2002). Does television viewing cultivate unrealistic expectations about marriage? *Journal of Communication*, 52, 247–263. doi:10.1111/j.1460-2466.2002.tb02543.x

Sherman, J. (2017). "Stress that I don't need": Gender expectations and relationship struggles among the poor. *Journal of Marriage and Family*, 79, 657–674. doi:10.1111/jomf.12387

Simons, R. L., Simons, L. G., Lei, M. K., & Landor, A. M. (2012). Relational schemas, hostile romantic relationships, and beliefs about marriage among young African American adults. *Journal of Social and Personal Relationships*, 29, 77–101. doi:10.1177/0265407511406897

Sprecher, S., Felmlee, D., Schmeeckle, M., & Shu, X. (2006). No breakup occurs on an island: Social networks and relationship dissolution. In M. A. Fine & J. H. Harvey (Eds.), *Handbook of Divorce and Relationship Dissolution* (pp. 457–478). Mahwah, NJ: Lawrence Erlbaum Associates Publishers.

Surra, C. A. (1985). Courtship types: Variations in interdependence between partners and social networks. *Journal of Personality and Social Psychology*, 49, 357–375. doi:10.1037/0022-3514.49.2.357

Surra, C. A. (1987). Reasons for changes in commitment: Variations by courtship type. *Journal of Social and Personal Relationships*, 4, 17–33. doi:10.1177/0265407587041002

Surra, C. A. (1995). *Reasons coding manual IV*. Unpublished manuscript, The University of Texas at Austin.

Surra, C. A., Arizzi, P., & Asmussen, L. A. (1988). The association between reasons for commitment and the development and outcome of marital relationships. *Journal of Social and Personal Relationships*, 5, 47–63. doi:10.1177/0265407588051003

Surra, C. A. & Gray, C. E. (2000). A typology of processes of commitment to marriage: Why do partners commit to problematic relationships? In L. J. Waite, C. Backrach, M. Hindin, E. Thomson, & A. Thornton (Eds.), *The Ties That Bind: Perspectives on Marriage and Cohabitation* (pp. 253–280). New York: Aldine de Gruyter.

Surra, C. A. & Hughes, D. K. (1997). Commitment processes in accounts of the development of premarital relationships. *Journal of Marriage and the Family*, 59, 5–21. doi:10.2307/353658

Surra, C. A., Hughes, D. K., & Jacquet, S. E. (1999). The development of commitment to marriage: A phenomenological approach. In J. M. Adams & W. H. Jones (Eds.), *Handbook of Interpersonal Commitment and Relationship Stability* (pp. 125–148). New York: Kluwer Academic/Plenum Press.

Surra, C. A. & Bartell, D. S. (2001) Attributions, communication, and the development of a marital identity, in V. Manusov & J. H. Harvey (Eds.), *Attribution, Communication Behavior, and Close Relationships* (pp. 93–114). Cambridge: Cambridge University Press.

Thibaut, J. W. & Kelley, H. H. (1959). *The Social Psychology of Groups*. New York: Wiley.

Towner, S. L., Dolcini, M. M., & Harper, G. W. (2015). Romantic relationship dynamics of urban African American adolescents: Patterns of monogamy, commitment, and trust. *Youth & Society*, 47, 343–373. doi:10.1177/0044118X12462591

Vannier, S. A. & O'Sullivan, L. F. (2017a). Great expectations: Examining unmet romantic expectations and dating relationship outcomes using an investment model framework. *Journal of Social and Personal Relationships*, 35, 1045–1066. doi:10.1177/0265407517703492

Vannier, S. A. & O'Sullivan, L. F. (2017b). Passion, connection, and destiny: How romantic expectations help predict satisfaction and commitment in young adults' dating relationships. *Journal of Social and Personal Relationships*, 34, 235–257. doi:10.1177/0265407516631156

Vaterlaus, J. M., Skogrand, L., Chaney, C., & Gahagan, K. (2017). Marital expectations in strong African American marriages. *Family Process*, 56, 883–899. doi:10.1111/famp.12263

16

Creating Closeness and Interdependence

*Results of Laboratory-Based Studies Involving
Getting-Acquainted Dyads*

SUSAN SPRECHER

Closeness and interdependence are considered to be essential components of any intimate relationship of significant duration. Closeness is a property that is synonymous with and encompasses other relationship phenomena including mutuality and attraction (Rusbult, Kumashiro, Coolsen, & Kirchner, 2004). Closeness also overlaps with the concept of interdependence, which refers both to an interaction pattern that develops between two people on the basis of their activities (e.g., Berscheid, Snyder, & Omoto, 1989; Kelley et al., 1983) and cognitive interdependence such as including the other in the self (Agnew, Loving, Le, & Goodfriend, 2004). Although closeness and interdependence are associated with intimate relationships (as discussed in many of the chapters of this volume), even an initial (or one-time) interaction between two strangers can be characterized by a pattern of interdependence, and the two strangers may feel a closeness to each other based on the brief interaction. Closeness and interdependence in an initial interaction – even if a relationship does not develop – can lead to other positive outcomes, including an increased sense of belonging and positive mood (Baumeister & Leary, 1995; Vittengl & Holt, 2000).

Many years ago, Aron, Melinat, Aron, Vallone, and Bator (1997) developed a closeness-generating exercise that was designed to create "a temporary feeling of closeness" and "an interconnectedness of self and other" (p. 364) within pairs of strangers. This exercise, also sometimes referred to as the Fast Friends procedure, has been used in various adaptations in many lines of research. Although Aron et al.'s "36 questions" may be the most popular (even highlighted in the *New York Times*), other self-disclosure exercises have also been developed (e.g., Sedikides, Campbell, Reeder, & Elliot, 1999). In fact, some get-acquainted exercises date back to the first self-disclosure studies conducted in the 1970s and 1980s, which often involved participants interacting with confederates (e.g., Collins & Miller, 1994). Most of the structured tasks that were developed to generate closeness between strangers required the participants to engage in self-disclosure; however, some researchers have had stranger pairs do other types of activities (e.g., a game, a humorous task) in addition to or instead of self-disclosure tasks, in order to create closeness.

This chapter focuses on the development of feelings of interdependence between strangers. The purpose of this chapter is first to describe the different tasks that have been developed to create a temporary feeling of closeness or interdependence in initial (mostly laboratory) interactions between strangers, and then to summarize illustrative findings from studies using these closeness-generating methods. There are certainly limits in the degree to which research findings based on temporary feelings of closeness generated between getting-acquainted individuals in a laboratory setting can generalize to the initial interactions of potential relationships that have a future in the "real world." Nonetheless, creating closeness and interconnectedness between strangers in a laboratory setting allows researchers to test the influence of various theoretical processes in a controlled setting. For example, researchers can examine the effects of individual characteristics (shyness), manipulations of relationship-relevant variables (the expectation of being liked), manipulations of the context of the interaction (length of discussion, medium of communication), and the role of mediators (e.g., responsiveness) on the degree to which closeness and interconnection are experienced after the task. Research has also examined how engaging in a closeness induction task (vs. another task) affects other social psychological phenomena likely to follow from interpersonal closeness.

TASKS TO INCREASE CLOSENESS AND INTERDEPENDENCE IN FIRST INTERACTIONS

Researchers have created several structured tasks to increase closeness and interdependence between previously unacquainted individuals in laboratory settings. This section reviews several such tasks, first describing the most commonly used closeness-generating task (Aron et al., 1997), second describing other illustrative self-disclosure tasks used to generate closeness, and third giving examples of other activities used in laboratory settings to generate closeness.

The Aron et al. Closeness-Generating Task

Aron et al. (1997) developed a procedure for inducing closeness between strangers under controlled conditions. Their goal was to develop a procedure that would generate a temporary feeling of closeness – an interconnection between self and other – which would give researchers the ability to test theoretical predictions about early stages of relationships in a laboratory or classroom setting. The procedure involves several self-disclosure topics divided into three sets that escalate in intimacy and personalism. An example question in the first set is "Given the choice of anyone in the world, whom would you want as a dinner guest?" An example item in the second set is "If a crystal ball could tell you the truth about yourself, your life, the future, or anything else, what would you want to know?" The third set, which had the most intimate questions, includes topics such as "If you were going to become a close friend with your partner, please share what would be important for him or her to know." The participants are directed to discuss each question one at a time in each set, and to alternate which partner reads the question aloud and goes first. Dyads are timed for each set of questions and directed when to move to the next set. The original procedure also included an additional intimacy step at the end, which was to stare into each other's eyes for three minutes, although this eye-gazing step has not generally been incorporated into the procedure in most subsequent studies.

As evidence of the validity of the closeness-generating task, Aron et al. (1997; Study 1) found that student dyads who were randomly assigned to engage in the closeness-inducing task reported higher scores on Aron, Aron, and Smollan's (1992) Inclusion of Other in Self (IOS) scale (which has seven pairs of circles representing self and other that overlap to varying degrees) and Berscheid et al.'s (1989) Subjective Closeness Index (which contains two items assessing closeness to the others) than did dyads randomly assigned to engage in a procedure that mimicked small talk. The small talk task was also divided into three sets, with such questions as: "Describe the last pet you owned," "What did you do this past summer?," and "What foreign country would you most like to visit and what attracts you to this place?"

In a majority of the studies using the Aron et al. (1997) procedure, only the closeness-generating task, and not also the small-talk task, is used (for example exceptions that included both tasks, see Slatcher [2010] and Kashdan & Wenzel [2005]). Some studies have used a brief version of the Aron et al. closeness task by selecting only some of the items and reducing the length of interaction (e.g., Boothby, Smith, Clark, & Bargh, 2016; Lundy & Drouin, 2016) or combining items from Aron et al. with those from other closeness-inducing tasks (e.g., Sprecher, Treger, & Wondra, 2012). Less common, but found in one line of research, an expanded version of the Aron et al. closeness task was used to allow for multi-session, get-acquainted interactions scheduled on different days (Mendoza-Denton & Page-Gould, 2008; Page-Gould, Mendoza-Denton, & Tropp, 2008).

Other Closeness-Generating Tasks Based on Self-Disclosure

Although the Aron et al. (1997) closeness-inducing task may be the most well-known, other self-disclosure tasks have also been developed. Sedikides et al.

(1999) created a structured closeness-inducing task for laboratory research that also involves reciprocal and escalating topics of self-disclosure. Similar to the Aron et al. (1997) task, the Sedikides et al. procedure includes three lists of questions, and the dyad members are instructed to take turns asking and answering the questions. There are fewer self-disclosure topics in the Sedikides et al. closeness task than in the Aron et al. procedure described, and the entire closeness procedure was designed to last only nine minutes (vs. forty-five minutes for the Aron et al. closeness task). Example items in the Sedikides et al. closeness task include: "What do you think you might major in?" (Set 1), "What is one thing happening in your life that makes you stressed out?" (Set 2), and "What is your happiest early childhood memory?" (Set 3). Sedikides et al. summarized validation information for their closeness task (including their own unpublished studies) and reported that "Participants [using the closeness procedure] report significantly higher levels of relationship closeness compared to a control group" (p. 2). (See also results in Sedikides, Campbell, Reeder, & Elliot, 1998.)

Other researchers have also created self-disclosure tasks for studies on the get-acquainted process. For example, self-disclosure tasks were created in the 1960s and 1970s within the *acquaintance paradigm* (Collins & Miller, 1994). Generally, the research conducted within this earlier paradigm did not include face-to-face interactions and was not focused on increasing closeness and interconnectedness specifically. In one such study, for example, Worthy, Gary, and Kahn (1969) created a list of seventy self-disclosure topics that were scaled for intimacy with a pretest sample and then divided into ten sets of seven questions each, with the questions in each set ordered from least to most intimate. Participants in their study became acquainted with other participants (in groups of four) by writing their answers to the self-disclosure topics and exchanging them, in multiple trials. One purpose of their research was to examine whether the participants self-disclosed more to those whom they liked more after a brief free-format introduction; results supported this prediction. In addition, the researchers found that the participants' final liking for the other participants in the study was affected by how much the others self-disclosed to them in the exchange of messages. Greater self-disclosure led to more liking. Other studies conducted within the acquaintance paradigm used similar lists of topics to examine how self-disclosure affected and was affected by initial liking, often with confederates engaged in scripted responses (for a review of this early research, see Collins & Miller, 1994).

More recently, and as another example of a self-disclosure task used in an initial interaction, Wright and Sinclair (2012) created a list of "Top 40 Getting to Know You Questions," including by obtaining many items from topics used at open-access dating websites. Example questions were: "In a general way, how would you describe yourself?," "Where did you grow up and what was it like?," and "What is your ideal romantic relationship/partner?" Wright and Sinclair used the list of getting-acquainted topics in a virtual dating game paradigm, where participants communicated online with two "bachelor(ette)s," although, unbeknownst to them, they were actually communicating with confederates who were given a script as to which questions to ask and how to answer the questions asked by the participants. A first impressions measure administered after a ten-minute exchange of communication within the structured self-disclosure task indicated that the participants reported liking the targets to whom they self-disclosed. In addition, if the participant was led to believe that their social network, and especially friends, approved of one of the "bachelor(ette)s," that target was liked even more.

Tasks That Involve Activities Other Than Self-Disclosure

In some studies, researchers have the participants engage in one or more activities (sometimes in addition to a self-disclosure task) in order to create closeness and interdependence or another phenomenon such as arousal. For example, Lewandowski and Aron (2004) had pairs of cross-sex strangers come into the laboratory and engage in four game-like activities. In one game, participants were at opposite sides of a circular target and had to bounce an unevenly weighted ball into the circular target so it could be caught by the partner on one bounce (to be counted as a success). The researchers had variations of the activities in order to manipulate both the challenge and the arousal of the activity. Although closeness *per se* was not measured as one of the dependent variables, the researchers administered a multiple-item measure of attraction, and found that the pairs of strangers who engaged in arousing activities reported more attraction to each other than did those who engaged in non-arousing activities (there was not a control group who did not engage in any activities).

Tasks designed to be fun and humorous have also been created to generate closeness in a laboratory setting between previously unacquainted pairs. For example, Fraley and Aron (2004) had stranger pairs engage in activities that were designed to be humorous (fun and likely to generate laughter) or were non-humorous comparable versions. They conducted extensive pilot testing to create the tasks, which included a ball-tossing task, a dance instructions task, and a charades game. In support of the researchers' predictions, the dyads who shared the humorous versions of the activities reported a greater sense of closeness after the activity than did those who engaged in the non-humorous versions. Similar results were found by Treger, Sprecher, and Erber (2013).

Other activities have also been developed to create closeness in stranger pairs. For example, in unpublished research, Beverley Fehr and her students have explored the role of watching sports (a hockey game) or engaging in a physically interactive game (playing hockey on Nintendo Wii) versus engaging in a structured self-disclosure task (either small talk or intimate) for enhancing closeness in existing male–male friendship pairs. Both the interactive activity and being in the condition of intimate self-disclosure resulted in enhanced friendship satisfaction ratings relative to being in a non-intimate self-disclosure condition or in the condition of watching a sport. Although Fehr and her students used the activity procedure with existing friendship pairs (to enhance their closeness), such a method could also be adapted for use to create closeness between previously unacquainted pairs.

Another activity used to generate closeness and interdependence in a laboratory setting is the game of Jenga^{TM}, in which dyad members take turns removing blocks from a stacked tower of blocks without the tower falling (e.g., Mendoza-Denton & Page-Gould, 2008; Reis, O'Keefe, & Lane, 2017, Study 3; Welker, Slatcher, Baker, & Aron, 2014). Welker et al. explained that they chose this activity to "build solidarity between couples and within couples by having them engage in mutual activities, which could help them feel closer to each other" (p. 696). It has also been identified as a superordinate activity that can increase bonding in stranger pairs (Mendoza-Denton & Page-Gould, 2008). Other activities have been used for participants assigned to the condition of less closeness, including shuffling cards (Welker et al., 2014).

In sum, in recognition that self-disclosure is a key ingredient for becoming acquainted and developing closeness, many researchers have developed structured self-disclosure tasks that guide the interaction between previously-unacquainted dyads in a laboratory context. In addition, various structured (non-disclosure) activities have been developed to generate interdependence and closeness. The alternative to structured tasks would be for dyads to have unstructured interactions or just receive the directions to "become acquainted." The unstructured approach has also been used in several research studies (e.g., Ickes, Bissonnette, Garcia, & Stinson, 1990; Sunnafrank, 1983), including in speed-dating research in which participants interact with several others very briefly and provide reactions to them (Tidwell, Eastwick, & Finkel, 2013). A summary of research with an unstructured approach is beyond the scope of this chapter, although for earlier reviews, see Eastwick and Finkel (2008) for speed-dating research and Ickes (2009) for research using an unstructured interaction paradigm.

FACTORS THAT ENHANCE (OR DIMINISH) CLOSENESS IN A
FIRST INTERACTION INVOLVING A STRUCTURED
CLOSENESS-INDUCING TASK

The structured tasks described in the previous section were designed to increase closeness and interdependence and related affiliative outcomes (attraction) in a first interaction between previously unacquainted individuals. One advantage of the closeness-generating procedures is that researchers can examine through carefully controlled laboratory designs how various factors, including the participants' personalities, particular pairings of individuals in the study, and manipulated variables, affect the level of closeness and other affiliative outcomes experienced after the structured interaction. The degree of closeness and other outcomes that are generated by a structured task to induce closeness is likely to vary as a function of factors that the researchers can measure or manipulate, and under controlled conditions (holding other factors constant). Such research can enhance our understanding of how these same factors may influence relationship development in naturally occurring situations, in which confounding variables and lack of experimental control can make it difficult to test the associations. In this section, I discuss findings from various studies that have used one of the closeness-generating tasks described above (or a variation) to examine how one or more factors (independent variables) enhance closeness, feelings of being interconnected, and other affiliative outcomes (e.g., liking) that result from engaging in the closeness task.

Effects of Relationship-Relevant Directions

In their original research to create a closeness-inducing task, Aron et al. (1997) manipulated two relationship-relevant expectations prior to having the dyads engage in the interaction. First, they included a manipulation (in their Study 2) referred to as expectations of mutual liking. Those in the expectation-of-mutual-liking condition received these instructions:

We have taken great care in matching partners. Based on our experience in previous research we expect that you and your partner will like one another – that is, you have been matched with someone we expect you will like and who will like you.

Those in the no-expectation-of-liking condition received the following instructions instead:

Partners in this study have been put together in ways that pair different categories of individuals. We are investigating the effect of different kinds of pairings. We have no special reason in your case to assume that you and your partner will like each other.

Aron et al. (1997) found no differences between participants in the two conditions in their scores on closeness after the interaction. The researchers speculated that the relationship-building aspect of the closeness task may have made an initial statement of expectation of liking less relevant.

In their Study 3, Aron et al. (1997) manipulated another expectation within the instructions – closeness as an explicit goal. The researchers assigned some participants to receive the directions, "This is a study of interpersonal closeness and your task ... is to get close to your partner ..." No such directions were provided for those in the other condition. Similar to the results reported for the effects of making expectations of liking explicit, no differences were found between participants in the two conditions. Aron et al. concluded that the lack of an effect of making closeness an explicit goal on closeness suggests that the closeness task works to generate closeness without any demand effects operating. However, Aron et al. found an interaction between these directions and the introversion/extroversion composition of the dyads, which will be discussed in the next section.

In sum, the results of Aron et al.'s (1997) original set of studies suggest that self-fulfilling prophecy effects of relationship-relevant instructions probably do not occur when participants participate in the highly engaging activity of the closeness-induction task.

Effects of Pre-Existing Individual Difference Variables on Closeness

As noted by Aron et al. (1997), one advantage of a closeness-generating task for studying the very early stage of relationship formation in a controlled laboratory setting is that the effects of pre-existing individual difference variables can be examined, including who is paired with whom, without leaving the selection process (of a partner) up to the participants. The effect of the pair members' pre-existing characteristics can be examined in three possible ways within the context of a closeness-inducing task in a laboratory study. First, pairs of strangers from a classroom or participant pool can be formed somewhat randomly (such as a function of schedule availability) and the degree to which the members' personal characteristics (measured prior to their interaction) are associated with experienced closeness and qualities of the interaction can be examined. The second way that the effects of pre-existing characteristics on closeness and other affiliative outcomes can be examined with this method is by measuring individual difference variables of the dyad members in advance of the research session, and then forming pairs that are similar versus dissimilar or low versus high on the theoretical characteristic of interest. The third way that the effects of the members' characteristics can be examined involves providing bogus information to the participants about their partner's characteristics, presented before the interaction begins. This last method, however, has rarely been used and would work only if the interaction task is conducted in a way that does not reveal the partner's actual characteristics. For example, if information about one or both members is fabricated, communication would need to occur over instant messaging, and possibly with a confederate (for an example, see MacInnis & Hodson, 2015).

Attachment Orientation One of the most commonly studied individual difference variables in the close relationships field is attachment orientation (Mikulincer & Shaver, 2018). Attachment orientation, including the dimensions of avoidance and anxiety, affect many aspects of relationships, from the very beginning stage to dissolution (Mikulincer & Shaver, 2013; Pietromonaco & Beck, 2015). Not surprisingly, research suggests that individuals with a high avoidance attachment orientation experience less closeness after engaging in the closeness task than individuals low in attachment avoidance.

Aron et al.'s (1997) original research that introduced their closeness induction task examined the effects of the participants' pre-existing attachment orientation on the closeness they experienced for an interaction partner as a consequence of the get-acquainted interaction. More specifically, in their Studies 1 and 2, participants completed Bartholomew and Horowitz's (1991) four-item attachment style measure. Combining the data across the two studies, Aron et al. found that avoidant/dismissive participants reported less closeness after the closeness-inducing interaction than did the other participants. Furthermore, the pairs that had at least one dismissive partner were least satisfied with the level of the closeness in the interaction.

In a more recent social interaction study, Ketay and Beck (2017) also examined the effects of the participants' attachment style on the closeness they experienced as a result of the interaction, as well as the level of closeness they desired. The participants completed measures upon arrival at the study, including Bartholomew and Horowitz's (1991) measure of attachment styles. The pairs, who were formed randomly (i.e., not based on their attachment scores), completed either the Aron et al. (1997) closeness task or another activity that was not designed to enhance closeness (e.g., taking turns giving each other directions to different places on campus). Participants with higher attachment avoidance reported less closeness to their partner. The researchers also found that the participants who were high in attachment anxiety or who were paired with someone high in attachment anxiety reported less closeness in the interaction and also desired less closeness, relative to participants who were lower in attachment anxiety (and/or had partners lower in attachment anxiety).

In a study that focused specifically on avoidant individuals' responses to social warmth versus social coldness, Philipp-Muller and MacDonald (2017) had participants engage in the Sedikides et al. (1999) closeness task with a confederate who was trained to respond either warmly (empathic responses with eye contact) or coldly (aloof with less eye contact). After the interaction, the participants completed an eight-item scale of closeness, which included such items as "How much do you feel you clicked with your partner?" A main effect was found for attachment scores (measured with the Feeney, Noller, & Hanrahan [1994] attachment questionnaire); those who scored high on the avoidant subscale reported less closeness to the other. In addition, and not surprisingly, participants felt more closeness to the warm confederate than to the cold confederate. However, the interaction between the participants' avoidance score and condition approached significance. Low avoidant participants felt closer to the warm confederate than to the cold confederate, whereas high avoidant participants did not differ in their levels of closeness in the two conditions.

Extroversion Personality characteristics included in the Big Five Personality Traits (McCrae & Costa, 2008) – particularly extroversion – have been found to affect the degree of closeness experienced after a structured self-disclosure task in an initial interaction. In their Study 3, Aron et al. (1997) had their classroom respondents (in advance of the session in which the closeness task was administered) indicate their introversion/extroversion type based on the Myers-Briggs type Indicator (Myers & McCaulley, 1985) that they had completed earlier in the semester. Then, based on the participants' responses to this measure, the researchers created extroverted pairs, introverted pairs, and mixed pairs. The researchers found a marginally significant result of the extroverted pairs reporting more closeness than the introverted pairs. However, they also found an interaction effect between type of pair and the instructions (mention of closeness vs. no mention of closeness, referred to above). The higher scores on closeness in extroverted pairs than introverted pairs was found only in the no-mention-of-closeness condition and not also in the condition in which the directions to become close were made explicit. The researchers concluded that even though introverted individuals may be generally less comfortable with social interaction, they have the skills to become close and can do so when it is made an explicit goal.

Social Anxiety The effect of social anxiety on the closeness experienced as a result of being in a structured self-disclosure task with another has also been examined. The results have been complicated and depend on the degree of similarity between the partners on social anxiety and the medium of communication.

For example, Kashdan and Wenzel (2005) randomly paired participants and had them complete a social anxiety scale (Mattick & Clarke, 1998). Then, the participants engaged in either the closeness task or the small talk task from Aron et al. (1997). Kashdan and Wenzel found no direct effects of own or partner's social anxiety levels on overall closeness experienced after the interaction. However, dyads composed of members who differed in their levels of social anxiety (i.e., one was socially anxious and one was not) reported less closeness than pairs in which the members were similar in social anxiety. Furthermore, as reported by the authors, "Across the full sample, low socially anxious individuals interacting with low socially anxious partners experienced the greatest levels of closeness." (p. 342)

Also examining the effects of social anxiety in a getting-acquainted interaction, Lundy and Drouin (2016) had dyads engage in an abbreviated version of the Aron et al. (1997) Fast Friends procedure in one of three conversation conditions – face-to-face, voice (Skype), or instant messaging. Their central hypothesis was that participants with high social anxiety would experience more interpersonal connectedness in the instant messaging condition, whereas low social anxiety individuals would report more interconnectedness in the face-to-face or voice conditions. There was slight evidence that those with low social anxiety experienced enhanced connectedness in face-to-face and voice conditions (compared to instant messaging). However, for high social anxiety participants, no differences were found in interpersonal connectedness across the three mediums.

In sum, research using the Aron et al. (1997) closeness task suggests that some individuals may experience more closeness than others after engaging in the task – particularly those who have a secure attachment orientation, are extroverted, and are not socially anxious. However, the differences in closeness experienced after a structured task based on pre-existing personal characteristics are not large, perhaps because of the salience of the task. More research is needed, though, to further examine the differences between Actor and Partner effects for individual characteristics, and to compare the effects of person characteristics (such as social anxiety) in a structured closeness task versus in an unstructured closeness task.

Effects of Conditions and Modes of the Interaction

A closeness-inducing task used in a laboratory setting can also allow the investigator to examine whether contextual factors affect the level of closeness experienced. In this section, I discuss the research that has included manipulations of aspects of the interaction, including conditions under which the closeness task is conducted.

Pattern of Reciprocity In the original Aron et al. (1997) self-disclosure task, participants were directed to take turns asking and answering questions. Thus, immediate (or tit-for-tat) self-disclosure reciprocity has been integral to the original self-disclosure task. Immediate reciprocity is also common in early stages of relationships in natural settings (Derlega, Winstead, & Greene, 2008; Jourard, 1971). However, in some situations, disclosure reciprocity occurs not immediately but over an extended time (Hill & Stull, 1982). This may occur for a variety of reasons, including due to modern forms of communication that are asynchronous. Research with a closeness-inducing task, as summarized in this section, indicates that immediate reciprocity leads to more closeness than asynchronous communication that may still be characterized as reciprocal, albeit over an extended period of time.

Several years ago, I began a line of research at Illinois State University to examine the get-acquainted process between strangers in a laboratory setting, which involved a structured closeness-generating task that combined disclosure topics from Aron et al.'s (1997) and Sedikides et al.'s (1999) procedures. In our first social interaction study (Sprecher et al., 2012), we distinguished between and examined the differential effects of the two sides of self-disclosure (giving/disclosing vs. receiving/listening) on experiencing closeness and other outcomes after the getting-acquainted interaction. In pairs of university students, one member of the dyad was randomly assigned to the disclosure role for a first twelve-minute segment, and therefore the other member of the dyad was automatically placed in the recipient role. The two participants then switched roles in a second twelve-minute interaction. The interactions occurred over Skype from two different university rooms, and the pair members could see and hear each other over a webcam.

After the first interaction and then again after the second interaction, the participants provided their reactions to each other and the interaction, including completing the Inclusion of Other in the Self (IOS) Scale (Aron et al., 1992). In the reaction measures completed after the first segment of interaction, participants in the recipient role of disclosure reported greater closeness (and other outcomes, such as liking) than did participants in the discloser role. After the dyad members switched roles in the second segment of interaction, the differences diminished although did not disappear completely. Initial disclosers who became recipients experienced moderate-sized increases in closeness, whereas the increase was smaller for those in the initial recipient role who then became disclosers. Although engaging in either side of self-disclosure (giving or receiving) – as manifested in the structured self-disclosure task – can lead to closeness, the process of receiving disclosure leads to knowledge and information-based familiarity of the other, which may be critical to the development of a close relationship.

In a second getting-acquainted study (Sprecher, Treger, Wondra, Hilaire, & Wallpe, 2013), we manipulated whether the dyad engaged in the structured self-disclosure task in an immediate turn-taking way (similar to how the closeness induction tasks were designed and how they are used in most studies) or as sequential self-disclosure (similar to Sprecher et al., 2012). We found that the dyads who engaged in (immediate) turn-taking reciprocity had a higher score on a composite measure that included closeness items than did the dyads who engaged in extended (sequential) reciprocity. Furthermore, in a later study (Sprecher & Treger, 2015) that was conducted in a similar way, we found that perceived responsiveness, enjoyment of the interaction, and perception of being liked each uniquely mediated the effect of the pattern of reciprocity (immediate vs. extended) on closeness and other affiliative outcomes. That is, dyads who engaged in the structured self-disclosure task in an immediate tit-for-tat fashion reported higher scores on these process mechanisms than did the dyads who were in the extended reciprocity condition. These results indicate that immediate reciprocity (turn-taking self-disclosure), characteristic of the original closeness-inducing task (Aron et al., 1997), is more conducive to generating closeness and other affiliative outcomes than a modification of it that includes taking longer turns at self-disclosure.

Length of the Interaction Aron et al.'s (1997) original closeness induction task was designed to last forty-five minutes, and a similar time frame has been used in several studies focused on the getting-acquainted process. However, in many studies, including those that I have conducted (e.g., Sprecher et al., 2012, 2013), the length of the interaction has been abbreviated. In addition, the Sedikides et al. (1999) closeness-inducing task was designed to last nine minutes. Does the length of the structured interaction task affect the closeness experienced? One would expect that a longer interaction (and more topics discussed) would be associated with greater closeness experienced. However, it is also possible that the mere engagement in the task, even if brief, is enough to generate the same level of closeness between strangers as would a longer getting-acquainted interaction. Indeed, there could even be the argument that a longer interaction could reduce a feeling of closeness and attraction because of the lure of ambiguity generated from less information (Norton, Frost, & Ariely, 2007).

A comparison in closeness and other affiliative outcomes across studies that have used different time lengths of a closeness-inducing task would be misleading as there are generally other differences beyond the length of the interaction across the studies, including the specific closeness induction task used, the mode of communication, and how closeness (as a dependent variable) is measured. However, in one of my social interaction studies (Sprecher, 2014b), dyads were randomly assigned to engage in the structured self-disclosure task over Skype for either six minutes or twelve minutes (after also having a brief, free-format get-acquainted interaction). Results indicated that dyads in the twelve-minute condition reported more closeness and other affiliative outcomes than did the dyads in the six-minute interaction.

Further evidence that the length of the structured self-disclosure task affects level of closeness experienced comes from a study by Reis, Maniaci, Caprariello, Eastwick, and Finkel (2011). In their Study 1, Reis et al. had same-sex pairs interact with each other using topics from both Sedikides et al. (1999) and Aron et al. (1997). Dyads were randomly assigned to either two or six topics to discuss, with each topic discussed by each dyad member for thirty seconds (thus, the procedure lasted two minutes or six minutes). Dyads in the six-topic condition had higher scores on a composite measure of attraction (which included the Aron et al. [1992] Inclusion of Other in Self Scale as an item of closeness) and partner responsiveness than the dyads in the two-topic condition.

Finally, when closeness has been measured at multiple time points in studies involving a closeness-inducing task – such as after each segment of interaction – feelings of closeness and other measures of connectedness have been found to significantly increase over the segments of the interaction (e.g., Lundy & Drouin, 2016; Page-Gould et al., 2008; Sprecher et al., 2012, 2013).

Medium of Communication The closeness-inducing tasks (Aron et al., 1997; Sedikides et al., 1999) were created in the 1990s, when online forms of communication were not in widespread use. Today, however, there are many ways to communicate online, including through asynchronous modes of communication (text messaging) and synchronous, Internet-based channels (Skype-video) (Yang, Brown, & Braun, 2014). Thus, not surprisingly, recent research has examined whether the mode of communication moderates the degree of closeness (and other affiliative outcomes) that dyads experience after engaging in a structured self-disclosure task.

In one such study, Mallen, Day, and Green (2003) had thirty-two dyads (mostly female–female dyads) discuss topics from the Aron et al. (1997) Closeness Inventory, either through a face-to-face chat or in an online interaction. The dyads who engaged in the structured task in a face-to-face condition reported more closeness (and other affiliative outcomes) than the dyads who did the same closeness task in a CMC-text condition. In another study that examined the effects of medium of communication on interaction, Ramirez and Burgoon (2004), although not using an existing closeness-induction task *per se*, assigned getting-acquainted same-sex dyads five topics to discuss (e.g., "What do you like or dislike about your classes?"). They manipulated the modality of the interaction and considered four: text-chat, audio, video, and face-to-face. Although the exact results depended on the valence of the information discussed (another manipulated variable in the study), overall the pairs in the text chat scored lowest on the outcome variables, which included a measure of mutuality. No strong differences in the outcomes were found among the other modalities.

In a study that I conducted (Sprecher & Hampton, 2017), getting-acquainted dyads engaged in a three-segment, structured self-disclosure task to become acquainted. Some dyads were randomly assigned to engage in all three segments of interaction entirely face-to-face. The other dyads did the first segment in computer-mediated-communication (instant messaging), the second segment in Skype-video, and the third segment face-to-face. After each segment of interaction, the participants provided their reactions to the interaction including a measure of how close they felt to the other ("How close do you feel toward the Other after this brief interaction?"). After the final interaction, additional reaction items were included, including the Aron et al. (1992) IOS Scale. We found that the dyads who experienced the closeness-induction task over CMC-text reported significantly less closeness than did the dyads in the face-to-face condition (even though the former dyads were given a little more time to converse). However, at the final assessment (after Segment 3) there were no differences in the reported closeness and other reactions as a function of whether the participants had been face-to-face the entire time or had progressed from text messages to face-to-face.

Combined, the studies that manipulated medium of communication in a social interaction study that included a closeness-inducing task suggest that if a closeness-inducing task is conducted over a text-based channel, less closeness is experienced relative to if it is done over a richer channel, either Skype or face-to-face (although see findings from Lundy & Drouin [2016] suggesting that this may be especially true of participants low in social anxiety). However, as long as the dyads switch to a richer channel while they are still engaged in the self-disclosure task, they can "catch up" in their felt closeness and other reactions (see also Sprecher, 2014b).

Effects of Hyperconnection Increasingly, people use communication technologies to begin relationships (Yang et al., 2014). The pervasiveness of phone texting and the Internet (email, Facebook), however, means that people can be connected to their social networks while they are simultaneously becoming acquainted with a new person, i.e., they experience hyperconnection (Rainie & Wellman, 2012). What are the implications for closeness and interconnection experienced in getting-acquainted interaction if communication devices are present or even used by the interaction pair? This has been referred to as "dual-front interactions" (Humphreys, 2005), in which individuals attend simultaneously to an immediate, face-to-face interaction partner while also attending to distant others through networking media.

Przybylski and Weinstein (2013) used a very brief form of the Aron et al. (1997) closeness generating task – actually only one topic (an interesting event that had occurred over the past month) – to generate closeness between two interacting strangers in the laboratory. Stranger–stranger dyads were asked to discuss the topic for ten minutes, and the researchers manipulated whether a cell phone or a pocket notebook was on a desk near the participants during the interaction. The dyads who engaged in the closeness task in the presence of a mobile phone – even though the phone did not belong to either of the participants – reported less closeness and lower relationship quality than did the dyads who interacted in the presence of a notebook (rather than a phone). In a follow-up study, Przybylski and Weinstein manipulated whether the dyads discussed for ten minutes the closeness topic or a topic from Aron et al.'s small-talk task (thoughts about plastic holiday trees). The presence of the cell phone continued to have a negative effect on their reactions to the interaction, but only for the dyads who were discussing a topic from the closeness task.

In a follow-up study to Przybylski and Weinstein (2013), Misra, Cheng, Genevie, and Yuan (2014) had trained research assistants approach pairs of individuals in coffee shops and cafes and asked them to discuss either a topic from Aron et al.'s (1997) closeness task or a more casual topic from their small talk list. As the pairs engaged in the conversations, the assistants unobtrusively observed whether they placed any mobile devices, including cell phones and laptops, on the table or in their hands. The dyads were then asked at the end of the interaction to complete a brief survey, which included measures of interpersonal connectedness during the conversation. The dyads who had a device visible during the conversation were found to report lower interconnectedness than did the dyads who did not have a device present. Explanations (Misra et al., 2014; Przybylski & Weinstein, 2013) offered for the negative effects of communication technologies on interactions focused on the detrimental effects of divided attention (Turkle, 2012) and on psychological discomfort due to potential norm violation of not giving full attention to each other in the interaction.

In a social interaction study that I conducted (Sprecher, Hampton, Heinzel, & Felmlee, 2016), we examined more directly whether being hyperconnected can interfere with the effectiveness of the structured self-disclosure task for generating closeness in get-acquainted interaction. The dyads in the study engaged in a twenty-one-minute structured self-disclosure task over Skype-video. We randomly assigned some dyads to be in the experimental condition and then further randomly selected one member of the experimental dyads to be able to have access to messages from their social network, received unobtrusively without their interaction partner being aware. To accomplish this, the participants in the hyperconnected (experimental) condition had their cell phones in silent mode on the desk in front of them and had Facebook open on half of their computer screen (with the Skype interaction on the other half of the screen). The list of questions provided to the participants in the experimental condition included frequent visual reminders to check their cell phone and refresh their Facebook posts. Access to the communication devices (i.e., being hyperconnected) had almost no effect on the participants' reactions to the interaction. For example, no differences were found in closeness experienced as a result of being hyperconnected (having access to messages on one's phone and on Facebook) versus being in the control condition and without access to messages from one's network. There were also no negative effects on the partner's reactions (including on closeness experienced), although it could be argued that more negative effects would likely be found if cell phones and Facebook connections are visible and intrusive during the interaction (due to the obvious reduced attention to one's interaction partner).

In sum, researchers have manipulated conditions of the context of a structured closeness-generating task, sometimes through a confederate, to examine how closeness experienced early in relationship development can be enhanced or diminished by the way that the closeness task is conducted, such as the mode and length of communication.

EFFECTS OF A CLOSENESS-INDUCING TASK ON OTHER PSYCHOLOGICAL PHENOMENA

While most of the research that has used a structured closeness-inducing task has examined how various factors (manipulated or pre-existing) affect the degree of closeness or other affiliative outcomes experienced after engaging in the task, a smaller number of studies have examined how the closeness generated from engaging in a closeness-inducing task affects other (non-relational) psychological phenomena. This section provides a brief summary of some of the other psychological factors that have been found to be affected by the enhanced closeness experienced as a result of engaging in a closeness-inducing task in a laboratory setting:

Reduction in Prejudice

In several studies, participants have been paired together to engage in a closeness task (e.g., Aron et al., 1997), either with someone of their ingroup (own race) or someone from an outgroup (different race). When the pairs are mixed-race, the members later expressed more positive intergroup attitudes, less anxiety about engaging in interaction with that specific outgroup, and more support for policies that help the other group (e.g., Page-Gould et al., 2008; Welker et al., 2014; Wright, Aron, McLaughlin-Volpe, & Ropp, 1997). In addition, the minority members in the mixed-raced dyads reported more satisfaction with the university (Mendoza-Denton & Page-Gould, 2008).

Attribution Biases

Sedikides et al. (1998) examined whether the self-serving attribution bias (e.g., taking credit for success), documented primarily in studies outside of a relational context, would also be found if stranger–stranger dyads became close in the laboratory. The stranger–stranger dyads in their study jointly engaged in a creative task and then received success or failure feedback. Stranger–stranger dyads who first jointly engaged in Sedikides et al.'s (1999) closeness-generating task and experienced temporary closeness were less likely to engage in a self-serving attribution bias of taking more credit on a successful joint task than participants who were paired with a new partner (someone with whom they had not just engaged in the closeness-inducing task).

Reduced Stress

Participants who engaged in Aron et al.'s (1997) closeness task with another participant and then were submitted to a stressful situation (a tape-stripping procedure on the skin) in the presence of that other person showed more improved skin recovery and reported less stress relative to participants in a control group who went through the tape-stripping activity alone (Robinson et al., 2017).

Reactions to Consumer Products

In the marketing research area, Dubois, Bonezzi, and De Angelis (2016; Study 2) found that the creation of closeness (Sedikides et al., 1999) between dyads in the lab contributed to the likelihood that the dyad members would be willing to transmit negative information to each other about a consumer product (their most recent meal in a restaurant). The authors interpreted these findings to indicate that interpersonal closeness contributes to a motive to protect others and decreases the motive to self-enhance. Tu, Shaw, and Fishbach (2015; Study 2) manipulated level of closeness (with the Sedikides et al. [1999] closeness induction task vs. superficial questions in a non-close condition) experienced by a participant and an online confederate, and then gave the participant the opportunity to choose between two gift packages that they and their interaction partner would receive. Those in the closeness condition were more likely to select the package that had a higher total benefit.

Reactions to Risky Types of Communication

Gorman and Jordan (2015; Study 2) found that members of female–female pairs who engaged in the Sedikides et al. (1999) closeness induction task responded more favorably to a staged tease by their interaction partner than did participants in the non-close condition (who discussed non-intimate topics). Sommer and Bernieri (2015) found that when participants were initially rejected by one person and then interacted with a new partner (by engaging in the Sedikides et al. closeness task), they reported lower levels of rapport as compared to the participants who had been initially accepted prior to the interaction with the new person, which the researchers interpreted as relational distancing and reducing the possibility of future rejection. However, the rejected participants were found to actually engage in more behaviors to increase closeness with their new partner, including matching the conversation content and engaging in mimicry. In research that examined the consequences of being forgotten by another (also a form of rejection or ostracism), Ray, Gomillion, Pintea, and Hamlin (2018) conducted a study that involved participants engaging in a closeness-inducing task (that included elements of both Aron et al.'s and Sedikides et al.'s closeness inducing task) with a confederate. Then, participants were asked to respond to an open-ended item on how much they recalled from the interaction and their ratings of liking of the other. Participants were then told this information would be shared with the other participant. The actual participants received a fabricated form that indicated moderately positive liking from the other and information that either indicated that the other had remembered the interaction well or had forgotten most of the interaction. The memory manipulation affected liking and closeness assessed after the exchange of information. Participants decreased in their liking and closeness (i.e., including other in self) from before to after the exchange of information in the condition of being forgotten.

Amplification of Shared Experiences

In extending past research on whether sharing an experience with a familiar other can amplify the experience, Boothby et al. (2016) had some participants engage in a brief version of Aron et al.'s (1997) closeness-inducing task for ten minutes with a confederate who provided scripted responses. When these participants then had a shared experience (simultaneously eating chocolate) with the confederate, the chocolate was rated more favorably, as compared to in a condition in which the participants did not get to know the other with whom they shared the chocolate-eating experience. Relatedly, Vacharkulksemsuk and Fredrickson (2012) found that same-sex dyads who completed an abbreviated version of Aron et al.'s (1997) self-disclosure task, as compared to dyads in a control condition (who jointly engaged in a manuscript-editing transcription task) were found to have greater behavioral synchrony (coordination of movement), as rated by outside observers of their video-taped interaction. The participants in the closeness condition also reported more positive rapport and mutuality in their self-reports, as compared to those in the control group.

Enhanced Productivity

Three-person groups who were assigned to engage in Sedikides' et al. (1999) closeness induction task collaboratively wrote stories that were later evaluated by outside judges as being more creative than the stories written by groups not assigned to the closeness induction (Oztop, Katsikopoulos, & Gummerum, 2018).

Ethical Group Decision-Making

In two studies, Nikolova, Lamberton, and Coleman (2017; Studies 2A and 2B) presented dyads and individuals with ethical decisions to make based on hypothetical scenarios (e.g., whether to lie to a job candidate about job security in order to receive a positive performance review). They randomly assigned some dyads to engage in the Sedikides et al. (1999) closeness induction task in order to become bonded. The decision-making by the bonded dyads in the hypothetical scenario was found to be more ethical than the decision-making in the non-bonded dyads, although was no more ethical than the individual decision-making (Study 2A). In Study 2B, the bonded dyads also engaged in more ethical behavior than the nonbonded dyads. The researchers argued that their findings support the idea that if there is not another opportunity to bond (such as through the closeness task) pairs or groups bond by acting unethically together (e.g., "partners in crime"). This research suggests that a closeness induction task used to create bonding in work groups may reduce the likelihood of ethical violations.

In sum, research has been conducted in diverse areas, ranging from consumer decisions to prejudice, to examine how the closeness and bonding experienced as a result of engaging in a closeness-inducing task in the laboratory can have implications for many other non-relational phenomena (e.g., degree of prejudice toward outgroup members, ethical decision-making). Often such studies are done in conjunction with studies with naturally occurring friendships or relationships. There are many other areas of psychology and social psychology that would benefit from incorporating the manipulation of a structured closeness task, including in the areas of group behavior, social cognition, and person perception. Many social psychological phenomena may operate differently in a relational context than when examined in isolation, and a closeness-inducing task provides the opportunity to examine this possibility in a controlled, laboratory setting.

CONCLUSIONS

Studying interdependence can be difficult. Structured, closeness-generating tasks, such as that of Aron et al. (1997) and Sedikides et al. (1999), were designed specifically to create closeness in a short period of time and in settings that allow for experimental manipulations. Since their introduction in the late 1990s, these two closeness-inducing tasks have been incorporated, in various forms, in many studies to examine the consequences of a temporary feeling of closeness. In addition, other activities have been used in some studies to enhance closeness and interdependence.

Certainly, such experimental research cannot take the place of studies of closeness and interdependence in naturally occurring, real-world relationships that extend across time and settings. However, research with the laboratory-based closeness-inducing tasks in stranger–stranger dyads can further our understanding of how interdependence develops early in the relationship, the myriad of factors that can influence the development of closeness and other affiliative outcomes, and how closeness and bonding generated in stranger–stranger pairs can influence other psychological phenomena that in the past were examined only at the individual level but now can be examined in a relational context in the laboratory.

REFERENCES

Agnew, C. R., Loving, T. J., Le, B., & Goodfriend, W. (2004). Thinking close: Measuring relational closeness as perceived self-other inclusion. In D. J. Mashek & A. Aron (Eds.), *Handbook of Closeness and Intimacy* (pp. 103–115). Mahwah, NJ: Erlbaum.

Aron, A., Aron, E. N., & Smollan, D. (1992). Inclusion of other in the self scale and the structure of interpersonal closeness. *Journal of Personality and Social Psychology*, 63, 596–612.

Aron, A., Melinat, E., Aron, E. N., Vallone, R. D., & Bator, R. J. (1997). The experimental generation of interpersonal closeness: A procedure and some preliminary findings. *Personality and Social Psychology Bulletin*, 23, 363–377.

Bartholomew, K. & Horowitz, L. M. (1991). Attachment styles among young adults: A test of a four-category model. *Journal of Personality and Social Psychology*, 61, 226–244.

Baumeister, R. F. & Leary, M. R. (1995). The need to belong: Desire for interpersonal attachments as a fundamental human motivation. *Psychological Bulletin*, 117, 497–529.

Berscheid, E., Snyder, M., & Omoto, A. M. (1989). The relationship closeness inventory: Assessing the closeness of interpersonal relationships. *Journal of Personality and Social Psychology*, 57, 792.

Boothby, E. J., Smith, L. K., Clark, M. S., & Bargh, J. A. (2016). Psychological distance moderates the amplification of shared experience. *Personality and Social Psychology Bulletin*, 42, 1431–1444.

Collins, N. L. & Miller, L. C. (1994). Self-disclosure and liking: A meta-analytic review. *Psychological Bulletin*, 116, 457–475.

Derlega, V. J., Winstead, B. A., & Greene, K. (2008). Self-disclosure and starting a close relationship. In S. Sprecher, A. Wenzel, & J. Harvey (Eds.), *Handbook of Relationship Initiation* (pp. 153–174). New York: Taylor & Francis.

Dubois, D., Bonezzi, A., & De Angelis, M. D. (2016). Sharing with friends versus strangers: How interpersonal closeness influences word-of-mouth valence. *Journal of Marketing Research*, 53, 712–727.

Eastwick, P. W. & Finkel, E. J. (2008). Speed-dating: A powerful and flexible paradigm for studying romantic relationship initiation. In S. Sprecher, A. Wenzel, & J. Harvey (Eds.), *Handbook of Relationship Initiation* (pp. 217–234). New York: Guildford.

Feeney, J. A., Noller, P., & Hanrahan, M. (1994). Assessing adult attachment. In M. Sperling & W. Berman (Eds.), *Attachment in Adults: Clinical and Developmental Perspectives* (pp. 128–152). New York: Guilford Press.

Fraley, B. & Aron, A. (2004). The effect of a shared humorous experience on closeness in initial encounters. *Personal Relationships*, 11, 61–78.

Gorman, G. & Jordan, C. H. (2015). "I know you're kidding": Relationship closeness enhances positive perceptions of teasing. *Personal Relationships*, 22, 173–187.

Hill, C. T. & Stull, D. E. (1982). Disclosure reciprocity: Conceptual and measurement issues. *Social Psychology Quarterly*, 45, 238–244.

Humphreys, L. (2005). Cellphones in public: Social interactions in a wireless era. *New Media & Society*, 7, 810–833.

Ickes, W. (2009). *Strangers in a Strange Lab: How Personality Shapes Our Initial Encounters with Others*. Oxford: Oxford University Press.

Ickes, W., Bissonnette, V., Garcia, S., & Stinson, L. L. (1990). Implementing and using the dyadic interaction paradigm. In C. Hendrick & M. S. Clark (Eds.), *Review of Personality and Social Psychology: Vol. 11. Research Methods in Personality and Social Psychology* (pp. 16–44). Newbury Park, CA: Sage.

Jourard, S. M. (1971). *The Transparent Self* (rev. ed.). New York: Van Nostrand Reinhold.

Kashdan, T. B. & Wenzel, A. (2005). A transactional approach to social anxiety and the genesis of interpersonal closeness: Self, partner, and social context. *Behavior Therapy*, 36, 335–346.

Kelley, H., Berscheid, E., Christensen, A., Harvey, J., Huston, T., Levinger, G., . . . Peterson, D. R. (1983). Analyzing close relationships. In H. Kelley, E. Berscheid, A. Christensen, J. Harvey, T. Huston, G. Levinger, . . . D. R. Peterson (Eds.), *Close Relationships* (pp. 20–67). New York: W. H. Freeman.

Ketay, S. & Beck, L. A. (2017). Attachment predicts cortisol response and closeness in dyadic social interaction. *Psychoneurendcrinology*, 80, 114–121.

Lewandowski, G. W. & Aron, A. P. (2004). Distinguishing arousal from novelty and challenge in initial romantic attraction between strangers. *Social Behavior and Personality: An International Journal*, 32, 361–372.

Lundy, B. L. & Drouin, M. (2016). From social anxiety to interpersonal connectedness: Relationship building within face-to-face, phone and instant messaging mediums. *Computers in Human Behavior*, 54, 271–277.

MacInnis, C. C. & Hodson, G. (2015). The development of online cross-group relationships among university students: Benefits of earlier (vs. later) disclosure of stigmatized group membership. *Journal of Social and Personal Relationships*, 32, 788–809.

Mallen, M. J., Day, S. X., & Green, M. A. (2003). Online versus face-to-face conversations: An examination of relational and discourse variables. *Psychotherapy: Theory, Research, Practice, Training*, 40, 155–163.

Mattick, R. P. & Clarke, J. C. (1998). Development and validation of measures of social phobia scrutiny fear and social interaction anxiety. *Behaviour Research and Therapy*, 36, 455–470.

McCrae, R. R. & Costa, P. T. (2008). The five-factor theory of personality. In O. P. John, R. W. Robins, & L. A. Pervin (Eds.), *Handbook of Personality: Theory and Research* (3rd ed., pp. 159–181). New York: Guilford Press.

Mendoza-Denton, R. & Page-Gould, E. (2008). Can cross-group friendships influence minority students' well-being at historically white universities? *Psychological Science*, 19, 933–939.

Mikulincer, M. & Shaver, P. R. (2013). The role of attachment security in adolescent and adult close relationships. In J. A. Simpson & L. Campbell (Eds.), *The Oxford Handbook of Close Relationships* (pp. 66–89). New York: Oxford University Press.

Mikulincer, M. & Shaver, P. R. (2018). Attachment theory as a framework for studying relationship dynamics and functioning. In A. L. Vangelisti & D. Perlman (Eds.), *The Cambridge Handbook of Personal Relationships* (pp. 175–185). Cambridge: Cambridge University Press.

Misra, S., Cheng, L., Genevie, J., & Yuan, M. (2014). The iPhone effect: The quality of in-person social interactions in the presence of mobile devices. *Environment and Behavior*, 48, 275–298.

Myers, I. B. & McCaulley, M. H. (1985). *Manual: A Guide to the Development and Use of the Myers-Briggs Type Indicator.* Palo Alto, CA: Consulting Psychologists.

Nikolova, H., Lamberton, C., & Coleman, N. V. (2017). Stranger danger: When and why consumer dyads behave less ethically than individuals. *Journal of Consumer Research*, 45, 90–108.

Norton, M. I., Frost, J. H., & Ariely, D. (2007). Less is more: The lure of ambiguity, or why familiarity breeds contempt. *Journal of Personality and Social Psychology*, 92, 97–105.

Oztop, P., Katsikopoulos, K., & Gummerum, M. (2018). Creativity through connectedness: The role of closeness and perspective taking n group creativity. *Creativity Research Journal*, 30, 266–275.

Page-Gould, E., Mendoza-Denton, R., & Tropp, L. R. (2008). With a little help from my cross-group friend: Reducing anxiety in intergroup contexts through cross-group friendship. *Journal of Personality and Social Psychology*, 95, 1080–1094.

Philipp-Muller, A. & MacDonald, G. (2017). Avoidant individuals may have muted responses to social warmth after all: An attempted replication of MacDonald and Borsook (2010). *Journal of Experimental Social Psychology*, 70, 272–280.

Pietromonaco, P. R. & Beck, L. A. (2015). Attachment processes in adult romantic relationships. In M. Mikulincer, P. R. Shaver, J. A. Simpson, & J. F. Dovidio (Eds.), *APA Handbook of Personality and Social Psychology, Vol. 3: Interpersonal Relations* (pp. 33–64). Washington, DC: American Psychological Association.

Przybylski, A. K. & Weinstein, N. (2013). Can you connect with me now? How the presence of mobile communication technology influences face-to-face conversation quality. *Journal of Social and Personal Relationships*, 30, 237–246.

Rainie, L. & Wellman, B. (2012). *Networked: The New Operating System.* Cambridge, MA: The MIT Press.

Ramirez, A. & Burgoon, J. K. (2004). The effect of interactivity on initial interactions: The influence of information valence and modality and information richness on computer-mediated interaction. *Communication Monographs*, 71, 422–447.

Ray, D. G., Gomillion, S., Pintea, A. I., & Hamlin, I. (2018). On being forgotten: Memory and forgetting serve as signals of interpersonal importance. *Journal of Personality and Social Psychology*, 116, 259–276.

Reis, H. T., Maniaci, M. R., Caprariello, P. A., Eastwick, P. W., & Finkel, E. J. (2011). Familiarity does indeed promote attraction in live interaction. *Journal of Personality and Social Psychology*, 101, 557–570.

Reis, H. T., O'Keefe, S. D., & Lane, R. D. (2017). Fun is more fun when others are involved. *Journal of Positive Psychology*, 12, 547–557.

Robinson, H., Ravikulan, A., Nater, U. M., Skoluda, N., Jarrett, P., & Broadbent, E. (2017). The role of social closeness during tape stripping to facilitate skin barrier recovery: Preliminary findings. *Health Psychology*, 36, 619.

Rusbult, C. E., Kumashiro, M., Coolsen, M. K., & Kirchner, J. L. (2004). Interdependence, closeness, and relationships. In D. J. Mashek & A. P. Aron (Eds.), *Handbook of Closeness and Intimacy* (pp. 137–161). Mahwah, NJ: Erlbaum.

Sedikides, C., Campbell, W. K., Reeder, G. D., & Elliot, A. J. (1998). The self-serving bias in relational context. *Journal of Personality and Social Psychology*, 74, 378–386.

Sedikides, C., Campbell, W. K., Reeder, G. D., & Elliot, A. J. (1999). The relationship closeness induction task. *Representative Research in Social Psychology*, 23, 1–4.

Slatcher, R. B. (2010). When Harry and Sally met Dick and Jane: Creating closeness between couples. *Personal Relationships*, 17, 279–297.

Sommer, K. L. & Bernieri, F. (2015). Minimizing the pain and probability of rejection: Evidence for relational distancing and proximity seeking within face-to-face interactions. *Social Psychological and Personality Science*, 6, 131–139.

Sprecher, S. (2014a). Effects of actual (manipulated) and perceived similarity on liking in get-acquainted interactions: The role of communication. *Communication Monographs*, 81, 4–27.

Sprecher, S. (2014b). Initial interactions online-text, online-audio, online-video, or face-to-face: Effects of modality on liking, closeness, and other interpersonal outcomes. *Computers in Human Behavior*, 31, 190–197.

Sprecher, S. & Hampton, A. J. (2017). Liking and other reactions after a get-acquainted interaction: A comparison of continuous face-to-face interaction versus interaction that progresses from text messages to face-to-face. *Communication Quarterly*, 65, 333–353.

Sprecher, S., Hampton, A. J., Heinzel, H. J., & Felmlee, D. (2016). Can I connect with both you and my social network? Access to network-salient communication technology and get-acquainted interactions. *Computers in Human Behavior*, 62, 423–432.

Sprecher, S. & Treger, S. (2015). The benefits of turn-taking reciprocal self-disclosure in get-acquainted interactions. *Personal Relationships*, 22, 460–475.

Sprecher, S., Treger, S., & Wondra, J. D. (2012). Effects of self-disclosure role on liking, closeness, and other impressions in get-acquainted interactions. *Journal of Social and Personal Relationships*, 30, 497–514.

Sprecher, S., Treger, S., Wondra, J. D., Hilaire, N., & Wallpe, K. (2013). Taking turns: Reciprocal self-disclosure promotes liking in initial interactions. *Journal of Experimental Social Psychology*, 49, 860–866.

Sunnafrank, M. (1983). Attitude similarity and interpersonal attraction in communication processes: In pursuit of an ephemeral influence. *Communications Monographs*, 50, 273–284.

Tidwell, N. D., Eastwick, P. W., & Finkel, E. J. (2013). Perceived, not actual, similarity predicts initial attraction in a live romantic context: Evidence from the speed-dating paradigm. *Personal Relationships*, 20, 199–215.

Treger, S., Sprecher, S., & Erber, R. (2013). Laughing and liking: Exploring the interpersonal effects of humor use in initial social interactions. *European Journal of Social Psychology*, 43, 532–543.

Tu, Y., Shaw, A., & Fishbach, A. (2015). The friendly taking effect: How interpersonal closeness leads to seemingly selfish yet jointly maximizing choice. *Journal of Consumer Research*, 42, 669–687.

Turkle, S. (2012). *Alone Together: Why We Expect More from Technology and Less from Each Other*. New York: Basic books.

Vacharkulksemsuk, T. & Fredrickson, B. L. (2012). Strangers in sync: Achieving embodied rapport through shared movements. *Journal of Experimental Social Psychology*, 48, 399–402.

Vittengl, J. R. & Holt, C. S. (2000). Getting acquainted: The relationship of self-disclosure and social attraction to positive affect. *Journal of Social and Personal Relationships*, 17, 53–66.

Welker, K. M., Slatcher, R. B., Baker, L., & Aron, A. (2014). Creating positive out-group attitudes through intergroup couple friendships and implications for compassionate love. *Journal of Social and Personal Relationships*, 31, 706–725.

Worthy, M., Gary, A. L., & Kahn, G. M. (1969). Self-disclosure as an exchange process. *Journal of Personality and Social Psychology*, 13, 59–63.

Wright, B. L. & Sinclair, H. C. (2012). Pulling the strings: Effects of friend and parent opinions on dating choices. *Personal Relationships*, 19, 743–758.

Wright, S. C., Aron, A., McLaughlin-Volpe, T., & Ropp, S. A. (1997). The extended contact effect: Knowledge of cross-group friendships and prejudice. *Journal of Personality and Social Psychology*, 73, 73.

Yang, C. C., Brown, B. B., & Braun, M. T. (2014). From Facebook to cell calls: Layers of electronic intimacy in college students' interpersonal relationships. *New Media & Society*, 16, 5–23.

INDEX

For EU product safety concerns, contact us at Calle de José Abascal, 56–1°,
28003 Madrid, Spain or eugpsr@cambridge.org.

www.ingramcontent.com/pod-product-compliance
Ingram Content Group UK Ltd.
Pitfield, Milton Keynes, MK11 3LW, UK
UKHW020455240426
470322UK00016B/357